CREATIVE HOMEOWNER®

BEST-SELLING

1-STORY HOME PLANS

CREATIVE
HOMEOWNER®

Book content provided by Design America, Inc., St. Louis, MO.

Printed in China

Third printing

Best-Selling 1-Story Home Plans
ISBN-13: 978-1-58011-567-4

Library of Congress Control Number: 2021939828

CREATIVE HOMEOWNER®
www.creativehomeowner.com

Creative Homeowner books are distributed by

Fox Chapel Publishing
903 Square Street
Mount Joy, PA 17552
www.FoxChapelPublishing.com

Note: The homes as shown in the photographs and renderings in this book may differ from the actual blueprints. When studying the house of your choice, please check the floor plans carefully. All plans appearing in this publication are protected under copyright law.

The homes on the cover are: Top, Plan #F08-144D-0023 on page 19; Bottom, left: Plan #F08-163D-0003 on page 50; Top, right: Plan #F08-011D-0526 on page 242; Bottom, right: Plan #F08-170D-0004 on page 99.

CONTENTS

Top to bottom: Plan #F08-111D-0060 on page 46; Plan #F08-051D-0970 on page 218; Plan #F08-011D-0526, on page 242; Plan #F08-011D-0311 on page 12; Plan #F08-101D-0125 on page 87; Plan #F08-011D-0007 on page 12.

what's the right PLAN for you?

Choosing a house design is exciting, but can be a difficult task. Many factors play a role in what home plan is best for you and your family. To help you get started, we have pinpointed some of the major factors to consider when searching for your dream home. Take the time to evaluate your family's needs and you will have an easier time sorting through all of the house designs offered in this book.

budget is the first thing to consider. Many items take part in this budget, from ordering the blueprints to the last doorknob purchased. When you find the perfect house plan, visit houseplansandmore.com and get a cost-to-build estimate to ensure that the finished home will be within your cost range. A cost-to-build report is a detailed summary that gives you the total cost to build a specific home in the zip code where you're wanting to build. It is interactive allowing you to adjust labor and material costs, and it's created on demand when ordered so all pricing is up-to-date. This valuable tool will help you know how much your dream home will cost before you buy plans (see page 282 for more information).

> **make a list!**
> Experts in the field suggest that the best way to determine your needs is to begin by listing everything you like or dislike about your current home.

family lifestyle After your budget is deciphered, you need to assess you and your family's lifestyle needs. Think about the stage of life you are in now, and what stages you will be going through in the future. Ask yourself questions to figure out how much room you need now and if you will need room for expansion. Are you married? Do you have children? How many children do you plan on having? Are you an empty-nester? How long do you plan to live in this home?

Incorporate into your planning any frequent guests you may have, including elderly parents, grandchildren or adult children who may live with you.

Does your family entertain a lot? If so, think about the rooms you will need to do so. Will you need both formal and informal spaces? Do you need a gourmet kitchen? Do you need a game room and/or a wet bar?

floor plan layouts When looking through these home plans, imagine yourself walking through the house. Consider the flow from the entry to the living, sleeping and gathering areas. Does the layout ensure privacy for the master bedroom? Does the garage enter near the kitchen for easy unloading? Does the placement of the windows provide enough privacy from any neighboring properties? Do you plan on using furniture you already have? Will this furniture fit in the appropriate rooms? When you find a plan you want to purchase, be sure to picture yourself actually living in it.

exterior spaces With many different home styles throughout ranging from Traditional to Contemporary, flip through these pages and find which 1-story home appeals to you the most and think about the neighborhood in which you plan to build. Also, think about how the house will fit on your site. Picture the landscaping you want to add to the lot. Using your imagination is key when choosing a home plan.

Choosing a house design can be an intimidating experience. Asking yourself these questions before you get started on the search will help you through the process. With our large selection of sizes and styles, we are certain you will find your dream home in this book.

10 steps to BUILDING your dream home

1 talk to a lender

If you plan to obtain a loan in order to build your new home, then it's best to find out first how much you can get approved for before selecting a home design. Knowing the financial information before you start looking for land or a home will keep you from selecting something out of your budget and turning a great experience into a major disappointment. Financing the home you plan to build is somewhat different than financing the purchase of an existing house. You're going to need thousands of dollars for land, labor, and materials. Chances are, you're going to have to borrow most of it. Therefore, you will probably need to obtain a construction loan. This is a short-term loan to pay for building your house. When the house is completed, the loan is paid off in full, usually out of the proceeds from your long-term mortgage loan.

2 determine needs

Selecting the right home plan for your needs and lifestyle requires a lot of thought. Your new home is an investment, so you should consider not only your current needs, but also your future requirements. Versatility and the potential for converting certain areas to other uses could be an important factor later on. So, although a home office may seem unnecessary now, in years to come, the idea may seem ideal. Home plans that include flex spaces or bonus rooms can really adapt to your needs in the future.

3 choose a home site

The site for your new home will have a definite impact on the design you select. It's a good idea to select a home that will complement your site. This will save you time and money when building. Or, you can then modify a design to specifically accommodate your site. However, it will most likely make your home construction more costly than selecting a home plan suited for your lot right from the start. For example, if your land slopes, a walk-out basement works perfectly. If it's wooded, or has a lake in the back, an atrium ranch home is a perfect style to take advantage of surrounding backyard views.

SOME IMPORTANT CRITERIA TO CONSIDER WHEN SELECTING A SITE:

- Improvements will have to be made including utilities, walks and driveways
- Convenience of the lot to work, school, shops, etc.
- Zoning requirements and property tax amounts
- Soil conditions at your future site
- Make sure the person or firm that sells you the land owns it free and clear

4 select a home design

We've chosen the "best of the best" of the 1-story home plans found at houseplansandmore.com to be featured in this book. With over 18,000 home plans from the best architects and designers across the country, this book includes the best variety of styles and sizes to suit the needs and tastes of a broad spectrum of homeowners.

5 get the cost to build

If you feel you have found "the" home, then before taking the step of purchasing house plans, order an estimated cost-to-build report for the exact zip code where you plan to build. Requesting this custom cost report created specifically for you will help educate you on all costs associated with building your new home. Simply order this report and gain knowledge of the material and labor cost associated with the home you love. Not only does the report allow you to choose the quality of the materials, you can also select options in every aspect of the project from lot condition to contractor fees. This report will allow you to successfully manage your construction budget in all areas, clearly see where the majority of the costs lie, and save you money from start to finish.

A COST-TO-BUILD REPORT WILL DETERMINE THE OVERALL COST OF YOUR NEW HOME INCLUDING THESE 5 MAJOR EXPENSE CATEGORIES:

- Land
- Foundation
- Materials
- General Contractor's fee - Some rules-of-thumb that you may find useful are: (a) the total labor cost will generally run a little higher than your total material cost, but it's not unusual for a builder or general contractor to charge 15-20% of the combined cost for managing the overall project.
- Site improvements - don't forget to add in the cost of your site improvements such as utilities, driveway, sidewalks, landscaping, etc.

6 hire a contractor

If you're inexperienced in construction, you'll probably want to hire a general contractor to manage the project. If you do not know a reputable general contractor, begin your search by contacting your local Home Builders Association to get references. Many states require building contractors to be licensed. If this is the case in your state, its licensing board is another referral source. Finding a reputable, quality-minded contractor is a key factor in ensuring that your new home is well constructed and is finished on time and within budget. It can be a smart decision to discuss the plan you like with your builder prior to ordering plans. They can guide you into choosing the right type of plan package option especially if you intend on doing some customizing to the design.

7 customizing

Sometimes your general contractor may want to be the one who makes the modifications you want to the home you've selected. But, sometimes they want to receive the plans ready to build. That is why we offer home plan modification services. Please see page 285 for specific information on the customizing process and how to get a free quote on the changes you want to make to a home before you buy the plans.

8 order plans

If you've found the home and are ready to order blueprints, we recommend ordering the PDF file format, which offers the most flexibility. A PDF file format will be emailed to you when you order, and it includes a copyright release from the designer, meaning you have the legal right to make changes to the plan if necessary as well as print out as many copies of the plan as you need for building the home one-time. You will be happy to have your blueprints saved electronically so they can easily be shared with your contractor, subcontractors, lender and local building officials. We do, however, offer several different types of plan package depending on your needs, so please refer to page 283 for the plan options available and choose the best one for your particular situation.

Another helpful component in the building process that is available for many of the house plans in this book is a material list. A material list includes not only a detailed list of materials, but it also indicates where various cuts of lumber and other building components are to be used. This will save your general contractor significant time and money since they won't have to create this list before building begins. See houseplansandmore.com for material list availability for any of the home featured in this book.

9 order materials

You can order materials yourself, or have your contractor do it. Nevertheless, in order to thoroughly enjoy your new home you will want to personally select many of the materials that go into its construction. Today, home improvement stores offer a wide variety of quality building products. Only you can decide what specific types of windows, cabinets, bath fixtures, etc. will make your new home yours. Spend time early on in the construction process looking at the materials and products available.

10 move in

With careful planning and organization, your new home will be built on schedule and ready for your move-in date. Be sure to have all of your important documents in place for the closing of your new home and then you'll be ready to move in and start living your dream.

Browse the pages of the Best-Selling 1-Story Home Plans book and discover over 360 designs offered in a huge variety of sizes and styles to suit many tastes. From Craftsman and Country, to Contemporary and Traditional, there is a home design here for everyone with all of the amenities and features homeowners are looking for in a home today. Start your search right now for the perfect 1-Story home!

Top, left: Plan #F08-163D-0003 on page 50; top, right: Plan #F08-101D-0118 on page 256; bottom, left: Plan #F08-155D-0047 on page 26; bottom, right: Plan #F08-056D-0120, on page 40.

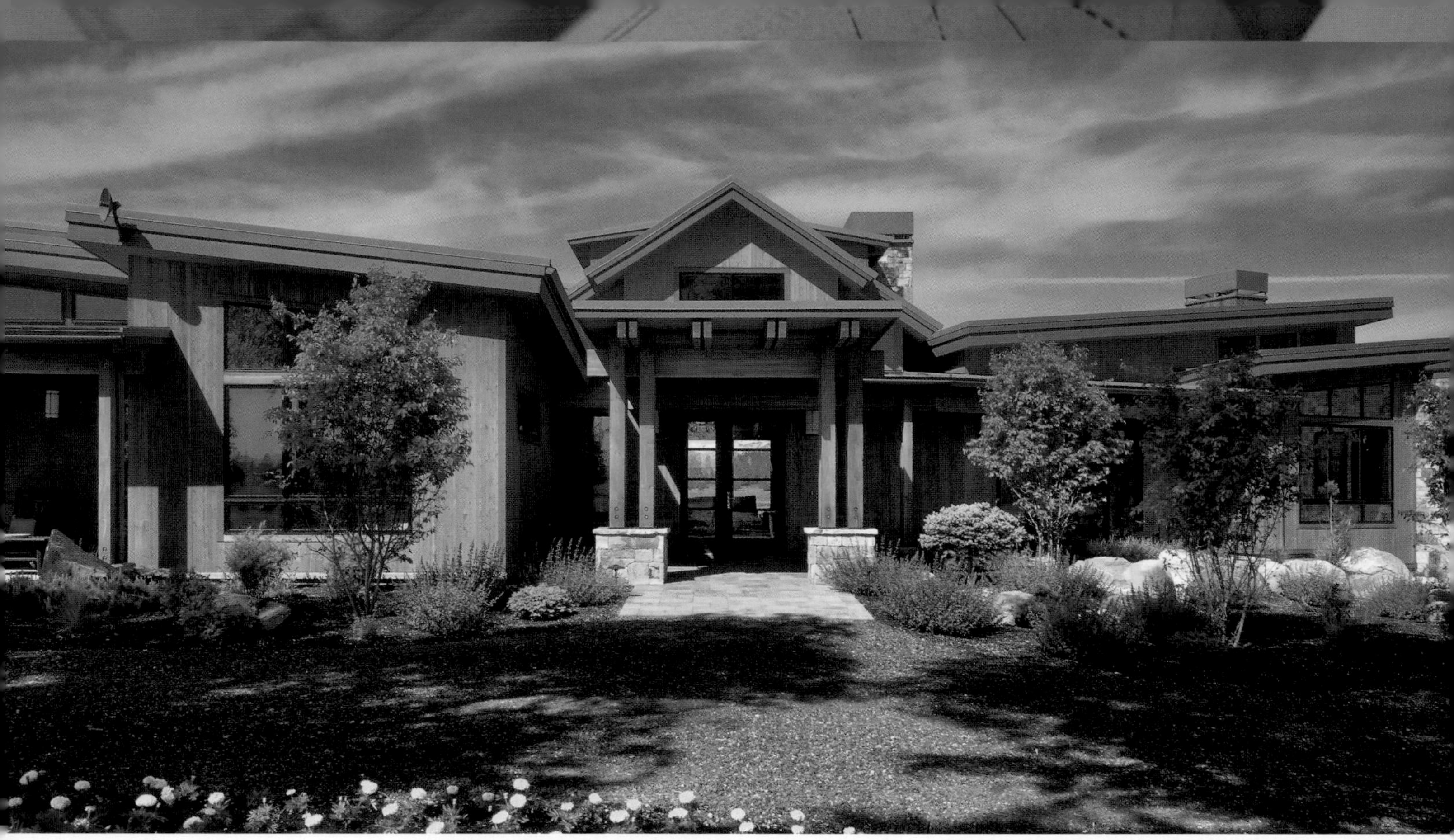

Plan #F08-161D-0001

Dimensions: 145'9" W x 93' D
Heated Sq. Ft.: 4,036
Bedrooms: 3 **Bathrooms:** 3½
Exterior Walls: 2" x 8"
Foundation: Crawl space or slab, please specify when ordering

See index for more information

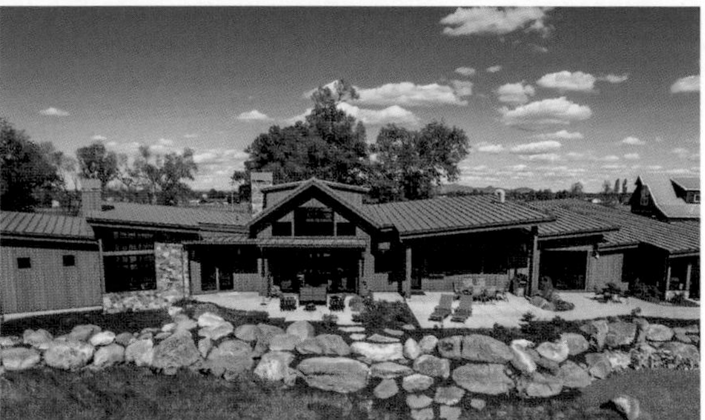

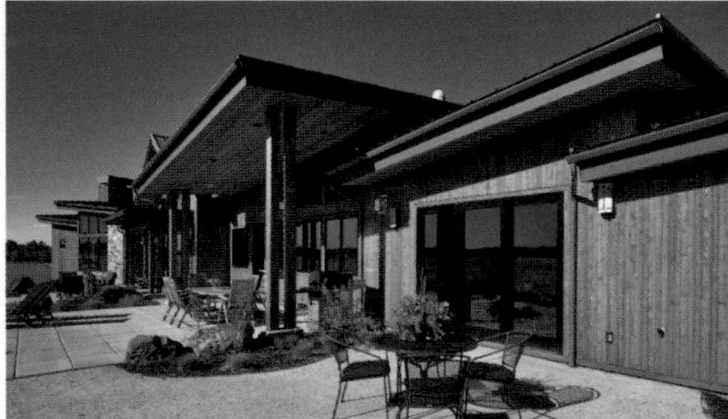

Images provided by designer/architect

Features

- Craftsman and modern style collide with this stunning rustic one-story home
- The open floor plan is ideal for maximizing square footage
- The master suite can be found in its own wing and it features a huge bath and two walk-in closets
- Built-ins and a walk-in pantry keep the kitchen sleek and clutter-free
- There is a flex space included int eh square footage that's perfect as a kid's playroom
- 3-car side entry garage

© Copyright by designer/architect

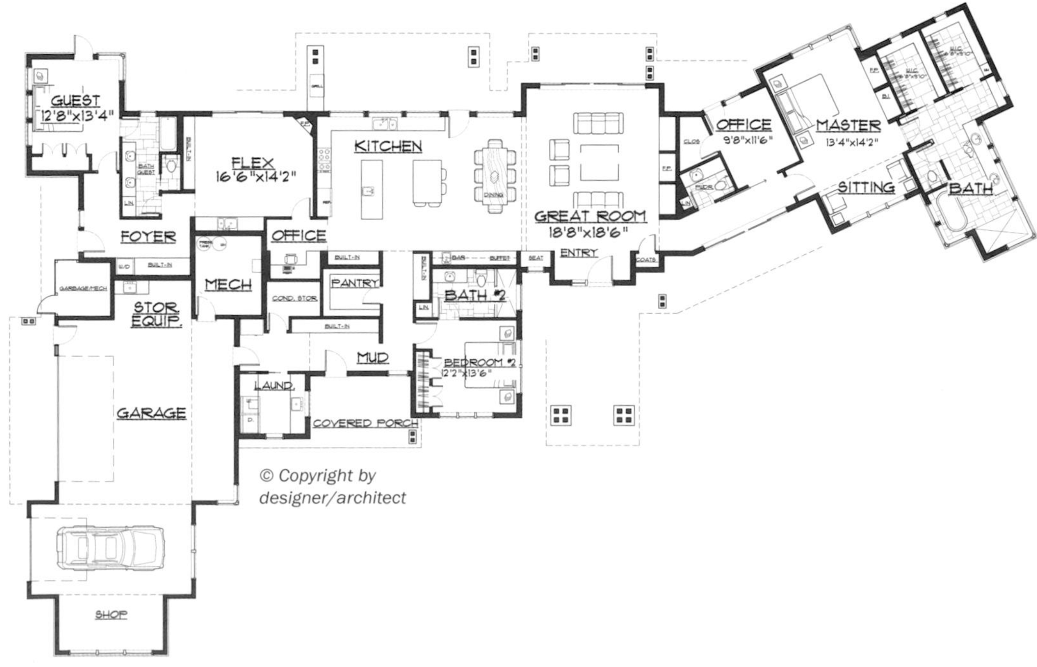

Images provided by designer/architect

Plan #F08-056D-0113

Dimensions: 58'6" W x 54' D
Heated Sq. Ft.: 1,997
Bonus Sq. Ft.: 1,869
Bedrooms: 2 **Bathrooms:** 3
Foundation: Basement standard; crawl space or slab for an additional fee

See index for more information

Features

- This charming rustic country home offers wonderful privacy and an oversized library perfect as a home office
- The cozy lodge room has a beamed ceiling, double doors onto the covered porch, and can be seen from the kitchen
- The kitchen enjoys a nearby bayed breakfast room and an enormous breakfast bar
- The master bedroom has a posh bath with a walk-in shower, an oversized tub, a double-bowl vanity, a separate toilet room, and a walk-in closet
- The optional lower level has an additional 1,869 square feet of living area and includes rec rooms, a wet bar, and a future bedroom and bath

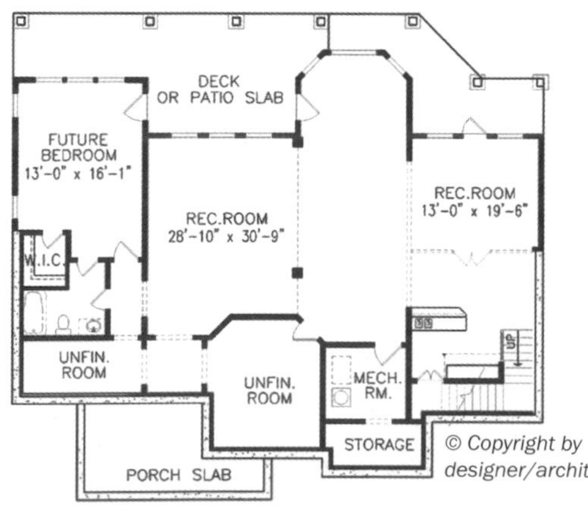

Optional Lower Level
1,869 sq. ft.

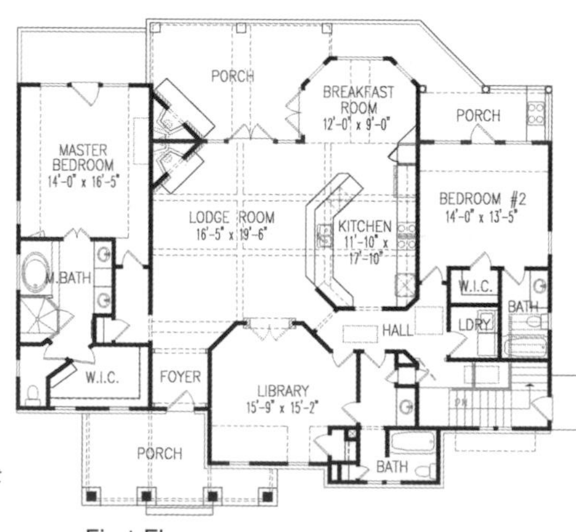

First Floor
1,997 sq. ft.

Plan #F08-055D-0748

Dimensions: 67'2" W x 55'10" D
Heated Sq. Ft.: 2,525
Bedrooms: 4 **Bathrooms:** 3
Foundation: Crawl space or slab standard; basement or daylight basement for an additional fee

See index for more information

Features

- This expansive one-story design has the split-bedroom floor plan everyone loves
- Stunning columns frame the foyer that leads into the open great room with fireplace, as well as the home theater/living room located right off of the foyer
- The formal dining room, casual breakfast room, and large grilling porch with fireplace provide an abundance of locations for dining opportunities
- Three bedrooms and two baths occupy one side of this home, while the master suite is secluded on the other
- 2-car front entry garage

Images provided by designer/architect

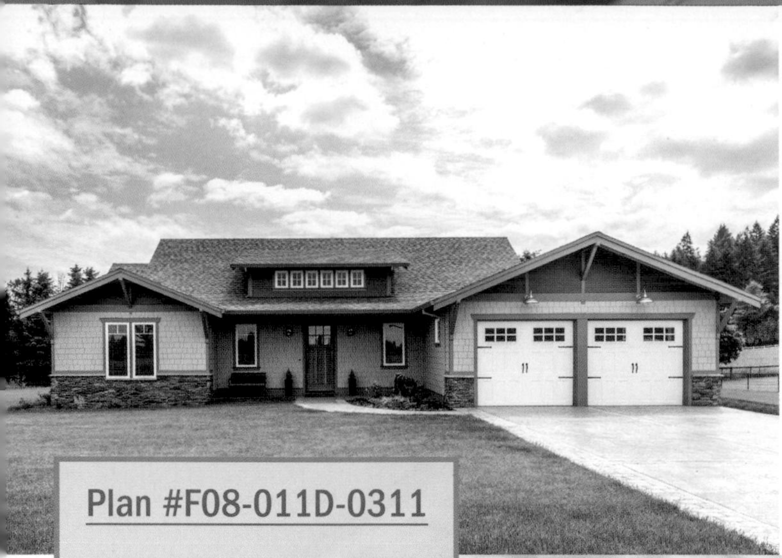

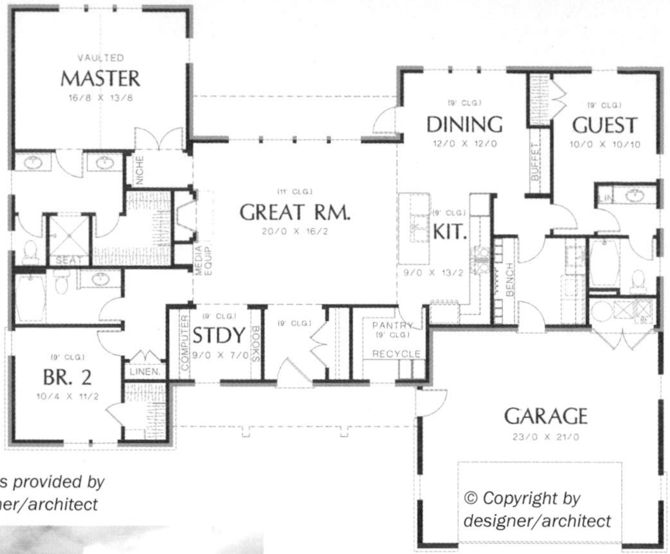

Images provided by designer/architect

© Copyright by designer/architect

Plan #F08-011D-0311

Dimensions: 64' W x 54' D
Heated sq. ft.: 1,988
Bedrooms: 3 **Bathrooms:** 3
Exterior Walls: 2" x 6"
Foundation: Crawl space or slab standard; basement for an additional fee

See index for more information

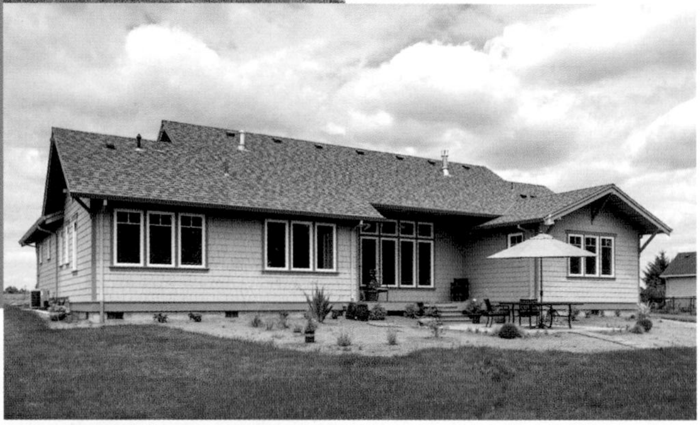

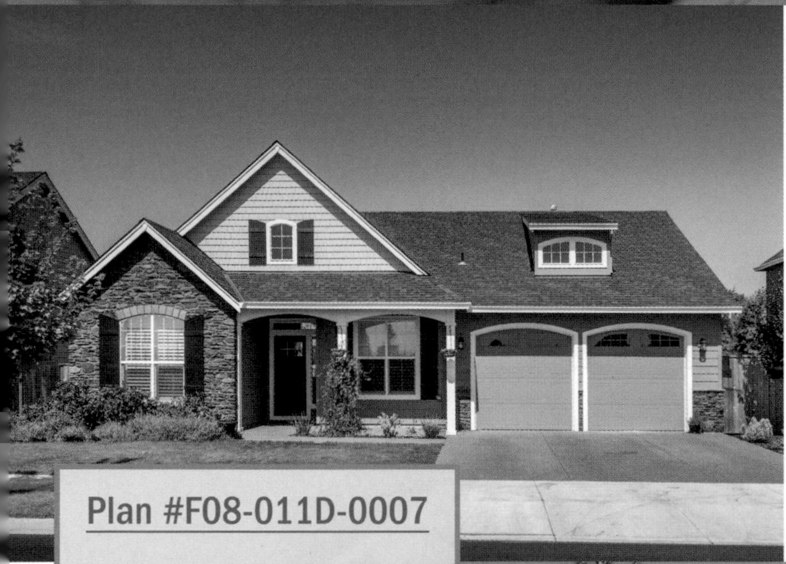

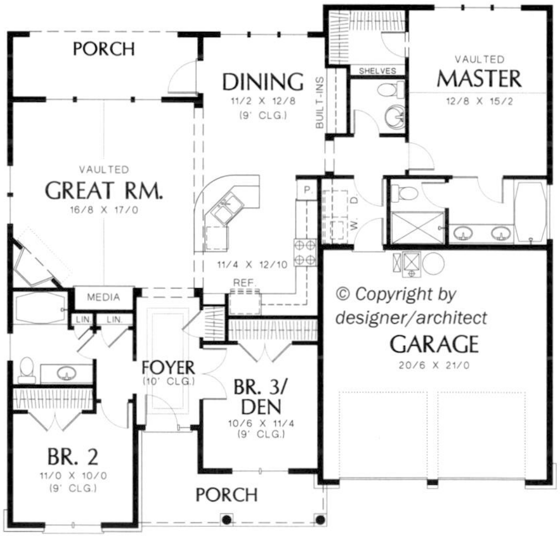

© Copyright by designer/architect

Images provided by designer/architect

Plan #F08-011D-0007

Dimensions: 50' W x 48' D
Heated Sq. Ft.: 1,580
Bedrooms: 3 **Bathrooms:** 2½
Exterior Walls: 2" x 6"
Foundation: Crawl space or slab standard; basement for an additional fee

See index for more information

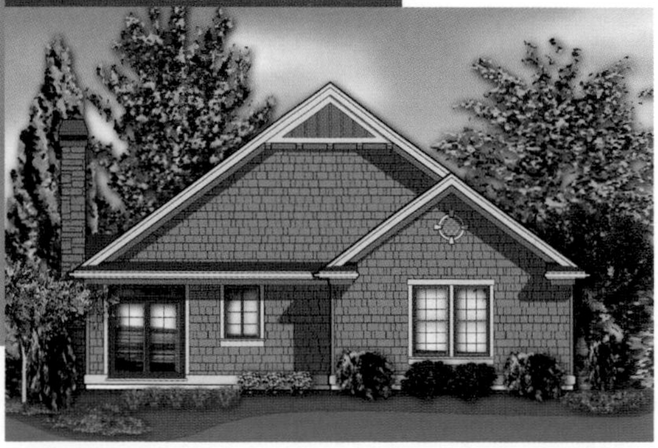

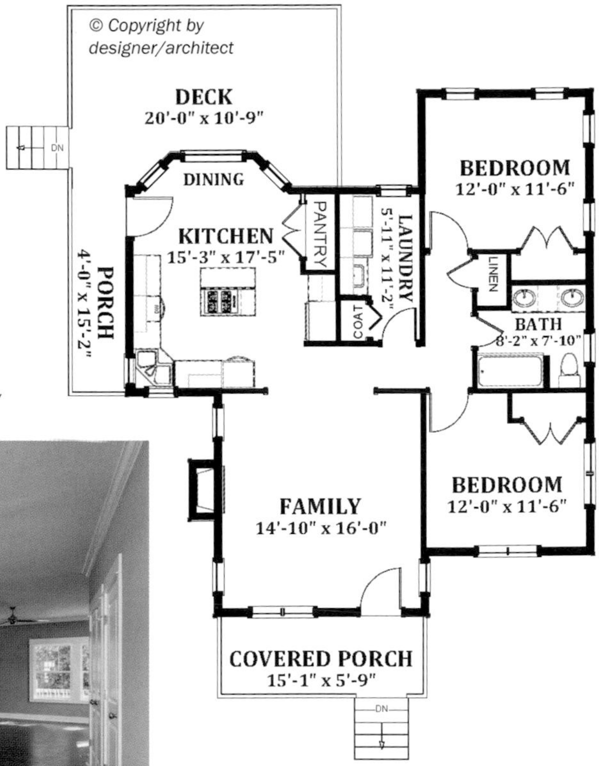

Images provided by designer/architect

Plan #F08-139D-0001

Dimensions: 39'7" W x 51'9" D
Heated Sq. Ft.: 1,068
Bedrooms: 2 **Bathrooms:** 1
Exterior Walls: 2" x 6"
Foundation: Crawl space standard; slab, basement, daylight basement or walk-out basement for an additional fee

See index for more information

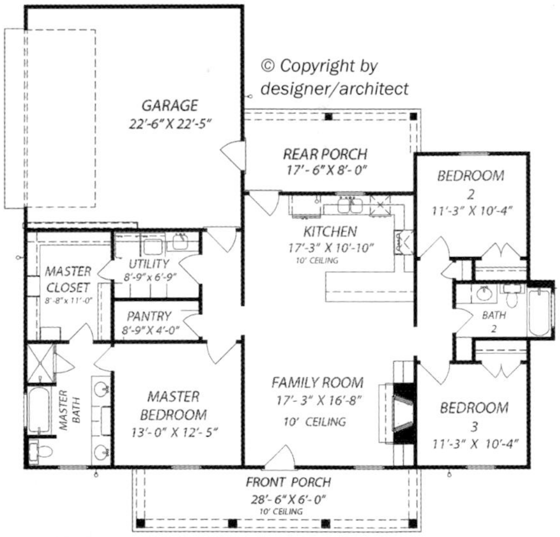

Images provided by designer/architect

Plan #F08-170D-0005

Dimensions: 54' W x 53' D
Heated Sq. Ft.: 1,422
Bedrooms: 3 **Bathrooms:** 2
Foundation: Slab or monolithic slab standard; crawl space, basement or daylight basement for an additional fee

See index for more information

Plan #F08-101D-0080

Dimensions: 79' W x 97'9" D
Heated Sq. Ft.: 2,682
Bonus Sq. Ft.: 1,940
Bedrooms: 2 **Bathrooms:** 2½
Exterior Walls: 2" x 6"
Foundation: Basement, daylight basement or walk-out basement, please specify when ordering

See index for more information

Images provided by designer/architect

Features

- This rambling ranch home typifies the best in design with unique architectural features
- A family can enjoy the outdoors with the expansive rear decks, one complete with a fireplace
- Private den with deck access is a secluded retreat
- The optional lower level has an additional 1,940 square feet of living area including three additional bedrooms, two baths, a laundry room, and rec room
- 3-car side entry garage

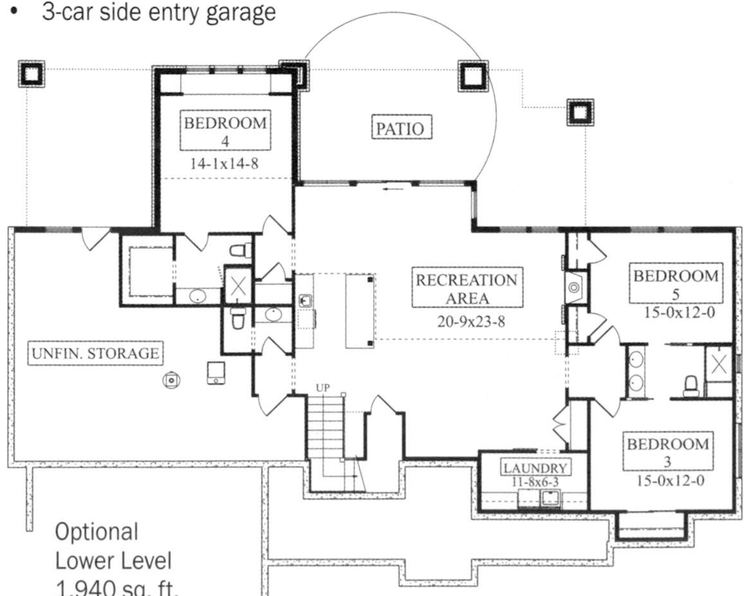

Optional
Lower Level
1,940 sq. ft.

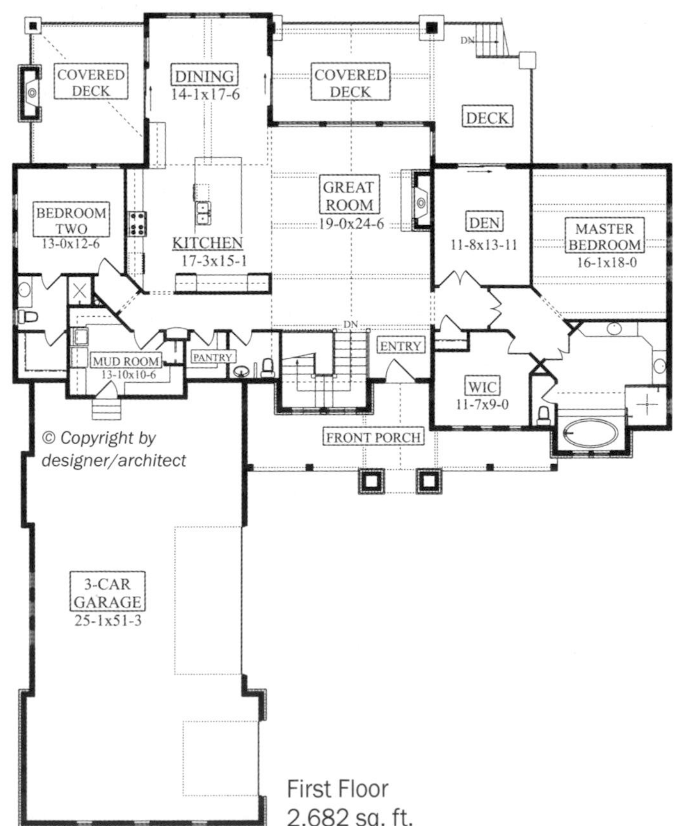

First Floor
2,682 sq. ft.

Plan #F08-032D-0813

Dimensions: 26' W x 26' D
Heated Sq. Ft.: 686
Bedrooms: 2 **Bathrooms:** 1
Exterior Walls: 2" x 6"
Foundation: Monolithic slab standard; crawl space or floating slab for an additional fee

See index for more information

Images provided by designer/architect

Plan #F08-170D-0001

Dimensions: 73' W x 73' D
Heated Sq. Ft.: 1,768
Bedrooms: 3 **Bathrooms:** 2
Foundation: Slab or monolithic slab standard; crawl space, basement or daylight basement for an additional fee

See index for more information

Images provided by designer/architect

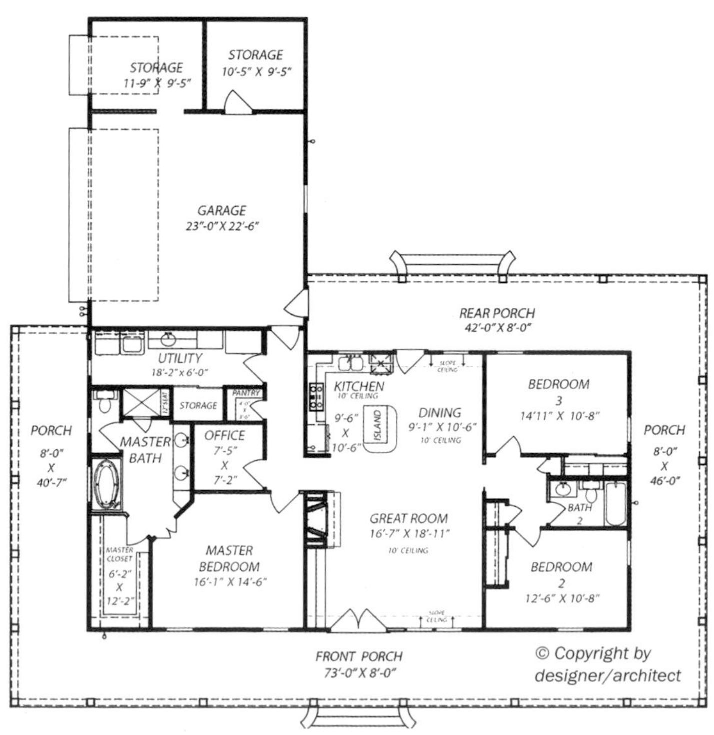

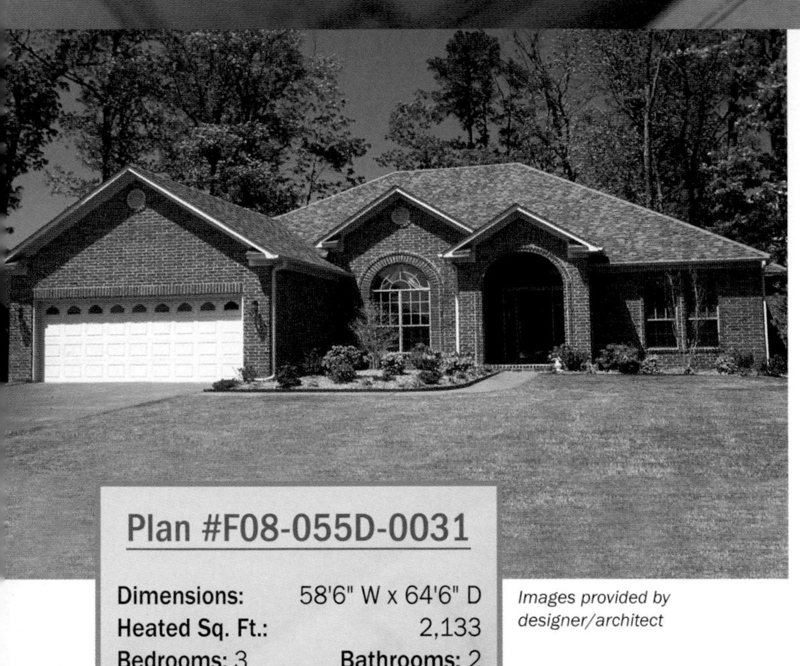

Plan #F08-055D-0031

Dimensions: 58'6" W x 64'6" D
Heated Sq. Ft.: 2,133
Bedrooms: 3 **Bathrooms:** 2
Foundation: Slab or crawl space standard; basement or daylight basement for an additional fee

See index for more information

Images provided by designer/architect

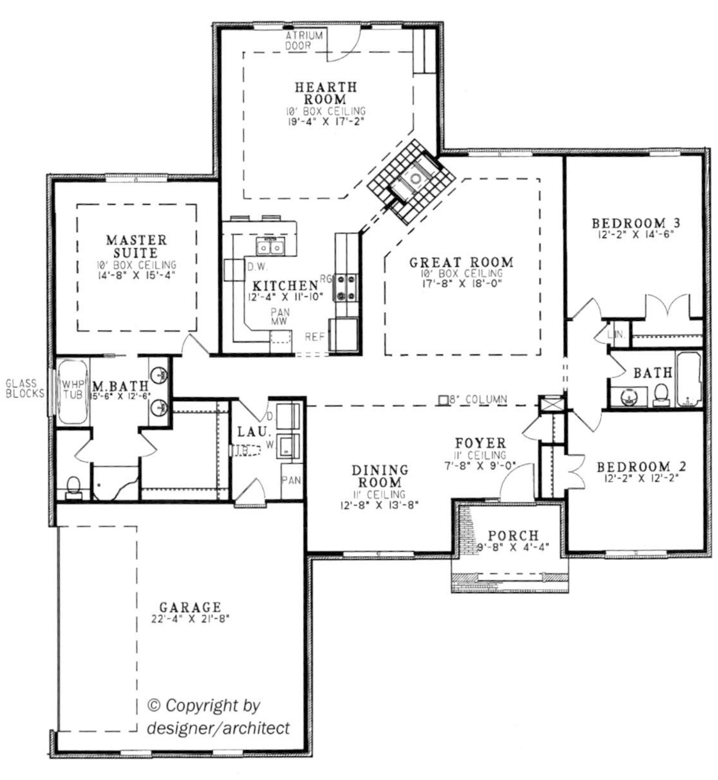

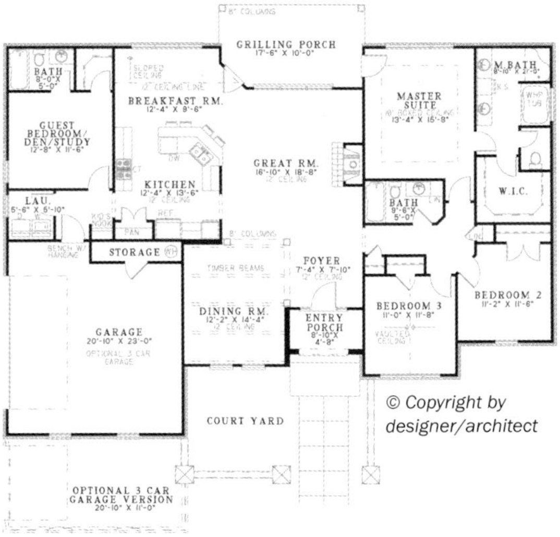

© Copyright by designer/architect

Plan #F08-055D-0790

Dimensions: 66' W x 52' D
Heated Sq. Ft.: 2,075
Bedrooms: 4 **Bathrooms:** 3
Foundation: Slab or crawl space standard; basement or daylight basement for an additional fee

See index for more information

Images provided by designer/architect

© Copyright by designer/architect

Plan #F08-019D-0046

Dimensions: 125'5" W x 76'1" D
Heated Sq. Ft.: 2,413
Bedrooms: 3 **Bathrooms:** 2½
Foundation: Slab standard; crawl space or basement for an additional fee

See index for more information

Images provided by designer/architect

Features

- This stunning Southwestern inspired home combines stone and stucco to create a home with tons of style and curb appeal
- The courtyard front entry offers a private escape for enjoying morning coffee or a cocktail at happy hour
- The grand great room is the main focal point as you enter the home thanks to its centered fireplace and tall ceiling with beams
- Off the kitchen is a handy flex room that could become a great home office, formal dining room or kid's play space
- The private master bedroom offers a luxurious environment for relaxing at the end of the day
- 3-car rear entry garage

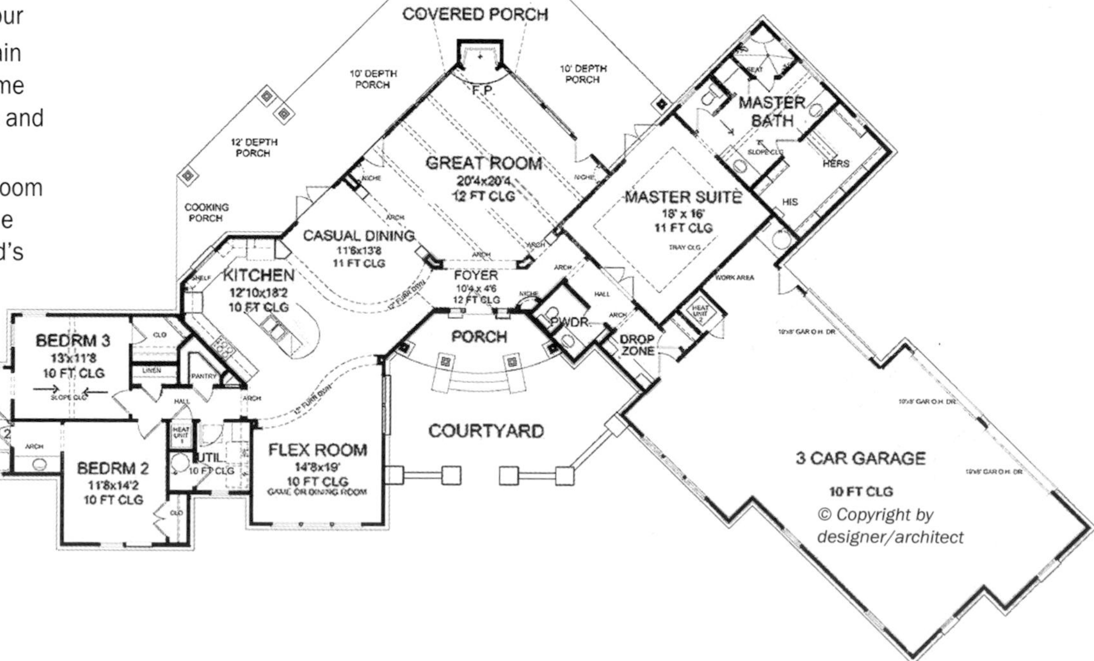

Plan #F08-144D-0023

Dimensions: 58' W x 32' D
Heated Sq. Ft.: 928
Bedrooms: 2 **Bathrooms:** 2
Exterior Walls: 2" x 6"
Foundation: Crawl space or slab, please specify when ordering

See index for more information

Features

- This Craftsman Modern home has an inviting entry with space for outdoor relaxation
- Enter the home and discover an open living room with a kitchen behind it
- The kitchen features a large breakfast bar with space for up to four people to dine comfortably
- To the right of the entry is the master bedroom with a large bath and walk-in closet
- A highly functional mud room/laundry area offers storage and convenience to the garage
- 2-car front entry garage

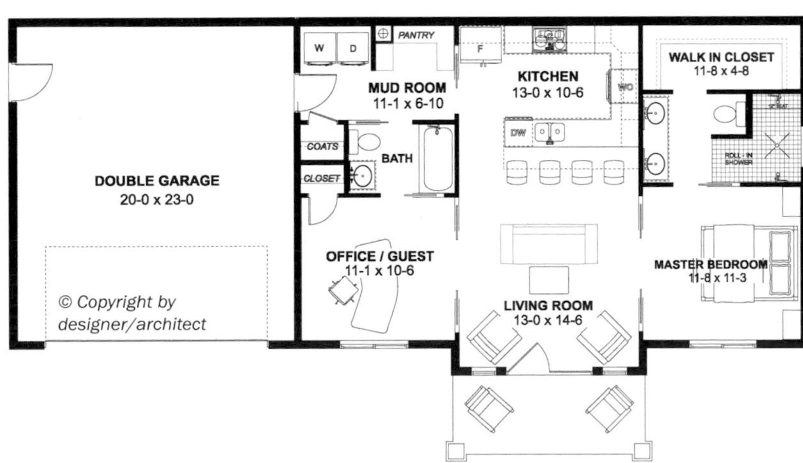

Images provided by designer/architect

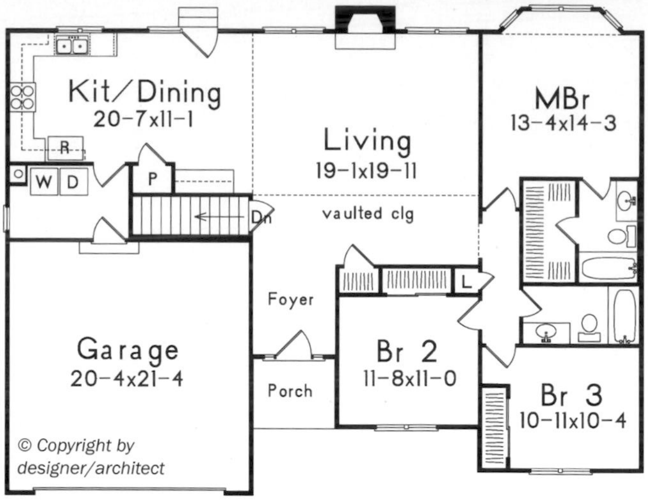

Kit/Dining
20-7x11-1
Living
19-1x19-11
vaulted clg
MBr
13-4x14-3
W D P R Dn
Foyer
Garage
20-4x21-4
Porch
Br 2
11-8x11-0
Br 3
10-11x10-4
L

© Copyright by designer/architect

Plan #F08-058D-0016

Dimensions: 54' W x 42' D
Heated Sq. Ft.: 1,558
Bedrooms: 3 **Bathrooms:** 2
Foundation: Basement

See index for more information

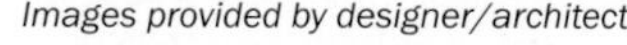

Images provided by designer/architect

OPTIONAL COVERED PATIO
Dining Area
$13^0 \times 11^0$
Family Room
$15^0 \times 18^4$
10'-0" CEILING
Owner's Suite
$13^0 \times 14^0$
10'-0" CEILING
R
Kit.
$13^0 \times 11^0$
P
DN
L
Br.3
$10^0 \times 11^0$
POCKET OFFICE
DROP ZONE
W D
Garage
$20^8 \times 22^0$
Br.2
$10^0 \times 12^0$

© Copyright by designer/architect

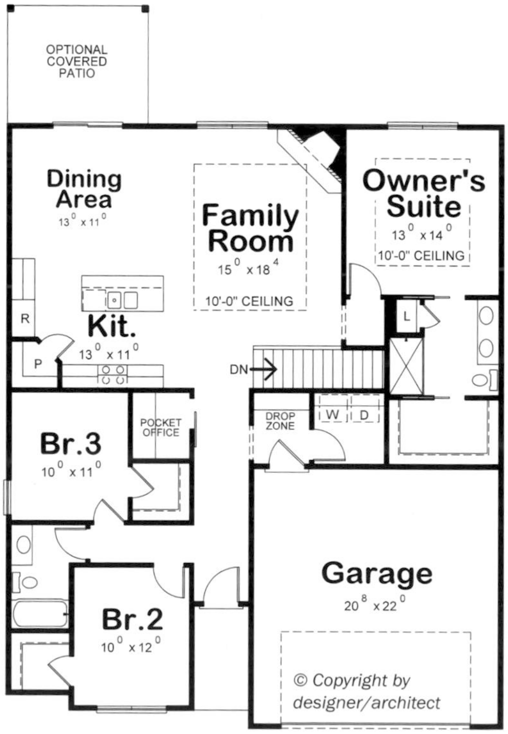

Plan #F08-026D-2091

Dimensions: 42' W x 51'4" D
Heated Sq. Ft.: 1,603
Bedrooms: 3 **Bathrooms:** 2
Foundation: Basement standard; crawl space, slab or walk-out basement for an additional fee

See index for more information

Images provided by designer/architect

© Copyright by designer/architect

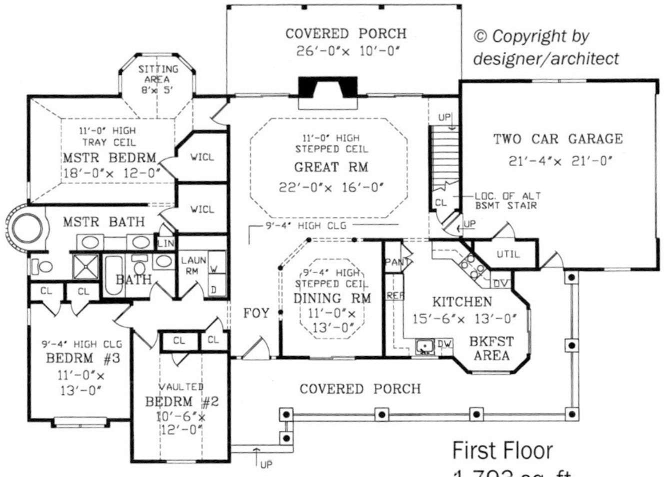

First Floor
1,793 sq. ft.

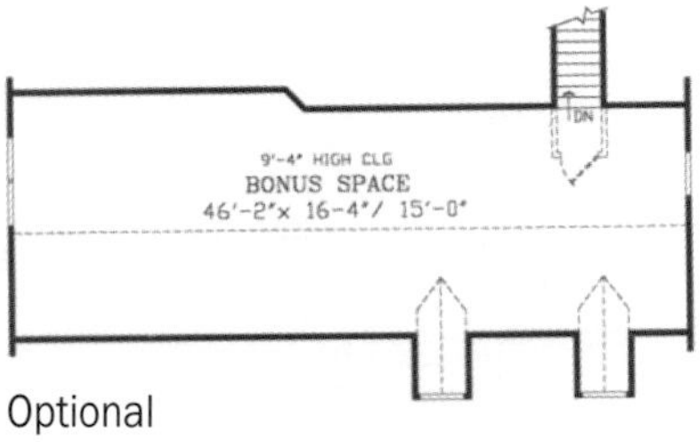

Optional Second Floor
779 sq. ft.

Images provided by designer/architect

Plan #F08-016D-0049

Dimensions: 69'10" W x 51'8" D
Heated Sq. Ft.: 1,793
Bonus Sq. Ft.: 779
Bedrooms: 3 **Bathrooms:** 2
Foundation: Crawl space or slab standard; basement for an additional fee

See index for more information

© Copyright by designer/architect

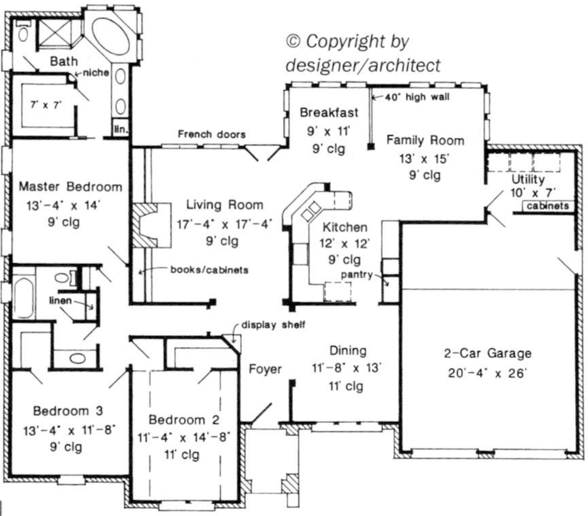

Plan #F08-137D-0223

Dimensions: 65'8" W x 56'6" D
Heated Sq. Ft.: 2,185
Bedrooms: 3 **Bathrooms:** 2
Foundation: Slab

Pricing subject to change

Images provided by designer/architect

Plan #F08-084D-0090

Dimensions: 73'6" W x 61' D
Heated Sq. Ft.: 2,221
Bonus Sq. Ft.: 403
Bedrooms: 4 **Bathrooms:** 2
Foundation: Slab standard; crawl space or basement for an additional fee

See index for more information

Images provided by designer/architect

Features

- If you're longing for today's hottest style home, then look no further, this is the home for you
- Step into the foyer and find a living/dining area open to the kitchen straight ahead
- On the left side of the home are three bedrooms and a full bath
- On the right side of the home you'll discover a private master bedroom and bath, a laundry room, and a mudroom for keeping everything organized
- The optional second floor has an additional 403 square feet of living area
- 2-car side entry garage

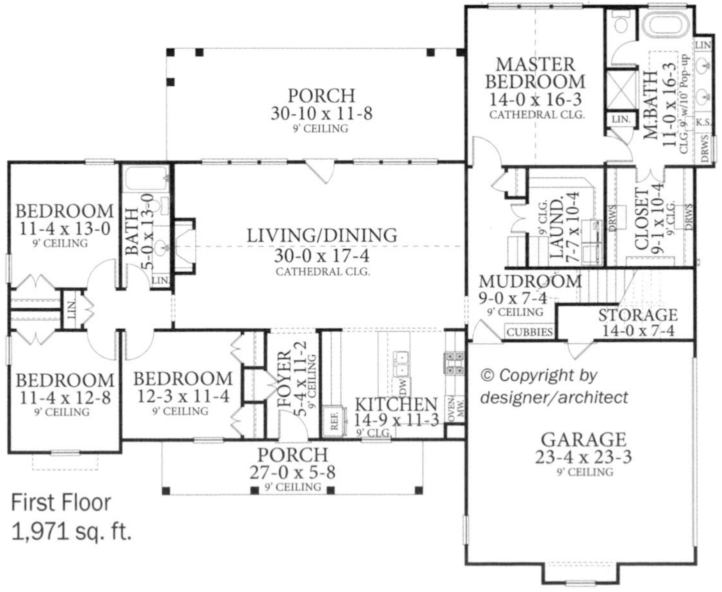

First Floor
1,971 sq. ft.

Optional
Second Floor
403 sq. ft.

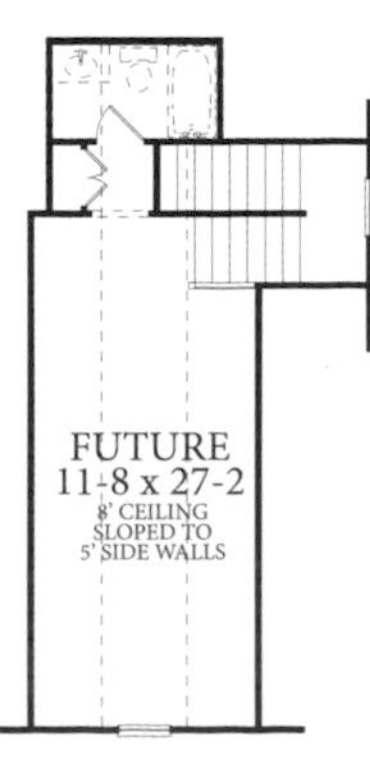

Plan #F08-170D-0006

Dimensions: 73'3" W x 84'8" D
Heated Sq. Ft.: 2,176
Bonus Sq. Ft.: 488
Bedrooms: 3 **Bathrooms:** 2
Foundation: Slab or monolithic slab standard; crawl space, basement or daylight basement for an additional fee

See index for more information

Images provided by designer/architect

Optional Second Floor
488 sq. ft.

First Floor
2,176 sq. ft.

Plan #F08-055D-0194

Dimensions: 38'4" W x 68'6" D
Heated Sq. Ft.: 1,379
Bedrooms: 3 **Bathrooms:** 2
Foundation: Crawl space or slab, please specify when ordering

See index for more information

Images provided by designer/architect

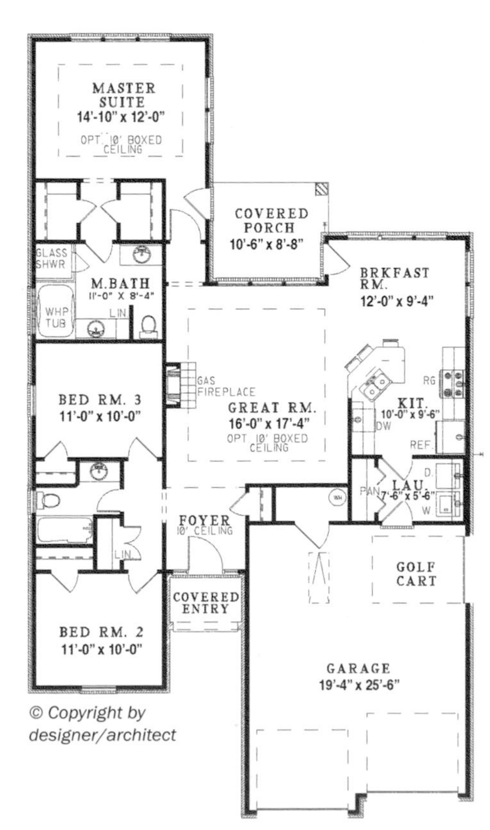

Plan #F08-111D-0032

Dimensions: 40' W x 37'6" D
Heated Sq. Ft.: 1,094
Bedrooms: 3 **Bathrooms:** 2
Foundation: Slab standard; crawl space or basement for an additional fee

See index for more information

Images provided by designer/architect

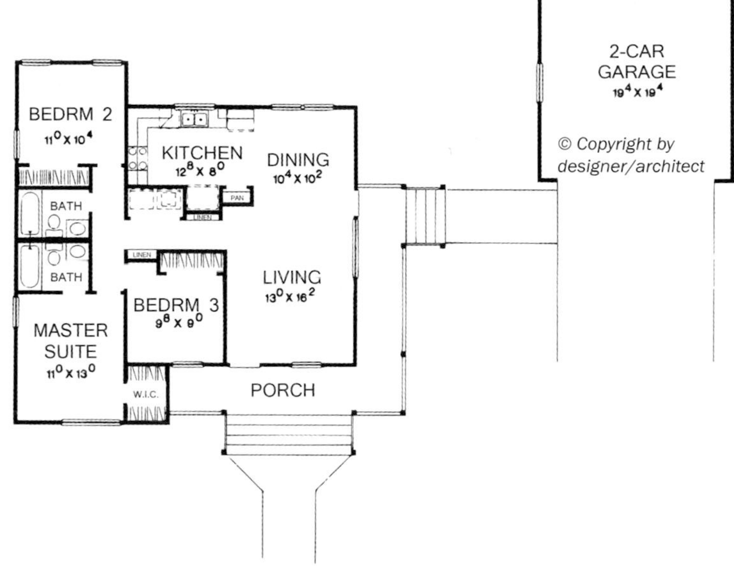

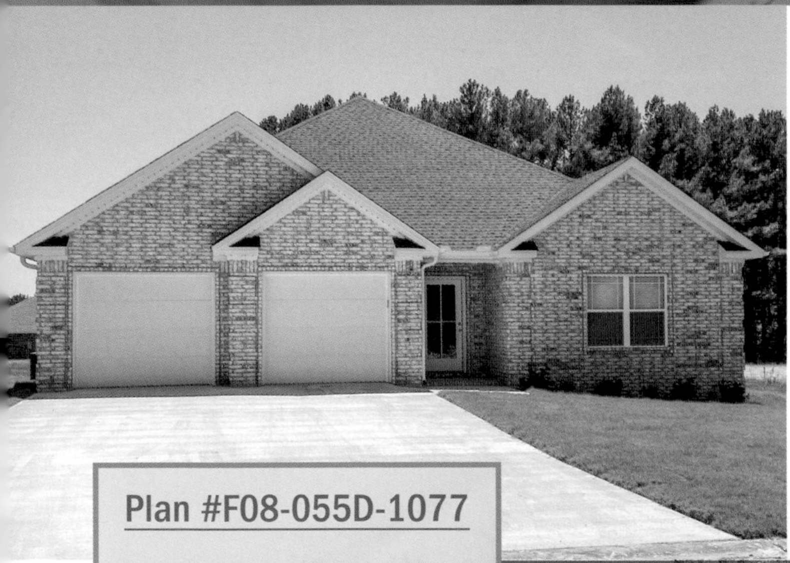

Plan #F08-055D-1077

Dimensions: 40'4" W x 60'2" D
Heated Sq. Ft.: 1,516
Bedrooms: 3 **Bathrooms:** 2
Foundation: Crawl space or slab standard; basement or daylight basement for an additional fee

See index for more information

Images provided by designer/architect

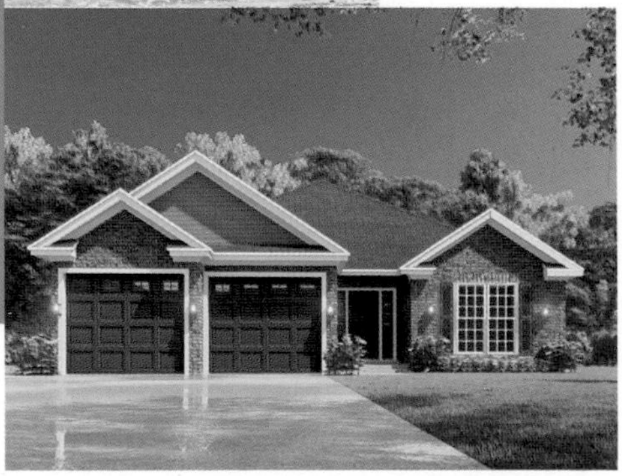

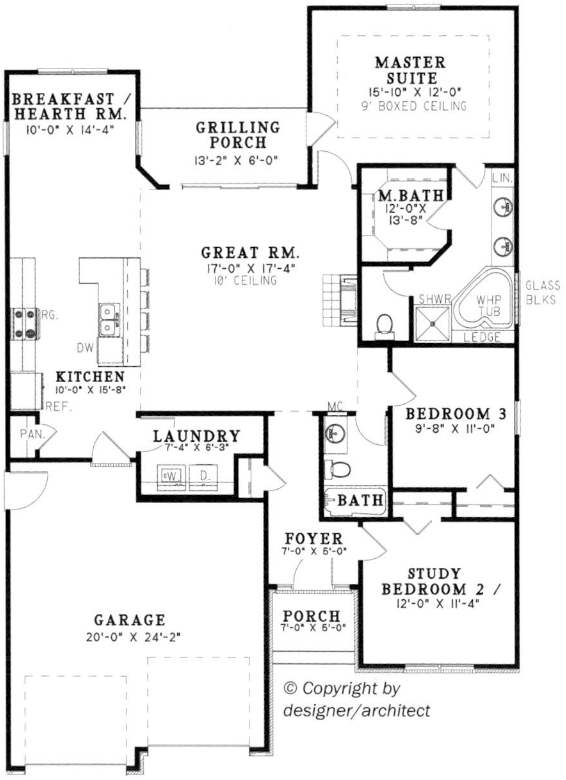

BREAKFAST / HEARTH RM.
10'-0" X 14'-4"
GRILLING PORCH
13'-2" X 6'-0"
MASTER SUITE
15'-10" X 12'-0"
9' BOXED CEILING
M.BATH
12'-0" X 13'-8"
LIN.
GREAT RM.
17'-0" X 17'-4"
10' CEILING
SHWR
WHP TUB
GLASS BLKS
LEDGE
RG.
DW
KITCHEN
10'-0" X 15'-8"
REF.
PAN.
LAUNDRY
7'-4" X 6'-3"
W D
MC
BEDROOM 3
9'-8" X 11'-0"
BATH
FOYER
7'-0" X 5'-0"
STUDY BEDROOM 2 /
12'-0" X 11'-4"
GARAGE
20'-0" X 24'-2"
PORCH
7'-0" X 5'-0"
© Copyright by designer/architect

Plan #F08-155D-0047

Dimensions: 60' W x 80'4" D
Heated Sq. Ft.: 2,500
Bonus Sq. Ft.: 354
Bedrooms: 3 **Bathrooms:** 2½
Foundation: Crawl space or slab, please specify when ordering

See index for more information

Features

- Modern Farmhouse touches grace the interior of this attractive rustic-looking ranch home
- The vaulted great room has a centered fireplace directly across from the island in the kitchen creating an intimate and cozy feel
- The master suite boasts a bath with a free-standing tub, a separate shower, a double-sink vanity, and a huge walk-in closet with built-ins
- Two additional bedrooms share a full bath
- The optional second floor has an additional 354 square feet of living area
- 2-car front entry garage

Optional
Second Floor
354 sq. ft.

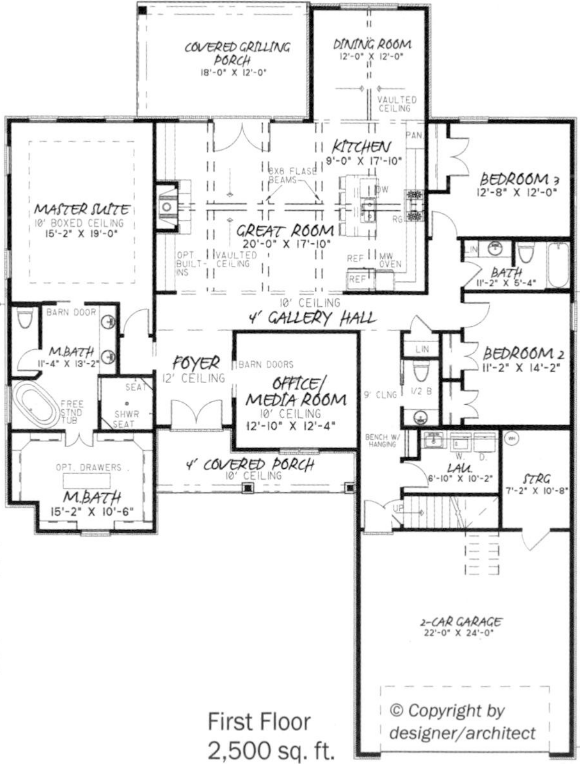

First Floor
2,500 sq. ft.

Images provided by designer/architect

Plan #F08-101D-0206

Dimensions: 78'6" W x 90'6" D
Heated Sq. Ft.: 2,766
Bonus Sq. Ft.: 1,340
Bedrooms: 2 **Bathrooms:** 2½
Foundation: Walk-out basement

See index for more information

Images provided by designer/architect

Features

- This home has an open interior that feels airy and spacious thanks to the large window wall in the great room
- The kitchen is equipped with a huge island overlooking the great room
- The owner's suite enjoys a private bath and walk-in closet
- Off the front hall is a notable den that's ideal for a quick zoom meeting or home office
- A massive walk-in pantry keeps the kitchen clutter-free which is always appreciated
- The optional lower level has an additional 1,340 square feet of living area including a family room with wet bar, a music room, and a guest bedroom with bath
- 1-car front entry garage, and a 2-car side entry garage

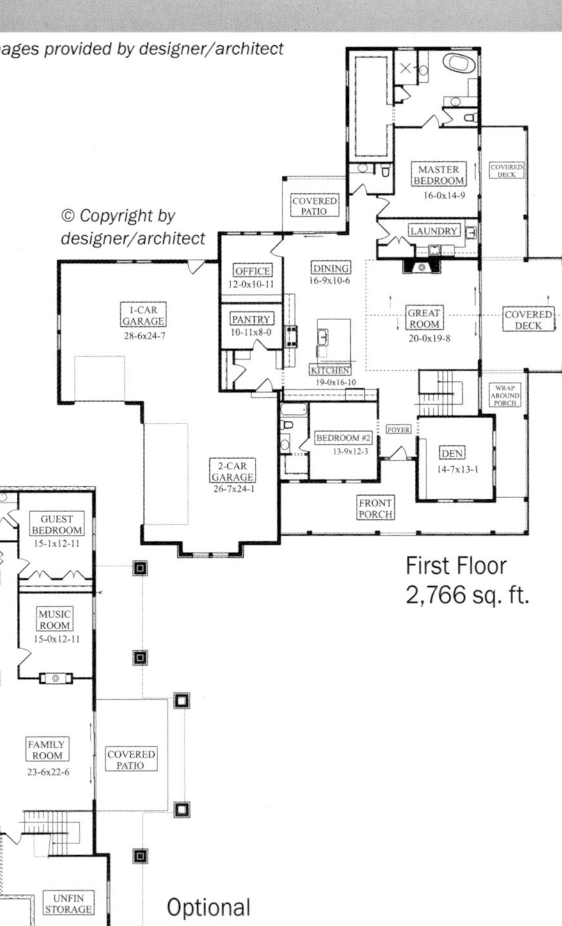

First Floor
2,766 sq. ft.

Optional
Lower Level
1,340 sq. ft.

Plan #F08-141D-0061

Dimensions: 46' W x 46' D
Heated Sq. Ft.: 1,273
Bedrooms: 2 **Bathrooms:** 2
Foundation: Crawl space standard; slab, basement or walk-out basement for an additional fee

See index for more information

Images provided by designer/architect

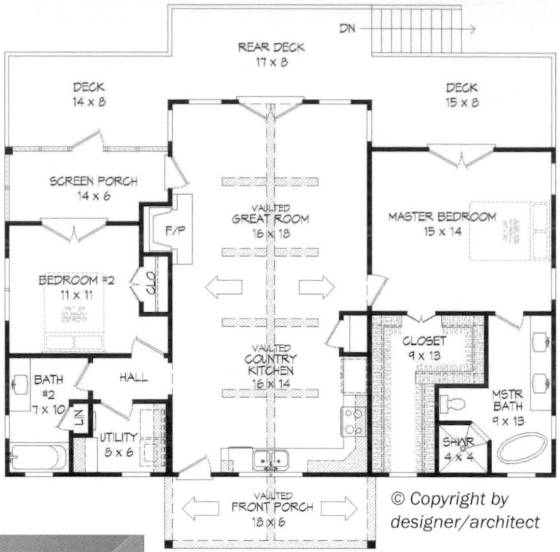

© Copyright by designer/architect

Plan #F08-084D-0016

Dimensions: 56' W x 45'8" D
Heated Sq. Ft.: 1,492
Bedrooms: 3 **Bathrooms:** 2
Foundation: Slab standard; crawl space or basement for an additional fee

See index for more information

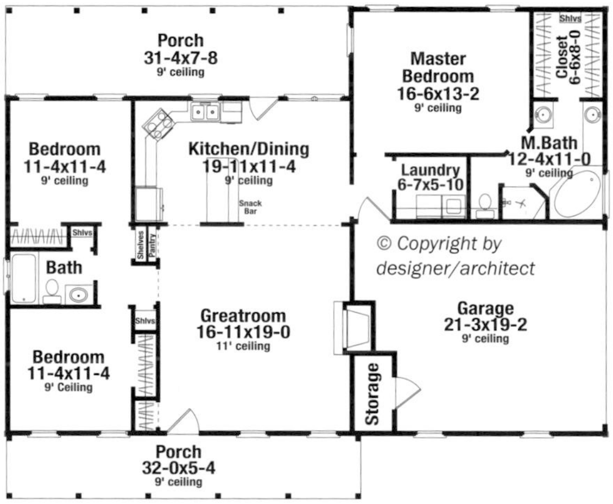

Images provided by designer/architect

© Copyright by designer/architect

Plan #F08-011D-0335

Images provided by designer/architect

Dimensions: 78' W x 62'6" D
Heated Sq. Ft.: 2,557
Bedrooms: 3 **Bathrooms:** 2½
Exterior Walls: 2" x 6"
Foundation: Crawl space or slab standard; basement for an additional fee

See index for more information

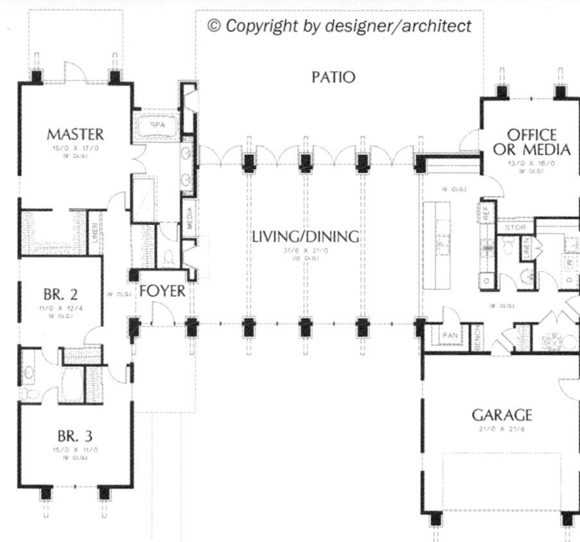

Plan #F08-111D-0058

Images provided by designer/architect

Dimensions: 38'11" W x 68'5" D
Heated Sq. Ft.: 1,674
Bedrooms: 3 **Bathrooms:** 2
Foundation: Slab standard; crawl space for an additional fee

See index for more information

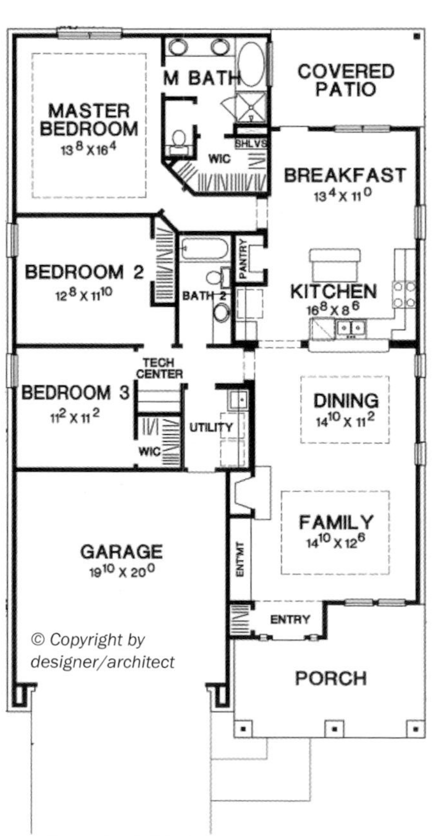

Plan #F08-019S-0008

Dimensions: 104'3" W x 80'8" D
Heated Sq. Ft.: 4,420
Bedrooms: 4
Bathrooms: 4 full, 2 half
Foundation: Slab standard; crawl space or basement for an additional fee

See index for more information

Features

- This sprawling Craftsman accented ranch has an open foyer that merges with the vaulted great room
- The study is near the entry foyer and convenient to a half bath
- The open island kitchen faces towards the great room and has a casual dining area to its side
- Behind the kitchen you'll find a media room for movie night and a game room perfect for playing cards or billiards
- A covered porch with a built-in kitchen and fireplace is bound to be everyone's favorite space regardless of the season
- The master bedroom and bath are filled with luxury including plenty of closetspace
- 3-car side entry garage

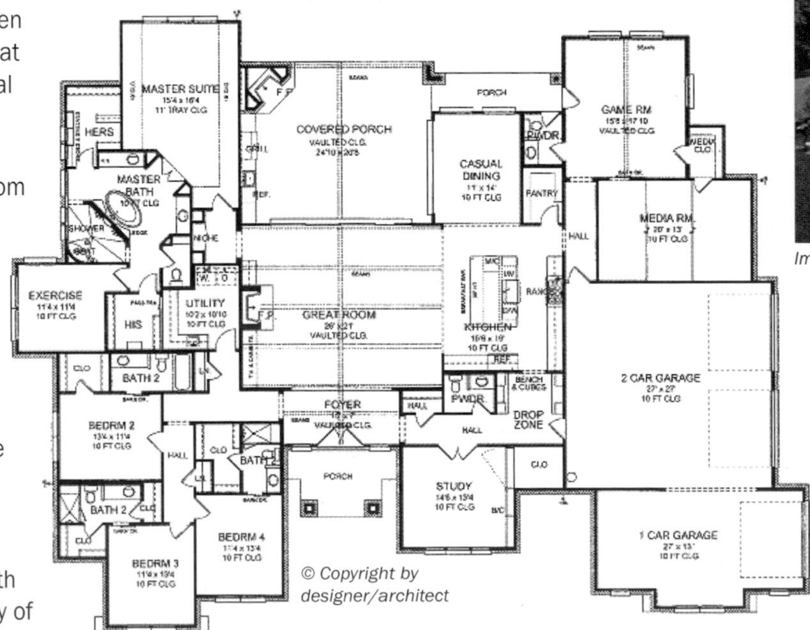

© Copyright by designer/architect

Images provided by designer/architect

Plan #F08-084D-0092

Dimensions:	58' W x 80'2" D
Heated Sq. Ft.:	2,366
Bonus Sq. Ft.:	809
Bedrooms: 3	**Bathrooms:** 2

Foundation: Slab standard; basement or crawl space for an additional fee

See index for more information

Images provided by designer/architect

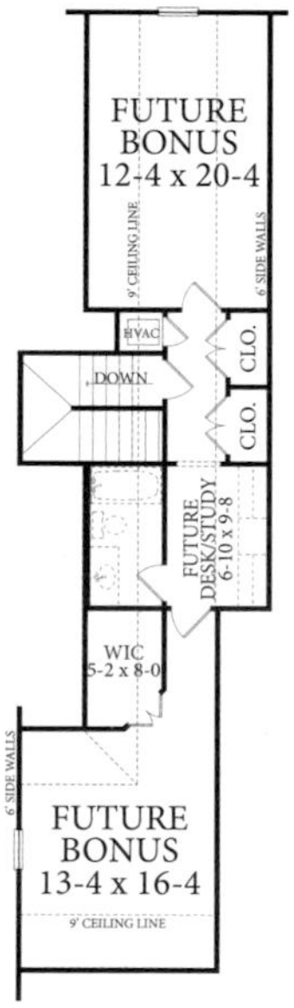

Optional Second Floor 809 sq. ft.

FUTURE BONUS 12-4 x 20-4

FUTURE DESK/STUDY 6-10 x 9-8

WIC 5-2 x 8-0

FUTURE BONUS 13-4 x 16-4

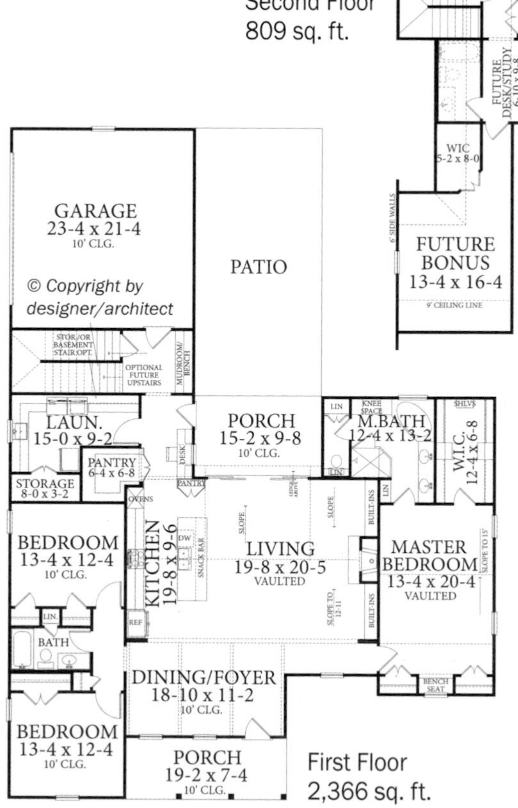

First Floor 2,366 sq. ft.

Features

- This stylish Farmhouse design has that wide open style floor plan that makes a home feel so much larger
- The kitchen island overlooks the vaulted living area for a great combined space for everyday relaxing or entertaining
- A large walk-in pantry and a spacious laundry room with storage add organization
- The master bedroom has a bench seat for character, a plush bath and a walk-in closet
- The optional second floor has an additional 809 square feet of living area
- 2-car side entry garage

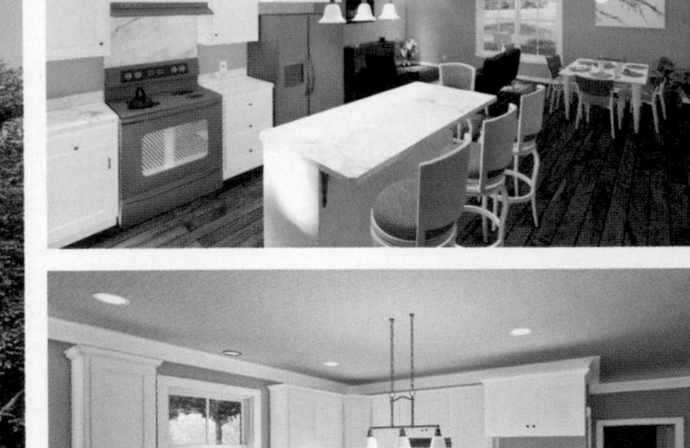

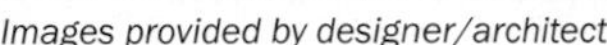

Images provided by designer/architect

Plan #F08-028D-0116

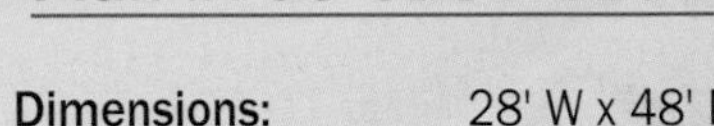

Dimensions: 28' W x 48' D
Heated Sq. Ft.: 1,120
Bedrooms: 2 **Bathrooms:** 2
Exterior Walls: 2" x 6"
Foundation: Floating slab standard; monolithic slab, crawl space, basement or walk-out basement for an additional fee

See index for more information

Features

- Spacious and open this home's interior feels much larger than its true size thanks to the absence of walls between spaces
- The kitchen features a sizable island with seating for up to four people
- Two symmetrical bedrooms and baths comprise the rear of the home and offer equal amenities
- The laundry room has a handy sink and outdoor access
- The great room/dining area extend off the kitchen and provide a quality open living concept

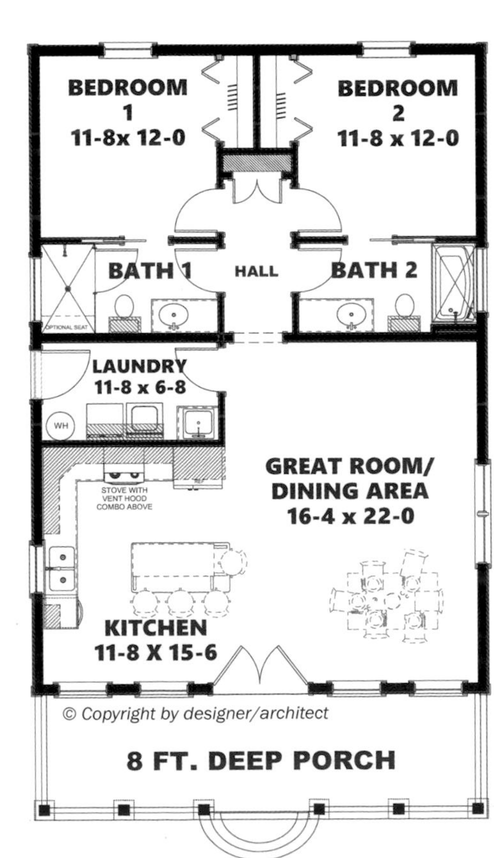

Plan #F08-032D-1124

Dimensions: 66' W x 50' D
Heated Sq. Ft.: 2,117
Bonus Sq. Ft.: 360
Bedrooms: 3 **Bathrooms:** 2
Exterior Walls: 2" x 6"
Foundation: Crawl space standard; floating slab, monolithic slab, basement or walk-out basement for an additional fee

See index for more information

Features

- This Modern Farmhouse inspired one-story has an open and split bedroom layout families love today
- Step into the foyer and be greeted by the formal dining room on the left and straight ahead the vaulted living room and open kitchen
- The master suite and bath enjoy two walk-in closets, a double vanity, a walk-in oversized shower and a freestanding tub as the focal point
- Two secondary bedrooms on the opposite side of the home share a full bath
- The optional second floor has an additional 360 square feet of living area
- 2-car front entry garage

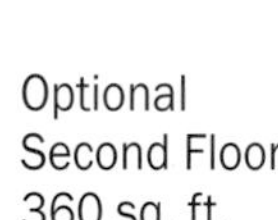

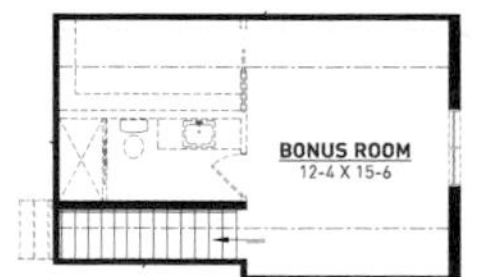

Optional
Second Floor
360 sq. ft.

First Floor
2,117 sq. ft.

Images provided by designer/architect

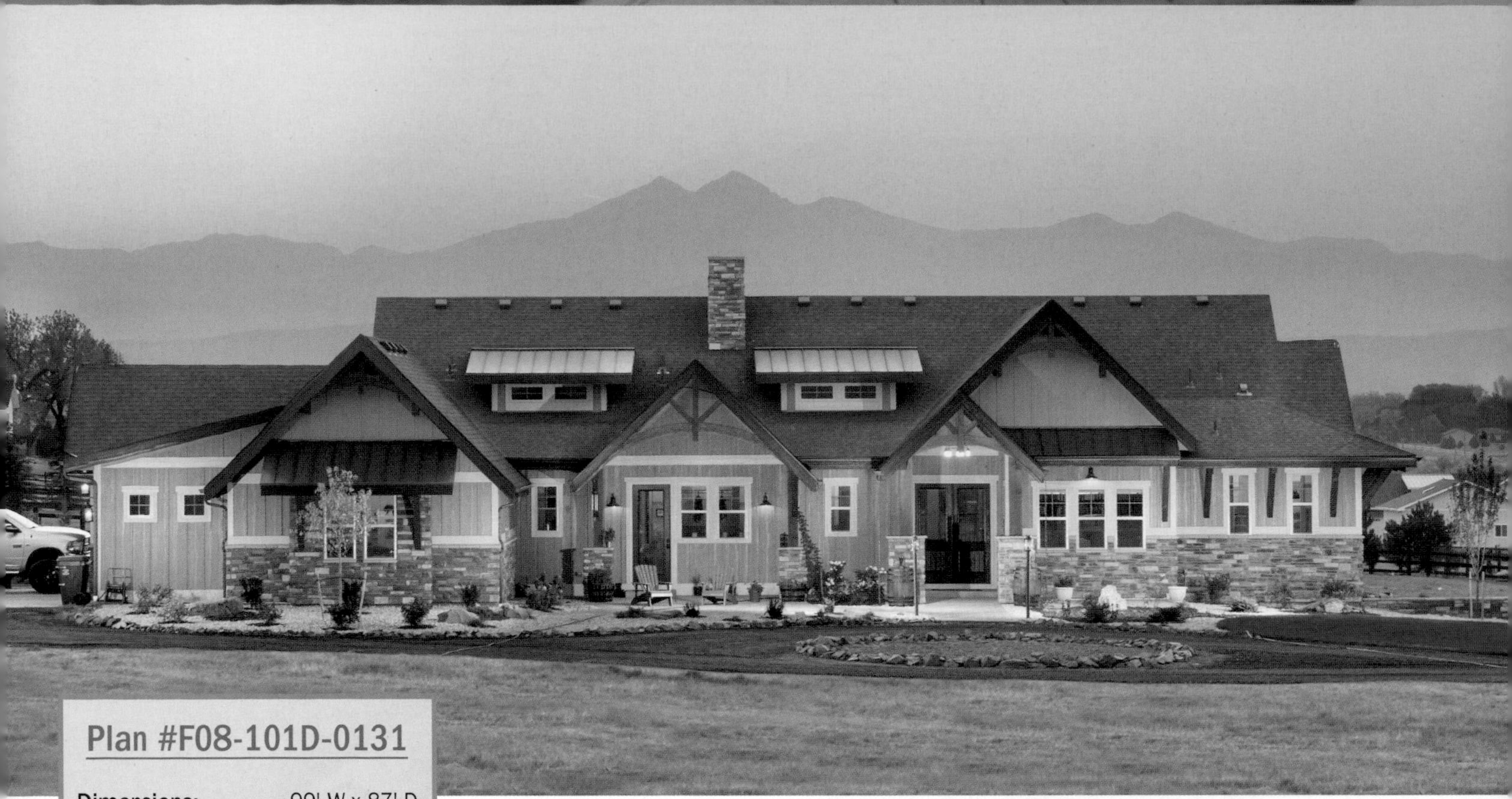

Plan #F08-101D-0131

Dimensions:	99' W x 87' D
Heated Sq. Ft.:	2,889
Bonus Sq. Ft.:	2,561
Bedrooms: 2	**Bathrooms:** 2½
Exterior Walls:	2" x 6"
Foundation:	Walk-out basement

See index for more information

Images provided by designer/architect

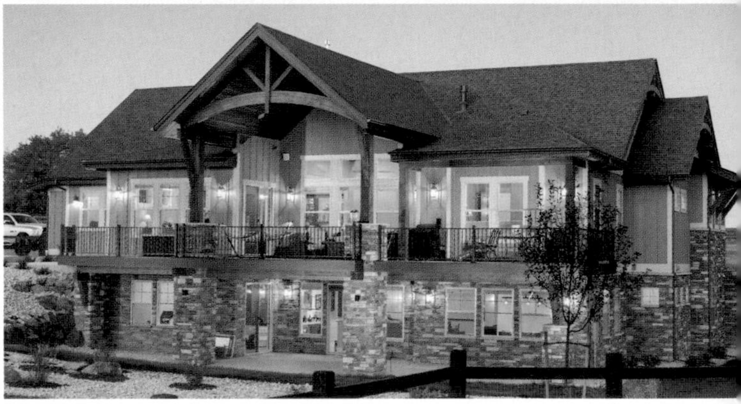

Features

- This gorgeous Craftsman home is stunning on the exterior, but just as beautiful on the interior with its rustic and modern twist
- The first floor has an open kitchen, living room and dining area, a private den and master bedroom suite, and an enormous mud room and pantry that will be the envy of the neighborhood
- The lower level has a bunk room, media area, bar, exercise room, and an extra laundry room
- The optional lower level has an additional 2,561 square feet of living area
- 3-car side entry garage

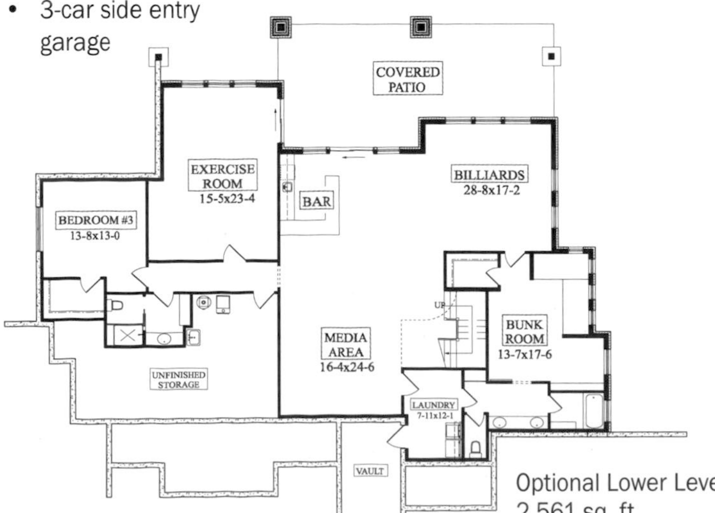

Optional Lower Level
2,561 sq. ft.

© Copyright by designer/architect

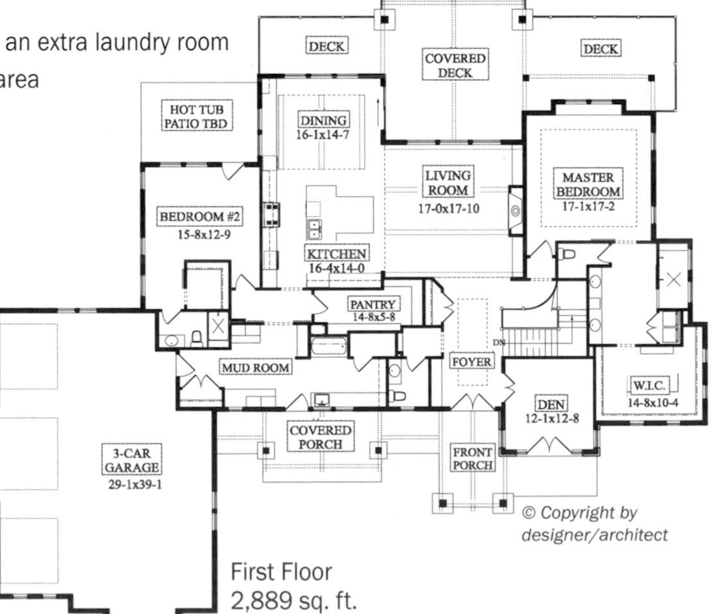

First Floor
2,889 sq. ft.

Plan #F08-056D-0102

Dimensions: 59' W x 52' D
Heated Sq. Ft.: 1,861
Bonus Sq. Ft.: 215
Bedrooms: 3 **Bathrooms:** 2
Foundation: Basement standard; crawl space or slab for an additional fee

See index for more information

Images provided by designer/architect

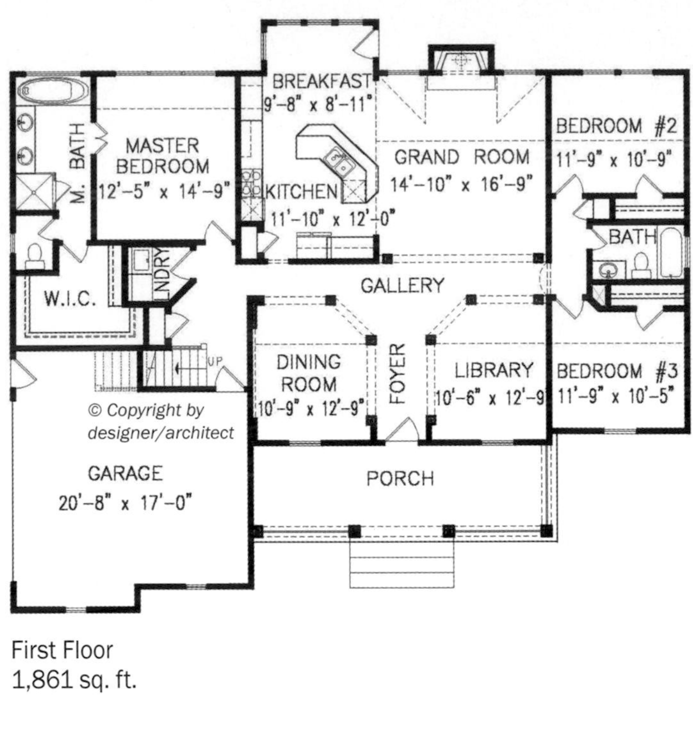

First Floor
1,861 sq. ft.

Optional
Second Floor
215 sq. ft.

Plan #F08-026D-1889

Dimensions: 62' W x 48' D
Heated Sq. Ft.: 1,763
Bedrooms: 3 **Bathrooms:** 2½
Foundation: Basement standard; crawl space, slab or walk-out basement for an additional fee

See index for more information

Images provided by designer/architect

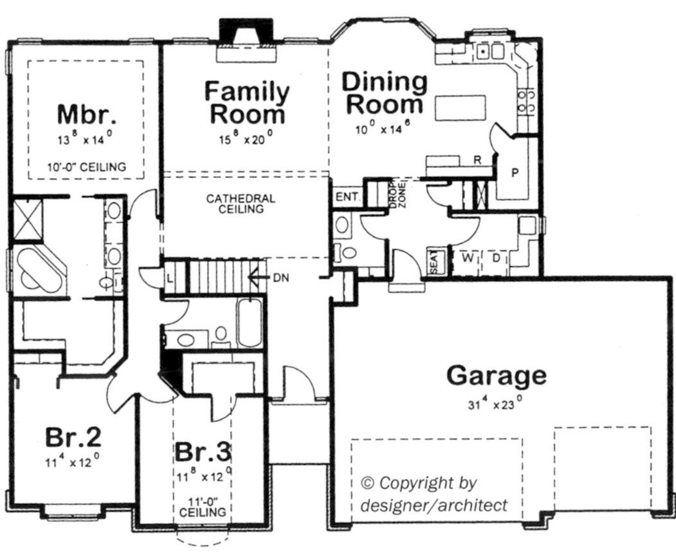

Plan #F08-013D-0022

Dimensions: 66'2" W x 62' D
Heated Sq. Ft.: 1,992
Bonus Sq. Ft.: 299
Bedrooms: 4 **Bathrooms:** 3
Foundation: Basement standard; crawl space or slab for an additional fee

See index for more information

Images provided by designer/architect

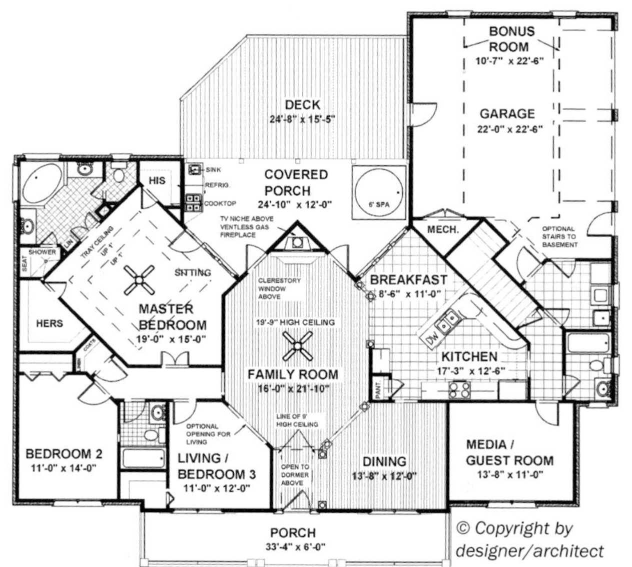

© Copyright by designer/architect

Plan #F08-052D-0160

Dimensions: 66' W x 64' D
Heated Sq. Ft.: 2,160
Bonus Sq. Ft.: 2,549
Bedrooms: 4 **Bathrooms:** 2
Foundation: Walk-out basement

See index for more information

Images provided by designer/architect

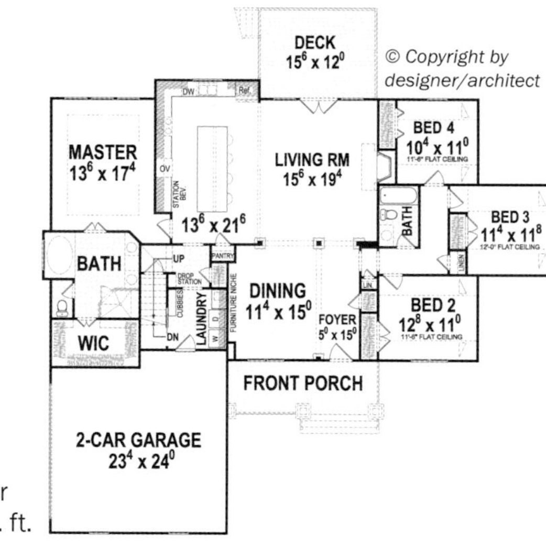

© Copyright by designer/architect

First Floor
2,160 sq. ft.

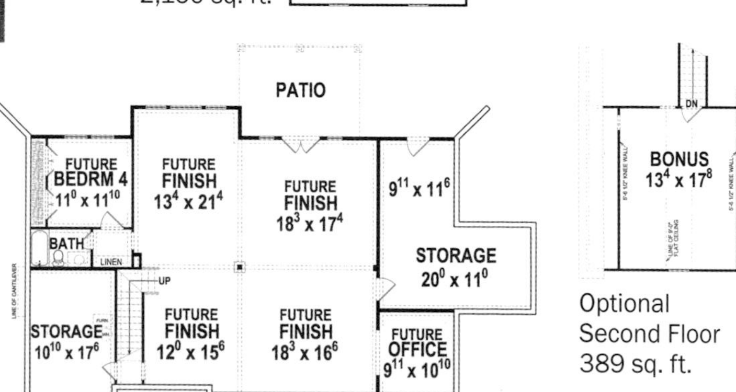

Optional Lower Level
2,160 sq. ft.

Optional Second Floor
389 sq. ft.

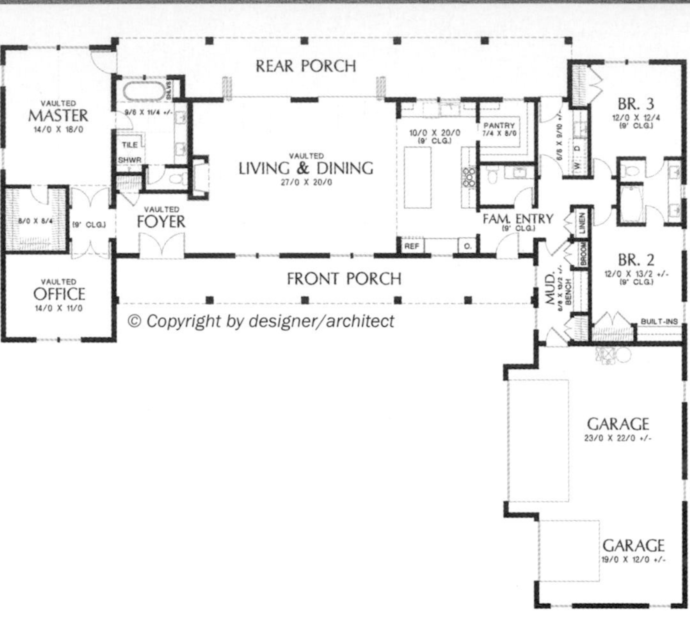

Plan #F08-011D-0630

Dimensions: 90' W x 75' D
Heated Sq. Ft.: 2,495
Bedrooms: 3 **Bathrooms:** 2½
Exterior Walls: 2" x 6"
Foundation: Crawl space or slab standard; basement for an additional fee

See index for more information

Images provided by designer/architect

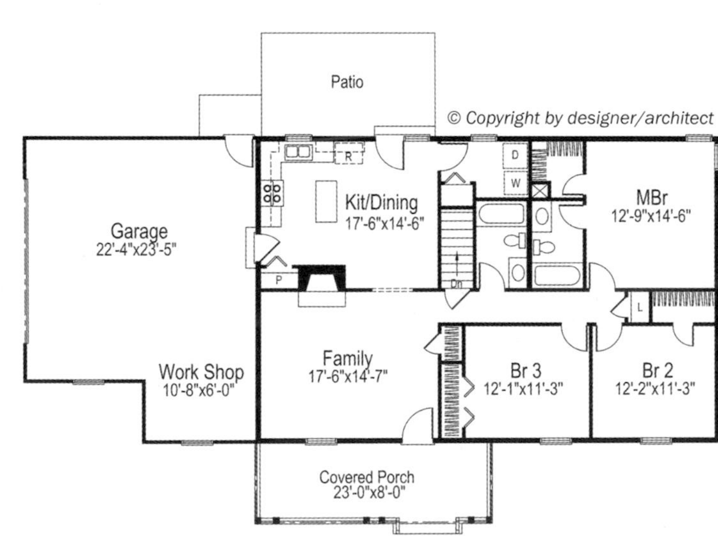

Plan #F08-001D-0024

Dimensions: 68' W x 38' D
Heated Sq. Ft.: 1,360
Bedrooms: 3 **Bathrooms:** 2
Foundation: Basement standard; slab or crawl space for an additional fee

See index for more information

Images provided by designer/architect

Plan #F08-013D-0134

Dimensions: 55' W x 58' D
Heated Sq. Ft.: 1,496
Bonus Sq. Ft.: 301
Bedrooms: 3 **Bathrooms:** 2
Foundation: Slab standard; crawl space or basement for an additional fee

See index for more information

Images provided by designer/architect

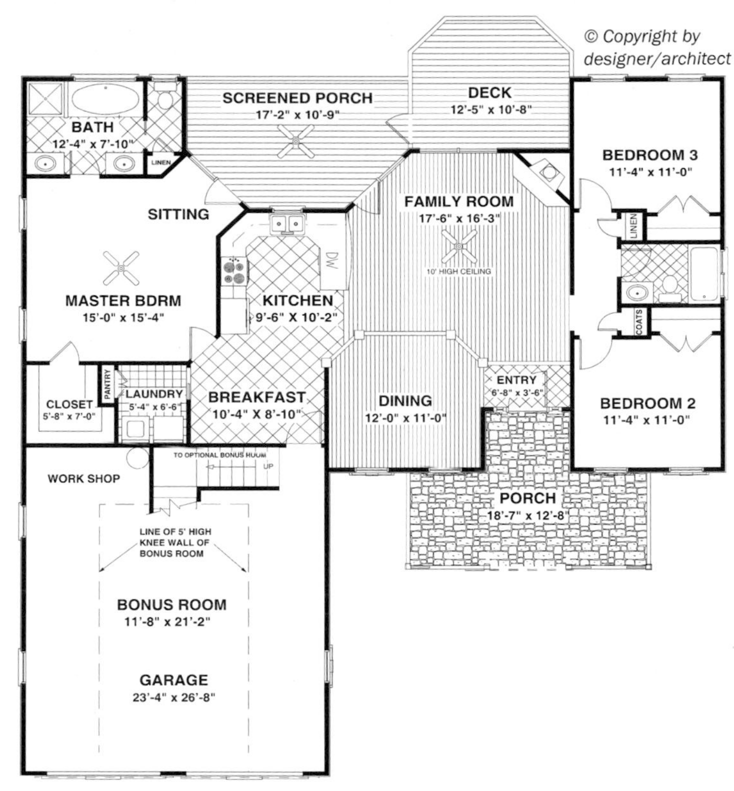

Plan #F08-121D-0046

Dimensions: 60' W x 61' D
Heated Sq. Ft.: 1,983
Bedrooms: 3 **Bathrooms:** 2½
Foundation: Basement standard; crawl space or slab for an additional fee

See index for more information

Images provided by designer/architect

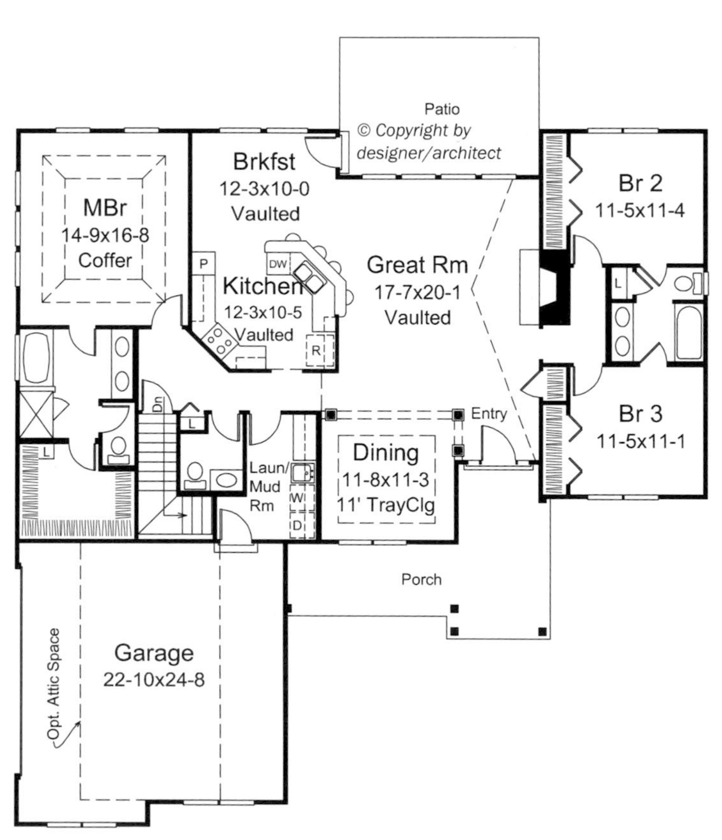

Plan #F08-056D-0120

Dimensions: 74'6" W x 65' D
Heated Sq. Ft.: 1,729
Bonus Sq. Ft.: 392
Bedrooms: 3 **Bathrooms:** 2
Foundation: Basement standard; crawl space or slab for an additional fee

See index for more information

Features

- The perfect sized Craftsman one-story home with privacy for the homeowners and plenty of space for guests or other family members
- Gorgeous rustic beams top the ceiling of the lodge room and provide an extra cozy atmosphere when paired with the fireplace
- The kitchen has an island overlooking the bayed breakfast area and beyond onto the covered porch with fireplace
- The master suite enjoys a beamed ceiling, and a posh bath with both an oversized tub and a walk-in shower
- The optional second floor has an additional 392 square feet of living area
- 2-car side entry garage

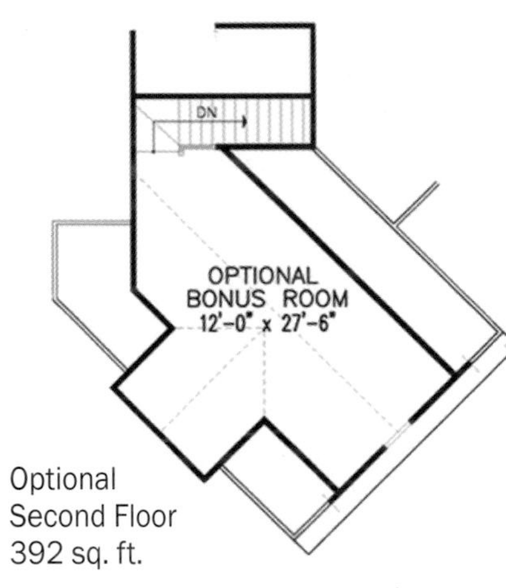

Optional
Second Floor
392 sq. ft.

Images provided by designer/architect

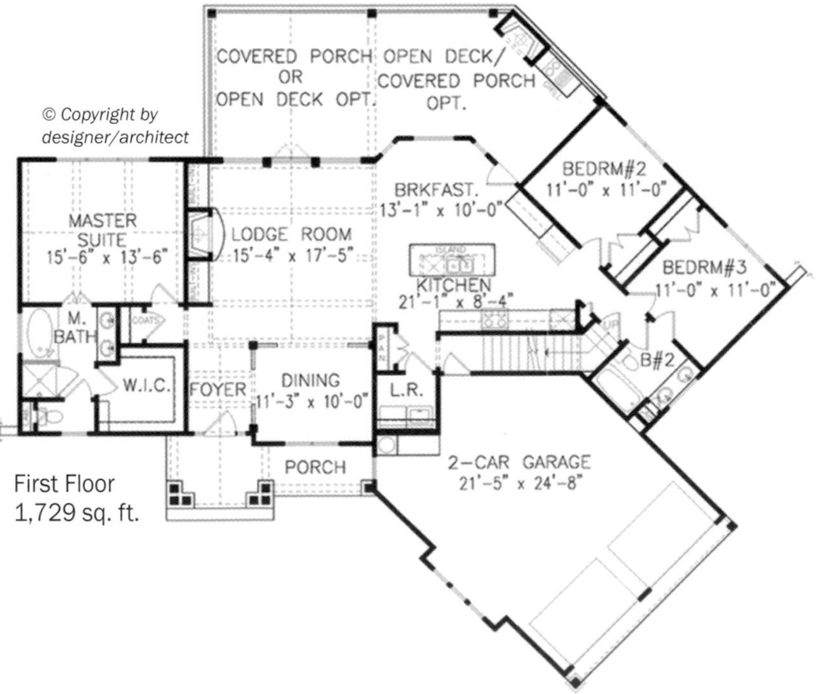

First Floor
1,729 sq. ft.

Images provided by designer/architect

Plan #F08-055D-1039

Dimensions: 91'6" W x 61'3" D
Heated Sq. Ft.: 2,661
Bonus Sq. Ft.: 602
Bedrooms: 4 **Bathrooms:** 3½
Foundation: Crawl space or slab standard; basement or daylight basement for an additional fee

See index for more information

Optional
Second Floor
602 sq. ft.

ATTIC STORAGE
BATH
10'-0" X 5'-0"
DN
OPT. ARCHED OPENING BALCONY
VAULTED CEILING BELOW
BONUS ROOM
18'-2" X 20'-2"
SLOPED CEILING
8' LINE
4' WALL
4' WALL

Features

- This stunning ranch home has a two-story vaulted and beamed ceiling in the great room and kitchen
- The outdoor living/grilling porch is adorned with a fireplace for extending your outdoor time into the colder months
- The master suite enjoys a private location and has a huge walk-in shower in the private bath
- The optional second floor has an additional 602 square feet of living area
- 2-car side entry garage, and a 1-car front entry garage

First Floor
2,688 sq. ft.

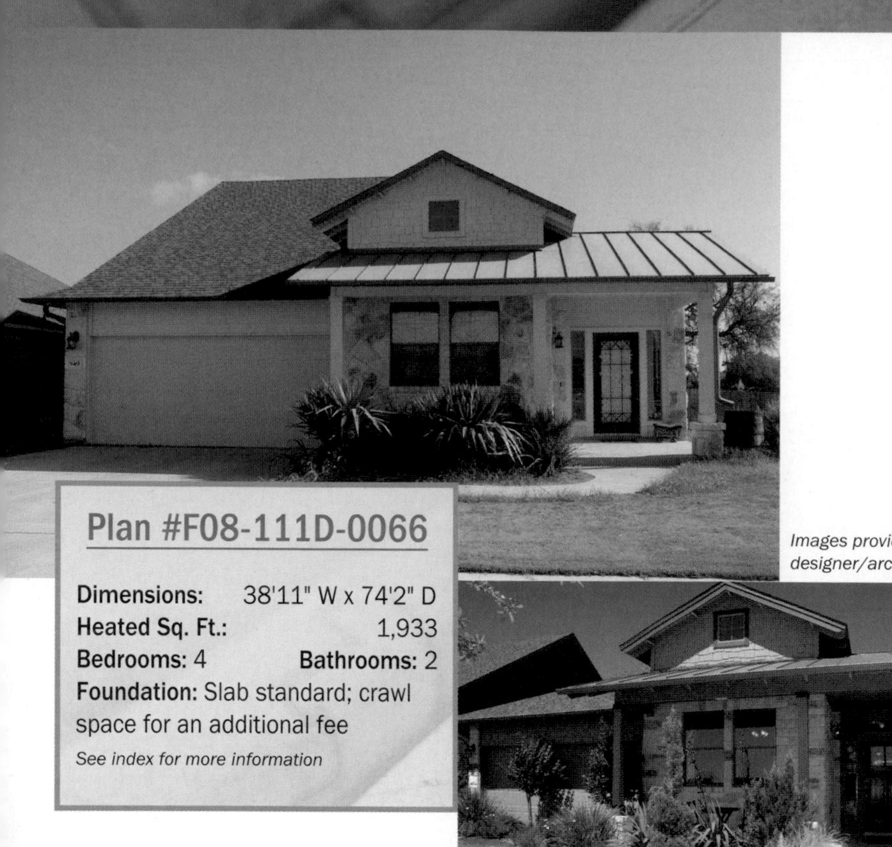

Plan #F08-111D-0066

Dimensions: 38'11" W x 74'2" D
Heated Sq. Ft.: 1,933
Bedrooms: 4 **Bathrooms:** 2
Foundation: Slab standard; crawl space for an additional fee

See index for more information

Images provided by designer/architect

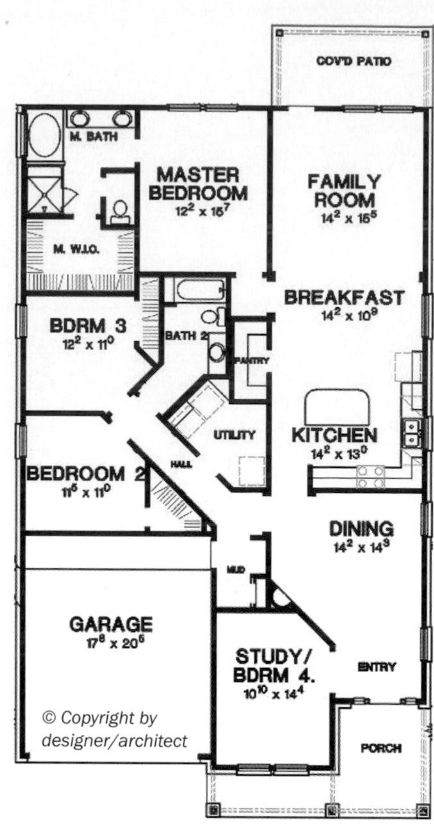

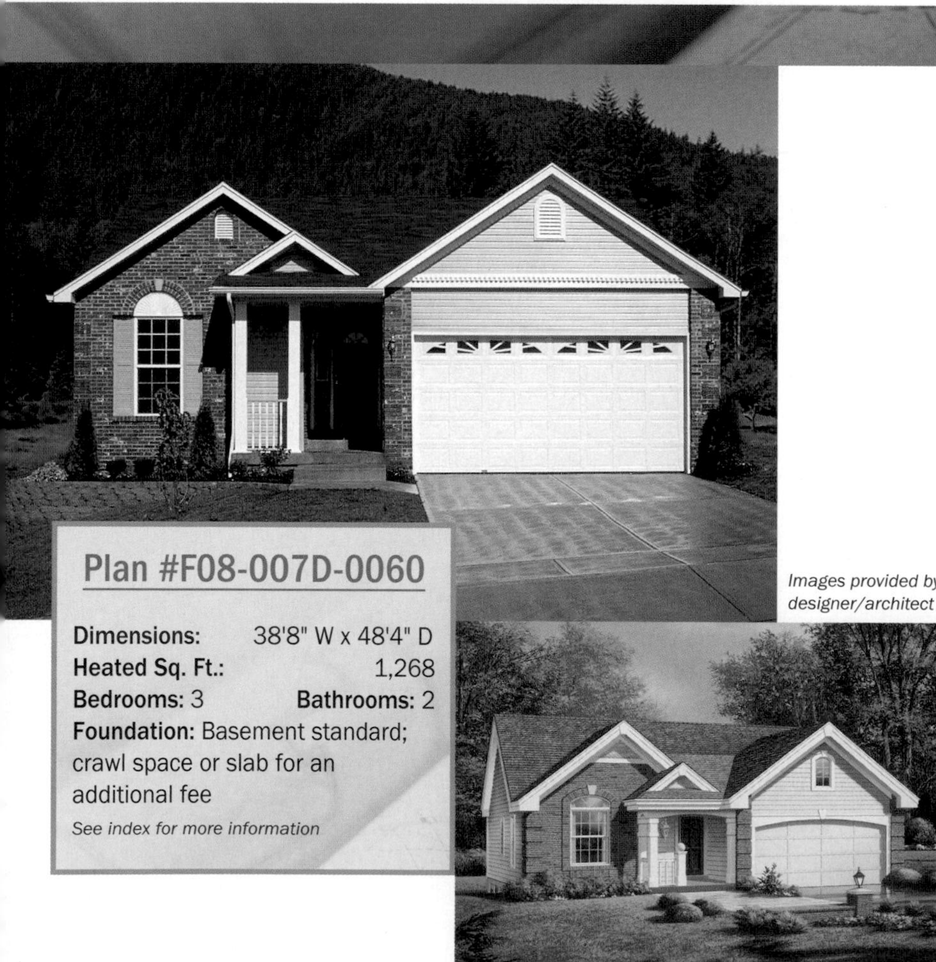

Plan #F08-007D-0060

Dimensions: 38'8" W x 48'4" D
Heated Sq. Ft.: 1,268
Bedrooms: 3 **Bathrooms:** 2
Foundation: Basement standard; crawl space or slab for an additional fee

See index for more information

Images provided by designer/architect

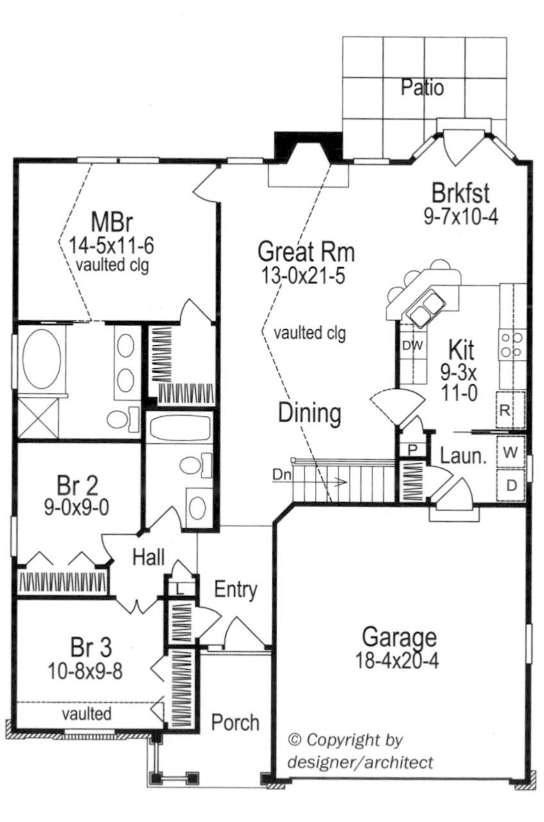

Images provided by designer/architect

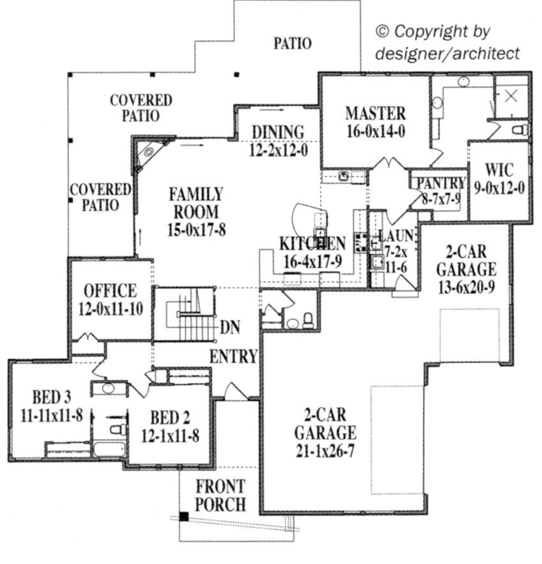

Plan #F08-101D-0116

Dimensions: 78'6" W x 66'3" D
Heated Sq. Ft.: 2,497
Bedrooms: 3 **Bathrooms:** 2½
Exterior Walls: 2" x 6"
Foundation: Basement

See index for more information

Images provided by designer/architect

DECK
9' CLG DINING RM 11'-0"× 15'-4"
KITCHEN 9'-0"× 10'-0"
OPTIONAL TWO CAR GARAGE 20'-0"× 20'-0"
BEDRM #3 11'-4"× 10'-0"
COV. PORCH
LAUN RM
UTIL
10' CLG GREAT RM 20'-0"× 15'-4"
WICL
MSTR BATH
BATH #2
BEDRM #2 11'-4"× 12'-4"
COV. PORCH
TRAY CEIL MSTR BEDRM 12'-0"× 16'-4"

© Copyright by designer/architect

Plan #F08-016D-0062

Dimensions: 48' W x 43'4" D
Heated Sq. Ft.: 1,380
Bonus Sq. Ft.: 385
Bedrooms: 3 **Bathrooms:** 2
Foundation: Slab or crawl space standard; basement walk-out basement for an additional fee

See index for more information

Images provided by designer/architect

Plan #F08-011D-0660

Dimensions: 52' W x 53' D
Heated Sq. Ft.: 1,704
Bedrooms: 3 **Bathrooms:** 2½
Exterior Walls: 2" x 6"
Foundation: Crawl space or slab standard; basement for an additional fee

See index for more information

Features

- Modern Farmhouse living has never been easier than with this perfectly-sized one-story
- The vaulted great room has a corner fireplace and windows on two walls for an airy atmosphere
- A large island in the kitchen faces towards the great room and provides casual dining space
- The secluded master bedroom enjoys a large walk-in closet, and a private bath
- 2-car side entry garage

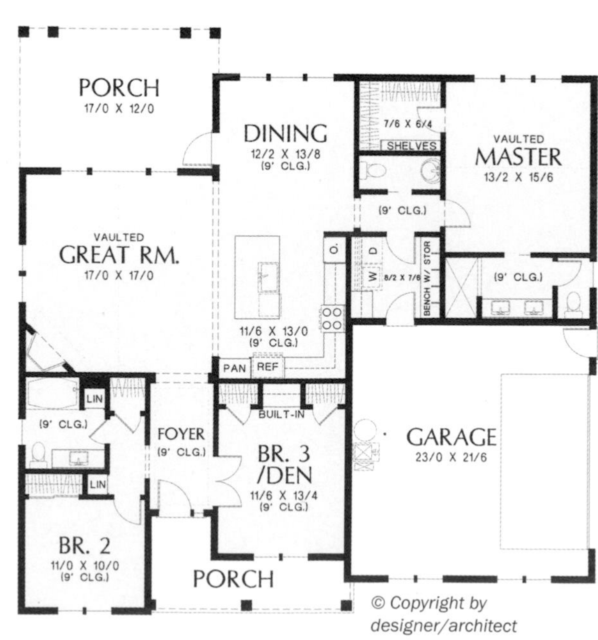

Plan #F08-155D-0126

Dimensions: 54'10" W x 62'8" D
Heated Sq. Ft.: 1,649
Bedrooms: 4 **Bathrooms:** 2
Foundation: Crawl space or slab standard; basement or daylight basement for an additional fee

See index for more information

Features

- This stylish one-story home draws inspiration from Prairie and Modern style architecture
- A barn-style door adorns the entrance into the media room/ bedroom 4
- The isolated master bedroom enjoys its privacy and a posh bath with a free-standing tub, a glass shower, and a walk-in closet
- The kitchen has a raised breakfast bar with space for four people that merges with the great room
- 2-car side entry garage

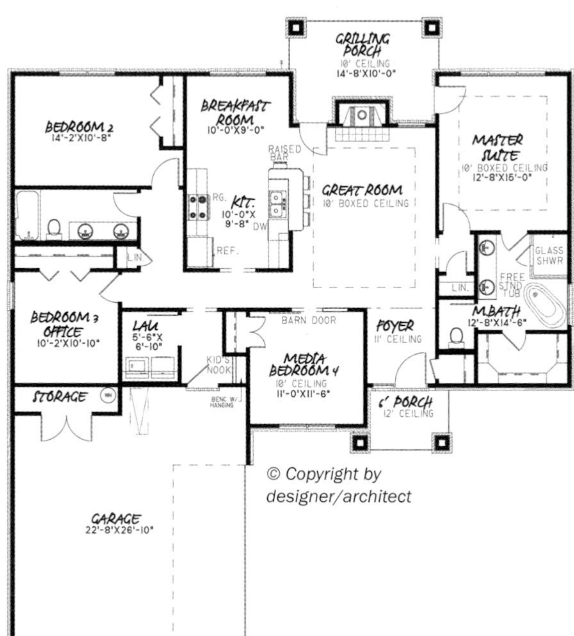

Images provided by designer/architect

Plan #F08-111D-0060

Dimensions: 38'11" W x 84' D
Heated Sq. Ft.: 1,768
Bedrooms: 3 **Bathrooms:** 2
Foundation: Slab standard; crawl space for an additional fee

See index for more information

Images provided by designer/architect

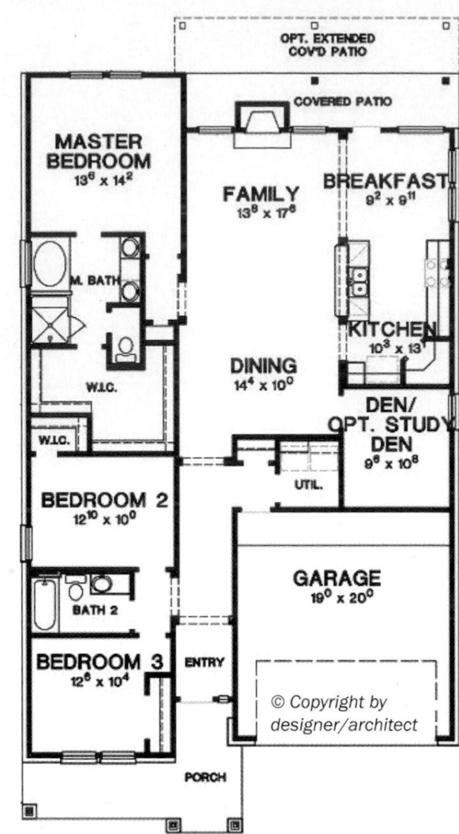

Plan #F08-007D-0207

Dimensions: 79'4" W x 61'4" D
Heated Sq. Ft.: 2,884
Bedrooms: 3 **Bathrooms:** 2½
Exterior Walls: 2" x 6"
Foundation: Walk-out basement

See index for more information

Images provided by designer/architect

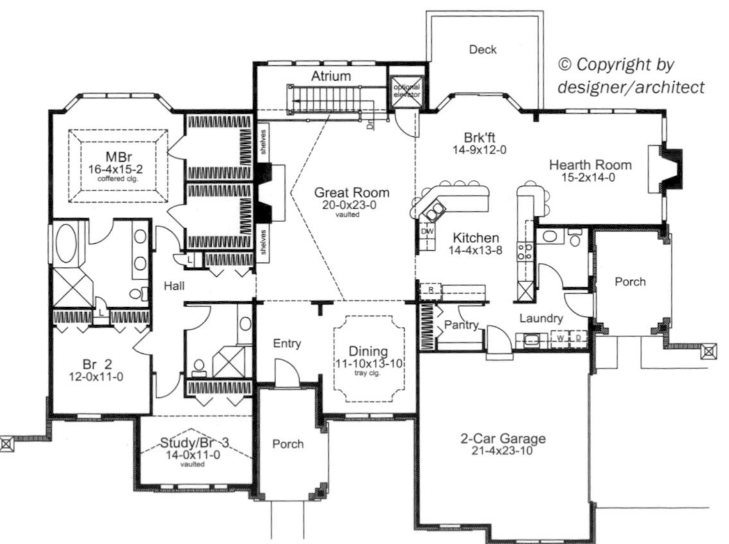

Plan #F08-026D-2017

Dimensions: 50' W x 58' D
Heated Sq. Ft.: 1,676
Bedrooms: 3 **Bathrooms:** 2
Foundation: Basement standard; crawl space, slab or walk-out basement for an additional fee

See index for more information

Images provided by designer/architect

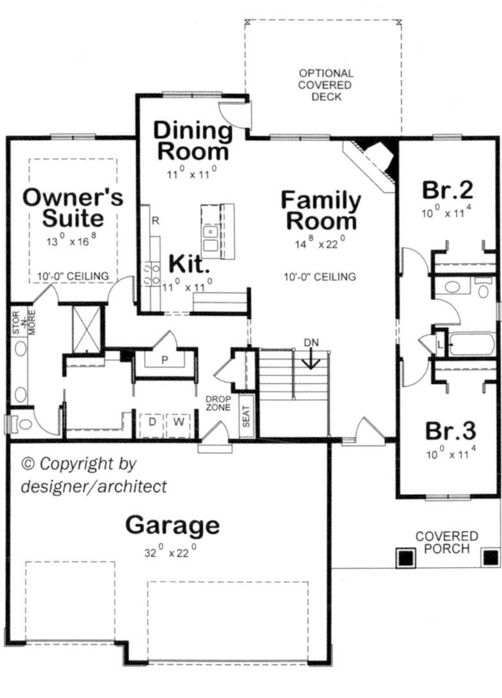

© Copyright by designer/architect

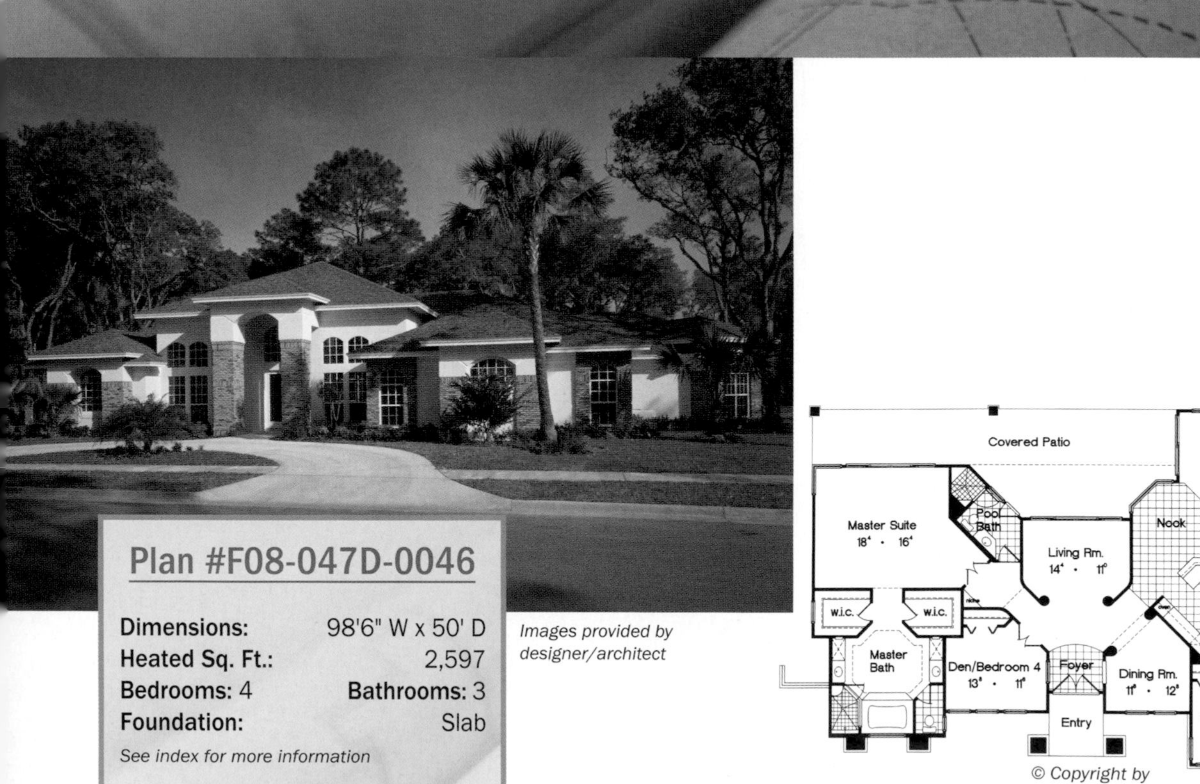

Plan #F08-047D-0046

Dimensions: 98'6" W x 50' D
Heated Sq. Ft.: 2,597
Bedrooms: 4 **Bathrooms:** 3
Foundation: Slab

See index for more information

Images provided by designer/architect

© Copyright by designer/architect

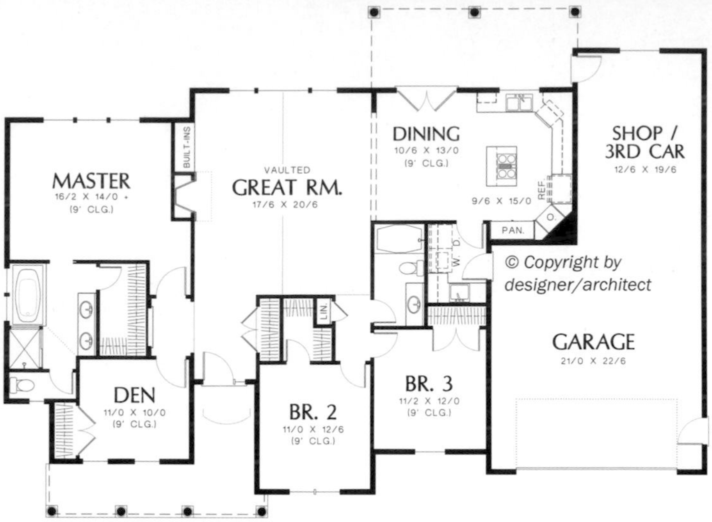

Plan #F08-011D-0006

Dimensions: 70' W x 51' D
Heated Sq. Ft.: 1,873
Bedrooms: 3 **Bathrooms:** 2
Exterior Walls: 2" x 6"
Foundation: Crawl space or slab standard; basement for an additional fee

See index for more information

Images provided by designer/architect

Plan #F08-076D-0238

Dimensions: 91'5" W x 79' D
Heated Sq. Ft.: 2,925
Bonus Sq. Ft.: 3,361
Bedrooms: 4 **Bathrooms:** 3½
Foundation: Slab or crawl space standard; basement for an additional fee

See index for more information

Optional Second Floor
432 sq. ft.

First Floor
2,925 sq. ft.

Optional Lower Level
2,929 sq. ft.

Images provided by designer/architect

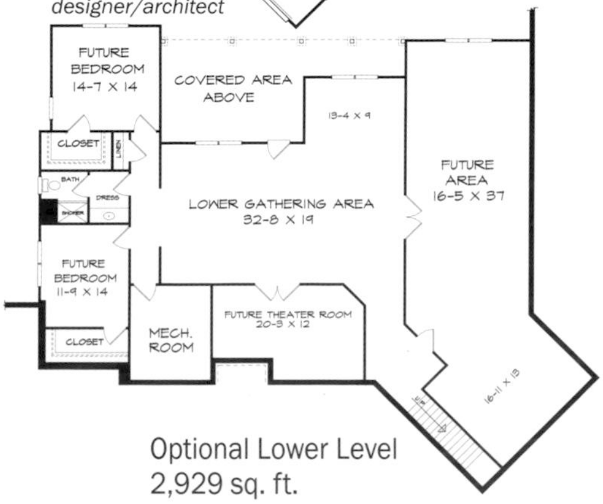

© Copyright by designer/architect

Plan #F08-013D-0025

Dimensions: 70'2" W x 59' D
Heated Sq. Ft.: 2,097
Bonus Sq. Ft.: 452
Bedrooms: 3 **Bathrooms:** 3
Foundation: Slab standard; crawl space or basement for an additional fee

See index for more information

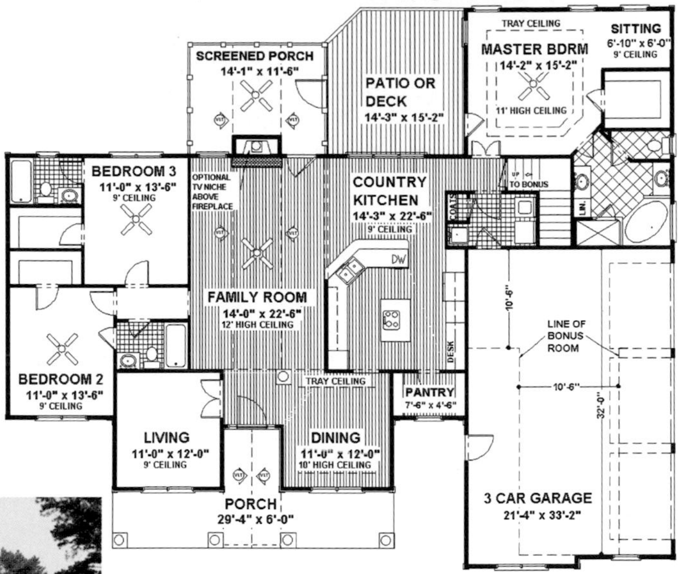

Images provided by designer/architect

Plan #F08-032D-1110

Dimensions: 64' W x 49' D
Heated Sq. Ft.: 1,704
Bonus Sq. Ft.: 1,704
Bedrooms: 3 **Bathrooms:** 2
Exterior Walls: 2" x 6"
Foundation: Basement standard; crawl space, floating slab or monolithic slab, for an additional fee

See index for more information

Images provided by designer/architect

© Copyright by designer/architect

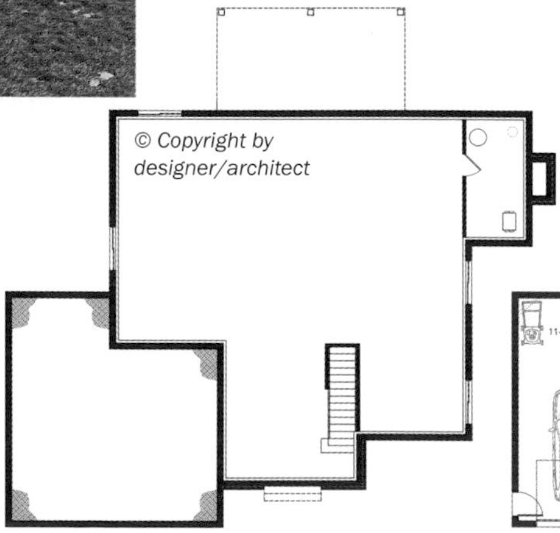

Optional Lower Level 1,704 sq. ft.

First Floor 1,704 sq. ft.

Plan #F08-163D-0003

Dimensions:	56' W x 40' D
Heated Sq. Ft.:	1,416
Bedrooms: 3	**Bathrooms:** 2
Exterior Walls:	2" x 6"
Foundation:	Crawl space

See index for more information

Images provided by designer/architect

Features

- The great room is open to both the kitchen and dining area on the left side of the house for an open, airy feel
- All three bedrooms are located on the right side of the house with the master suite having a private sitting porch
- The laundry room is conveniently located just off of the kitchen
- A lovely covered back porch is the perfect way to enjoy the outdoors

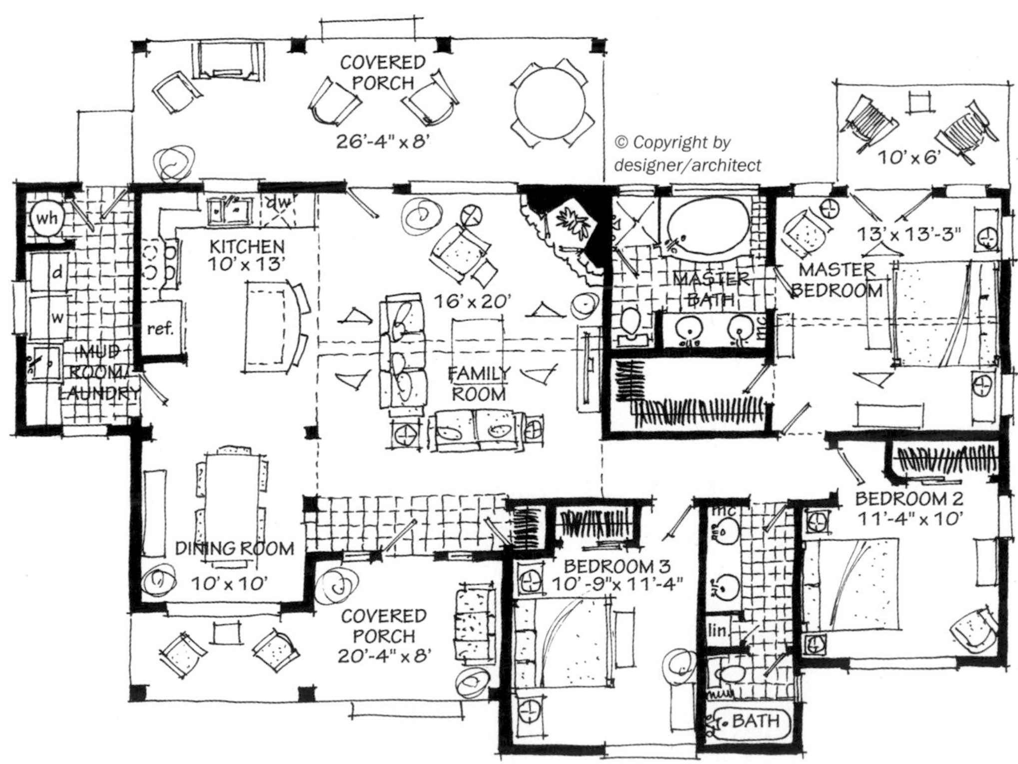

WOOD CABINS

a place of refuge is the wave of the future

There's a lot of irony in today's home building trends. Today's homeowners are constantly searching for the next "big thing" especially when it comes to smart home technology. At the same time, they're wanting to feel secure and back to nature with a sharp focus on ways to live more simply and purposeful. Is it safe to say homeowners want it all? Is today's ideal home one with The Jetsons-like technology, but also with that inviting feel like Grandma's house? In many ways, the answer is yes!

Trends in all areas of life are born from the unique combination of the current environment, economy and demographics. So, no place or time in history is ever exactly the same, and although it may seem as though trends resurface all of the time, they are never exactly the same as they were before. Today's trends in home design are a result of several lifestyle factors that include our intense need to feel connected, while also wanting or needing to be able to detach from the world. Since the pandemic, not only have we had to adapt to lifestyle changes, but many of our wants and needs in a home have changed, So, home designers have their work cut out for them! Homeowners are sensible and are no longer as wasteful. And, because information on every topic imaginable is available at their fingertips anytime of day, they are smarter than ever before. And, because of their ability to research anything at anytime they feel as though anything they see can be attainable.

From Baby Boomers to Millennials, homeowners are taking today's technology and mixing it with yesterday's vintage furnishings, retro design elements, and reclaimed natural materials that once had another purpose entirely. Homeowners have become resourceful, imaginative, and driven to live in a home that offers them refuge from their busy lives, while spotlighting their personality and interests. The current home design trends speak volumes on how today's homeowners want to live.

Today's these home design trends offer solutions for homeowners, while also providing comfort and security.

Although social media allows us to feel connected, people are yearning for ways to feel more connected face-to-face especially since the pandemic. Because of this need for community, many generations of family are choosing to live together. This living style is trending since many generations of family were separated during the pandemic. Whether it's for convenience or community, homes are being universally designed so they are comfortable and accessible for all ages. Having adult children at home, a parent or an in-law requires a thoughtful floor plan that combines openness and privacy for everyone. Split bedroom floor plans have become the most popular option meaning the master suite is separated from the other bedrooms for privacy. Gone are the days of all of the bedrooms doors being side-by-side down one small hallway. Now, master suites are hidden in one side of the house and the other bedrooms are scattered in other areas or placed near each other on the opposite side of the house.

Unless noted, images are copyright of designer/architect. Page 52 top: Plan #F08-101D-0056 on page 268, Warren Diggles Photography; bottom: Plan #F08-161D-0001 on page 8; Page 53 top: Plan #011S-0192; left, Plan #F08-101D-0115 on page 63; For more photos or to purchase plans, visit houseplanandmore.com

Other popular design options include one-level living with a finished lower level featuring an in-law suite. Keep in mind however, that as the older individual continues to age accessibility to another level of the home will get even more difficult. So, it's very important to plan for the future when choosing a layout. A few other options are being designed to offer even more privacy. Home designers are developing home layouts with apartments connected, or inside of the home. Apartment garages and tiny homes are also a popular choice and offer alternative ways in creating privacy, while adding additional living space to your home's living conditions or property.

not against the grain

With sustainability continuing to be popular, it comes as no surprise that texture and wood grain are trending in home design. The use of sustainable materials such as cork and bamboo also are included in the mix. With both cork and bamboo being highly renewable resources, they are great options for those wanting to make less of an impact on the environment when building or remodeling a home. These natural and textured materials are being used in a variety of creative ways from exposed ceiling beams, flooring, wall covering ("think ship lap"), and one-of-a-kind hearths. Even vintage wood furniture pieces are becoming unique bathroom vanities, kitchen islands, or desks in home offices. With natural elements filling our homes again, taupe and gray-beige called "greige" are the new gray. It appears people are craving warmth once again and so beige and other warmer tone colors are making a comeback.

Although white never goes out of style, even today's hottest kitchen designs are featuring lots of white with rough sewn timber shelving, or a wood butcher-block countertop adding a warmer element to the starkness of the white. With homeowners searching for a cozy, natural and warm living environment it only makes sense beige is becoming the color of choice again.

Unless noted, all images copyright by designer/architect; Page 54 top: Plan #F08-101D-0052 on page 232, Damon Searles, photographer; left: Plan #F08-101D-0192; Page 55, top right clockwise: Plan #101D-0199; Plan #011S-0196, Bob Greenspan, photographer; Plan #F08-101D-0047 on page 162, Warren Diggles Photography; Plan #011S-0196, Bob Greenspan, photographer; Backyard putting green, Sport Court St. Louis; Plan #F08-101D-0045 on page 91, Warren Diggles Photography. To see more photos or purchase plans, visit houseplansandmore.com

all work and no play?

We're spending more time than ever before working. Even with all of the technology that should be simplifying life for us, before the pandemic we were spending more time away from home than ever before. With people working longer and harder, including many delaying retirement, or starting a second career, homes are becoming more playful by offering ways to decompress. With little free time in most people's lives, being able to do things you love under your own roof is important. Areas that encourage people to relax and unwind are topping new homeowner's wish lists, while on the flip side home offices and computer spaces are becoming a necessity. From exercise and meditation rooms, to libraries and reading areas designed purposely with or without technology, homeowners are making a statement that technology is important, but not in all aspects of their lives. In order to truly decompress and unplug, many want a refuge that frees them from the never-ending noise technology creates. However, technology is a necessary evil that allows a homeowner to easily work from anywhere when set-up properly. To add an element of fun, playful extras are being added to homes today including sports rooms, pools and putting greens. And, for those who enjoy cooking, pizza ovens. Outdoor living spaces are now a must-have since they offer a refuge in nature. Outdoor rooms are an extension of the interior and provide space for dining, relaxing and include fireplaces, kitchens and other functions.

why
separate spaces
with walls?

honest spaces

Homes may be getting smarter, but there's a reason, they have to! Today's new homes are smaller; so space is in high demand and that means great function is a necessity. With people choosing to live with less space, the space they do have must be able to handle all of a person's or family's needs. Architects and residential designers are catering specifically to a person's wants and needs rather than creating floor plans without their personality in mind. With every square foot so important, no corner can be wasted. If a home is designed to cater to a larger audience, then it's being designed with flexible spaces that can be adapted to many different scenarios from dining rooms to home offices. The birth of the open floor plan solves smaller home issues by offering one large, open space that integrates gathering, working, cooking and dining. However, since the pandemic, open floor plans can create a challenge when multiple family members are needing their own space to perform work or school-related tasks. Even still, open floor plans are the most popular since they promote spaciousness and a sense of community with family members. Wood beams, vaulted ceilings, and large windows combines today's best trends creating a comfortable and inviting living space.

Unless noted, all images copyright by designer/architect; Page 56, top: Plan #F08-032D-0887 on page 90; bottom, Plan #F08-101D-0195; Page 57 top: Plan #101D-0149; middle: Plan #011S-0189; bottom, right: Plan #011S-0195; bottom, left: Technology drawer, ClosetMaid®; bottom, right: For more photos or to purchase plans, please visit houseplansandmore.com.

green feels clean

Green building is remaining an important factor in new home design, but many home buyers and designers are initially choosing less costly surface upgrades using efficient green materials rather than overhauling all of the appliances and the HVAC system for more efficient models. But, people are more mindful than ever of toxic indoor chemicals and materials we're exposed to everyday that are affecting our home's air and water quality. From water purifiers to low VOC paint brands, all of these subtle choices result in a healthier home for all who dwell there. This trend continues to expand with essential oils allowing indoor environments to be filled with scents that can calm, or energize. There are even new light fixtures that will mimic natural circadian sleep patterns promoting better quality sleep. Home buyers are leaving no stone unturned when it comes to their health, so even fireplaces have become vent-less, or being more commonly built for outdoor use on covered patios or porches.

work-life balance achieved

As we maintain our position on how important a playful home refuge is, it is also very important there is a place within today's homes for work especially since the pandemic. More people work from home than ever before and there must be a place that promotes effective and productive work free from noise and distraction, while encouraging a healthier work-life balance. However, thanks to the literally shrinking size of our technology, we need less space than ever for work tasks. So, don't picture a huge study or home office any longer, a small computer niche off the mud room or kitchen can easily suffice. In fact, many homes are now including a technology center where additional outlets, charging stations, and storage spaces for safely housing smart phones, hand held devices, and other popular electronic necessities we all seem to believe we can't live without can be kept. Typically, this technology center is designed near the laundry room, mud room, or a rear foyer, so these items can easily be grabbed on your way out the door.

make
furniture multi-functional, sometimes it's a home office, sometimes it's just a place to sort mail, and pay bills.

power play

Look for furniture that has built-in USB ports and smart phone chargers and eliminate all of those wires!

Today's home design trends are so much more than features within a house. The features homeowners desire provide therapy from our non-stop lives outside our home; they shelter us from dangerous chemicals in the environment; and they promote a feeling of contentment and togetherness we're all craving now more than ever. Today's home designs provide sanity and peace and a life better lived.

TAKE-AWAYS: 5 HOME DECORATING TRENDS

everything old is new again

Vintage, retro and reclaimed is the thing. Re-purposed and refurbished home furnishings and materials are continuing to see new life again. Styles from the 50s, 60s, and 70s including velvet, tapered legs, geometric accents, and curved back seating are becoming popular once again. So, stray away from overly matching décor and opt for a playful furniture addition from the 50s, 60s, or 70s. Not only is vintage in, but it's also a great way to use older furniture pieces in a whole new light. Even appliances are having fun with this hot trend and refrigerators and kitchen appliances have gone retro and can be found in styles reminiscent of the 50s in bold candy-colored colors sure to add personality to kitchens of any size.

go for the bold

When it comes to color, think bold. Not only will turquoise and green colors remain popular, so will jewel tones in plum and red. Also, with all of the use of wood, like previously mentioned beige is back. And don't be surprised to see close to neon colors being used for outdoor furniture. Bold patterned wallpaper especially in tropical prints is being seen in rooms creating little need for adding expensive artwork.

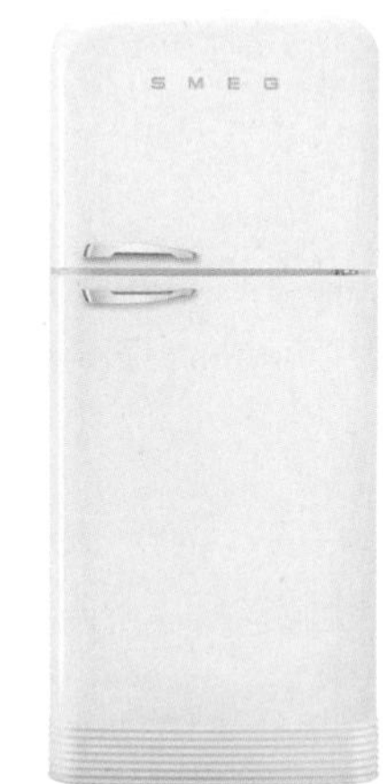

things are looking up

Embellished ceilings are a popular focal point in decorating. Don't be surprised to see ceilings painted in bold colors, architecturally enhanced ceiling designs with beams, and other natural textures and materials using herringbone patterns. Quirky and fun statement lighting fixtures are everywhere and add a unique look. Hang a fun light fixture in an unexpected place such as a bedroom, bathroom or even a closet.

keep it simple

As home sizes decrease, the need for keeping things organized and in their place increases. It is essential to have an organized home when it's smaller, so anything that can be functional while helping you organize is popular right now. Kitchen islands, banquettes and integrated office spaces keep everything organized and functional. Kitchen storage walls also do just that and require little space. Smart home features like smart phone charging technology built into furniture and pop-up outlets including USB ports promote less clutter, too.

easy being green

While "living green" may not exactly be a new trend, it is one that is here to stay. Now that people are more educated on how even the little things can greatly and positively impact the environment, homeowners continue to be drawn to recycled or reused products for their homes. Homeowners have learned that LED lighting, eco-friendly light bulbs and other simple swaps are worth every penny in the end.

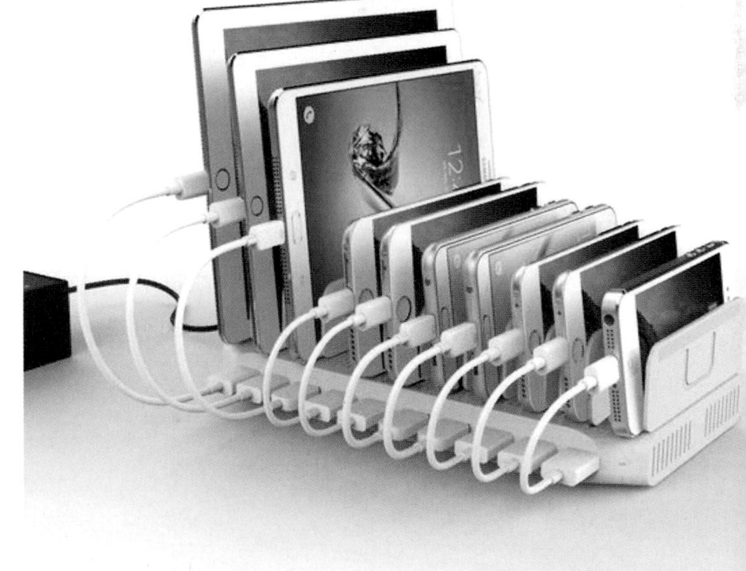

Unless noted, all images copyright by designer/architect; Page 58 top, left: Plan #F08-101D-0056 on page 268, Warren Diggles Photography; bottom, left: Plan #128D-0006; top, right: Smeg 50's Retro Style Aesthetic Refrigerator Item# FAB50URPB3, smeg.com; bottom, right: bright mud room, southern living.com, styled by Page Mullins, Hector Sanchez, photographer; Page 59 top, left: Plan #101D-0195; top, right: Selje Nightstand with wireless charging, Item#: 690.949.54, ikea.com; middle: Mockett Pop-Up Kitchen Power™, Item #PCS77-23G, mockett.com; bottom, right: UNITEK 96W/2.4A 10-Port USB Charging Station with Quick Charge 3.0, amazon.com. To see more photos or to purchase plans, please visit houseplansandmore.com.

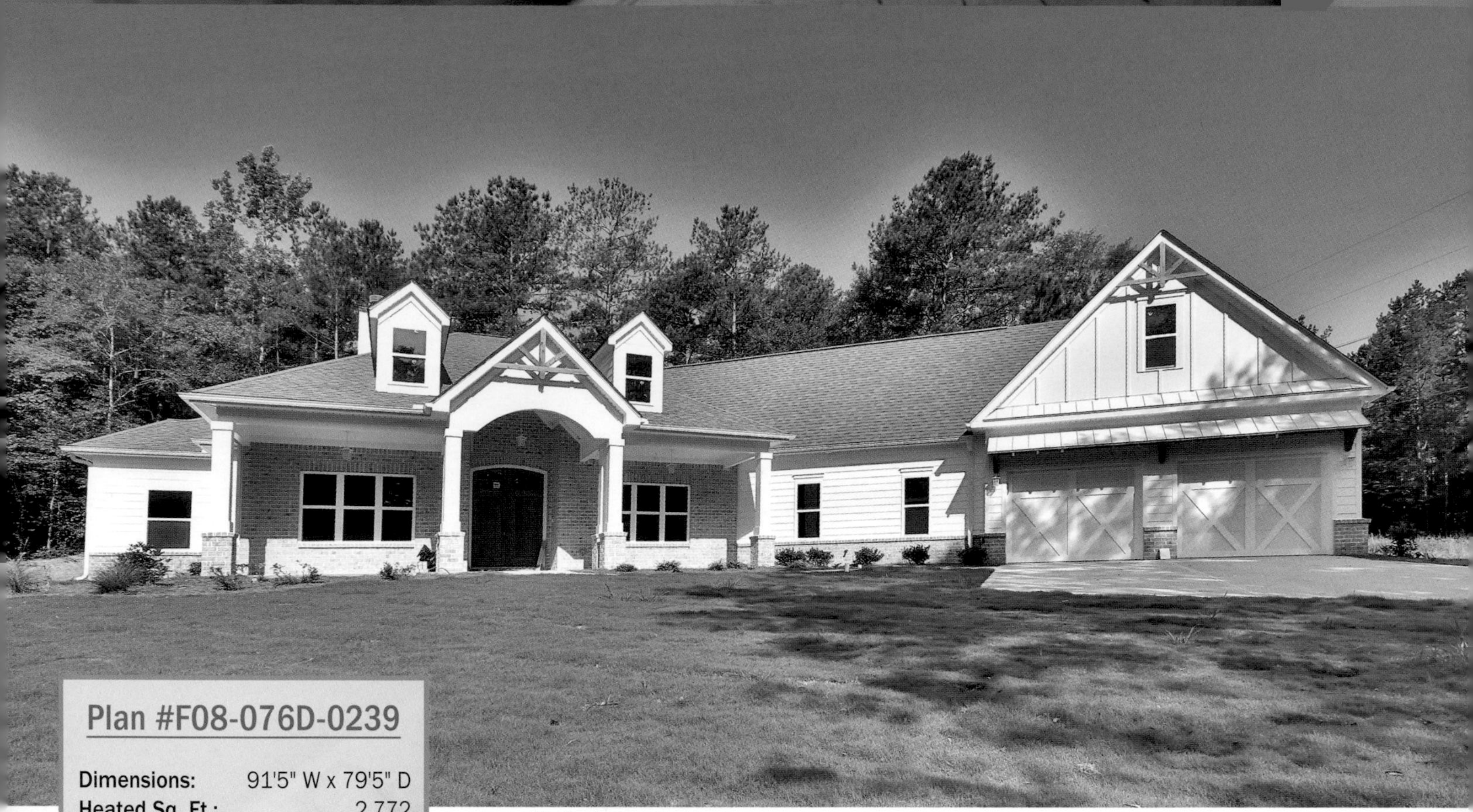

Plan #F08-076D-0239

Dimensions: 91'5" W x 79'5" D
Heated Sq. Ft.: 2,772
Bonus Sq. Ft.: 433
Bedrooms: 4 **Bathrooms:** 2½
Foundation: Crawl space or slab, please specify when ordering

See index for more information

Images provided by designer/architect

Features

- The vaulted beamed family room is open and inviting with the kitchen island able to be a part of the family room activity
- The kitchen enjoys a sizable walk-in pantry for keeping the highly visible kitchen free of clutter and excess appliances
- The master suite has a remote location and provides the homeowners with a dressing room style closet space and a private bath
- The bonus room on the second floor has an additional 433 square feet of living area
- 2-car front entry garage

© Copyright by designer/architect

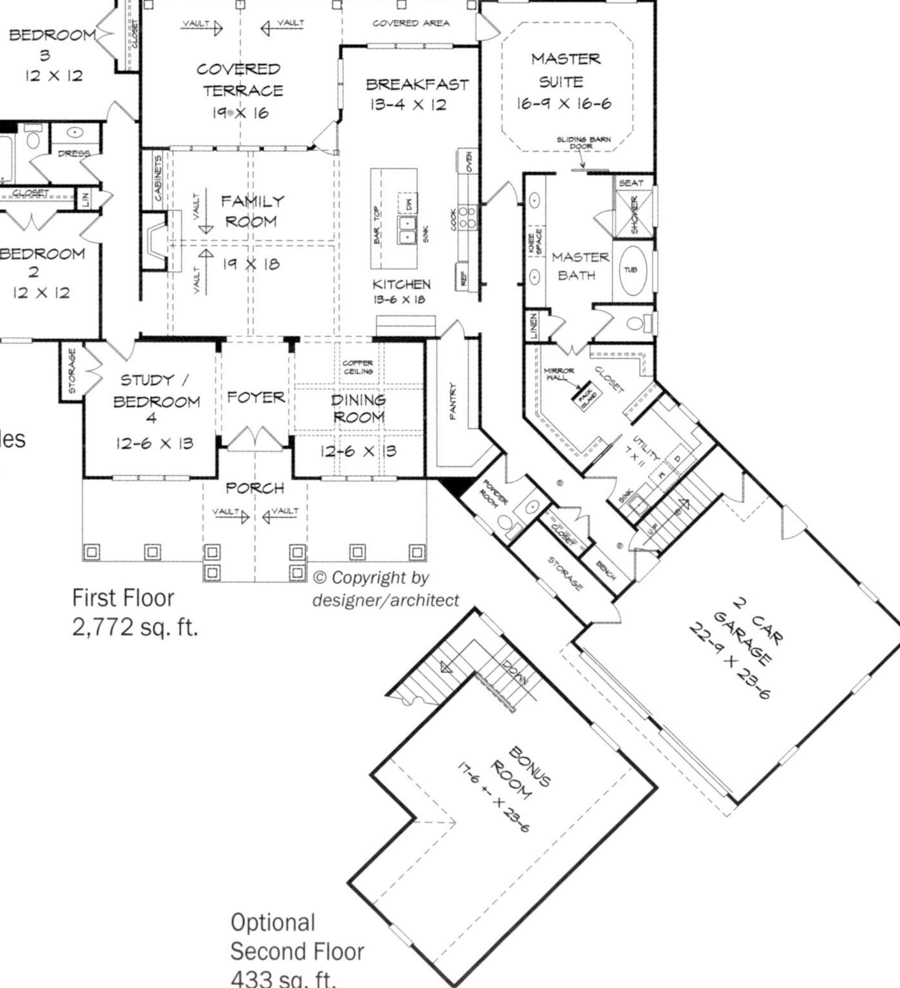

First Floor
2,772 sq. ft.

Optional
Second Floor
433 sq. ft.

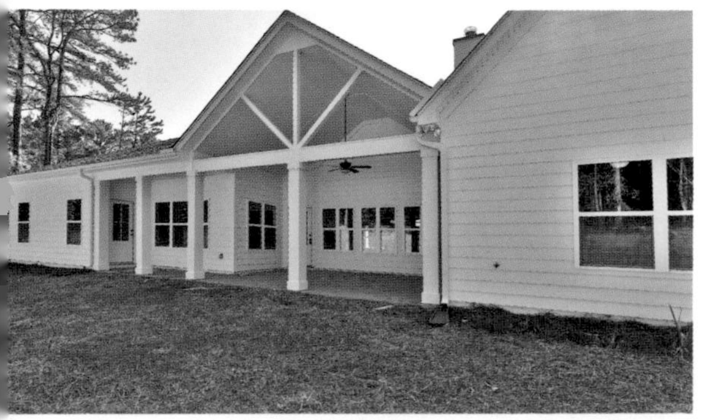

Images provided by designer/architect

Plan #F08-026D-1890

Dimensions: 69' W x 68' D
Heated Sq. Ft.: 2,449
Bedrooms: 3 **Bathrooms:** 2½
Foundation: Slab standard; crawl space, basement or walk-out basement for an additional fee

See index for more information

Features

- The bedrooms are placed for privacy in a wing to themselves
- Both the entry foyer and great room feature 11' ceilings that add volume and grandeur to this home
- Combining the kitchen, dining and great room is family living at its best
- Located as you enter through the garage is a drop zone, lockers, shelves and a closet that work together to keep clutter out of the kitchen and add organization to a homeowner's busy schedule
- 2-car side entry garage, and an optional 1-car front entry garage

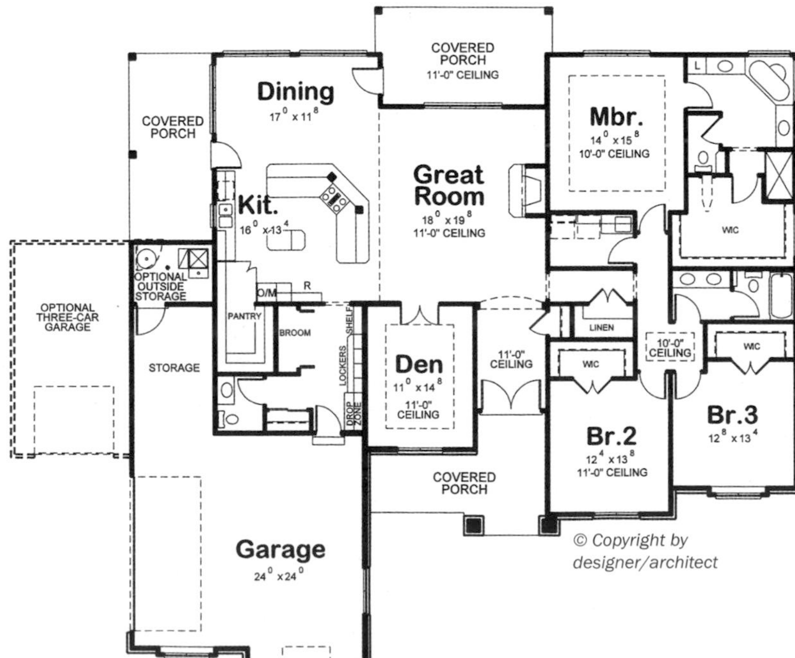

© Copyright by designer/architect

Plan #F08-101D-0115

Dimensions: 60' W x 76' D
Heated Sq. Ft.: 2,251
Bonus Sq. Ft.: 1,109
Bedrooms: 3 **Bathrooms:** 2½
Exterior Walls: 2" x 6"
Foundation: Basement or daylight basement, please specify when ordering

See index for more information

Images provided by designer/architect

Features

- This stylish rustic home has a great size for easy maintenance and a floor plan that offers privacy for all those who live there
- The great room with fireplace is open to the kitchen and dining area
- Study/bedroom #3 is a versatile space that can adapt to your needs
- A lovely covered deck extends off the great room
- The optional lower level has an additional 1,109 square feet of living area including a rec room, bar, an extra bedroom, and a bath
- 3-car front entry garage

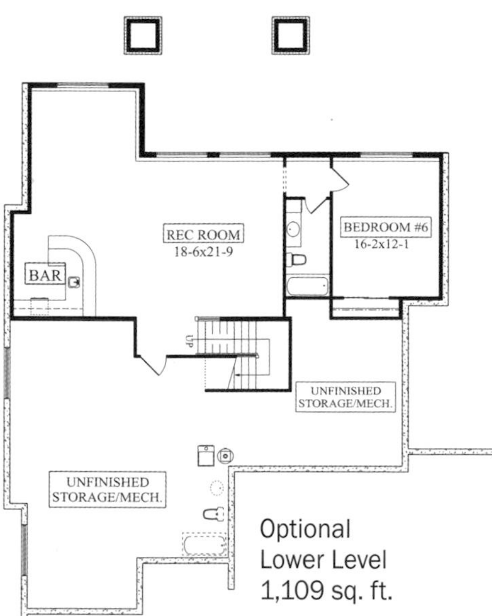

Optional Lower Level 1,109 sq. ft.

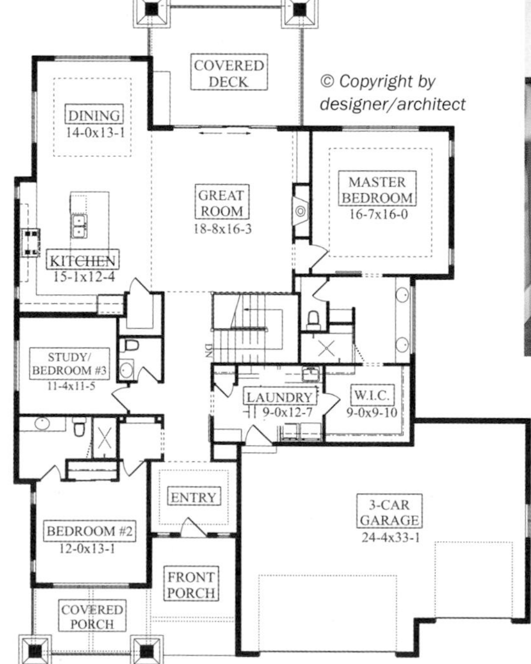

First Floor 2,251 sq. ft.

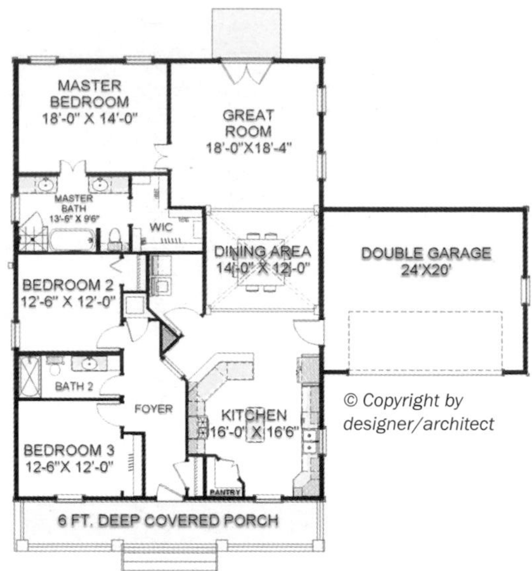

© Copyright by designer/architect

Images provided by designer/architect

Plan #F08-028D-0097

Dimensions: 60' W x 53' D
Heated Sq. Ft.: 1,908
Bedrooms: 3 **Bathrooms:** 2
Exterior Walls: 2" x 6"
Foundation: Floating slab standard; monolithic slab, crawl space, basement or walk-out basement for an additional fee

See index for more information

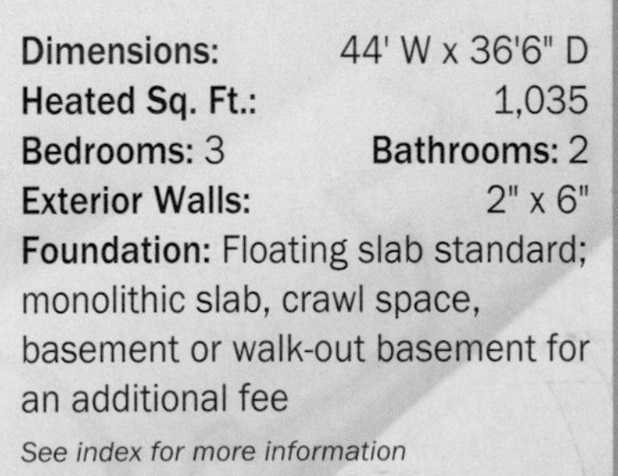

Images provided by designer/architect

Plan #F08-028D-0115

Dimensions: 44' W x 36'6" D
Heated Sq. Ft.: 1,035
Bedrooms: 3 **Bathrooms:** 2
Exterior Walls: 2" x 6"
Foundation: Floating slab standard; monolithic slab, crawl space, basement or walk-out basement for an additional fee

See index for more information

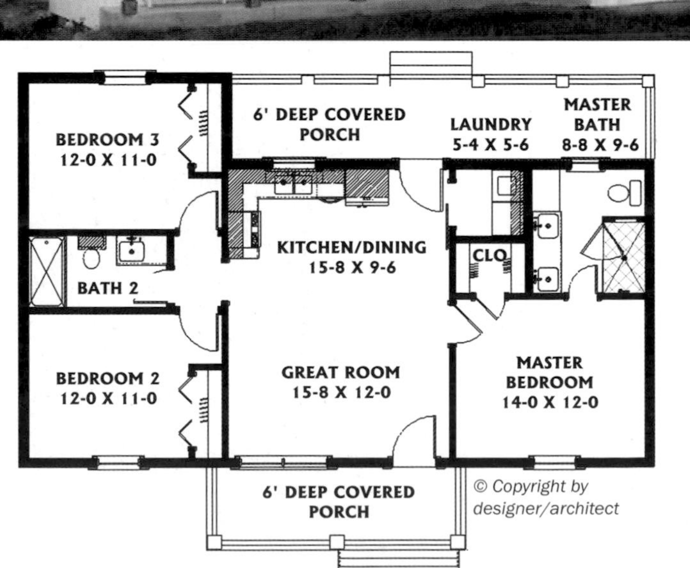

© Copyright by designer/architect

Plan #F08-170D-0010

Dimensions: 58'6" W x 77'10" D
Heated Sq. Ft.: 1,824
Bedrooms: 3 **Bathrooms:** 2
Foundation: Slab or monolithic slab standard; crawl space, basement or daylight basement for an additional fee

See index for more information

Images provided by designer/architect

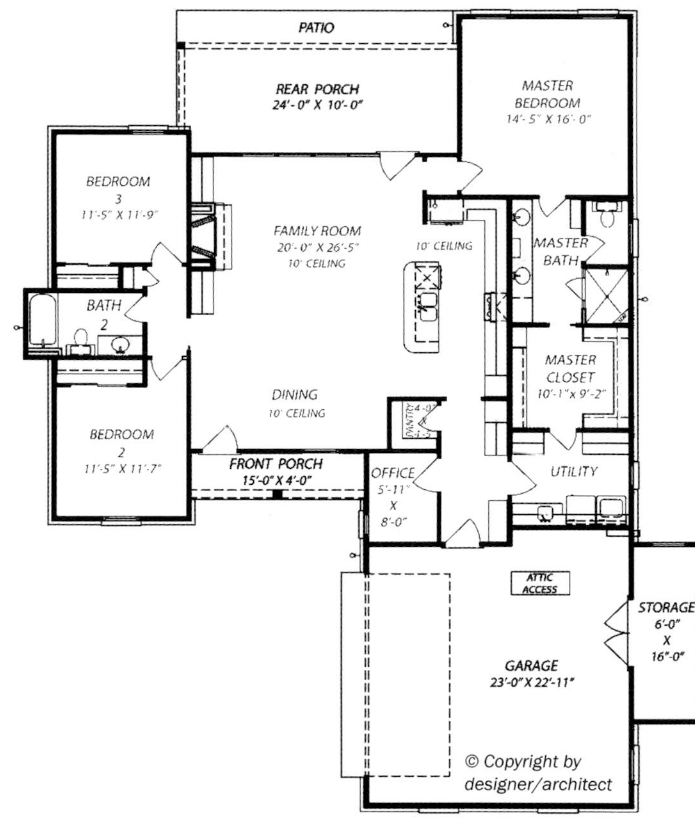

© Copyright by designer/architect

Plan #F08-111D-0065

Dimensions: 61'7" W x 68'6" D
Heated Sq. Ft.: 1,919
Bedrooms: 3 **Bathrooms:** 2
Foundation: Slab standard; crawl space or basement for an additional fee

See index for more information

Images provided by designer/architect

© Copyright by designer/architect

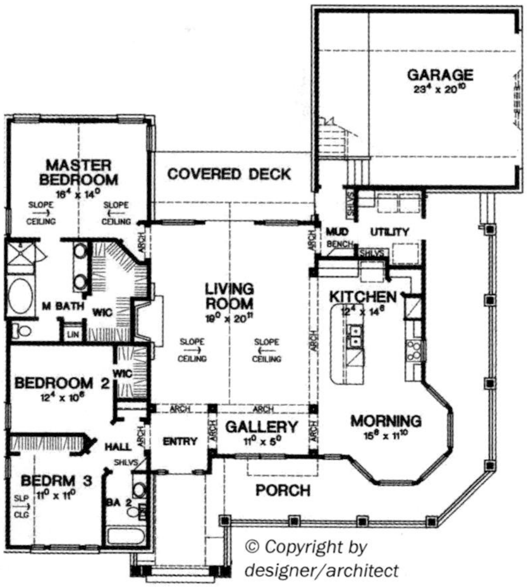

Plan #F08-077D-0002

Dimensions: 72'8" W x 51' D
Heated Sq. Ft.: 1,855
Bonus Sq. Ft.: 416
Bedrooms: 3 **Bathrooms:** 2½
Foundation: Basement, crawl space or slab, please specify when ordering

See index for more information

Images provided by designer/architect

First Floor
1,855 sq. ft.

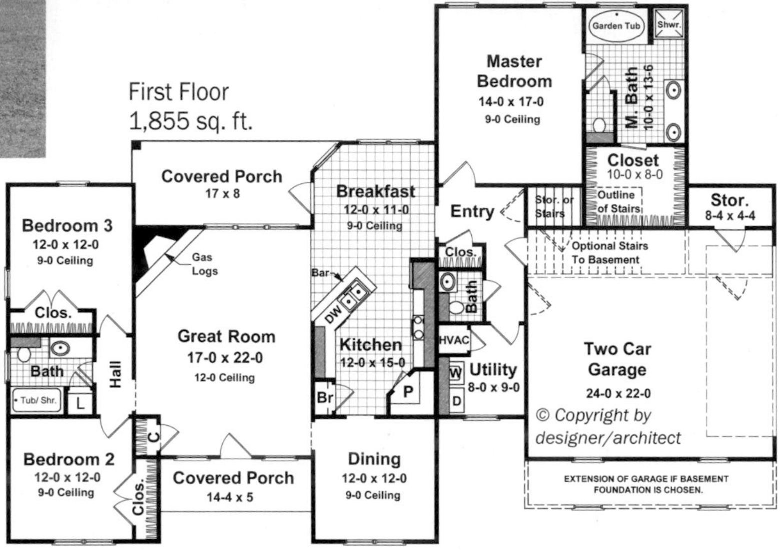

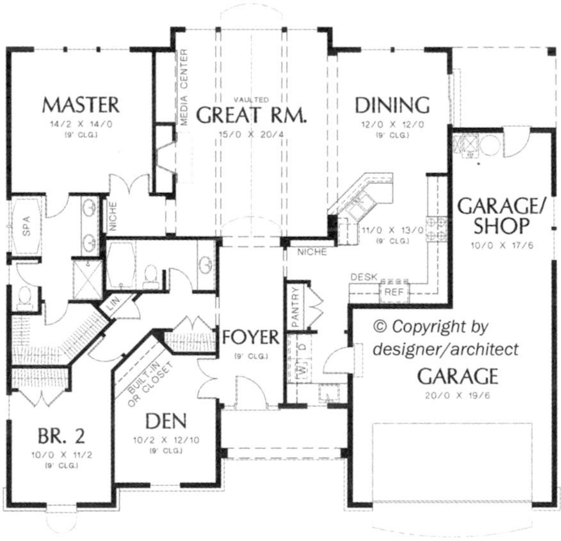

Optional
Second Floor
416 sq. ft.

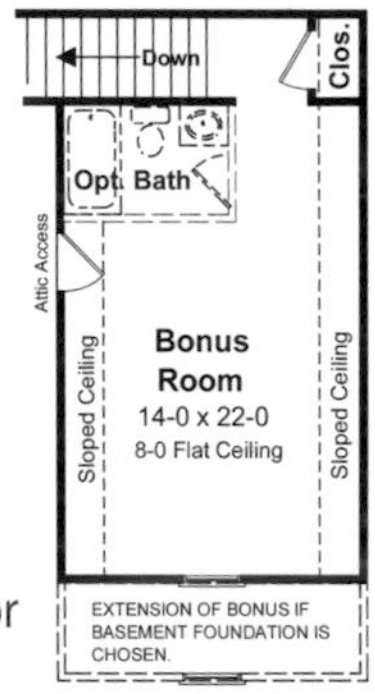

© Copyright by designer/architect

Plan #F08-011D-0008

Dimensions: 55' W x 48' D
Heated sq. ft.: 1,728
Bedrooms: 2 **Bathrooms:** 2
Exterior Walls: 2" x 6"
Foundation: Crawl space or slab standard; basement for an additional fee

See index for more information

Images provided by designer/architect

© Copyright by designer/architect

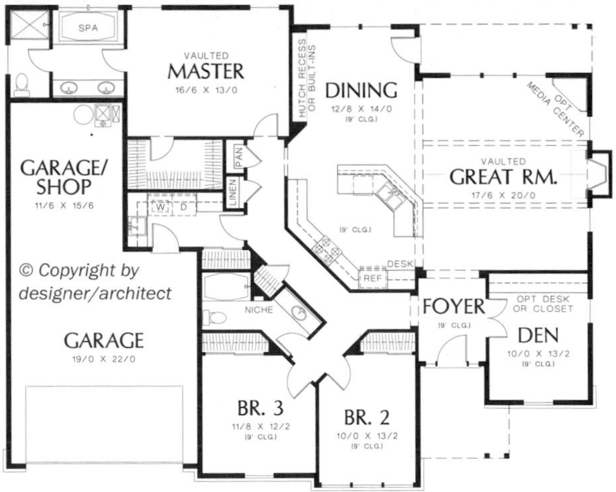

Plan #F08-011D-0013

Dimensions: 60' W x 50' D
Heated Sq. Ft.: 2,001
Bedrooms: 3 **Bathrooms:** 2
Exterior Walls: 2" x 6"
Foundation: Crawl space or slab standard; basement for an additional fee

See index for more information

Images provided by designer/architect

Plan #F08-013D-0053

Dimensions: 71'4" W x 74'8" D
Heated Sq. Ft.: 2,461
Bonus Sq. Ft.: 518
Bedrooms: 3 **Bathrooms:** 3½
Foundation: Basement standard; crawl space or slab for an additional fee

See index for more information

Images provided by designer/architect

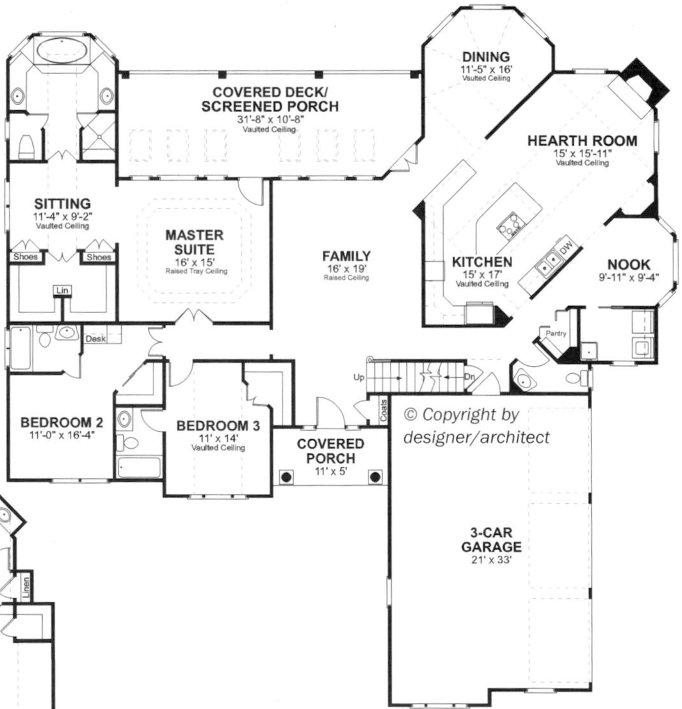

First Floor
2,461 sq. ft.

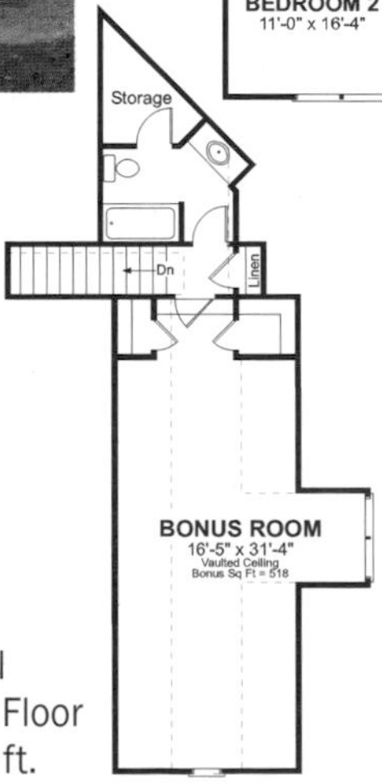

Optional
Second Floor
518 sq. ft.

Plan #F08-032D-0825

Dimensions: 70' W x 38'4" D
Heated sq. ft.: 1,313
Bedrooms: 2 **Bathrooms:** 1
Exterior Walls: 2" x 6"
Foundation: Basement standard; crawl space, floating slab or monolithic slab for an additional fee

See index for more information

Images provided by designer/architect

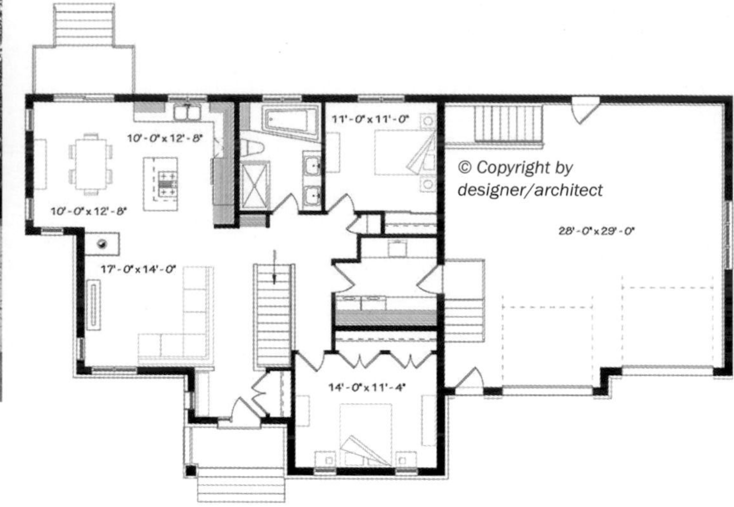

Plan #F08-159D-0004

Dimensions: 73' W x 44' D
Heated Sq. Ft.: 1,655
Bonus Sq. Ft.: 1,219
Bedrooms: 3 **Bathrooms:** 2
Exterior Walls: 2" x 6"
Foundation: Walk-out basement

See index for more information

Images provided by designer/architect

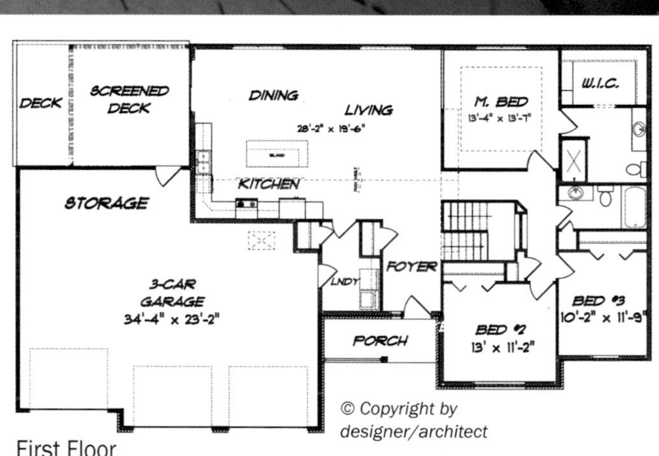

First Floor
1,655 sq. ft.

BED 4
12' x 11'-4"
FAMILY ROOM
38'-9" x 17'-3"
MECH / STORAGE
FLEX ROOM
14'-6" x 17'
UNEXCAVATED
UNEXCAVATED

Optional
Lower Level
1,219 sq. ft.

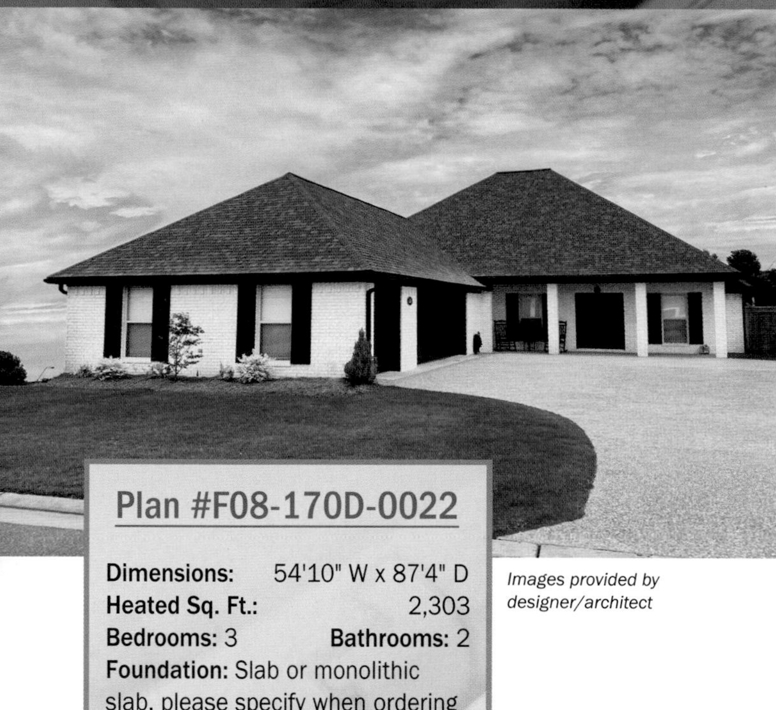

Plan #F08-170D-0022

Dimensions: 54'10" W x 87'4" D
Heated Sq. Ft.: 2,303
Bedrooms: 3 **Bathrooms:** 2
Foundation: Slab or monolithic slab, please specify when ordering

See index for more information

Images provided by designer/architect

PATIO
MASTER BEDROOM
13'-4" X 16'-1"
REAR PORCH
12'-0" X 5'-0"
SUNROOM
16'-5" X 10'-0"
BEDROOM 3
11'-0" X 14'-0"
EATING
12'-0" X 11'-0"
10' CEILING
MASTER BATH
KITCHEN
ISLAND
FAMILY ROOM
16'-5" X 18'-1"
10' CEILING
BATH 2
11'-11" X 11'-0"
10' CEILING
HALL
FOYER
6'-5" X 10'-5"
10' CEILING
MASTER CLOSET
ISLAND
13'-4" X 9'-7"
PANTRY
DINING
10'-0" X 10'-5"
10' CEILING
BEDROOM 2
11'-0" X 11'-0"
HALL
OFFICE
6'-7" X 8'-6"
UTILITY
13'-4" x 8'-7"
FRONT PORCH
27'-0" X 6'-0"
10' CEILING
STORAGE
GARAGE
25'-0" X 23'-9"
GOLFCART GARAGE
25'-0" X 9'-8"

© Copyright by designer/architect

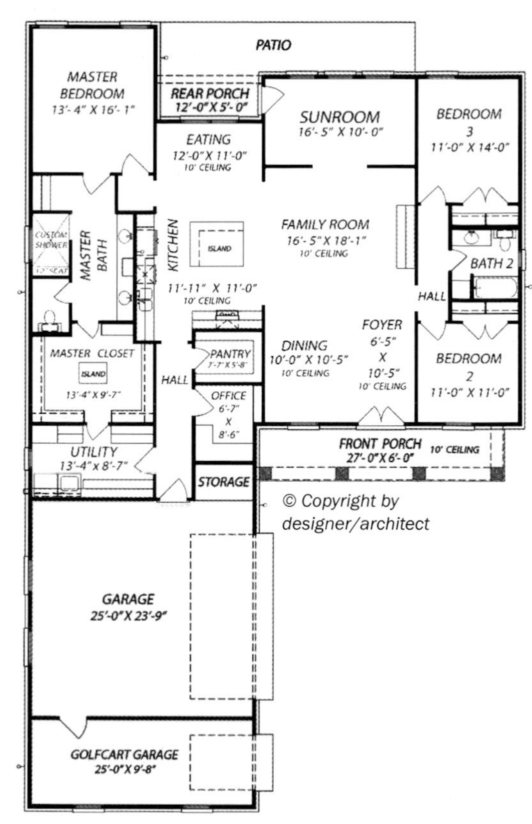

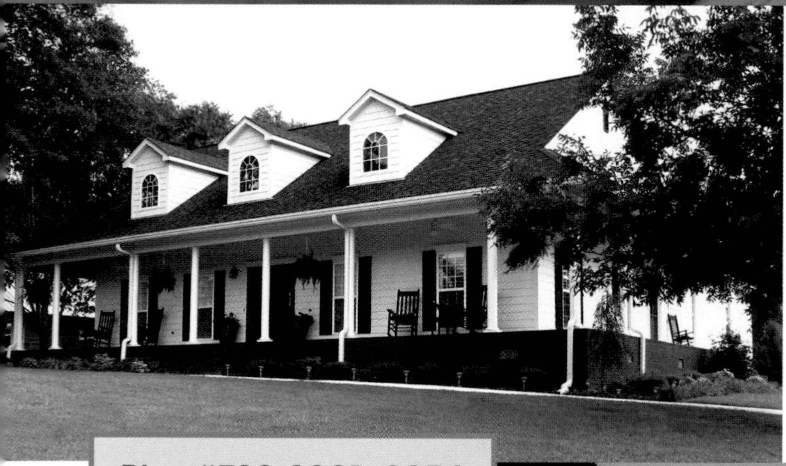

Plan #F08-028D-0054

Dimensions: 60' W x 76' D
Heated Sq. Ft.: 2,123
Bedrooms: 3 **Bathrooms:** 2½
Foundation: Floating slab standard; monolithic slab, crawl space, basement or walk-out basement for an additional fee

See index for more information

Images provided by designer/architect

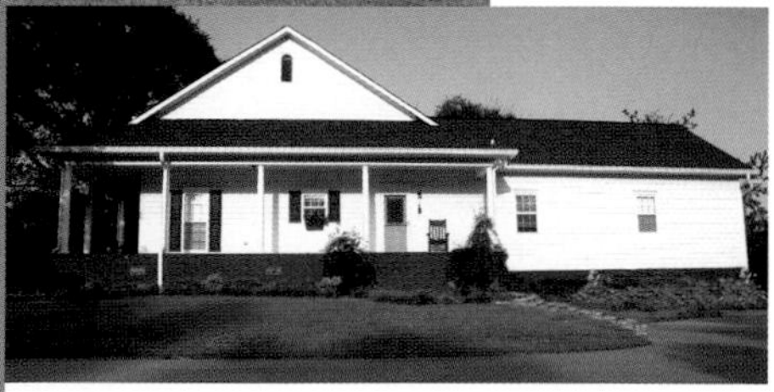

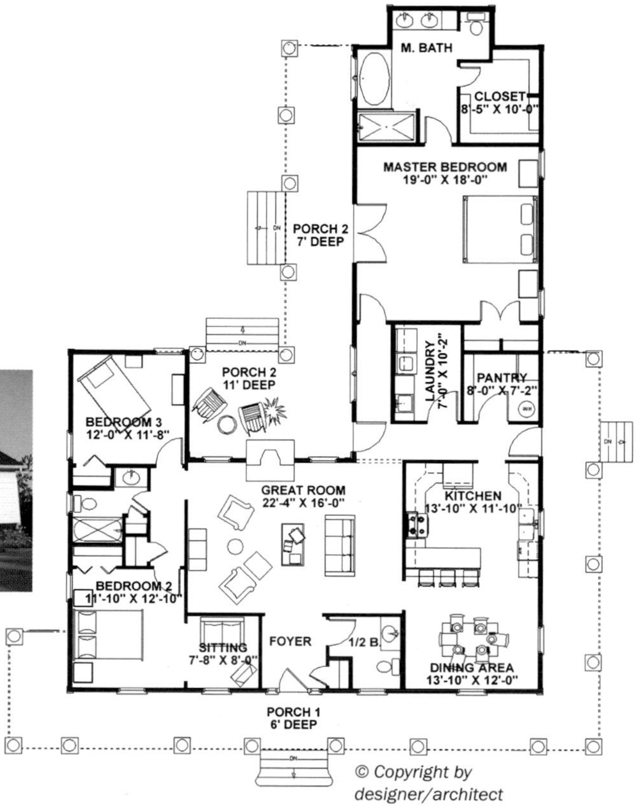

M. BATH
CLOSET
8'-5" X 10'-0"
MASTER BEDROOM
19'-0" X 18'-0"
PORCH 2
7' DEEP
PORCH 2
11' DEEP
LAUNDRY
7'-0" X 10'-2"
PANTRY
8'-0" X 7'-2"
BEDROOM 3
12'-0" X 11'-8"
GREAT ROOM
22'-4" X 16'-0"
KITCHEN
13'-10" X 11'-10"
BEDROOM 2
11'-10" X 12'-10"
SITTING
7'-8" X 8'-0"
FOYER
1/2 B.
DINING AREA
13'-10" X 12'-0"
PORCH 1
6' DEEP

© Copyright by designer/architect

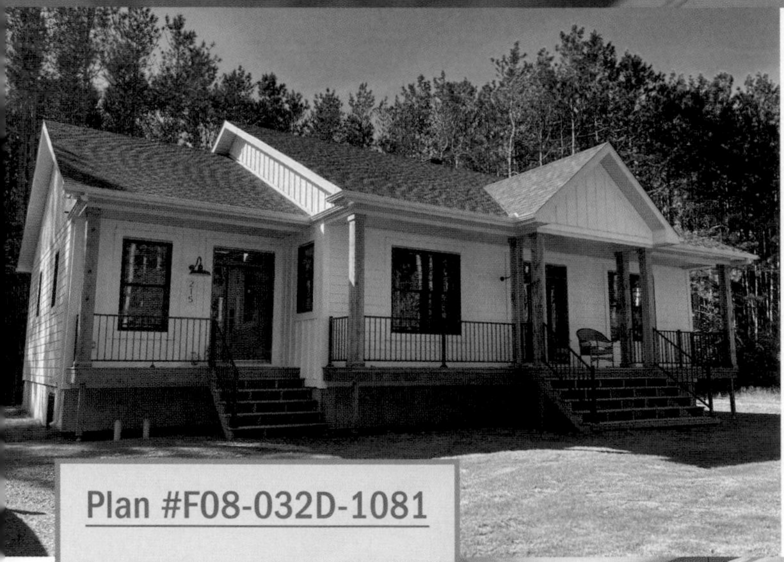

Plan #F08-032D-1081

Dimensions: 50' W x 38' D
Heated Sq. Ft.: 1,604
Bedrooms: 2 **Bathrooms:** 2
Exterior Walls: 2" x 6"
Foundation: Basement standard; crawl space, floating slab or monolithic slab for an additional fee

See index for more information

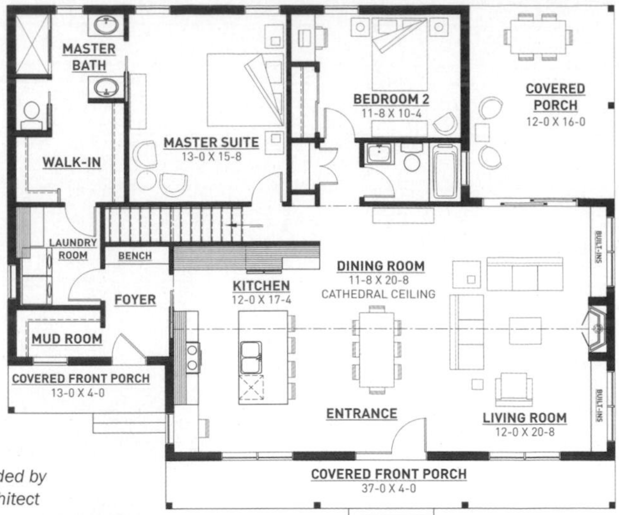

MASTER BATH
WALK-IN
MASTER SUITE
13-0 X 15-8
BEDROOM 2
11-8 X 10-4
COVERED PORCH
12-0 X 16-0
LAUNDRY ROOM
BENCH
FOYER
MUD ROOM
KITCHEN
12-0 X 17-4
DINING ROOM
11-8 X 20-8
CATHEDRAL CEILING
BUILT-INS
COVERED FRONT PORCH
13-0 X 4-0
ENTRANCE
LIVING ROOM
12-0 X 20-8
COVERED FRONT PORCH
37-0 X 4-0

Images provided by designer/architect

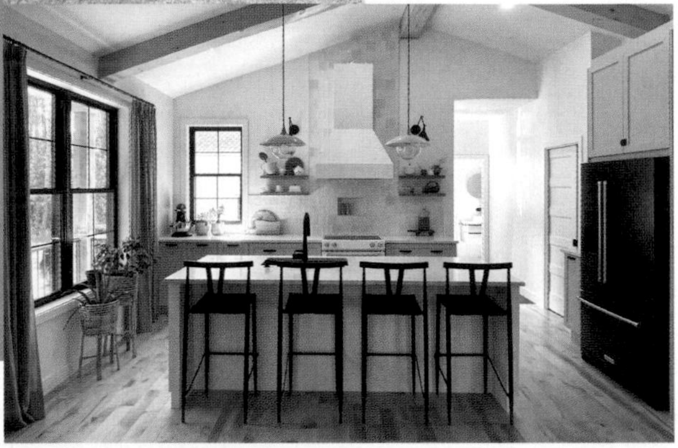

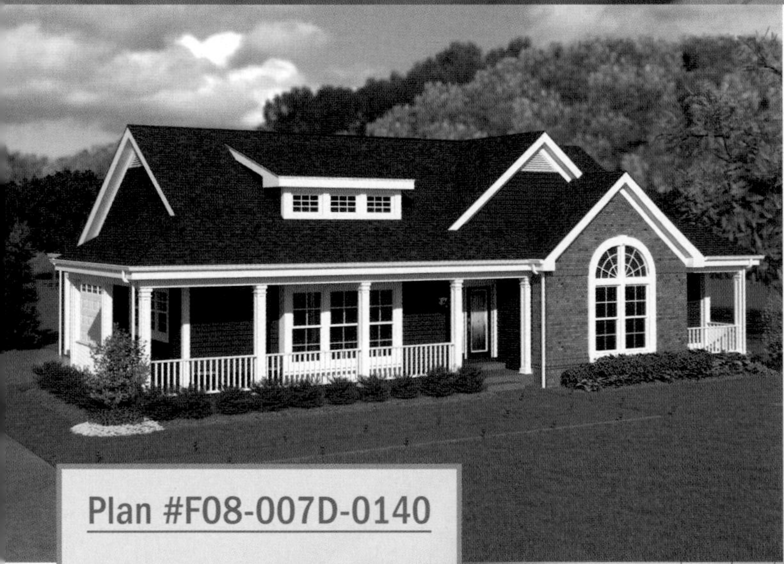

Plan #F08-007D-0140

Dimensions: 62' W x 45' D
Heated Sq. Ft.: 1,591
Bedrooms: 3 **Bathrooms:** 2
Foundation: Basement standard; crawl space or slab for an additional fee

See index for more information

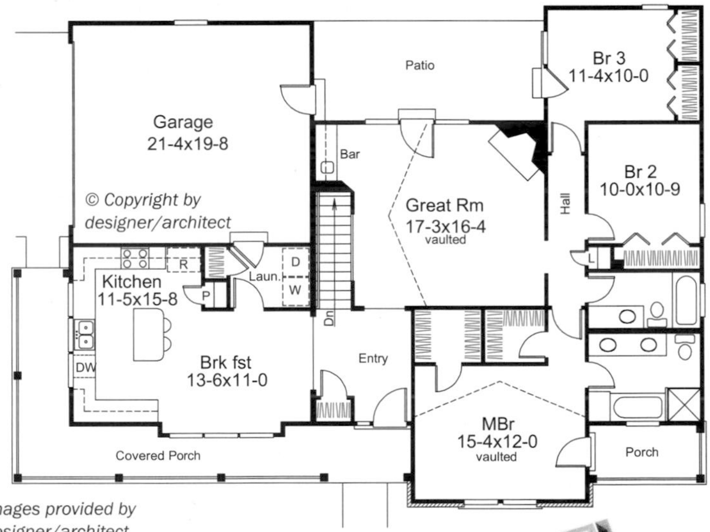

Patio
Br 3
11-4x10-0
Garage
21-4x19-8
Bar
Great Rm
17-3x16-4
vaulted
Br 2
10-0x10-9
Hall
© Copyright by designer/architect
Kitchen
11-5x15-8
R
P
Laun.
D
W
DW
Dn
L
Brk fst
13-6x11-0
Entry
MBr
15-4x12-0
vaulted
Covered Porch
Porch

Images provided by designer/architect

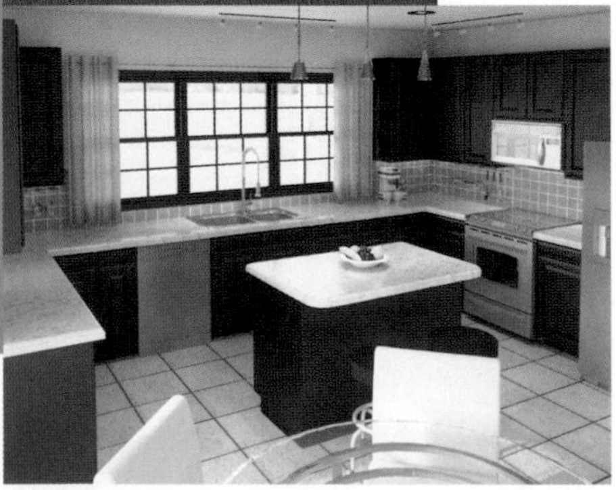

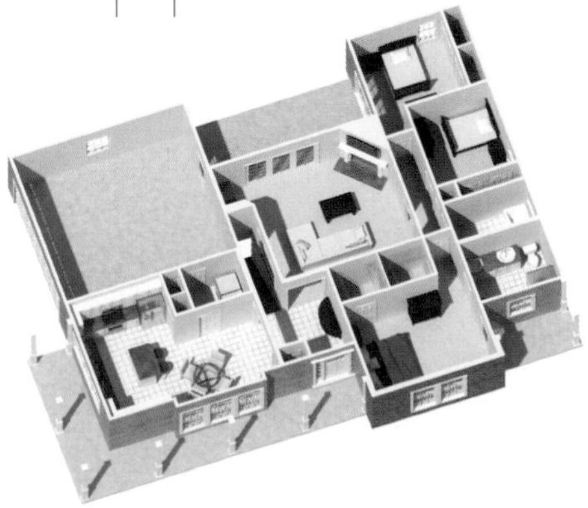

Images provided by designer/architect

Plan #F08-077D-0293

Dimensions: 58' W x 58'6" D
Heated Sq. Ft.: 1,800
Bedrooms: 3 **Bathrooms:** 2
Foundation: Crawl space or slab, please specify when ordering

See index for more information

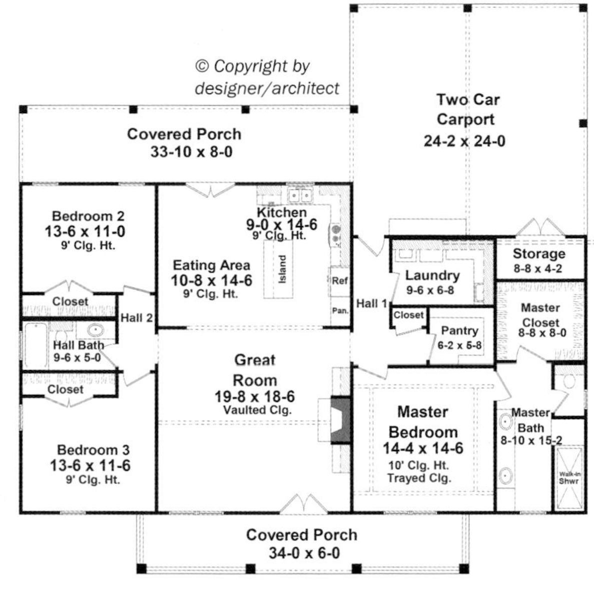

Images provided by designer/architect

Plan #F08-159D-0005

Dimensions: 58'10" W x 54' D
Heated Sq. Ft.: 1,660
Bonus Sq. Ft.: 1,340
Bedrooms: 3 **Bathrooms:** 2
Exterior Walls: 2" x 6"
Foundation: Walk-out basement

See index for more information

Optional Lower Level 1,340 sq. ft.

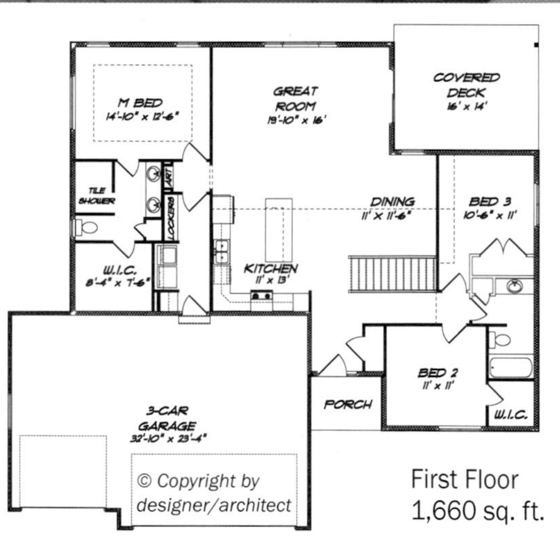

First Floor 1,660 sq. ft.

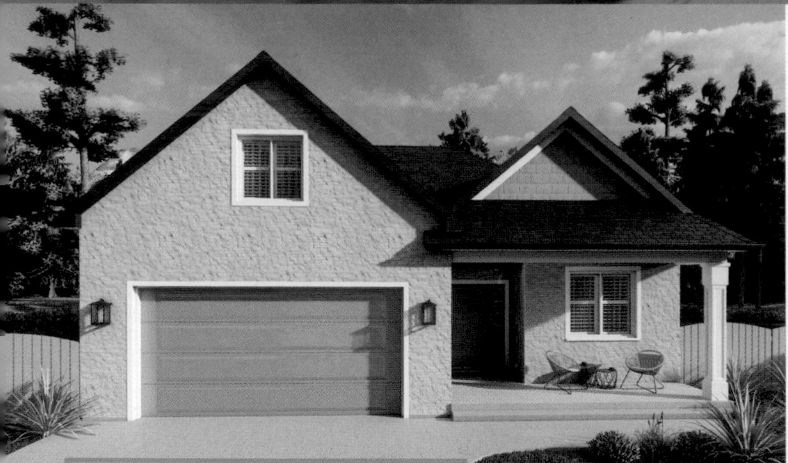

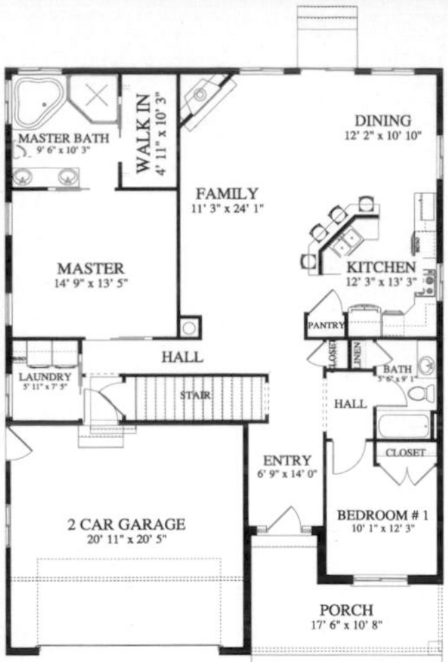

First Floor
1,545 sq. ft.

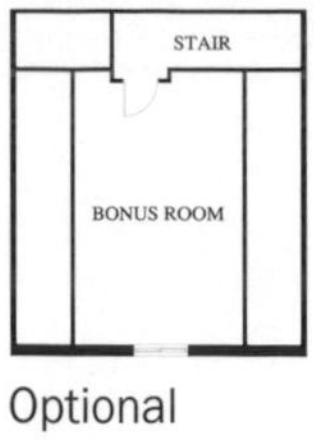

Optional
Second Floor
330 sq. ft.

Optional
Lower Level
1,680 sq. ft.

© Copyright by
designer/architect

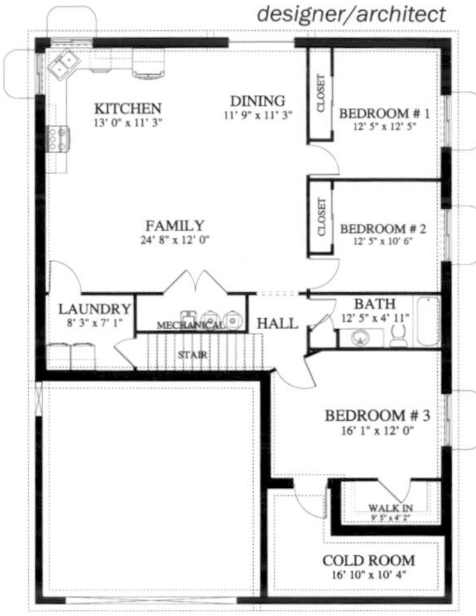

Plan #F08-172D-0065

Dimensions: 39'6" W x 54' D
Heated Sq. Ft.: 1,545
Bonus Sq. Ft.: 2,010
Bedrooms: 2 **Bathrooms:** 2
Exterior Walls: 2" x 6"
Foundation: Basement standard; slab, stem wall slab, crawl space, daylight basement or walk-out basement for an additional fee

See index for more information

Images provided by designer/architect

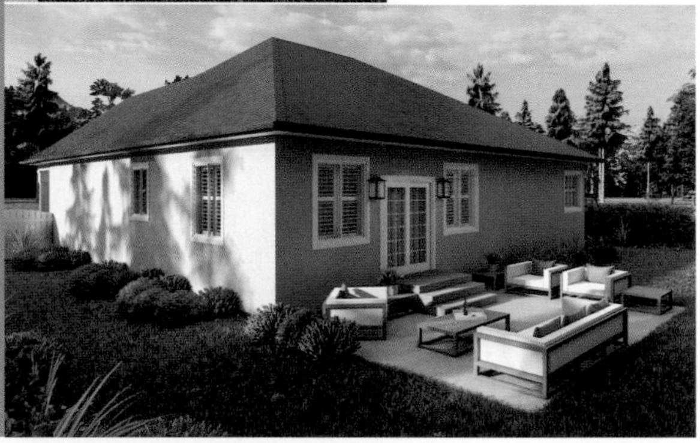

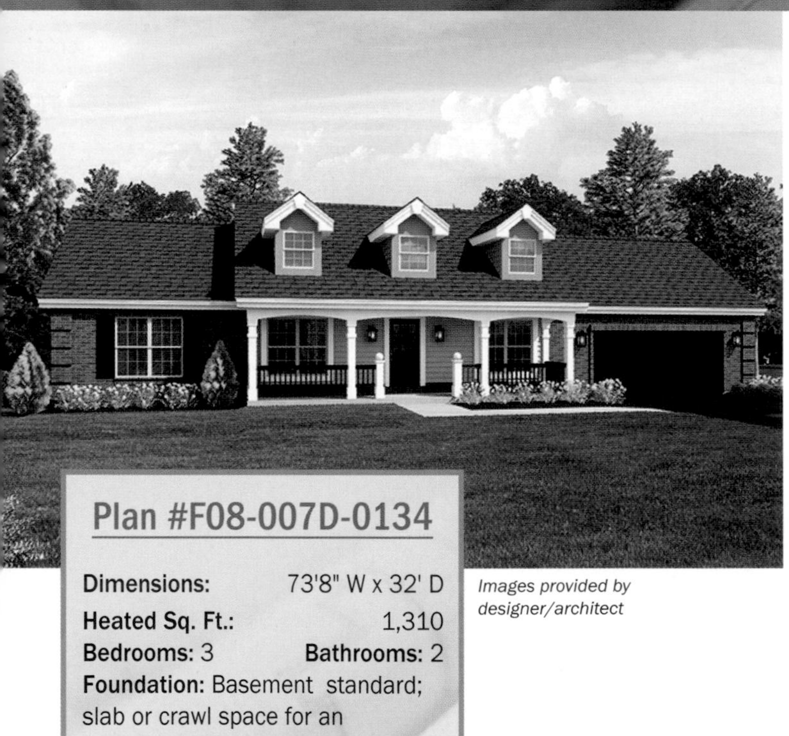

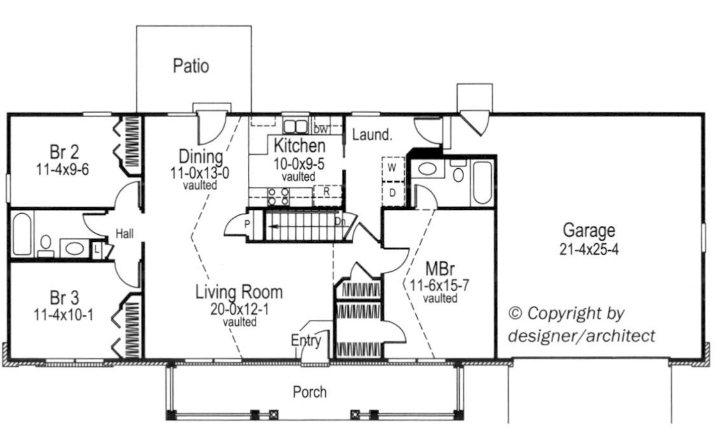

Plan #F08-007D-0134

Dimensions: 73'8" W x 32' D
Heated Sq. Ft.: 1,310
Bedrooms: 3 **Bathrooms:** 2
Foundation: Basement standard; slab or crawl space for an additional fee

See index for more information

Images provided by designer/architect

© Copyright by
designer/architect

Plan #F08-141D-0578

Dimensions: 93' W x 52' D
Heated Sq. Ft.: 1,787
Bonus Sq. Ft.: 1,650
Bedrooms: 2 **Bathrooms:** 2
Foundation: Walk-out basement standard; slab, crawl space or basement for an additional fee

See index for more information

Images provided by designer/architect

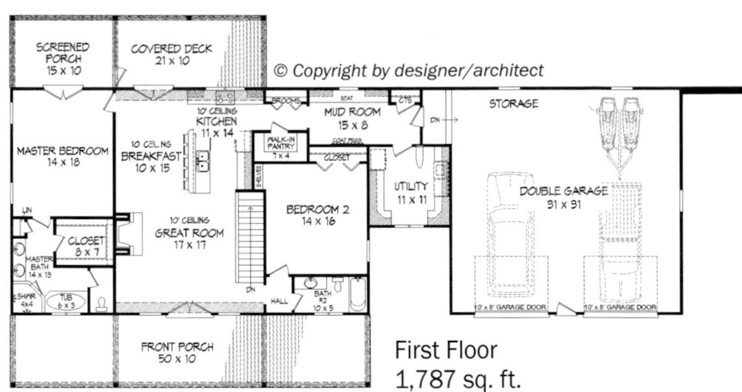

First Floor
1,787 sq. ft.

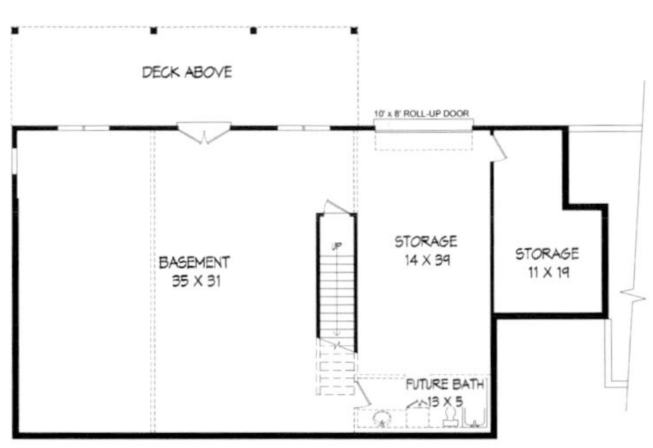

Optional
Lower Level
1,650 sq. ft.

Plan #F08-011D-0617

Dimensions: 69' W x 58' D
Heated Sq. Ft.: 2,104
Bonus Sq. Ft.: 268
Bedrooms: 3 **Bathrooms:** 2½
Exterior Walls: 2" x 6"
Foundation: Crawl space or slab standard; basement for an additional fee

See index for more information

Images provided by designer/architect

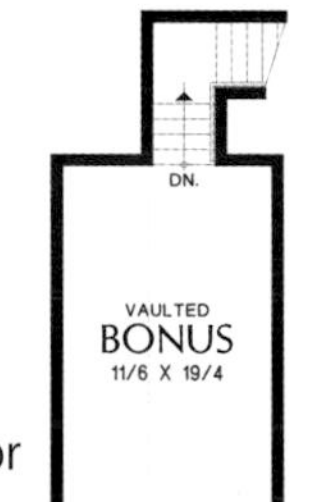

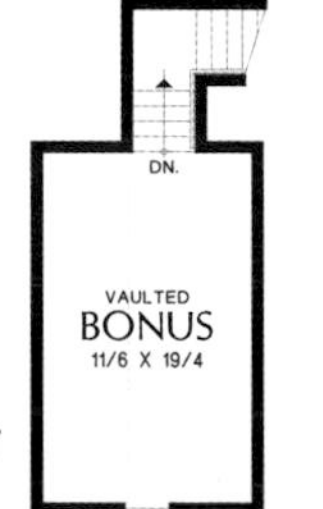

Optional
Second Floor
268 sq. ft.

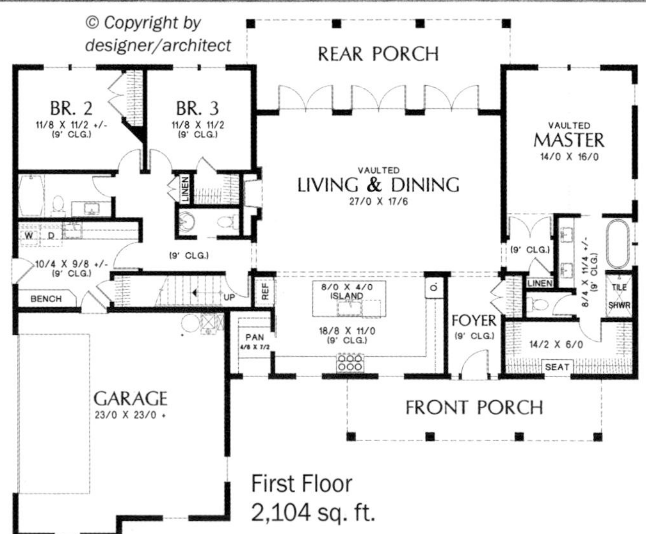

First Floor
2,104 sq. ft.

8-0 DEEP COVERED PORCH
BEDROOM 3 14-0 X 12-9
KITCHEN/DINING 20-0 X 12-0
LAUNDRY 16-0 X 6-8
TWO CAR GARAGE 22 X 24
BATH 2 10 X 8
CLO 6X6
BATH 10-0 X 9-4
GREAT ROOM 20-0 X 18-0
BEDROOM 2 14-0 X 12-9
MASTER BEDROOM 16-0 X 14-0
6-0 DEEP COVERED PORCH

© Copyright by designer/architect

Plan #F08-028D-0128

Dimensions: 72' W x 44' D
Heated Sq. Ft.: 1,629
Bedrooms: 3 **Bathrooms:** 2
Exterior Walls: 2" x 6"
Foundation: Floating slab standard; monolithic slab, crawl space, basement or walk-out basement for an additional fee

See index for more information

Images provided by designer/architect

Images provided by designer/architect

OWNER'S SUITE 14'11"X13'7"
DINING 11'10"X10'3"
SCREENED PORCH
GREAT ROOM 16'8" X 18'3"
BED 3 12'4" X 11'0"
O'S BATH
KITCHEN
BATH
WIC
WIC 1
WIC 2
UTIL.
FOYER
STUDY 11'1"X11'7"
BED 2 12'4"X11'0"
GARAGE 24'5" X 22'0"
FRONT PORCH

© Copyright by designer/architect

Plan #F08-167D-0001

Dimensions: 59'6" W x 60' D
Heated Sq. Ft.: 2,017
Bedrooms: 3 **Bathrooms:** 3
Exterior Walls: 2" x 6"
Foundation: Crawl space standard; slab for an additional fee

See index for more information

Plan #F08-065D-0062

Dimensions: 50' W x 55'8" D
Heated Sq. Ft.: 1,390
Bedrooms: 3 **Bathrooms:** 2
Foundation: Walk-out basement standard; crawl space or slab for an additional fee

See index for more information

Images provided by designer/architect

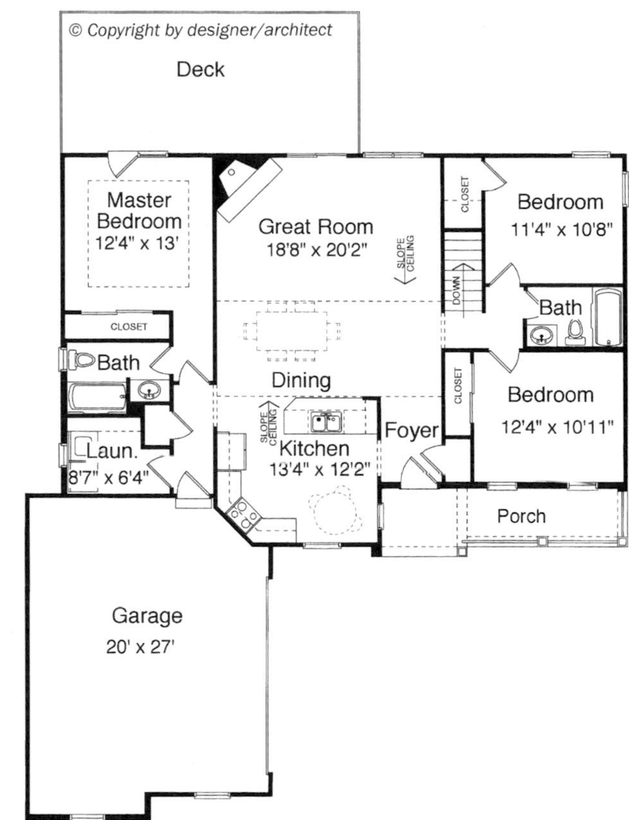

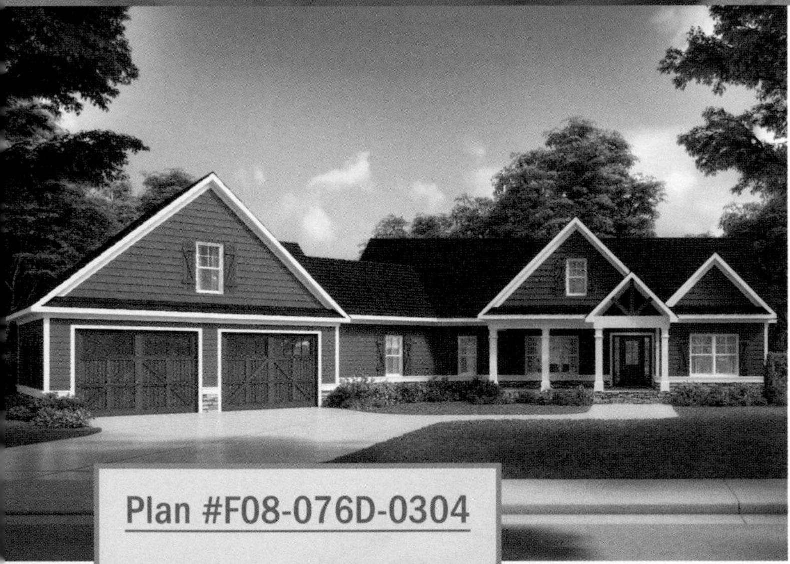

Plan #F08-076D-0304

Dimensions: 89' W x 76'4" D
Heated Sq. Ft.: 2,162
Bonus Sq. Ft.: 412
Bedrooms: 3 **Bathrooms:** 2½
Foundation: Slab

See index for more information

Images provided by designer/architect

© Copyright by designer/architect

COVERED TERRACE 18-3 X 14

MASTER SUITE 13-6 X 16

M. BATH 11 X 16-6

FAMILY ROOM 18-3 X 16-6

KITCHEN 11-6 X 16-6

BEDROOM 3 13 X 12

CLOSET 9-8 X 10-9

PANTRY 7-6 X 4-6

DINING ROOM 14-6 X 13

FOYER 7-3 X 13

UTILITY 11 X 7-6

PORCH

BEDROOM 2 13 X 12

2 CAR GARAGE 26 X 22-6

BONUS ROOM 15-6 X 22-6

First Floor
2,162 sq. ft.

Optional
Second Floor
412 sq. ft.

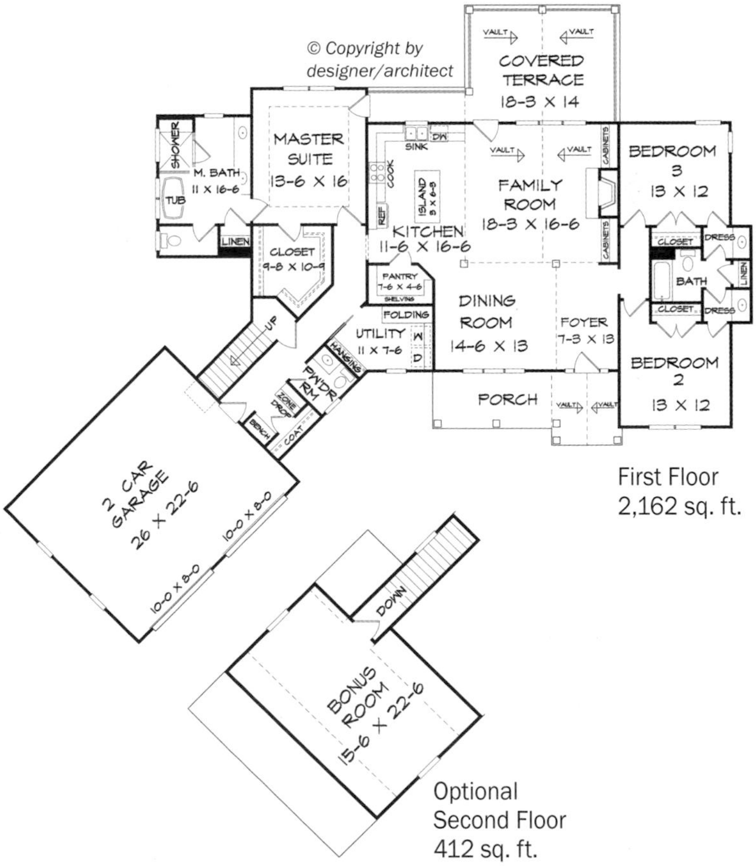

Plan #F08-130D-0396

Dimensions: 31' W x 57' D
Heated Sq. Ft.: 1,420
Bedrooms: 3 **Bathrooms:** 2
Exterior Walls: 2" x 6"
Foundation: Slab standard; crawl space or basement for an additional fee

See index for more information

Images provided by designer/architect

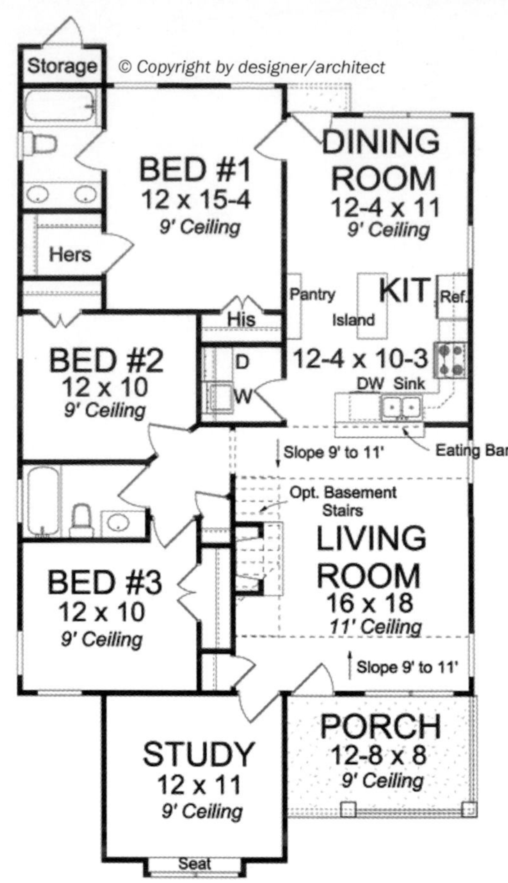

Plan #F08-065D-0355

Dimensions: 60' W x 55'1" D
Heated Sq. Ft.: 1,791
Bedrooms: 3 **Bathrooms:** 2
Foundation: Basement standard; crawl space or slab for an additional fee

See index for more information

Images provided by designer/architect

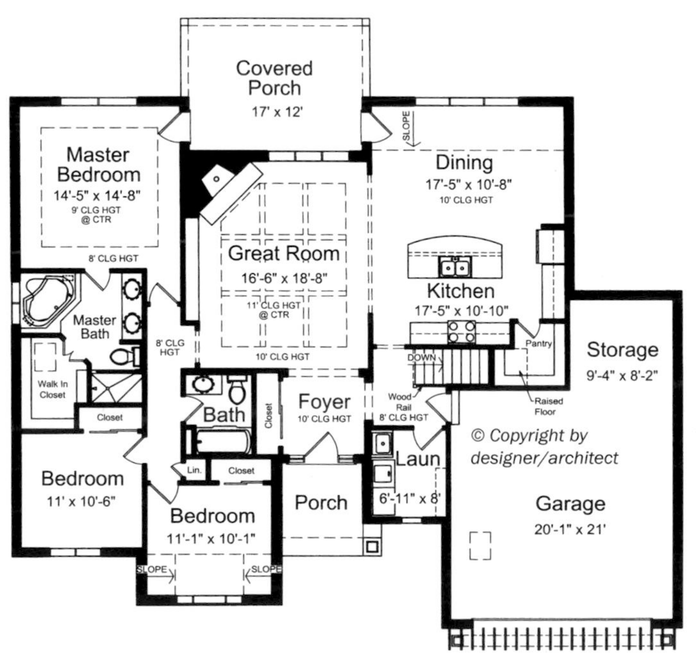

Plan #F08-028D-0100

Dimensions: 46' W x 42'6" D
Heated Sq. Ft.: 1,311
Bedrooms: 3 **Bathrooms:** 2
Exterior Walls: 2" x 6"
Foundation: Floating slab standard; monolithic slab, crawl space, basement or walk-out basement for an additional fee

See index for more information

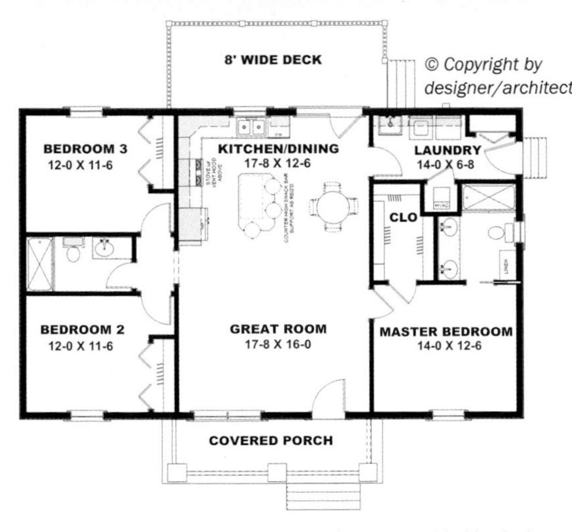

Images provided by designer/architect

Plan #F08-005D-0001

Dimensions: 72' W x 34'4" D
Heated Sq. Ft.: 1,400
Bedrooms: 3 **Bathrooms:** 2
Foundation: Basement standard; crawl space or slab for an additional fee

See index for more information

Images provided by designer/architect

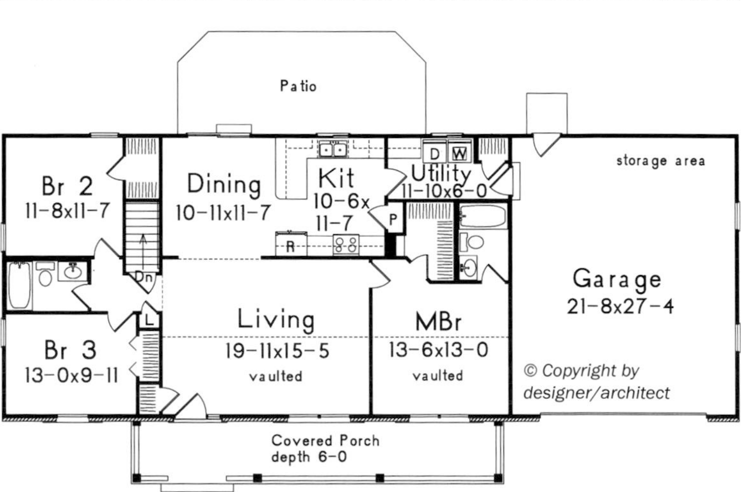

Plan #F08-013D-0154

Dimensions: 36' W x 42'4" D
Heated Sq. Ft.: 953
Bedrooms: 2 **Bathrooms:** 1½
Foundation: Crawl space standard; slab or basement for an additional fee

See index for more information

Images provided by designer/architect

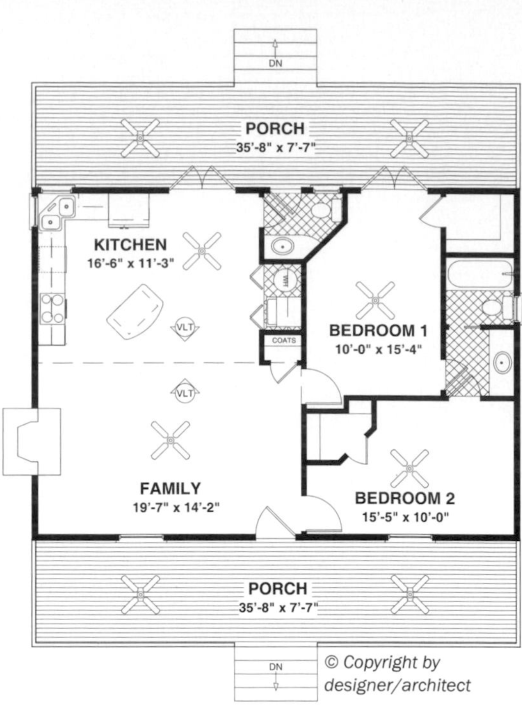

© Copyright by designer/architect

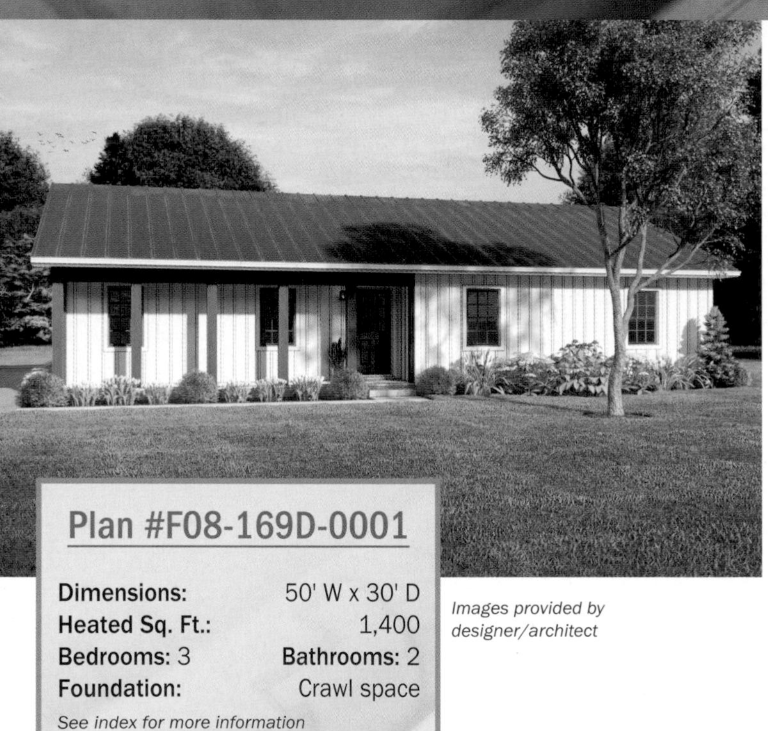

Plan #F08-169D-0001

Dimensions: 50' W x 30' D
Heated Sq. Ft.: 1,400
Bedrooms: 3 **Bathrooms:** 2
Foundation: Crawl space

See index for more information

Images provided by designer/architect

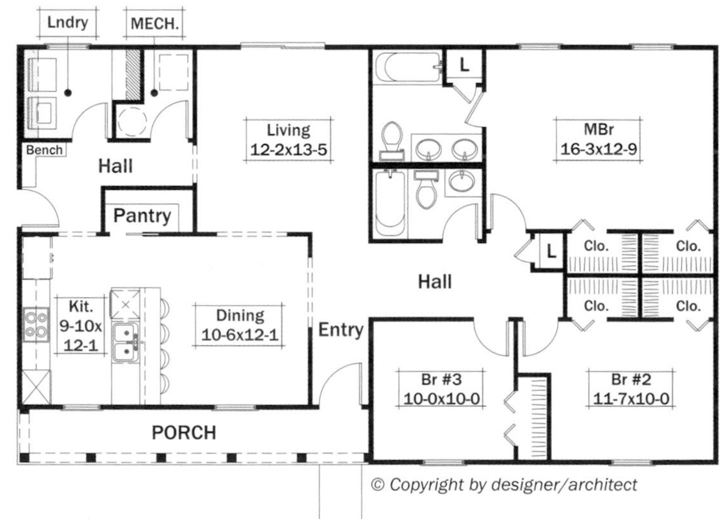

© Copyright by designer/architect

Plan #F08-130D-0368

Dimensions: 31' W x 53' D
Heated Sq. Ft.: 1,277
Bedrooms: 3 **Bathrooms:** 2
Foundation: Slab standard; crawl space or basement for an additional fee

See index for more information

Images provided by designer/architect

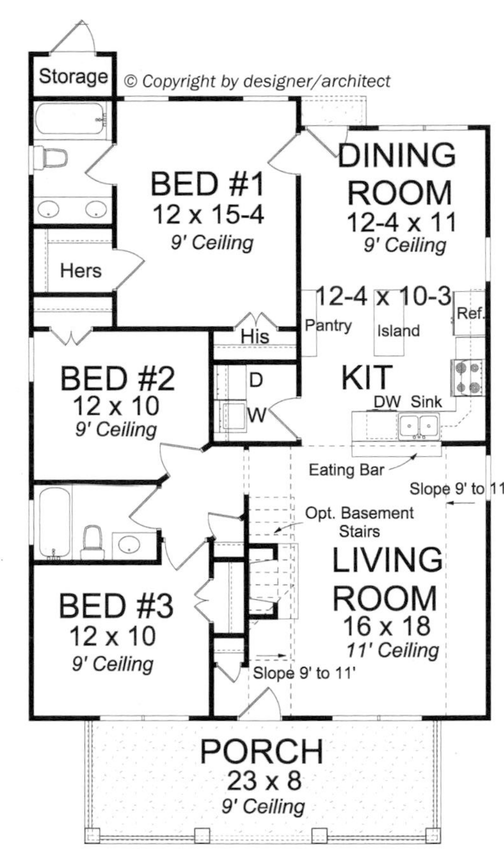

Plan #F08-013D-0198

Dimensions: 61'9" W x 37'3" D
Heated Sq. Ft.: 1,399
Bedrooms: 3 **Bathrooms:** 2
Foundation: Slab standard; crawl space or basement for an additional fee

See index for more information

Images provided by designer/architect

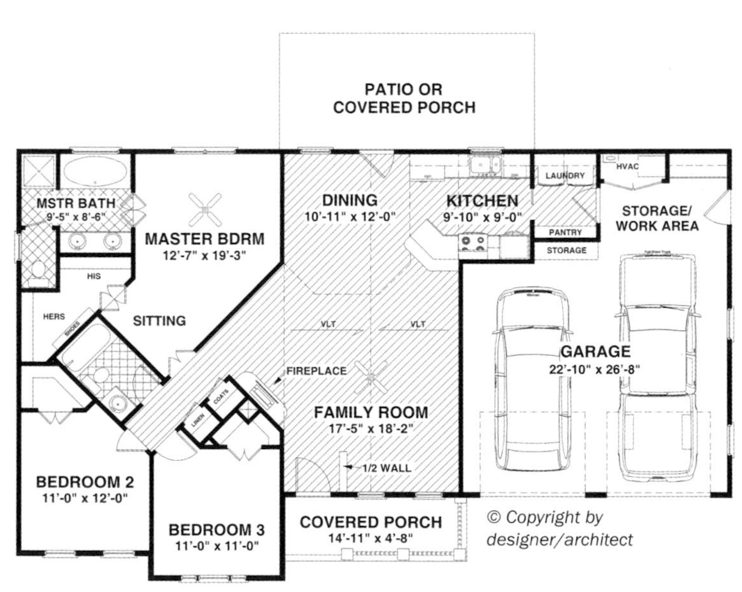

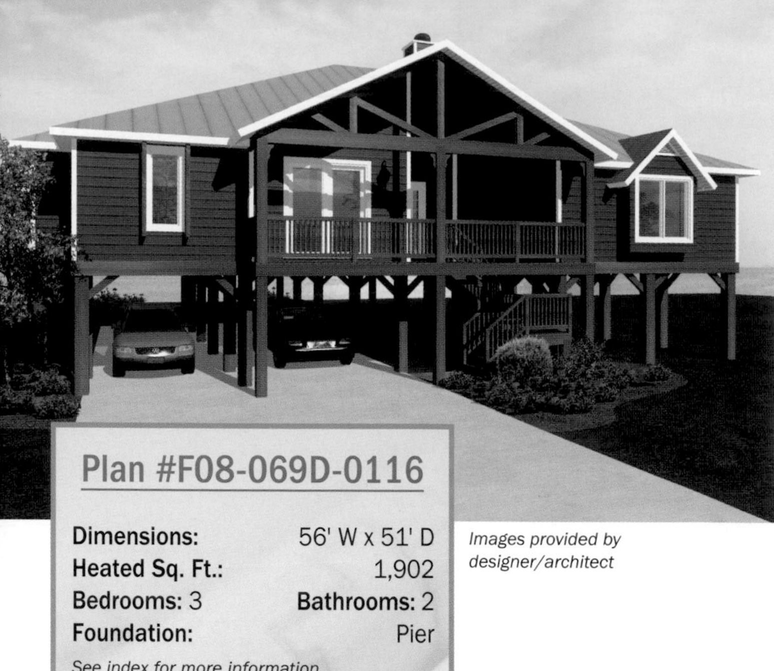

Plan #F08-069D-0116

Dimensions: 56' W x 51' D
Heated Sq. Ft.: 1,902
Bedrooms: 3 **Bathrooms:** 2
Foundation: Pier

See index for more information

Images provided by designer/architect

PORCH
10 x 44
© Copyright by designer/architect
10' STEP UP CEIL
MASTER SUITE
14 X 19
KITCHEN
11 X 13
10' CEIL
GREAT ROOM
17 X 19
10' CEIL
BEDROOM
12 X 12
CLOSET
A/C
WASH
DRY
DINING RM
11 X 12
10' CEIL
F/P
FOYER
10' CEIL
UTILITY
8 x 9
CLOSET
7 x 11
DRESS.
ENTRY
ELEVATOR
BATH
STUDIO
11 X 12
BEDROOM
12 X 12
GARDEN TUB
BATH
CLOSET
PORCH
6 x 16
SEAT
DOWN
PARKING UNDER

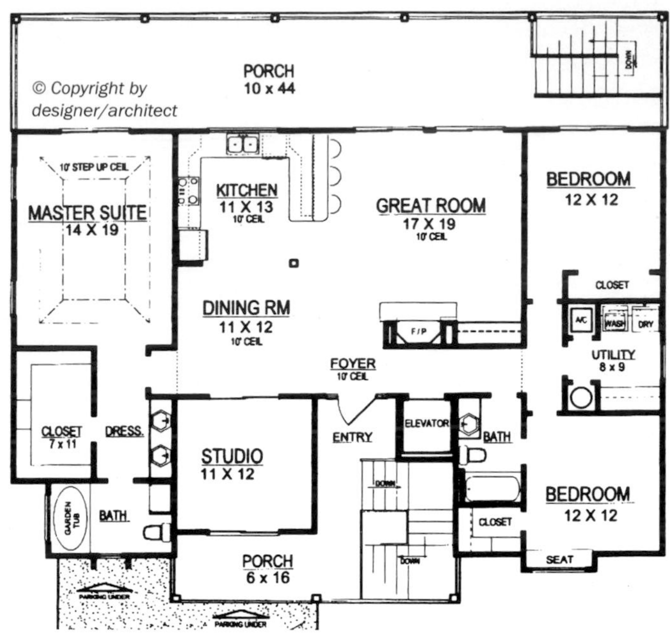

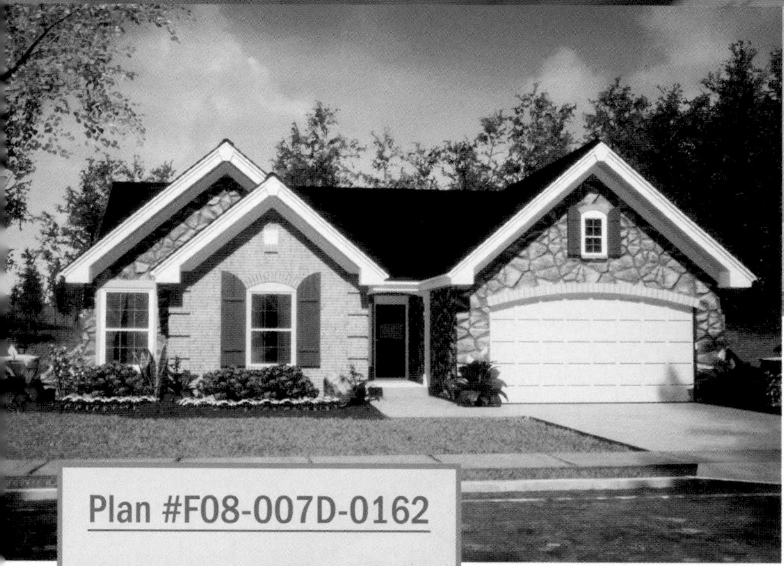

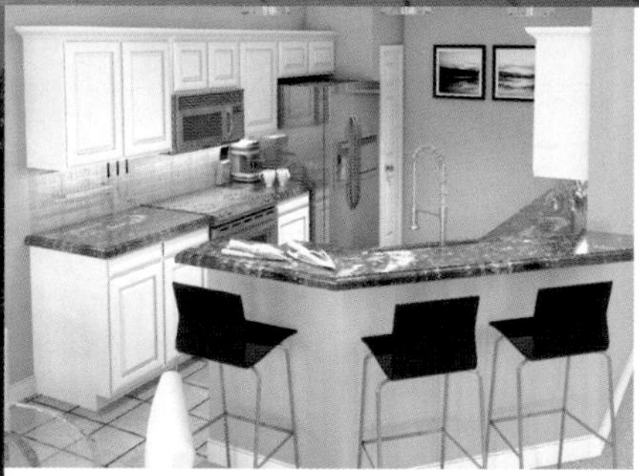

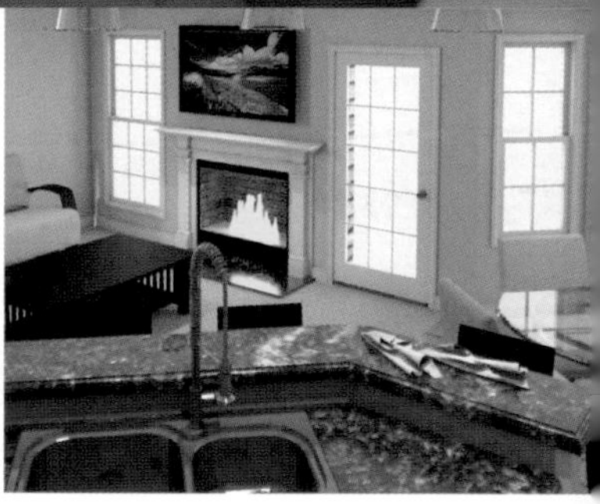

Plan #F08-007D-0162

Dimensions: 47'8" W x 47'4" D
Heated Sq. Ft.: 1,519
Bedrooms: 4 **Bathrooms:** 2
Foundation: Crawl space standard; slab or basement for an additional fee

See index for more information

Images provided by designer/architect

Patio
Br 2
12-0x12-0
Br 3
10-4x12-0
Living Rm
13-1x18-5
vaulted
Dining
10-3x12-8
vaulted
Hall
Plant Shelf Above
DW
Kit
10-0x
13-0
vaulted
Entry
Laundry
Study/Br 4
10-0x9-0
Porch
MBr
15-0x14-0
Sitting
Garage
19-4x20-4
© Copyright by designer/architect

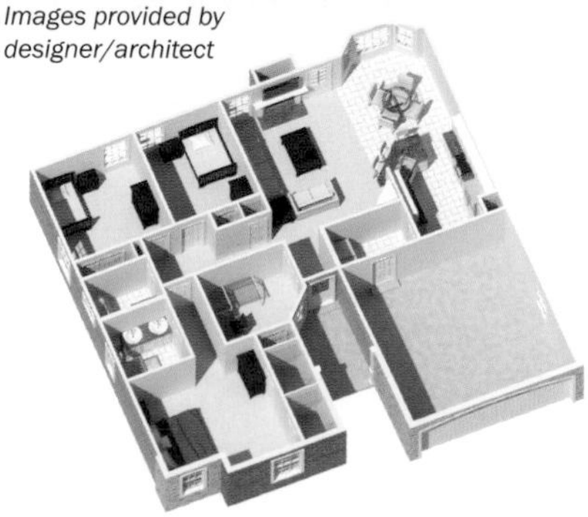

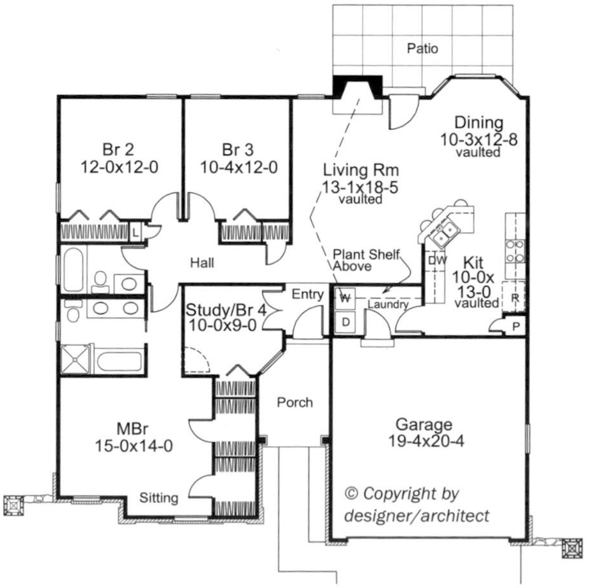

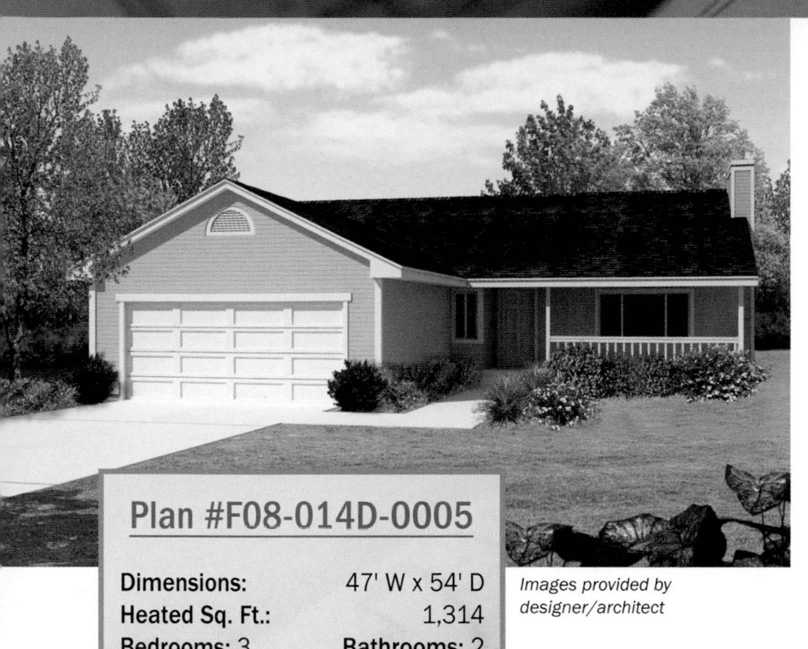

Plan #F08-014D-0005

Dimensions:	47' W x 54' D
Heated Sq. Ft.:	1,314
Bedrooms: 3	**Bathrooms:** 2
Exterior Walls:	2" x 6"
Foundation:	Basement

See index for more information

Images provided by designer/architect

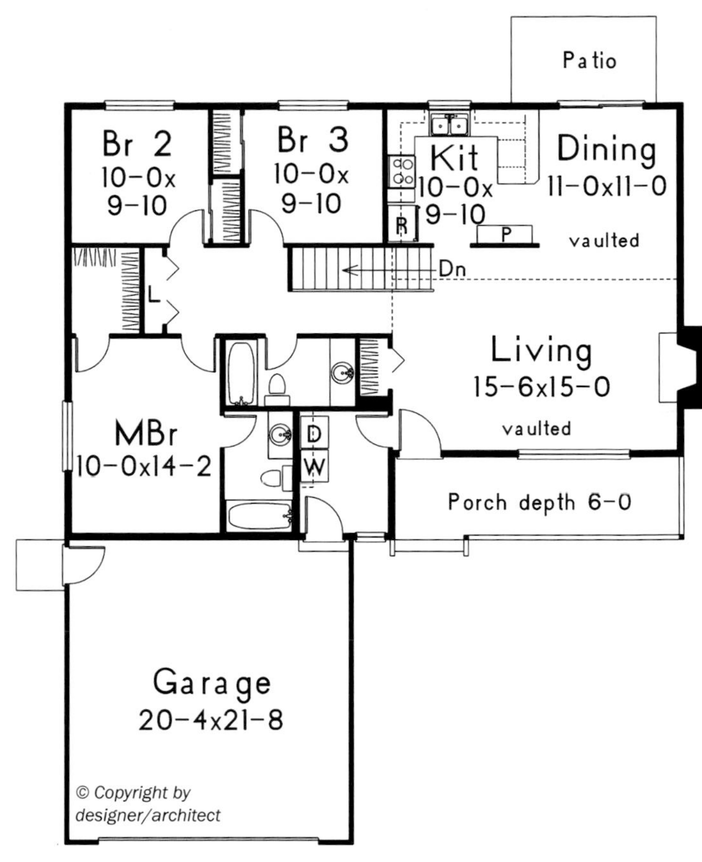

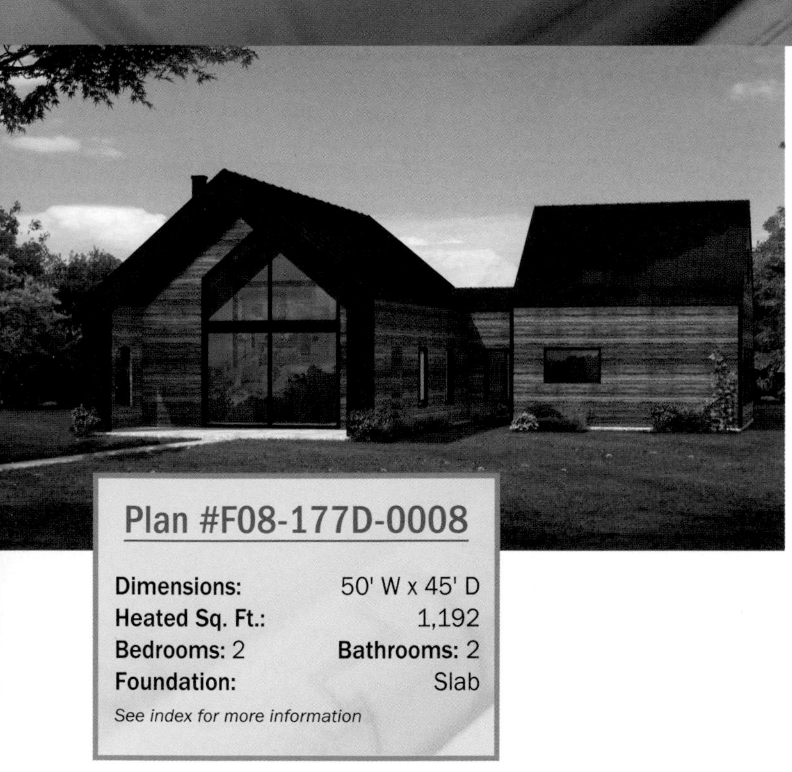

Plan #F08-177D-0008

Dimensions:	50' W x 45' D
Heated Sq. Ft.:	1,192
Bedrooms: 2	**Bathrooms:** 2
Foundation:	Slab

See index for more information

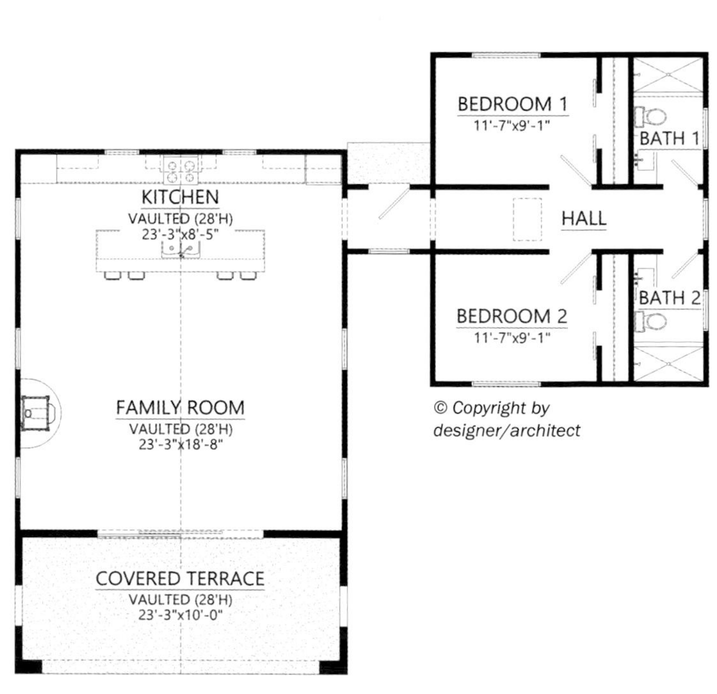

Plan #F08-011D-0347

Dimensions: 113'4" W x 62'8" D
Heated Sq. Ft.: 2,910
Bedrooms: 3 **Bathrooms:** 3
Exterior Walls: 2" x 6"
Foundation: Crawl space or slab standard; basement for an additional fee

See index for more information

Images provided by designer/architect

Features

- The foyer of this country ranch house plan has 11' ceilings with wood columns into the vaulted great room straight ahead for an open and rustic interior
- The vaulted great room has gorgeous exposed beams, and a fireplace with built-ins
- An open floor plan combines the great room, kitchen, and dining room into one big "family triangle," with no walls to cramp the space
- The kitchen has an island with a double sink, 10' ceilings, and plenty of counterspace
- 3-car side entry garage

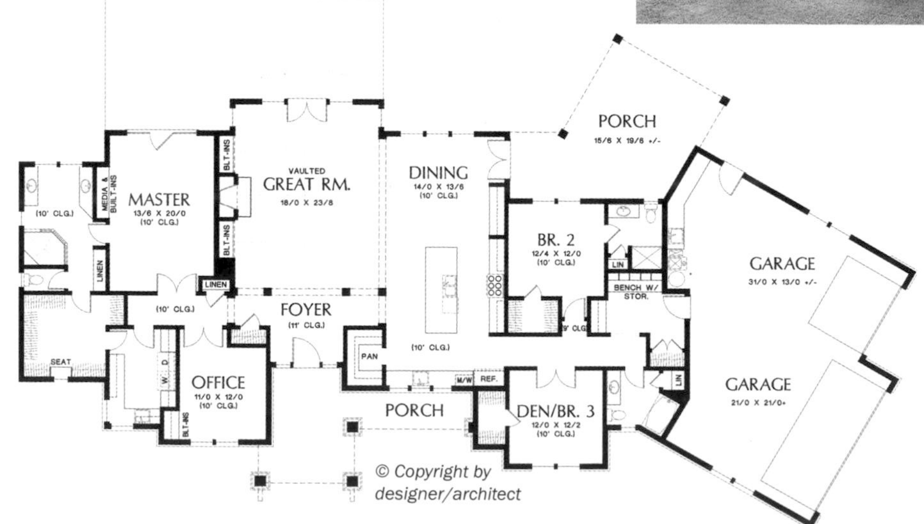

Plan #F08-101D-0121

Dimensions: 116'6" W x 62' D
Heated Sq. Ft.: 3,380
Bonus Sq. Ft.: 2,027
Bedrooms: 2 **Bathrooms:** 2½
Exterior Walls: 2" x 6"
Foundation: Basement, daylight basement or walk-out basement, please specify when ordering

See index for more information

Images provided by designer/architect

Features

- This stunning Modern home has a touch of a Modern Farmhouse feel
- This unique floor plan has a separate apartment style suite that features its own living room, a separate entrance, a covered patio and a kitchen with an island
- The main home offers an open kitchen with massive island, a cozy great room with fireplace, a casual dining space, a laundry room and a master bedroom and bath in a private location
- There's also a first floor study, ideal as a home office
- The lower level has an additional 2,027 square feet of living area and features a rec room, media area, bar, an exercise room, two bedrooms and two full baths
- 3-car side entry garage

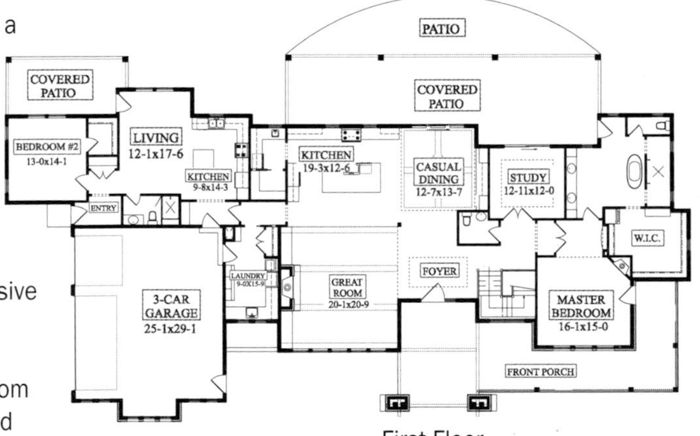

First Floor
3,380 sq. ft.

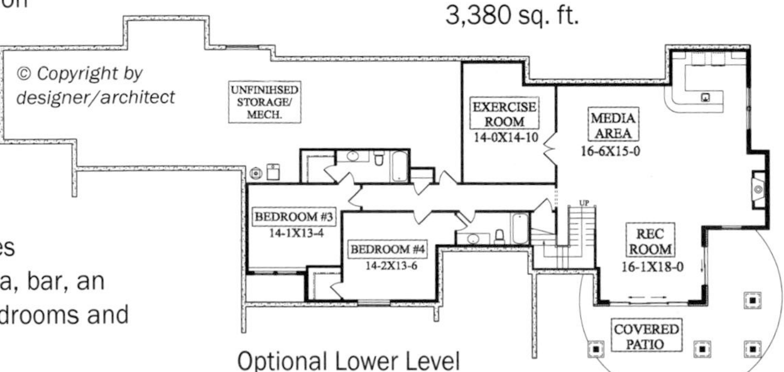

Optional Lower Level
2,027 sq. ft.

Plan #F08-086D-0149

Dimensions: 50' W x 56'4" D
Heated Sq. Ft.: 1,837
Bonus Sq. Ft.: 1,721
Bedrooms: 2 **Bathrooms:** 2½
Foundation: Basement

See index for more information

Images provided by designer/architect

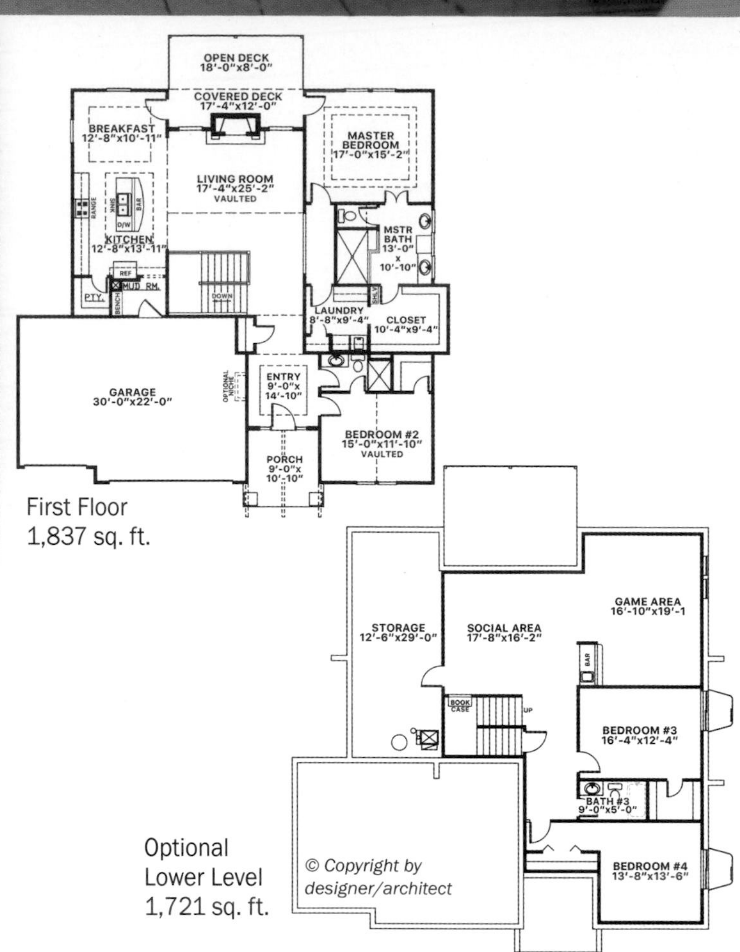

First Floor
1,837 sq. ft.

Optional
Lower Level
1,721 sq. ft.

Plan #F08-001D-0041

Dimensions: 40' W x 25' D
Heated Sq. Ft.: 1,000
Bedrooms: 3 **Bathrooms:** 1
Foundation: Crawl space standard; slab or basement for an additional fee

See index for more information

Images provided by designer/architect

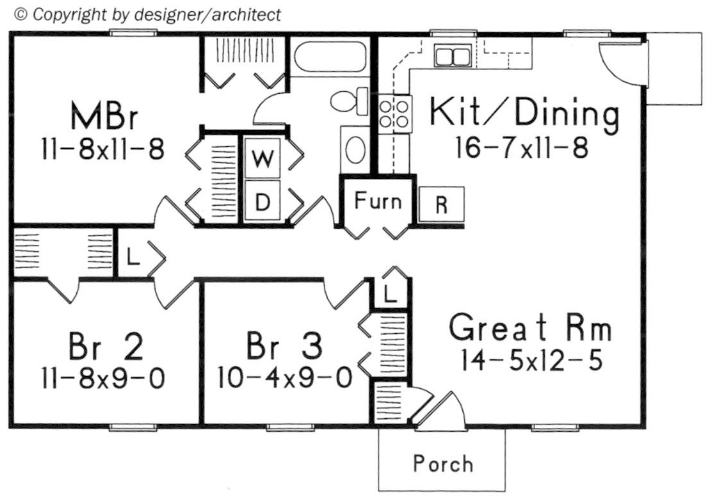

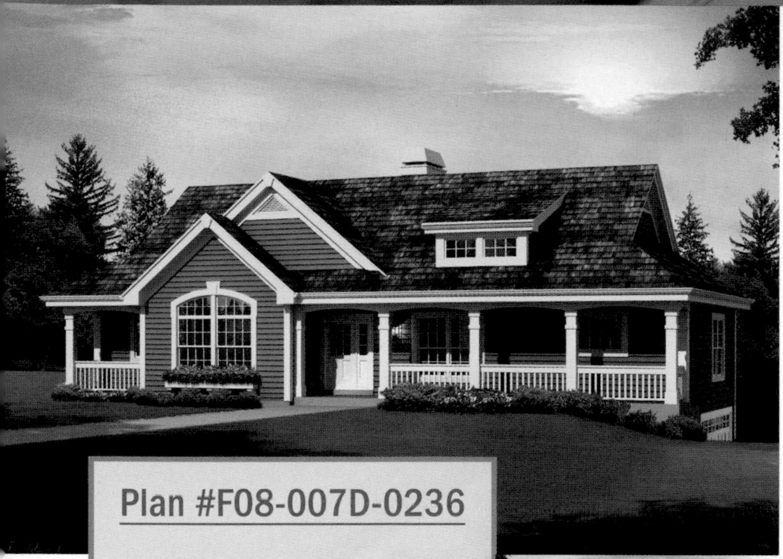

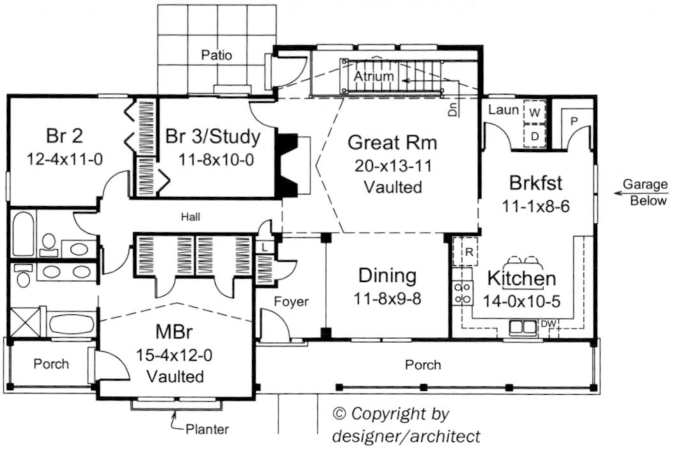

Patio
Atrium
Dn
Laun
W
D
P
Br 2
12-4x11-0
Br 3/Study
11-8x10-0
Great Rm
20-x13-11
Vaulted
Brkfst
11-1x8-6
Garage
Below
Hall
L
R
Dining
11-8x9-8
Kitchen
14-0x10-5
Foyer
DW
MBr
15-4x12-0
Vaulted
Porch
Porch
Planter
© Copyright by
designer/architect

Plan #F08-007D-0236

Dimensions:	59' W x 36' D
Heated Sq. Ft.:	1,676
Bedrooms: 3	**Bathrooms:** 2
Foundation:	Basement

See index for more information

Images provided by designer/architect

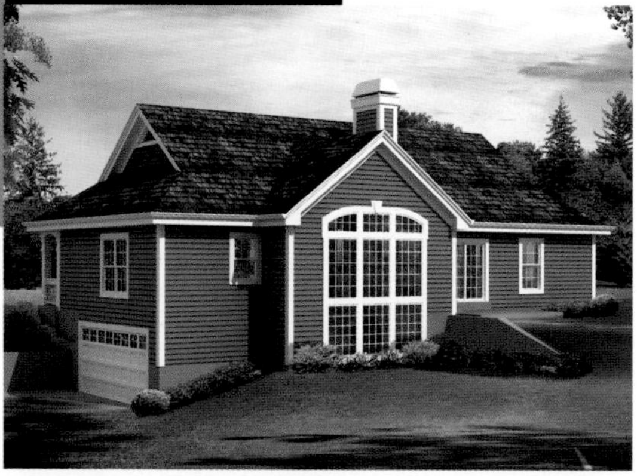

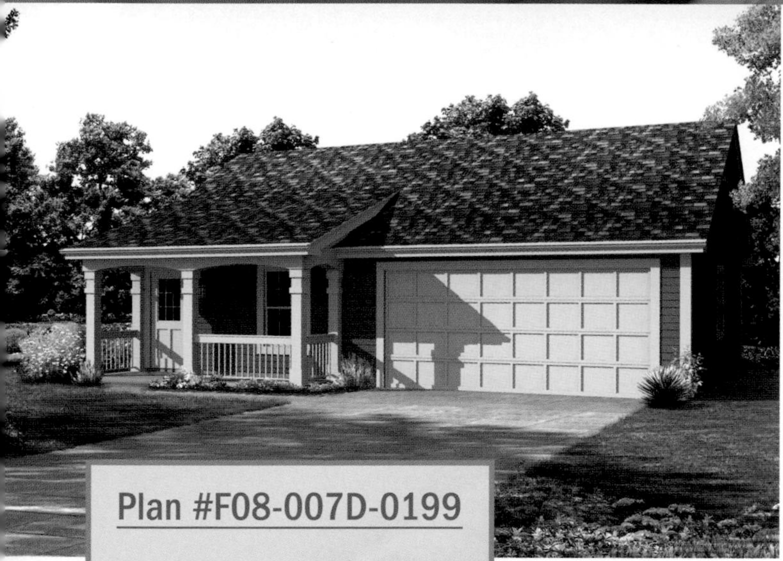

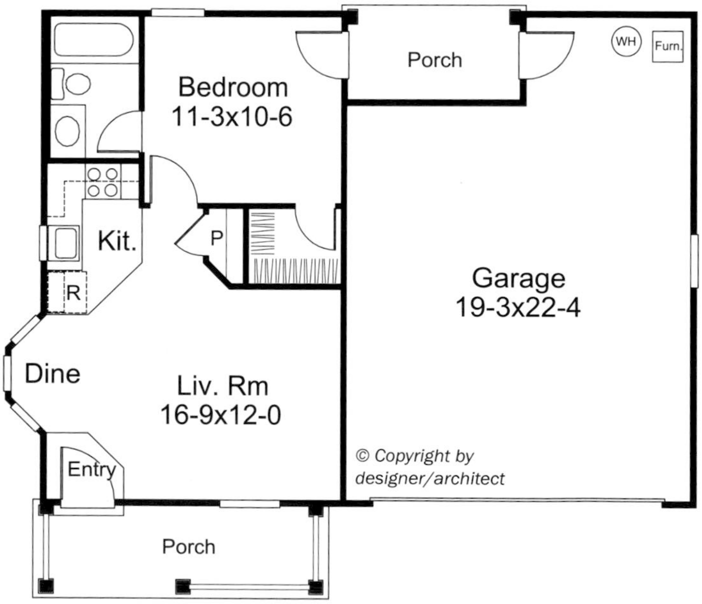

Porch
WH
Furn.
Bedroom
11-3x10-6
Kit.
P
R
Garage
19-3x22-4
Dine
Liv. Rm
16-9x12-0
Entry
© Copyright by
designer/architect
Porch

Plan #F08-007D-0199

Dimensions:	39' W x 33' D
Heated Sq. Ft.:	496
Bedrooms: 1	**Bathrooms:** 1
Foundation:	Slab

See index for more information

Images provided by designer/architect

Images provided by designer/architect

Plan #F08-011D-0342

Dimensions: 63' W x 61'6" D
Heated Sq. Ft.: 2,368
Bedrooms: 3 **Bathrooms:** 2½
Exterior Walls: 2" x 6
Foundation: Crawl space or slab standard; basement for an additional fee

See index for more information

Features

- This Craftsman home's curb appeal will make it a standout in any neighborhood with its tasteful combination of stone, siding and multiple gables
- The chef of the family will love the island in the kitchen, the walk-in pantry, and the spacious snack bar space
- The nearby laundry room is bright and cheerful, with plenty of counterspace for folding clothes
- The secluded office could serve as a guest room, or a place for hobbies
- The well-appointed master suite features a vaulted ceiling, and a lovely window arrangement with transoms above that overlooks the backyard
- A sit-down shower anchors the posh master bath, which also includes a toilet space, dual sinks and a walk-in closet
- 3-car front entry garage

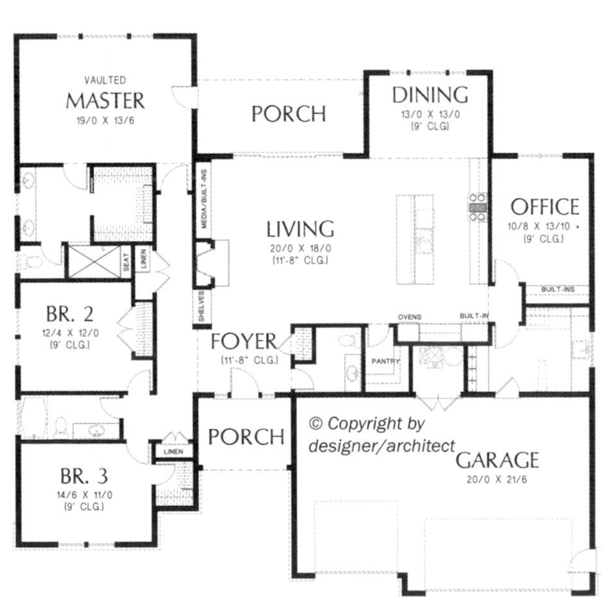

Plan #F08-101D-0125

Dimensions: 118'3" W x 70' D
Heated Sq. Ft.: 2,970
Bonus Sq. Ft.: 2,014
Bedrooms: 2 **Bathrooms:** 2½
Exterior Walls: 2" x 6"
Foundation: Walk-out basement

See index for more information

Features

- This stunning rustic Modern Craftsman home is loaded with curb appeal and intrigue
- Step into the foyer and discover an awe-inspiring vaulted great room that is the focal point of the home
- The kitchen faces the great room and has a massive island with dining space
- Behind the kitchen there is a large walk-in pantry, and a mud room for staying organized
- There's also a guest room with direct access to a full bath
- The master suite has a beamed ceiling, covered deck access, and a luxury bath with a freestanding tub, walk-in shower and a huge walk-in closet
- The optional lower level has an additional 2,014 square feet of living area includes a huge rec room with a bar, a game nook, three additional bedrooms, a half bath and two full baths
- 2-car front entry garage, and a 1-car side entry garage

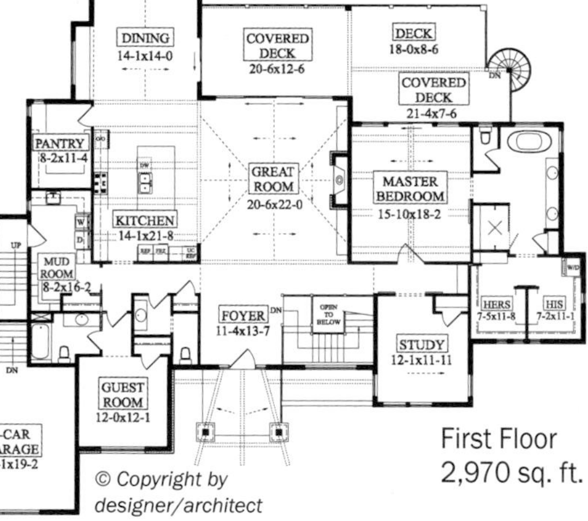

© Copyright by designer/architect

First Floor
2,970 sq. ft.

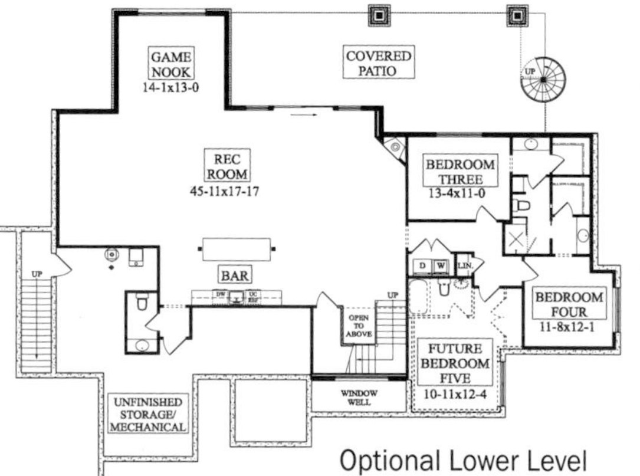

Optional Lower Level
2,014 sq. ft.

Images provided by designer/architect

Plan #F08-007D-0105

Dimensions: 35' W x 40'8" D
Heated Sq. Ft.: 1,084
Bedrooms: 2 **Bathrooms:** 2
Foundation: Basement standard; crawl space or slab for an additional fee

See index for more information

Images provided by designer/architect

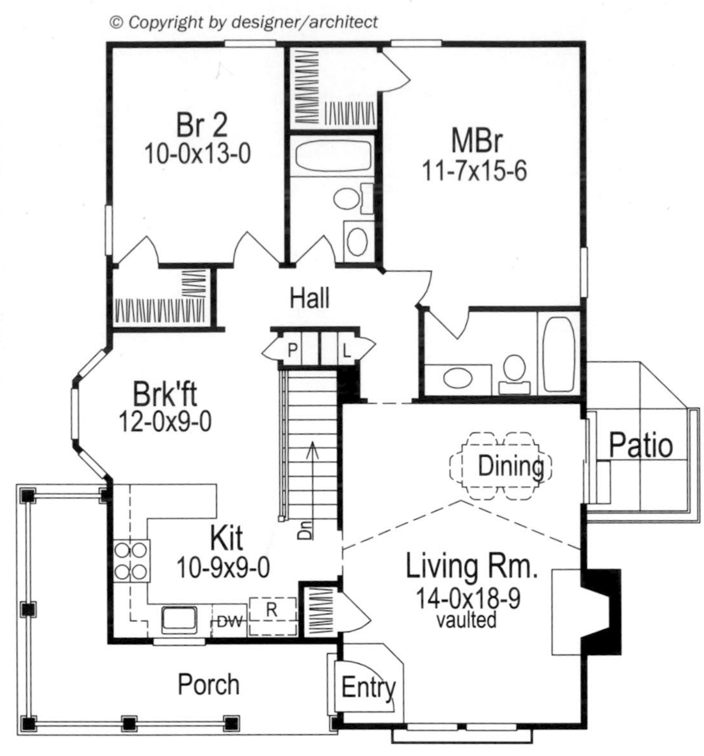

Plan #F08-007D-0192

Dimensions: 75'8" W x 32' D
Heated Sq. Ft.: 1,420
Bedrooms: 3 **Bathrooms:** 2
Foundation: Basement standard; crawl space or slab for an additional fee

See index for more information

Images provided by designer/architect

Patio
MBr 15-0x12-1
Kitchen 9-4x12-1
Dining 10-8x12-4
Pantry
W D
Laun
Garage 20-0x25-4
Hall
Br 2 12-1x11-0
Br 3 10-0x9-6
Living Rm 23-4x13-0
Entry
Porch

© Copyright by designer/architect

Plan #F08-130D-0408

Dimensions: 32' W x 65'10" D
Heated Sq. Ft.: 1,772
Bedrooms: 3 **Bathrooms:** 2
Foundation: Slab standard; crawl space or basement for an additional fee

See index for more information

Images provided by designer/architect

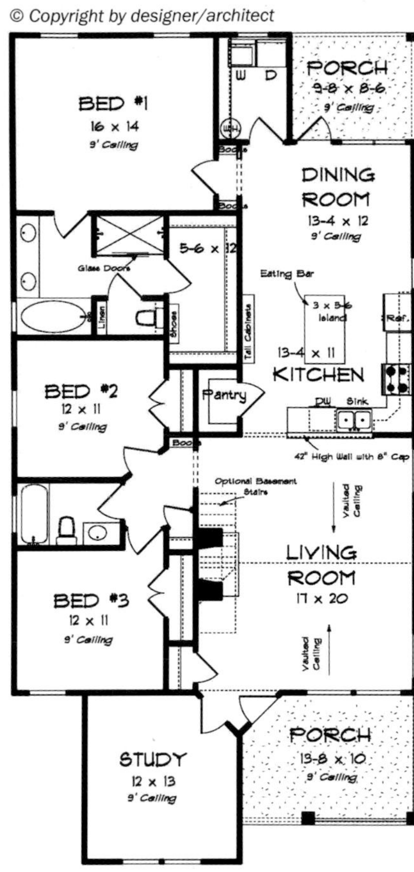

Plan #F08-065D-0412

Dimensions: 59'5" W x 58'4" D
Heated Sq. Ft.: 1,894
Bedrooms: 3 **Bathrooms:** 2½
Foundation: Basement

See index for more information

Images provided by designer/architect

First Floor
1,894 sq. ft.

Covered Porch 22'-0" x 12'-0"
Master Bedroom 12'-2" x 16'-7"
Mstr Bath
Walk-in Closet
Dining 10'-10" x 15'-10"
Great Room 14'-3" x 20'-10" Irr.
Bedroom 11'-0" x 12'-4"
Laun. 8'-4" x 8'-6"
Bath
Pwdr.
Kitchen 17'-4" x 12'-7"
Foyer
Garage 20'-0" x 27'-0" Irr.
Porch
Bedroom 11'-0" x 12'-4"

Unexcavated
Unfinished Basement
Future Bath
Unexcavated
Unexcavated

© Copyright by designer/architect

Optional Lower Level
1,894 sq. ft.

Plan #F08-032D-0887

Dimensions: 42' W x 40' D
Heated Sq. Ft.: 1,212
Bonus Sq. Ft.: 1,212
Bedrooms: 2 **Bathrooms:** 1
Exterior Walls: 2" x 6"
Foundation: Basement standard; crawl space, floating slab or monolithic slab for an additional fee

See index for more information

Images provided by designer/architect

Features

- This highly efficient home offers an open floor plan with beamed ceilings above adding a tremendous amount of architectural interest to the interior
- A fireplace acts like a partition between the bedrooms and the gathering spaces
- The large covered porch is a wonderful extension of the interior living spaces
- The island in the kitchen includes casual dining space and a double basin sink and dishwasher
- The optional lower level has an additional 1,212 square feet of living area

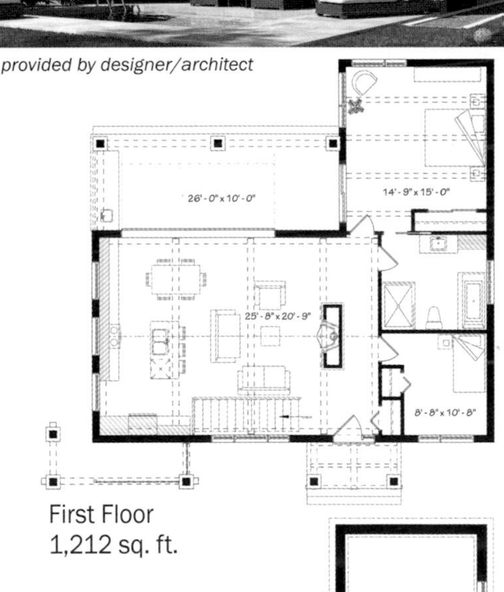

First Floor
1,212 sq. ft.

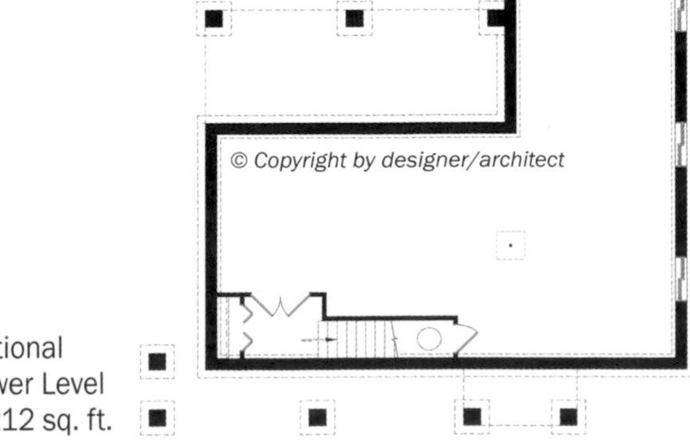

Optional
Lower Level
1,212 sq. ft.

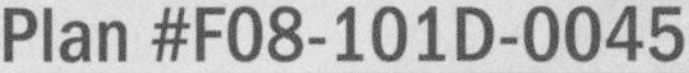

Plan #F08-101D-0045

Dimensions:	69' W x 68'3" D
Heated Sq. Ft.:	1,885
Bedrooms: 2	**Bathrooms:** 2½
Exterior Walls:	2" x 6"
Foundation:	Basement

See index for more information

Features

- The open floor plan maximizes space creating a flowing open layout
- A dual fireplace warms the family room as well as the outdoor covered patio
- The spacious and private master suite has includes its own bath and walk-in closet
- Guests will never want to leave the guest bedroom with its own bath and large walk-in closet
- 3-car front entry garage

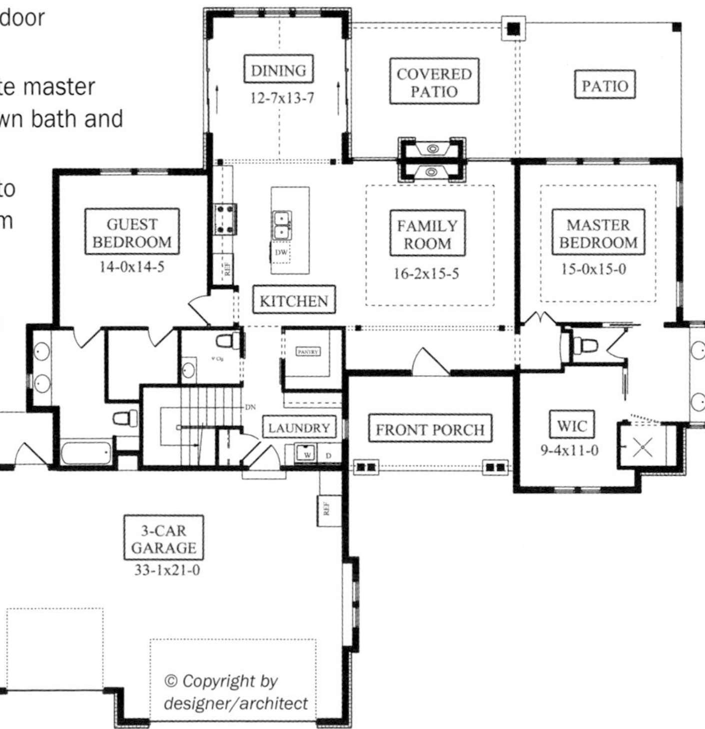

Images provided by designer/architect

Plan #F08-148D-0047

Dimensions:	30' W x 24' D
Heated Sq. Ft.:	720
Bonus Sq. Ft.:	720
Bedrooms: 1	**Bathrooms:** 1
Exterior Walls:	2" x 6"
Foundation:	Basement

See index for more information

Images provided by designer/architect

First Floor
720 sq. ft.

Optional
Lower Level
720 sq. ft.

Plan #F08-077D-0310

Dimensions:	40' W x 68' D
Heated Sq. Ft.:	2,000
Bedrooms: 4	**Bathrooms:** 3

Foundation: Crawl space, slab or basement for an additional fee

See index for more information

Images provided by designer/architect

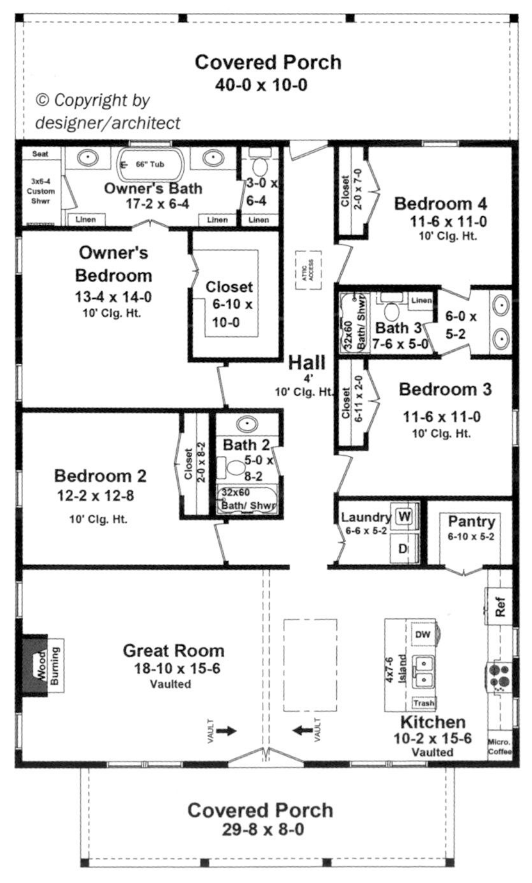

Plan #F08-177D-0001

Dimensions: 26' W x 31' D
Heated Sq. Ft.: 651
Bedrooms: 1 **Bathrooms:** 1
Foundation: Slab standard; crawl space for an additional fee

See index for more information

Images provided by designer/architect

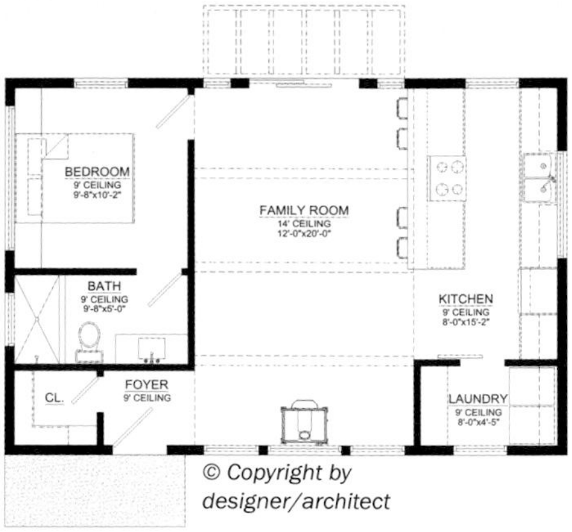

BEDROOM 9' CEILING 9'-8"x10'-2"
FAMILY ROOM 14' CEILING 12'-0"x20'-0"
BATH 9' CEILING 9'-8"x5'-0"
KITCHEN 9' CEILING 8'-0"x15'-2"
CL.
FOYER 9' CEILING
LAUNDRY 9' CEILING 8'-0"x4'-5"

© Copyright by designer/architect

Plan #F08-077D-0019

Dimensions: 54' W x 47' D
Heated Sq. Ft.: 1,400
Bedrooms: 3 **Bathrooms:** 2
Foundation: Crawl space, slab, basement or walk-out basement, please specify when ordering

See index for more information

Images provided by designer/architect

© Copyright by designer/architect

PATIO 19-8 x 11-6
Garden Tub
Bath
Master Bedroom 15-8 x 14-8 8-0 Ceiling
Kitchen 9-10 x 12-0
Dining 9-10 x 12-0 8-0 Ceiling
Bedroom 2 12-2 x 11-0 8-0 Ceiling
Clos.
Bath
Clos.
Utility
Entry
Great Room 19-8 x 15-6 8-0 Ceiling
Hall
Hall Bath
Tub/ Shr.
Clos.
Stor.
OPTIONAL STAIRS TO BASEMENT
Bedroom 3 12-2 x 11-0 8-0 Ceiling
Covered Porch 19-8 x 5
Two Car Garage 22-2 x 25-0
NOTE: ALL DASHED WALLS INDICATE OPTIONAL WALL LOCATIONS IF BASEMENT OPTION IS CHOSEN.

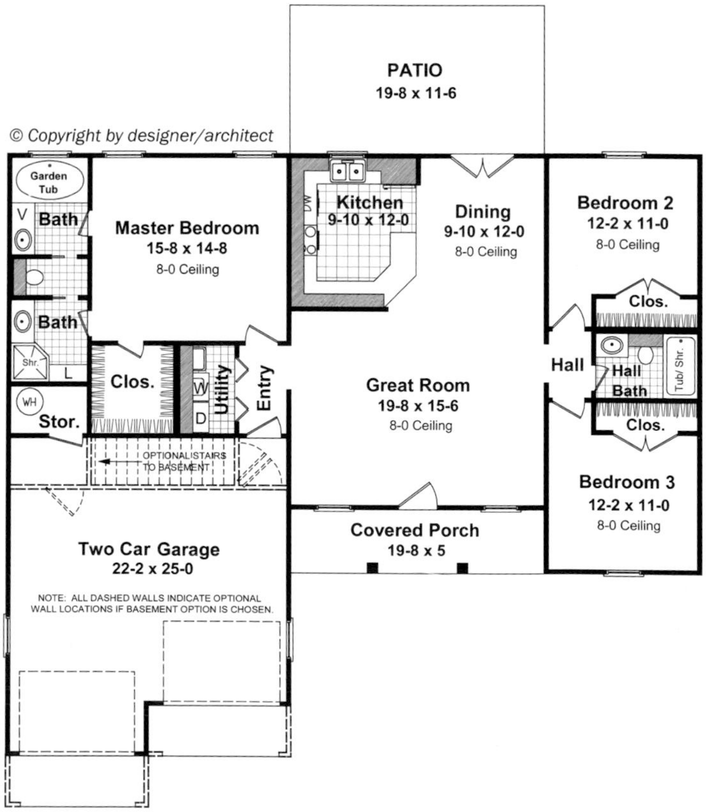

Plan #F08-155D-0198

Dimensions: 36'4" W x 91' D
Heated Sq. Ft.: 1,365
Bedrooms: 3 **Bathrooms:** 2
Foundation: Crawl space or slab standard; basement or daylight basement for an additional fee

See index for more information

Images provided by designer/architect

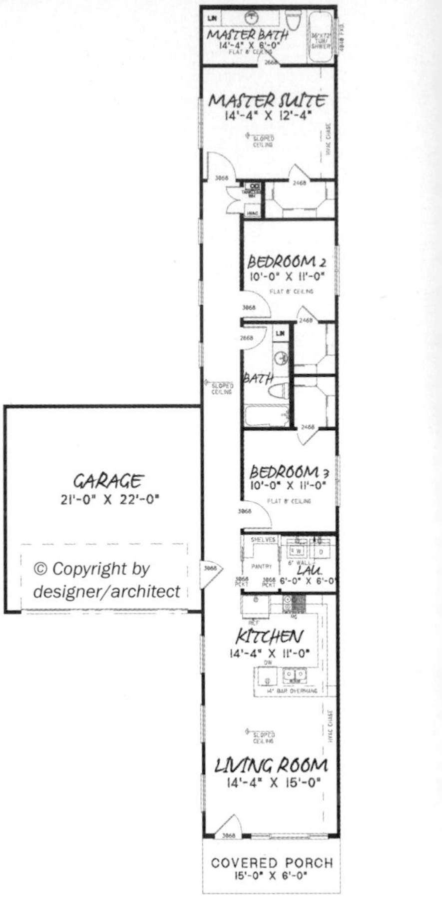

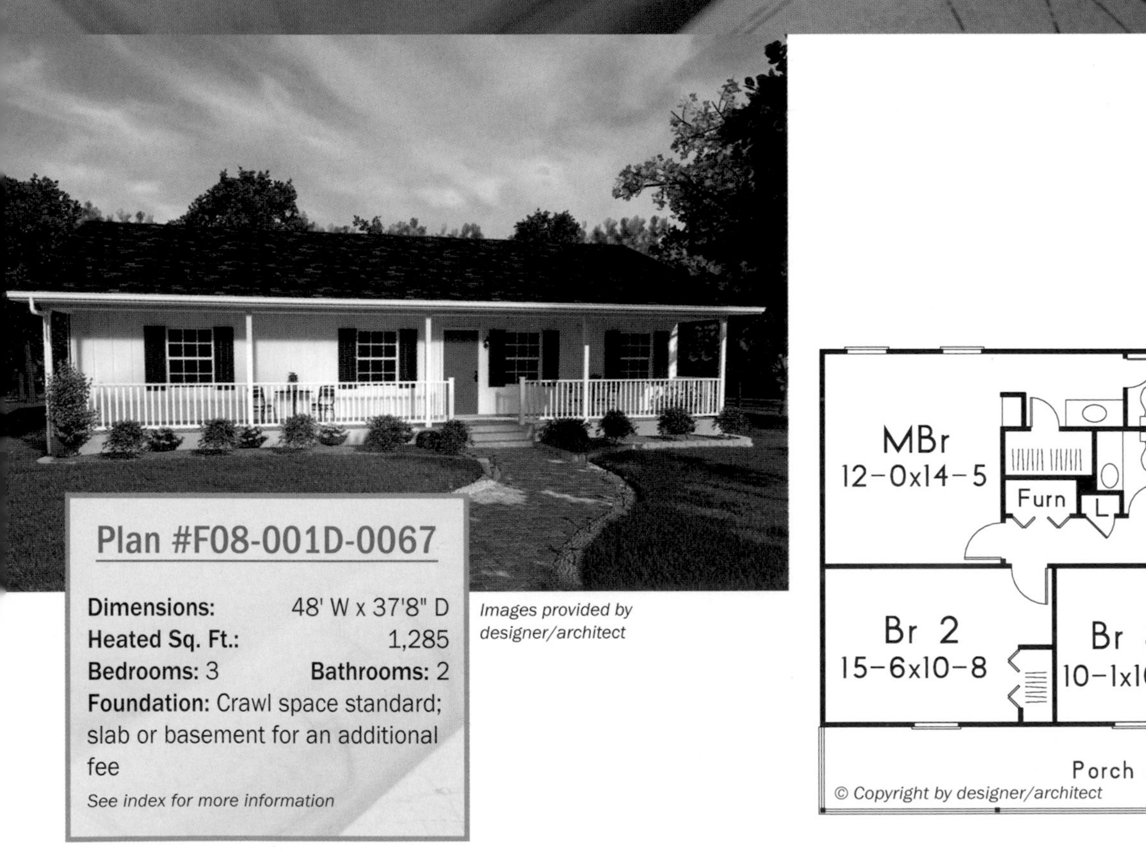

Plan #F08-001D-0067

Dimensions: 48' W x 37'8" D
Heated Sq. Ft.: 1,285
Bedrooms: 3 **Bathrooms:** 2
Foundation: Crawl space standard; slab or basement for an additional fee

See index for more information

Images provided by designer/architect

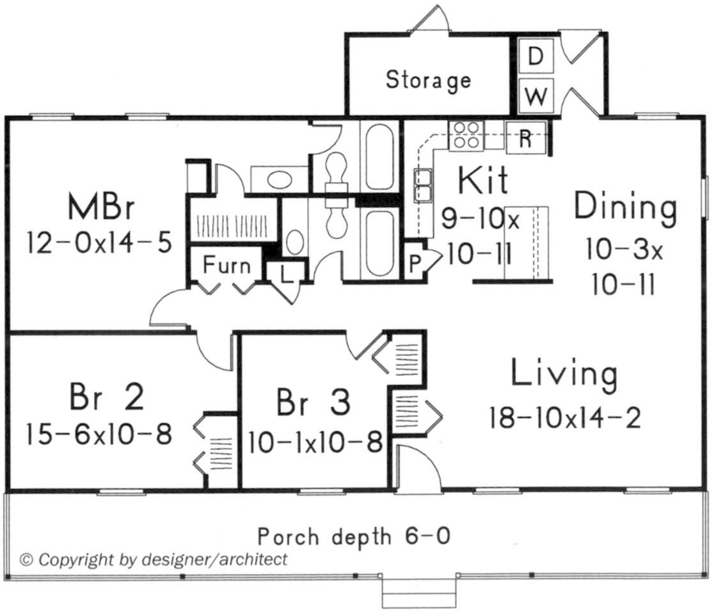

Plan #F08-007D-0146

Dimensions: 68' W x 49'8" D
Heated Sq. Ft.: 1,929
Bedrooms: 4 **Bathrooms:** 3
Foundation: Crawl space standard; slab or basement for an additional fee

See index for more information

Images provided by designer/architect

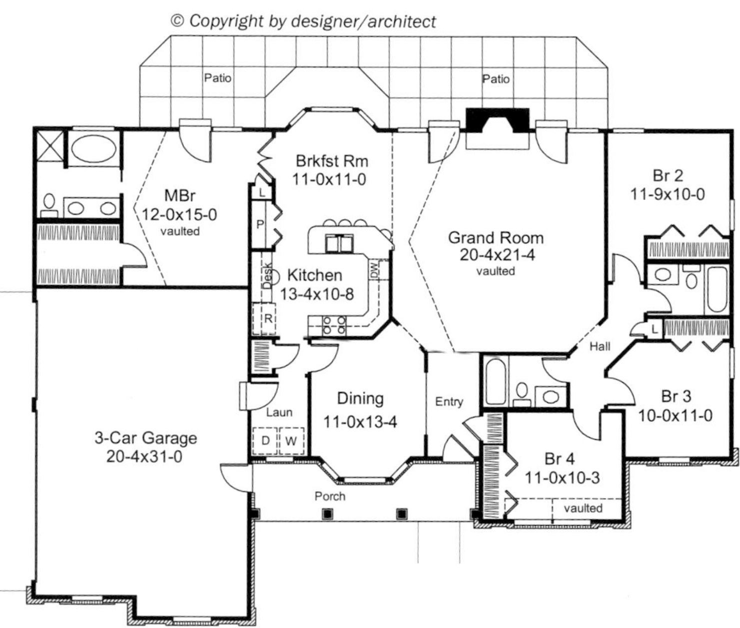

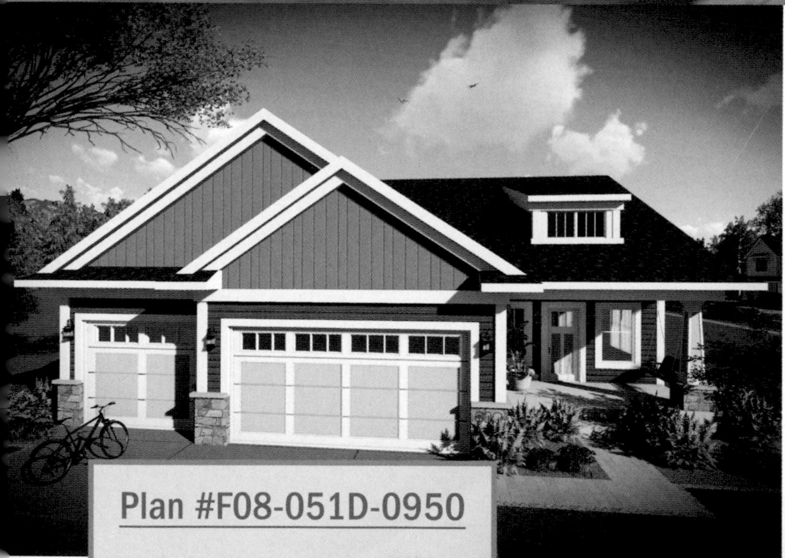

Plan #F08-051D-0950

Dimensions: 50' W x 57'8" D
Heated Sq. Ft.: 1,681
Bedrooms: 3 **Bathrooms:** 2
Exterior Walls: 2" x 6"
Foundation: Basement standard; crawl space or slab for an additional fee

See index for more information

Images provided by designer/architect

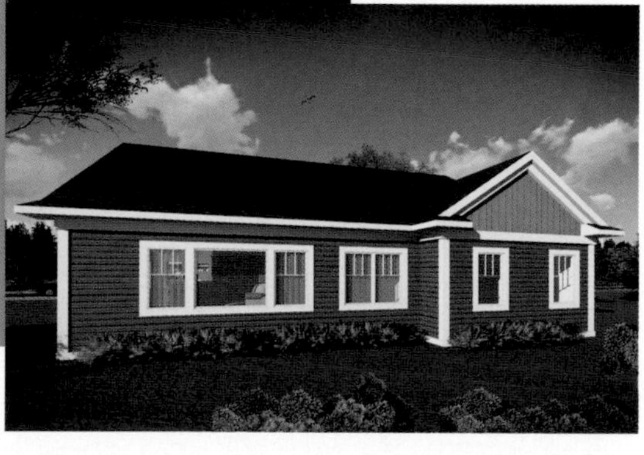

© Copyright by designer/architect

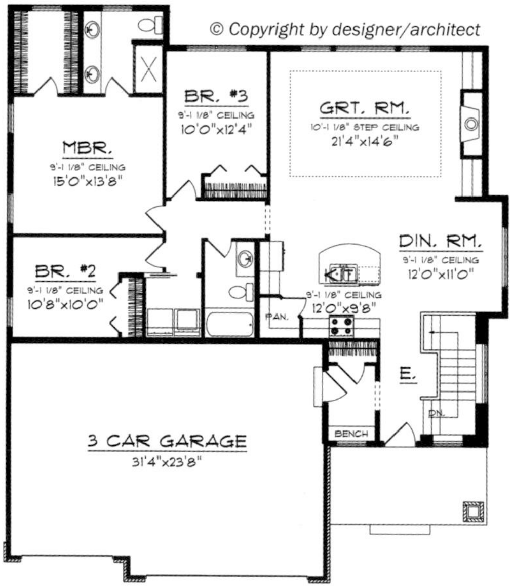

BR. #3 9'-1 1/8" CEILING 10'0"x12'4"
GRT. RM. 10'-1 1/8" STEP CEILING 21'4"x14'6"
MBR. 9'-1 1/8" CEILING 15'0"x13'8"
DIN. RM. 9'-1 1/8" CEILING 12'0"x11'0"
BR. #2 9'-1 1/8" CEILING 10'8"x10'0"
KIT. 9'-1 1/8" CEILING 12'0"x9'8"
PAN.
E.
DN.
BENCH
3 CAR GARAGE 31'4"x23'8"

Plan #F08-077D-0042

Dimensions: 64' W x 45'10" D
Heated Sq. Ft.: 1,752
Bedrooms: 3 **Bathrooms:** 2
Foundation: Slab, crawl space or basement, please specify when ordering

See index for more information

Images provided by designer/architect

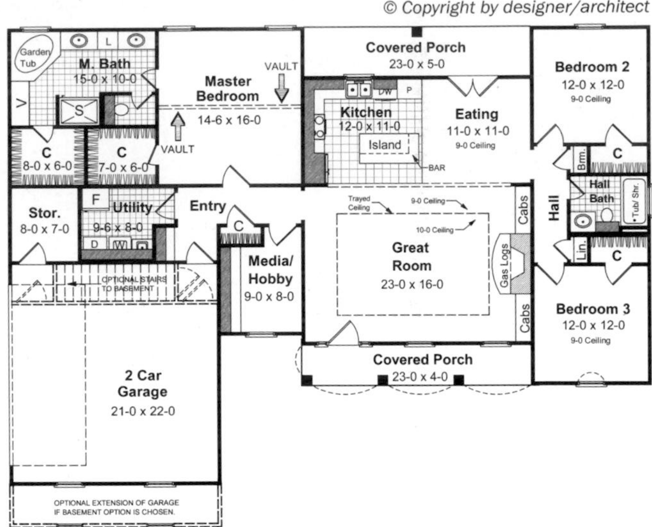

Plan #F08-032D-0841

Dimensions: 48' W x 58' D
Heated Sq. Ft.: 1,525
Bedrooms: 3 **Bathrooms:** 1½
Exterior Walls: 2" x 6"
Foundation: Floating slab standard; crawl space or monolithic slab for an additional fee

See index for more information

Images provided by designer/architect

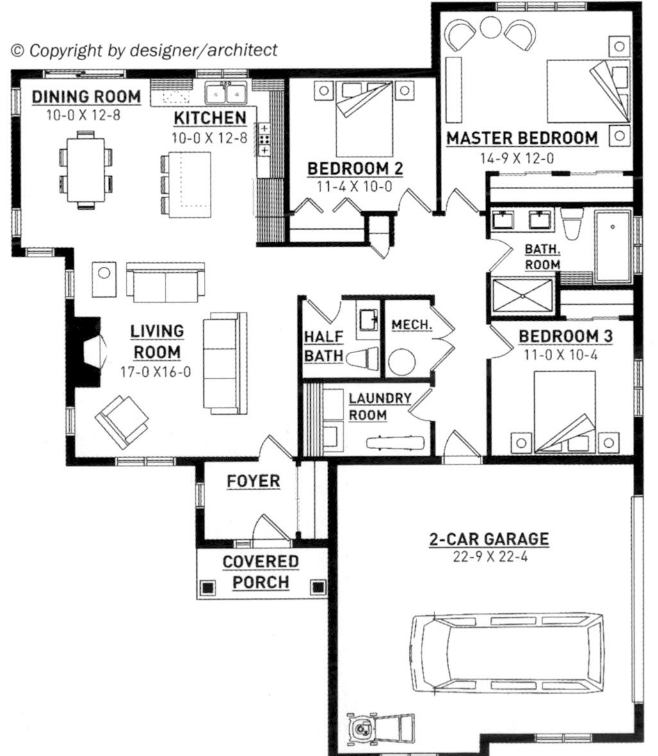

Plan #F08-121D-0039

Dimensions: 61' W x 40'4" D
Heated Sq. Ft.: 1,624
Bedrooms: 3 **Bathrooms:** 2
Foundation: Basement standard; crawl space or slab for an additional fee

See index for more information

Images provided by designer/architect

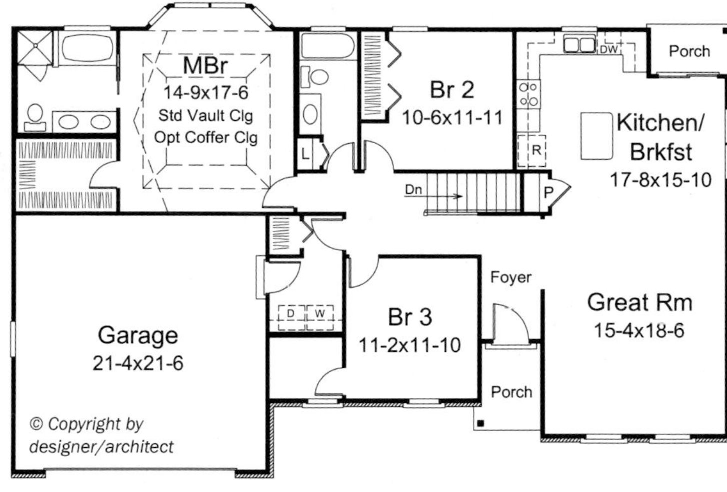

Plan #F08-076D-0210

Dimensions: 91'9" W x 76'4" D
Heated Sq. Ft.: 2,650
Bonus Sq. Ft.: 900
Bedrooms: 3 **Bathrooms:** 2½
Foundation: Basement, crawl space or slab, please specify when ordering

See index for more information

Images provided by designer/architect

© Copyright by designer/architect

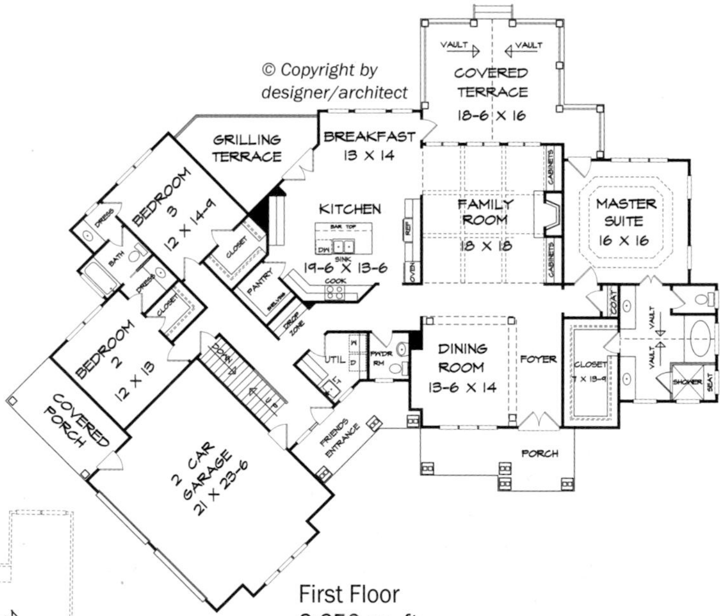

First Floor
2,650 sq. ft.

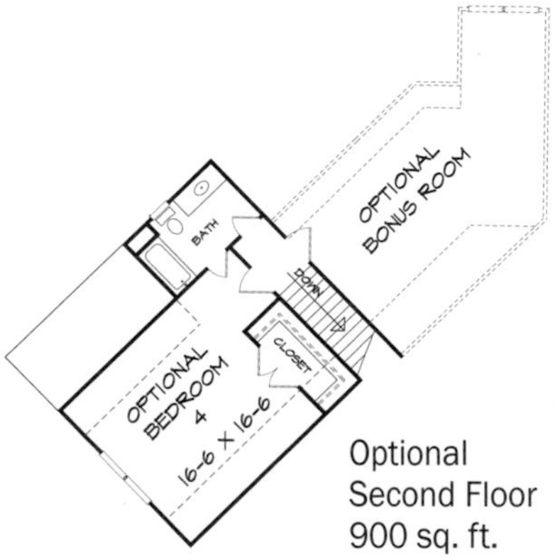

Optional
Second Floor
900 sq. ft.

Images provided by designer/architect

Plan #F08-051D-0981

Dimensions: 55'4" W x 71'8" D
Heated Sq. Ft.: 2,005
Bedrooms: 3 **Bathrooms:** 2
Exterior Walls: 2" x 6"
Foundation: Basement standard; crawl space or slab for an additional fee

See index for more information

Features

- The master suite is located just off the great room and boasts dual sinks and a generously sized walk-in closet in its private bath
- There is easy access to the laundry room from the master closet which makes tackling dirty laundry a breeze
- The kitchen island looks out into the open great room and dining area giving a very open feeling
- The second and third bedrooms are situated in the front left of the house, with the master bedroom in the back right for privacy
- You can walk out onto the covered porch from the dining room for a view of the backyard
- 3-car front entry garage

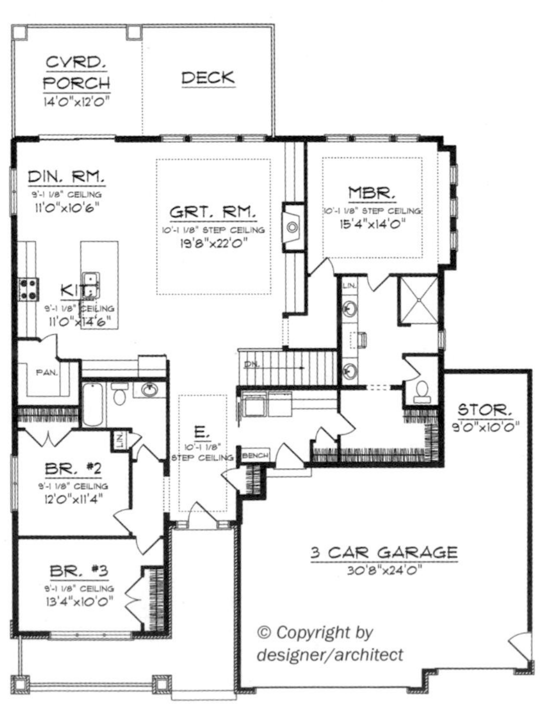

Plan #F08-170D-0004

Dimensions: 48'4" W x 66'4" D
Heated Sq. Ft.: 1,581
Bedrooms: 3 **Bathrooms:** 2
Foundation: Slab or monolithic slab standard; crawl space, basement or daylight basement for an additional fee

See index for more information

Images provided by designer/architect

Features

- This modest sized one-story home offers many great features for today's family
- A side entry garage gives the exterior added curb appeal
- When entering from the garage you'll find lockers on the right and a utility room on the left
- The kitchen has a very open feel and includes an island with dining space
- The family room enjoys a cozy corner fireplace and an entire wall of windows that overlook the rear covered porch and beyond to the patio
- The master bedroom and bath include a large walk-in closet
- Two secondary bedrooms share the full bath between them
- 2-car side entry garage

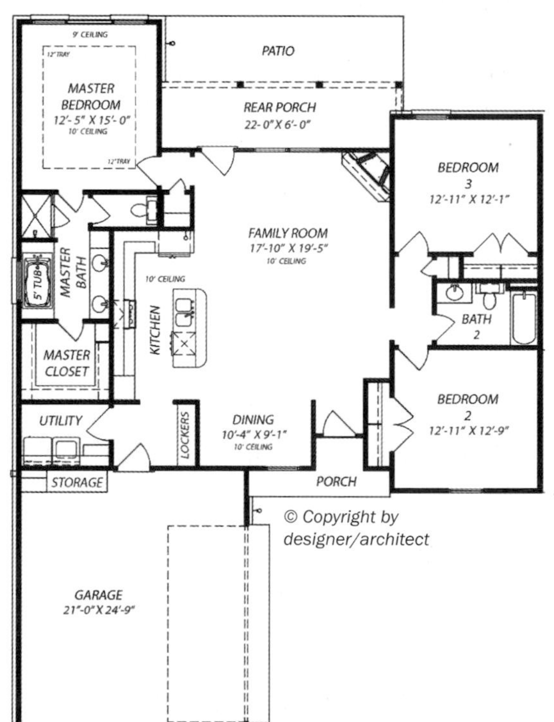

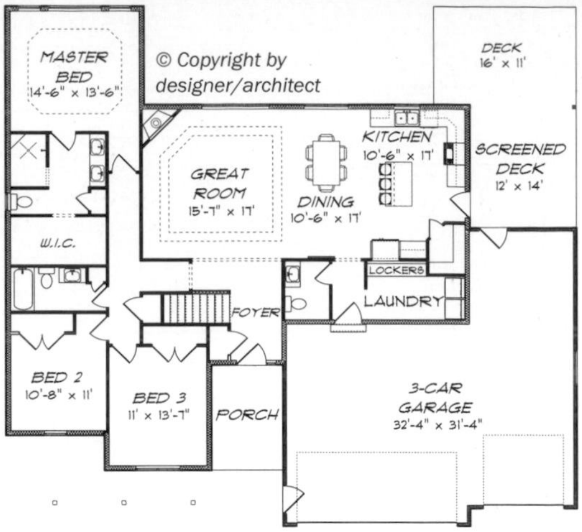

Plan #F08-159D-0007

Dimensions: 64' W x 59' D
Heated Sq. Ft.: 1,850
Bonus Sq. Ft.: 1,300
Bedrooms: 3 **Bathrooms:** 2½
Exterior Walls: 2" x 6"
Foundation: Walk-out basement

See index for more information

Images provided by designer/architect

© Copyright by designer/architect

First Floor
1,850 sq. ft.

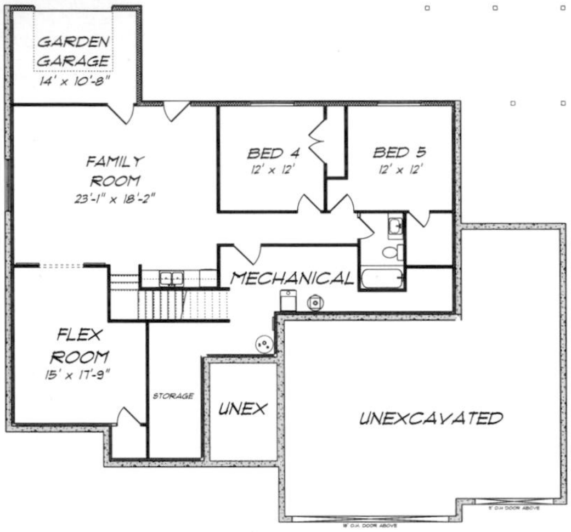

Optional
Lower Level
1,300 sq. ft.

Plan #F08-032D-1142

Dimensions: 46' W x 32' D
Heated Sq. Ft.: 1,209
Bonus Sq. Ft.: 1,209
Bedrooms: 2 **Bathrooms:** 1
Exterior Walls: 2" x 6"
Foundation: Basement standard; crawl space, floating slab or monolithic slab for an additional fee

See index for more information

Images provided by designer/architect

© Copyright by designer/architect

First Floor
1,209 sq. ft.

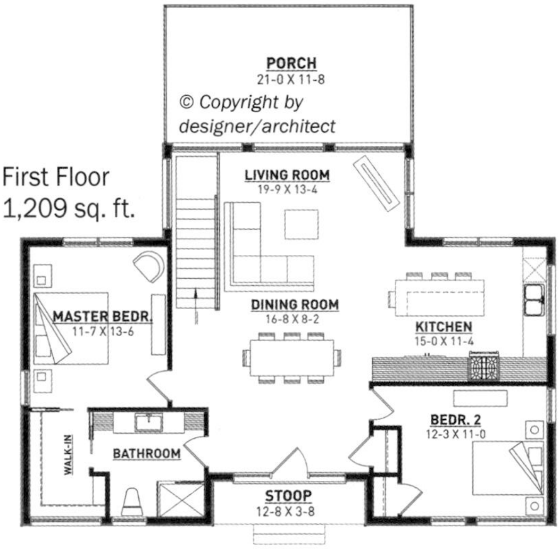

Optional
Lower Level
1,209 sq. ft.

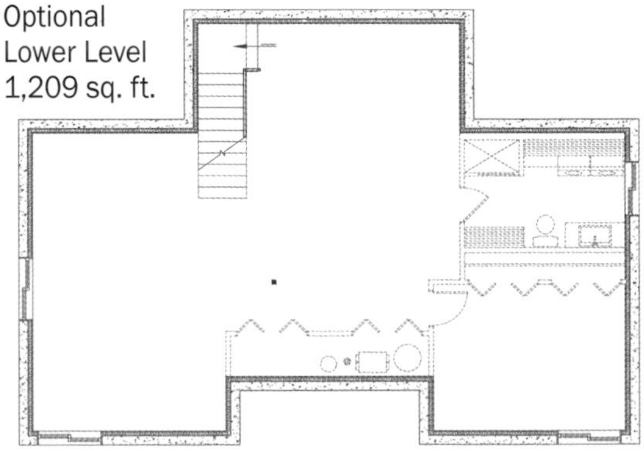

Images provided by designer/architect

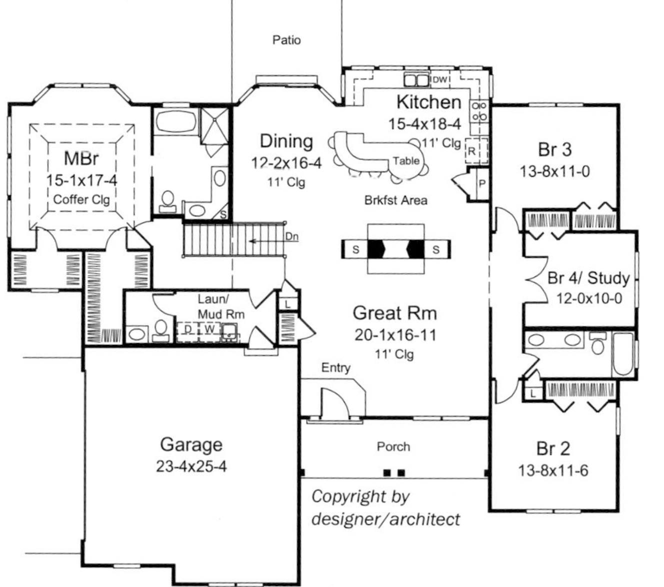

Copyright by designer/architect

Plan #F08-121D-0011

Dimensions: 68'4" W x 56' D
Heated Sq. Ft.: 2,241
Bedrooms: 4 **Bathrooms:** 2½
Foundation: Basement standard; crawl space or slab for an additional fee

See index for more information

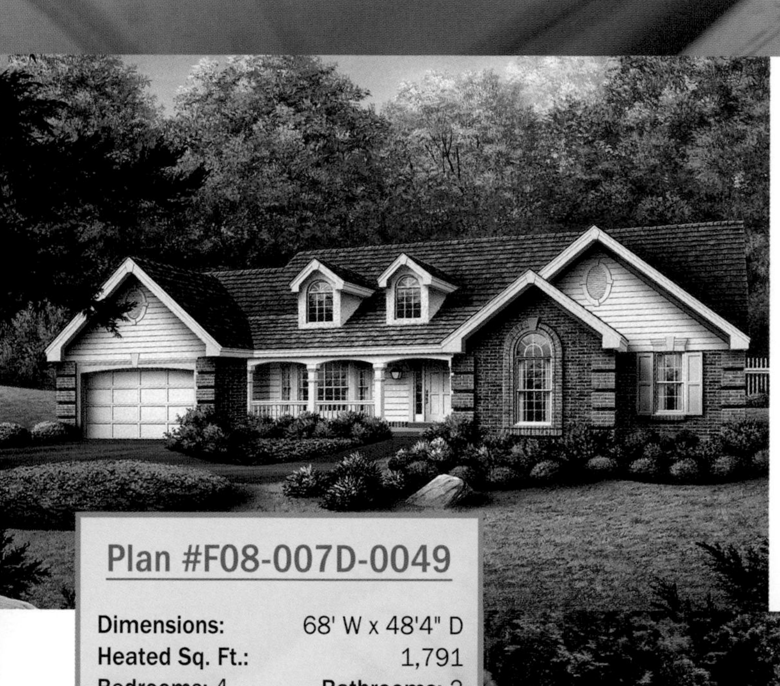

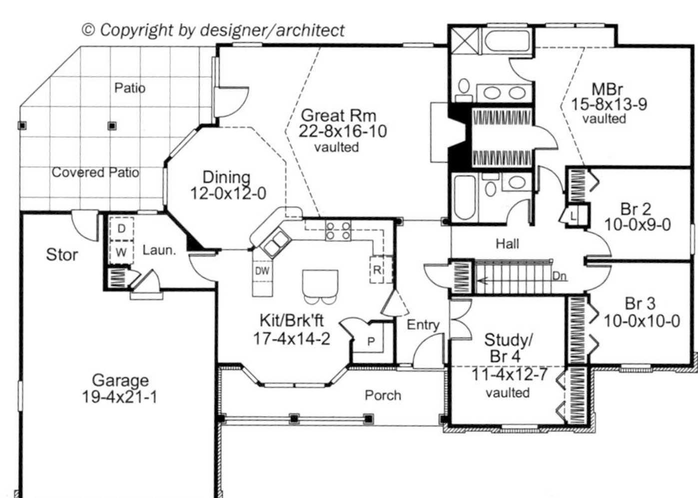

Images provided by designer/architect

Plan #F08-007D-0049

Dimensions: 68' W x 48'4" D
Heated Sq. Ft.: 1,791
Bedrooms: 4 **Bathrooms:** 2
Foundation: Basement standard; crawl space or slab for an additional fee

See index for more information

Plan #F08-032D-1139

Dimensions: 71' W x 46' D
Heated Sq. Ft.: 1,948
Bonus Sq. Ft.: 1,948
Bedrooms: 2 **Bathrooms:** 2½
Exterior Walls: 2" x 6"
Foundation: Partial basement/crawl space standard; crawl space, floating slab or monolithic slab for an additional fee

See index for more information

Images provided by designer/architect

First Floor
1,948 sq. ft.

Optional
Lower Level
1,948 sq. ft.

Features

- Sleek and simple Modern Farmhouse creates an exterior with tons of curb appeal for today's home buyers
- This unique floor plan offers a mother-in-law studio apartment on the left with its own bath, kitchen and living room plus a side covered porch private entrance
- The right side of the home has lovely living an dining rooms, an open kitchen, a laundry room and a spacious and luxurious master bedroom
- The optional lower level has an additional 1,948 square feet of living area
- 1-car side entry garage

Plan #F08-019S-0007

Dimensions: 103'6" W x 88'5" D
Heated Sq. Ft.: 3,886
Bedrooms: 4 **Bathrooms:** 3½
Foundation: Slab standard; crawl space or basement for an additional fee

See index for more information

Images provided by designer/architect

Features

- Interesting angles accentuate the exterior of this rustic Craftsman home
- A massive beamed great room connects to a sunny casual dining area and both space surround a huge kitchen with an angled double island design
- A fun game room off the casual dining area has a designated card playing area and a nearby powder room
- The rear patio has a unique circular shape where you can find a built-in fire pit
- The master suite enjoys its privacy away from the other bedrooms and has a posh bath and plenty of closetspace
- 3-car side entry garage, and a 1-car rear entry garage workshop

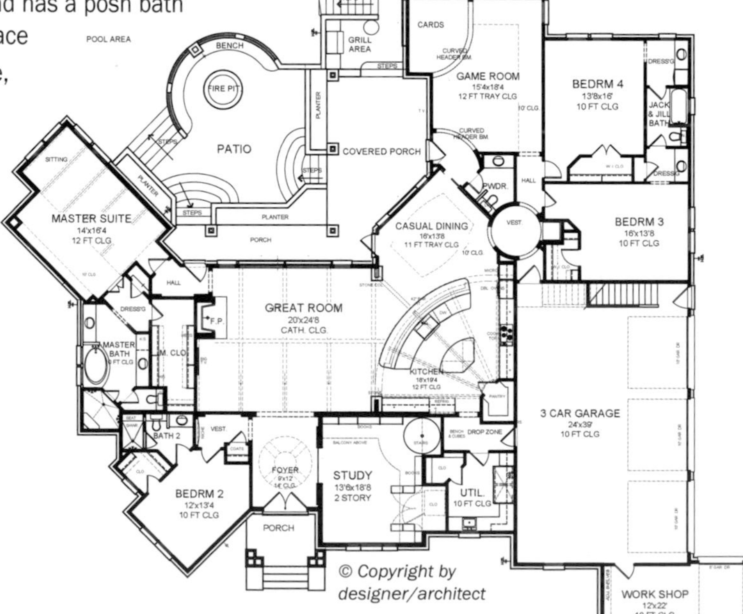

Plan #F08-032D-1136

Dimensions: 42' W x 48' D
Heated Sq. Ft.: 1,440
Bonus Sq. Ft.: 1,440
Bedrooms: 2 **Bathrooms:** 2
Exterior Walls: 2" x 6"
Foundation: Basement standard; crawl space, floating slab or monolithic slab for an additional fee

See index for more information

Features

- This home has a functional and easy-to-maintain size, but is packed with great features
- The kitchen, living and dining rooms combine to form the core of the home
- A walk-in pantry, mud room and a laundry room all add great function and storage
- The optional lower level has an additional 1,440 square feet of living area
- 1-car front entry garage

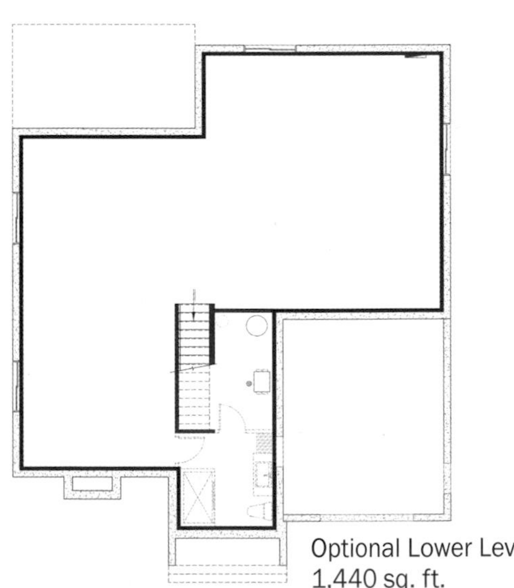

Optional Lower Level
1,440 sq. ft.

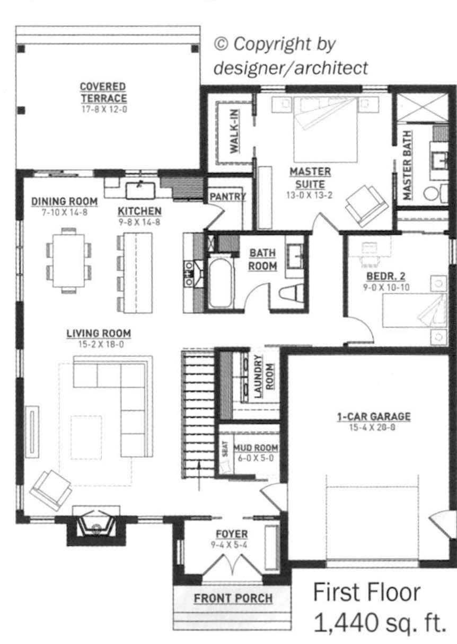

First Floor
1,440 sq. ft.

Images provided by designer/architect

Plan #F08-011D-0649

Dimensions: 49' W x 53' D
Heated Sq. Ft.: 1,605
Bedrooms: 3 **Bathrooms:** 2
Exterior Walls: 2" x 6"
Foundation: Crawl space or slab standard; basement for an additional fee

See index for more information

Images provided by designer/architect

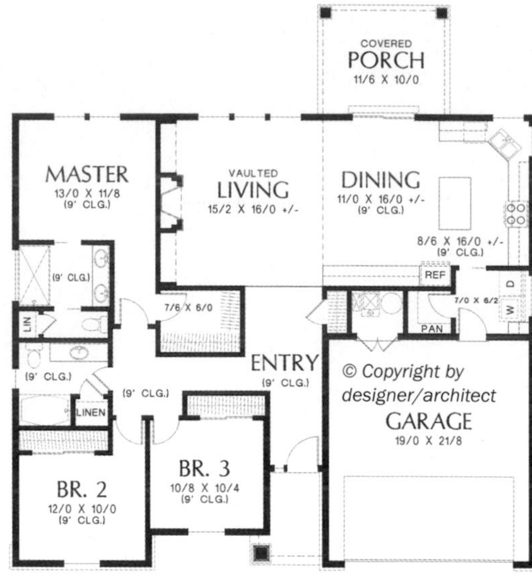

Plan #F08-026D-2187

Dimensions: 64'4" W x 63'8" D
Heated Sq. Ft.: 2,176
Bedrooms: 3 **Bathrooms:** 2
Exterior Walls: 2" x 6"
Foundation: Slab standard; crawl space, basement or walk-out basement for an additional fee

See index for more information

Images provided by designer/architect

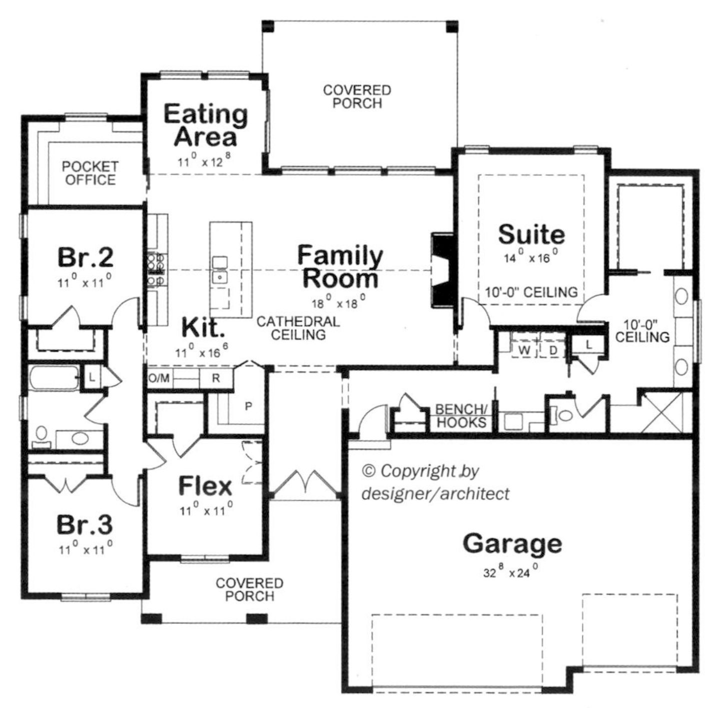

Plan #F08-130D-0407

Dimensions: 37'4" W x 64'4" D
Heated Sq. Ft.: 1,577
Bedrooms: 3 **Bathrooms:** 2
Foundation: Slab standard; crawl space or basement for an additional fee
See index for more information

Images provided by designer/architect

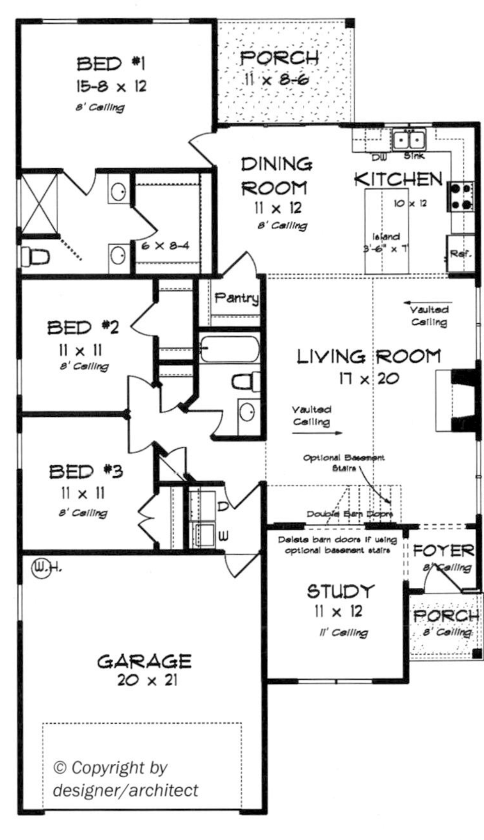

Plan #F08-007D-0181

Dimensions: 38' W x 52'8" D
Heated Sq. Ft.: 1,140
Bedrooms: 3 **Bathrooms:** 2
Foundation: Basement standard; crawl space or slab for an additional fee
See index for more information

Images provided by designer/architect

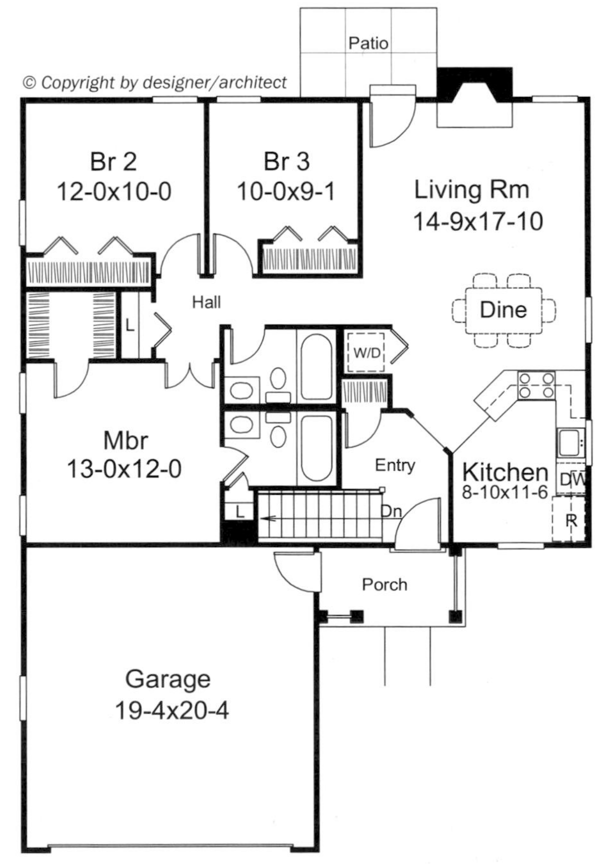

Plan #F08-051D-0960

Dimensions: 117' W x 50'8" D
Heated Sq. Ft.: 2,784
Bedrooms: 3 **Bathrooms:** 2
Exterior Walls: 2" x 6"
Foundation: Basement standard; crawl space or slab for an additional fee

See index for more information

Images provided by designer/architect

Features

- This Traditional ranch home design is sure to win you over with a very classy exterior
- You are welcomed into the home with eleven-foot ceilings that top the great room and kitchen
- All three bedrooms, including the master bedroom, are located to the right in the house
- The master bedroom includes a bath with a spa style tub, dual sinks, as well as a spacious walk-in closet
- The three-stall garage is located on the left side of the house with a large screened-in porch behind it
- 3-car front entry garage

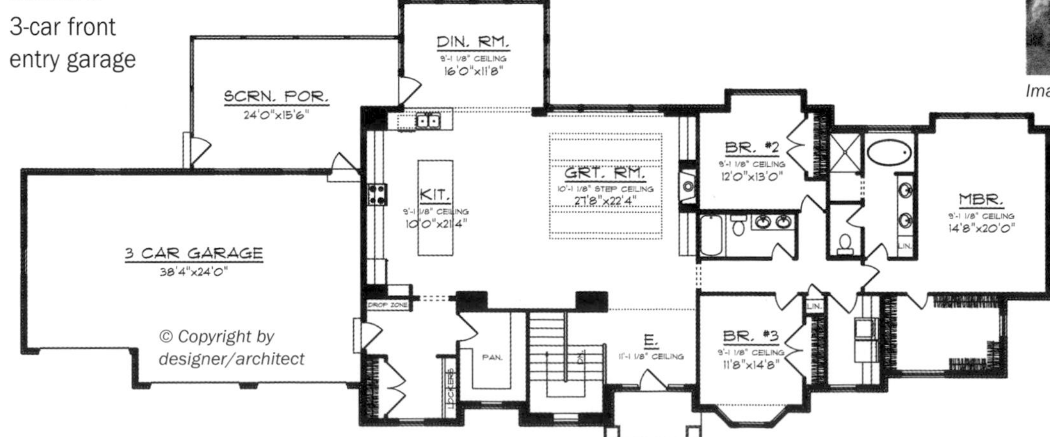

Plan #F08-077D-0294

Dimensions: 56' W x 62'4" D
Heated Sq. Ft.: 1,600
Bedrooms: 3 **Bathrooms:** 2
Foundation: Crawl space, slab, basement or daylight basement, please specify when ordering

See index for more information

Images provided by designer/architect

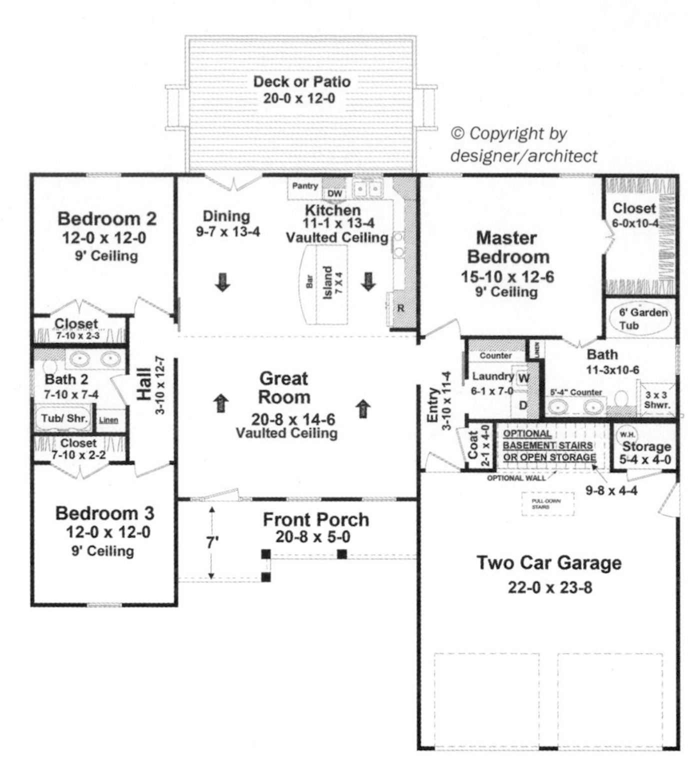

Plan #F08-121D-0021

Dimensions: 65' W x 46'4" D
Heated Sq. Ft.: 1,562
Bedrooms: 3 **Bathrooms:** 2
Foundation: Basement standard; crawl space or slab for an additional fee

See index for more information

Images provided by designer/architect

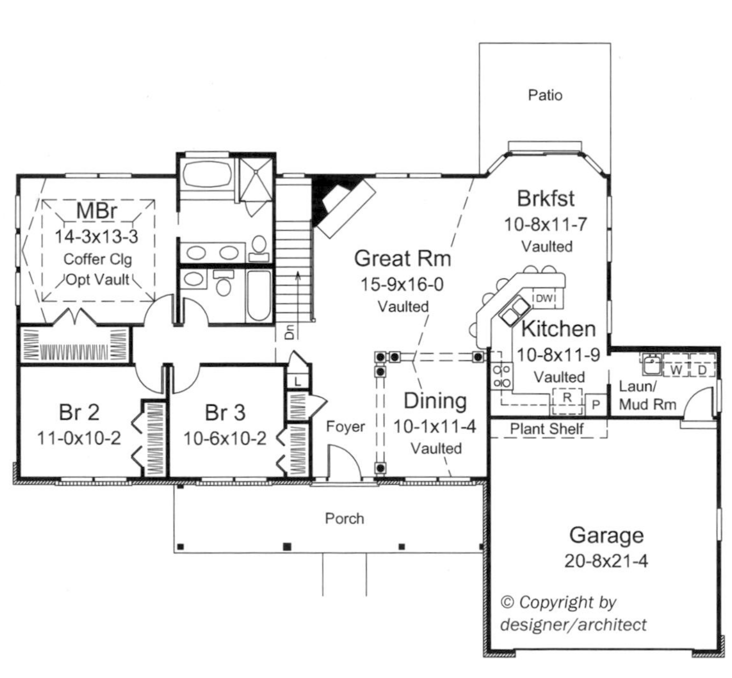

Plan #F08-084D-0095

Dimensions: 64'4" W x 74'1" D
Heated Sq. Ft.: 2,298
Bedrooms: 4 **Bathrooms:** 2½
Foundation: Slab standard; crawl space for an additional fee

See index for more information

Images provided by designer/architect

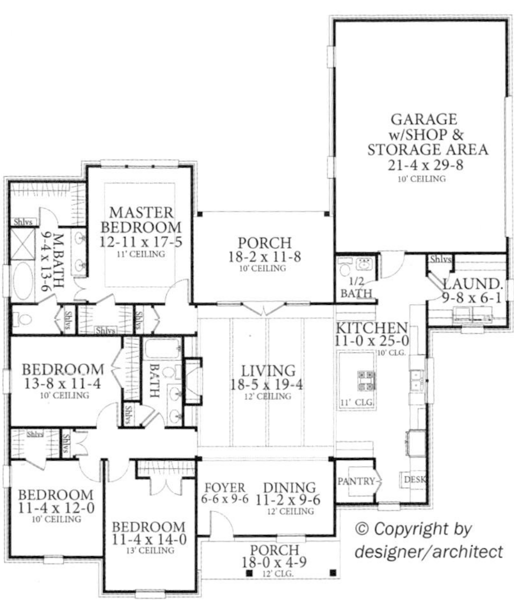

Br 2 9-1x11-1
Br 1 11-6x11-1
R
F
Kit/Dining 11-8x15-9
Living 11-8x22-0 vaulted clg
Covered Deck 24-0x8-0

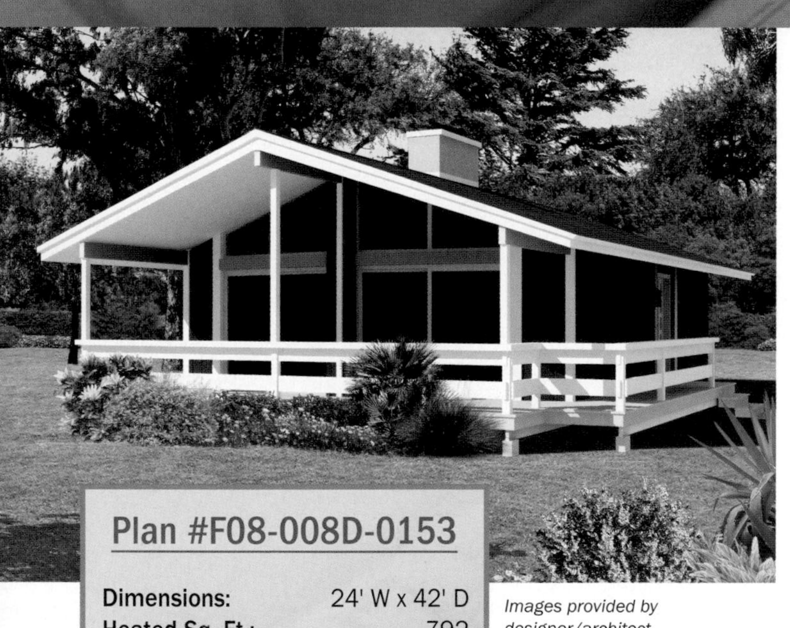

Plan #F08-008D-0153

Dimensions: 24' W x 42' D
Heated Sq. Ft.: 792
Bedrooms: 2 **Bathrooms:** 1
Foundation: Crawl space standard; slab for an additional fee

See index for more information

Images provided by designer/architect

Plan #F08-101D-0138

Dimensions:	109'8" W x 81'5" D
Heated Sq. Ft.:	2,767
Bonus Sq. Ft.:	2,259
Bedrooms: 2	**Bathrooms:** 2½
Exterior Walls:	2" x 6"
Foundation:	Walk-out basement

See index for more information

Images provided by designer/architect

Features

- The first floor has an open floor plan, a vaulted den, the master suite and bath, and bedroom 2 with a full bath outside its door
- The mud room and laundry area are something special and provide the space you need to stay organized on a daily basis
- The kitchen has a coveted oversized island and an open floor plan
- The optional lower level has an additional 2,259 square feet of living area and a recreation area with a wet bar, a game nook, a patio, three additional bedrooms and two full baths
- 2-car side entry garage, and a 2-car front entry garage

Plan #F08-101D-0072

Dimensions:	154'4" W x 81' D
Heated Sq. Ft.:	3,623
Bonus Sq. Ft.:	2,080
Bedrooms: 2	**Bathrooms:** 2½
Exterior Walls:	2" x 6"
Foundation:	Basement

See index for more information

Features

- The great room is topped with a beamed ceiling and has a gorgeous stone fireplace
- The kitchen enjoys two islands both facing the great room and a walk-in pantry around the corner
- A home office is located in a private spot
- The optional lower level has an additional 2,080 square feet of living area and a wine cellar, rec and media areas and a spacious guest bedroom with a full bath
- 3-car side entry garage

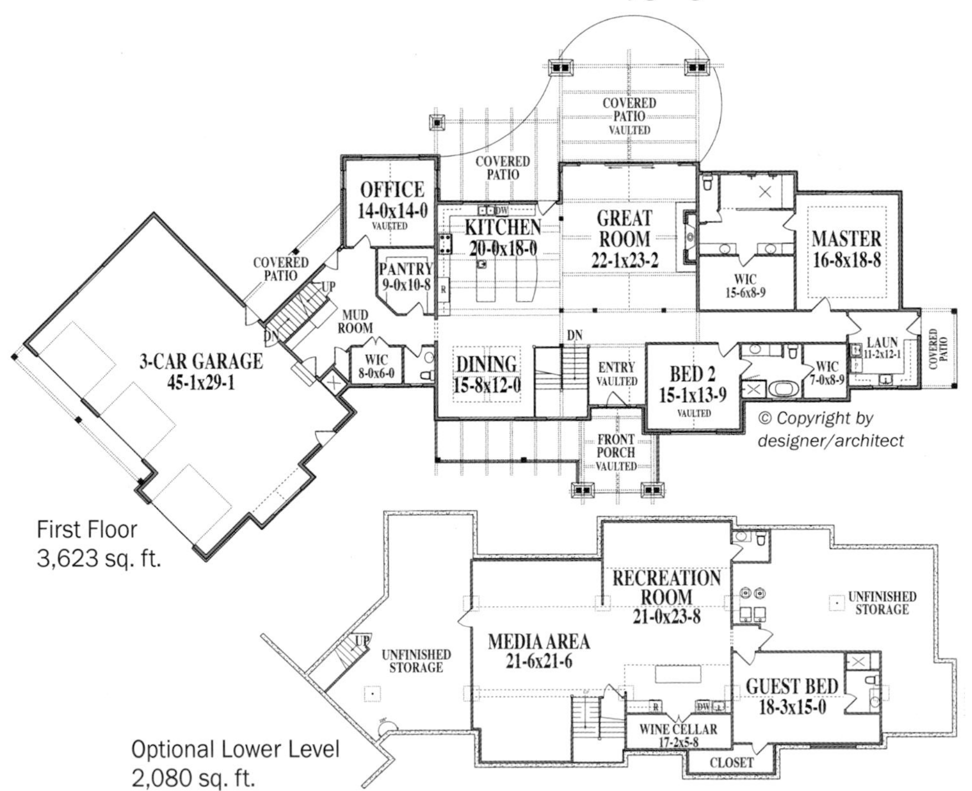

First Floor
3,623 sq. ft.

Optional Lower Level
2,080 sq. ft.

Images provided by designer/architect

Plan #F08-026D-1985

Dimensions: 40' W x 70'8" D
Heated Sq. Ft.: 1,886
Bedrooms: 3 **Bathrooms:** 2½
Exterior Walls: 2" x 6"
Foundation: Basement standard; crawl space, slab or walk-out basement for an additional fee

See index for more information

Images provided by designer/architect

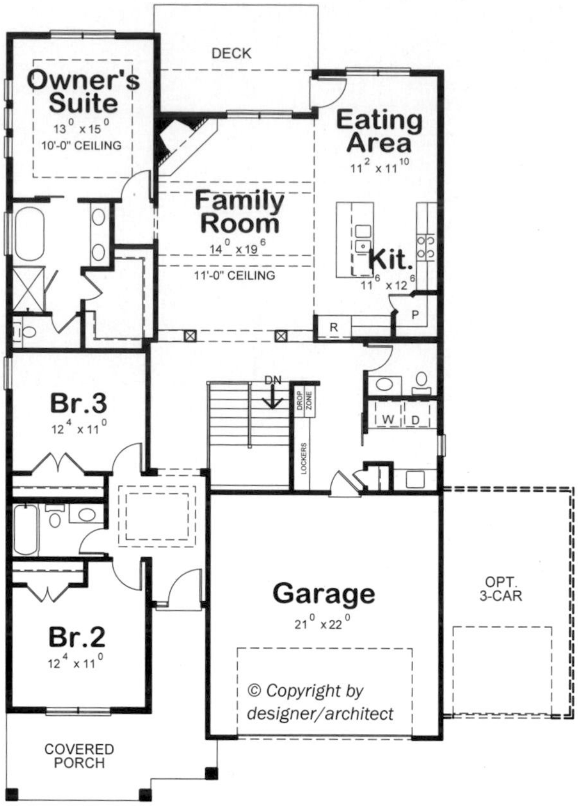

Plan #F08-013D-0156

Dimensions: 63' W x 73' D
Heated Sq. Ft.: 1,800
Bonus Sq. Ft.: 503
Bedrooms: 3 **Bathrooms:** 3
Foundation: Slab standard; basement or crawl space for an additional fee

See index for more information

Images provided by designer/architect

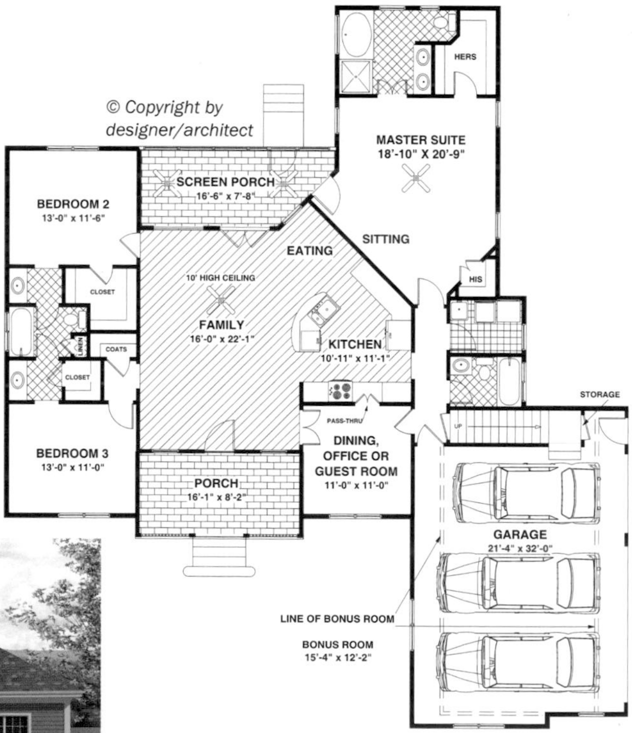

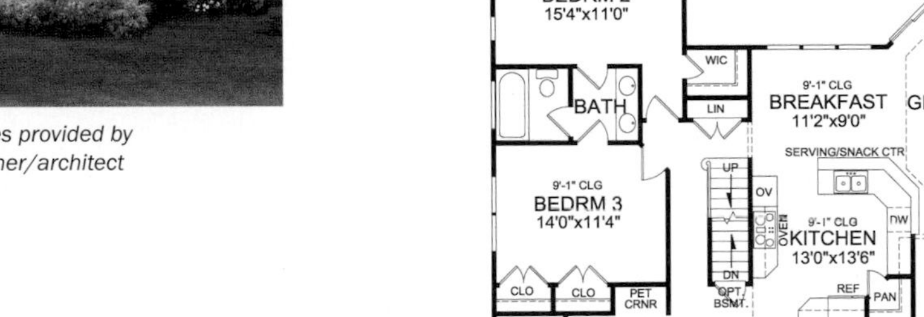

Plan #F08-016D-0106

Dimensions: 61'6" W x 66'10" D
Heated Sq. Ft.: 2,233
Bonus Sq. Ft.: 645
Bedrooms: 3 **Bathrooms:** 2½
Foundation: Slab or crawl space standard; basement for an additional fee

See index for more information

Images provided by designer/architect

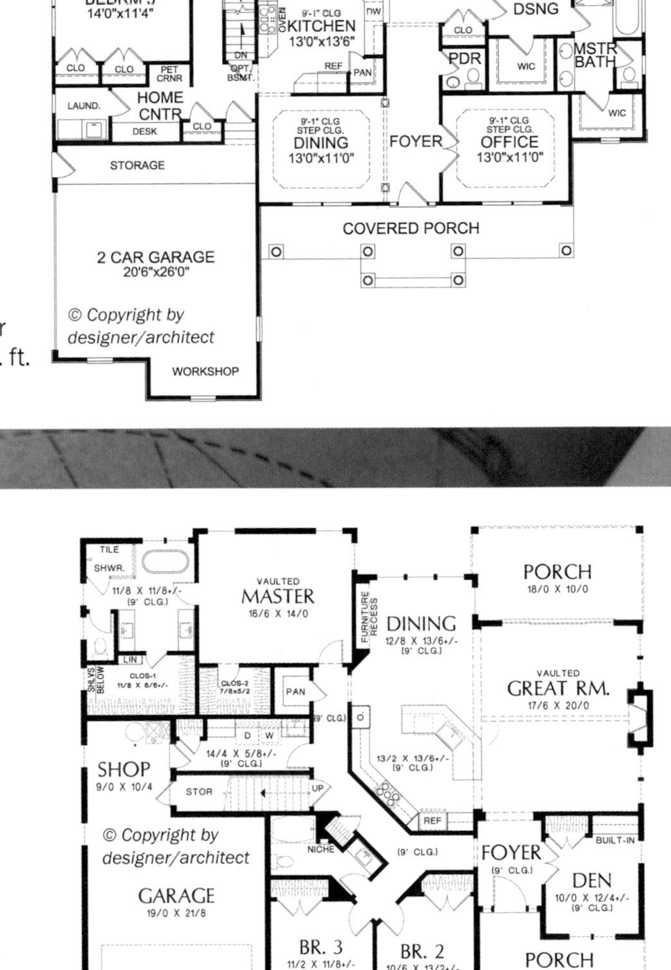

Optional Second Floor
645 sq. ft.

First Floor
2,233 sq. ft.

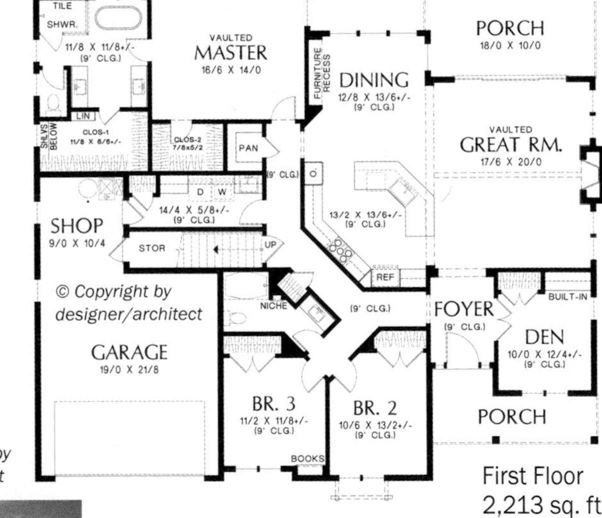

First Floor
2,213 sq. ft.

Images provided by designer/architect

Plan #F08-011D-0650

Dimensions: 60' W x 53' D
Heated Sq. Ft.: 2,213
Bonus Sq. Ft.: 442
Bedrooms: 3 **Bathrooms:** 2
Exterior Walls: 2" x 6"
Foundation: Crawl space or slab standard; basement for an additional fee

See index for more information

Optional Second Floor
442 sq. ft.

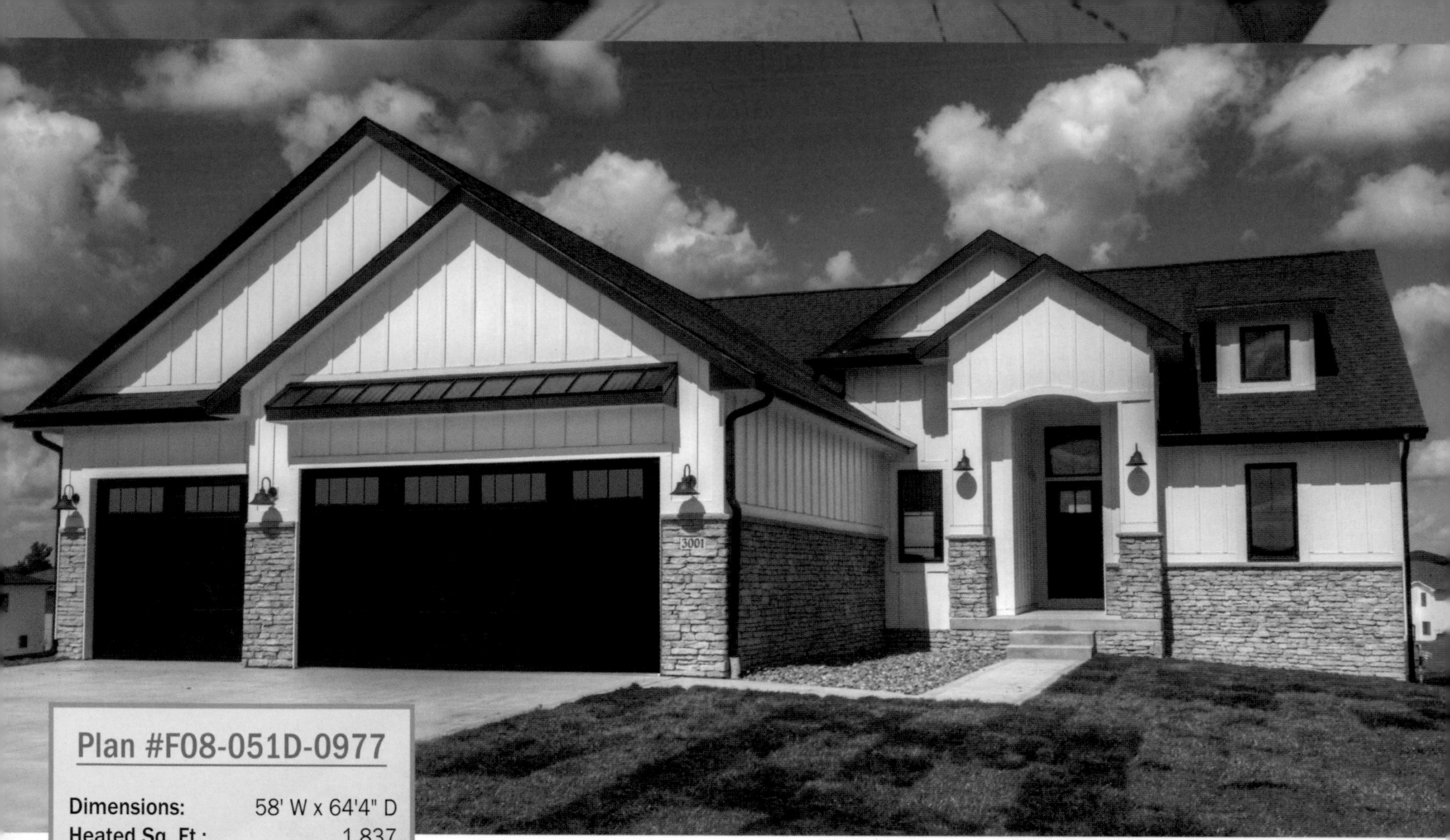

Plan #F08-051D-0977

Dimensions: 58' W x 64'4" D
Heated Sq. Ft.: 1,837
Bedrooms: 3 **Bathrooms:** 2
Exterior Walls: 2" x 6"
Foundation: Basement standard; crawl space or slab for an additional fee

See index for more information

Images provided by designer/architect

© Copyright by designer/architect

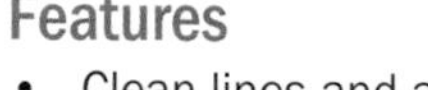

Features

- Clean lines and an attention to detail create an exterior that's timeless and modern at the same time
- The covered entrance opens into the great room with its impressive 11' ceiling, fireplace and large windows for a great view of the covered porch and deck
- An appealing split bedroom home that offers privacy from the central living space
- The kitchen features a large hidden pantry, nearby lockers and laundry space, as well as unique curved breakfast bar and dining space
- 3-car front entry garage

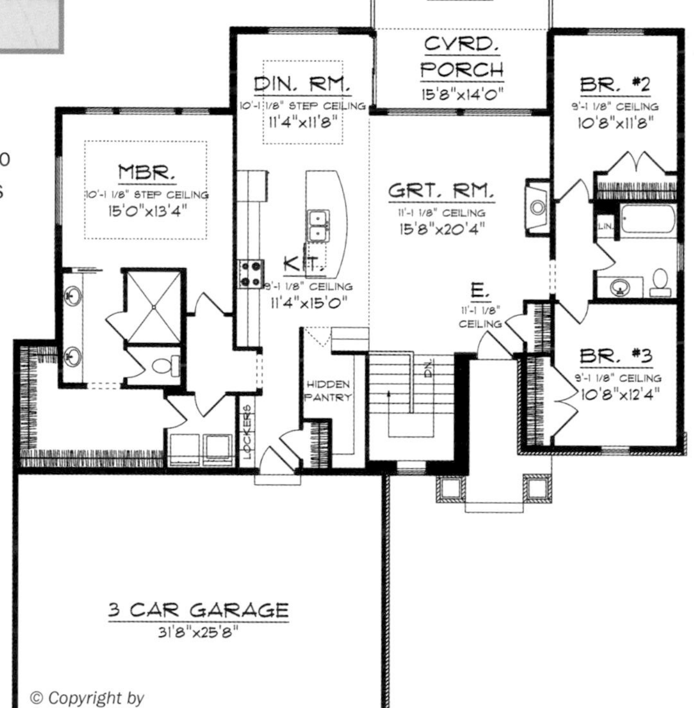

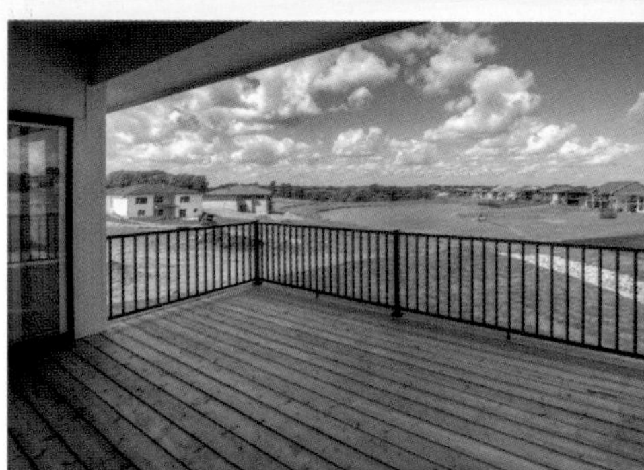

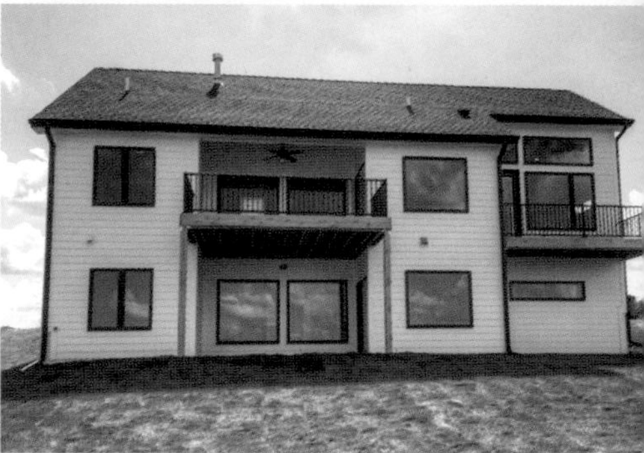

Plan #F08-155D-0039

Dimensions: 52'6" W x 57'10" D
Heated Sq. Ft.: 1,640
Bonus Sq. Ft.: 281
Bedrooms: 3 **Bathrooms:** 2
Foundation: Slab or crawl space, please specify when ordering

See index for more information

Images provided by designer/architect

First Floor
1,640 sq. ft.

BONUS RM
13'-2"X20'-0"

Optional
Second Floor
281 sq. ft.

Plan #F08-126D-1012

Dimensions: 30' W x 30' D
Heated Sq. Ft.: 815
Bedrooms: 1 **Bathrooms:** 1
Exterior Walls: 2" x 6"
Foundation: Basement

See index for more information

Images provided by designer/architect

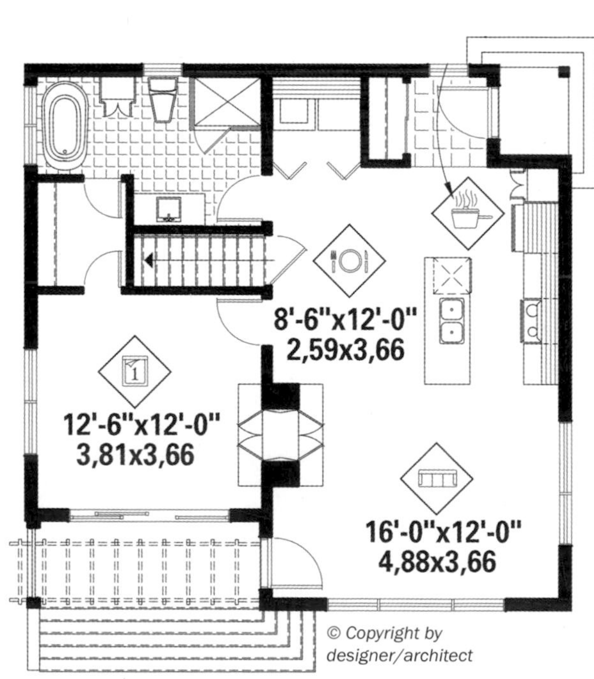

© Copyright by designer/architect

Plan #F08-007D-0163

Dimensions: 50'8" W x 50'4" D
Heated Sq. Ft.: 1,580
Bedrooms: 3 **Bathrooms:** 2
Foundation: Crawl space standard; slab or basement for an additional fee

See index for more information

Images provided by designer/architect

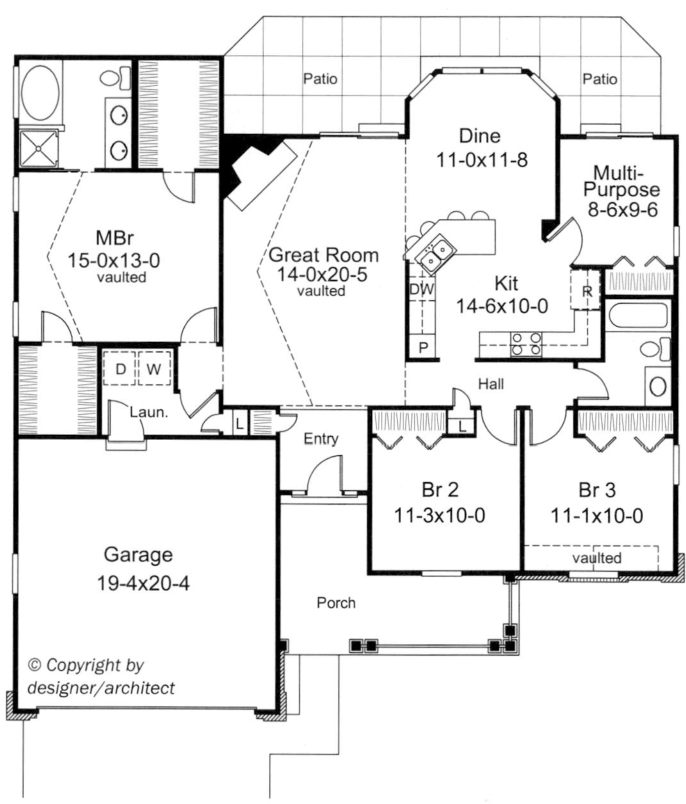

Plan #F08-058D-0219

Dimensions: 54'4" W x 50'4" D
Heated Sq. Ft.: 1,684
Bedrooms: 3 **Bathrooms:** 2
Foundation: Basement

See index for more information

Images provided by designer/architect

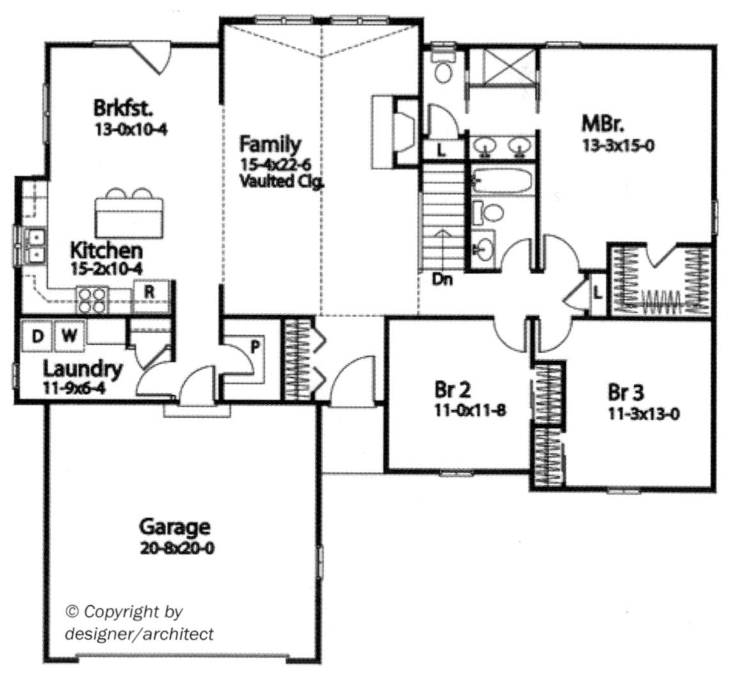

Images provided by designer/architect

Plan #F08-077D-0142

Dimensions: 70' W x 56' D
Heated Sq. Ft.: 2,067
Bonus Sq. Ft.: 379
Bedrooms: 3 **Bathrooms:** 2½
Foundation: Slab or crawl space, please specify when ordering; for basement foundation version, see Plan #077D-0164 at houseplansandmore.com

See index for more information

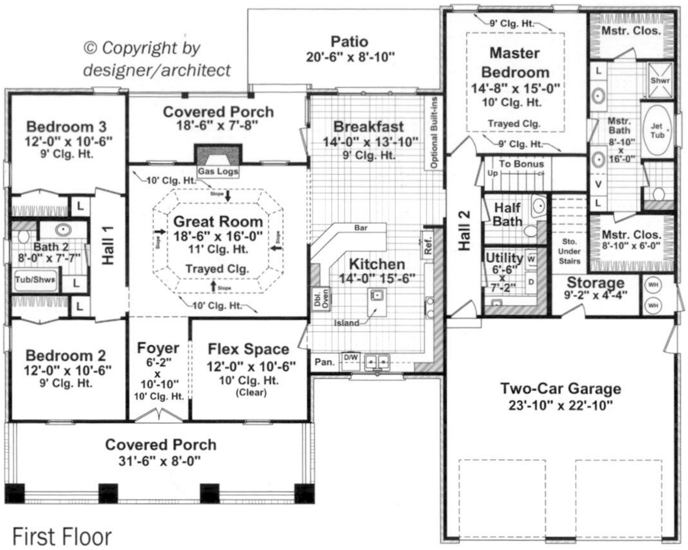

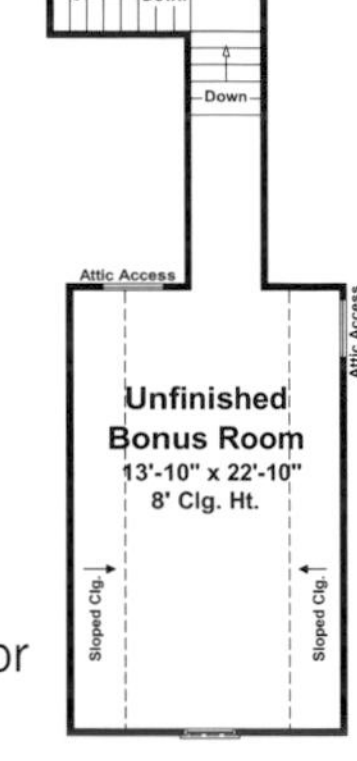

Optional Second Floor
379 sq. ft.

First Floor
2,067 sq. ft.

Plan #F08-155D-0197

Dimensions: 48' W x 68' D
Heated Sq. Ft.: 1,598
Bedrooms: 3 **Bathrooms:** 2
Foundation: Crawl space or slab standard; basement or daylight basement for an additional fee

See index for more information

Images provided by designer/architect

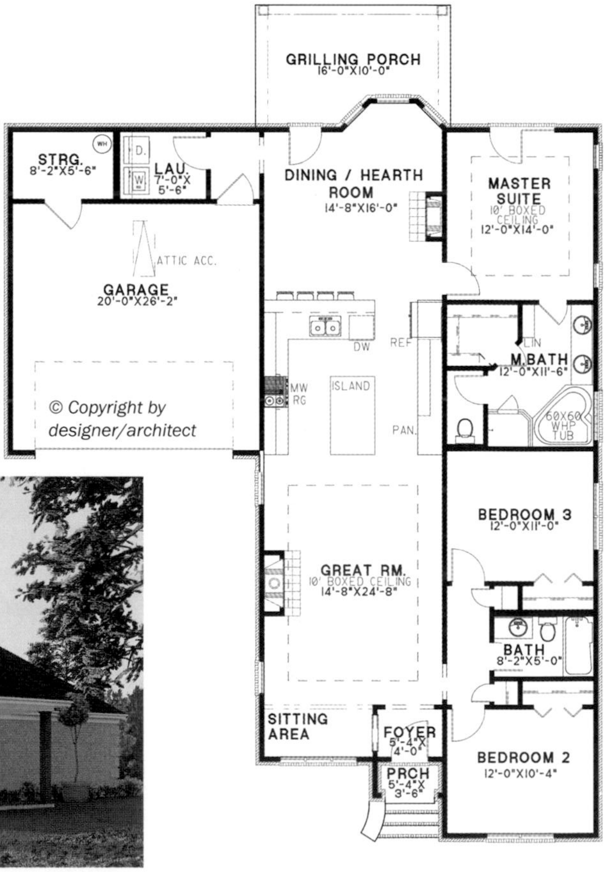

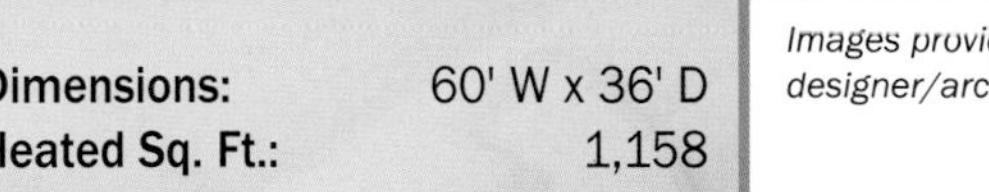

Plan #F08-058D-0231

Dimensions: 60' W x 36' D
Heated Sq. Ft.: 1,158
Bedrooms: 3 **Bathrooms:** 2
Foundation: Basement

See index for more information

Images provided by designer/architect

© Copyright by designer/architect

M. Bedrm 11-8x12-10
Brkfst 8-9x11-4
Kitchen 9-6x11-4
Dn
Garage 19-8x23-2
Family 16-1x14-2
Bedrm 2 10-1x10-8
Bedrm 3 10-1x10-8
16'x7' Door
Covered Porch 15-0x6-0

Plan #F08-077D-0058

Dimensions: 64'6" W x 61'4" D
Heated Sq. Ft.: 2,002
Bedrooms: 3 **Bathrooms:** 2
Exterior Walls: 2" x 6"
Foundation: Slab, crawl space, basement or walk-out basement, please specify when ordering

See index for more information

Images provided by designer/architect

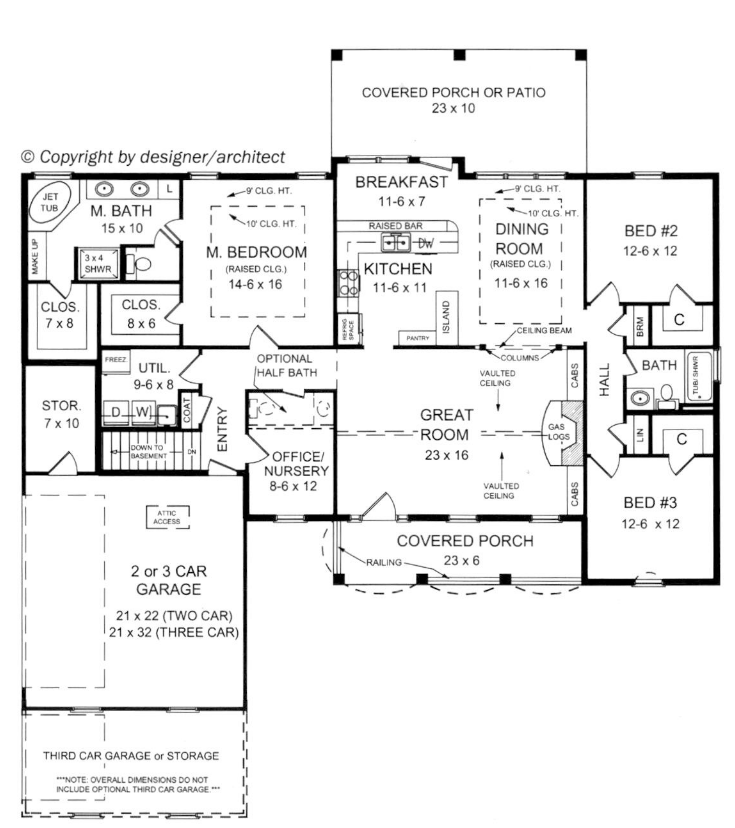

Plan #F08-011D-0662

Dimensions: 76' W x 62' D
Heated Sq. Ft.: 2,460
Bedrooms: 3 **Bathrooms:** 2½
Exterior Walls: 2" x 6"
Foundation: Crawl space or slab standard; basement for an additional fee

See index for more information

Images provided by designer/architect

Features

- Stunning curb appeal can be noted upon seeing this stylish one-story home
- The covered front porch welcomes you into the interior where you will find a formal dining room right off the foyer
- The vaulted great room enjoys direct access to the amazing vaulted outdoor living area with a fireplace, an outdoor kitchen and a sunny patio
- The bayed breakfast nook right off the kitchen will enjoy views of the outdoors
- The private master suite has a posh bath and a spacious walk-in closet with direct laundry room access
- Two additional bedrooms and a bath complete this home
- 2-car side entry garage

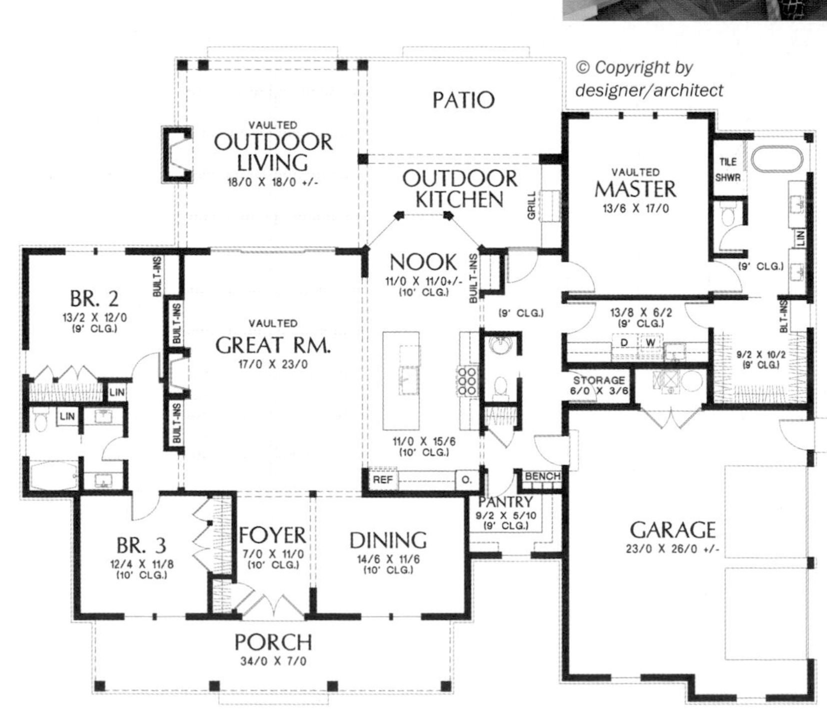

Plan #F08-084D-0086

Dimensions: 45'4" W x 76' D
Heated Sq. Ft.: 1,725
Bedrooms: 3 **Bathrooms:** 2
Foundation: Slab standard; crawl space for an additional fee

See index for more information

Images provided by designer/architect

Features

- This stylish ranch home offers a great split bedroom layout for a more narrow lot
- The open living area enjoys beautiful views of the outdoor living space that features an outdoor fireplace
- The kitchen enjoys a snack bar, a center work island, tons of storage floor-to-ceiling and even a built-in desk
- A cheerful dining area is surrounded in windows
- The private master bedroom features a luxury bath with two walk-in closets, a double-bowl vanity, an oversized tub and walk-in easy access shower
- 2-car front entry garage

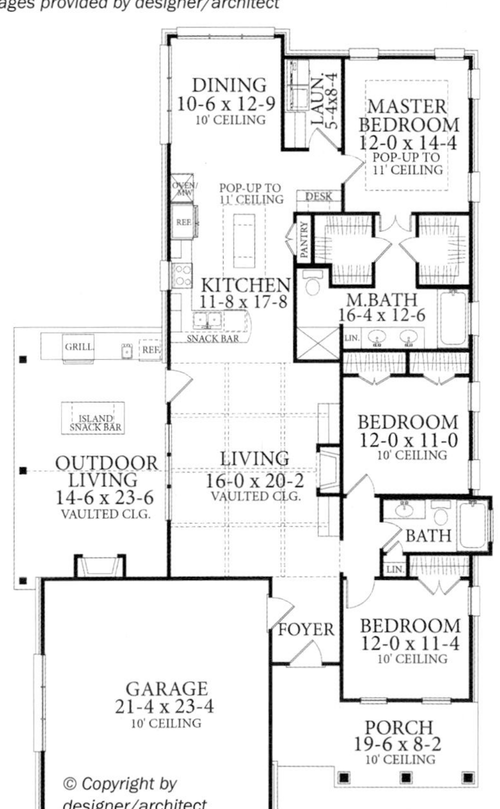

Plan #F08-169D-0002

Dimensions: 41' W x 60'4" D
Heated Sq. Ft.: 1,762
Bedrooms: 3 **Bathrooms:** 2
Foundation: Basement standard; crawl space or slab for an additional fee
See index for more information

Images provided by designer/architect

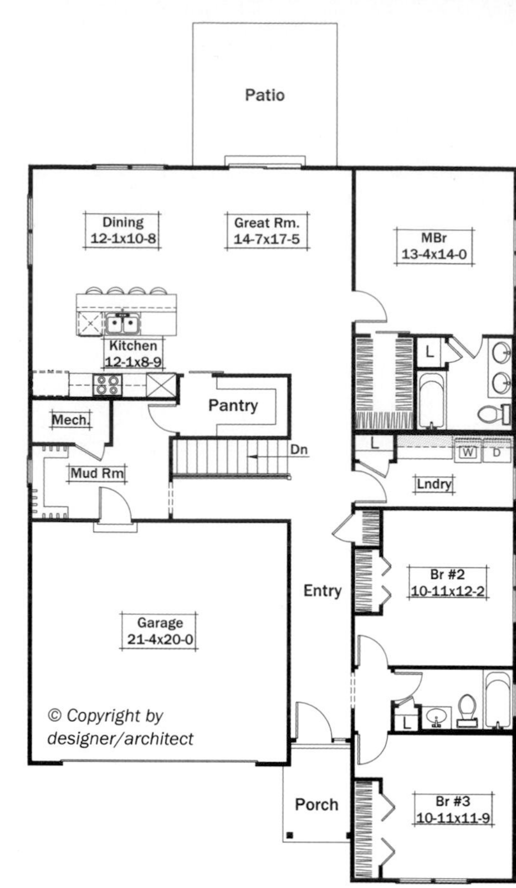

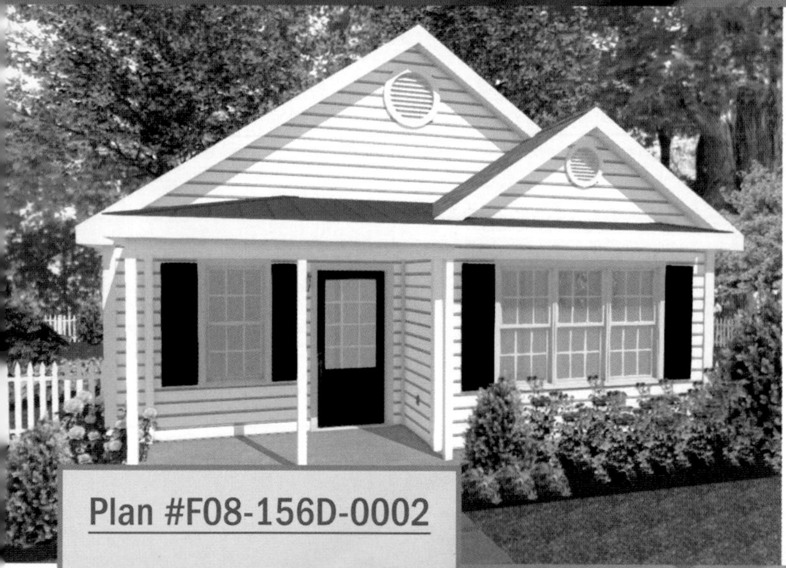

Plan #F08-156D-0002

Dimensions: 24' W x 27'6" D
Heated Sq. Ft.: 576
Bedrooms: 1 **Bathrooms:** 1
Foundation: Slab standard; crawl space for an additional fee
See index for more information

Images provided by designer/architect

Util.
3' x 3'
Clos.
2'-4" x 6'-1"
Bedroom
11'-6" x 10'
8' clg.
Bath
5'-5" x 10'
8' clg.
W/D
Hall
4'-11" x 3'-7"
Raised ceiling - 10'
Kitchen
11'-8" x 11'
Living
11'-8" x 15'
Porch
10'-6" x 5'-4"

© Copyright by designer/architect

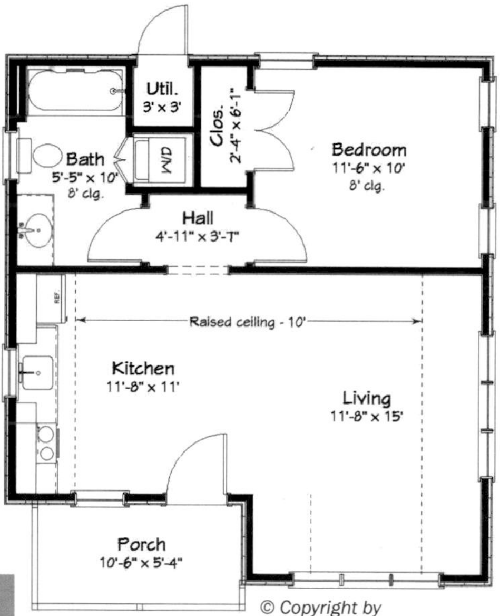

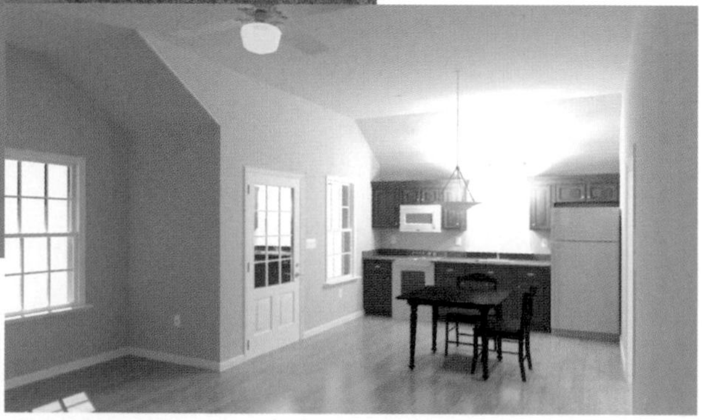

Plan #F08-086D-0143

Dimensions: 45' W x 55' D
Heated Sq. Ft.: 1,562
Bedrooms: 3 **Bathrooms:** 2
Foundation: Basement

See index for more information

Images provided by designer/architect

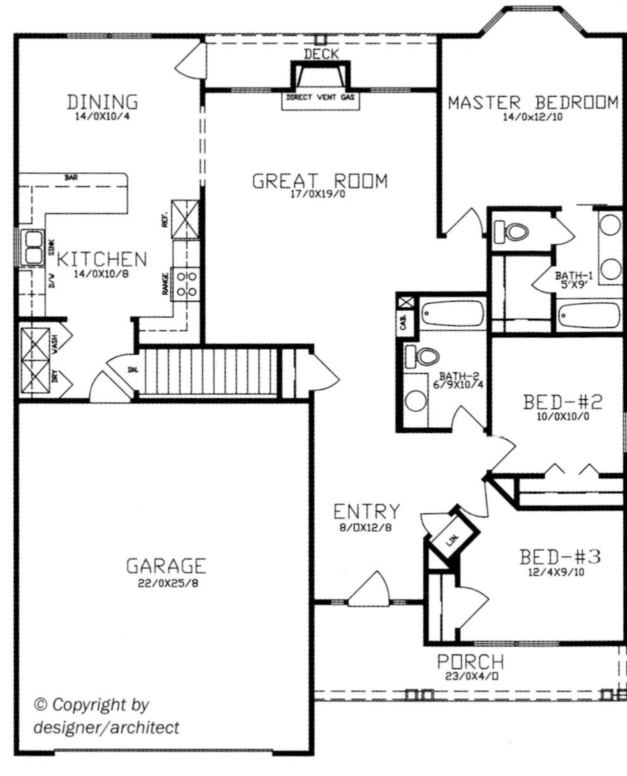

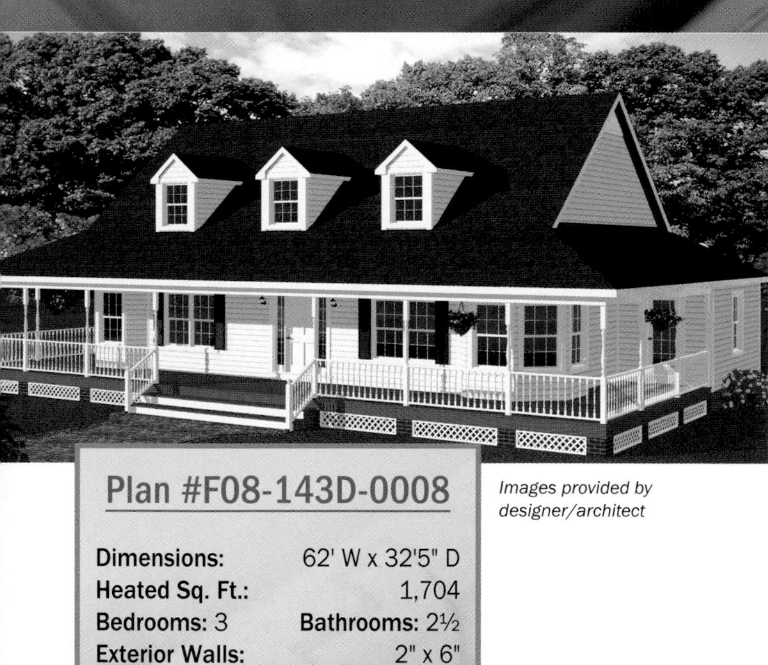

Plan #F08-143D-0008

Dimensions: 62' W x 32'5" D
Heated Sq. Ft.: 1,704
Bedrooms: 3 **Bathrooms:** 2½
Exterior Walls: 2" x 6"
Foundation: Basement, crawl space or slab, please specify when ordering

See index for more information

Images provided by designer/architect

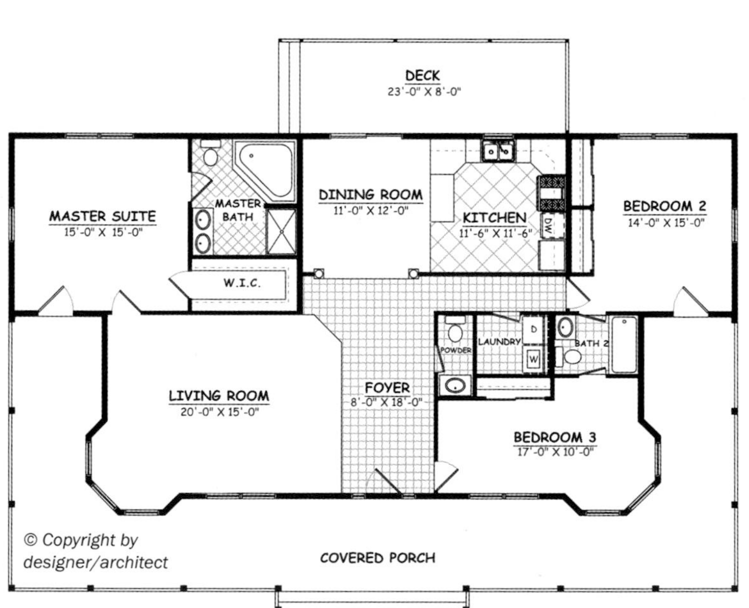

Plan #F08-051D-0974

Dimensions: 60' W x 73' D
Heated Sq. Ft.: 1,736
Bedrooms: 2 **Bathrooms:** 2
Exterior Walls: 2" x 6"
Foundation: Basement standard; crawl space or slab for an additional fee

See index for more information

Features

- A deep Craftsman style porch greets all those who enter this home and has enough space for a swing or rocking chairs
- The ever-popular open floor plan reigns in this home featuring sunny dining and great rooms with a kitchen overlooking it all
- The kitchen has a unique and functional hidden pantry that seamlessly blends with the rest of the cabinets
- The super-private master bedroom enjoys a spacious walk-in closet extending from the bath
- 3-car front entry garage

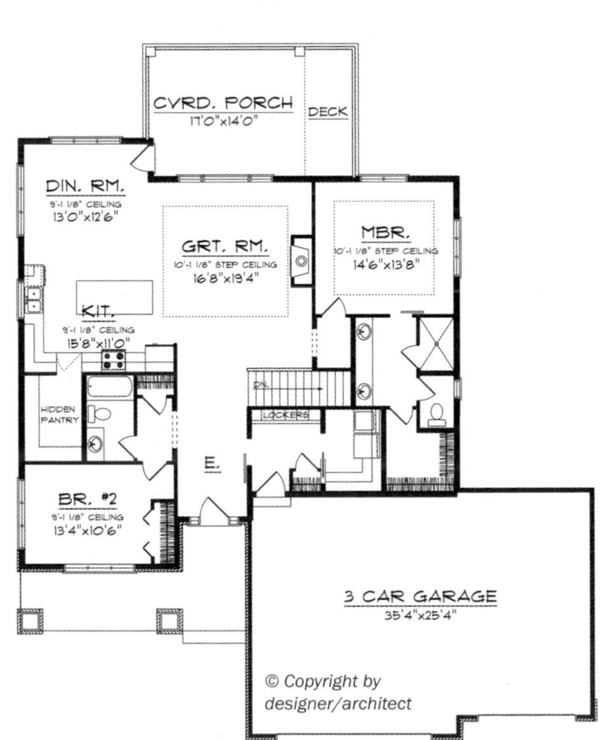

Images provided by designer/architect

Plan #F08-101D-0192

Dimensions: 118' W x 63' D
Heated Sq. Ft.: 3,224
Bonus Sq. Ft.: 2,324
Bedrooms: 2 **Bathrooms:** 2½
Exterior Walls: 2" x 6"
Foundation: Basement

See index for more information

Images provided by designer/architect

Features

- Symmetrically pleasing to the eye, this one-story home enjoys an open-concept layout, cheerful dining space, and a chef's gourmet kitchen at mealtime
- The master bedroom and guest bedroom are separated for privacy making entertaining house guests more enjoyable for everyone
- A huge workshop is found off the garage and is ideal for the homeowner who always has "projects" in progress
- The optional lower level has an additional 2,324 square feet of living area that features a wet bar, rec room, home theater, craft room, two bedrooms, a second laundry room, two full baths and a half bath
- 4-car side entry garage

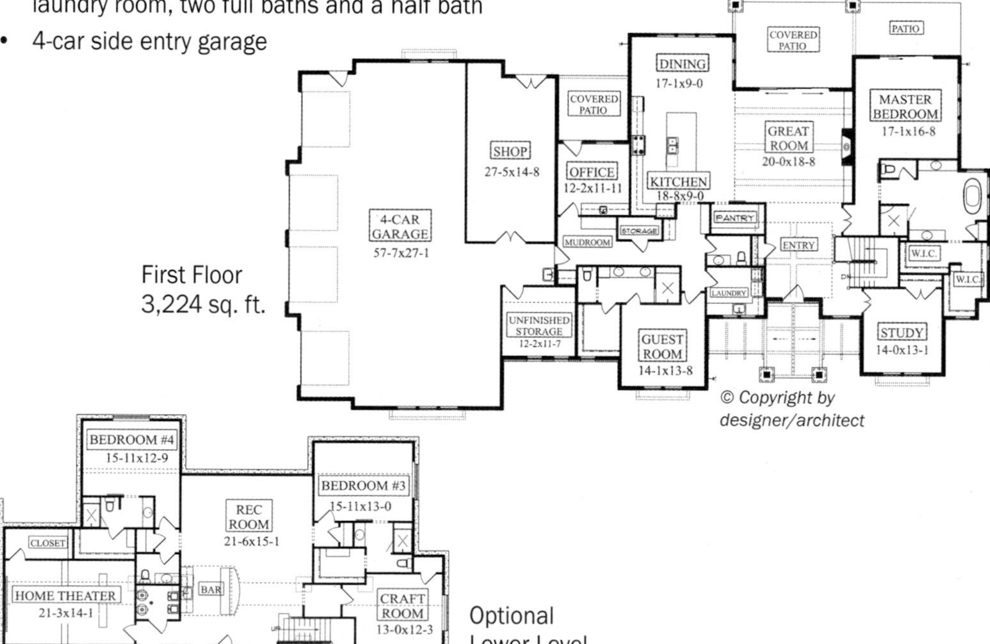

First Floor
3,224 sq. ft.

Optional
Lower Level
2,324 sq. ft.

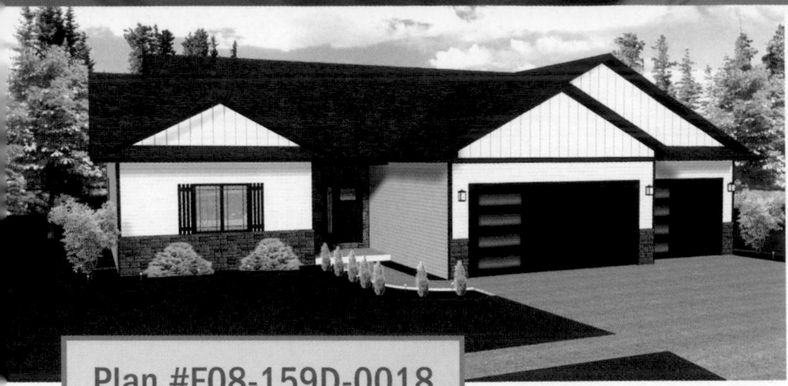

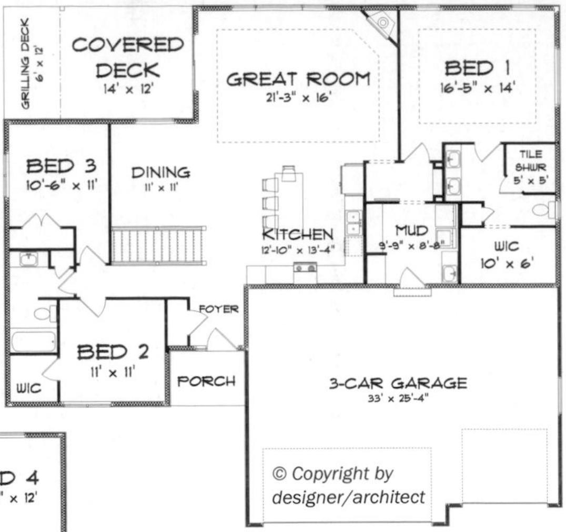
GRILLING DECK
6' x 12'
COVERED DECK
14' x 12'
GREAT ROOM
21'-3" x 16'
BED 1
16'-5" x 14'
BED 3
10'-6" x 11'
DINING
11' x 11'
TILE SHWR
5' x 5'
KITCHEN
12'-10" x 13'-4"
MUD
9'-9" x 8'-8"
WIC
10' x 6'
FOYER
BED 2
11' x 11'
PORCH
WIC
3-CAR GARAGE
33' x 25'-4"
© Copyright by
designer/architect

Images provided by designer/architect

First Floor
1,818 sq. ft.

Plan #F08-159D-0018

Dimensions: 59' W x 56' D
Heated Sq. Ft.: 1,818
Bonus Sq. Ft.: 1,507
Bedrooms: 3 **Bathrooms:** 2
Exterior Walls: 2" x 6"
Foundation: Walk-out basement

See index for more information

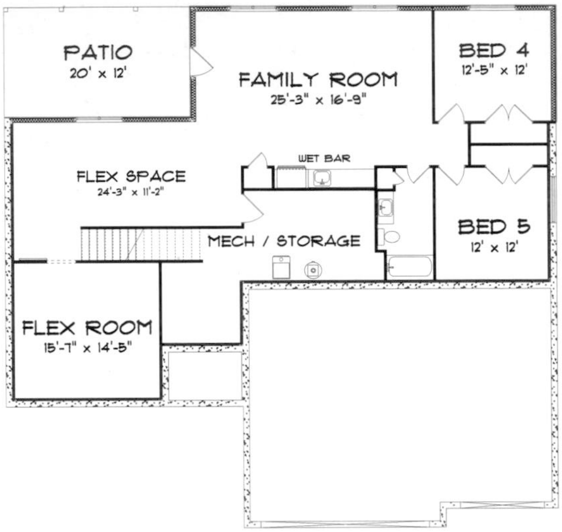
PATIO
20' x 12'
FAMILY ROOM
25'-3" x 16'-9"
BED 4
12'-5" x 12'
WET BAR
FLEX SPACE
24'-3" x 11'-2"
MECH / STORAGE
BED 5
12' x 12'
FLEX ROOM
15'-7" x 14'-5"

Optional
Lower Level
1,507 sq. ft.

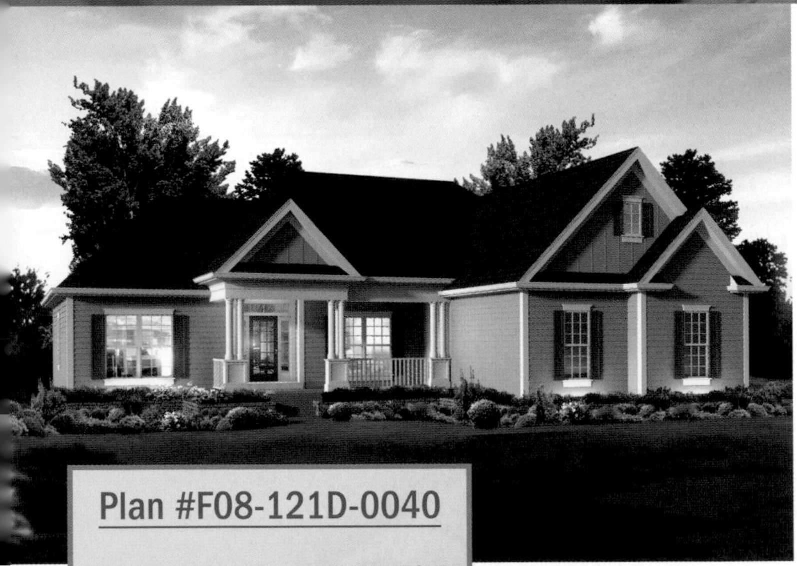

Plan #F08-121D-0040

Dimensions: 58' W x 58' D
Heated Sq. Ft.: 1,863
Bedrooms: 3 **Bathrooms:** 2½
Foundation: Basement standard; crawl space or slab for an additional fee

See index for more information

Images provided by designer/architect

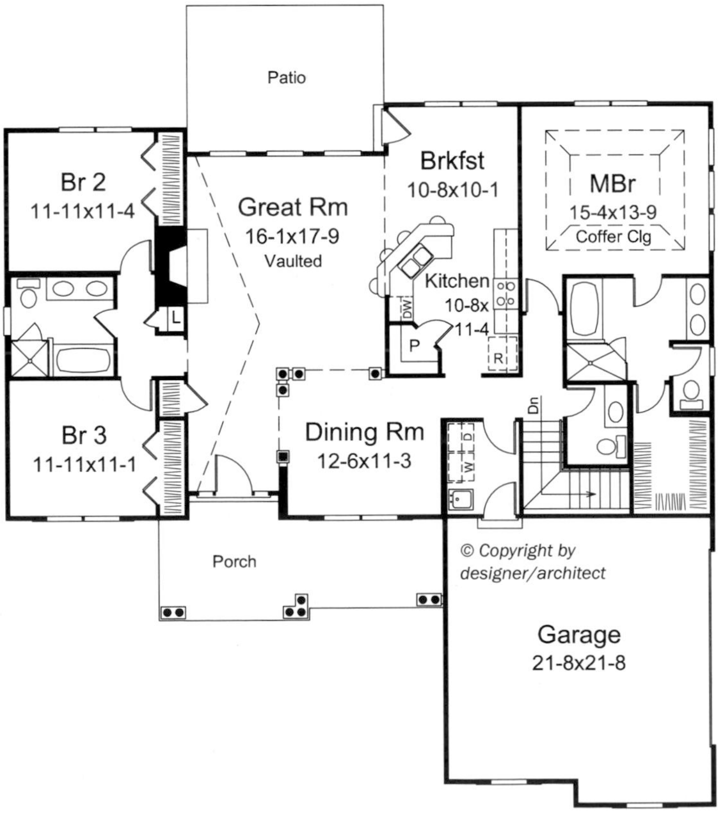
Patio
Br 2
11-11x11-4
Great Rm
16-1x17-9
Vaulted
Brkfst
10-8x10-1
MBr
15-4x13-9
Coffer Clg
Kitchen
10-8x
11-4
DW
P
R
L
Br 3
11-11x11-1
Dining Rm
12-6x11-3
Dn
W
D
Porch
© Copyright by
designer/architect
Garage
21-8x21-8

Plan #F08-033D-0012

Dimensions:	60' W x 43' D
Heated Sq. Ft.:	1,546
Bedrooms: 3	**Bathrooms:** 2
Foundation:	Basement

See index for more information

Images provided by designer/architect

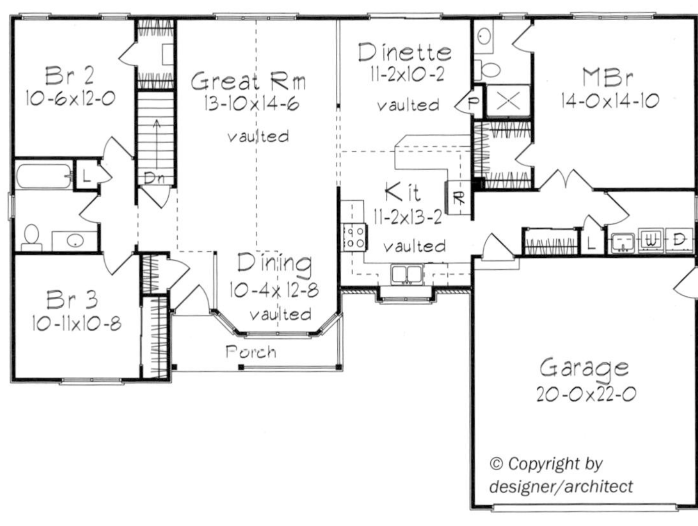

Plan #F08-141D-0315

Dimensions:	25' W x 40' D
Heated Sq. Ft.:	750
Bedrooms: 1	**Bathrooms:** 1
Exterior Walls:	2" x 6"
Foundation:	Pier

See index for more information

Images provided by designer/architect

© Copyright by designer/architect

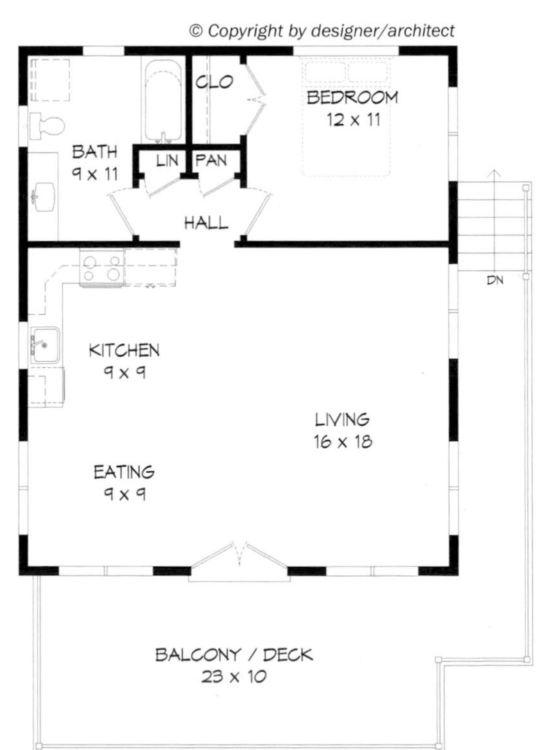

Plan #F08-121D-0023

Dimensions: 41' W x 60'4" D
Heated Sq. Ft.: 1,762
Bedrooms: 3 **Bathrooms:** 2
Foundation: Basement standard; crawl space or slab for an additional fee

See index for more information

Images provided by designer/architect

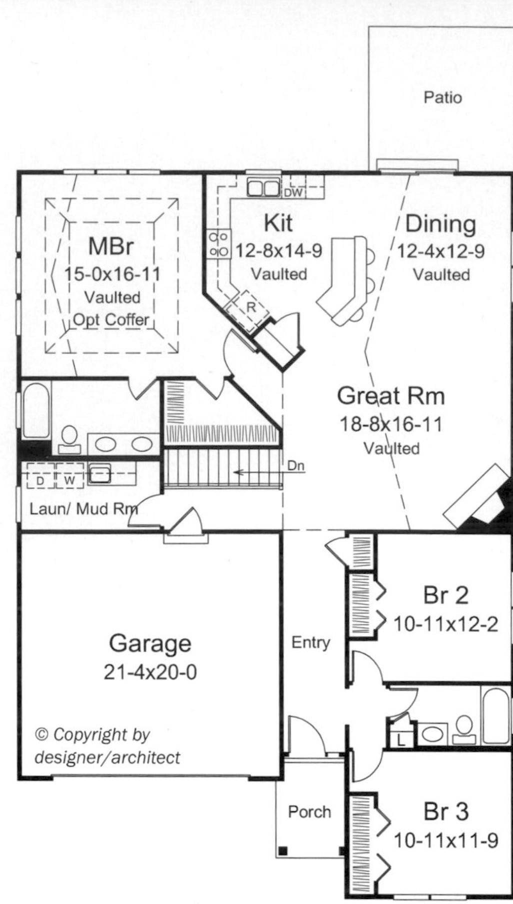

Plan #F08-155D-0192

Dimensions: 64'10" W x 67'4" D
Heated Sq. Ft.: 2,509
Bedrooms: 4 **Bathrooms:** 2½
Foundation: Crawl space or slab standard; basement or daylight basement for an additional fee

See index for more information

Images provided by designer/architect

Plan #F08-011D-0670

Dimensions: 69' W x 58' D
Heated Sq. Ft.: 2,104
Bonus Sq. Ft.: 268
Bedrooms: 3 **Bathrooms:** 2½
Exterior Walls: 2" x 6"
Foundation: Crawl space or slab standard; basement for an additional fee

See index for more information

Images provided by designer/architect

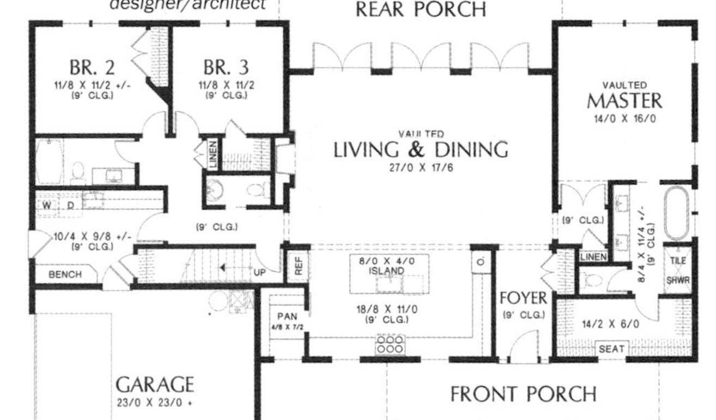

Optional Second Floor
268 sq. ft.

First Floor
2,104 sq. ft.

Plan #F08-058D-0240

Dimensions: 55' W x 46' D
Heated Sq. Ft.: 1,594
Bedrooms: 3 **Bathrooms:** 2
Foundation: Basement

See index for more information

Images provided by designer/architect

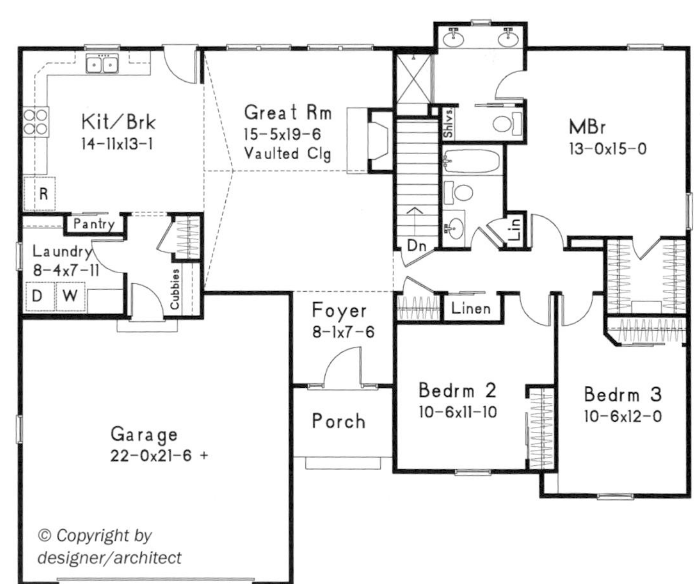

Plan #F08-028D-0064

Dimensions: 38' W x 52' D
Heated Sq. Ft.: 1,292
Bedrooms: 2 **Bathrooms:** 2
Exterior Walls: 2" x 6"
Foundation: Monolithic slab standard; floating slab, crawl space, basement or walk-out basement for an additional fee

See index for more information

Images provided by designer/architect

Features

- Two large covered porches in the front and back offer plenty of desirable outdoor living space with their wide design
- The combined kitchen/dining area is open to the sunny great room making this the main gathering place in this home
- A large laundry room provides plenty of space for household chores and has direct access to the outdoors
- Each of the two bedrooms includes ample walk-in closetspace for keeping things organized

homemade

homemade

WELCOME TO THE LAKE

bonus rooms & basements

finding flexibility within your home

You found it – the perfect dream home! It has the exact number of bedrooms and bathrooms. The open floor plan is great. The kitchen is spacious, the mud room ideal, and the storage is awesome. You even have a bonus room. Now, what to do with that space? Here lies the beauty of this space – you can do whatever you like! From newlyweds to families of five, the bonus room holds numerous possibilities for every homeowner to customize their design as they see fit. Many one-story homes today are designed with bonus or flex spaces that give families that wiggle room when additional space is needed. Let your imagination run wild! There are so many opportunities to make this your area for fun, fitness, work or relaxation; you name it.

think big

Maximize your home's fun quotient by finishing your flex or bonus space for a big time fun spot everyone will love! Better yet, your basement may be below ground, but there's nothing sub-par about these ideas!

Unless noted, copyright by designer/architect; Page 134, top, left: Plan #101D-0092; above: Plan #011S-0189; Page 135, clockwise from top: Plan #011S-0018; Bonus room playroom, Plan #011S-0192; Plan #F08-101D-0198; Plan #101S-0019; For more photos or to order plan, please visit houseplansandmore.com.

here's some favorites

play room

Every mom wishes she had a place where she could put those extra toys, keeping them from clashing with her living room décor, or ending up under her feet while she tries to fix dinner. So why not put that bonus room to good use as a designated play room? Organizational systems of cubbies, baskets, and shelves will keep an unruly collection of toys organized, while providing enough space to enjoy playing with them. Bean bag chairs and play rugs in bright colors keep the room fun and functional. You could even break the room down into stations – an art area with chalkboard paint walls for your budding Van Gogh, a reading corner with special pillows and lighting, or a block table for the young architect. Keep this room child-friendly and fun and your kids will flock there, all while keeping the mess out of the rest of the house.

the home theater

To turn your bonus room into your own personal theater experience, you need surprisingly few items. A quality television, proper media players, and surround sound are the best setup. Now that your theater is functional it's time to personalize your movie watching experience. Are you going to put in oversized reclining chairs and couches, or movie theater seats? Will you put in dimming ambient lights? How about a popcorn machine? After all, the primary reason you have a home theater is to enjoy cinema entertainment in unsurpassed comfort. Some homeowners with serious theater systems choose to have professional input and installation. Whether home designed or professionally outfitted, the home theater is a bonus room design enjoyed by all.

the family gathering spot

Often called a recreation or game room, this family gathering spot is the place where family can get together and relax. Filled with games, movies, and perhaps a snack area or wet bar, this bonus room use is great for families that need an informal space to hang out in that doesn't necessarily need to be kept perfect like the highly visible great room. Keep this space cozy and inviting for making family memories.

the home gym

We all know someone who has purchased home workout equipment only to realize that the plan was not thought out. Bulky equipment is a pain to set up and take down everyday, so it often goes unused. If the equipment is left out, those machines always manage to take up awkward amounts of space. Even small free weights often find themselves in the way, causing stubbed toes and storage woes. Turning your bonus room into a home gym, or exercise room creates a designated space for all that equipment, plus it allows options of customized flooring or built-in sound systems. It will definitely make exercising less of a chore since you won't have to leave the house!

the home office

If you choose to work from home, there is no more valuable a space than a bonus room that's been turned into a home office. Remember that your home office is a reflection of you and the work you produce. Make it a priority to keep the space efficient and eye-appealing with necessary storage, noise buffers, and organizational systems. Keeping this room working for you makes working from home a pleasant affair and ensures the bonus room is never a wasted space.

double your square footage + customize your basement into something special

Many of today's one-story homes like the ones featured in this book are designed with an optional lower level. Offering flexibility if additional square footage is needed or desired, finishing a lower level can instantly increase a home's square footage providing added bedrooms, gathering space, or whatever you need to make your home more functional and work for you. Gone are the days of a home's basement being only used as a place for old boxes. The basements, or lower levels of today are nothing in comparison. Basement storage is being transformed into finished family spaces. The most popular options are best broken into specialized areas. From gaming to movie theaters, much like a bonus or flex room, your basement can be designed to your unique desires.

Unless noted, copyright by designer/architect; Page 136, top to bottom, left: Plan #055D-0817; Plan #011S-0196, Bob Greenspan, photographer; Plan #011S-0191, Bob Greenspan, photographer; bottom, right: Plan #101D-0114, © 2017 Diggles Creative Warren Diggles, photographer; Page 137, top: Plan #071S-0001; middle: Plan #101D-0091, Rebecca of Sunnybrook Photo, photographer; bottom: Plan #101D-0121.

need ideas?

game on

What you do with your dedicated game room depends on the game to be played. Families may choose to have a special table for game play, with shelves installed to organize their extensive board game collections. Poker, or Texas Hold'em are popular and if you love to play, then a personalized table, chips, and cards would be great additions to this space. Pool tables, air hockey, shuffleboard, and even full-scale arcade games are also available for purchase, allowing fans to recreate their favorite gaming experiences – without worrying about their high scores being challenged!

media coverage

As family lifestyles become more hectic, the free time they spend together is often wanted at home. The availability of flat screen smart televisions, surround sound (often wireless), and multiple video, audio, gaming systems and apps allow any media experience to be enjoyed at full capacity without ever leaving home. Specialized lighting can add the appropriate ambiance when movie watching or having gaming tournaments with just a click of the remote.

lounging around

For some families, extra space is best outfitted with the amenities needed to relax. Cozy furniture, warm lighting, blankets and bookshelves create a desirable place to retreat to while enjoying one another's company.

Many families choose to mix and match the different suggestions, creating zones of activity within the basement. Additionally, refreshment centers are becoming more popular in finished basements, adding to the level of comfort. These can be uniquely designed, ranging from full-scale kitchens to specialized wet bars. Wine cellars and humidors are also popular in many households. Keep in mind that with refreshments usually come bathrooms. Full baths, saunas, hot tubs, and even guest rooms are prevalent in basements when resources allow.

When it comes to decorating and creating a specific atmosphere, it may be best to consider a theme. This works particularly well for dedicated rooms. If you are choosing to outfit your basement for multiple uses, stick to something that will be enjoyed by everyone without overshadowing any particular area. Your basement is one more opportunity to show how creative you are – so, don't hold back!

Attempt to use as much of the space as you can. Vertical shelves are great for visible, neat storage, while also giving you further places to display pictures and other treasures while also promoting a feeling of spaciousness with their height.

hot tip

Make your finished basement feel like an extension of your main level. Use the same finishes and remove the doors that separate each floor and now you have twice the house with twice the personality and comfort!

hit the floor

Flooring is important, and the basement will likely be exposed to heavy traffic flow. Durability and comfort are both vital in addition to stain resistance and sound proofing. Cork flooring is growing in popularity for these reasons. Another popular choice is luxury vinyl laminate, or ceramic tile. Both of these options can look exactly like stone or wood flooring, but are entirely waterproof, perfect for damper environments like basements and areas where there will be plenty of entertaining and the chance for frequent spills.

let there be light

Recessed lighting eliminates overhead and wasting floor space, but can be expensive. Sconces are another idea to prevent wasting precious entertainment space, but try to include as much natural light as possible to avoid the feeling of being underground. Today, many areas have code requirements for egress windows in basements, these windows are larger than their traditional counterparts and allow much more natural light to filter into the space. They alleviate the feeling of a dark, damp basement instantly, and they also allow any bedroom designed into a basement space to be considered a true bedroom when you plan to resell your home. Per code, a bedroom must have a proper escape method if there's a fire, and an egress window is large enough for just that.

make it multi-task

Some homeowners like the idea of multiple uses but really desire the peace of reading a book without overhearing the poker game going on across the room. Don't give up the hope of having both a flexible and functional recreation room. Curtain rails and bi-fold doors/walls can be installed, sectioning off areas in use or opening up the room to its greatest space potential, perfect for privacy or parties.

As you ponder finishing your basement with a festive and fun game room, or a tranquil spa and meditation area, keep in mind the space allowed as well as your budget, time constrictions and future needs. Measure the area and plan for traffic flow and adequate seating. It will be beneficial to pick a large space and plot the exact layout you desire. Homeowners are often surprised to find that a simple ping-pong table can take up a third of a room's floor space when unfolded. It is essential to have a defined plan for what amenities you definitely need to include in your new basement, in addition to where they will be located. Then, discuss your desires with your contractor. They can re-evaluate your design, ensuring the availability of your preferences. Although tempting, avoid purchasing items until your contractor has agreed to a layout. If you already own specific items, inform your contractor of their existence so those components are not ruled out when adjustments are made. With a little creativity, your former damp, dark basement will become the family's favorite gathering place, or the much-needed comfortable guest or living quarters you've always wanted.

Plan #F08-055S-0036

Dimensions: 89' W x 104' D
Heated Sq. Ft.: 4,121
Bonus Sq. Ft.: 1,826
Bedrooms: 3 **Bathrooms:** 3
Foundation: Crawl space or slab standard; basement or daylight basement for an additional fee

See index for more information

Images provided by designer/architect

Features

- An 11' boxed ceiling, a media center, a wet bar, and a cozy corner fireplace make the hearth room/ den the center of activity
- The master suite is full of amenities including a corner fireplace, a luxury bath, an exercise room, and a unique reinforced storm closet for shelter
- A home office is available for working remotely off the hall by the master suite
- The optional second floor has an additional 734 square feet of living area and includes a home theater or game room and bonus room providing space for entertaining and fun for the whole family
- 3-car front entry garage

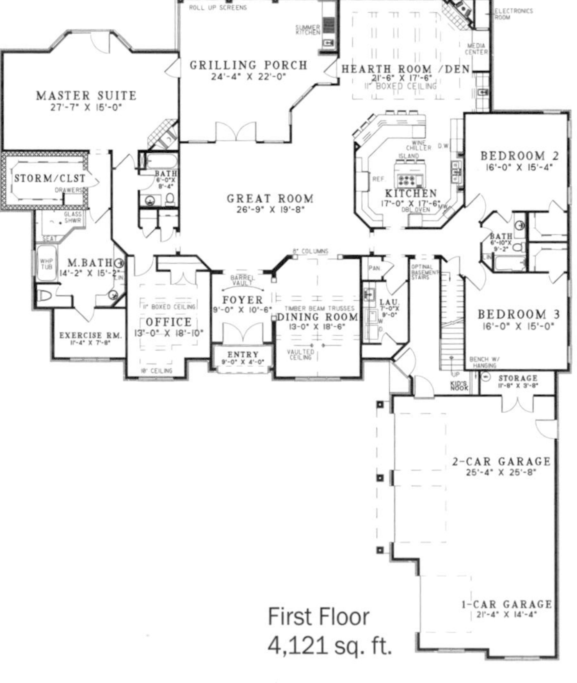

First Floor
4,121 sq. ft.

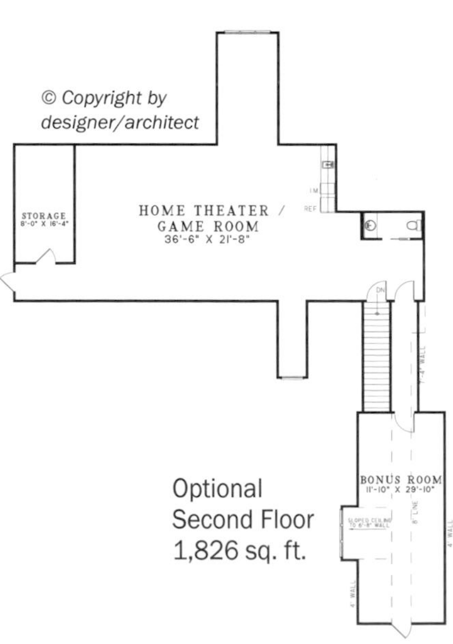

Optional
Second Floor
1,826 sq. ft.

Plan #F08-020D-0348

Dimensions: 70' W x 64' D
Heated Sq. Ft.: 2,342
Bedrooms: 4 **Bathrooms:** 3½
Foundation: Slab standard; crawl space for an additional fee

See index for more information

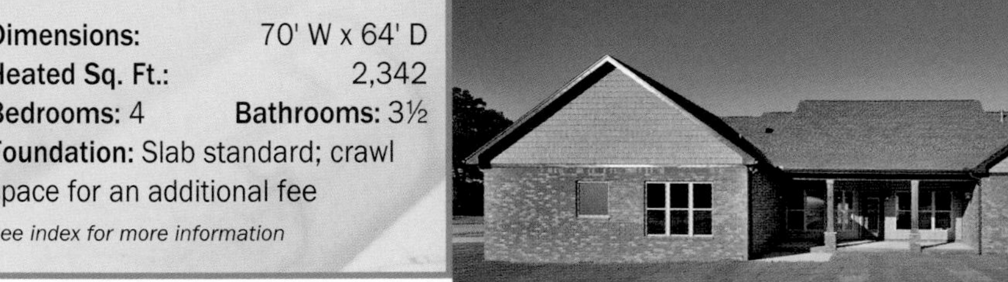

Features

- Rustic Craftsman appeal makes this home feel inviting and casual
- Portions of the front covered porch are large enough to create outdoor living areas
- Once inside, discover a formal dining room to the right that can easily be reached by the kitchen
- The split bedroom floor plan is the most popular and has the master suite in a private location away from the other bedrooms
- A swing room offers flexibility families need and could be turned into a nursery, an in-law suite, a home office, or playroom
- 2-car side entry garage

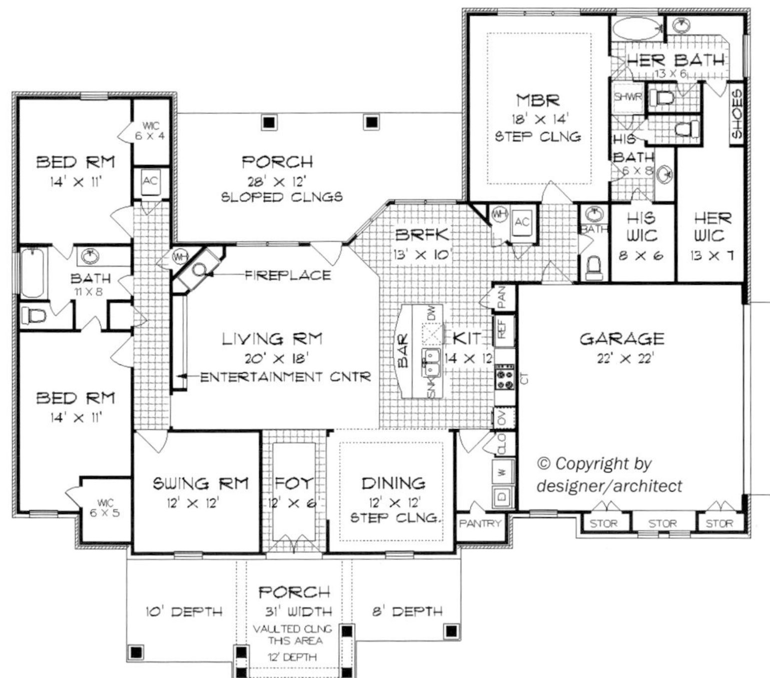

Images provided by designer/architect

Plan #F08-123D-0202

Dimensions: 64' W x 89' D
Heated Sq. Ft.: 1,856
Bonus Sq. Ft.: 1,032
Bedrooms: 2 **Bathrooms:** 2
Foundation: Walk-out basement standard; crawl space, slab or basement for an additional fee

See index for more information

Images provided by designer/architect

Features

- This home is ideal for lake living thanks to its wrap-around covered porch, huge covered patio, and screened deck area
- The huge beamed great room has a built-in fireplace and kitchen on the opposite end with an island for casual dining
- The private master bedroom has rear views and covered deck access, and a private bath
- A convenient guest suite on the first floor has direct access to a full bath
- The optional lower level has an additional 1,032 square feet of living area and has a family room with wet bar, game table area, half bath accessible from the outdoors, a bedroom, bunk room, and a full bath
- 2-car side entry garage

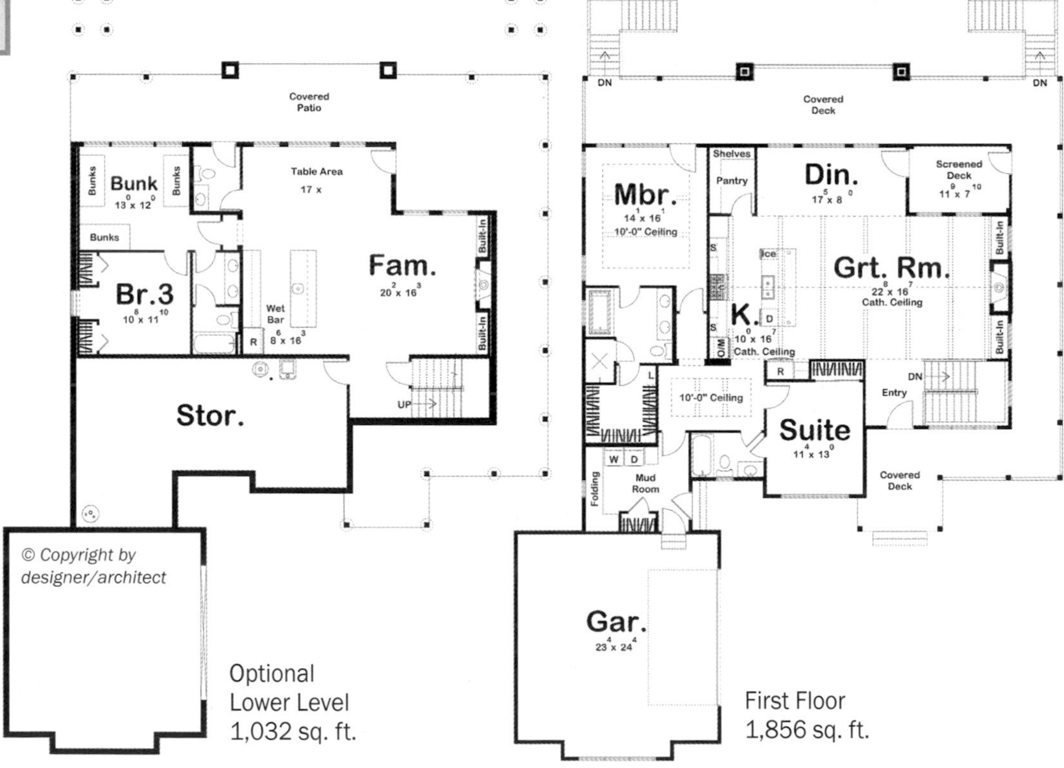

Optional Lower Level 1,032 sq. ft.

First Floor 1,856 sq. ft.

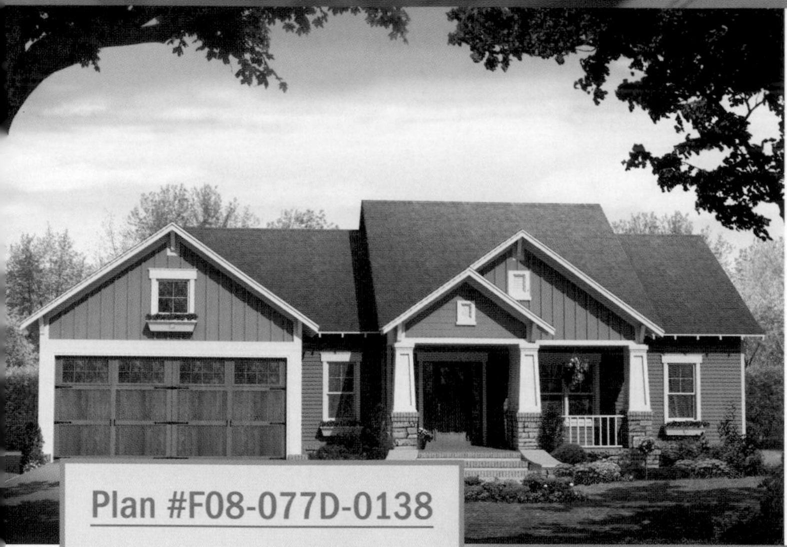

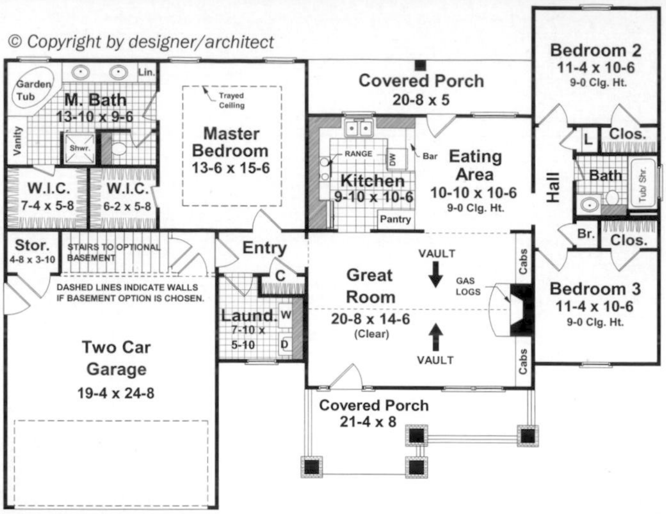

© Copyright by designer/architect

Garden Tub
M. Bath 13-10 x 9-6
Lin.
Vanity
Shwr.
W.I.C. 7-4 x 5-8
W.I.C. 6-2 x 5-8
Trayed Ceiling
Master Bedroom 13-6 x 15-6
Covered Porch 20-8 x 5
Range
DW
Bar
Kitchen 9-10 x 10-6
Pantry
Eating Area 10-10 x 10-6 9-0 Clg. Ht.
Bedroom 2 11-4 x 10-6 9-0 Clg. Ht.
L
Clos.
Hall
Bath
Tub/ Shr.
Br.
Clos.
Stor. 4-8 x 3-10
STAIRS TO OPTIONAL BASEMENT
DASHED LINES INDICATE WALLS IF BASEMENT OPTION IS CHOSEN.
Entry
C
Laund. 7-10 x 5-10
W
D
Great Room 20-8 x 14-6 (Clear)
VAULT
GAS LOGS
Cabs
VAULT
Cabs
Bedroom 3 11-4 x 10-6 9-0 Clg. Ht.
Two Car Garage 19-4 x 24-8
Covered Porch 21-4 x 8

Plan #F08-077D-0138

Dimensions: 61' W x 47'4" D
Heated Sq. Ft.: 1,509
Bedrooms: 3 **Bathrooms:** 2
Foundation: Slab, basement or crawl space, please specify when ordering

See index for more information

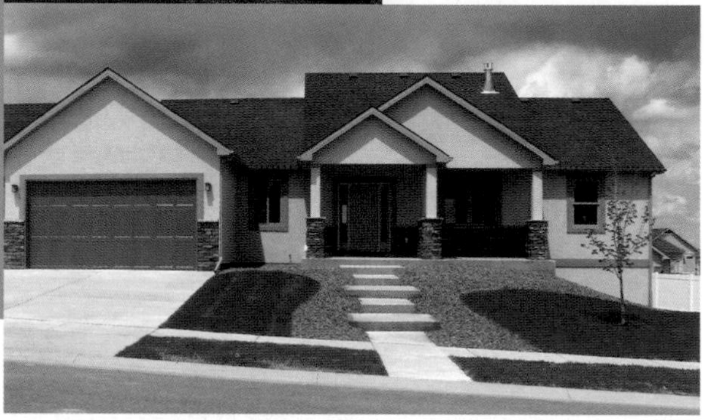

Images provided by designer/architect

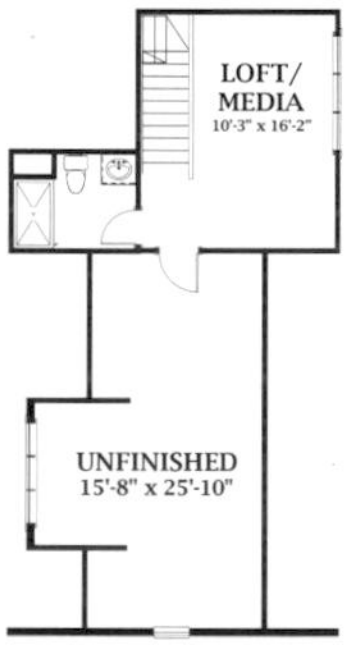

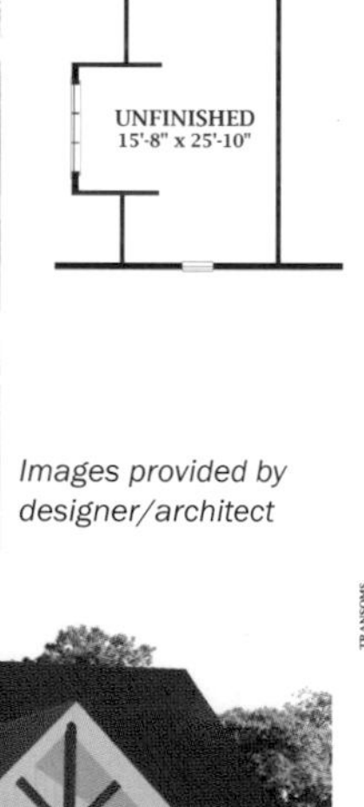

Optional Second Floor
632 sq. ft.

Images provided by designer/architect

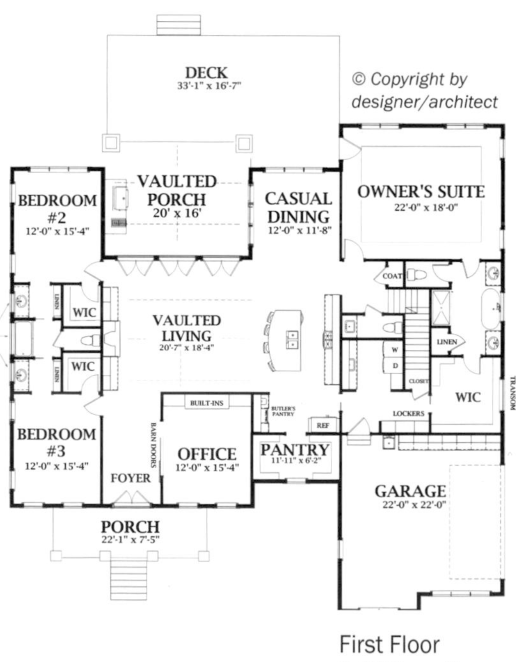

First Floor
2,838 sq. ft.

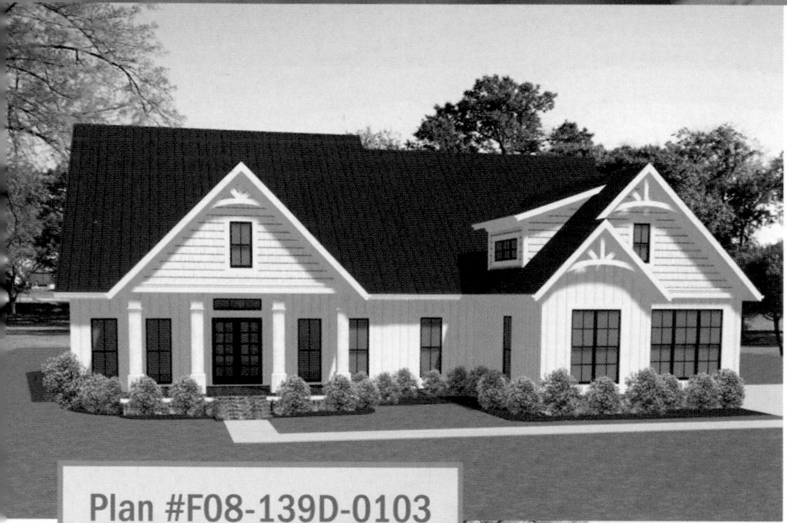

Plan #F08-139D-0103

Dimensions: 68'6" W x 80'5" D
Heated Sq. Ft.: 2,838
Bonus Sq. Ft.: 632
Bedrooms: 3 **Bathrooms:** 2½
Exterior Walls: 2" x 6"
Foundation: Crawl space standard; slab, basement, daylight basement or walk-out basement for an additional fee

See index for more information

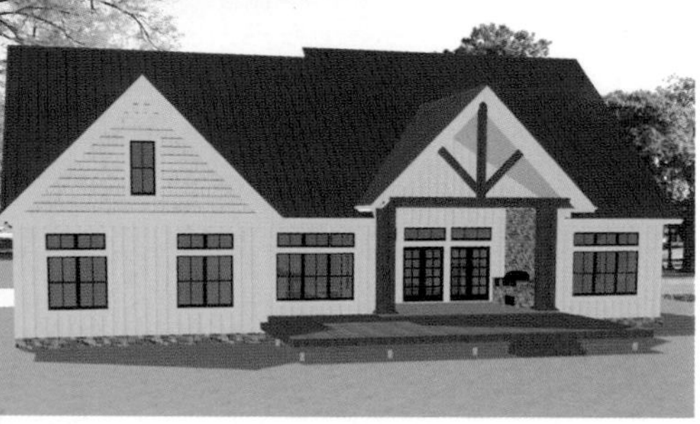

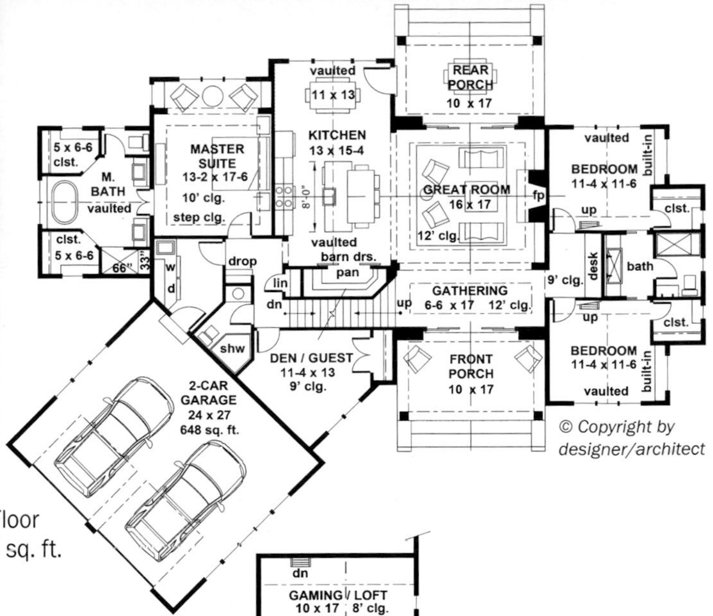

Plan #F08-091D-0511

Dimensions: 78'11" W x 65'5" D
Heated Sq. Ft.: 2,150
Bonus Sq. Ft.: 733
Bedrooms: 4 **Bathrooms:** 3
Exterior Walls: 2" x 6"
Foundation: Basement or crawl space standard; slab, daylight basement or walk-out basement for an additional fee

See index for more information

Images provided by designer/architect

First Floor
2,150 sq. ft.

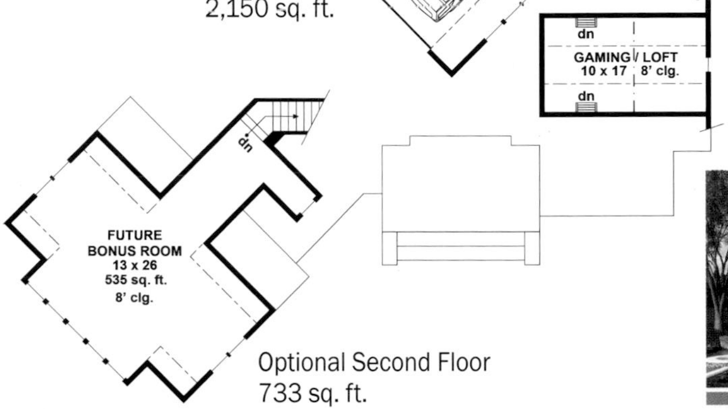

Optional Second Floor
733 sq. ft.

© Copyright by designer/architect

Plan #F08-013D-0202

Dimensions: 63' W x 62'8" D
Heated Sq. Ft.: 2,000
Bonus Sq. Ft.: 495
Bedrooms: 4 **Bathrooms:** 2½
Foundation: Basement standard; crawl space or slab for an additional fee

See index for more information

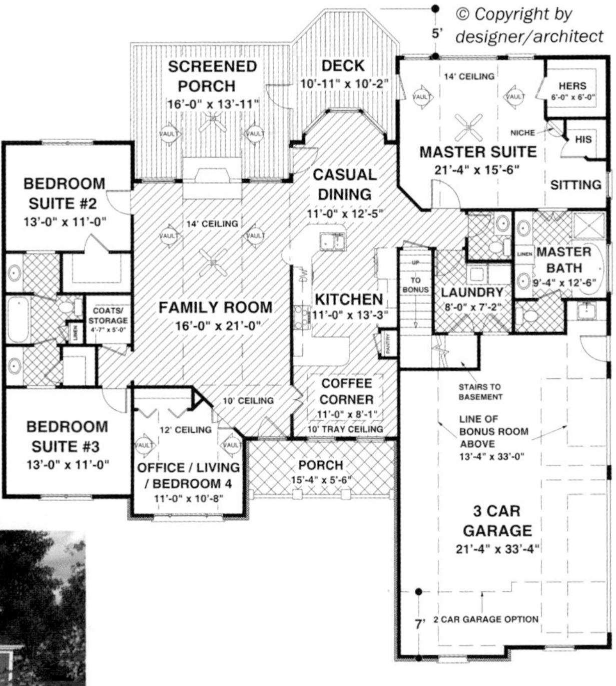

© Copyright by designer/architect

Images provided by designer/architect

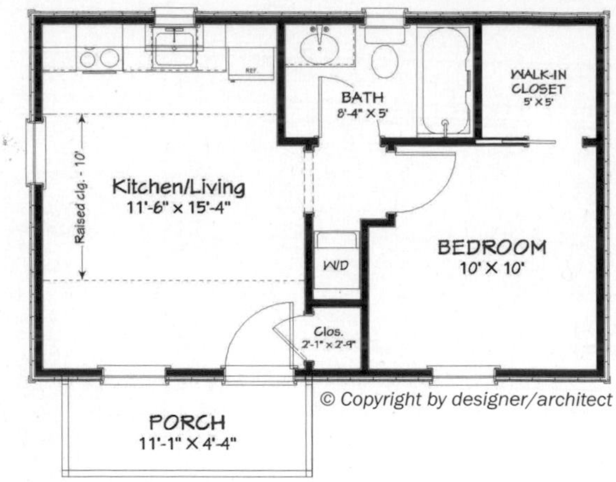

Plan #F08-156D-0008

Dimensions: 25' W x 20'6" D
Heated Sq. Ft.: 400
Bedrooms: 1 **Bathrooms:** 1
Foundation: Slab standard; crawl space for an additional fee

See index for more information

Kitchen/Living 11'-6" x 15'-4"
Raised clg. - 10'
BATH 8'-4" X 5'
WALK-IN CLOSET 5' X 5'
BEDROOM 10' X 10'
W/D
Clos. 2'-1" x 2'-9"
PORCH 11'-1" X 4'-4"

© Copyright by designer/architect

Images provided by designer/architect

Plan #F08-001D-0013

Dimensions: 60'10" W x 51'2" D
Heated Sq. Ft.: 1,882
Bedrooms: 3 **Bathrooms:** 2
Foundation: Basement standard; crawl space or slab for an additional fee

See index for more information

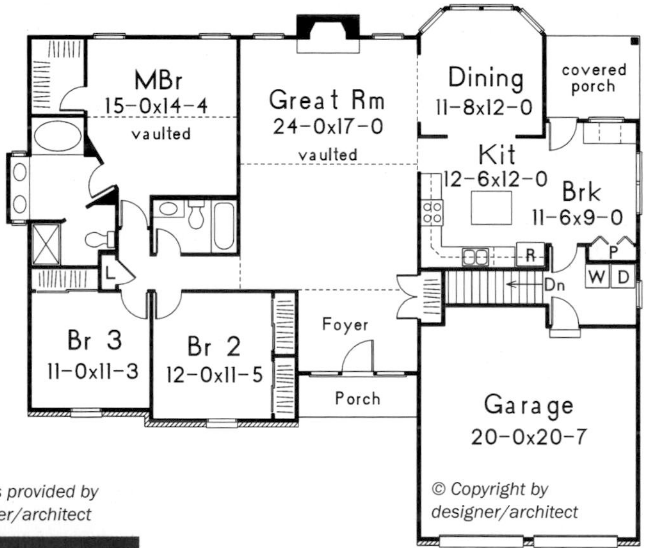

MBr 15-0x14-4 vaulted
Great Rm 24-0x17-0 vaulted
Dining 11-8x12-0
covered porch
Kit 12-6x12-0
Brk 11-6x9-0
Br 3 11-0x11-3
Br 2 12-0x11-5
Foyer
Porch
Garage 20-0x20-7

© Copyright by designer/architect

Images provided by designer/architect

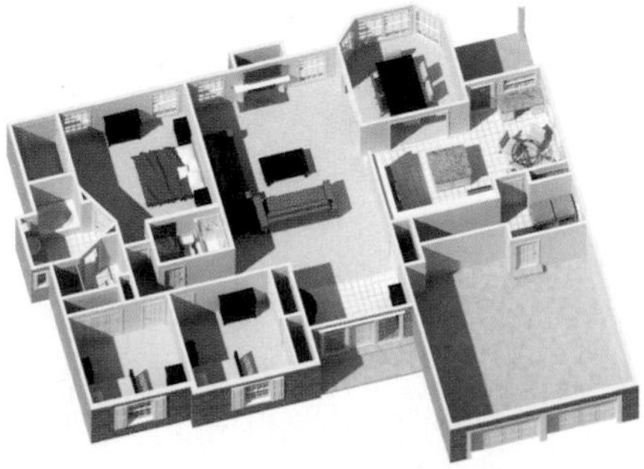

Plan #F08-091D-0522

Dimensions: 64' W x 60'4" D
Heated Sq. Ft.: 2,148
Bonus Sq. Ft.: 387
Bedrooms: 3 **Bathrooms:** 2½
Exterior Walls: 2" x 6"
Foundation: Crawl space standard; slab, basement or walk-out basement for an additional fee

See index for more information

Images provided by designer/architect

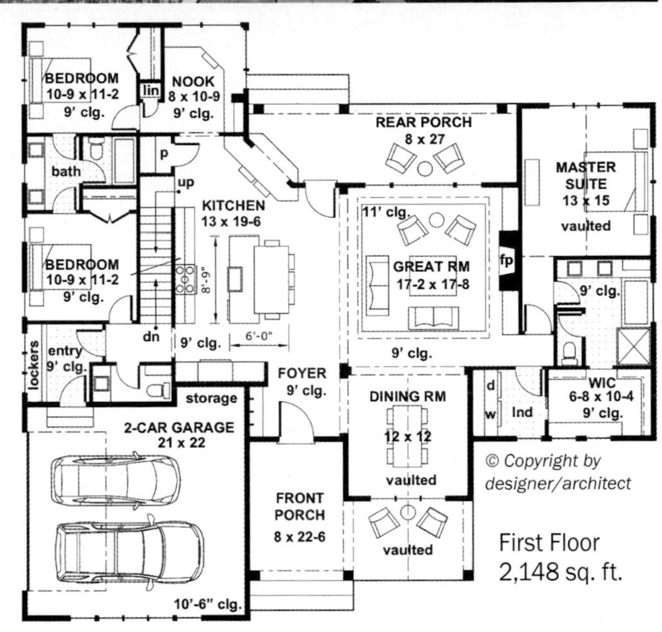

Optional Second Floor 387 sq. ft.

First Floor 2,148 sq. ft.

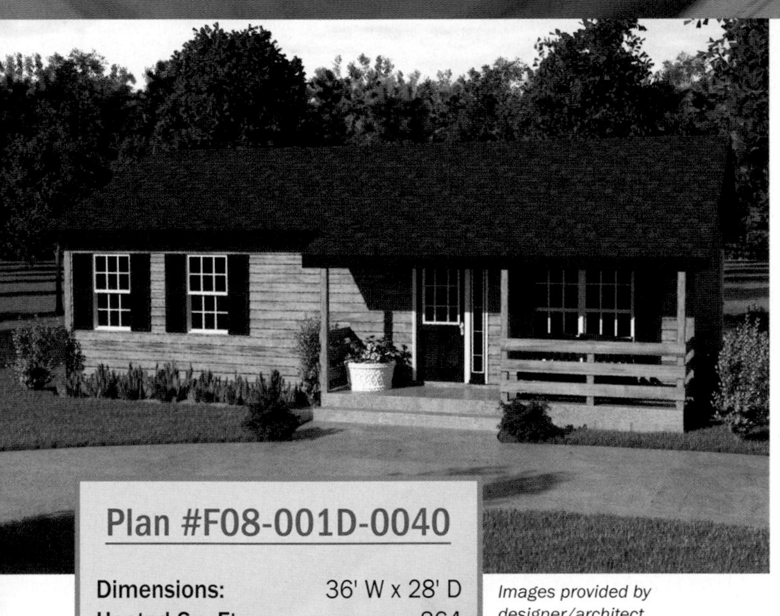

Plan #F08-001D-0040

Dimensions: 36' W x 28' D
Heated Sq. Ft.: 864
Bedrooms: 2 **Bathrooms:** 1
Foundation: Crawl space standard; basement or slab for an additional fee

See index for more information

Images provided by designer/architect

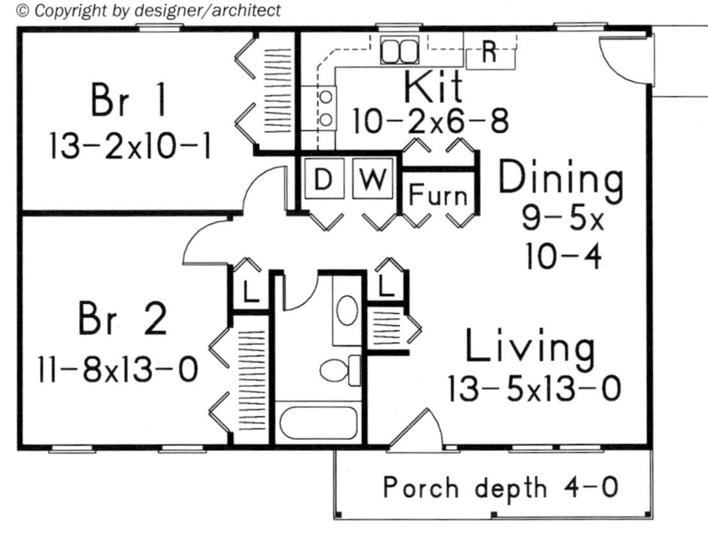

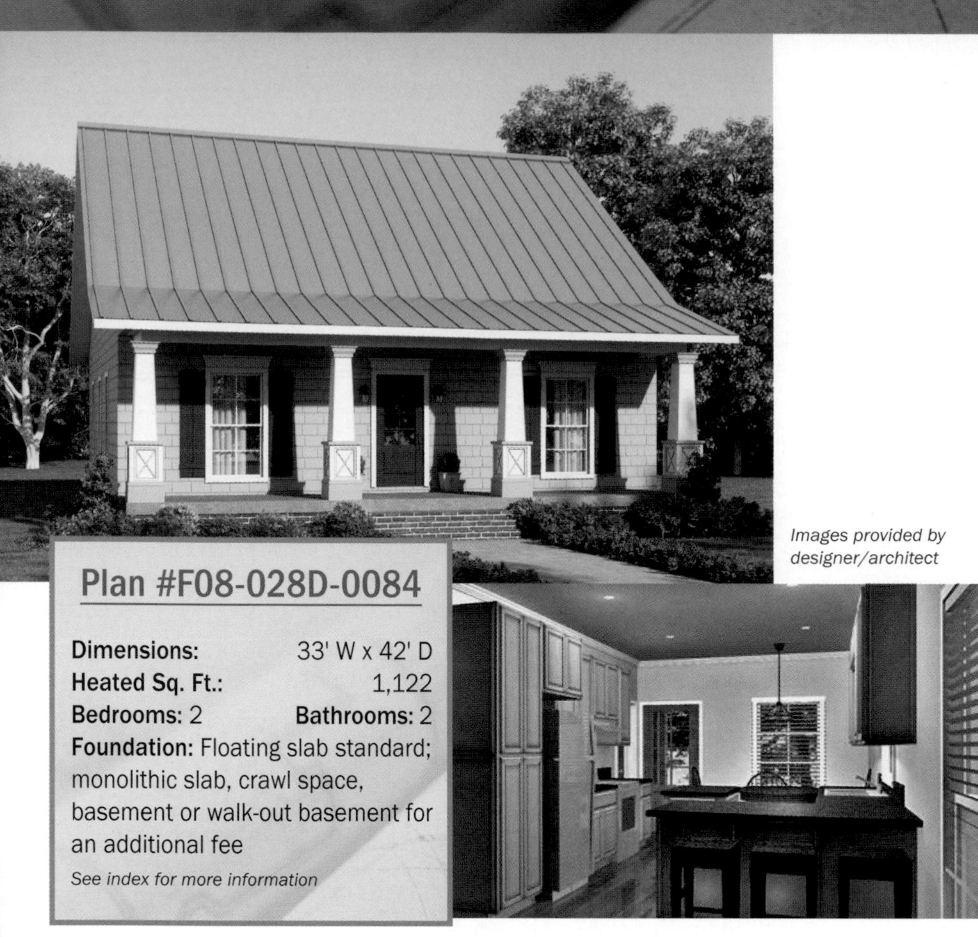

Images provided by designer/architect

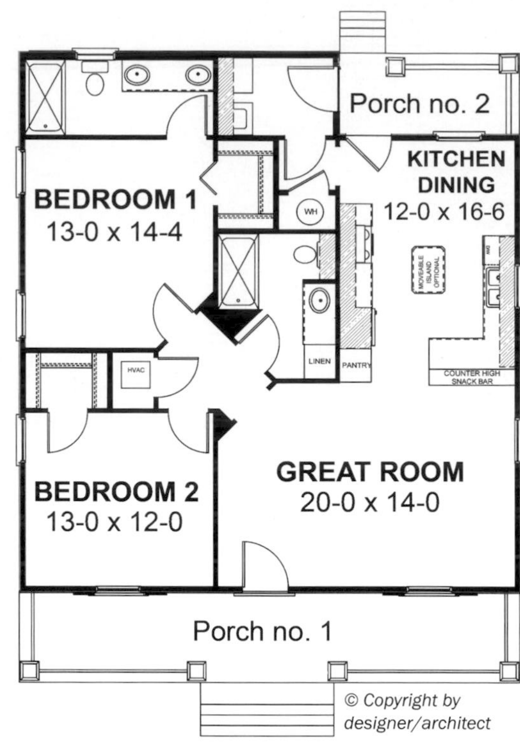

© Copyright by designer/architect

Plan #F08-028D-0084

Dimensions: 33' W x 42' D
Heated Sq. Ft.: 1,122
Bedrooms: 2 **Bathrooms:** 2
Foundation: Floating slab standard; monolithic slab, crawl space, basement or walk-out basement for an additional fee

See index for more information

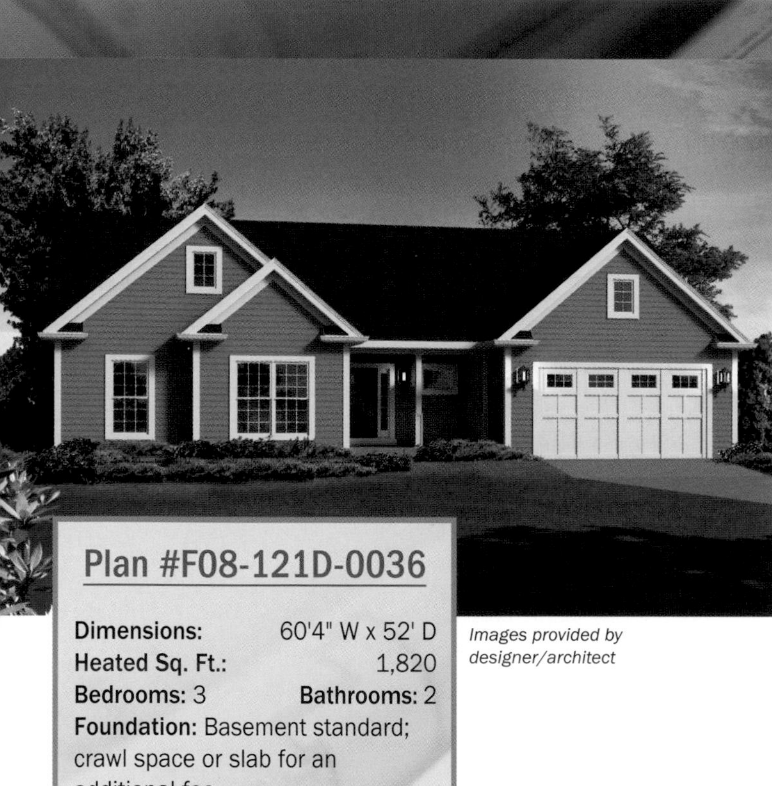

Images provided by designer/architect

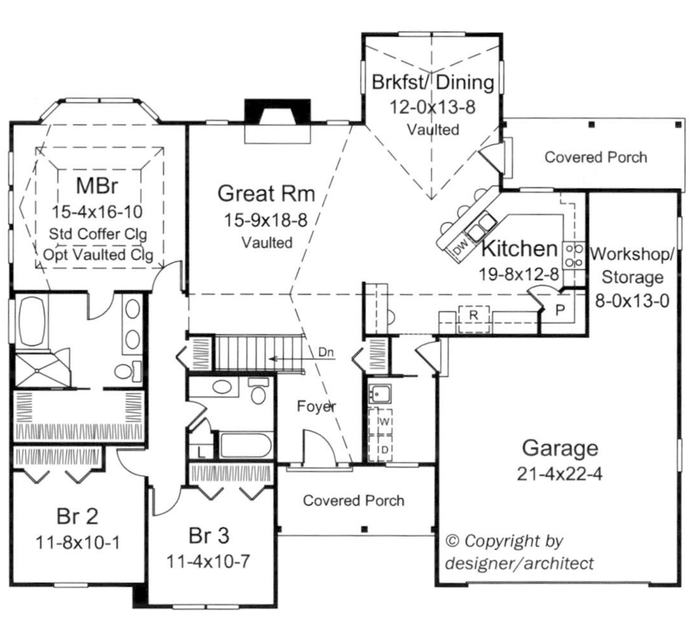

© Copyright by designer/architect

Plan #F08-121D-0036

Dimensions: 60'4" W x 52' D
Heated Sq. Ft.: 1,820
Bedrooms: 3 **Bathrooms:** 2
Foundation: Basement standard; crawl space or slab for an additional fee

See index for more information

Plan #F08-020D-0397

Dimensions: 59' W x 50' D
Heated Sq. Ft.: 1,608
Bedrooms: 3 **Bathrooms:** 2
Exterior Walls: 2" x 6"
Foundation: Crawl space standard; slab for an additional fee

See index for more information

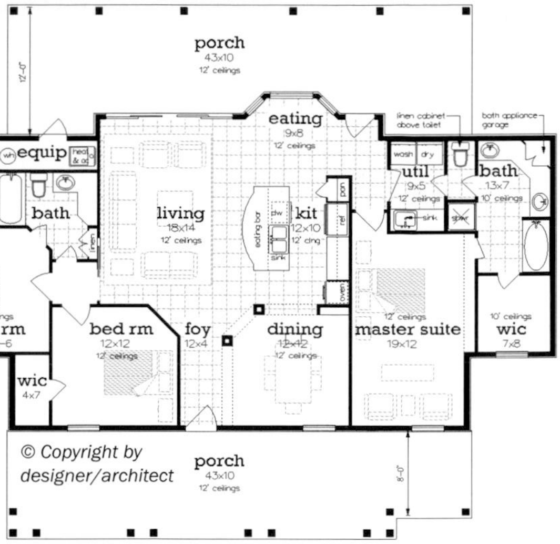

Images provided by designer/architect

Plan #F08-051D-0954

Dimensions: 65'4" W x 59'4" D
Heated Sq. Ft.: 2,096
Bonus Sq. Ft.: 410
Bedrooms: 2 **Bathrooms:** 2½
Exterior Walls: 2" x 6"
Foundation: Basement standard; crawl space or slab for an additional fee

See index for more information

Images provided by designer/architect

First Floor
2,096 sq. ft.

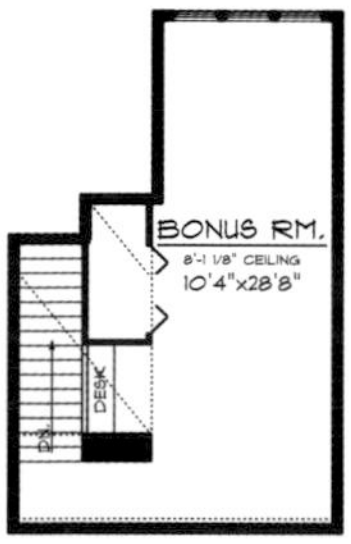

Optional
Second Floor
410 sq. ft.

Plan #F08-141D-0223

Dimensions: 52'10" W x 67'2" D
Heated Sq. Ft.: 2,095
Bedrooms: 3 **Bathrooms:** 2½
Exterior Walls: 2" x 6"
Foundation: Crawl space or slab standard; basement or walk-out basement for an additional fee

See index for more information

Images provided by designer/architect

© Copyright by designer/architect

Plan #F08-007D-0174

Dimensions: 82'4" W x 49'4" D
Heated Sq. Ft.: 2,322
Bedrooms: 4 **Bathrooms:** 3
Foundation: Basement standard; crawl space or slab for an additional fee

See index for more information

Images provided by designer/architect

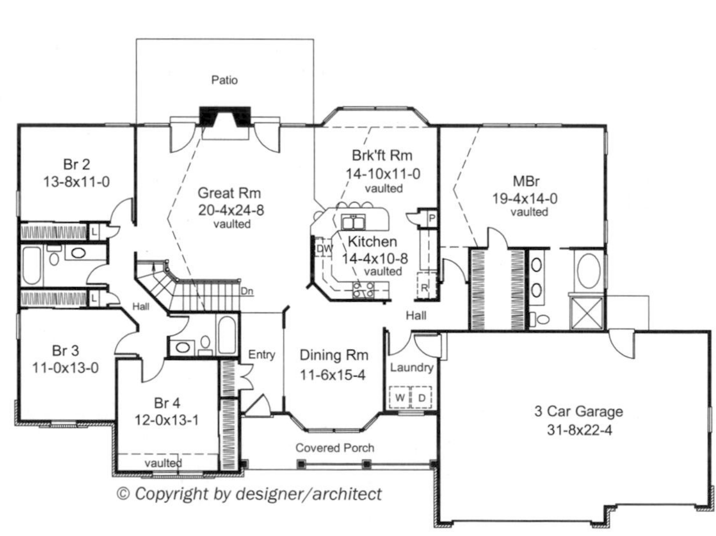

© Copyright by designer/architect

Plan #F08-011D-0676

Dimensions: 40' W x 55'6" D
Heated Sq. Ft.: 1,196
Bedrooms: 3 **Bathrooms:** 2
Exterior Walls: 2" x 6"
Foundation: Crawl space or slab standard; basement for an additional fee

See index for more information

Images provided by designer/architect

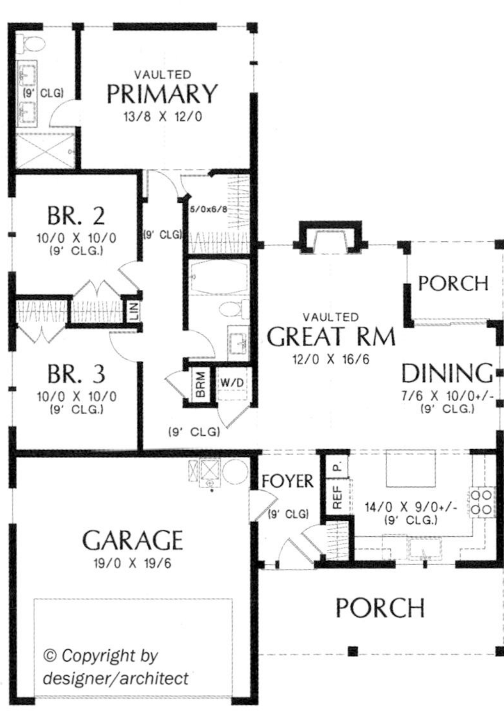

Plan #F08-007D-0124

Dimensions: 65' W x 51' D
Heated Sq. Ft.: 1,944
Bedrooms: 3 **Bathrooms:** 2
Foundation: Basement standard; crawl space or slab for an additional fee

See index for more information

Images provided by designer/architect

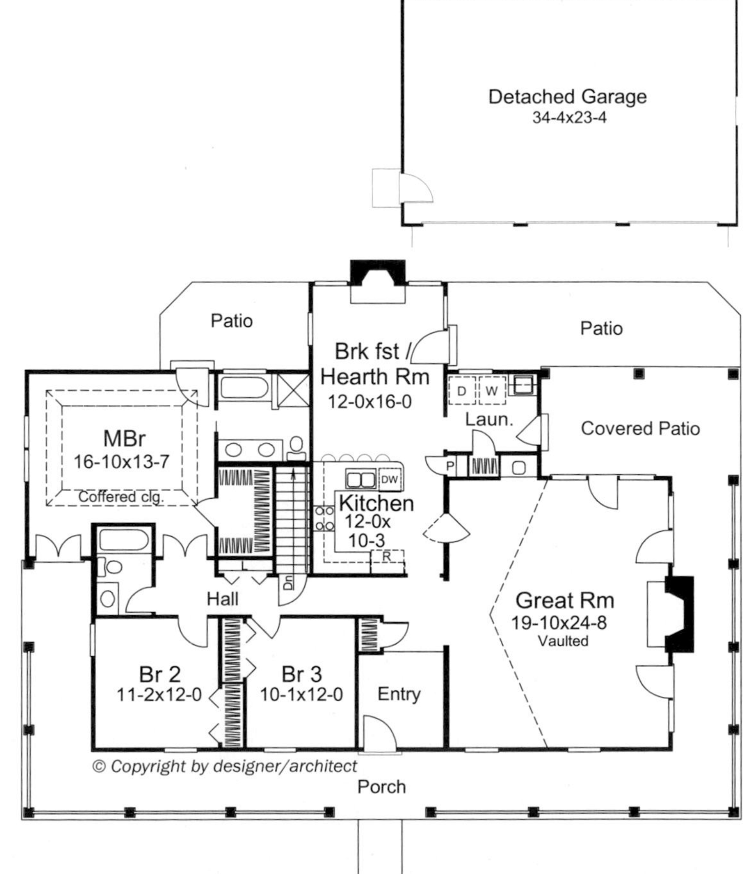

Plan #F08-026D-2134

Dimensions: 38' W x 55' D
Heated Sq. Ft.: 1,387
Bedrooms: 2 **Bathrooms:** 2
Foundation: Basement standard; crawl space, slab or walk-out basement for an additional fee

See index for more information

Images provided by designer/architect

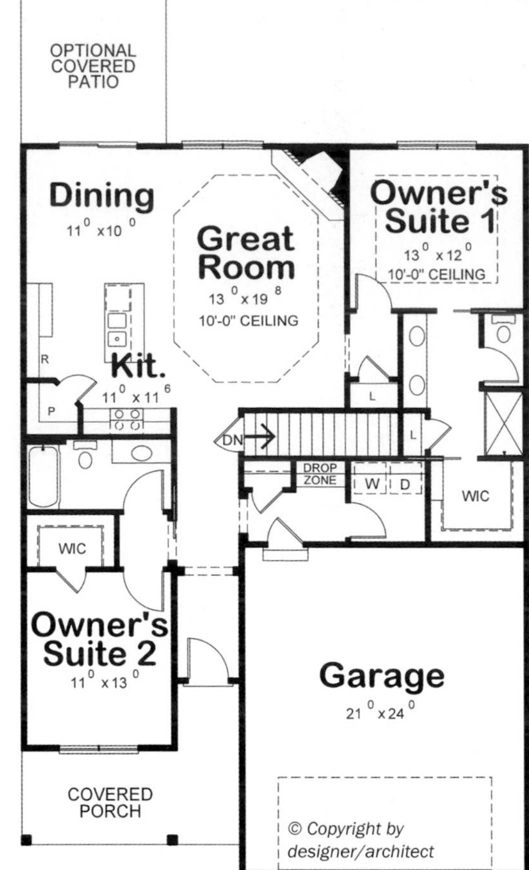

Plan #F08-013D-0209

Dimensions: 58'7" W x 41' D
Heated Sq. Ft.: 1,457
Bedrooms: 3 **Bathrooms:** 2
Foundation: Slab standard; crawl space or basement for an additional fee

See index for more information

Images provided by designer/architect

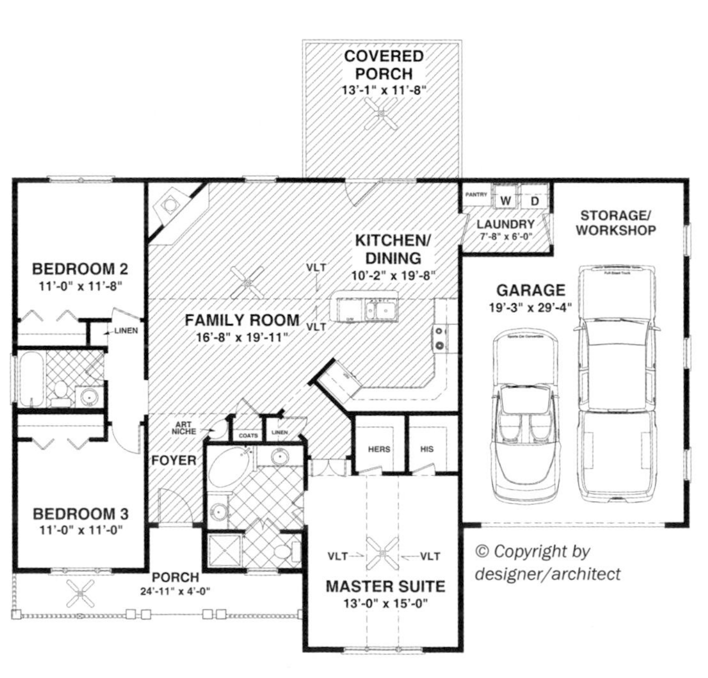

Plan #F08-007D-0010

Dimensions: 83' W x 42'4" D
Heated Sq. Ft.: 1,845
Bonus Sq. Ft.: 889
Bedrooms: 3 **Bathrooms:** 2
Foundation: Walk-out basement standard; crawl space or slab for an additional fee

See index for more information

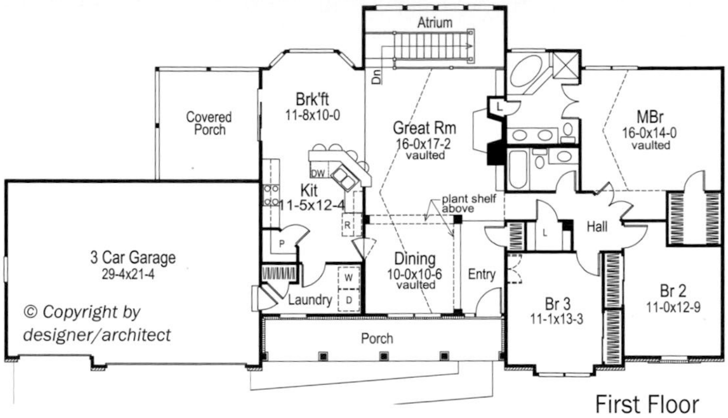

Images provided by designer/architect

First Floor
1,845 sq. ft.

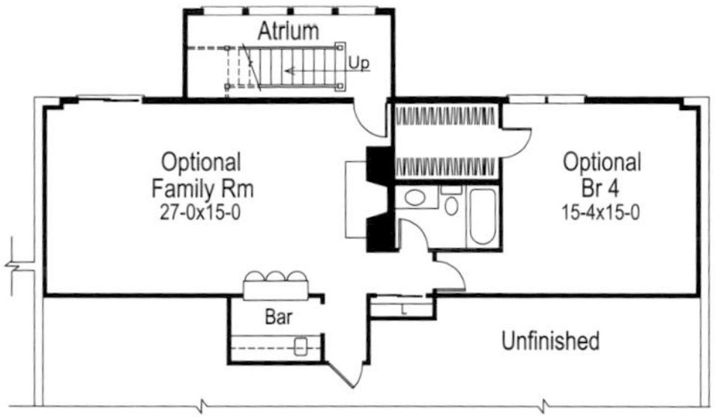

Optional Lower Level
889 sq. ft.

Plan #F08-007D-5060

Dimensions: 38' W x 48'4" D
Heated Sq. Ft.: 1,344
Bedrooms: 3 **Bathrooms:** 2
Foundation: Basement standard; crawl space or slab for an additional fee

See index for more information

Images provided by designer/architect

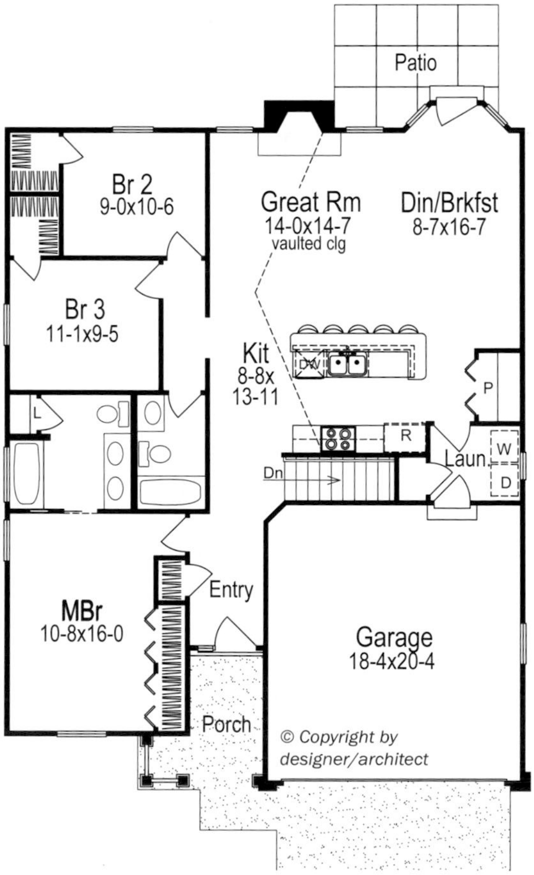

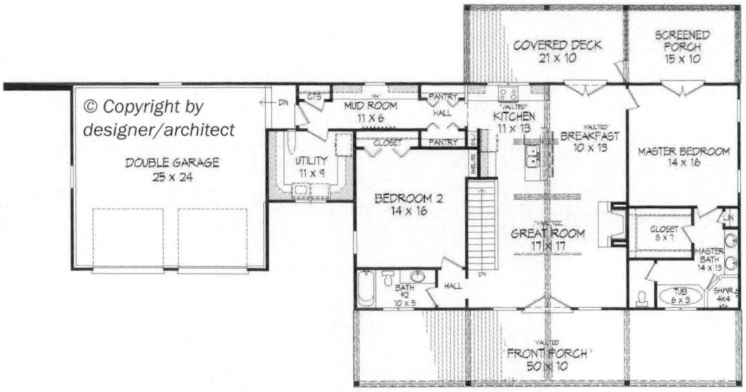

Plan #F08-141D-0064

Dimensions: 86'9" W x 50' D
Heated Sq. Ft.: 1,650
Bedrooms: 2 **Bathrooms:** 2
Foundation: Slab standard; crawl space, basement or walk-out basement for an additional fee

See index for more information

COVERED DECK 21 x 10
SCREENED PORCH 15 x 10
MUD ROOM 11 X 6
PANTRY
HALL
KITCHEN 11 x 13
BREAKFAST 10 x 13
MASTER BEDROOM 14 x 16
DOUBLE GARAGE 25 x 24
UTILITY 11 x 9
CLOSET
BEDROOM 2 14 x 16
GREAT ROOM 17 x 17
CLOSET 8 x 7
MASTER BATH 14 x 13
TUB
BATH #2
HALL
FRONT PORCH 50 x 10

Images provided by designer/architect

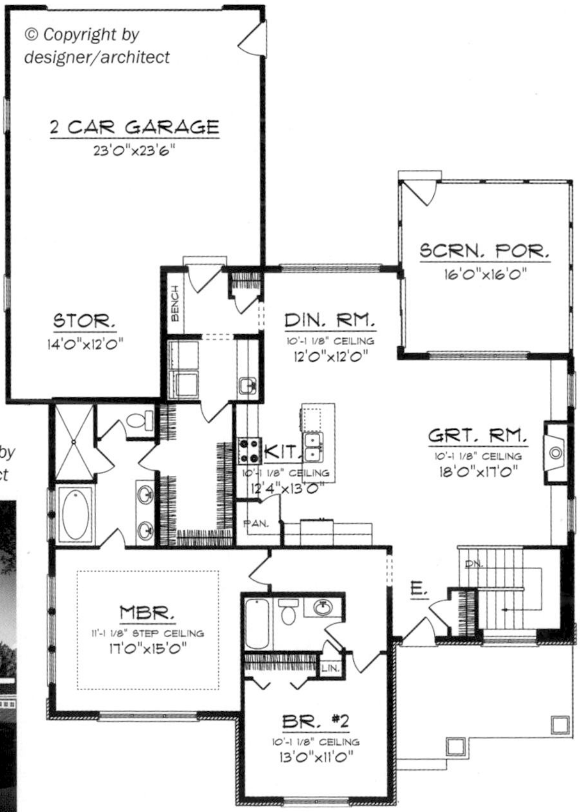

Plan #F08-051D-0952

Dimensions: 52' W x 73'4" D
Heated Sq. Ft.: 1,730
Bedrooms: 2 **Bathrooms:** 2
Exterior Walls: 2" x 6"
Foundation: Basement standard; crawl space or slab for an additional fee

See index for more information

2 CAR GARAGE 23'0"x23'6"
STOR. 14'0"x12'0"
BENCH
DIN. RM. 10'-1 1/8" CEILING 12'0"x12'0"
SCRN. POR. 16'0"x16'0"
KIT. 10'-1 1/8" CEILING 12'4"x13'0"
GRT. RM. 10'-1 1/8" CEILING 18'0"x17'0"
PAN.
MBR. 11'-1 1/8" STEP CEILING 17'0"x15'0"
LIN.
E.
BR. #2 10'-1 1/8" CEILING 13'0"x11'0"

Images provided by designer/architect

Images provided by designer/architect

Plan #F08-167D-0006

Dimensions: 68'11" W x 69'10" D
Heated Sq. Ft.: 2,939
Bedrooms: 4 **Bathrooms:** 3½
Exterior Walls: 2" x 6"
Foundation: Slab standard; crawl space for an additional fee

See index for more information

© Copyright by designer/architect

Plan #F08-055D-0192

Dimensions: 69'2" W x 74'10" D
Heated Sq. Ft.: 2,096
Bedrooms: 3 **Bathrooms:** 2½
Foundation: Crawl space or slab standard; basement or daylight basement for an additional fee

See index for more information

Images provided by designer/architect

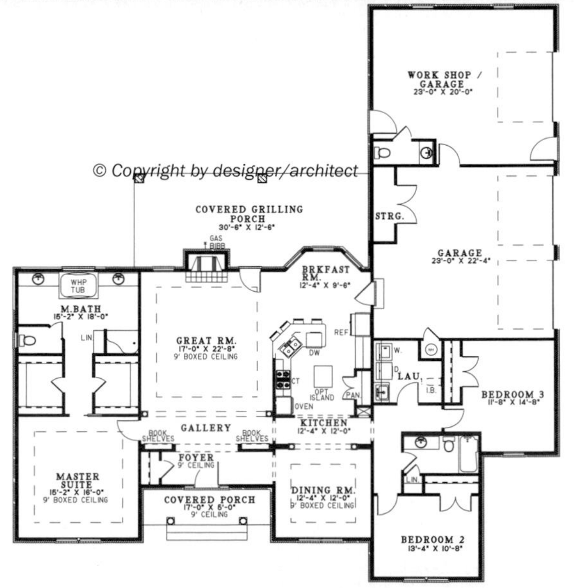

Plan #F08-011D-0661

Dimensions: 76' W x 62' D
Heated Sq. Ft.: 2,508
Bedrooms: 3 **Bathrooms:** 2½
Exterior Walls: 2" x 6"
Foundation: Crawl space or slab standard; basement for an additional fee

See index for more information

Images provided by designer/architect

Features

- This one-story Modern Farmhouse style home design has great features at every turn
- The covered front porch greets guests as they approach this charming home
- The formal dining room has an open feel to the entry foyer
- The vaulted great room has a fireplace, a huge glass sliding door and views of the vaulted outdoor living area with fireplace
- The outdoor living area with a fireplace has an outdoor kitchen and a patio
- The private master suite has a lavish bath featuring a freestanding tub, two sinks, a large tile shower, and a toilet room
- The kitchen has a bayed breakfast nook, a large island overlooking the great room, and a walk-in pantry
- Two additional bedrooms share a bath
- 2-car side entry garage

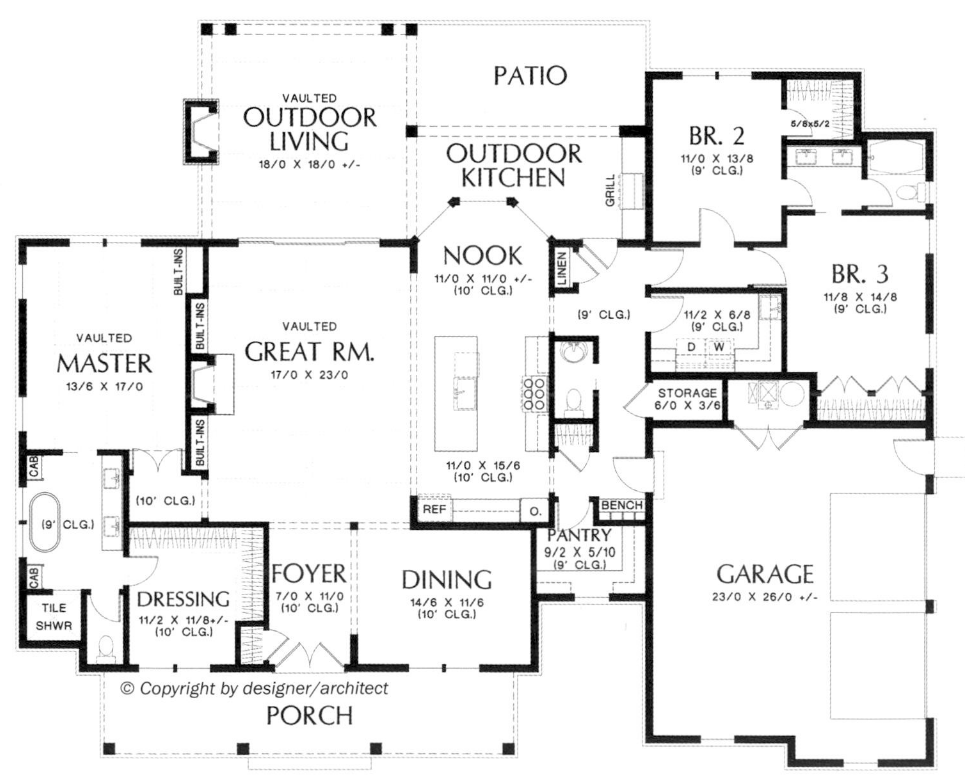

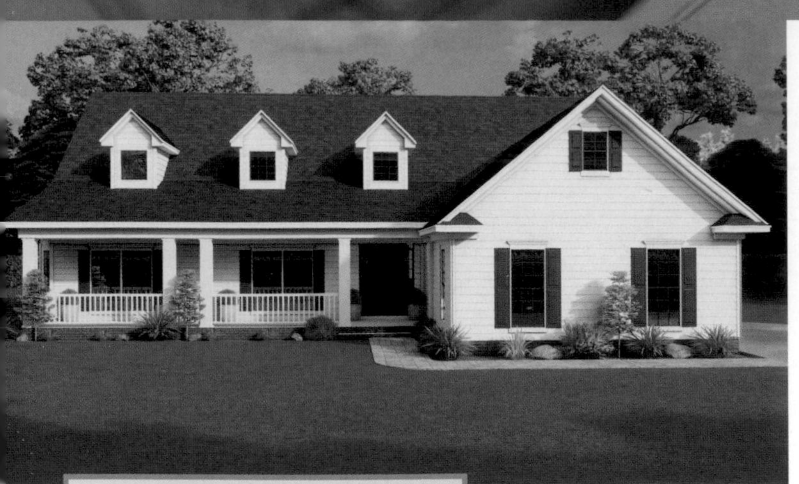

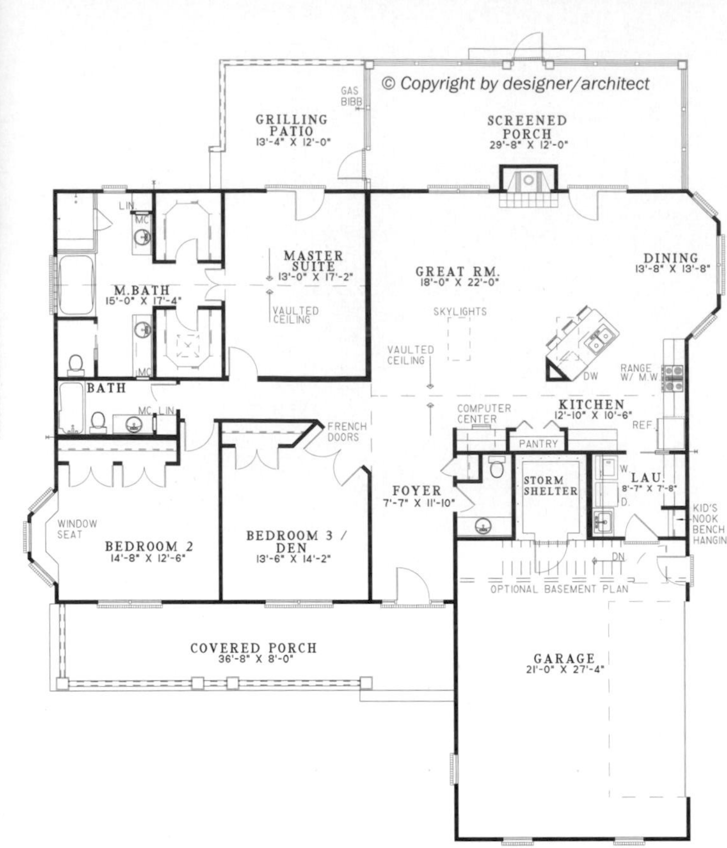

© Copyright by designer/architect
GAS BIBB
GRILLING PATIO
13'-4" X 12'-0"
SCREENED PORCH
29'-8" X 12'-0"
LIN
MC
MASTER SUITE
13'-0" X 17'-2"
VAULTED CEILING
M.BATH
15'-0" X 17'-4"
GREAT RM.
18'-0" X 22'-0"
SKYLIGHTS
VAULTED CEILING
DINING
13'-8" X 13'-8"
DW
RANGE W/ M.W.
BATH
MC LIN
COMPUTER CENTER
KITCHEN
12'-10" X 10'-6"
REF.
FRENCH DOORS
PANTRY
FOYER
7'-7" X 11'-10"
STORM SHELTER
LAU.
8'-7" X 7'-8"
KID'S NOOK BENCH / HANGING
WINDOW SEAT
BEDROOM 2
14'-8" X 12'-6"
BEDROOM 3 / DEN
13'-6" X 14'-2"
DN
OPTIONAL BASEMENT PLAN
COVERED PORCH
36'-8" X 8'-0"
GARAGE
21'-0" X 27'-4"

Plan #F08-055D-0193

Images provided by designer/architect

Dimensions: 63'10" W x 72'2" D
Heated Sq. Ft.: 2,129
Bedrooms: 3 **Bathrooms:** 2½
Foundation: Slab or crawl space, standard; basement or daylight basement for an additional fee

See index for more information

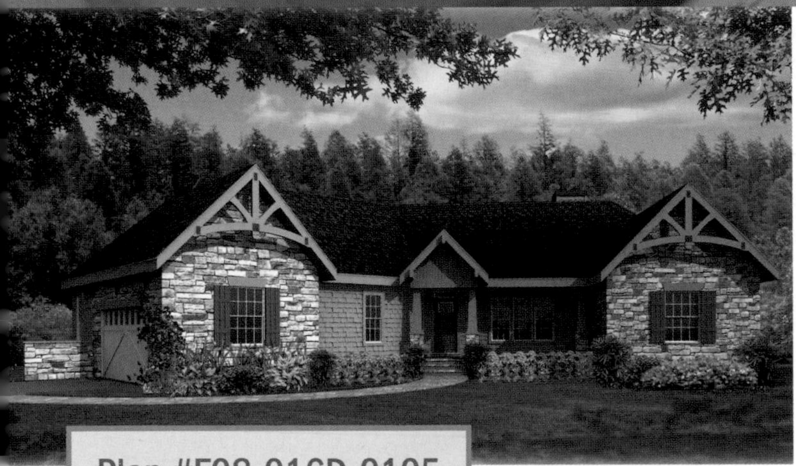

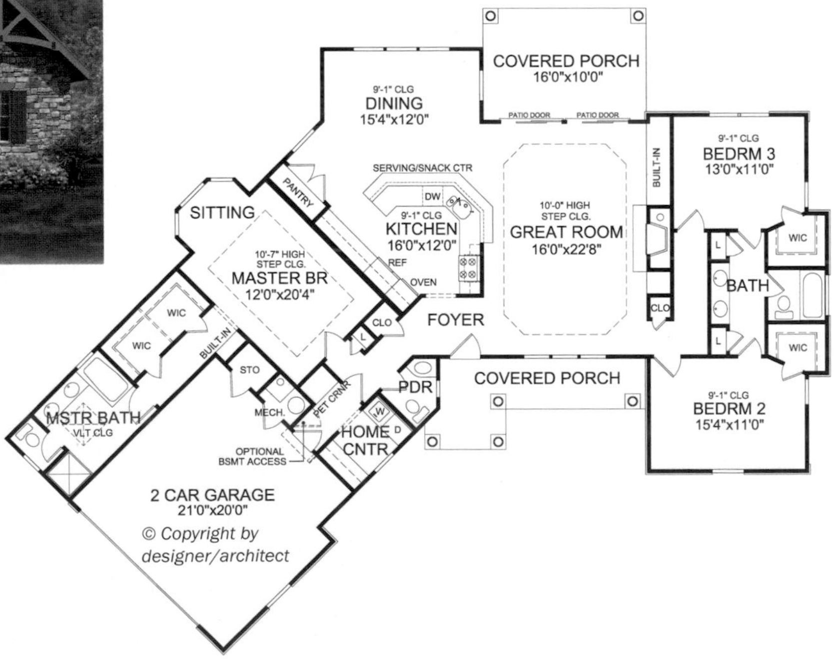

COVERED PORCH
16'0"x10'0"
9'-1" CLG
DINING
15'4"x12'0"
PATIO DOOR
PATIO DOOR
SERVING/SNACK CTR
DW
PANTRY
9'-1" CLG
KITCHEN
16'0"x12'0"
REF
OVEN
10'-0" HIGH STEP CLG.
GREAT ROOM
16'0"x22'8"
BUILT-IN
9'-1" CLG
BEDRM 3
13'0"x11'0"
WIC
BATH
CLO
WIC
SITTING
10'-7" HIGH STEP CLG.
MASTER BR
12'0"x20'4"
WIC
WIC
BUILT-IN
CLO
FOYER
STO
MECH.
PET CRNR
PDR
COVERED PORCH
9'-1" CLG
BEDRM 2
15'4"x11'0"
MSTR BATH
VLT CLG
OPTIONAL BSMT ACCESS
HOME CNTR
2 CAR GARAGE
21'0"x20'0"
© Copyright by designer/architect

Plan #F08-016D-0105

Images provided by designer/architect

Dimensions: 81'3" W x 63'8" D
Heated Sq. Ft.: 2,065
Bedrooms: 3 **Bathrooms:** 2½
Foundation: Crawl space or slab standard; basement for an additional fee

See index for more information

Plan #F08-121D-0035

Dimensions: 45'8" W x 72'4" D
Heated Sq. Ft.: 1,759
Bedrooms: 3 **Bathrooms:** 2
Foundation: Basement standard; crawl space or slab for an additional fee

See index for more information

Images provided by designer/architect

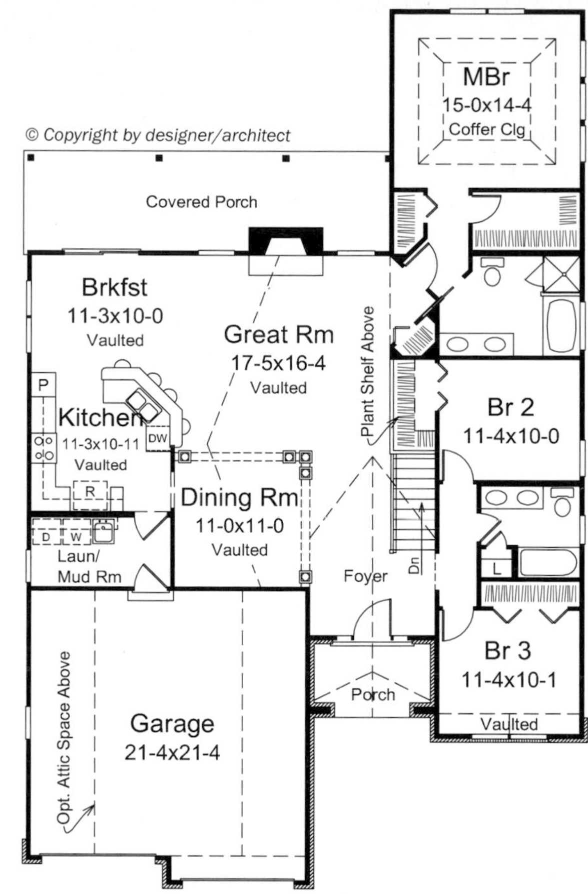

Plan #F08-051D-0971

Dimensions: 50' W x 50' D
Heated Sq. Ft.: 1,484
Bedrooms: 2 **Bathrooms:** 2
Exterior Walls: 2" x 6"
Foundation: Basement standard; crawl space or slab for an additional fee

See index for more information

Images provided by designer/architect

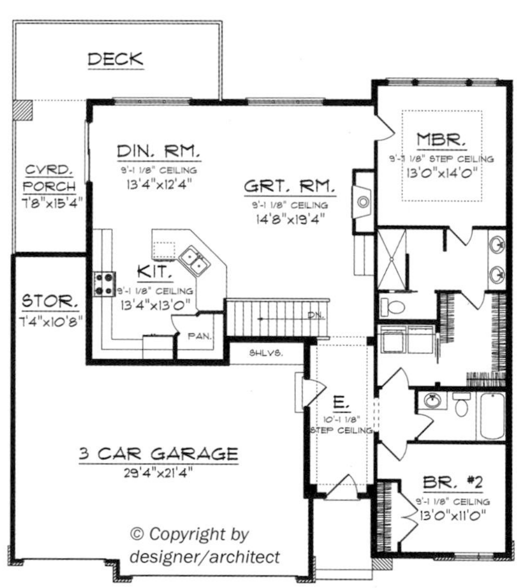

Plan #F08-076D-0218

Images provided by designer/architect

Dimensions: 91'9" W x 81'7" D
Heated Sq. Ft.: 2,818
Bonus Sq. Ft.: 468
Bedrooms: 3 **Bathrooms:** 2½
Foundation: Basement, crawl space or slab, please specify when ordering

See index for more information

First Floor
2,818 sq. ft.

Optional
Second Floor
468 sq. ft.

Plan #F08-144D-0005

Images provided by designer/architect

Dimensions: 48' W x 58' D
Heated Sq. Ft.: 1,506
Bedrooms: 3 **Bathrooms:** 2
Exterior Walls: 2" x 6"
Foundation: Daylight basement standard; crawl space, slab, basement or walk-out basement for an additional fee

See index for more information

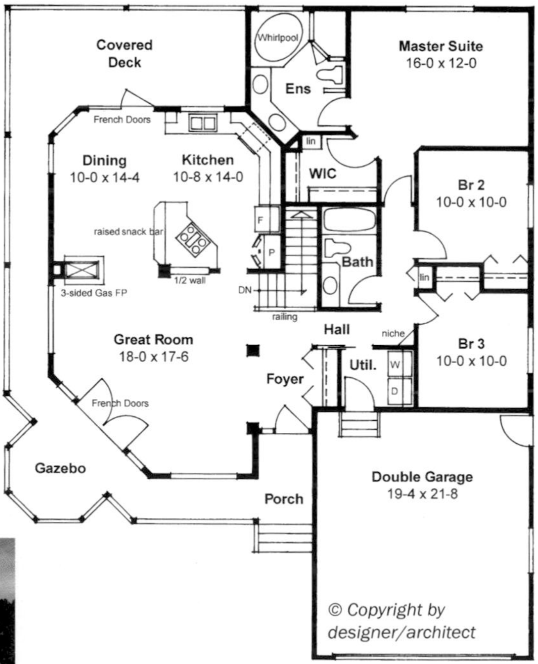

Plan #F08-056D-0104

Dimensions: 63'1" W x 41'10" D
Heated Sq. Ft.: 1,925
Bedrooms: 3 **Bathrooms:** 2½
Foundation: Slab

See index for more information

Images provided by designer/architect

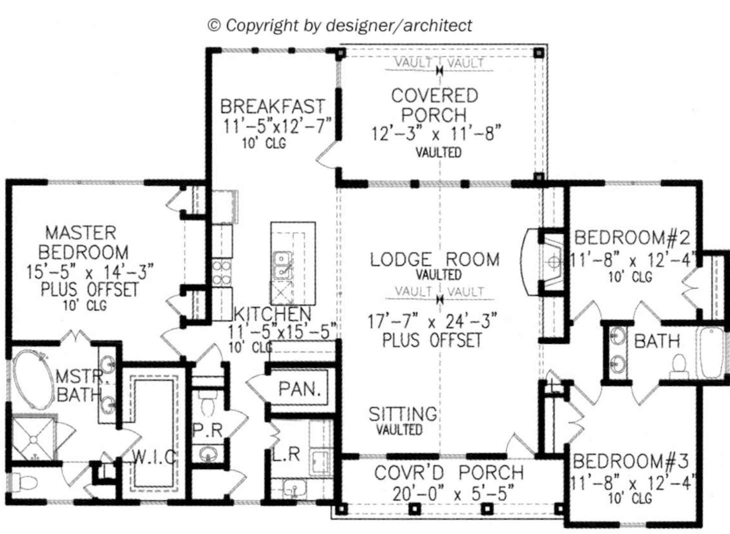

Plan #F08-026D-2072

Dimensions: 45' W x 62' D
Heated Sq. Ft.: 1,619
Bedrooms: 3 **Bathrooms:** 2
Exterior Walls: 2" x 6"
Foundation: Slab standard; crawl space, basement or walk-out basement for an additional fee

See index for more information

Images provided by designer/architect

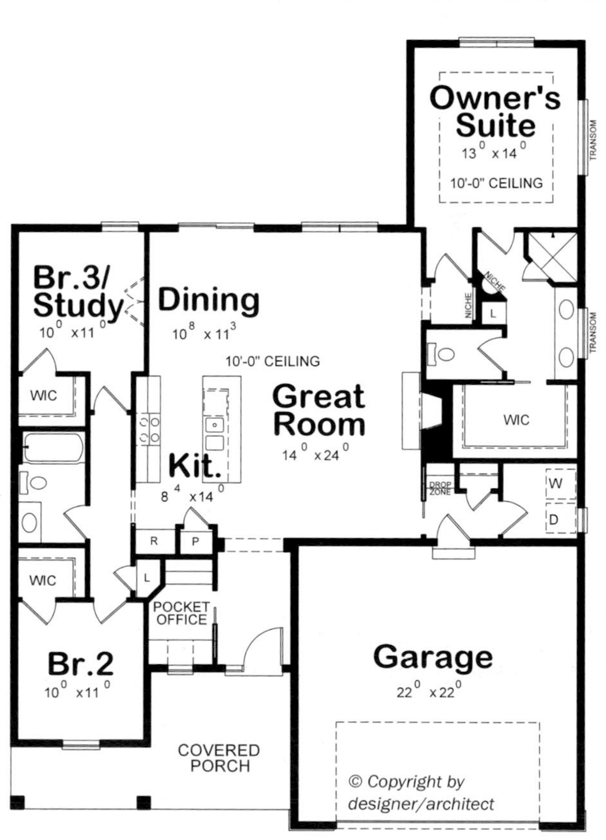

Plan #F08-101D-0047

Dimensions:	99' W x 81' D
Heated Sq. Ft.:	2,478
Bonus Sq. Ft.:	1,795
Bedrooms: 2	**Bathrooms:** 2½
Exterior Walls:	2" x 6"
Foundation:	Walk-out basement

See index for more information

Images provided by designer/architect

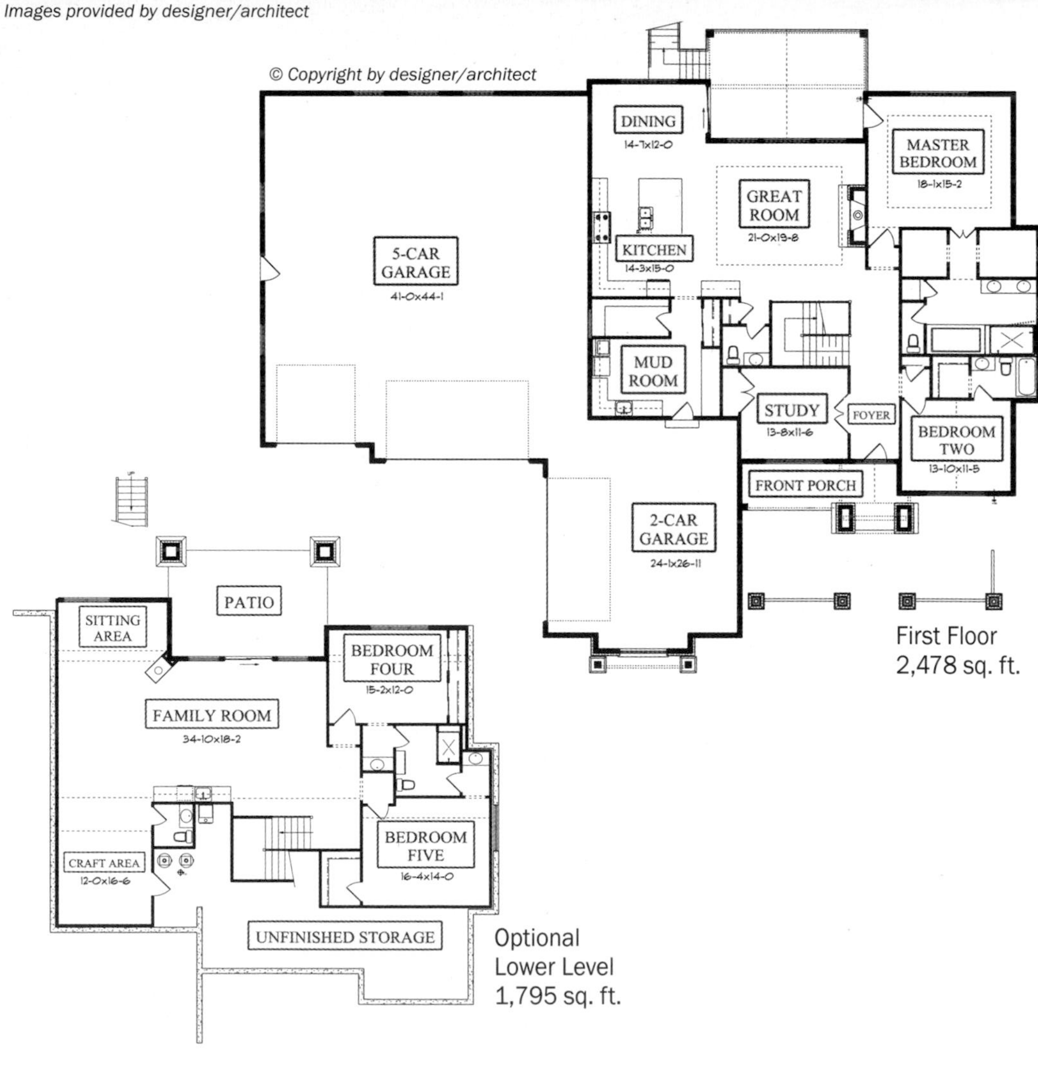

First Floor
2,478 sq. ft.

Optional Lower Level
1,795 sq. ft.

Features

- The architectural style of this home has interesting features and great curb appeal
- The master bedroom features double walk-in closets, separate tub and shower and double bowl vanity
- Open living at its finest with the combination of the great room, kitchen and dining area creating a relaxed and open atmosphere
- Directly off the foyer is a study that is private and could easily be converted to a home office
- The optional lower level has an additional 1,795 square feet of living area and features a craft area, sitting area, family room, and two additional bedrooms and a bath
- Oversized 5-car front entry tandem garage, and a 2-car side entry garage

mike's hard lemonade
BEND PAK

Plan #F08-007D-0030

Dimensions: 46' W x 32' D
Heated Sq. Ft.: 1,140
Bedrooms: 3 **Bathrooms:** 2
Foundation: Basement standard; crawl space or slab for an additional fee

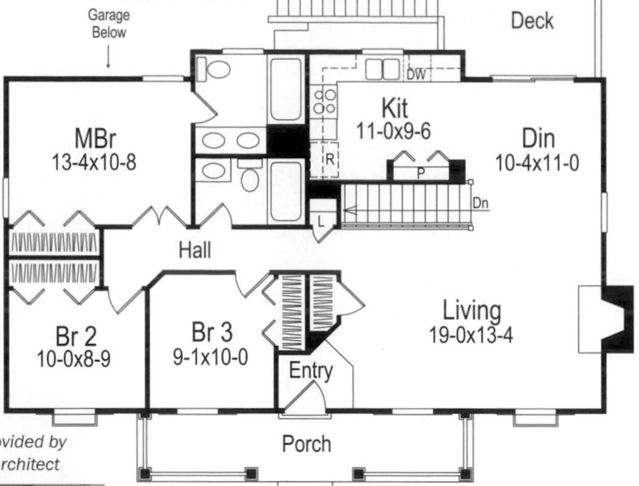

See index for more information

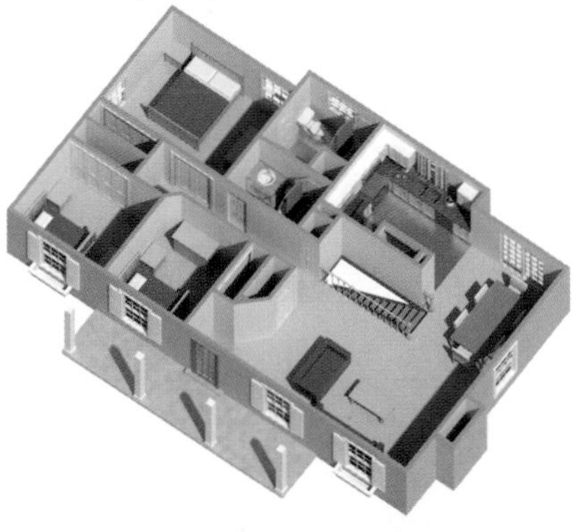

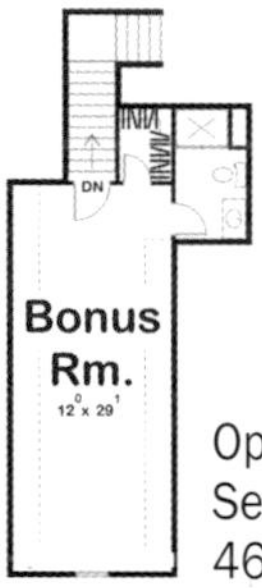

Images provided by designer/architect

© Copyright by designer/architect

Plan #F08-123D-0146

Dimensions: 66' W x 62' D
Heated Sq. Ft.: 2,309
Bonus Sq. Ft.: 1,706
Bedrooms: 4 **Bathrooms:** 3½
Foundation: Basement standard; crawl space, slab or walk-out basement for an additional fee

Pricing subject to change

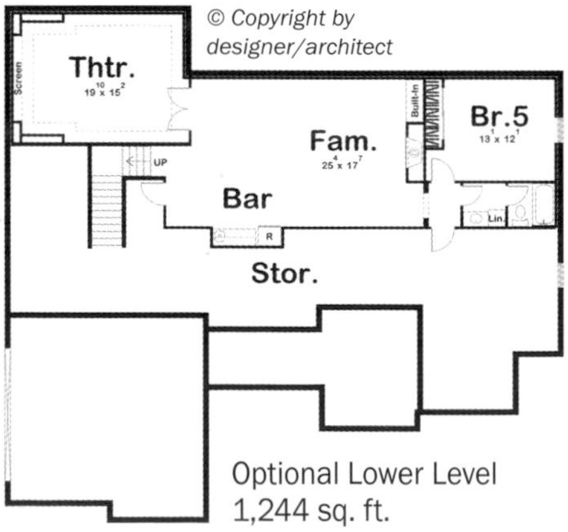

Images provided by designer/architect

© Copyright by designer/architect

Optional Second Floor
462 sq. ft.

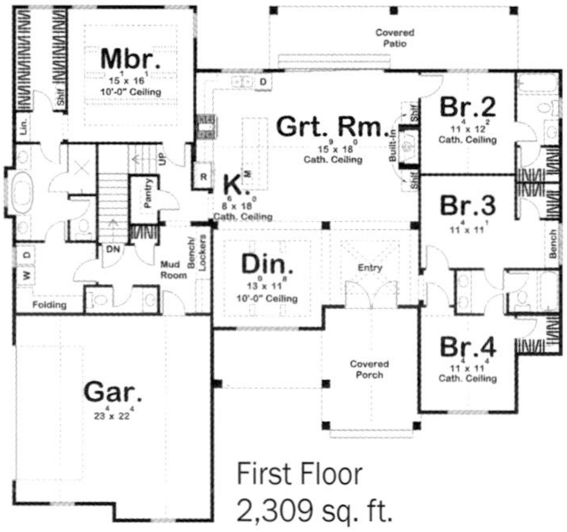

First Floor
2,309 sq. ft.

Optional Lower Level
1,244 sq. ft.

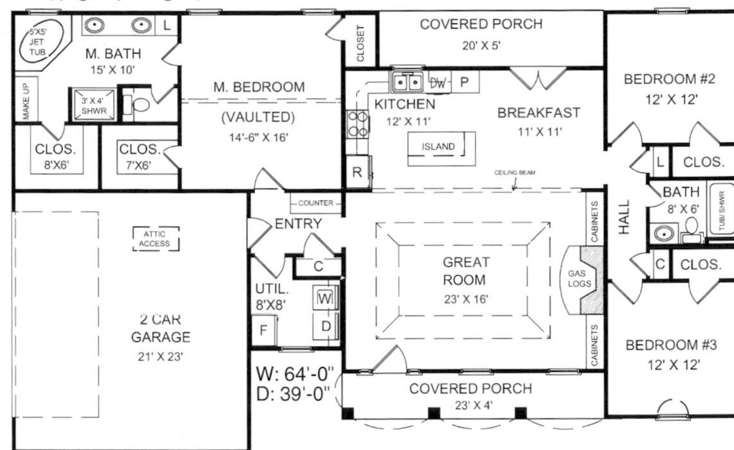

Images provided by designer/architect

Plan #F08-077D-0039

Dimensions: 64' W x 39' D
Heated sq. ft.: 1,654
Bedrooms: 3 **Bathrooms:** 2
Foundation: Slab, crawl space, basement or daylight basement please specify when ordering

See index for more information

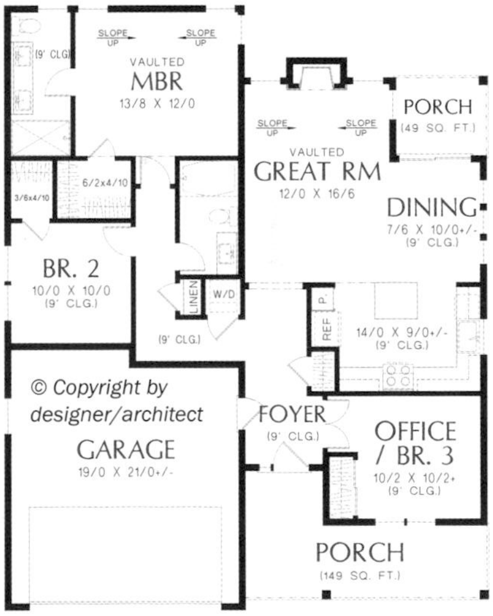

© Copyright by designer/architect

Images provided by designer/architect

Plan #F08-011D-0745

Dimensions: 40' W x 50' D
Heated Sq. Ft.: 1,251
Bedrooms: 3 **Bathrooms:** 2
Exterior Walls: 2" x 6"
Foundation: Crawl space or slab standard; basement for an additional fee

See index for more information

Plan #F08-076D-0230

Dimensions: 66'10" W x 67'7" D
Heated Sq. Ft.: 2,298
Bonus Sq. Ft.: 439
Bedrooms: 3 **Bathrooms:** 2½
Foundation: Crawl space or slab, please specify when ordering

See index for more information

Images provided by designer/architect

Features

- 11' ceiling heights top the family and breakfast rooms creating the most open and inviting feeling
- The kitchen is combined with both the family and breakfast rooms and includes a huge island with dining space, a double basin sink and a dishwasher
- The private master suite has an amazing amount of closetspace in addition to a luxurious bath with an oversized whirlpool tub and separate walk-in shower
- The vaulted covered patio is ideal for relaxing outdoors in any kind of weather
- The optional second floor has an additional 439 square feet of living area
- 2-car side entry garage

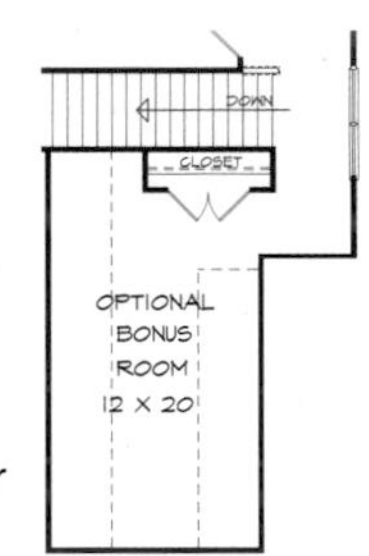

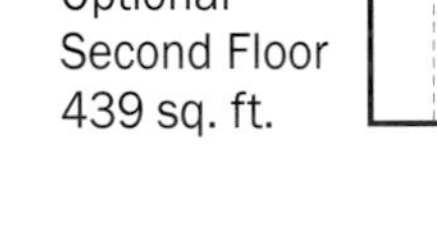

Optional Second Floor
439 sq. ft.

First Floor
2,298 sq. ft.

Images provided by designer/architect

Plan #F08-011D-0229

Dimensions: 60' W x 111' D
Heated Sq. Ft.: 2,904
Bedrooms: 3 **Bathrooms:** 3½
Exterior Walls: 2" x 6"
Foundation: Crawl space or slab standard; basement for an for an additional fee

See index for more information

Features

- This stunning one-story has all of the essentials for great family living
- The kitchen features an island facing out over the dining area with a nearby sitting and great room
- The bedrooms are all in close proximity to one another for convenience
- A cozy vaulted den has a fireplace and a bay window
- The outdoor living space has a fireplace and built-in grill
- 3-car side entry garage

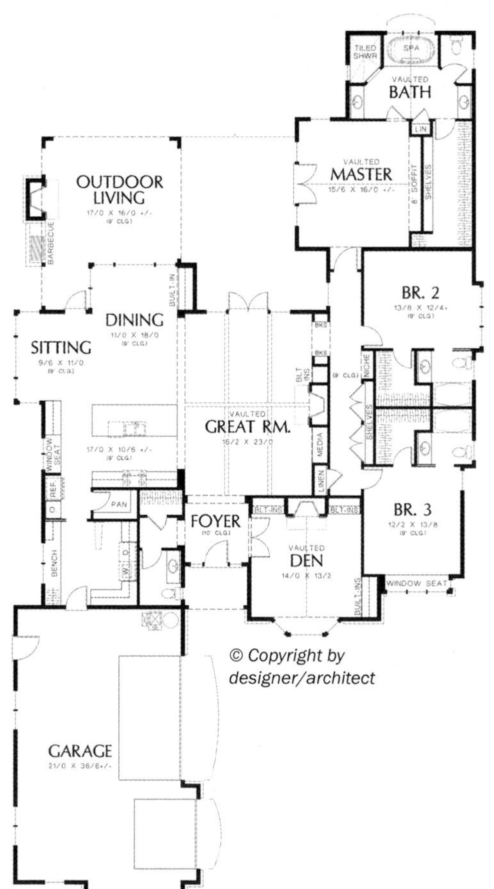

Plan #F08-007D-0117

Dimensions: 76'8" W x 57'6" D
Heated Sq. Ft.: 2,695
Bedrooms: 3 **Bathrooms:** 2½
Foundation: Basement standard; crawl space or slab for an additional fee

See index for more information

Images provided by designer/architect

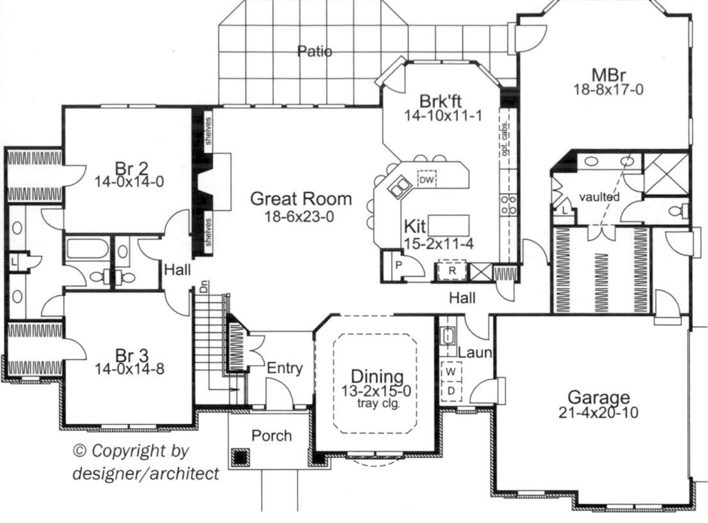

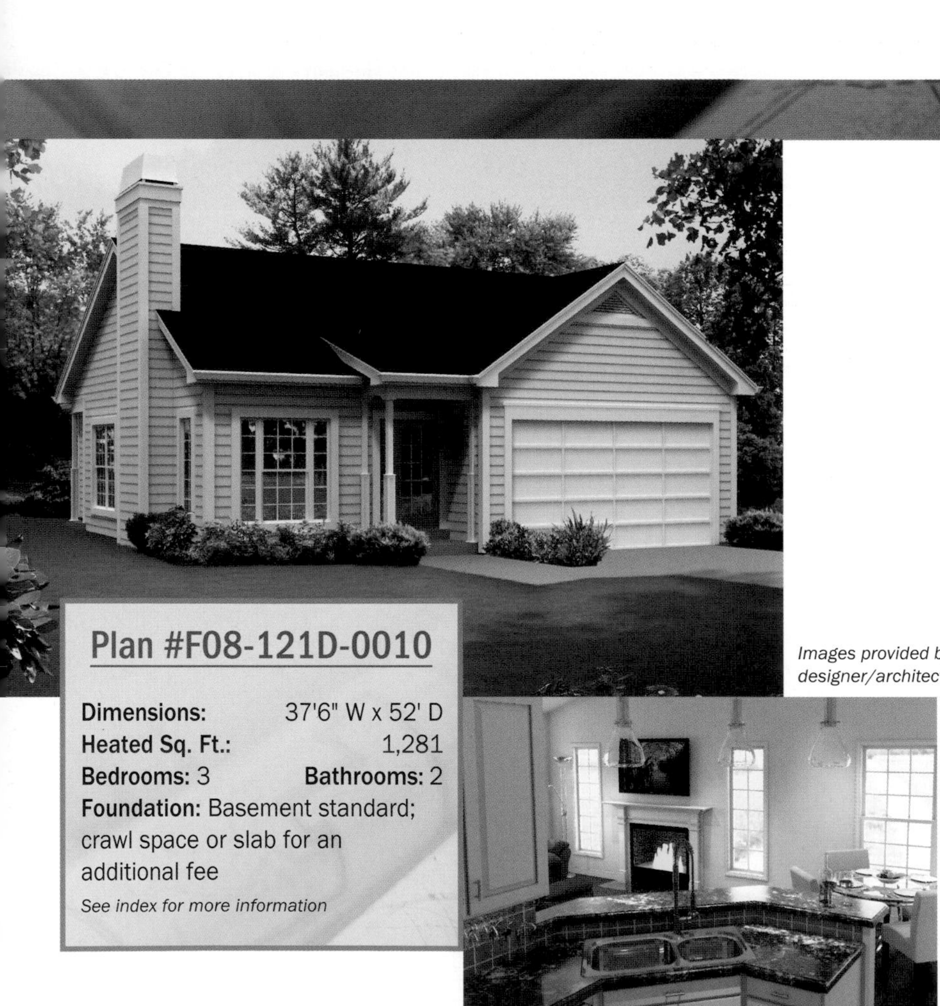

Plan #F08-121D-0010

Dimensions: 37'6" W x 52' D
Heated Sq. Ft.: 1,281
Bedrooms: 3 **Bathrooms:** 2
Foundation: Basement standard; crawl space or slab for an additional fee

See index for more information

Images provided by designer/architect

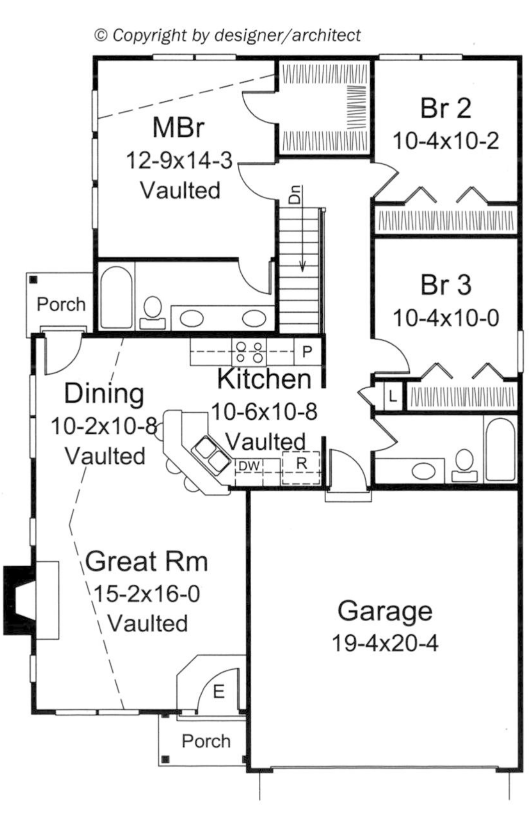

Images provided by designer/architect

Plan #F08-167D-0007

Dimensions: 72' W x 76'9" D
Heated Sq. Ft.: 3,016
Bedrooms: 4 **Bathrooms:** 3
Exterior Walls: 2" x 6"
Foundation: Slab standard; crawl space for an additional fee

See index for more information

Images provided by designer/architect

Plan #F08-101D-0128

Dimensions: 76'5" W x 82' D
Heated Sq. Ft.: 3,170
Bonus Sq. Ft.: 1,983
Bedrooms: 2 **Bathrooms:** 2½
Exterior Walls: 2" x 6"
Foundation: Walk-out basement

See index for more information

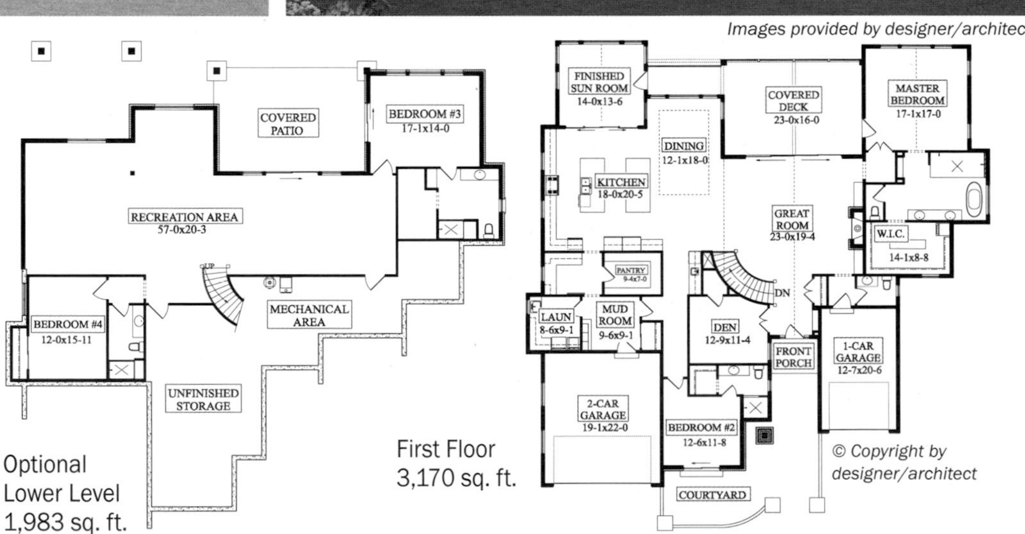

Optional Lower Level 1,983 sq. ft.

First Floor 3,170 sq. ft.

Plan #F08-161D-0013

Images provided by designer/architect

Dimensions: 99'4" W x 87'10" D
Heated Sq. Ft.: 3,264
Bedrooms: 3 **Bathrooms:** 3½
Exterior Walls: 2" x 6"
Foundation: Crawl space

See index for more information

Features

- This stunning modern home offers the open floor plan and high ceilings homeowners want today
- The split bedroom floor plan has the master suite tucked behind the kitchen and near a quiet study
- There are lovely outdoor spaces in the front as well as the back of the home
- The great room enjoys a sleek fireplace that can also be seen by the kitchen and dining space.
- 3-car side entry garage

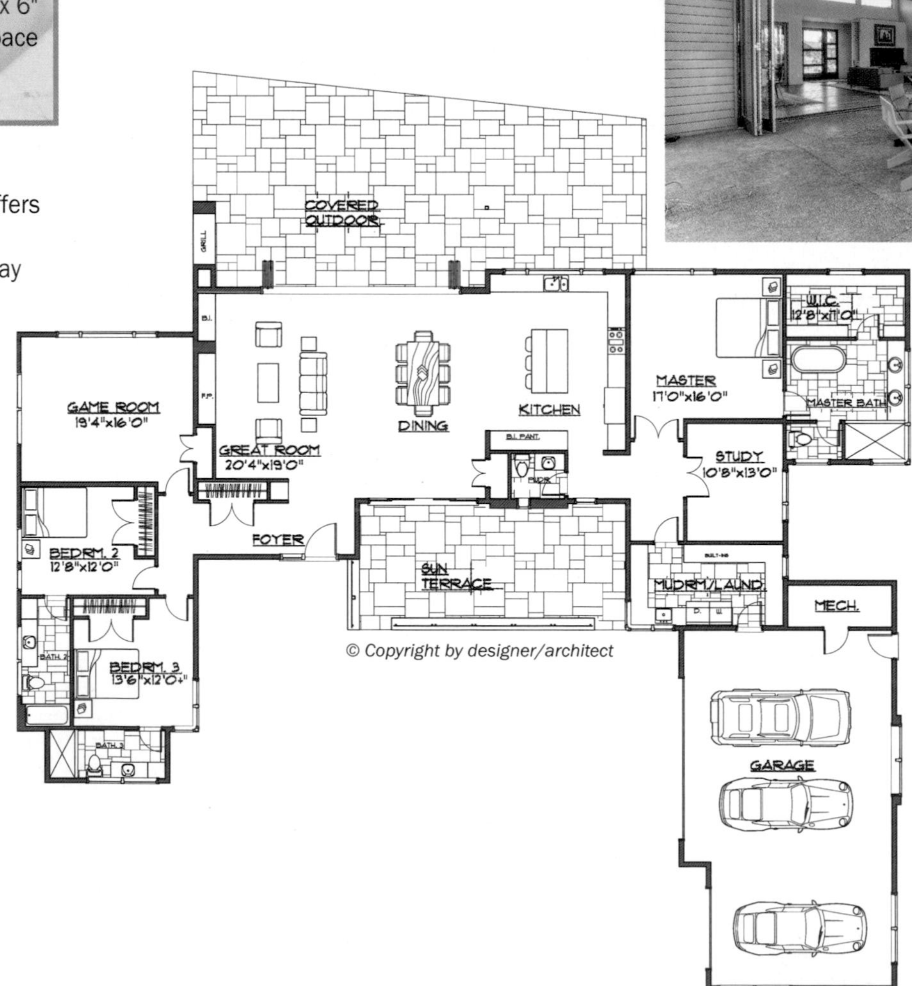

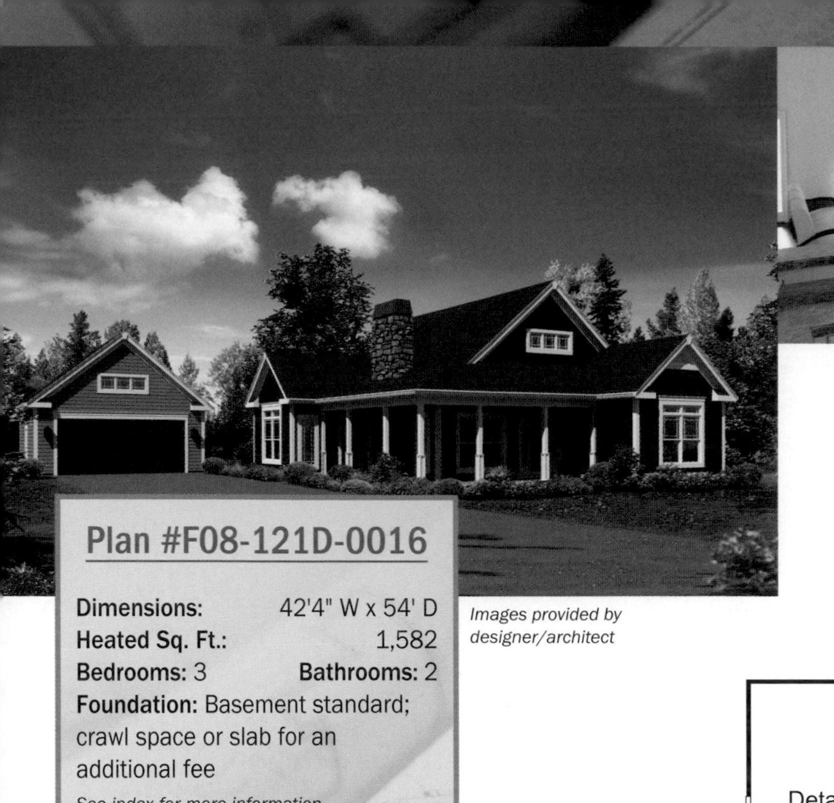

Plan #F08-121D-0016

Dimensions: 42'4" W x 54' D
Heated Sq. Ft.: 1,582
Bedrooms: 3 **Bathrooms:** 2
Foundation: Basement standard; crawl space or slab for an additional fee

See index for more information

Images provided by designer/architect

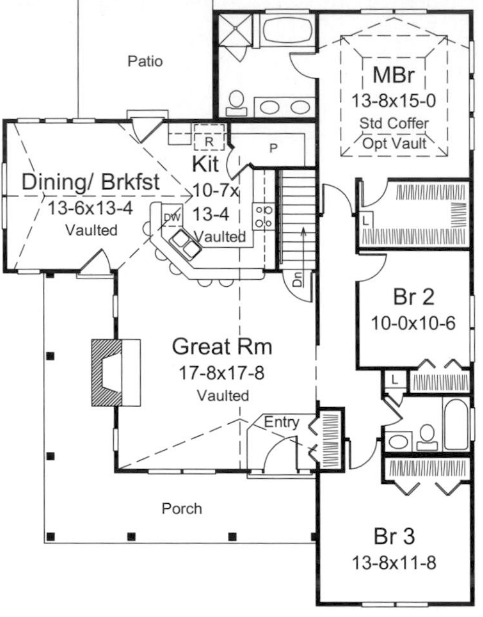

Plan #F08-026D-2051

Dimensions: 40' W x 62' D
Heated Sq. Ft.: 1,511
Bedrooms: 3 **Bathrooms:** 2
Exterior Walls: 2" x 6"
Foundation: Basement standard; crawl space, slab or walk-out basement for an additional fee

See index for more information

Images provided by designer/architect

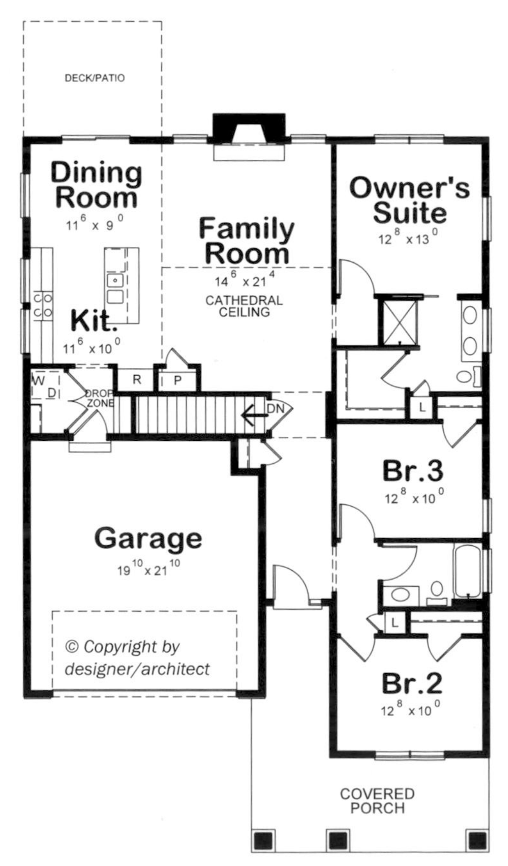

Plan #F08-032D-1080

Dimensions: 40' W x 36' D
Heated Sq. Ft.: 1,212
Bonus Sq. Ft.: 1,212
Bedrooms: 1 **Bathrooms:** 1½
Exterior Walls: 2" x 6"
Foundation: Basement standard; crawl space, floating slab or monolithic slab for an additional fee

See index for more information

Images provided by designer/architect

PORCH 18-0 X 8-0
DINING ROOM 13-4 X 12-10
LIVING ROOM 13-4 X 13-0
MASTER BATH
WALK-IN
MASTER SUITE 11-8 X 13-0
PANTRY
LAUNDRY ROOM
KITCHEN 12-0 X 12-6
FOYER/ MUD ROOM 9-8 X 9-0
PWD. ROOM
FRONT PORCH 8-0 X 6-0

© Copyright by designer/architect

First Floor 1,212 sq. ft.

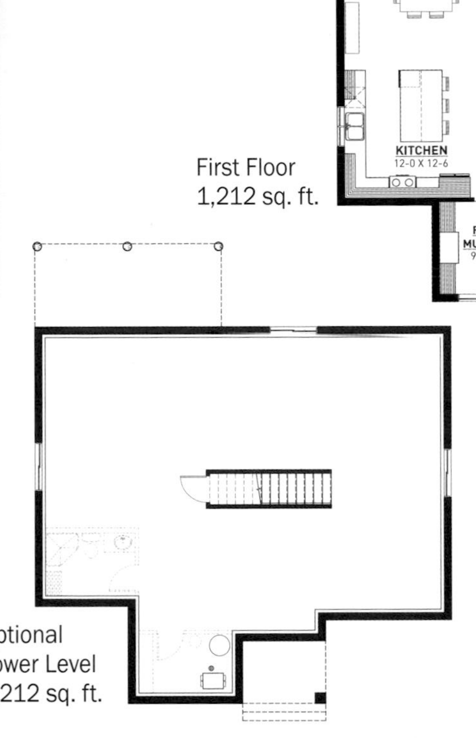

Optional Lower Level 1,212 sq. ft.

Plan #F08-007D-0055

Dimensions: 67' W x 51'4" D
Heated Sq. Ft.: 2,029
Bedrooms: 3 **Bathrooms:** 2
Foundation: Basement standard; crawl space or slab for an additional fee

See index for more information

Images provided by designer/architect

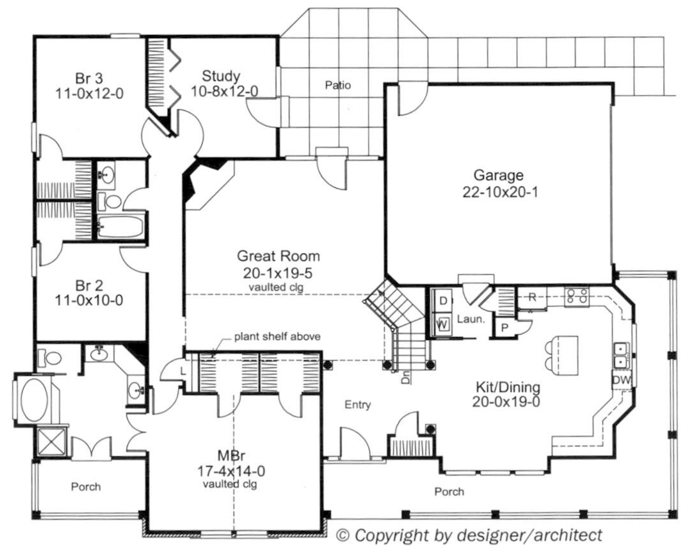

© Copyright by designer/architect

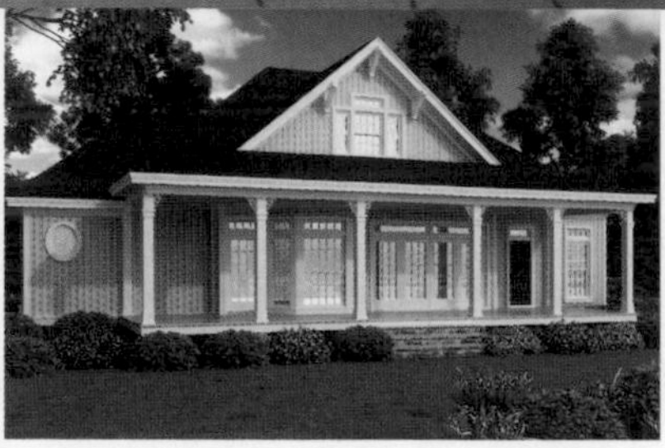

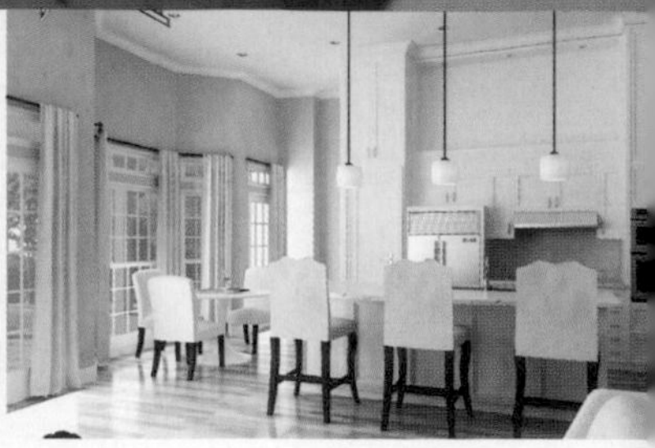

Plan #F08-020D-0358

Dimensions: 58' W x 50' D
Heated Sq. Ft.: 1,516
Bedrooms: 2 **Bathrooms:** 2
Exterior Walls: 2" x 6"
Foundation: Crawl space standard; slab for an additional fee

See index for more information

Images provided by designer/architect

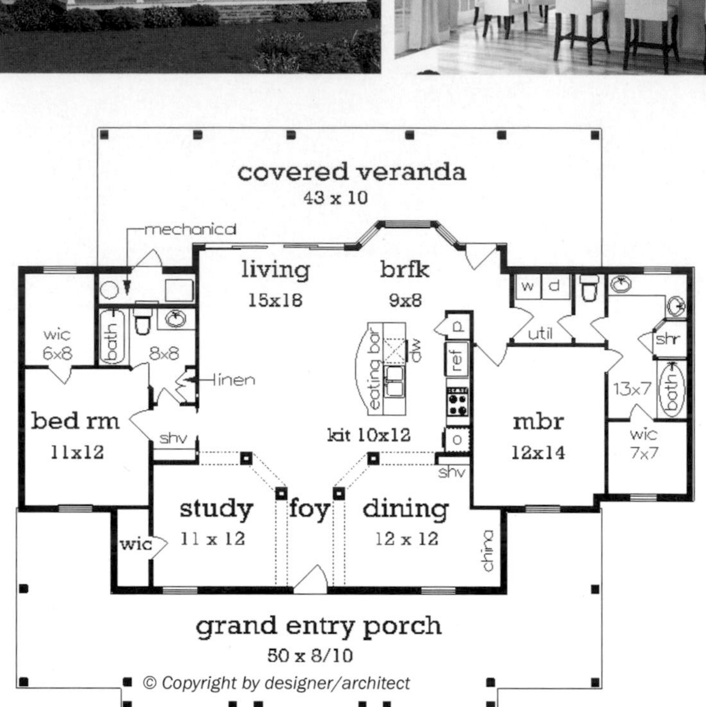

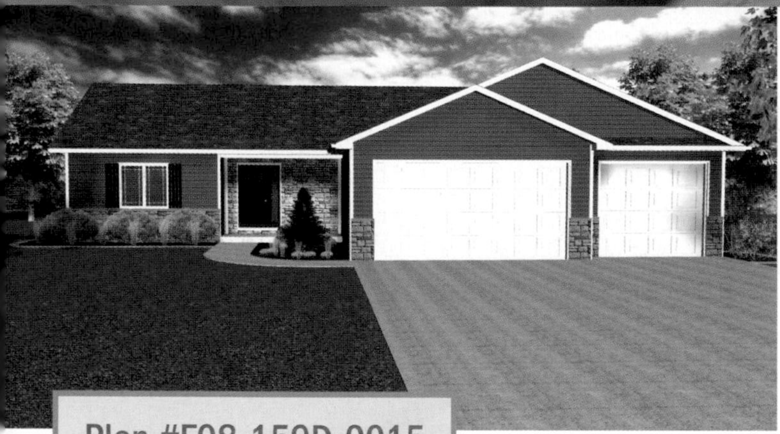

Plan #F08-159D-0015

Dimensions: 60' W x 48' D
Heated Sq. Ft.: 1,518
Bonus Sq. Ft.: 1,076
Bedrooms: 3 **Bathrooms:** 2
Exterior Walls: 2" x 6"
Foundation: Walk-out basement

See index for more information

Images provided by designer/architect

DECK
12' x 12'
BED 2
12' x 10'-6"
LIVING
DINING
M BED
14' x 13'-4"
W.I.C.
KITCHEN
PANTRY
BED 3
12' x 10'-4"
FOYER
LNDRY
STORAGE
14'-8" x 6'-5"
PORCH
3-CAR
GARAGE
31'-4" x 21'-8"

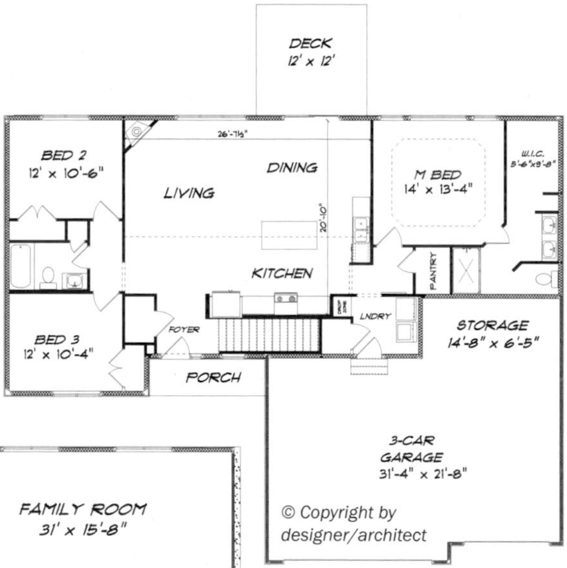

© Copyright by designer/architect

First Floor
1,518 sq. ft.

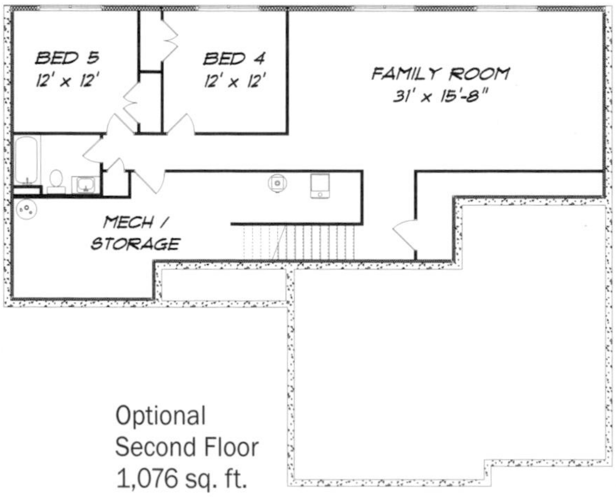

BED 5
12' x 12'
BED 4
12' x 12'
FAMILY ROOM
31' x 15'-8"
MECH /
STORAGE

Optional
Second Floor
1,076 sq. ft.

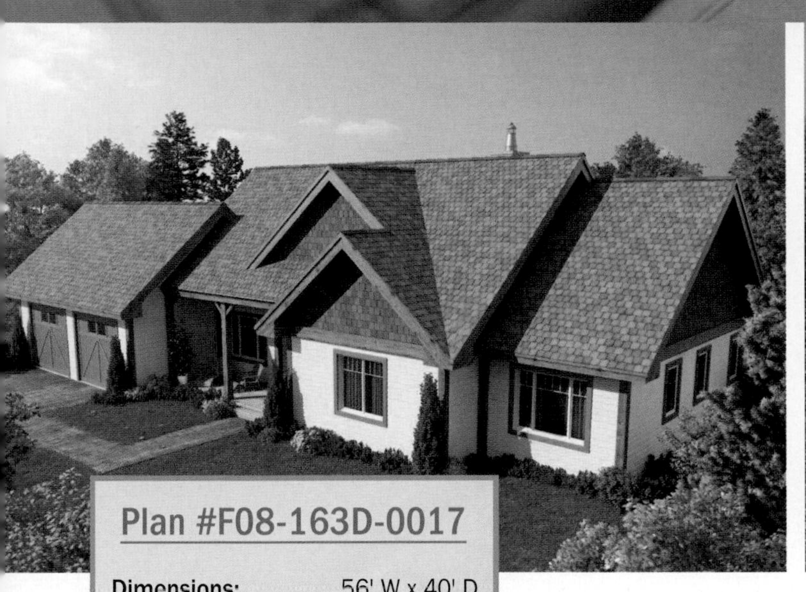

Images provided by designer/architect

Plan #F08-163D-0017

Dimensions: 56' W x 40' D
Heated Sq. Ft.: 1,416
Bedrooms: 3 **Bathrooms:** 2
Exterior Walls: 2" x 6"
Foundation: Crawl space

See index for more information

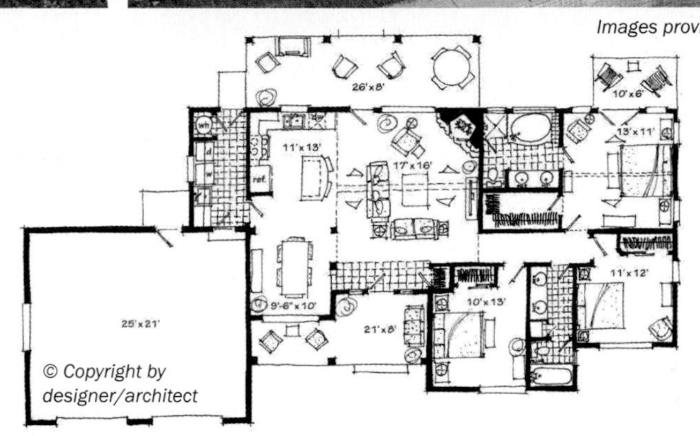

Images provided by designer/architect

Plan #F08-076D-0259

Dimensions: 46' W x 57'2" D
Heated Sq. Ft.: 1,730
Bonus Sq. Ft.: 312
Bedrooms: 3 **Bathrooms:** 2
Foundation: Slab

See index for more information

DOWN
BONUS ROOM 12-3 X 19-9

Optional
Second Floor
312 sq. ft.

LINEN
SHOWER
MASTER BATH
HER
VAULT
COVERED TERRACE
BREAKFAST 11 X 12
DW
KITCHEN
REF
COOK TOP
PAN
11'-0" HIGH CLG
FAMILY ROOM 18 X 20
MASTER BEDROOM 15 X 14
BEDROOM 3 12 X 12
LIN
CLOSET
BATH
HIM
W
D
UTIL
UP
SEAT
FOYER
GARAGE 21-6 X 22
PORCH
CLOSET
BEDROOM 2 12 X 12

© Copyright by designer/architect

First Floor
1,730 sq. ft.

Plan #F08-101D-0057

Dimensions:	58' W x 90' D
Heated Sq. Ft.:	2,037
Bonus Sq. Ft.:	1,330
Bedrooms: 1	**Bathrooms:** 1½
Exterior Walls:	2" x 6"
Foundation:	Walk-out basement

See index for more information

Images provided by designer/architect

Features

- Enjoy the outdoors on both levels of this home with upper and lower covered patios and decks
- The front porch opens to an entry hall with formal dining and a staircase to the lower level nearby
- The large U-shaped kitchen features space for casual dining as well as a wet bar for entertaining
- The master bedroom is in a wing to itself and features a stepped ceiling, a luxurious bath, and a large walk-in closet
- The optional lower level has an additional 1,330 square feet of living area and offers two additional bedrooms with baths, an office, an open recreation space as well as a safe room and unfinished storage
- 3-car side entry garage

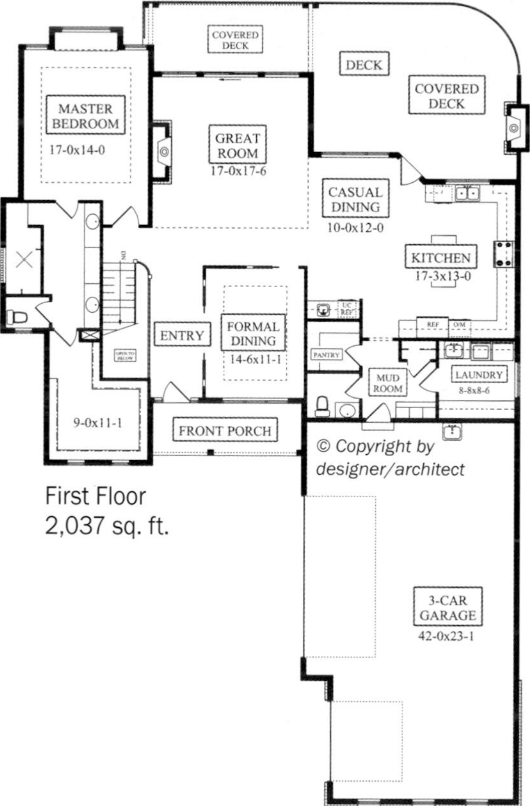

First Floor
2,037 sq. ft.

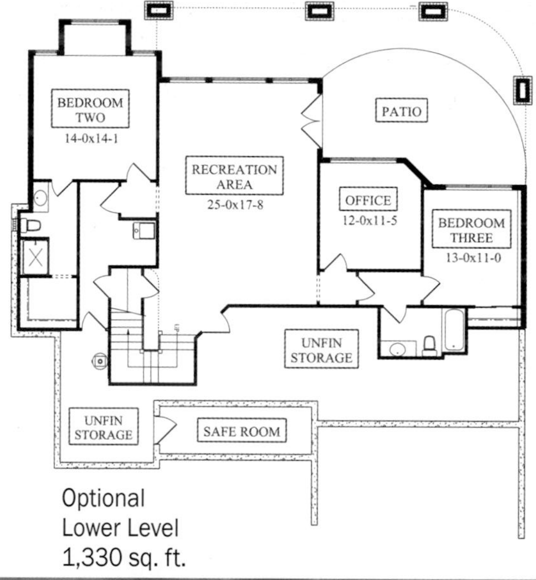

Optional
Lower Level
1,330 sq. ft.

Plan #F08-076D-0323

Dimensions: 54'4" W x 53'6" D
Heated Sq. Ft.: 1,530
Bonus Sq. Ft.: 284
Bedrooms: 3 **Bathrooms:** 3
Exterior Walls: 2" x 6"
Foundation: Slab

See index for more information

Images provided by designer/architect

OPTIONAL BONUS ROOM 14 X 18-9
DOWN

Optional Second Floor 284 sq. ft.

DECK OR PATIO
VAULT VAULT
MASTER BEDROOM 13 X 13-4
MASTER BATH
VAULT
SHOWER
LINEN
BRK'FST 10-9 X 14
SINK DW
RANGE KITCHEN
REF ISLAND
BEDROOM 3 12-3 X 10
COAT W D UTILITY
CLOSET 8-4 X 8-3
UP
CLOSET LIN
BATH
12'-0" HIGH CLG FAMILY ROOM 14 -8 X 17
STORAGE WH STORAGE
11'-0" HIGH CLG BEDROOM 2 9-9 X 11-6
CLOSET
ENTRY
PORCH
GARAGE 21 X 22

© Copyright by designer/architect

First Floor 1,530 sq. ft.

Plan #F08-007D-0172

Dimensions: 56'4" W x 61'4" D
Heated Sq. Ft.: 1,646
Bedrooms: 2 **Bathrooms:** 2
Foundation: Basement standard; crawl space or slab for an additional fee

See index for more information

Images provided by designer/architect

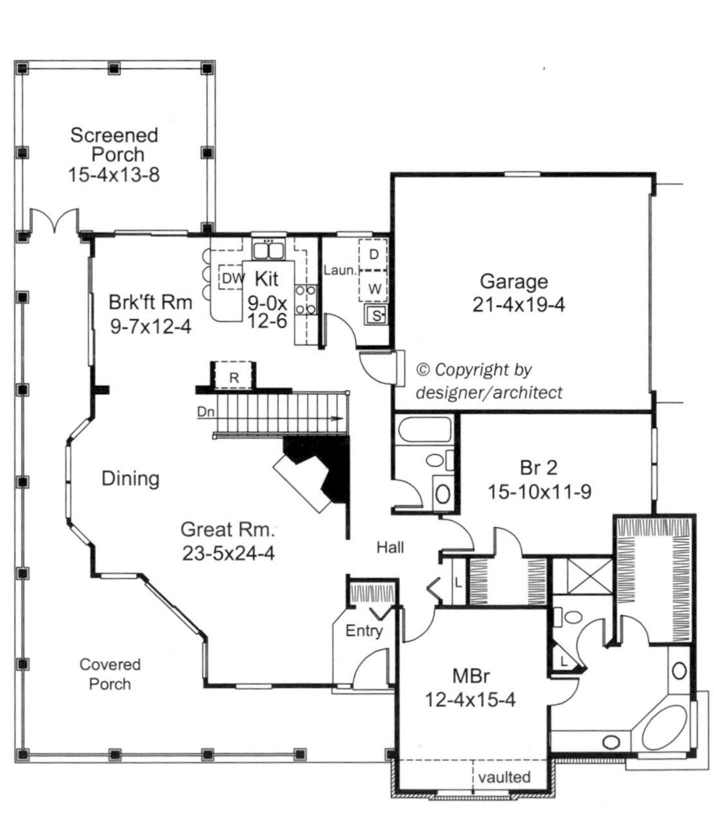

Plan #F08-121D-0025

Dimensions: 50' W x 34'6" D
Heated Sq. Ft.: 1,368
Bedrooms: 3 **Bathrooms:** 2
Foundation: Basement standard; crawl space or slab for an additional fee
See index for more information

Images provided by designer/architect

Garage
23-4x23-4
© Copyright by designer/architect

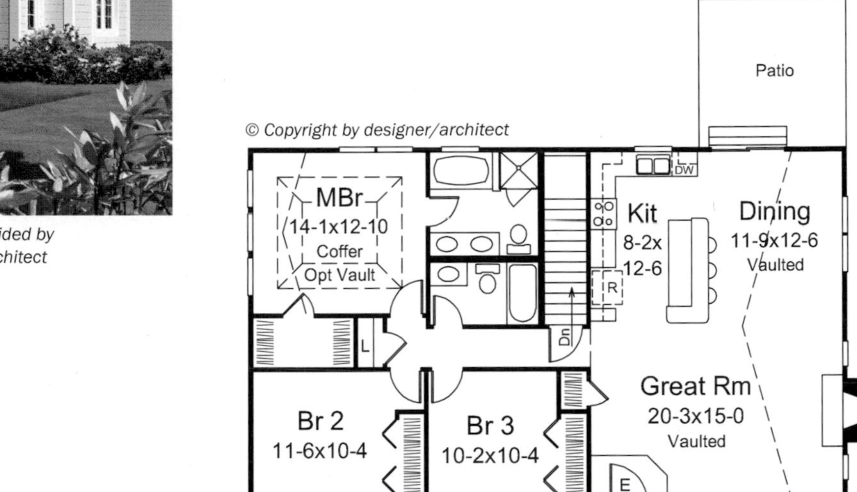

Plan #F08-011D-0742

Dimensions: 17' W x 29' D
Heated Sq. Ft.: 442
Bedrooms: 1 **Bathrooms:** 1
Exterior Walls: 2" x 6"
Foundation: Crawl space or slab standard; basement for an additional fee
See index for more information

Images provided by designer/architect

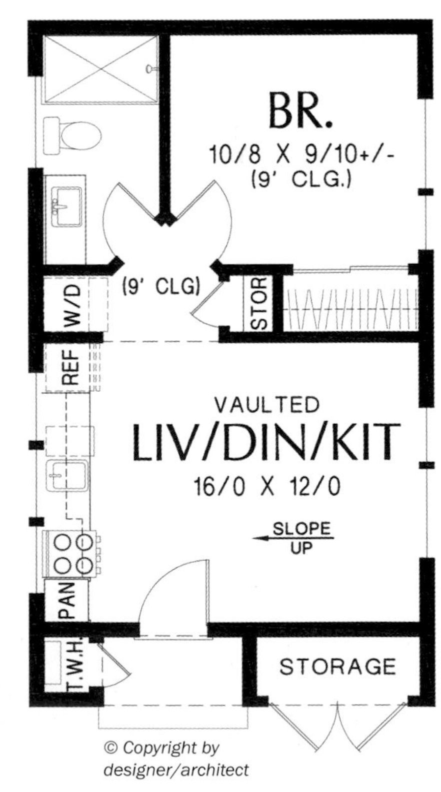

© Copyright by designer/architect

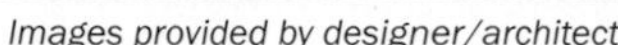
Images provided by designer/architect

Plan #F08-144D-0024

Dimensions: 32' W x 32' D
Heated Sq. Ft.: 1,024
Bedrooms: 1 **Bathrooms:** 1½
Exterior Walls: 2" x 6"
Foundation: Crawl space, slab or basement standard; walk-out basement for an additional fee

See index for more information

Features

- This smaller sized dwelling has a great layout for a mother-in-law home, vacation spot or anyone looking to downsize
- The U-shaped kitchen has a breakfast bar and seating for up to four people to comfortably dine
- Just off the kitchen is a laundry room with a closet and only steps away is also a large walk-in pantry both utilizing space-saving pocket doors
- The living room is open to the kitchen creating plenty of room when entertaining
- The master bedroom is spacious and features a large walk-in closet, private bath with a double bowl vanity, and a huge tile shower that has been designed to handle a roll-in wheelchair

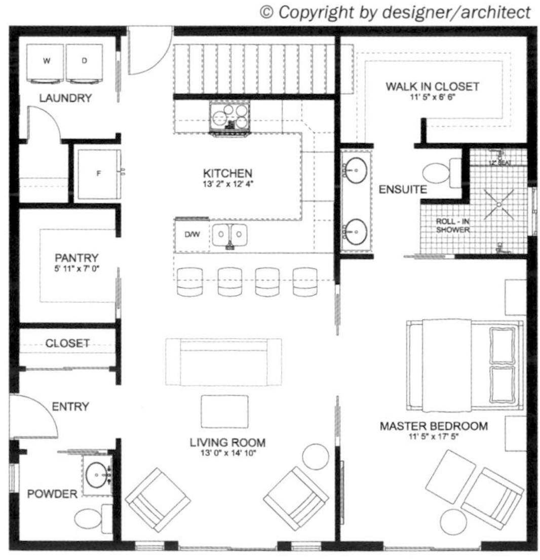

Plan #F08-028D-0112

Dimensions: 56' W x 52' D
Heated Sq. Ft.: 1,611
Bedrooms: 3 **Bathrooms:** 2
Exterior Walls: 2" x 6"
Foundation: Floating slab standard; monolithic slab, crawl space, basemen tor walk-out basement for an additional fee

See index for more information

Features

- This Craftsman one-story home has timeless farmhouse appeal
- The cozy great room with fireplace has built-ins on each side for added storage and style
- The kitchen and dining area enjoy a snack bar, great when entertaining in the great room
- The master bedroom enjoys its privacy, and its own bath and walk-in closet
- Two additional bedrooms share the full bath between them
- 2-car side entry garage

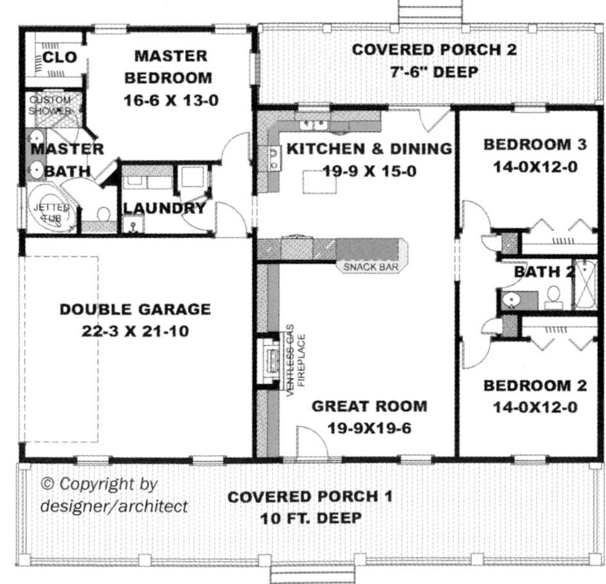

Images provided by designer/architect

the social kitchen

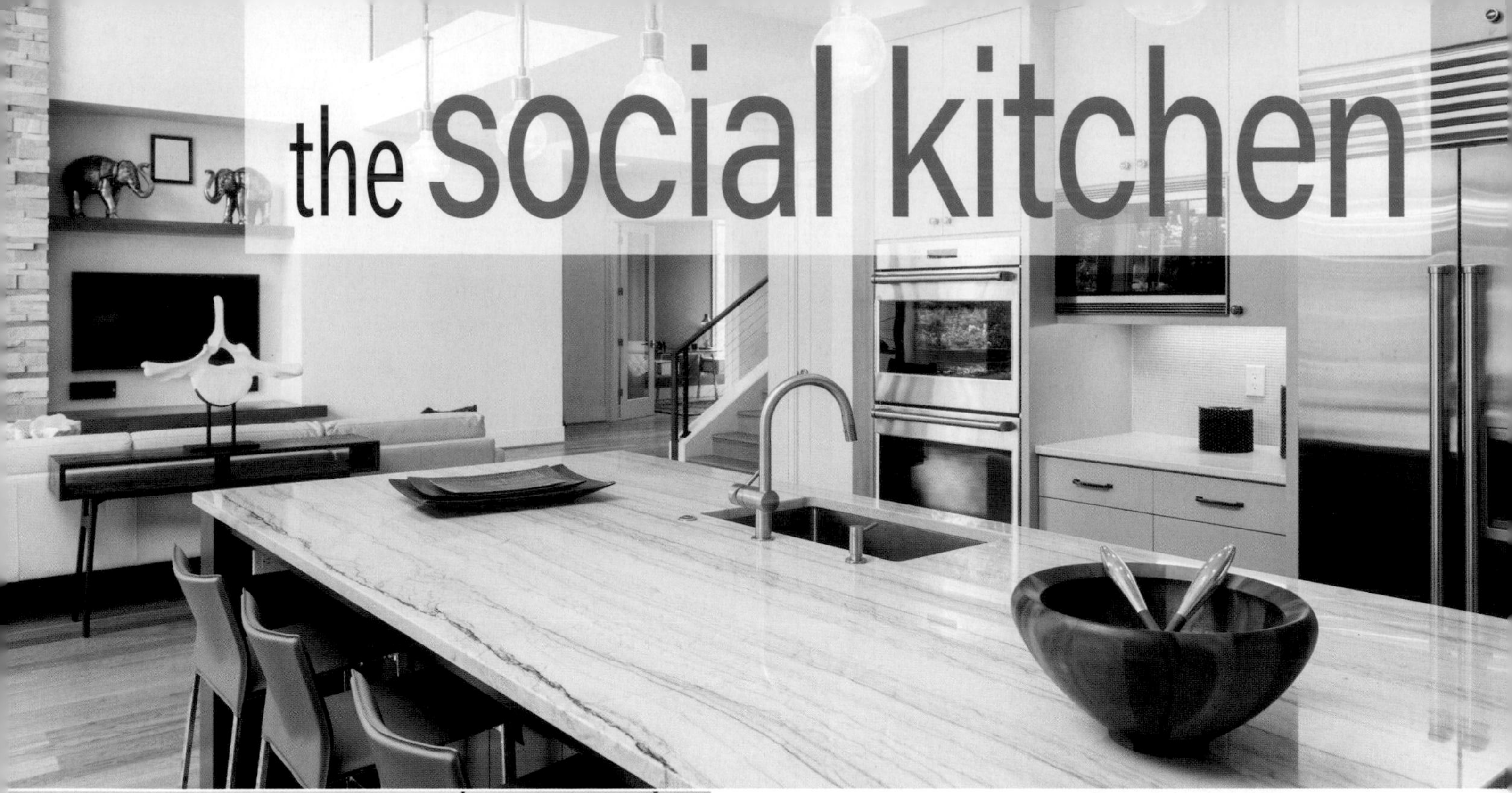

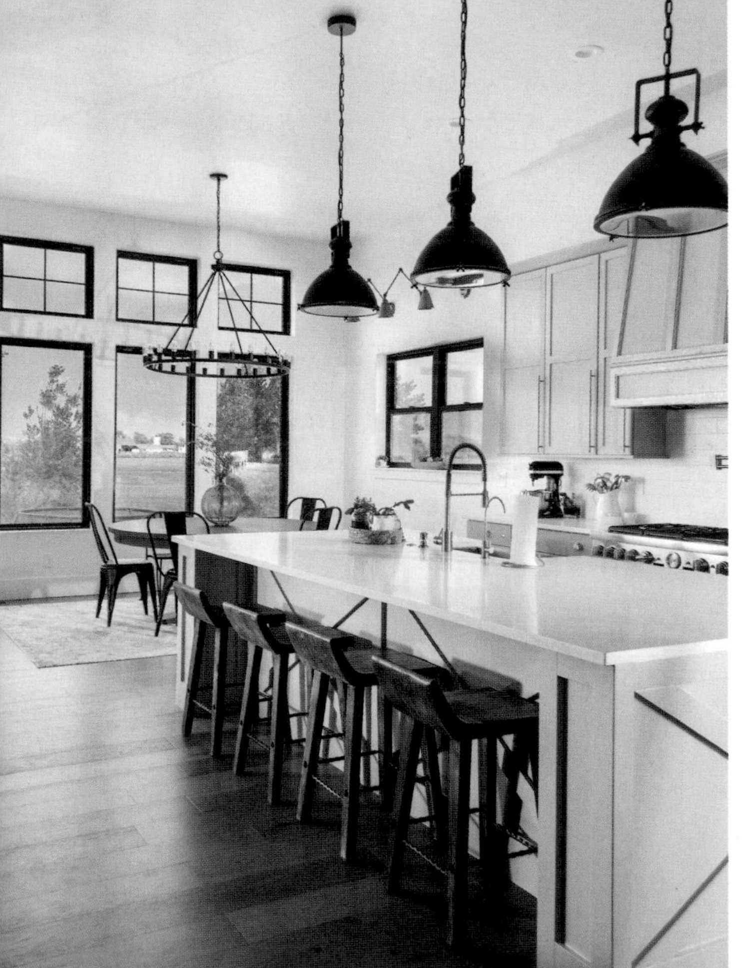

You have just put the finishing touches on a beautiful table centerpiece, and the spread of hors d'oeuvres and the other delectable culinary treats for your gathering. The utmost attention to detail has been made to the great room, dining area and all the gathering places in your home. You want to make sure your guests feel pampered, comfortable, and completely at ease. But, no matter how inviting your living space may be, why does it always seem everyone ends up gathering in the kitchen?

Kitchens seem to be magnets for everyone who enters a home. Maybe it's the flurry of activity always taking place there, or the scrumptious aromas that fill the air making guests want to investigate what possibly could be cooking. Whatever the reason, kitchens are everyone's favorite gathering spots in the home. So, instead of fighting it, give in and make your kitchen a socially inviting place that is comfortable, fun and also allows you to get everything done even if people are lingering about. There are many ways to create social spots that keep everyone in the kitchen, while allowing him or her to feel welcome and comfortable in participating in the activities.

Thankfully, today's floor plans are taking this into consideration now more than ever. Most homes being designed today utilize an open floor plan that easily integrates the kitchen into the gathering spaces seamlessly. So, no longer is the kitchen hidden behind a swinging door. It's actually a stunning focal point filled with many design elements that enhance the entire gathering area including seating, dining space and other amenities.

Unless noted, copyright by designer/architect; Page 182 top: Plan #011S-0192; bottom: Plan #101D-0132; Page 183 top: Kohler Crevasse sink, kohler.com; Plan #101D-0123; For more photos or to purchase plans, please visit houseplansandmore.com.

The kitchen is the center of your home; where you do the most work, where you entertain friends, where you gather as a family, and where life happens. It is hands-down the busiest area of the home and needs to be carefully planned for function as well as style.

A home's kitchen tends to be a place that quickly turns into a dumping ground. With the daily mail, homework projects, laundry, food storage and office work finding its way there, the kitchen can often have an identity crisis since there are so many different activities being carried out in the same space. Well, these habits will never change most likely, so instead of letting them aggravate you, embrace them and learn how to incorporate all of your family's favorite activities into this one wonderful place within your home.

One way to create an inviting feeling with function within your kitchen is to create a chopping and chatting spot. Whether it's a breakfast bar counter, an island, workbench or table, guests and family will need a spot that can function as a place for dining, prepping a meal, or finishing the homework that's due tomorrow. A decent space for gathering around will become a beacon and will keep everyone right where the action is, but out of the cooking space. An important thing to remember when creating this special gathering spot is that you don't want to crowd your kitchen with too many tables, or an island that is too oversized. It shouldn't affect the natural traffic flow, or act as a barrier at all. So, pick a piece of furniture, or a space that facilitates function, storage and possibly workspace, plus a spot where people feel they can just hang out and not be in the chef's way.

Another important factor to include when creating a social kitchen is to make sure there is plenty of seating. Use stools, benches and other seating options to offer plenty of places for your guest to "pop a squat." Of course, you may be thinking that your dining table has chairs and that should be enough, but think of other types of seating that can be tucked away (under a counter, for example) and can remain out of sight. That is also why the idea of a bench is great. It can provide a handy place to drop things the minute you come in the door, plus when company arrive, it's an instant spot for chatting with the chef. Everyone enjoys gathering in the kitchen and enjoying chips and dip, while watching the cook finish up their meal time tasks. Having some comfortable stools, benches, and other seating options will ensure your guests remain comfortable for their entire stay. Even better, stick with wood, plastic or other low-maintenance options for this seating and if spills occur, clean up will be a breeze.

Adding a variety of lighting in the kitchen is another way to make this space feel inviting, warm and comfortable for all those who enter it. Add lighting under the cabinets, recessed lighting into the ceiling and over tables and work zones so that all the bases are covered. That way, when the family cozies up around the table playing games, you can just light the table area and its nearby surroundings for a warmer feel. Plus, light sources can really play with the mood of the space.

So, when entertaining, use soft, low lighting and when cooking or prepping, turn up the lighting so it's safer for everyone involved with these tasks. Even soft candlelight on a countertop or dining table adds warmth and dimension to the space making it feel intimate and less institutional.

A great way to inexpensively allow you to change the amount of light in your kitchen is to install dimmer switches on many of the light sources. That way, the light above the sink can be bright enough for kitchen tasks at mealtime and then turned down much lower and used as a night light after everyone has gone off to bed. Dimmers allow great versatility and keep you from having an overabundance of lighting that may make your kitchen feel too busy, distracting or tense.

A kitchen filled entirely of glass cabinetry would be a little distressing don't you think? With all those kitchen gadgets being seen by everyone who came into the space, all of the clutter would make for a busy space that would be unnerving for most. But, strategically placing a couple of glass front cabinets in your kitchen can really become a focal point. If you have a great collection of vases or rustic wooden bowls, glass front cabinets or even the popular trend of open shelving can give you the perfect opportunity to display away. Not only will they add some great character to your kitchen interior, but they will surely become conversation starters.

Just remember that less is more. Select just a few key items to be seen in these cabinets and avoid the temptation of showing a huge collection. It will make your kitchen instantly cluttered and less interesting than just giving them a glimpse of your special collection.

Making some minor adjustments with the layout, seating options, lighting, and cabinetry can add scores of points when family and guests gather in your kitchen. Instead of trying to find ways to keep everyone out while you cook away, invite them in and let the party begin!

Unless notes, copyright by designer/architect; Page 184 top, left: Plan #155D-0115; top, right: Plan #F08-155D-0047 on page 24; middle: Plan #F08-051D-0960 on page 108, Jason Ickowitz, photographer; Plan #032D-1104; Page 185: Plan #101D-0120; To see more photos or purchase plans, please visit houseplansandmore.com.

your dream kitchen wish list

If you're designing the ultimate kitchen, trying to make your kitchen more functional for entertaining, or building a new home and trying to remember the things to take into consideration with a kitchen layout, it is important to remember that it is one of the best home investments you can make so make sure it meets all your needs right from the start.

The three main appliances in the kitchen are the sink, the refrigerator, and the stove. Make sure you arrange them so the workspace flows.

sink or swim Of the three appliances, the sink gets the most use. Place it in an area of the kitchen that is visually appealing to its user. So, don't push it up against a wall without a view. Place it in front of a window with a view to the outdoors, or in an island that overlooks the other areas of the home. It is also important to place the dishwasher to either side of the sink so that loading dishes is convenient. Many kitchens have a second sink, one for preparing food and another for dishes. Some kitchens also feature a second dishwasher, one for gently washing breakables and another for power scrubbing pots and pans.

shut the fridge When it comes to the refrigerator there are many basic options such as brand, color, size and finish. But, also think about the various styles including a freezer/fridge combination, side-by-side doors, a top and bottom door style, a style with an ice and water dispenser in the door, a smart fridge with technology that allows you to see what's inside it from your smart phone, and now the fun retro refrigerators meant to make a bold decorating statement and be a focal point. Also showing resurgence, refrigerators with the same cabinet style treatment added to the door so they don't stand out in your kitchen, are becoming quite popular again. Shiny stainless steel finishes are becoming less popular as the new appliances being introduced have a matte finish. Whatever option you choose make sure you leave plenty of room for the doors to open completely. If the fridge is placed near a wall make sure the doors and drawers open freely without hitting the wall. It is a good idea to check with the manufacturer for specific installation dimensions. And, becoming extremely popular especially if a kitchen is small are counter the depth refrigerators. These slightly smaller sized models offer a seamless look to your kitchen that feels custom since the appliance doesn't stick out further than the countertops. It easily adds square footage to your kitchen without it being obvious.

too hot in the kitchen The options available for stoves go way beyond gas or electric. There are cooktops, double ovens, oven and microwave combinations, burners and griddle tops, convection and even warming drawers. When making a decision it is important to think about the type of cooking you plan to do and how much space you have to work with. The cooking surface needs to be planned to allow for workspace that is easily accessible and safe.

The selection process isn't over just yet...now, it's time to think about cabinets, shelving, countertops, pantry units, closets, a planning center, electronics, a center island, and eating space!

cabinets, shelving & countertops

You can never have enough storage and this is especially true when it comes to the kitchen and all of the gadgets that need to be stored. Most common are cabinets with closed fronts but also available are open cabinets where plates can be stored on end and open fronts where objects are quickly within reach. It is also a good idea to consider cabinets that go all the way up to the ceiling. The top shelf can easily be reached with a step stool and can hold the items that are not used on a daily basis. Countertops need to be durable and accent the cabinetry. There can be built-in items such as cutting boards and seamless sinks. There are many surfaces available and the biggest decision will be how long you want it to last and how much you want to spend. Granite has long been a favorite, but many new homeowners are also opting for quartz, concrete, or recycled glass countertops.

pantries, storage walls, & closets

Pantries are a great way to store all of your food in one place. They are typically wider than a standard cabinet and have additional shelves for storage. If space allows, a built-in pantry closet is a wonderful addition to any kitchen. These can be placed in the general vicinity of the kitchen and custom shelving can be added to meet your storage needs. Storage walls in kitchens are very popular now too, and typically linger in the area near the stove. Often shelves are mounted on a wall near the stove and include spices, measuring cups, oils, vinegars and other cooking essentials. Or, kitchen storage walls are found on another wall often floor-to-ceiling and include an assortment of china, ceramic bowls, glassware and other items that look nice displayed together. Both decorative and functional, these kitchen walls can really show off your personality, while providing the extra storage always needed in the kitchen.

Unless noted, copyright by designer/architect; Page 186 top: Plan #101D-0106, Warren Diggles, photographer; bottom: Plan #F08-101D-0052 on page 232, Damon Searles, photographer; Page 187 top, left: Do-It-Yourself Decorative Charging Box, centsationalgirl.com; Organized mud room, nextluxury.com; Plan #101D-0108; right: Mockett® Convenience Kitchen Outlet, Item #PCS39/EE/HW, mockett.com; To see more photos or purchase plans, please visit houseplansandmore.com.

planning and/or technology center

Growing in popularity, the planning or technology center is basically a simplified "home office" located in the kitchen or adjacent to it. It can consist of a desk with surrounding cabinets and storage, space for a computer or ipad®, a charging station with additional USB ports, an area to organize bills and other important papers, cubbies or bins for every family member to stay organized, and a family schedule.

kitchen electronics

There are so many items that are used in the kitchen that need to be plugged in, make sure there are plenty of electrical outlets so you don't have to run extension cords. Mockett® simplifies the need for electrical outlets everywhere in the kitchen with this pop-up kitchen outlet design. Simply, click it and it ascends from the countertops to reveal additional outlets that can be used when additional seldom used appliances are needed.

kitchen island

An island in the kitchen can function as an eating bar, additional workspace, or can house the cooktop or sink. Whatever the function, it usually ends up being the focal point of the kitchen and can be accented with dramatic lighting, or hanging kitchen racks that will creatively hold your pots and pans while reclaiming valuable cabinet space. Designing it with different colors than the other cabinets and countertops is a popular trend and makes it even more of a focal point.

eating space

This can be a nook, breakfast bar, banquette or island and for many families on the go it is where most of the meals are served. If you plan on having an eat-in kitchen, make sure there is enough stools so everyone has a place to sit.

If you're trying to design or plan the layout of a new kitchen the options are a little overwhelming, but it is important to remember that it needs to be well-organized and efficient, as well as beautiful since it is everyone's favorite spot. After all, it is the place you live, entertain and most importantly – cook! From cabinetry to appliances, it is important to create the perfect gathering space so that the chef, as well as family and friends, are always happy when they enter.

Plan #F08-155D-0116

Dimensions: 107'8" W x 57'10" D
Heated Sq. Ft.: 3,277
Bonus Sq. Ft.: 603
Bedrooms: 5 **Bathrooms:** 3½
Foundation: Crawl space or slab, please specify when ordering

See index for more information

Features

- This totally unique barn-style home has a central gathering space and bedrooms on each side
- The great room and kitchen blend together to form the core of this home
- A huge laundry/mud room includes a shower, a sink, and a walk-in pantry
- The master suite is comprised of a private bath and two large walk-in closets
- The optional second floor has an additional 603 square feet of living area and can be accessed from a spiral staircase in the great room
- 2-car front entry garage

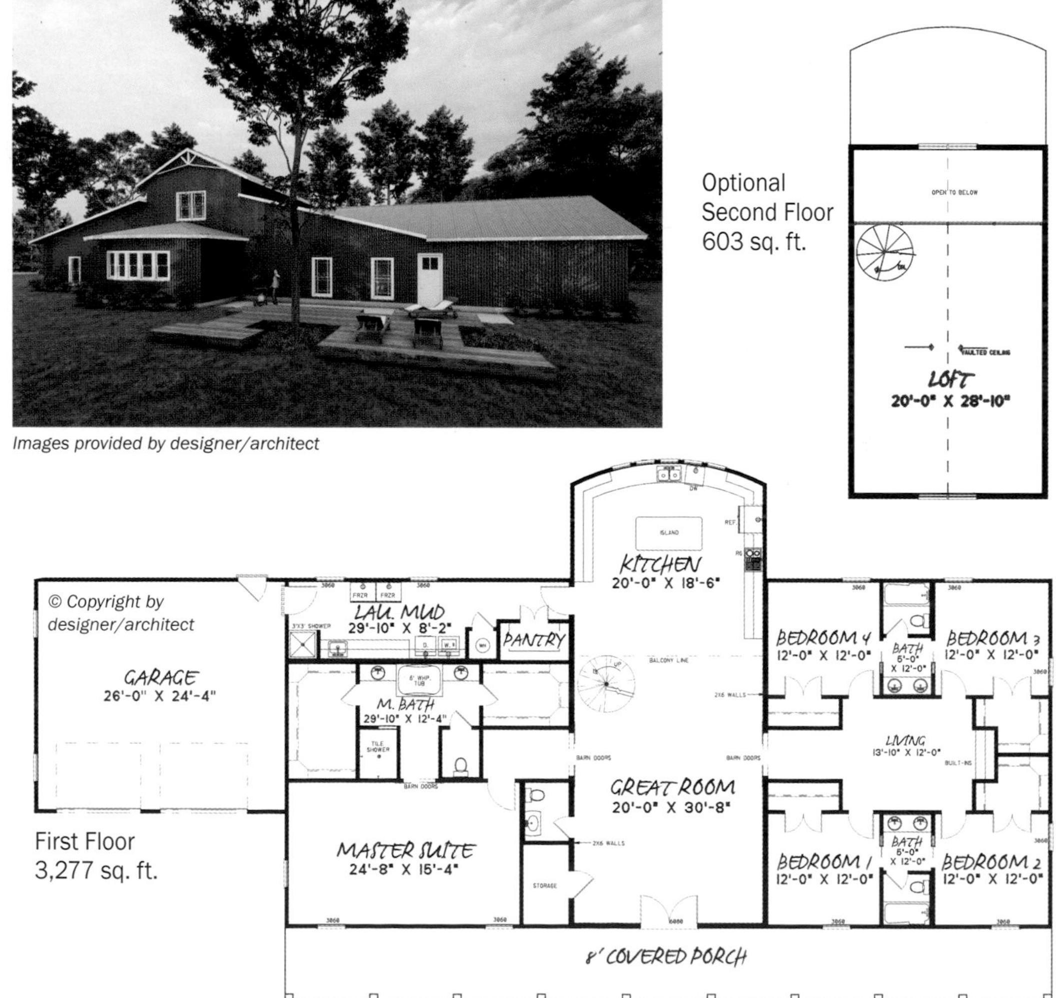

Images provided by designer/architect

Optional Second Floor
603 sq. ft.

First Floor
3,277 sq. ft.

Plan #F08-028D-0119

Dimensions: 56' W x 52' D
Heated Sq. Ft.: 2,096
Bedrooms: 4 **Bathrooms:** 3
Exterior Walls: 2" x 6"
Foundation: Floating slab standard; monolithic slab, crawl space, basement or walk-out basement for an additional fee

See index for more information

Images provided by designer/architect

Features

- This home's large great room has built-in cabinets/shelves and a ventless gas fireplace
- A large kitchen/dining area shares a counter-high snack bar with the great room
- The kitchen has lots of storage with a long island, dual pantry cabinets, and French doors in the dining area
- This plan has two master suites which is ideal for many family living situations or guests
- Master suite 1 is located in the back of the house for privacy and contains a walk-in closet with a spa style bath
- Master suite 2 is large and contains a walk-in closet, and a private bath
- The laundry room accesses the rear covered porch and has room for a farmhouse sink, washer/dryer area and cabinets with rustic shelves above for extra storage

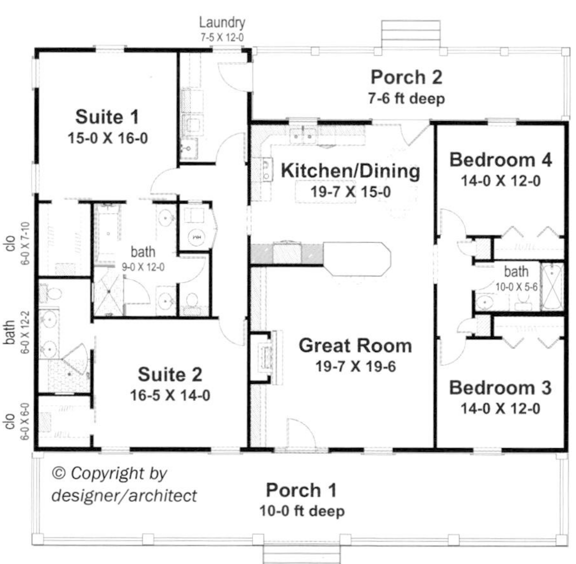

Plan #F08-161D-0022

Dimensions: 104'10" W x 93'10" D
Heated Sq. Ft.: 3,338
Bedrooms: 3 **Bathrooms:** 3½
Exterior Walls: 2" x 6"
Foundation: Crawl space

See index for more information

Features

- The perfect open floor plan for today's family focuses on plenty of windows and private bedrooms for every family member
- A massive great room, dining area, and kitchen form the main hub of this home
- A private master suite has a sun-filled bath with a free-standing tub and separate shower
- A fun game room is tucked between two secondary bedrooms, perfect for kid's play area
- 3-car side entry garage

Images provided by designer/architect

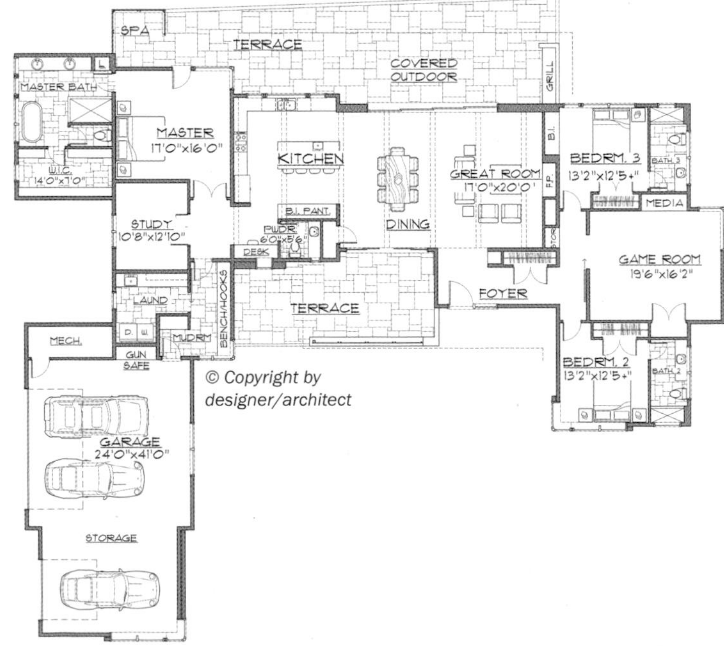

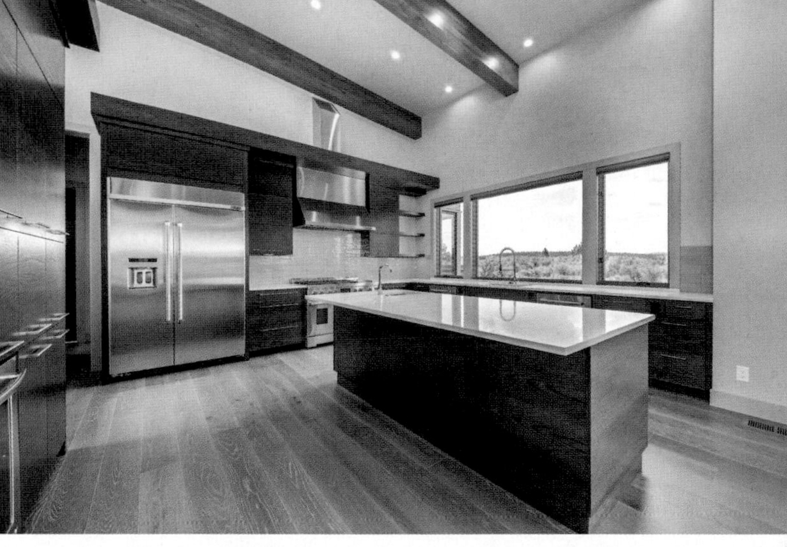

Plan #F08-011D-0655

Dimensions: 60' W x 62' D
Heated Sq. Ft.: 2,707
Bonus Sq. Ft.: 375
Bedrooms: 4 **Bathrooms:** 2½
Exterior Walls: 2" x 6"
Foundation: Walk-out basement

See index for more information

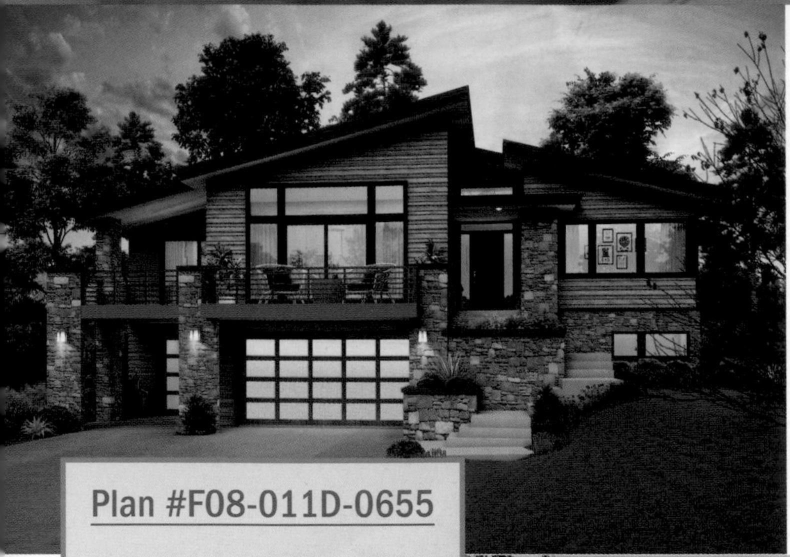

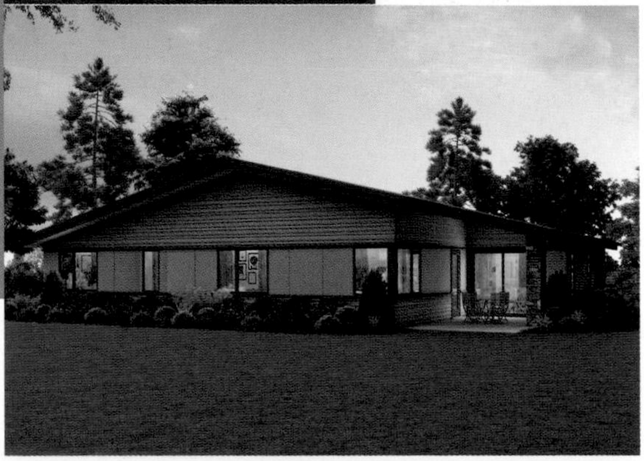

First Floor
2,549 sq. ft.

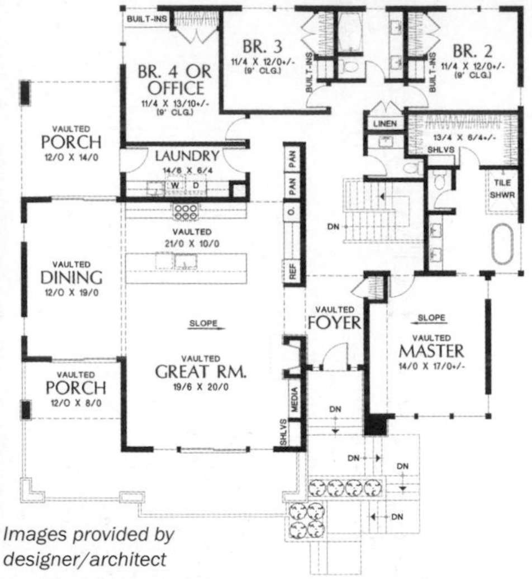

Images provided by designer/architect

Lower Level
158 sq. ft.

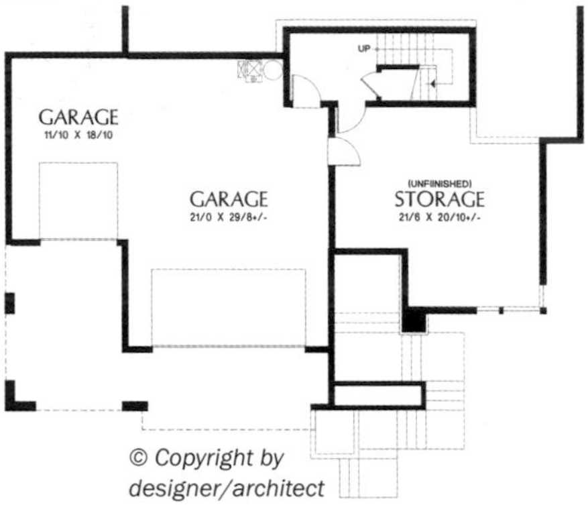

© Copyright by designer/architect

Plan #F08-007D-0113

Dimensions: 66' W x 66' D
Heated Sq. Ft.: 2,547
Bedrooms: 4 **Bathrooms:** 2½
Foundation: Basement standard; crawl space or slab for an additional fee

See index for more information

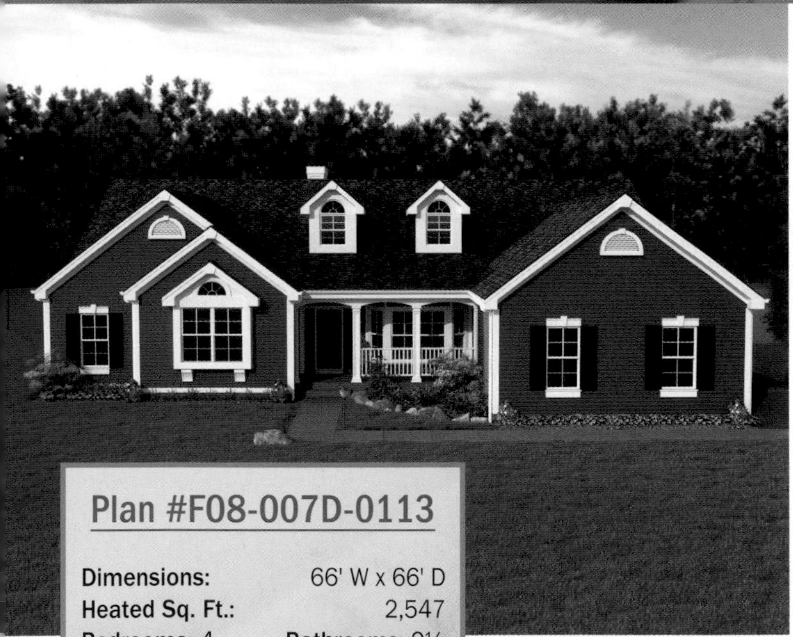

Images provided by designer/architect

© Copyright by designer/architect

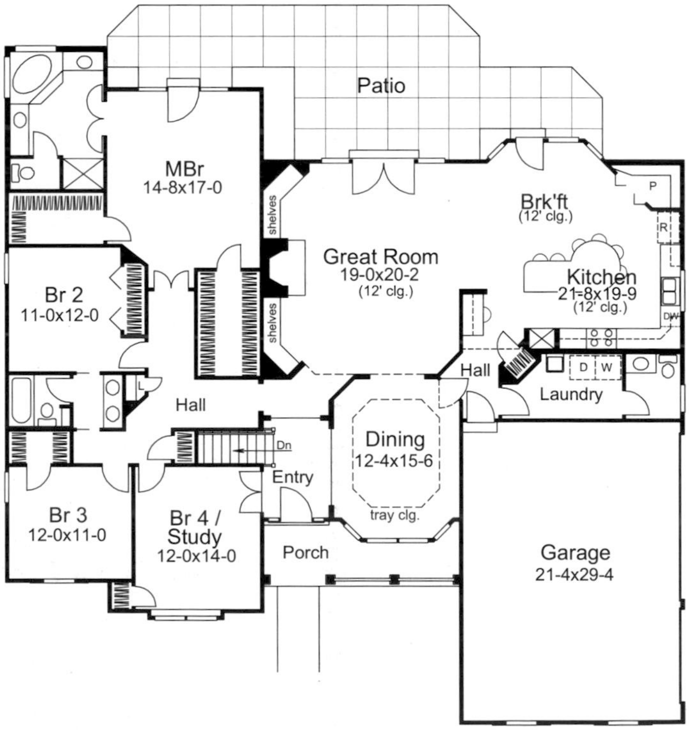

Plan #F08-058D-0232

Dimensions: 44' W x 62' D
Heated Sq. Ft.: 1,650
Bedrooms: 3 **Bathrooms:** 2½
Foundation: Basement

See index for more information

Images provided by designer/architect

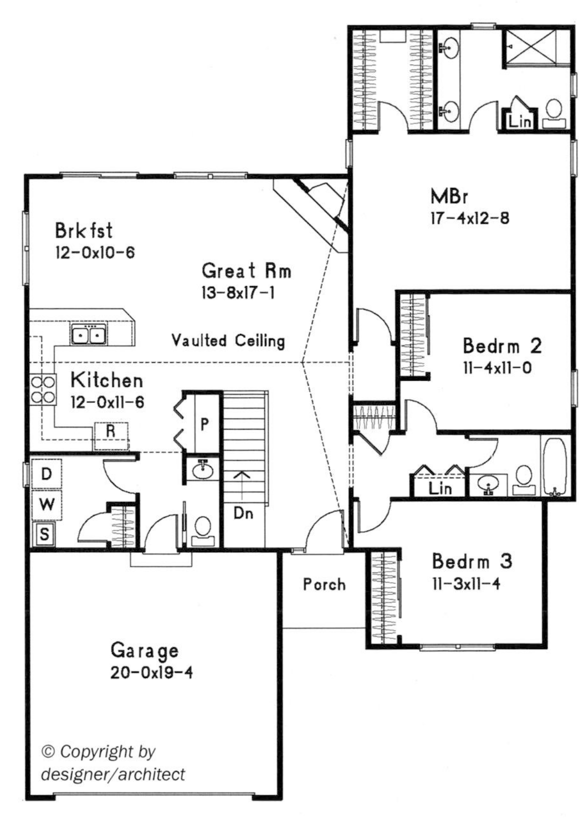

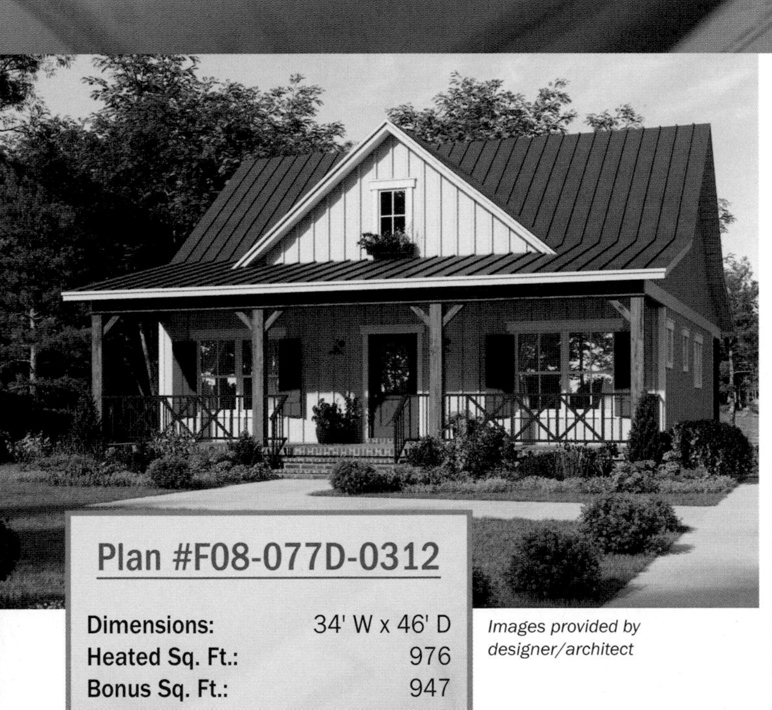

Plan #F08-077D-0312

Dimensions: 34' W x 46' D
Heated Sq. Ft.: 976
Bonus Sq. Ft.: 947
Bedrooms: 2 **Bathrooms:** 2
Foundation: Walk-out basement, crawl space or slab, please specify when ordering

See index for more information

Images provided by designer/architect

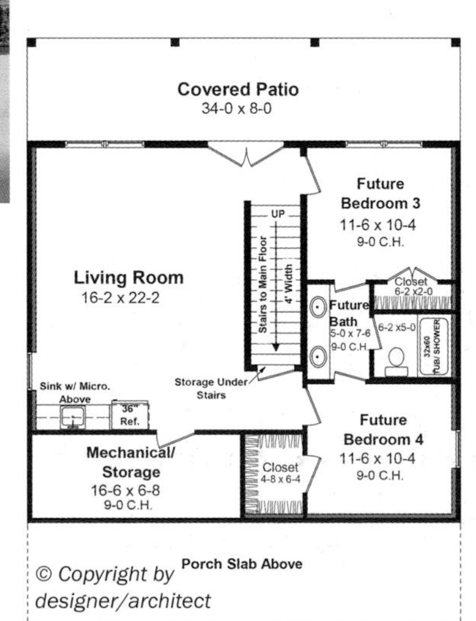

Optional Lower Level
947 sq. ft.

First Floor
976 sq. ft.

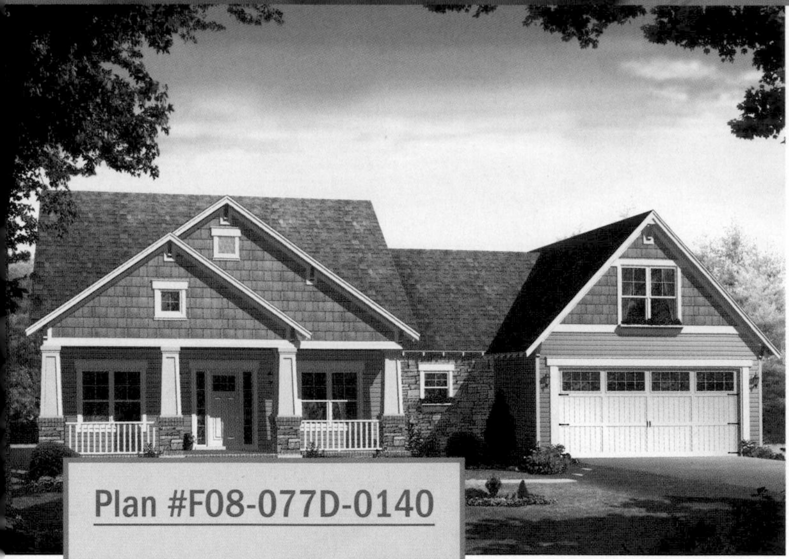

Plan #F08-077D-0140

Dimensions: 65' W x 56'8" D
Heated Sq. Ft.: 1,800
Bonus Sq. Ft.: 326
Bedrooms: 3 **Bathrooms:** 2
Foundation: Slab or crawl space, please specify when ordering; for basement version, see Plan #077D-0187 at houseplansandmore.com

See index for more information

Images provided by designer/architect

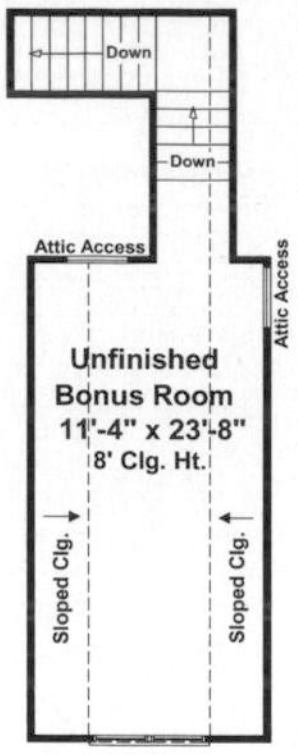

Optional Second Floor
326 sq. ft.

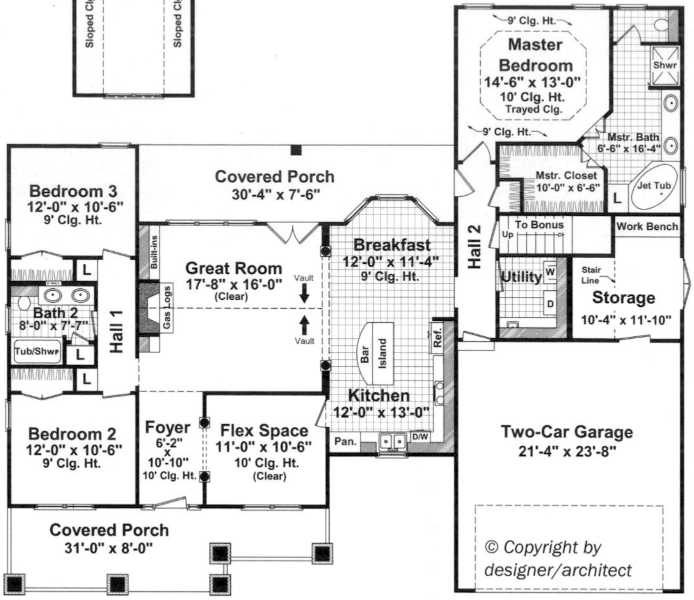

First Floor
1,800 sq. ft.

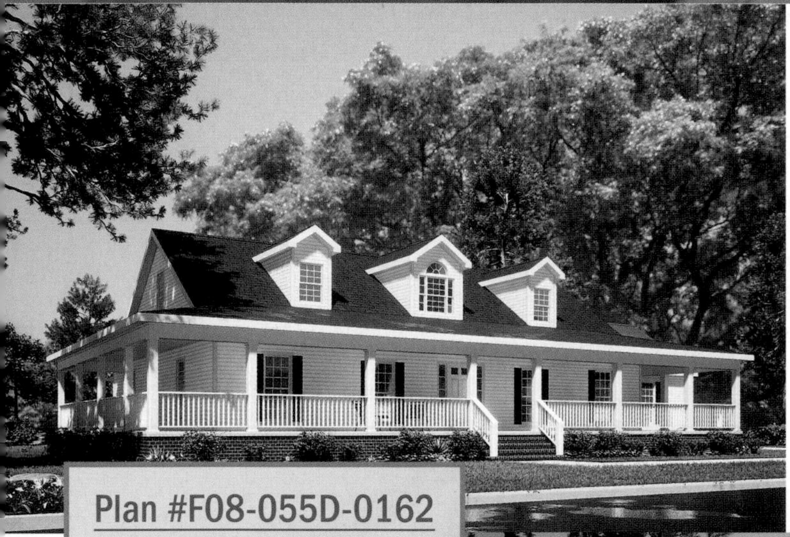

Plan #F08-055D-0162

Dimensions: 84' W x 55'6" D
Heated Sq. Ft.: 1,921
Bonus Sq. Ft.: 812
Bedrooms: 3 **Bathrooms:** 2
Foundation: Crawl space or slab standard; basement or daylight basement for an additional fee

See index for more information

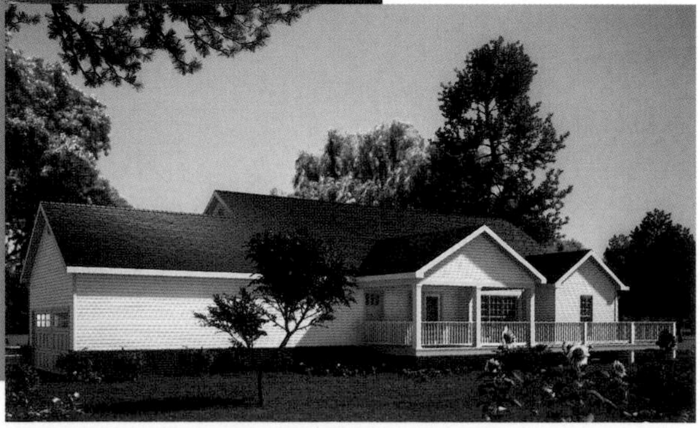

Images provided by designer/architect

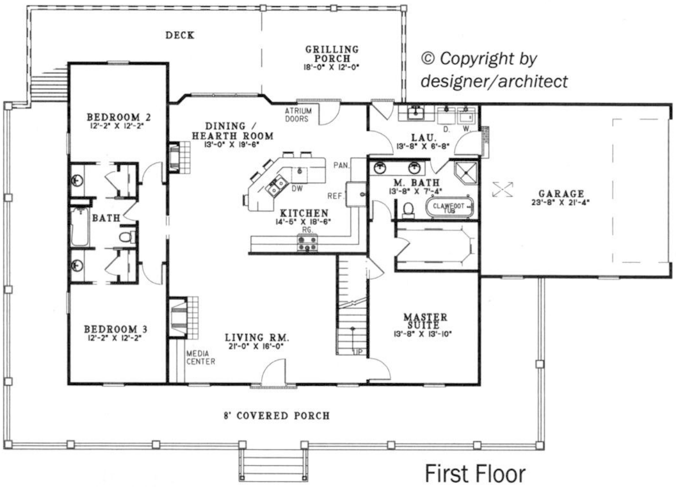

© Copyright by designer/architect

First Floor
1,921 sq. ft.

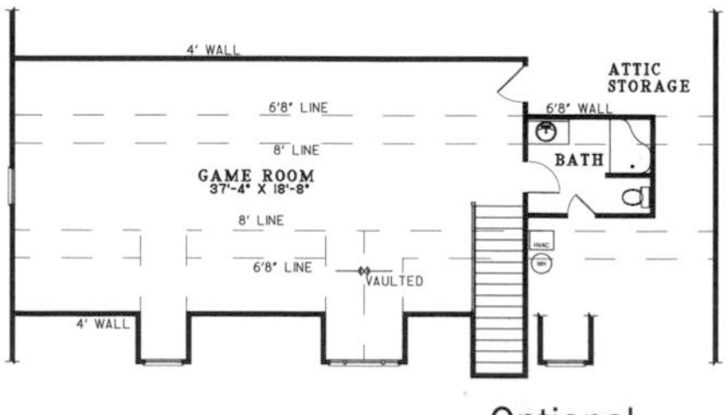

Optional Second Floor
812 sq. ft.

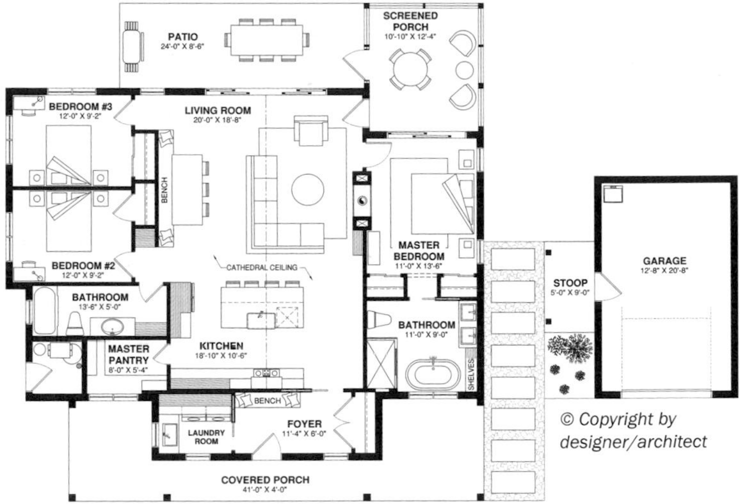

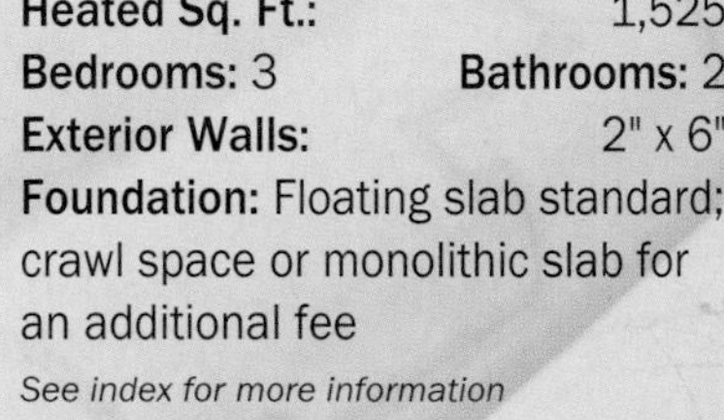

Plan #F08-032D-1192

Dimensions: 47'4" W x 36'10" D
Heated Sq. Ft.: 1,525
Bedrooms: 3 **Bathrooms:** 2
Exterior Walls: 2" x 6"
Foundation: Floating slab standard; crawl space or monolithic slab for an additional fee

See index for more information

Images provided by designer/architect

© Copyright by designer/architect

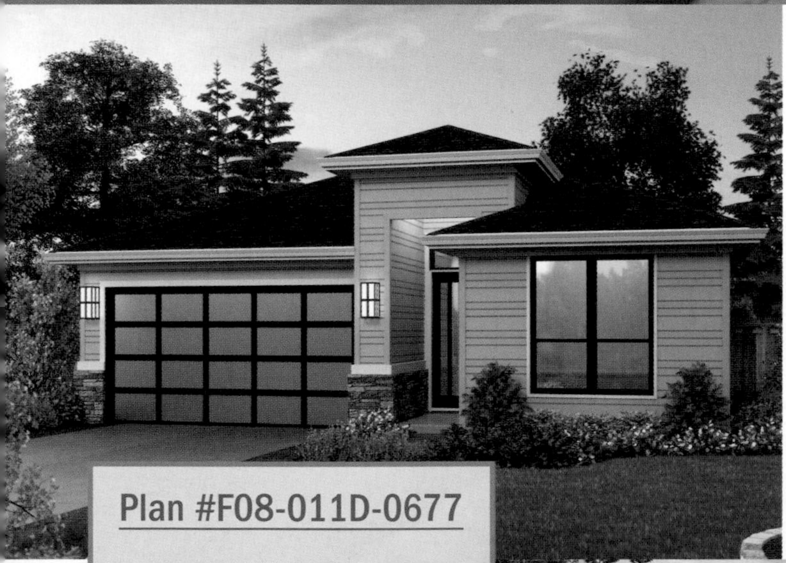

Plan #F08-011D-0677

Dimensions: 38' W x 72' D
Heated Sq. Ft.: 1,922
Bedrooms: 3 **Bathrooms:** 2
Exterior Walls: 2" x 6"
Foundation: Crawl space or slab standard; basement for an additional fee

See index for more information

Images provided by designer/architect

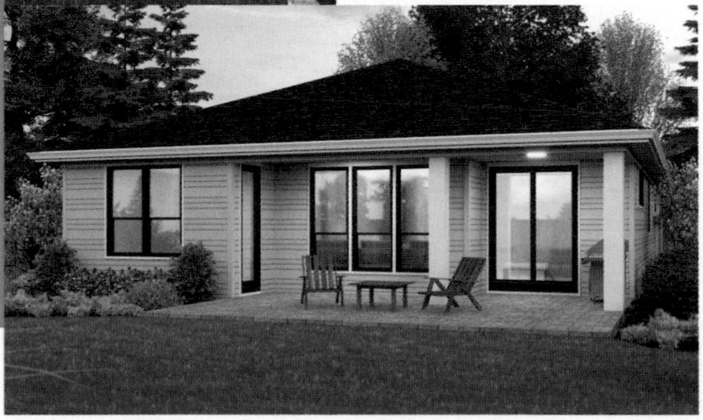

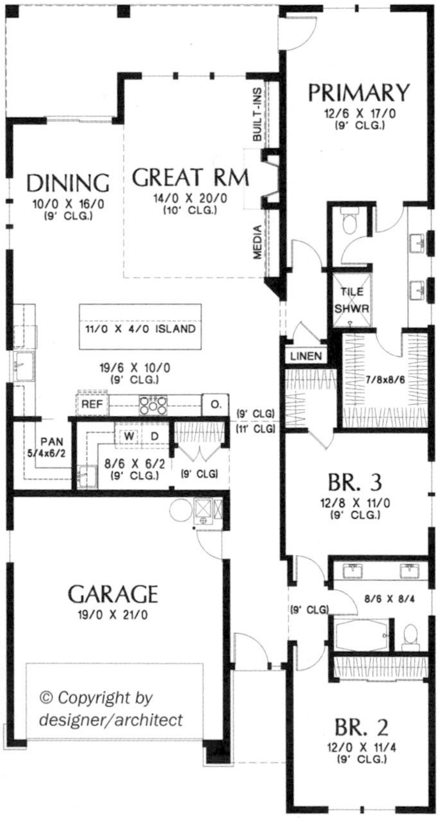

PRIMARY
12/6 X 17/0
(9' CLG.)
DINING
10/0 X 16/0
(9' CLG.)
GREAT RM
14/0 X 20/0
(10' CLG.)
BUILT-INS
MEDIA
TILE SHWR
11/0 X 4/0 ISLAND
19/6 X 10/0
(9' CLG.)
LINEN
7/8x8/6
REF
PAN
5/4x6/2
W D
8/6 X 6/2
(9' CLG.)
(9' CLG)
(11' CLG)
BR. 3
12/8 X 11/0
(9' CLG.)
GARAGE
19/0 X 21/0
8/6 X 8/4
BR. 2
12/0 X 11/4
(9' CLG.)

© Copyright by designer/architect

Plan #F08-130D-0337

Dimensions: 48' W x 63' D
Heated Sq. Ft.: 2,107
Bedrooms: 4 **Bathrooms:** 3½
Foundation: Slab standard; crawl space or basement for an additional fee

See index for more information

Images provided by designer/architect

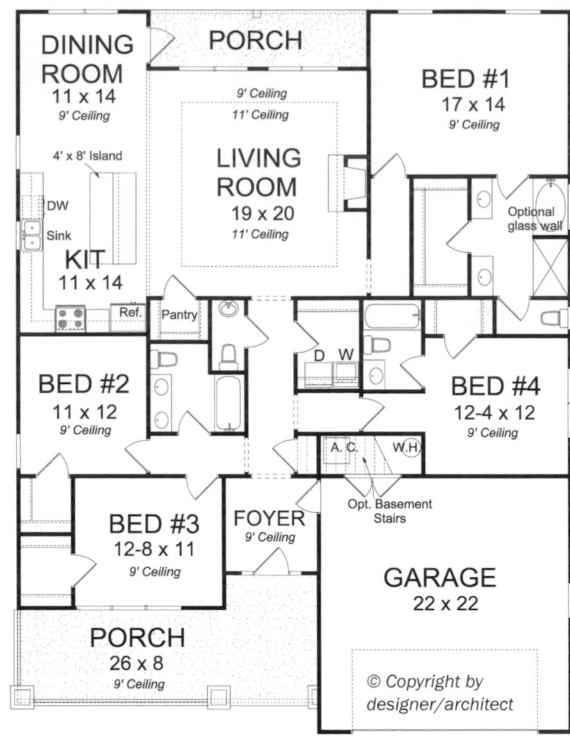

Plan #F08-139D-0066

Dimensions: 39'5" W x 65'11" D
Heated Sq. Ft.: 1,770
Bedrooms: 3 **Bathrooms:** 2
Exterior Walls: 2" x 6"
Foundation: Crawl space standard; slab, basement, daylight basement or walk-out basement for an additional fee

See index for more information

Images provided by designer/architect

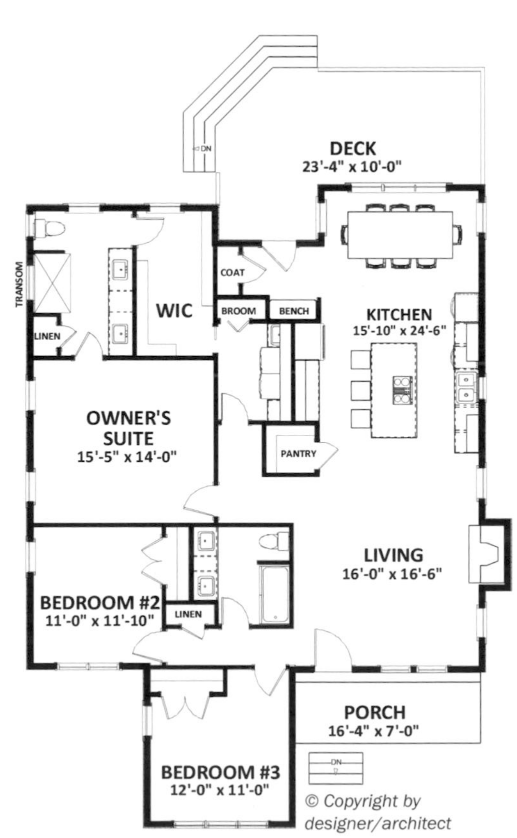

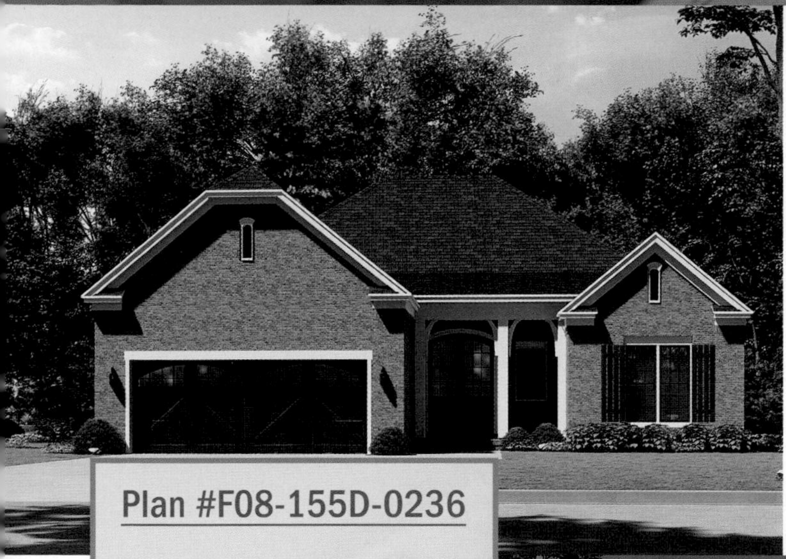

Plan #F08-155D-0236

Dimensions: 47' W x 54'4" D
Heated Sq. Ft.: 1,783
Bedrooms: 4 **Bathrooms:** 2
Foundation: Crawl space or slab standard; basement or daylight basement for an additional fee

See index for more information

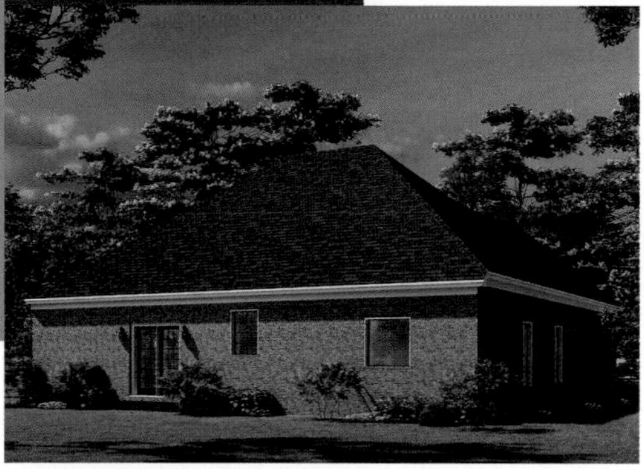

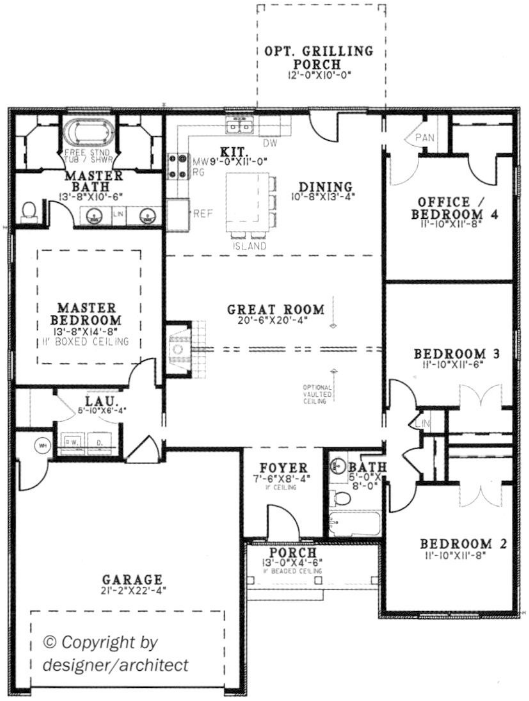

OPT. GRILLING PORCH
12'-0"X10'-0"
FREE STND TUB / SHWR
MASTER BATH
13'-8"X10'-6"
LIN
KIT.
MW 9'-0"X11'-0"
RG
DW
REF
ISLAND
DINING
10'-8"X13'-4"
PAN
OFFICE / BEDROOM 4
11'-10"X11'-8"
MASTER BEDROOM
13'-8"X14'-8"
11' BOXED CEILING
GREAT ROOM
20'-6"X20'-4"
OPTIONAL VAULTED CEILING
BEDROOM 3
11'-10"X11'-6"
LAU.
5'-10"X6'-4"
WH
W.
D.
LIN
FOYER
7'-6"X8'-4"
11' CEILING
BATH
5'-0"X 8'-0"
PORCH
13'-0"X4'-6"
11' BEADED CEILING
BEDROOM 2
11'-10"X11'-8"
GARAGE
21'-2"X22'-4"
© Copyright by designer/architect

Images provided by designer/architect

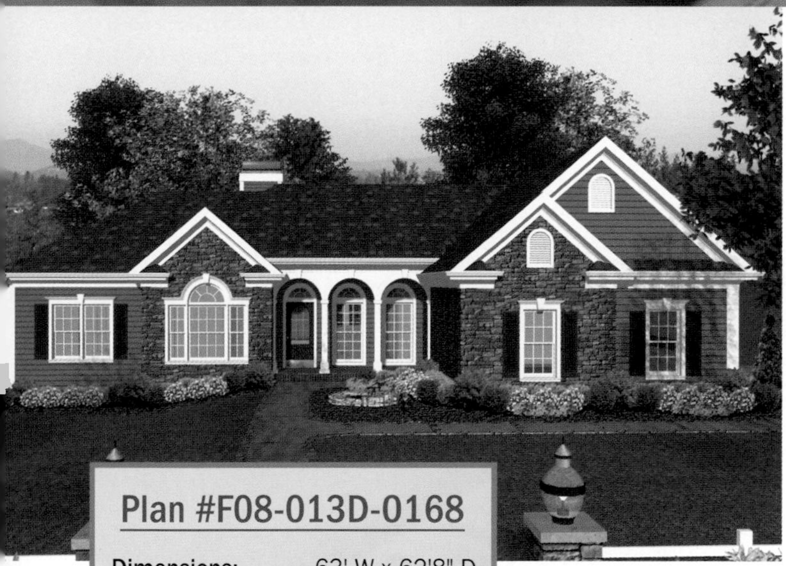

Plan #F08-013D-0168

Dimensions: 63' W x 62'8" D
Heated Sq. Ft.: 2,000
Bonus Sq. Ft.: 503
Bedrooms: 3 **Bathrooms:** 3½
Foundation: Slab standard; crawl space or basement for an additional fee

See index for more information

Images provided by designer/architect

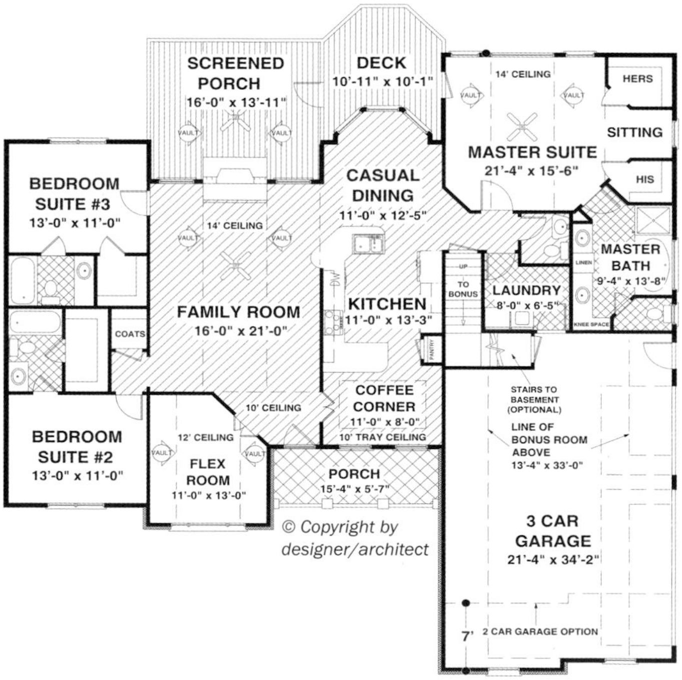

SCREENED PORCH
16'-0" x 13'-11"
VAULT
DECK
10'-11" x 10'-1"
14' CEILING
HERS
SITTING
MASTER SUITE
21'-4" x 15'-6"
HIS
BEDROOM SUITE #3
13'-0" x 11'-0"
CASUAL DINING
11'-0" x 12'-5"
14' CEILING
MASTER BATH
9'-4" x 13'-8"
LINEN
UP
TO BONUS
LAUNDRY
8'-0" x 6'-5"
KNEE SPACE
DW
FAMILY ROOM
16'-0" x 21'-0"
KITCHEN
11'-0" x 13'-3"
COATS
PANTRY
STAIRS TO BASEMENT (OPTIONAL)
COFFEE CORNER
11'-0" x 8'-0"
10' TRAY CEILING
10' CEILING
12' CEILING
LINE OF BONUS ROOM ABOVE
13'-4" x 33'-0"
BEDROOM SUITE #2
13'-0" x 11'-0"
FLEX ROOM
11'-0" x 13'-0"
PORCH
15'-4" x 5'-7"
3 CAR GARAGE
21'-4" x 34'-2"
© Copyright by designer/architect
7'
2 CAR GARAGE OPTION

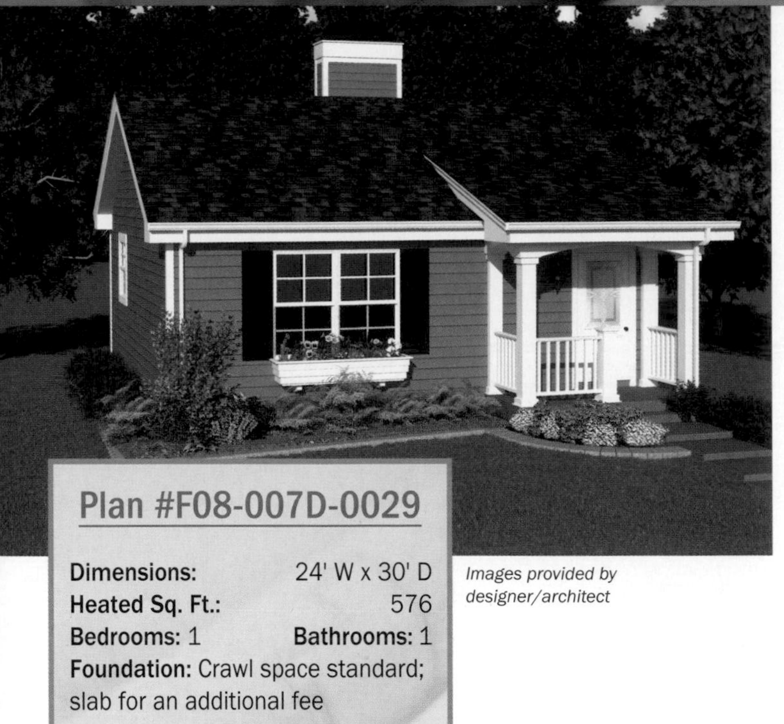

Plan #F08-007D-0029

Dimensions: 24' W x 30' D
Heated Sq. Ft.: 576
Bedrooms: 1 **Bathrooms:** 1
Foundation: Crawl space standard; slab for an additional fee

See index for more information

Images provided by designer/architect

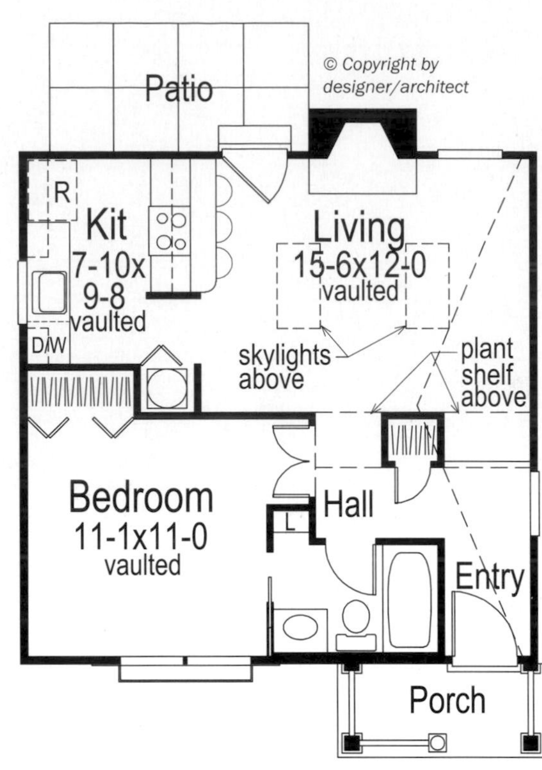

Plan #F08-065D-0307

Dimensions: 80'2" W x 44'6" D
Heated Sq. Ft.: 2,246
Bedrooms: 3 **Bathrooms:** 2
Foundation: Basement standard; crawl space or slab for an additional fee

Pricing subject to change

Images provided by designer/architect

Plan #F08-077D-0128

Dimensions: 69' W x 59'10" D
Heated Sq. Ft.: 2,000
Bonus Sq. Ft.: 359
Bedrooms: 3 **Bathrooms:** 2½
Foundation: Slab or crawl space, please specify when ordering; for basement version, see Plan #077D-0131 at houseplansandmore.com

See index for more information

Images provided by designer/architect

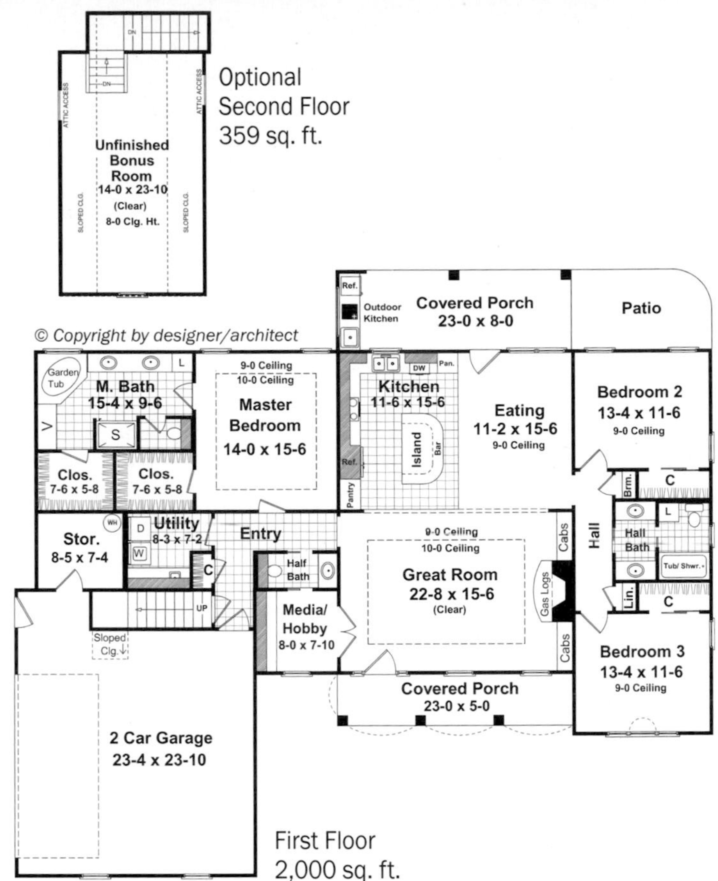

Plan #F08-155D-0222

Dimensions: 24' W x 53'2" D
Heated Sq. Ft.: 921
Bedrooms: 2 **Bathrooms:** 1
Foundation: Crawl space or slab, please specify when ordering

See index for more information

Images provided by designer/architect

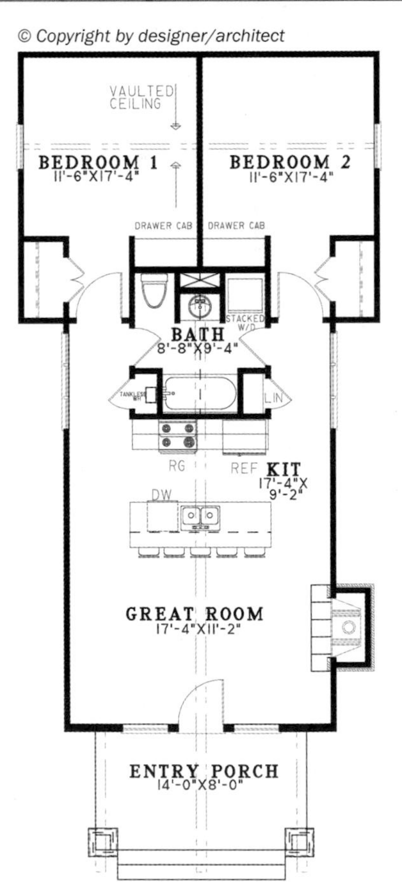

Images provided by designer/architect

Plan #F08-155D-0179

Dimensions: 60'8" W x 73'10" D
Heated Sq. Ft.: 2,382
Bedrooms: 3 **Bathrooms:** 2
Foundation: Crawl space or slab standard; basement or daylight basement for an additional fee

See index for more information

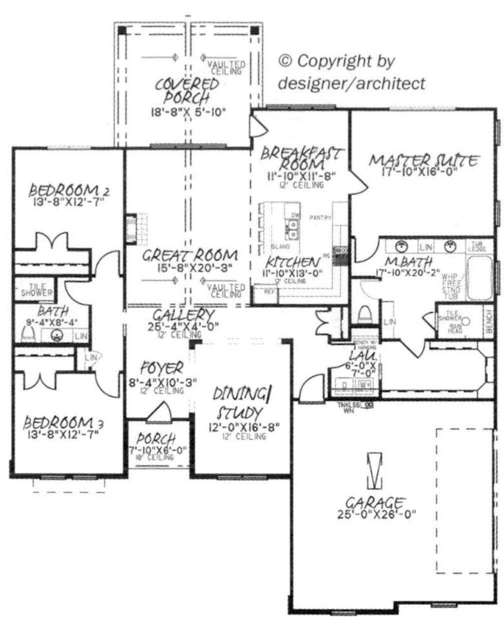

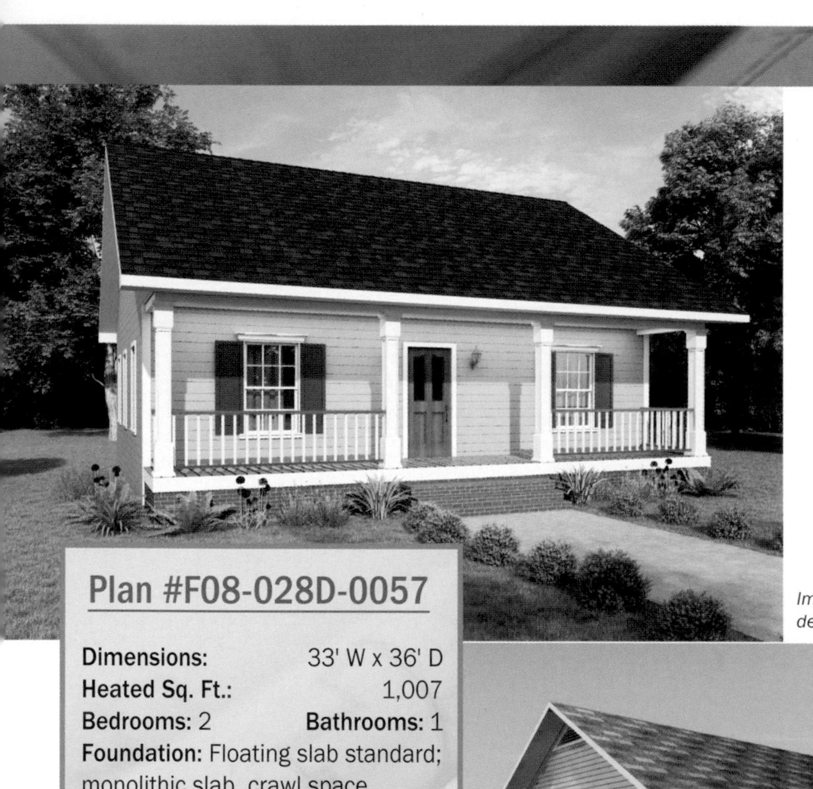

Images provided by designer/architect

Plan #F08-028D-0057

Dimensions: 33' W x 36' D
Heated Sq. Ft.: 1,007
Bedrooms: 2 **Bathrooms:** 1
Foundation: Floating slab standard; monolithic slab, crawl space, basement or walk-out basement for an additional fee

See index for more information

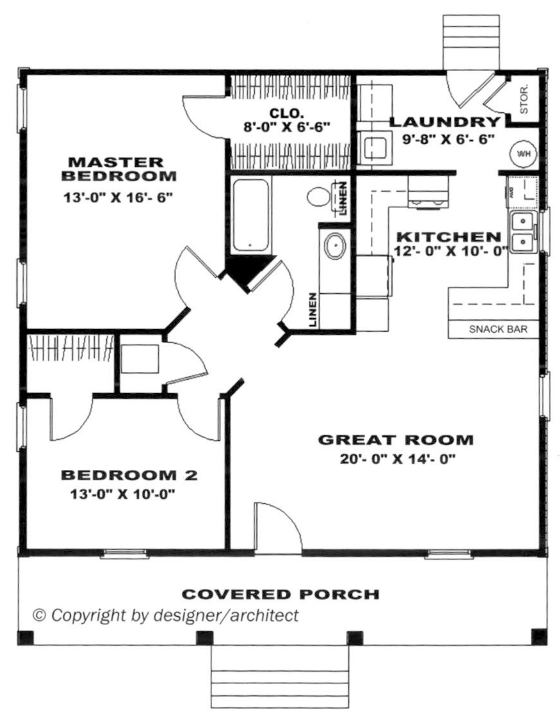

Plan #F08-077D-0008

Dimensions: 31'8" W x 26' D
Heated Sq. Ft.: 600
Bedrooms: 1 **Bathrooms:** 1
Foundation: Basement, crawl space or slab, please specify when ordering

See index for more information

Images provided by designer/architect

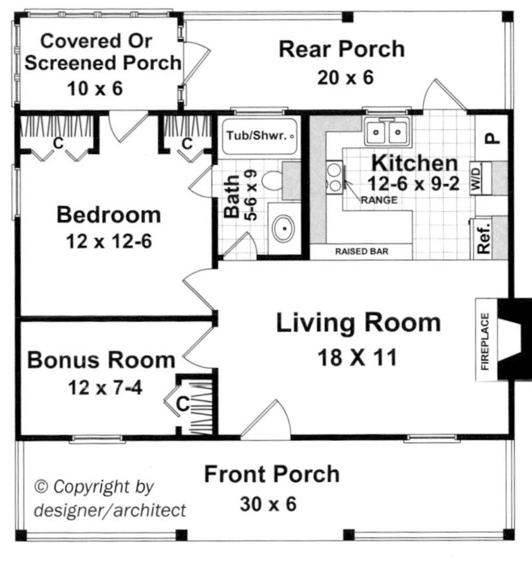

Plan #F08-141D-0013

Dimensions: 50' W x 33' D
Heated Sq. Ft.: 1,200
Bedrooms: 2 **Bathrooms:** 1
Foundation: Slab standard; crawl space, basement or walk-out basement for an additional fee

See index for more information

© Copyright by designer/architect

Images provided by designer/architect

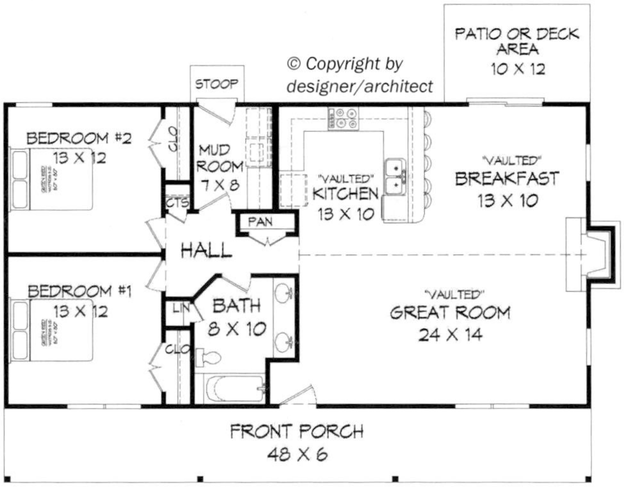

Plan #F08-028D-0022

Images provided by designer/architect

Dimensions: 70' W x 80' D
Heated Sq. Ft.: 3,029
Bonus Sq. Ft.: 288
Bedrooms: 4 **Bathrooms:** 3
Foundation: Floating slab standard; monolithic slab, crawl space, basement or walk-out basement for an additional fee

See index for more information

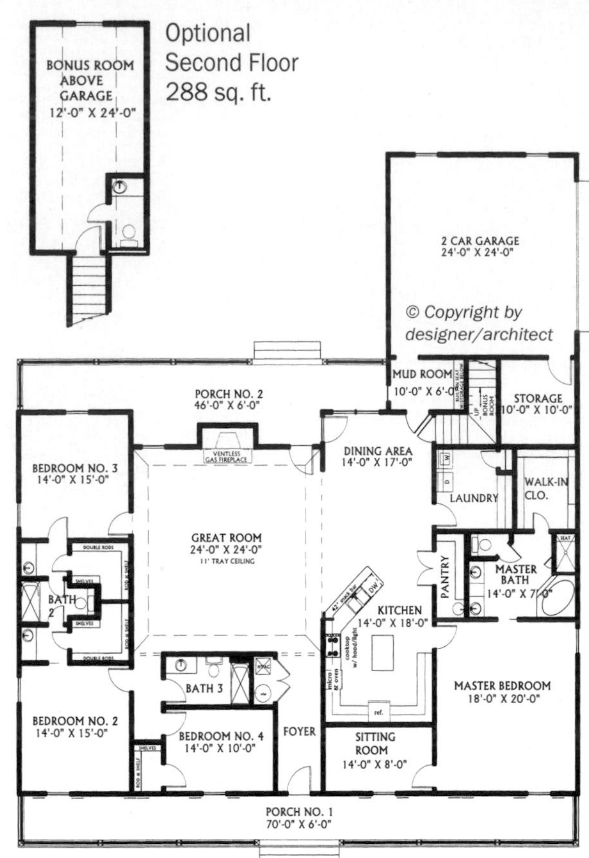

First Floor
3,029 sq. ft.

Plan #F08-144D-0013

Images provided by designer/architect

Dimensions: 24' W x 36' D
Heated Sq. Ft.: 624
Bedrooms: 1 **Bathrooms:** 1
Exterior Walls: 2" x 6"
Foundation: Crawl space or slab, please specify when ordering

See index for more information

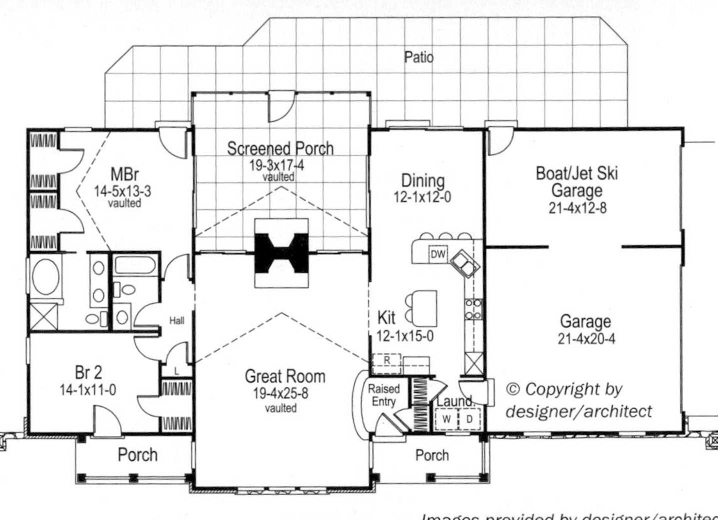

Images provided by designer/architect

Plan #F08-007D-0137

Dimensions: 72'8" W x 44'4" D
Heated Sq. Ft.: 1,568
Bedrooms: 2 **Bathrooms:** 2
Foundation: Crawl space standard; slab for an additional fee

See index for more information

Plan #F08-147D-0001

Dimensions: 40'8" W x 49'4" D
Heated Sq. Ft.: 1,472
Bedrooms: 3 **Bathrooms:** 2
Foundation: Basement, slab or crawl space, please specify when ordering

See index for more information

Images provided by designer/architect

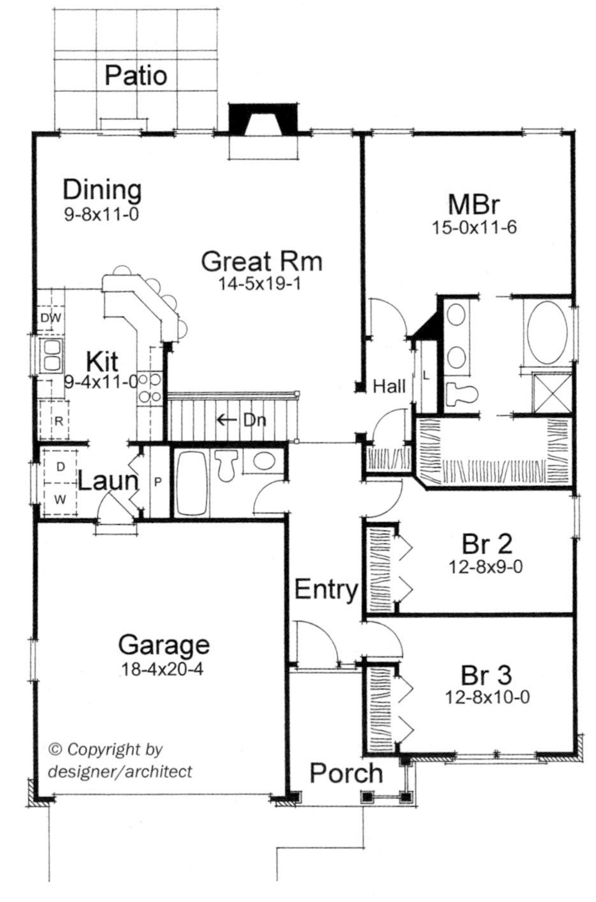

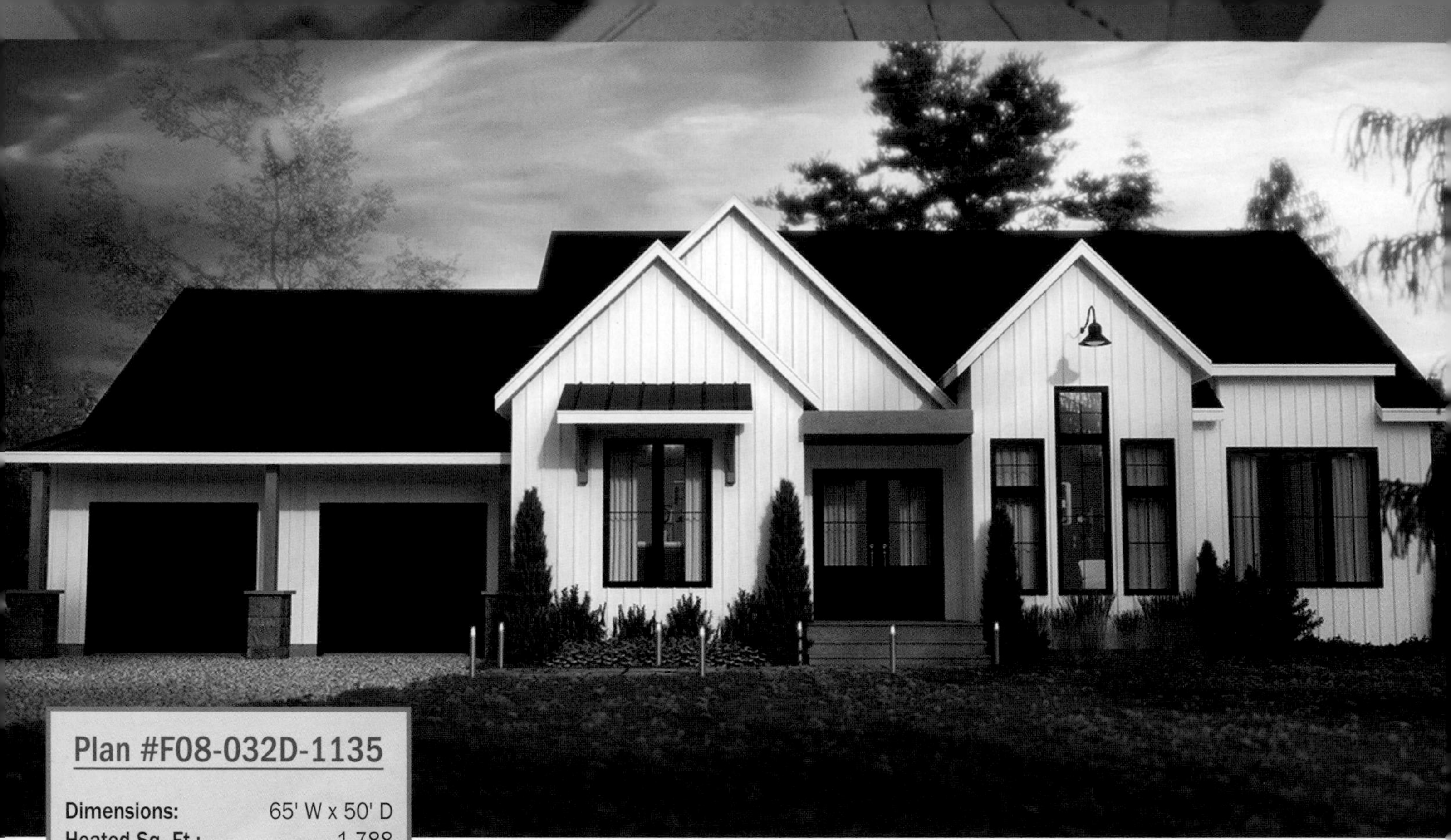

Plan #F08-032D-1135

Dimensions: 65' W x 50' D
Heated Sq. Ft.: 1,788
Bonus Sq. Ft.: 1,788
Bedrooms: 2 **Bathrooms:** 2
Exterior Walls: 2" x 6"
Foundation: Basement standard; crawl space, floating slab or monolithic slab for an additional fee

See index for more information

Features

- A cozy office/den has enough space for two work stations and a vaulted ceiling
- The laundry room is near the master bedroom for convenience and has a stylish barn door entry
- The open kitchen with island overlooks the living room with a fireplace
- The master suite has two walk-in closets and a bath with a freestanding tub
- The mud room connects to the garage
- The optional lower level has an additional 1,788 square feet of living are
- 2-car front entry garage

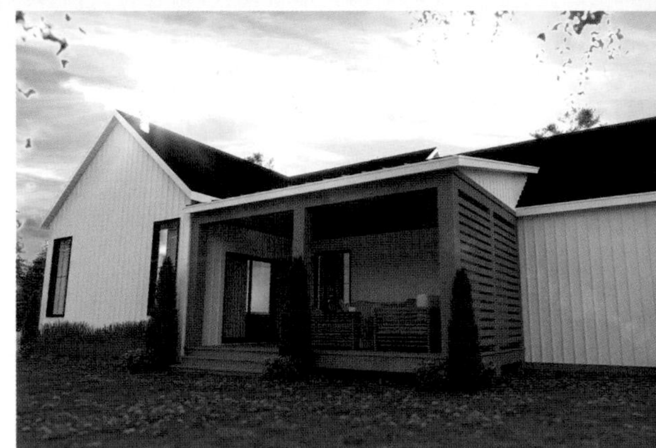

Images provided by designer/architect

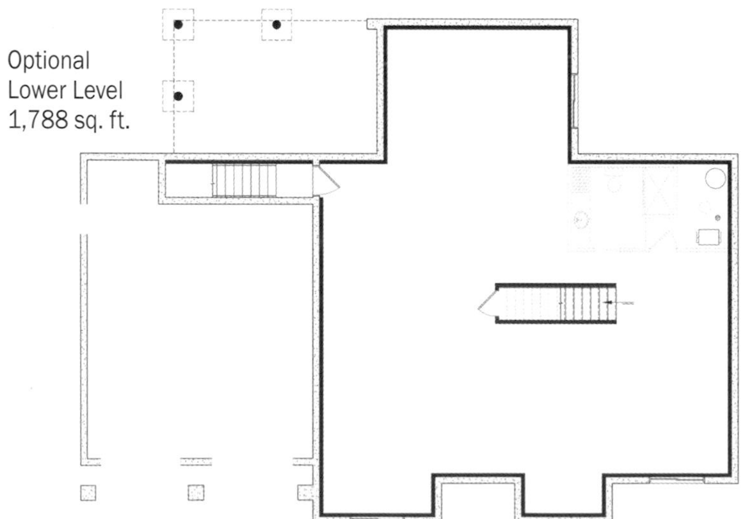

Optional Lower Level
1,788 sq. ft.

© Copyright by designer/architect

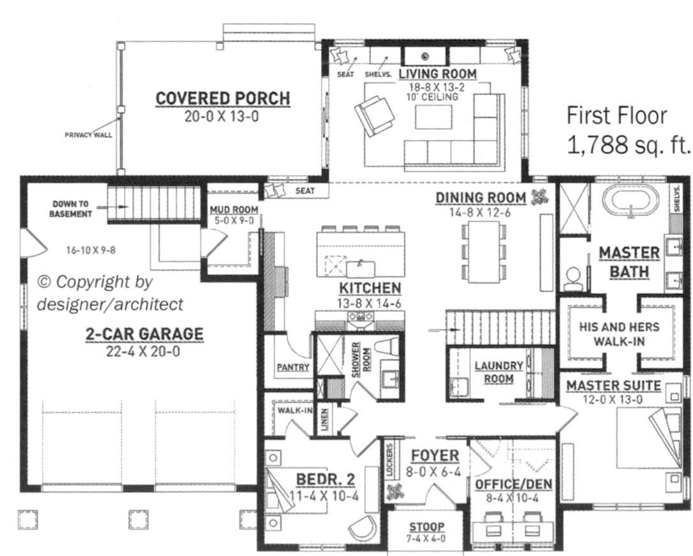

First Floor
1,788 sq. ft.

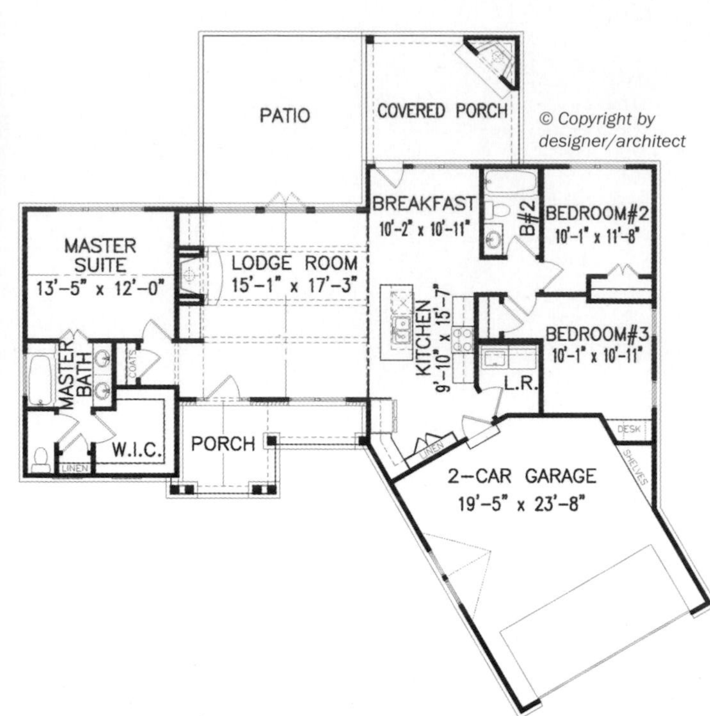

© Copyright by designer/architect

Plan #F08-056D-0122

Images provided by designer/architect

Dimensions: 63'9" W x 63'6" D
Heated Sq. Ft.: 1,338
Bedrooms: 3 **Bathrooms:** 2
Foundation: Slab standard; crawl space for an additional fee

See index for more information

Plan #F08-084D-0087

Images provided by designer/architect

Dimensions: 78' W x 80' D
Heated Sq. Ft.: 3,507
Bonus Sq. Ft.: 716
Bedrooms: 4 **Bathrooms:** 3
Foundation: Slab standard; crawl space or basement for an additional fee

See index for more information

Optional Second Floor
716 sq. ft.

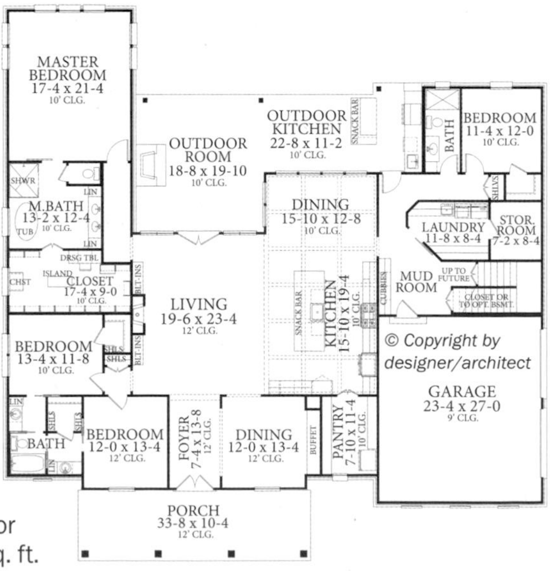

© Copyright by designer/architect

First Floor
3,507 sq. ft.

Plan #F08-077D-0024

Dimensions: 54' W x 48' D
Heated Sq. Ft.: 1,488
Bedrooms: 3 **Bathrooms:** 2
Foundation: Basement or daylight basement, please specify when ordering; for the crawl space or slab version, see Plan #077D-0023 at houseplansandmore.com

See index for more information

Images provided by designer/architect

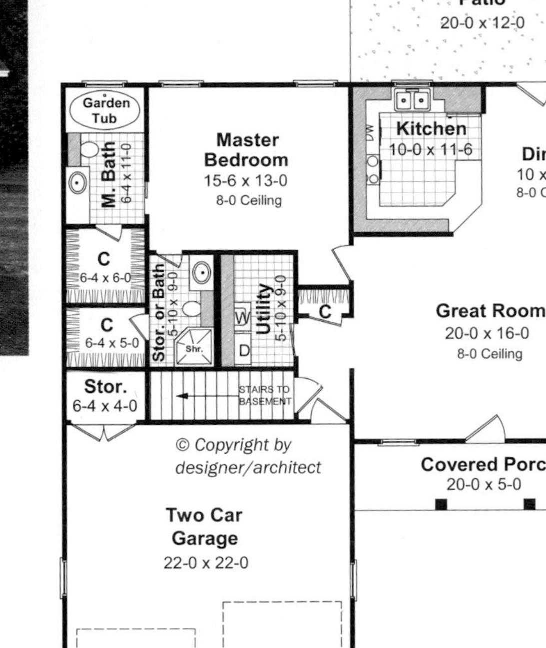

Plan #F08-001D-0085

Dimensions: 28' W x 38' D
Heated Sq. Ft.: 720
Bedrooms: 2 **Bathrooms:** 1
Foundation: Crawl space standard; slab for an additional fee

See index for more information

Images provided by designer/architect

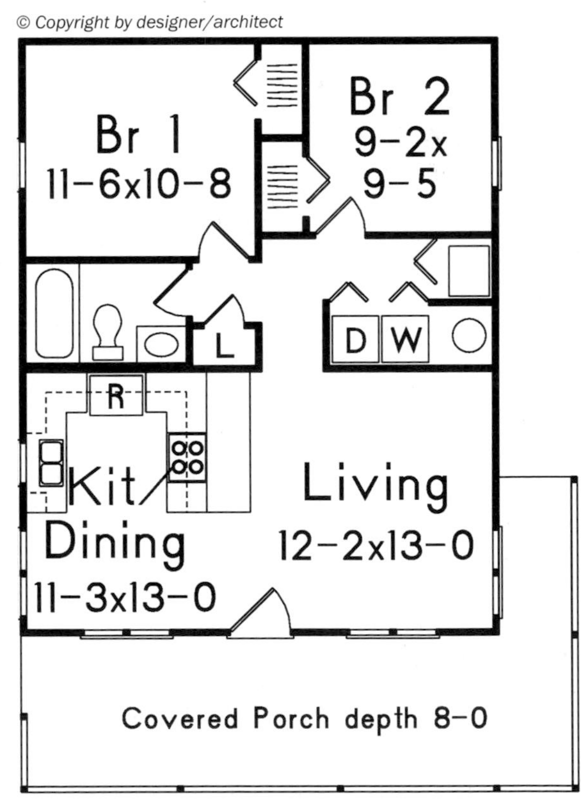

Plan #F08-143D-0010

Dimensions: 56' W x 27'6" D
Heated Sq. Ft.: 1,538
Bedrooms: 3 **Bathrooms:** 2
Exterior Walls: 2" x 6"
Foundation: Slab, crawl space or basement, please specify when ordering
See index for more information

Images provided by designer/architect

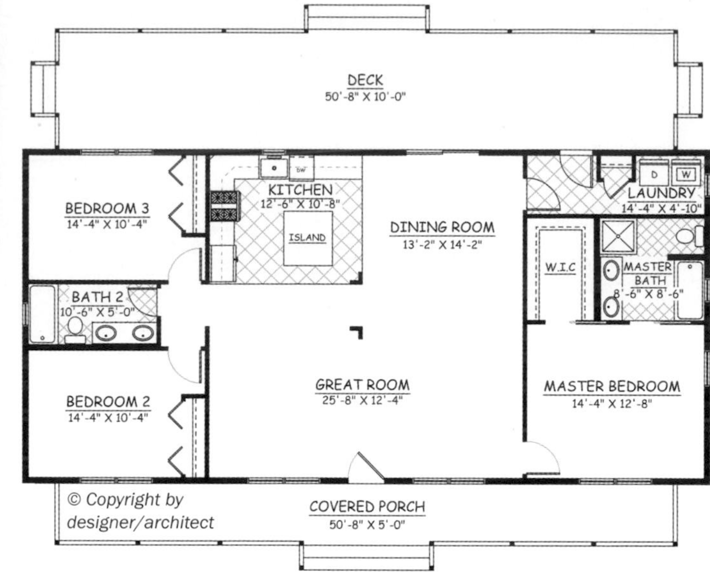

Plan #F08-007D-0178

Dimensions: 42' W x 48'8" D
Heated Sq. Ft.: 1,203
Bedrooms: 4 **Bathrooms:** 2½
Foundation: Basement standard; crawl space or slab for an additional fee
See index for more information

Images provided by designer/architect

Dn
Walk
P
DW
R
Kit
9-11x
13-9
vaulted
Br 2
10-0x10-1
Mbr
11-0x13-6
L
Dn
Patio
Dine
Plant Shelf
Above
Hall
Br 3
9-6x10-1
Br 4
11-2x10-1
Living Rm.
15-9x17-6
vaulted
Dn
E
Porch
Garage
19-4x20-4
© Copyright by
designer/architect

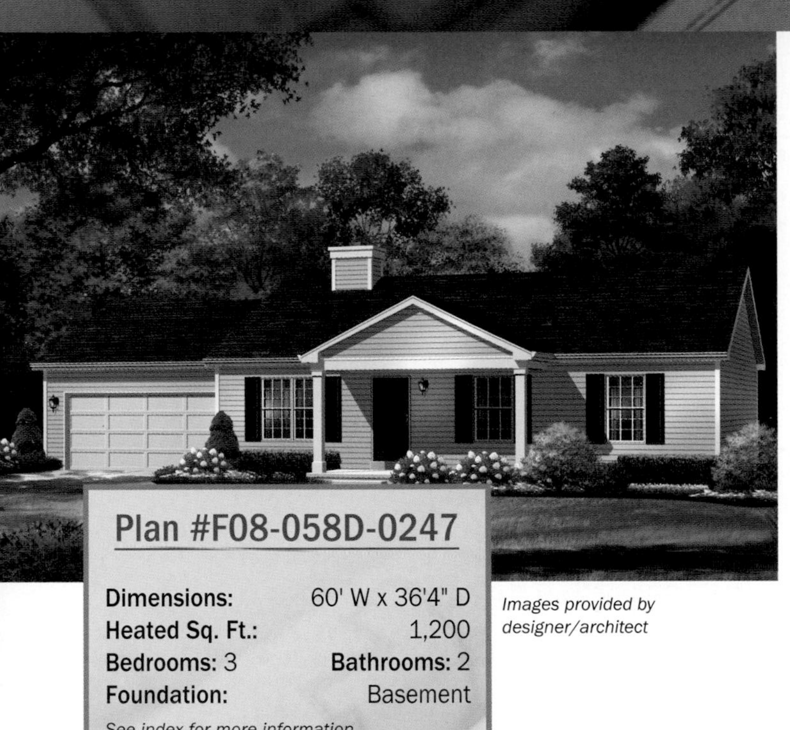

Plan #F08-058D-0247

Dimensions:	60' W x 36'4" D
Heated Sq. Ft.:	1,200
Bedrooms: 3	**Bathrooms:** 2
Foundation:	Basement

See index for more information

Images provided by designer/architect

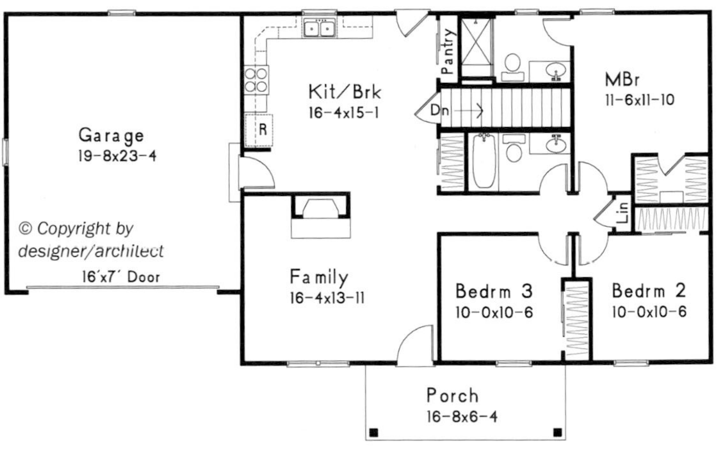

Plan #F08-058D-0010

Dimensions:	26' W x 32' D
Heated Sq. Ft.:	676
Bedrooms: 1	**Bathrooms:** 1
Foundation:	Crawl space

See index for more information

Images provided by designer/architect

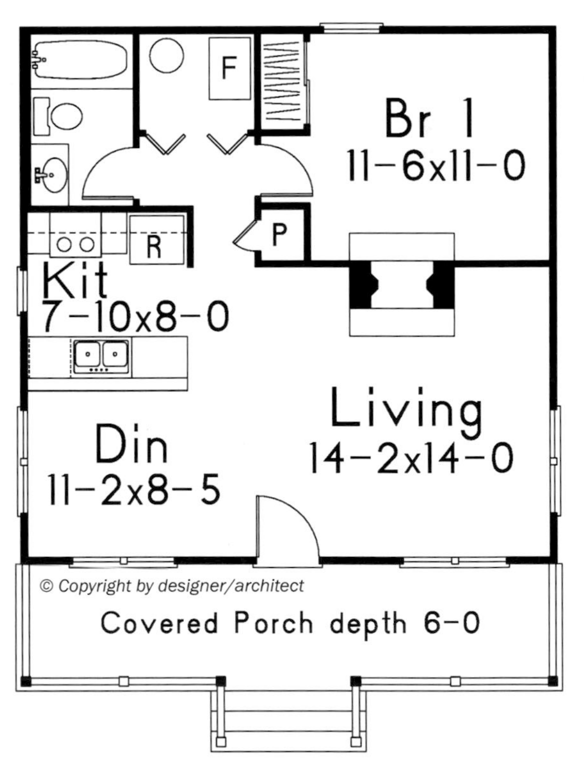

Plan #F08-084D-0091

Dimensions: 59' W x 68'2" D
Heated Sq. Ft.: 1,936
Bedrooms: 3 **Bathrooms:** 2
Foundation: Slab standard; crawl space for an additional fee

See index for more information

Features

- The perfect stylish ranch home with a split bedroom layout
- Enter the dining/foyer and find a beamed ceiling for added interest and it opens to the vaulted living area with a centered fireplace
- The kitchen enjoys an open feel and has an island and a mud room entrance from the garage
- The vaulted master bedroom has a built-in bench for added character plus a walk-in closet, and a private bath with an oversized tub and a walk-in shower with seat
- Two additional bedrooms share a full bath
- 2-car side entry garage

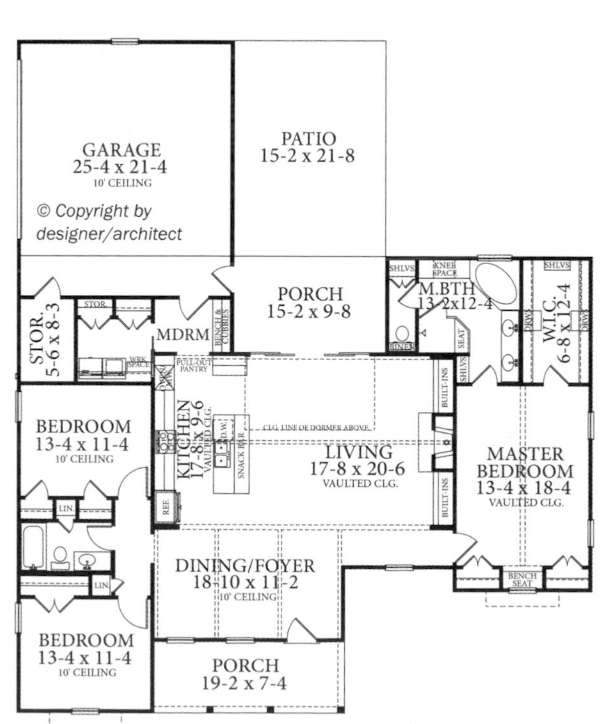

Images provided by designer/architect

Images provided by designer/architect

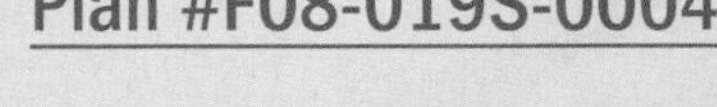

Plan #F08-019S-0004

Dimensions: 81'3" W x 101'4" D
Heated Sq. Ft.: 3,381
Bedrooms: 3 **Bathrooms:** 4
Foundation: Slab standard; crawl space or basement for an additional fee

See index for more information

Features

- This luxury one-story home offers ultra private bedrooms and plenty of spaces for entertaining in style
- As you enter the foyer you are greeted by a wine bar to the left
- The spacious great room enjoys covered porch views and a cozy corner fireplace
- The open kitchen has an island with a breakfast bar extension, a drop zone from the garage and a walk-in pantry
- A friend's entry off the side of the home has the office steps away creating an easy way for clients or business partners to access the office space
- The master suite enjoys an oversized bath with all of the amenities, a huge walk-in closet with utility room access and a nearby exercise room
- A fun game room is near the secondary bedrooms and offers plenty of space for billiards, a gaming area or a card table
- 3-car side entry garage

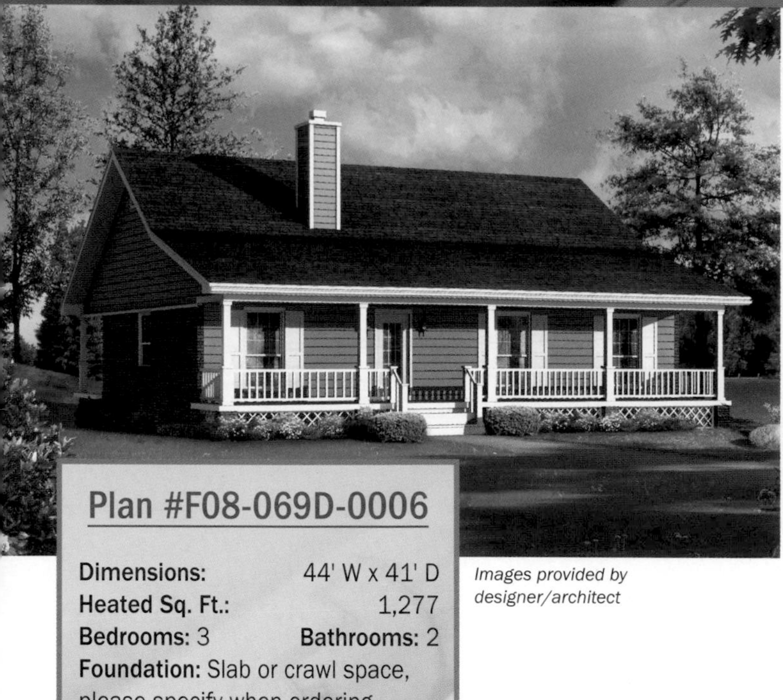

Plan #F08-069D-0006

Dimensions: 44' W x 41' D
Heated Sq. Ft.: 1,277
Bedrooms: 3 **Bathrooms:** 2
Foundation: Slab or crawl space, please specify when ordering

See index for more information

Images provided by designer/architect

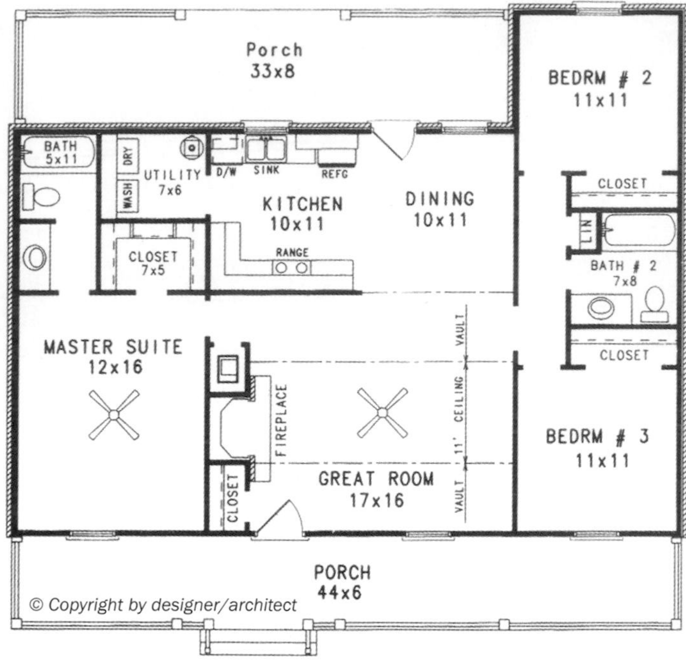

Plan #F08-069D-0117

Dimensions: 38' W x 40' D
Heated Sq. Ft.: 1,094
Bedrooms: 2 **Bathrooms:** 2
Foundation: Slab or crawl space, please specify when ordering

See index for more information

Images provided by designer/architect

Plan #F08-051D-0921

Dimensions: 50' W x 53'8" D
Heated Sq. Ft.: 1,583
Bedrooms: 3 **Bathrooms:** 2
Exterior Walls: 2" x 6"
Foundation: Basement standard; crawl space or slab for an additional fee

See index for more information

Images provided by designer/architect

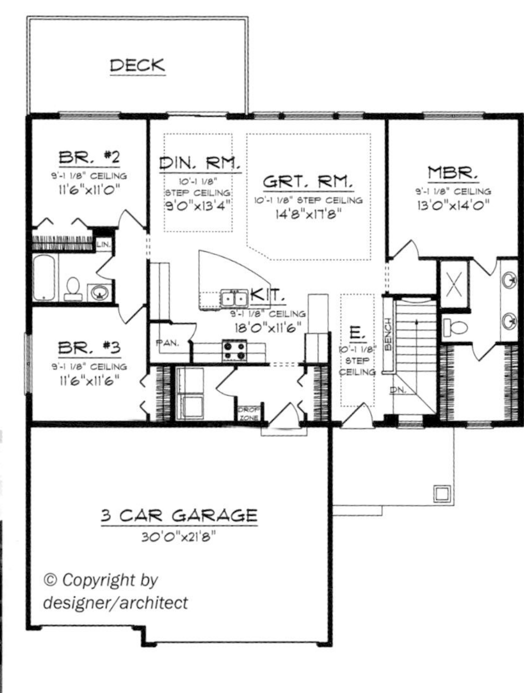

© Copyright by designer/architect

Plan #F08-028D-0140

Dimensions: 60' W x 70' D
Heated Sq. Ft.: 2,160
Bedrooms: 3 **Bathrooms:** 2½
Exterior Walls: 2" x 6"
Foundation: Floating slab

See index for more information

Images provided by designer/architect

© Copyright by designer/architect

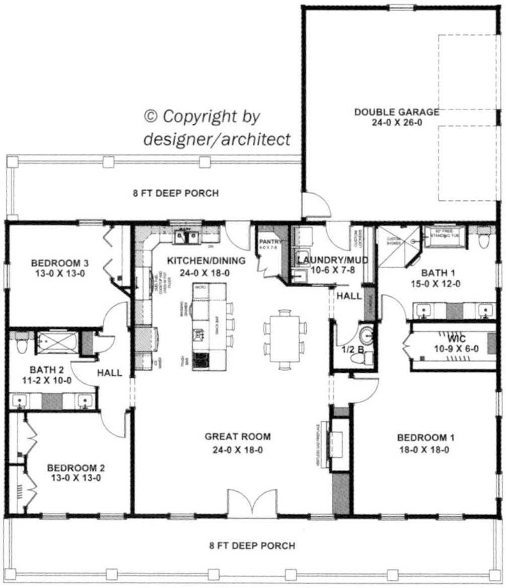

Plan #F08-011D-0738

Dimensions: 59' W x 59'4" D
Heated Sq. Ft.: 2,117
Bedrooms: 3 **Bathrooms:** 2½
Exterior Walls: 2" x 6"
Foundation: Crawl space or slab standard; basement for an additional fee

See index for more information

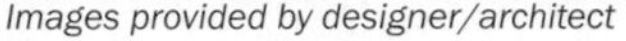

Images provided by designer/architect

Features

- Contemporary style one-story has an open-concept floor plan that's works well for many homeowners
- Enter the foyer and discover a great room with fireplace to the left and just beyond is a kitchen with a large centered island, great for meal prepping and casual dining
- A small, efficient office is right off the foyer on the right
- A sunny dining area is found at the back of the home and enjoys covered porch access
- The master bedroom has large corner windows, a walk-in closet and a private bath with a free-standing tub, separate shower and double-bowl vanity
- Two additional bedrooms share a Jack and Jill style bath
- 3-car front entry garage

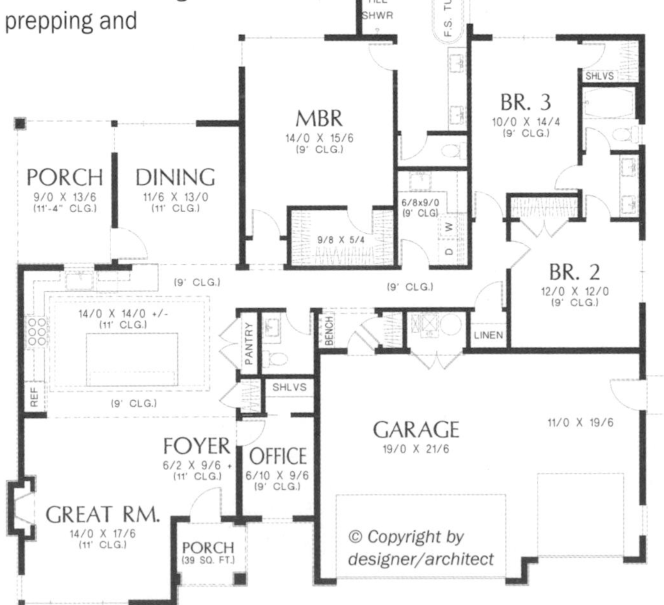

Plan #F08-011D-0627

Dimensions: 52' W x 61' D
Heated Sq. Ft.: 1,878
Bedrooms: 3 **Bathrooms:** 2
Exterior Walls: 2" x 6"
Foundation: Crawl space or slab standard; basement for an additional fee

See index for more information

Features

- Upon entering the foyer that is flanked by benches, there is a soaring 16' ceiling allowing for plenty of natural light to enter the space
- Beautiful family-friendly design with a centrally located great room, dining room and kitchen combination and the sleeping quarters in a private wing
- The master suite is complete with the amenities of a walk-in closet, a double-bowl vanity and separate tub and shower units in the private bath
- Enjoy outdoor living on the covered rear patio that has a built-in barbecue grill and cabinets for ease when cooking outdoors
- 2-car front entry garage

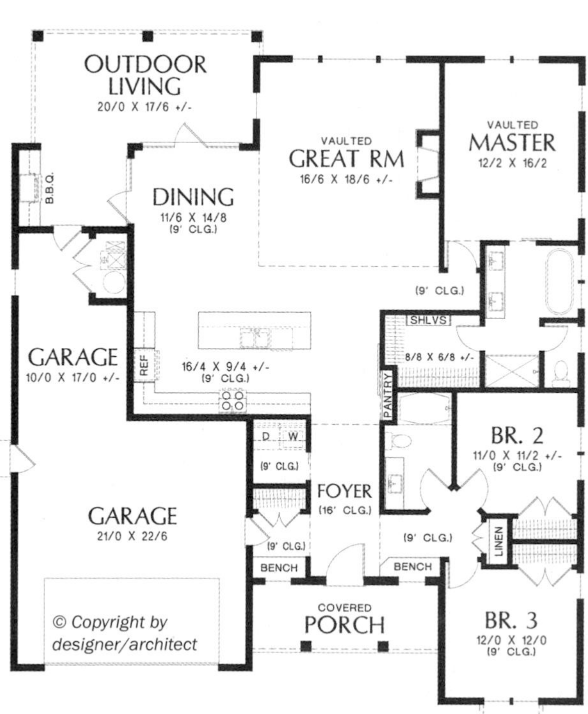

Images provided by designer/architect

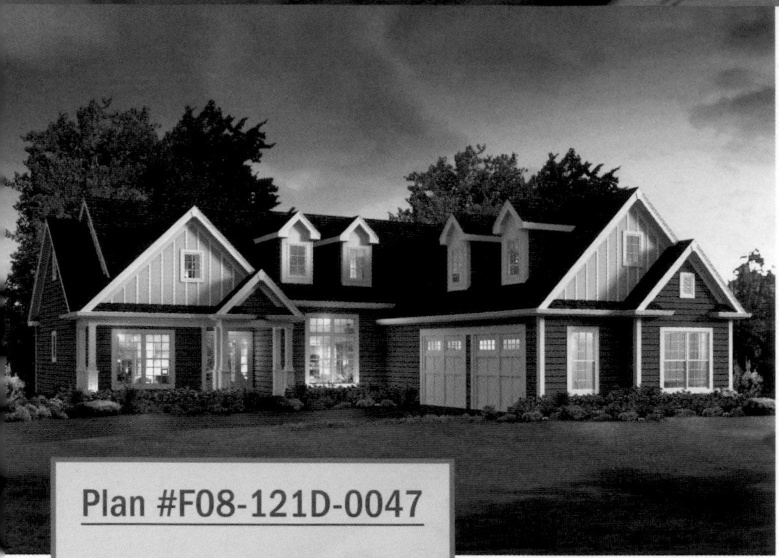

Plan #F08-121D-0047

Dimensions: 60' W x 70' D
Heated Sq. Ft.: 1,983
Bonus Sq. Ft.: 404
Bedrooms: 3 **Bathrooms:** 2
Foundation: Basement standard; crawl space or slab for an additional fee

See index for more information

Images provided by designer/architect

Bonus Rm
12-0x31-8

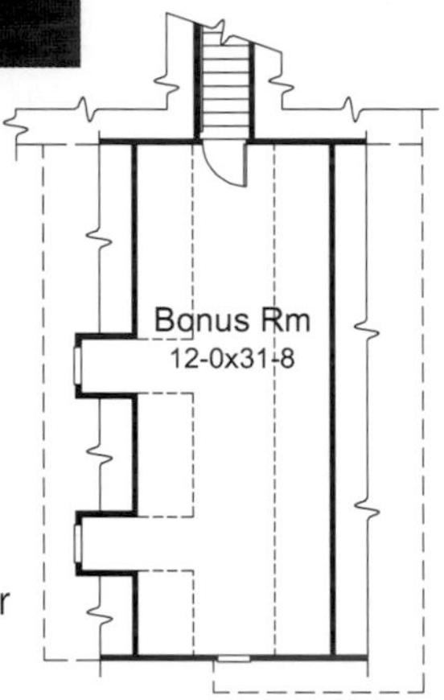

Optional
Second Floor
404 sq. ft.

Patio
Br 2
11-5x11-4
Brkfst
12-3x10-0
Vaulted
MBr
14-9x16-8
Std Coffer
Opt Vault
Great Rm
17-7x20-1
Vaulted
DW
Kitchen
12-3x10-5
Vaulted
R
L
Br 3
11-5x11-1
Entry
P
Dn
Up
Dining
11-8x10-7
13' Clg
Laun/
Mud
Rm
W
D
L
Porch
Workshop Area
Garage
22-8x33-8
© Copyright by
designer/architect

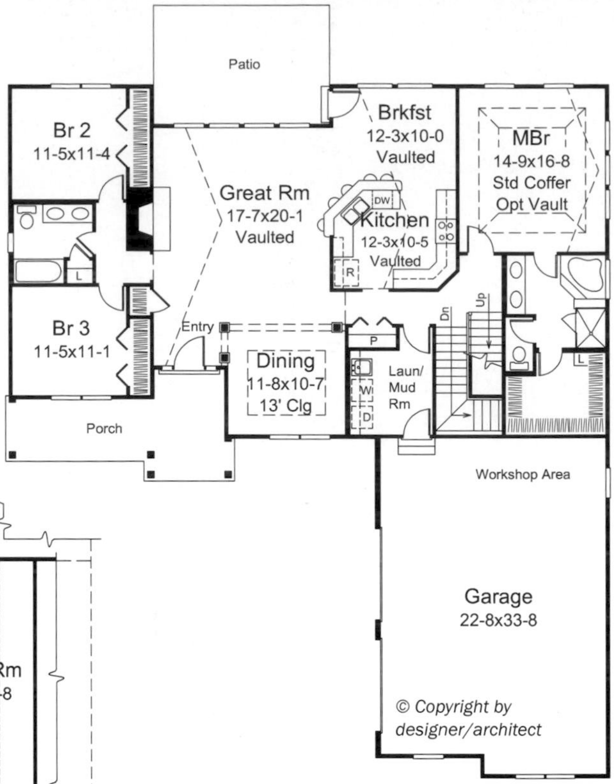

First Floor
1,983 sq. ft.

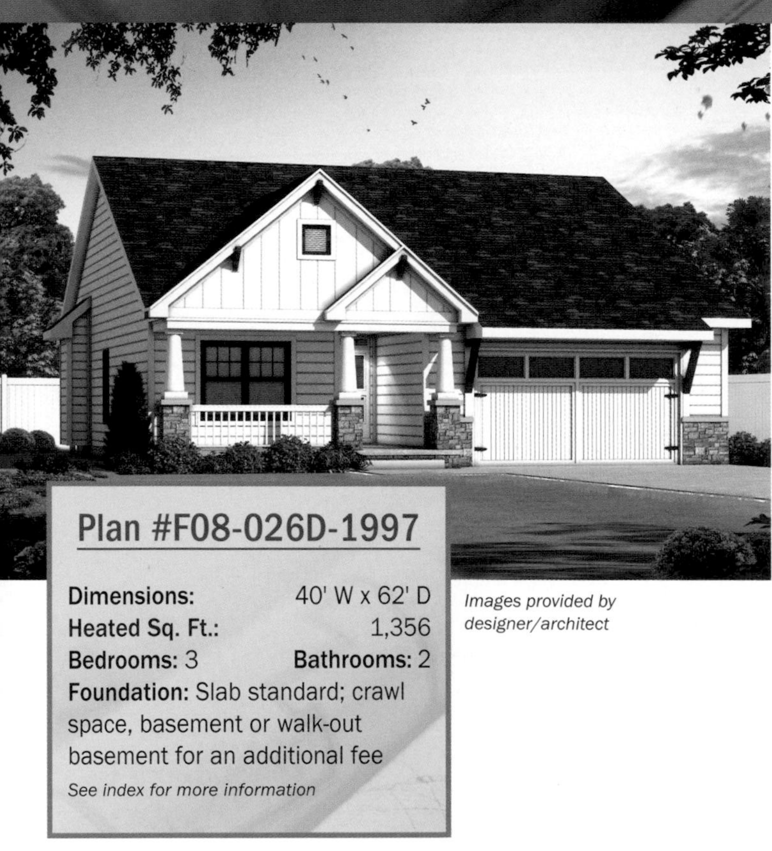

Plan #F08-026D-1997

Dimensions: 40' W x 62' D
Heated Sq. Ft.: 1,356
Bedrooms: 3 **Bathrooms:** 2
Foundation: Slab standard; crawl space, basement or walk-out basement for an additional fee

See index for more information

Images provided by designer/architect

Br.2
10⁴ x 10⁰
COVERED
PATIO
Dining
Room
10⁰ x 10⁰
10'-0" CEILING
Family
Room
18⁸ x 14⁰
10'-0" CEILING
R
L
Kit.
10⁰ x 11⁰
P
Br.3
10⁴ x 10⁰
D
W
NICHE
GALLERY
L
NICHE
GALLERY
Garage
20⁸ x 22⁰
Mbr.
12⁰ x 14⁰
10'-0" CEILING
© Copyright by
designer/architect
COVERED
PORCH

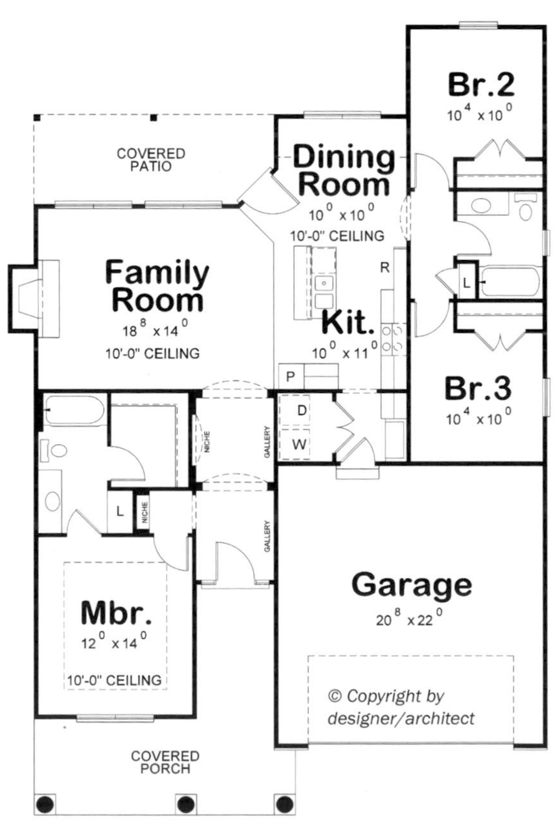

Plan #F08-001D-0031

Dimensions: 48' W x 66' D
Heated Sq. Ft.: 1,501
Bedrooms: 3 **Bathrooms:** 2
Foundation: Basement standard; crawl space or slab for an additional fee

See index for more information

Images provided by designer/architect

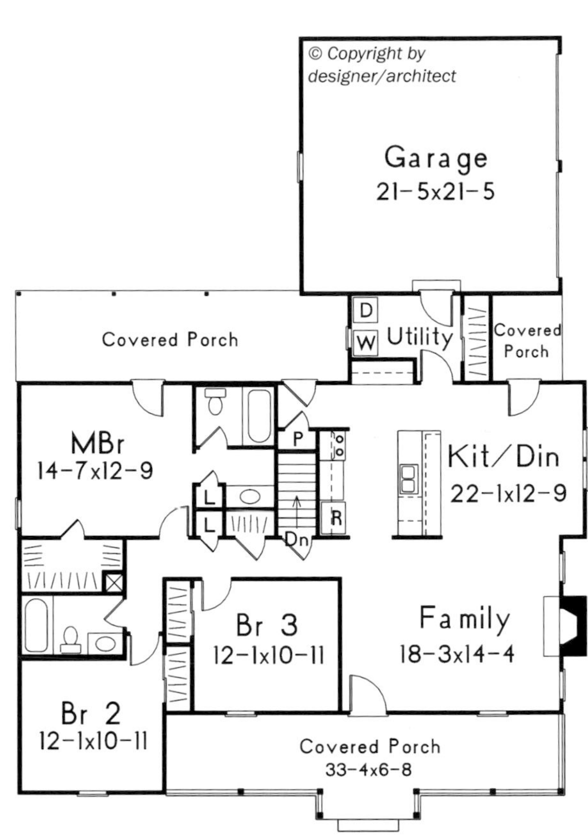

Plan #F08-077D-0043

Dimensions: 64' W x 45'10" D
Heated Sq. Ft.: 1,752
Bedrooms: 3 **Bathrooms:** 2
Foundation: Crawl space, slab, basement, daylight basement or walk-out basement, please specify when ordering

See index for more information

Images provided by designer/architect

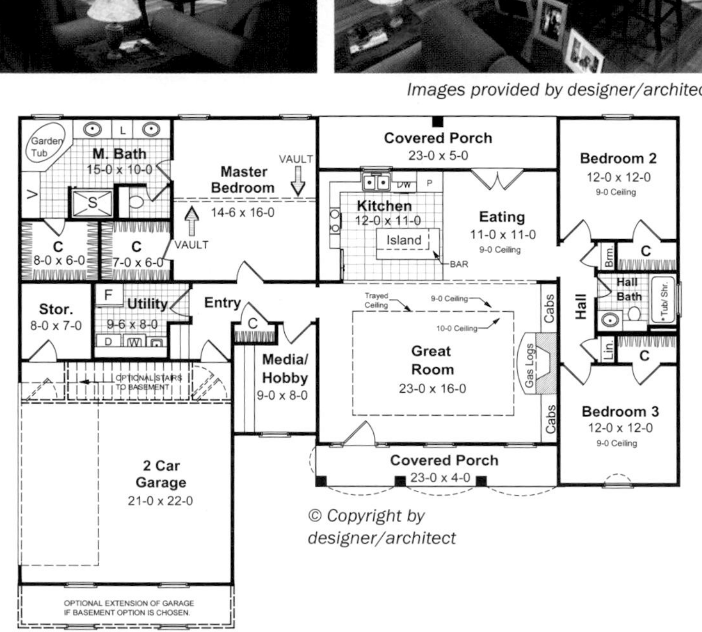

Plan #F08-051D-0970

Dimensions: 37' W x 68' D
Heated Sq. Ft.: 1,354
Bedrooms: 2 **Bathrooms:** 2
Exterior Walls: 2" x 6"
Foundation: Basement standard; crawl space or slab for an additional fee

See index for more information

Images provided by designer/architect

Features

- Small and stylish, this home offers the layout everyone loves in an easy-to-maintain size
- The covered front porch is large enough for relaxing, while the rear has a screened porch with access onto an open deck, perfect when grilling
- The private master bedroom has a private bath with an oversized walk-in shower, a double-bowl vanity, and a spacious walk-in closet
- Bedroom #2 is just steps away from a full bath
- 2-car front entry garage

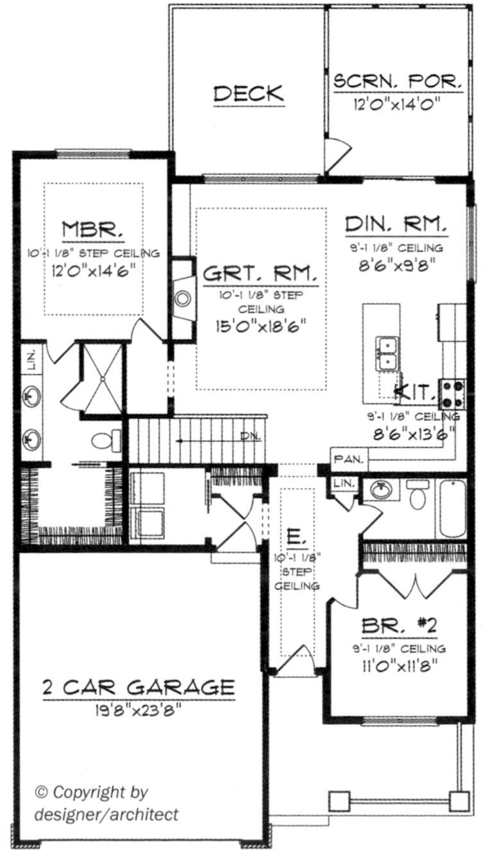

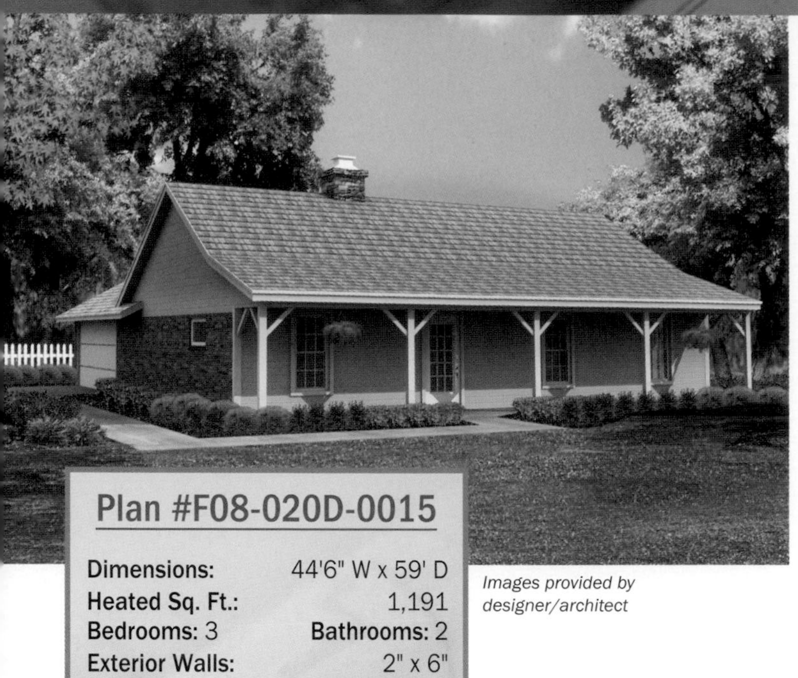

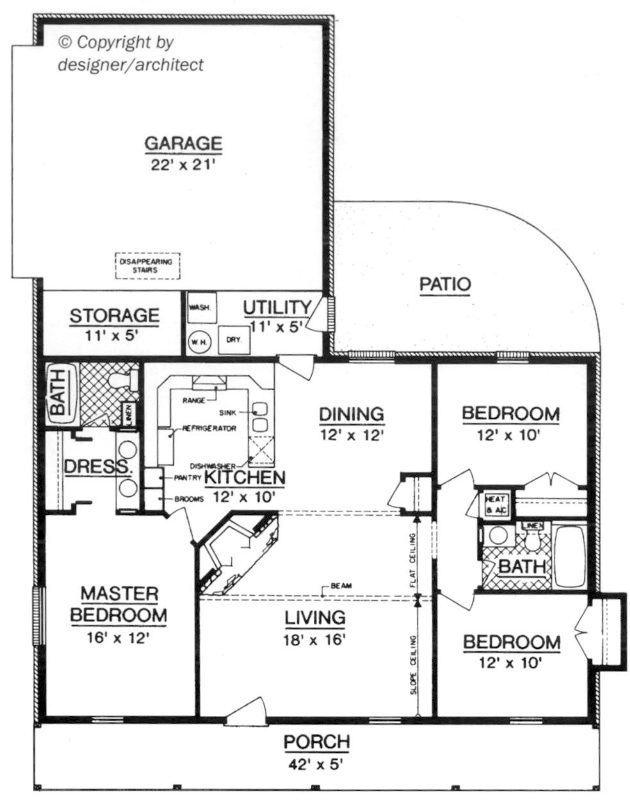

Plan #F08-020D-0015

Dimensions: 44'6" W x 59' D
Heated Sq. Ft.: 1,191
Bedrooms: 3 **Bathrooms:** 2
Exterior Walls: 2" x 6"
Foundation: Slab standard; crawl space or basement for an additional fee

See index for more information

Images provided by designer/architect

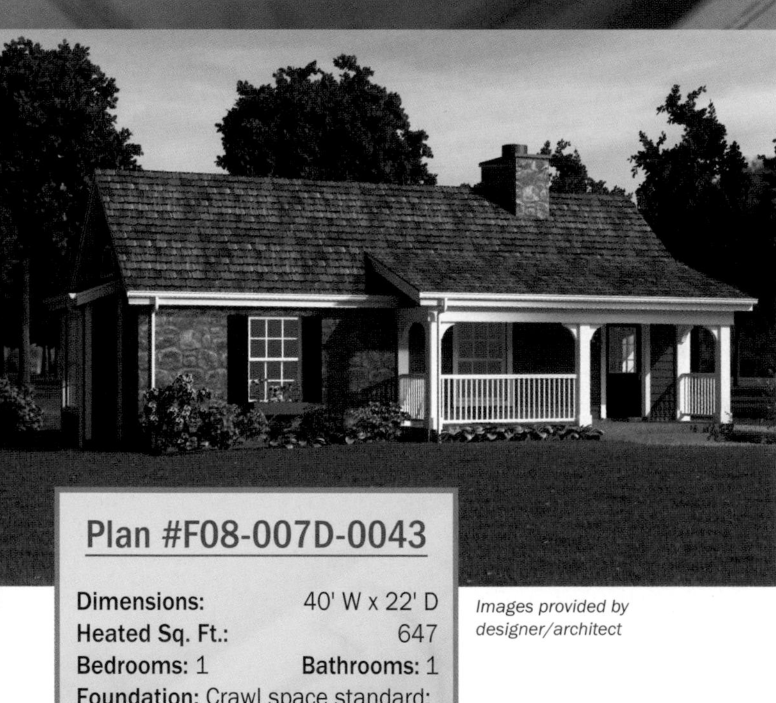

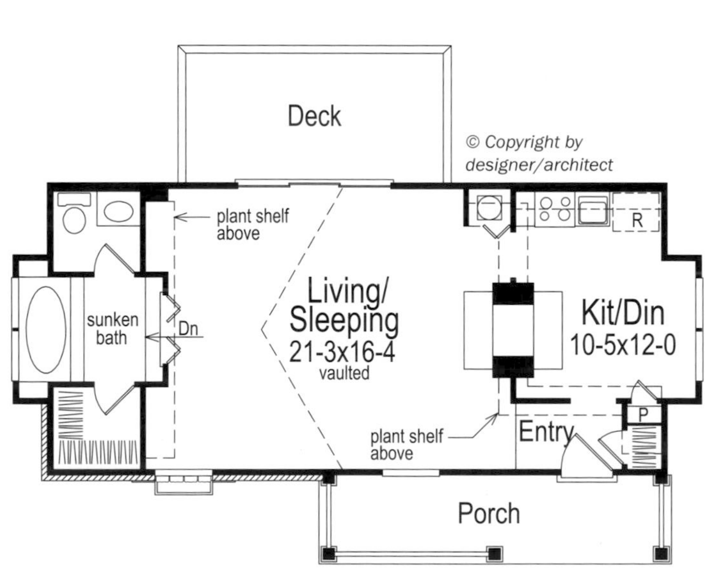

Plan #F08-007D-0043

Dimensions: 40' W x 22' D
Heated Sq. Ft.: 647
Bedrooms: 1 **Bathrooms:** 1
Foundation: Crawl space standard; slab for an additional fee

See index for more information

Images provided by designer/architect

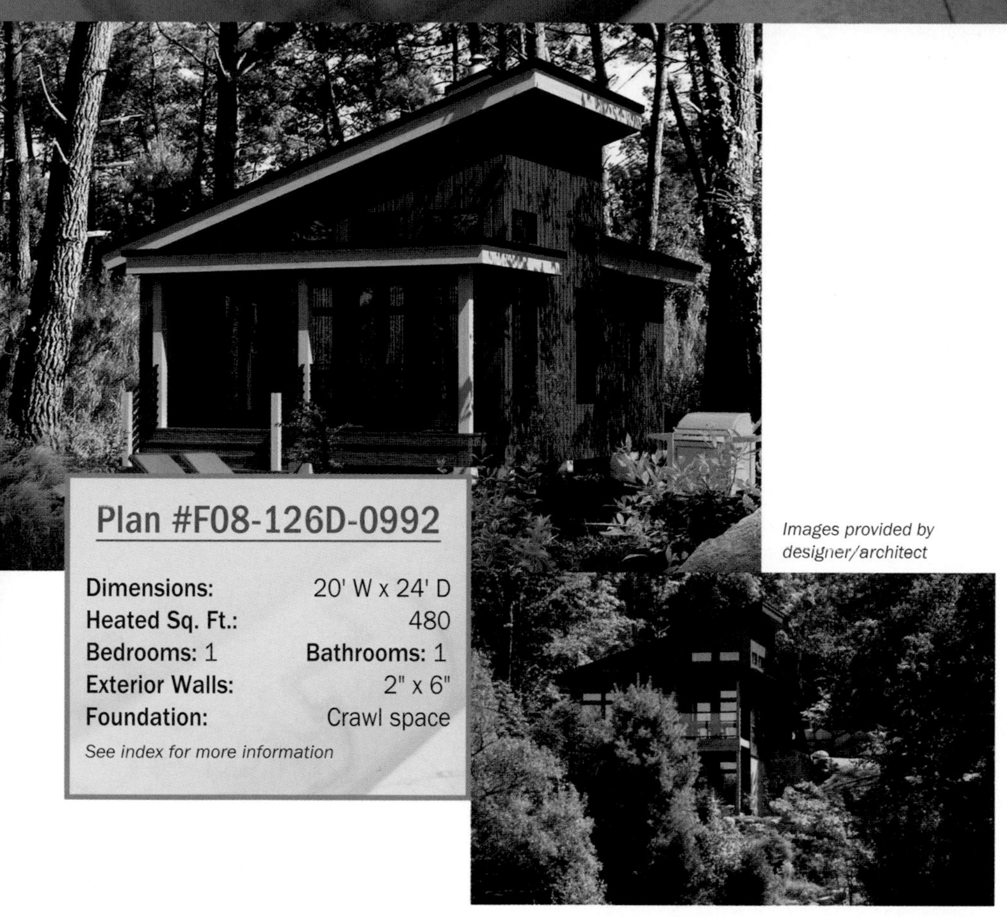

Images provided by designer/architect

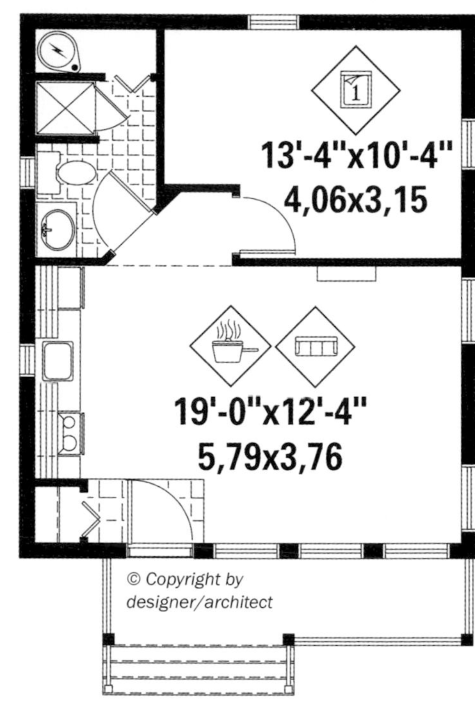

Plan #F08-126D-0992

Dimensions: 20' W x 24' D
Heated Sq. Ft.: 480
Bedrooms: 1 **Bathrooms:** 1
Exterior Walls: 2" x 6"
Foundation: Crawl space

See index for more information

Images provided by designer/architect

Plan #F08-091D-0510

Dimensions: 76' W x 60'2" D
Heated Sq. Ft.: 2,125
Bonus Sq. Ft.: 427
Bedrooms: 3 **Bathrooms:** 2½
Exterior Walls: 2" x 6"
Foundation: Crawl space standard; slab, basement, daylight basement or walk-out basement for an additional fee

See index for more information

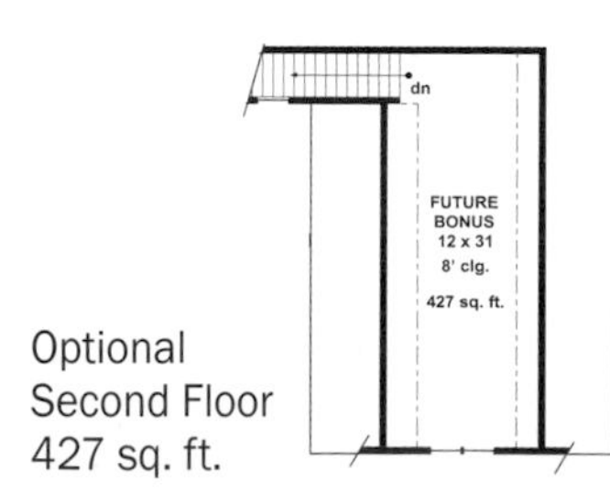

Optional Second Floor 427 sq. ft.

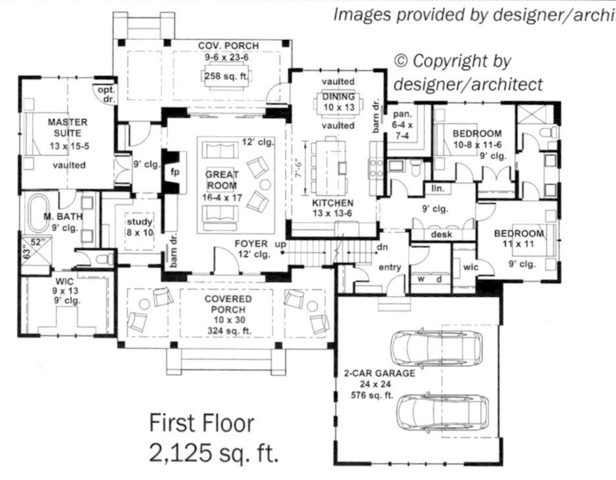

First Floor 2,125 sq. ft.

Plan #F08-055D-1083

Dimensions: 39' W x 70' D
Heated Sq. Ft.: 1,608
Bedrooms: 3 **Bathrooms:** 2
Foundation: Crawl space or slab standard; basement or daylight basement for an additional fee

See index for more information

Images provided by designer/architect

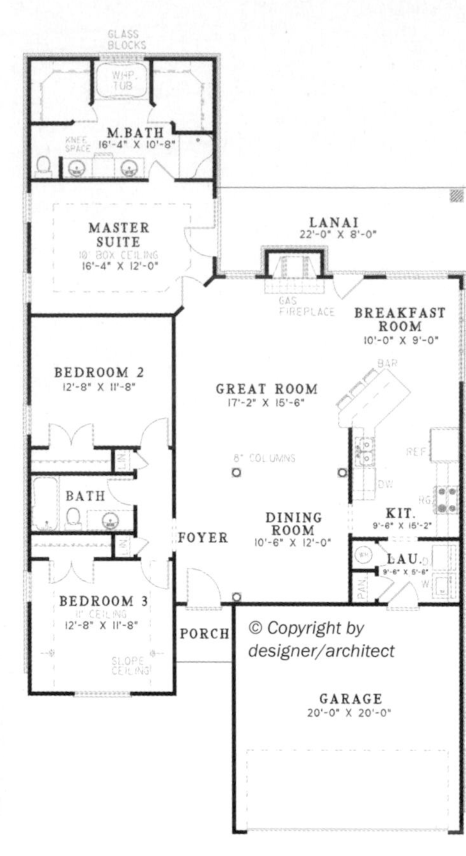

Plan #F08-011D-0674

Dimensions: 40' W x 60'6" D
Heated Sq. Ft.: 1,552
Bedrooms: 3 **Bathrooms:** 2
Exterior Walls: 2" x 6"
Foundation: Crawl space or slab standard; basement for an additional fee

See index for more information

Images provided by designer/architect

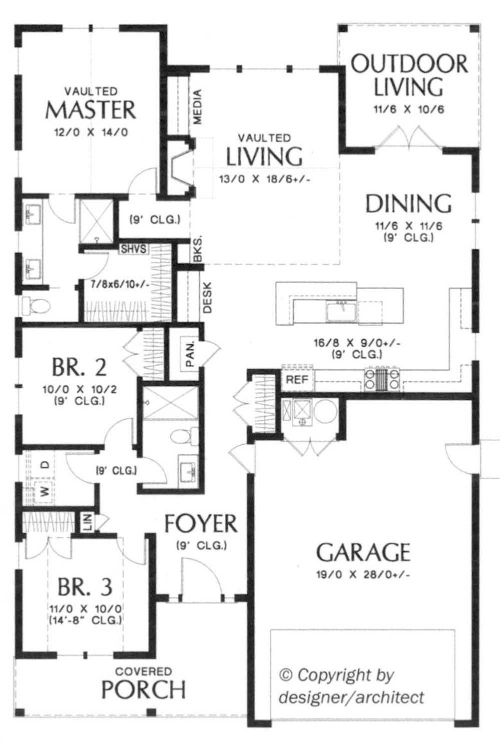

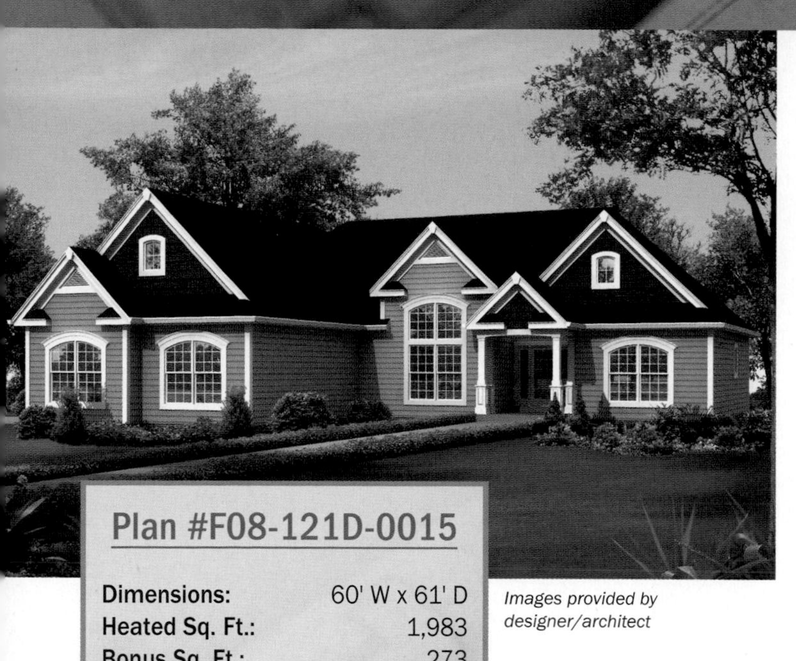

Plan #F08-121D-0015

Dimensions: 60' W x 61' D
Heated Sq. Ft.: 1,983
Bonus Sq. Ft.: 273
Bedrooms: 3 **Bathrooms:** 2½
Foundation: Basement standard; crawl space or slab for an additional fee

See index for more information

Images provided by designer/architect

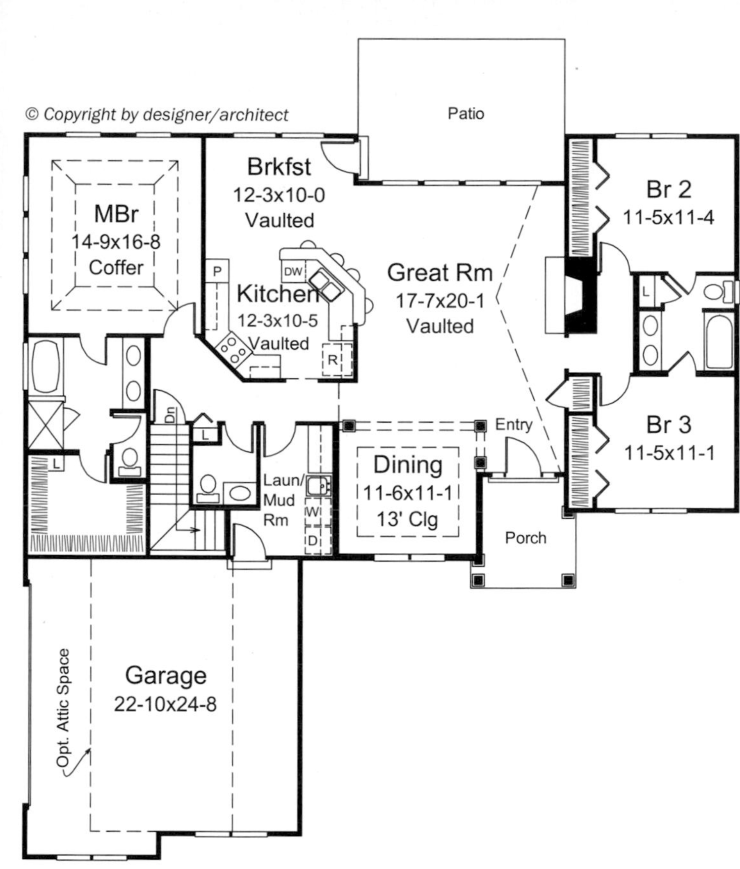

Plan #F08-058D-0171

Dimensions: 51' W x 50'4" D
Heated Sq. Ft.: 1,635
Bedrooms: 3 **Bathrooms:** 2½
Foundation: Basement

See index for more information

Images provided by designer/architect

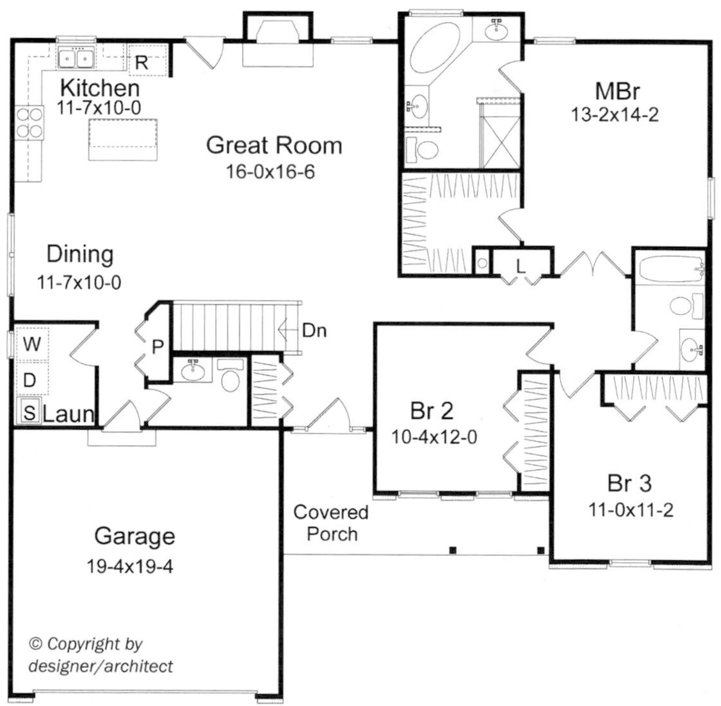

Plan #F08-028D-0099

Dimensions: 30' W x 49' D
Heated Sq. Ft.: 1,320
Bedrooms: 3 **Bathrooms:** 2
Exterior Walls: 2" x 6"
Foundation: Monolithic slab standard; floating slab, crawl space, basement or walk-out basement for an additional fee

See index for more information

Features

- In a sensible size, this cottage can easily incorporate popular Modern Farmhouse style trends into its floor plan with a barn style door from the master bedroom into the bath
- The great room and kitchen/dining area blend together making the interior feel larger than its true size
- Three bedrooms are located near each other for convenience
- A laundry room is centrally located adding ease with this frequent chore

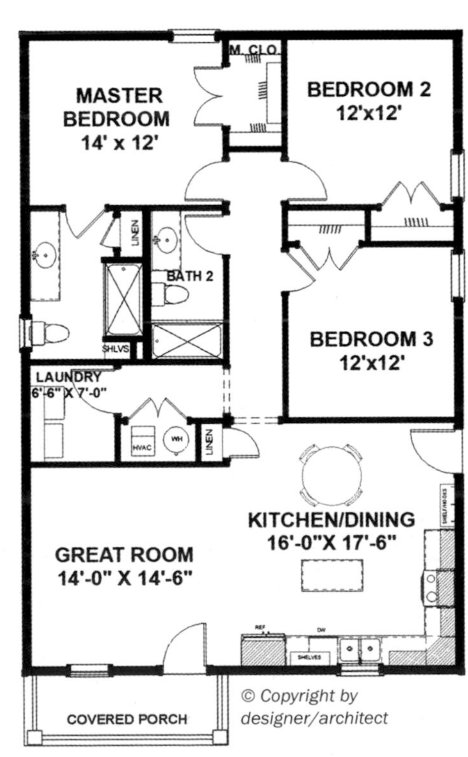

Images provided by designer/architect

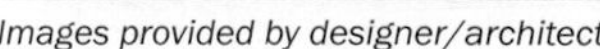

Images provided by designer/architect

Plan #F08-020D-0398

Dimensions: 36' W x 57' D
Heated Sq. Ft.: 1,062
Bedrooms: 1 **Bathrooms:** 1½
Exterior Walls: 2" x 6"
Foundation: Crawl space standard; slab for an additional fee

See index for more information

Features

- This little home can serve a variety of needs whether you need a guest house, or you just want to downsize
- The interior is open, spacious and full of light with lots of glass and volume ceilings in the living room
- The kitchen is fully appointed and has an island with lots of bar seating for casual dining
- The adjoining dining area has a built in buffet server which is an extension of the kitchen cabinets and further enhances the size of the kitchen
- A side porch connects the back porch to a half bath which also serves as a mud room since it includes the washer and dryer tucked behind louvered bi-folding doors
- The adjoining bath has twin vanities, an appliance garage, shower and a linen storage cabinet

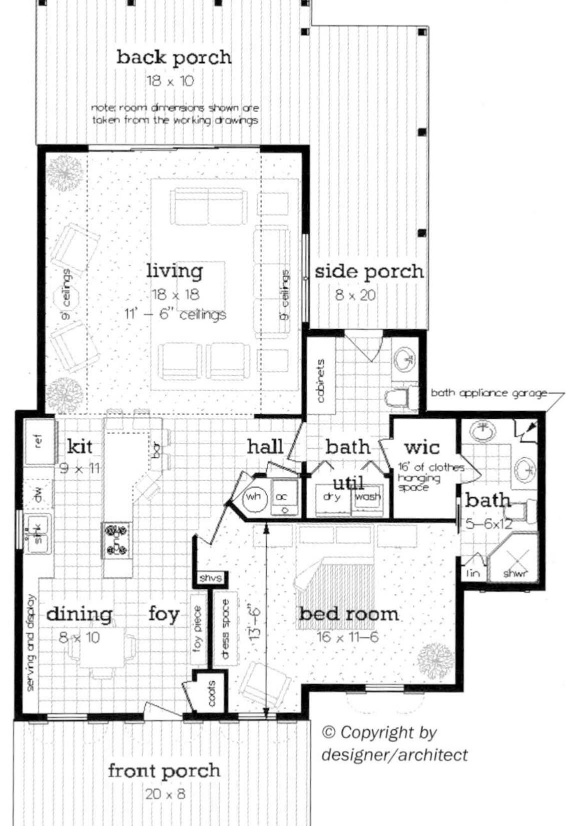

Plan #F08-170D-0032

Dimensions: 80'10" W x 87'8" D
Heated Sq. Ft.: 2,526
Bonus Sq. Ft.: 508
Bedrooms: 4 **Bathrooms:** 2½
Foundation: Slab or monolithic slab, please specify when ordering
See index for more information

Images provided by designer/architect

GARAGE 26'-0" X 12'-6"
GARAGE 26'-0" X 23'-7"
PATIO
MASTER BEDROOM 18'-5" X 14'-0"
KEEPING ROOM 15'-5" X 14'-3" 10' CEILING
REAR PORCH 31'-6" X 10'-0"
UTILITY 8'-9" X 9'-9"
MASTER CLOSET 6'-0" X 15'-5"
MASTER BATH 11'-4" X 15'-5"
1/2 BATH
LIVING 21'-0" X 20'-4" 12' CEILING
KITCHEN 15'-1" X 16'-4" 10' CEILING
BATH 2
BEDROOM 3 12'-5" X 13'-9"
PANTRY
STUDY/ BEDROOM 4 13'-7" X 11'-0"
FOYER 7'-0" X 11'-2" 12' CEILING
BEDROOM 2 13'-11" X 11'-2"
FRONT PORCH 36'-0" X 8'-0" 12' CEILING

© Copyright by designer/architect

Plan #F08-155D-0333

Dimensions: 85'6" W x 67'5" D
Heated Sq. Ft.: 2,679
Bonus Sq. Ft.: 678
Bedrooms: 4 **Bathrooms:** 3
Foundation: Crawl space or slab standard; basement or daylight basement for an additional fee
See index for more information

Images provided by designer/architect

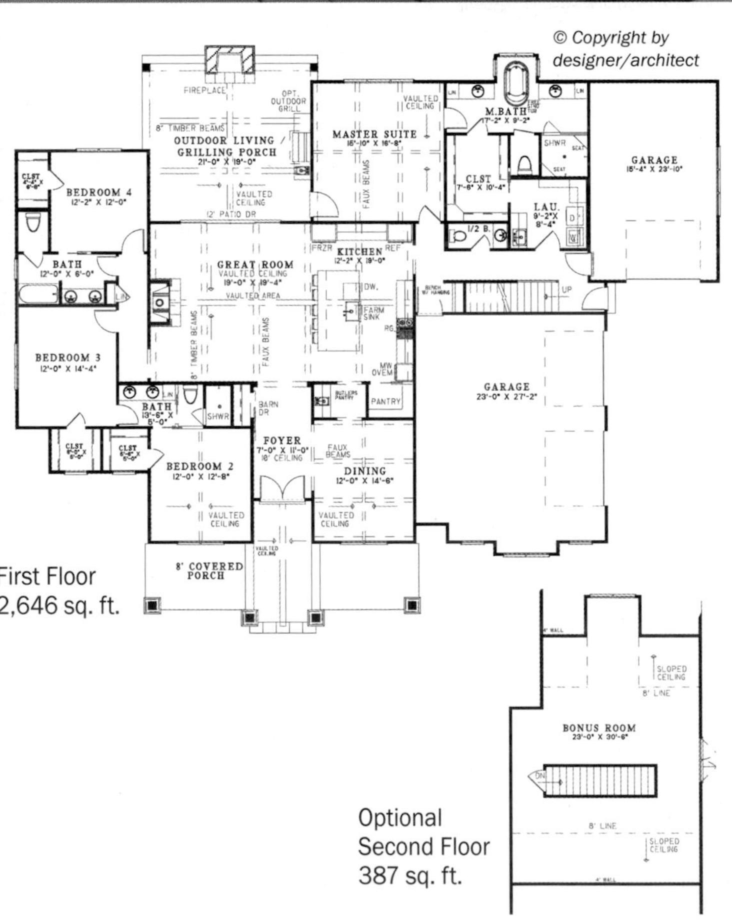

© Copyright by designer/architect

First Floor 2,646 sq. ft.

Optional Second Floor 387 sq. ft.

Plan #F08-007D-0108

Dimensions: 25' W x 60' D
Heated Sq. Ft.: 983
Bedrooms: 3 **Bathrooms:** 2
Foundation: Crawl space standard; slab for an additional fee

See index for more information

Images provided by designer/architect

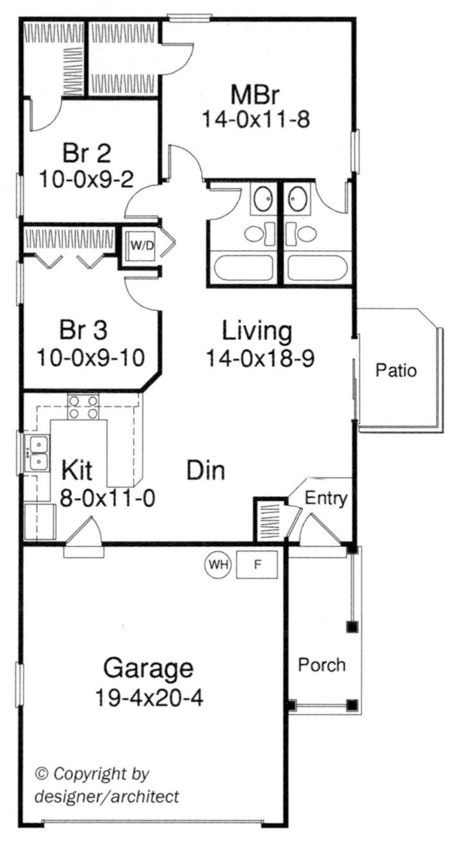

Plan #F08-051D-0850

Dimensions: 38' W x 52' D
Heated Sq. Ft.: 1,334
Bedrooms: 2 **Bathrooms:** 2
Exterior Walls: 2" x 6"
Foundation: Basement standard; crawl space or slab for an additional fee

See index for more information

Images provided by designer/architect

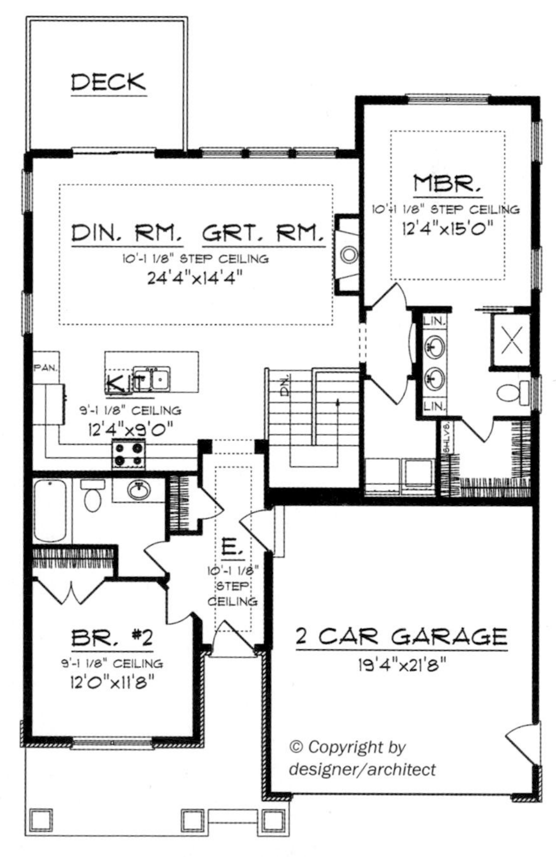

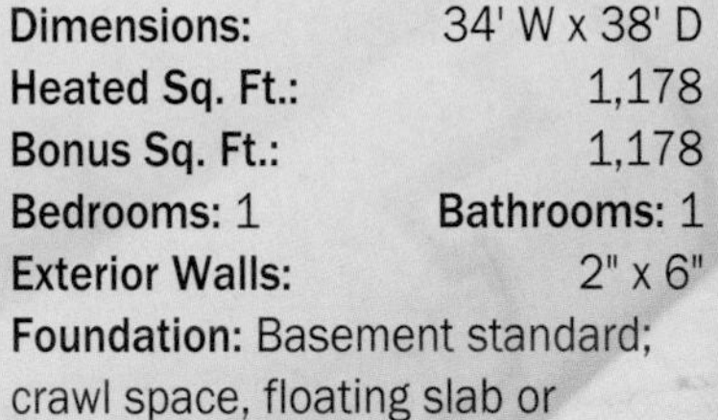

Plan #F08-032D-0963

Dimensions: 34' W x 38' D
Heated Sq. Ft.: 1,178
Bonus Sq. Ft.: 1,178
Bedrooms: 1 **Bathrooms:** 1
Exterior Walls: 2" x 6"
Foundation: Basement standard; crawl space, floating slab or monolithic slab for an additional fee

See index for more information

Images provided by designer/architect

Features

- This small Modern Farmhouse inspired home takes simplicity and style to a new level
- Step into the entry from the covered front porch and discover an oversized walk-in closet for
- The open-concept floor plan has the kitchen and dining area blended perfectly
- The kitchen has a large walk-in pantry with a barn style door for a farmhouse feel
- The bedroom enjoys close proximity to the pampering bath that features a shower as well as a free-standing tub in one corner
- The optional lower level has an additional 1,178 square feet of living area

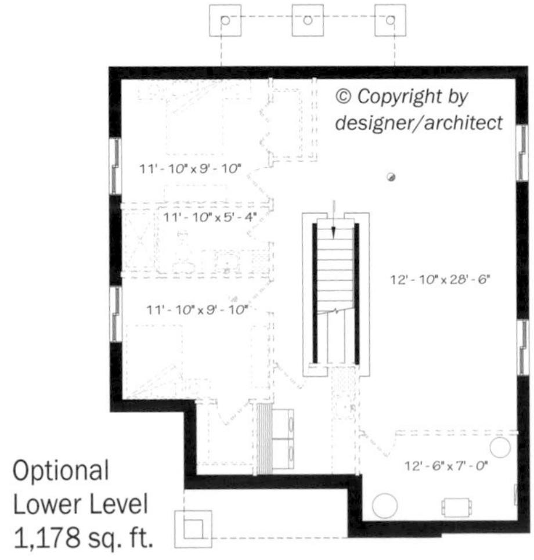

Optional Lower Level
1,178 sq. ft.

First Floor
1,178 sq. ft.

Plan #F08-032D-0835

Dimensions: 40' W x 30' D
Heated Sq. Ft.: 1,146
Bedrooms: 2 **Bathrooms:** 1
Exterior Walls: 2" x 6"
Foundation: Basement standard; floating slab for an additional fee

See index for more information

Images provided by designer/architect

Features

- You'll never want to leave this stunning rustic cabin
- The interior is open and airy with tons of windows in the kitchen, dining and living area to capture surrounding views
- The floor plan is open and offers optimal use of the square footage
- The two bedrooms are convenient to the full bath featuring a walk-in shower and a separate tub

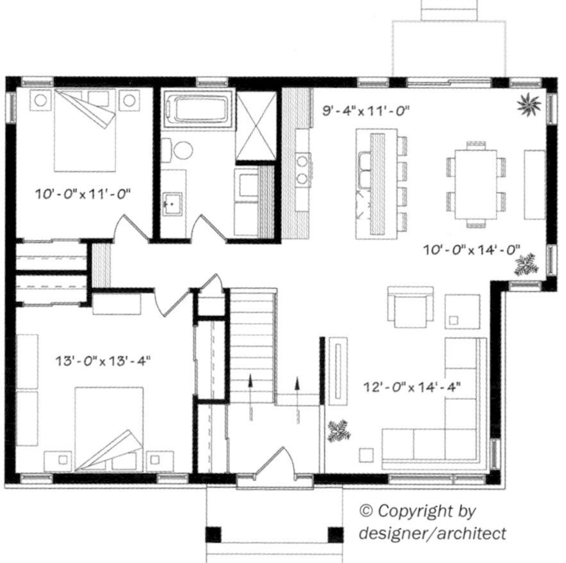

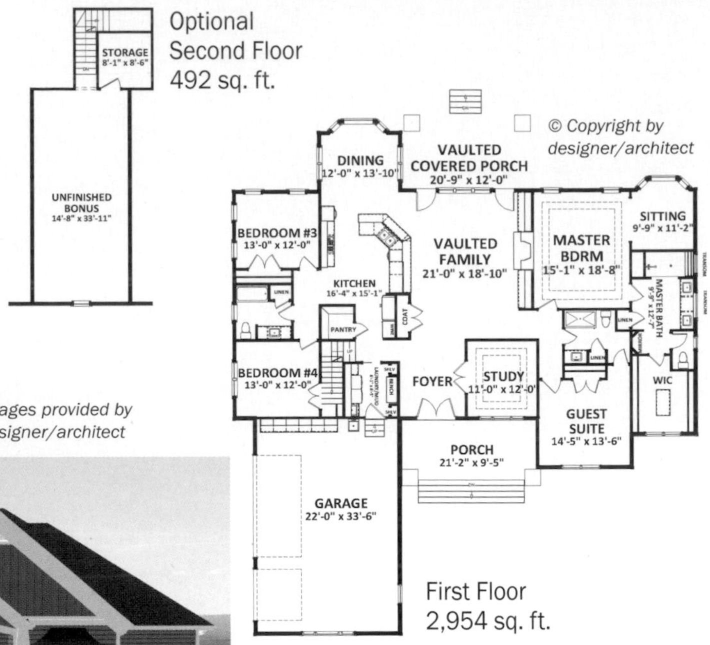

Plan #F08-139D-0009

Dimensions: 73' W x 80' D
Heated Sq. Ft.: 2,954
Bonus Sq. Ft.: 492
Bedrooms: 4 **Bathrooms:** 3
Exterior Walls: 2" x 6"
Foundation: Crawl space standard; slab, basement, daylight basement or walk-out basement for an additional fee

See index for more information

Images provided by designer/architect

Optional Second Floor 492 sq. ft.

STORAGE 8'-1" x 8'-6"
UNFINISHED BONUS 14'-8" x 33'-11"

© Copyright by designer/architect

DINING 12'-0" x 13'-10"
VAULTED COVERED PORCH 20'-9" x 12'-0"
BEDROOM #3 13'-0" x 12'-0"
KITCHEN 16'-4" x 15'-1"
VAULTED FAMILY 21'-0" x 18'-10"
MASTER BDRM 15'-1" x 18'-8"
SITTING 9'-9" x 11'-2"
MASTER BATH
BEDROOM #4 13'-0" x 12'-0"
FOYER
STUDY 11'-0" x 12'-0"
WIC
GUEST SUITE 14'-5" x 13'-6"
PORCH 21'-2" x 9'-5"
GARAGE 22'-0" x 33'-6"

First Floor 2,954 sq. ft.

Plan #F08-007D-0161

Dimensions: 70' W x 36' D
Heated Sq. Ft.: 1,480
Bedrooms: 2 **Bathrooms:** 2
Exterior Walls: 2" x 6"
Foundation: Slab

See index for more information

Images provided by designer/architect

Stor.
Study 10-0x11-0
Kit 9-0 x 13-0 vaulted
Dining Rm 10-0x13-0 vaulted
Laundry
Storage
Hall
MBr 13-0x15-0
Br 2 10-5x11-4
Living Rm 18-0x15-0 vaulted
Entry
Garage 20-8x22-0
Porch

© Copyright by designer/architect

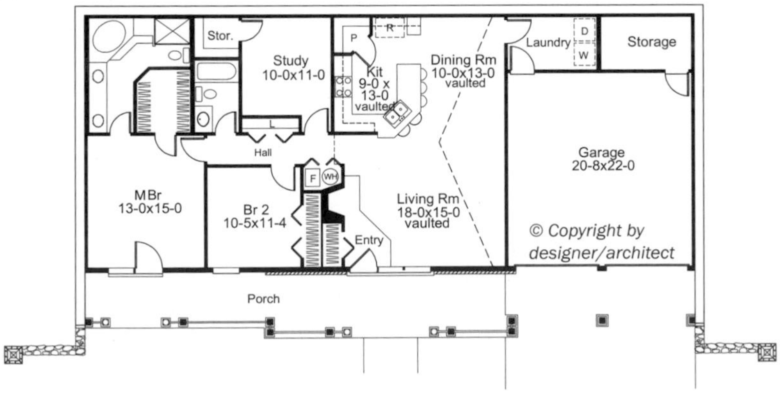

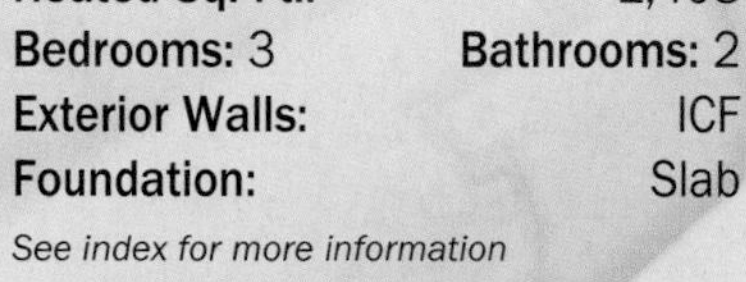

Plan #F08-088D-0118

Dimensions:	44' W x 32' D
Heated Sq. Ft.:	1,408
Bedrooms: 3	**Bathrooms:** 2
Exterior Walls:	ICF
Foundation:	Slab

See index for more information

Images provided by designer/architect

MSTR. STE.
12⁰ X 14¹⁰
KITCHEN
9⁶ X 14¹⁰
DINING ROOM
11⁸ X 14¹⁰
LIVING ROOM
16⁰ X 14¹⁰
BDRM. #2
12⁰ X 11⁴
BDRM. #3
11⁰ X 11⁴
LIN.
ATTIC ACCESS
FURNACE ABOVE
DW
PAN
WH

Plan #F08-007D-0135

Dimensions:	57' W x 36'4" D
Heated Sq. Ft.:	801
Bedrooms: 2	**Bathrooms:** 1
Foundation:	Slab

See index for more information

Images provided by designer/architect

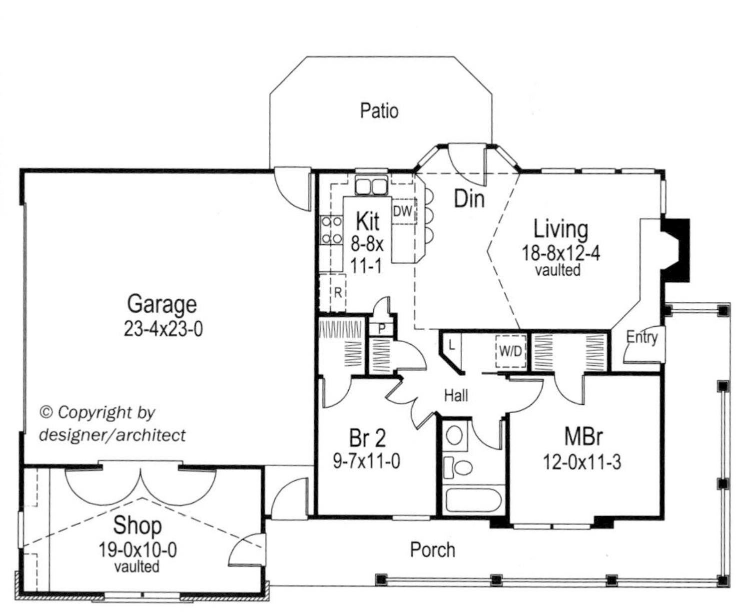

Plan #F08-101D-0052

Dimensions: 129'8" W x 70'8" D
Heated Sq. Ft.: 2,611
Bonus Sq. Ft.: 2,456
Bedrooms: 2 **Bathrooms:** 2½
Exterior Walls: 2" x 6"
Foundation: Walk-out basement

See index for more information

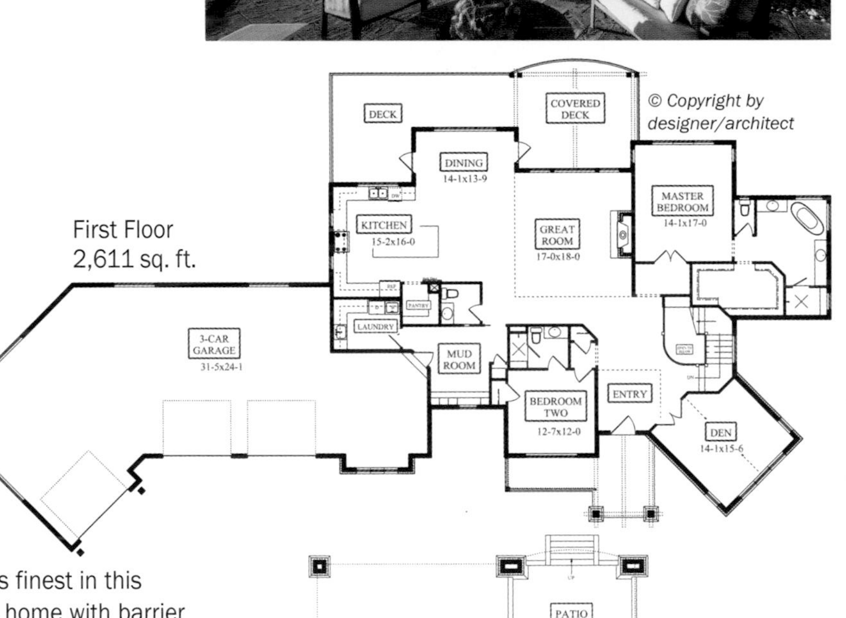

First Floor
2,611 sq. ft.

PATIO
BEDROOM THREE 14-1x13-6
GAME NOOK 14-1x10-2
BEDROOM TWO 12-6x16-2
EXERCISE ROOM 14-1x17-3
RECREATION AREA 20-4x36-9
Storage
THEATER 17-6x13-0
VAULT

Optional Lower Level
2,456 sq. ft.

Images provided by designer/architect

Features

- Open living at its finest in this Craftsman style home with barrier free living spaces
- An angled den off the foyer creates a private home office
- Highlighting the U-shaped kitchen is the large center island
- Convenient mud room and laundry as you enter from the garage
- The optional lower level has an additional 2,456 square feet of living area
- 3-car front entry garage

Plan #F08-013D-0015

Dimensions: 55'8" W x 56'6" D
Heated Sq. Ft.: 1,787
Bonus Sq. Ft.: 263
Bedrooms: 3 **Bathrooms:** 2
Foundation: Slab standard; crawl space or basement for an additional fee

See index for more information

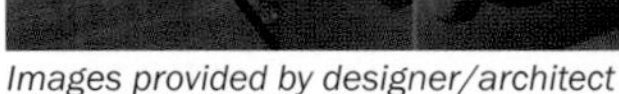

Images provided by designer/architect

Features

- Skylights brighten the screen porch that connects to the family room, master bedroom, and the deck outdoors
- The master bedroom features a comfortable sitting area, a large private bath, and a huge walk-in closet
- The kitchen has a serving bar that extends dining into the family room
- The bonus room above the garage has an additional 263 square feet of living area
- 2-car side entry garage

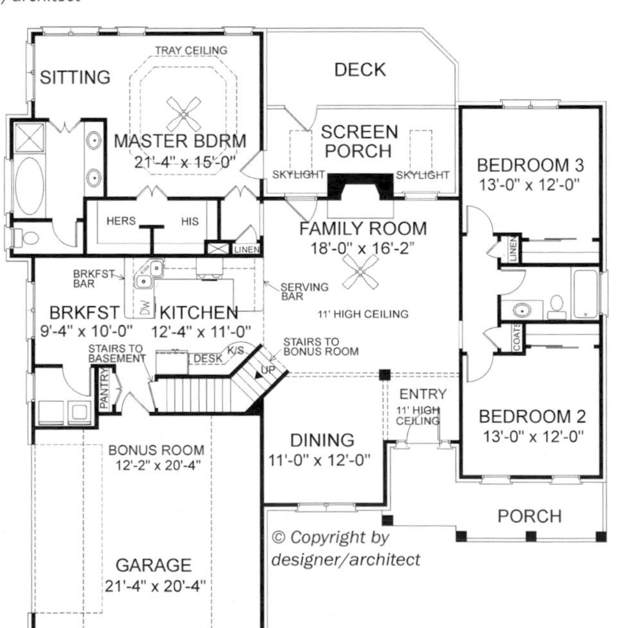

take living OUTDOORS

You wake to a perfectly sunny day. After a long stretch to awaken your senses you head to the French doors and swing them open to reveal an amazing oasis with stunning gardens, patios, and a waterfall. No, you are not on vacation – you are experiencing and living the luxury of your very own outdoor living area!

It seems homeowners have taken the idea of a "staycation" to a whole new level. Instead of jetting off to pricey tropical vacation destinations all the time, now more homeowners than ever are looking to invest their income into something more gratifying, their home. Why not invest in something you can truly enjoy every single day? Homeowners are enjoying staying at home more, and that includes entertaining on a more regular basis. With many home designs being designed smaller, more compact, and efficient, it seems only natural that entertaining and everyday living is now heading outdoors. The line between the interior spaces and the exterior ones has been blurred now more than ever before.

Both home and landscape designers have seen a huge desire for homeowners to bring an indoor entertainment experience to the outdoors. Through adding things like fireplaces, fire pits, outdoor kitchens, televisions, sound systems, etc., the party has moved to the outdoors.

Think of your outdoor space as another room in your home. Gone are the days of rickety old rusted patio furniture and a wilted plant in one corner of the concrete slab patio. The best outdoor living areas rival the interior ones by creating an open flow that encourages easy entertaining, dining and relaxing.

Unless noted, copyright by designer/architect; Page 234, top: Plan #047D-0083; bottom: Sunset Cottage, designed by Bob Chatham, bobchatham.com; Page 235 top: 2006 ASLA Award Winner, Marmol Radziner and Associates, Los Angeles, California, photo by John Ellis; middle: Bayside Living designed by Bob Chatham, built by Peter Gaillard of Gaillard Builders, Bailey Chastang, photographer; Bottom, left: Plan #101D-0107, Robert Yone, photographer; Bottom, right: Providence Pointe designed by Bob Chatham, built by Achee Builders, Inc., Bailey Chastang, photographer; To see more photos or to purchase plans, visit houseplansandmore.com.

get started!

List some features you want to incorporate into your outdoor area so you can determine what the focal point should be.

Do you love the idea of an outdoor kitchen? Then, make that one of the focal points. If your budget or area is small, maybe a deluxe grill is all you need to get the area ready for entertaining. Or, if you plan to spare no expense, then there are countless amenities available including: built-in grills, stovetops, refrigerators, and even a pizza oven can be a family fun spot that no doubt will be a conversation starter when friends are over for memorable get-togethers.

There are two other popular features being added to outdoor spaces all across the country - one being a fire source, and the other being a water element. Both mesmerizing as well as relaxing, fire and water features are quickly gaining popularity in climates of all types. When it comes to fire - fire pits, outdoor fireplaces, and even barbecue grills fall into this popular category. Often evoking memories of childhood campfires and family time, adding a place where everyone can gather around a fire pit, or outdoor fireplace is bound to become a favorite backyard destination especially when the weather starts to cool down. This feature is an excellent way to extend your time in the outdoors earlier into the spring and later into the fall and early winter. Whether it's an intimate gathering with couples enjoying some wine on a fall evening, or a lively night with the entire family roasting marshmallows, one thing is for sure; a backyard fireplace or fire pit is bound to create countless memories.

Another focal point cropping up in outdoor spaces everywhere are water features. From waterfalls and fountains, to hot tubs and swimming pools, a water feature is a welcomed amenity that appeals to the senses. Nothing says refreshing like the cool, crystal blue waters of a swimming pool. And, the bubbling sound of a fountain or waterfall instantly refreshes and relaxes the soul. So, whatever your budget, there is a water solution for your outdoor space.

how to create a seamless feel from your outdoor room to the indoor spaces of your home:

select a finish for your patio that mimics your interior flooring and instantly expand your living space visually. Homeowners are taking a lot of time and putting a lot of thought into treating and decorating outdoor patios like indoor rooms – again, sort of bringing the look and feel of the home's interior to its outdoor spaces creating a cohesive experience between the indoors and the outdoors. While many homeowners may stick with traditional concrete or stamped concrete that comes in a variety of colors, what some designers believe is more aesthetically pleasing are pavers and flagstone products. These have also proven to be a wiser investment in terms of long term value and durability. So, start with the floor and select a beautiful foundation that mirrors your interior spaces. It will create a solid design anchor that will merge your indoor and outdoor rooms seamlessly. If your outdoor space is covered like many are today, you may even wish to use ceramic tile, or other stone tile surfaces that can be used both indoors and outdoors for the ultimate seamless look.

select furniture that resembles the interior style when it comes to colors and textures. This will further enhance the open feel of these merging spaces naturally and will keep the areas from looking disjointed. When investing in outdoor furniture, it is sometimes best to stick to natural neutral colors such as brown, beige, white, and other earth tones. These are timeless colors that make the perfect backdrop for highlighting outdoor artwork, textiles such as pillows, and other exciting colorful accessories. However, although neutral furniture is a wise investment, current trends in outdoor spaces show wildly bright and neon colored furniture gaining popularity. Regardless of its color, group furniture pieces creating several types of spaces for dining, intimate conversation spots, and seating areas for larger parties. If you have a special focal point in nature, don't forget to arrange a seating area so this can be enjoyed to its fullest. If you're lucky enough to have panoramic ocean or lake views, arrange one seating area so it completely enjoys this scenic vista with little or no visual distractions.

Unless noted, copyright by designer/architect; Page 236, top: Plan #Copper Creek Cottage, designed by Bob Chatham, built by Jeff Frostholm Construction, Bailey Chastang, photographer; bottom: Plan #011S-0189; Page 237 top: Plan #101D-0106, Warren Diggles, photographer; middle: Plan #101D-0121; Bottom: istockphotos.com; To see more photos or purchase plans, visit houseplansandmore.com.

fire or rain?

What would you choose for your outdoor living area? Fire, water, or both? Why?

Last, don't forget to incorporate lighting that highlights all of the amazing features and design ideas you have added to your own outdoor paradise. Not only will "lightscaping" call attention to a focal point like a water feature, it can designate a space. For example, a chandelier or statement light fixture can spotlight a special dining spot, or a unique side table lamp will make an intimate outdoor space even more cozy and comfortable.

Don't let another season go by without finding a way to smoothly transition your indoor and outdoor spaces into something truly spectacular. Use some or all of these great outdoor design trends to provide a year-round outdoor oasis that creates a sanctuary for your senses just steps from your home's interior.

select color including vibrant colors that have really made a comeback recently and add a tremendous amount of personality to any space both indoors and out. So, choose three to four colors for your scheme and have fun! Rich reds, bold oranges, vivid blues or garden-inspired greens all offer personality. Then, pair up some plants and flowers native to your area for easy maintenance. Select matching or contrasting colors and you'll have an outdoor area that exudes your own personal style.

eat, play & live: using your outdoor space

Outdoor living is a trend that is here to stay. For many homeowners the opportunity to have a backyard paradise is too good to be true. However, as thoughts of swimming pools, gardens, outdoor televisions, fireplaces, gorgeous stonework, kitchens, fabrics and furniture swirl through the mind, it can create a sense of overwhelming confusion causing you to see major dollar signs. Sure, outdoor living space is great, but beyond the grill, where do you even start? How extensive is this outdoor project going to be?

below are some tips for planning your outdoor living expansion:

1 Remember, outdoor living can be made as simple or as grand as you desire.

2 Set a budget. This will also help determine what outdoor living components can become a reality and are must-haves.

3 Evaluate the space. A small patio for hosting dinner parties with friends and family may be closer to reality than a huge swimming pool and spa. Will it be better to have one multi-purpose area or designated zones for dining, resting, and play? Take note of the space available and determine which amenities are most important to your lifestyle.

today's most popular options include:

outdoor kitchens are the most popular feature in outdoor living spaces right now. People naturally tend to gather in the kitchen anyway, so combining hosting and cooking with the pleasure of visiting with guests in an outdoor setting is truly a winning combination. To ensure function, look at how the outdoor kitchen will be used with your lifestyle. The basic outdoor kitchen is an extension of the home and typically contains a small prep sink, grill, and limited counter space for small tasks. Close proximity to the indoor kitchen allows easy transport of ingredients, dishes, and drinks not stored outdoors. On the other end of the spectrum, an outdoor kitchen can be fully independent from the one inside the home and can include a dishwasher, refrigerator, cooktop, and storage. These elaborate kitchens are typically L- or U-shaped with an island, creating a work atmosphere with similar distinct zones for food preparation and cooking like an indoor kitchen utilizes. These outdoor kitchens are ideal for hosting large groups. Outdoor kitchens of any size can be fully built-in with massive grills and impressive hardware, or comprised of rolling carts that move when necessary. Permanent versus flexible kitchen options are often determined by budget and local climate.

good to know...

Many homeowners are choosing container gardens in plant varieties native to their local climate for easy maintenance. Or, fill your pots with fragrant herbs, vegetables, or small fruit bearing trees and reap the extra reward of fresh homegrown organic produce right in your own outdoor kitchen!

outdoor social spaces fill the need for a place to retreat to. The options are endless when it comes to creating a space that is perfect for private or social use. Again, determined by budget and need, outdoor living rooms can be sprawling extensions of the indoors, full of cozy couches and chairs, fireplaces, and even outdoor media centers. There can be separate dining and resting spaces, or these can be combined into one multi-purpose space with a few well-chosen pieces of furniture. The choice is up to you, but either option can be a haven of comfort. Part of keeping outdoor living spaces functional is keeping them comfortable. Outdoor fans and fireplaces add decorative touches with practical purposes. Outdoor fans are the same as indoor fans since they circulate the air, provide a light breeze, and help shoo away disruptive bugs. Whether placed over dining or sitting areas, outdoor fans are rated for damp or wet use, meaning they can be placed in partially uncovered situations.

Outdoor fireplaces come in numerous shapes and sizes, and are the perfect accessory for any outdoor space. Two-sided fireplaces can be placed in the home's exterior wall and enjoyed both inside and out. Chimineas are freestanding pot-bellied fireplaces, perfect for smaller patios and situations that may require mobility. Fire pits can be permanent or portable and radiate warmth from all sides. These are the most popular choices in today's homes. Lastly, is the built-in outdoor fireplace. These are permanent masterpieces of masonry, fully constructed like indoor fireplaces with surrounds and mantles. Stunning and functional, built-in fireplaces can be prohibitively expensive and do require regular maintenance, but they are a stunning addition to any backyard landscape.

outdoor play reminds us that the outdoors is a place for fun and maintaining an active, healthy lifestyle, too. While outdoor living areas are typically ideal for creating a relaxing paradise close to home; they usually only designate space for dining and resting. Keep in mind, the need for play space is equally important. Many families are choosing to include outdoor sport courts into their landscape. Whether tennis is your game, or a quick game of hoops with your rising star basketball player, sport courts can handle active families and their need for a variety of the active options they crave. And, not just for looks, a backyard swimming pool is beautiful, but it also provides a healthy active option for people of all ages even during the hottest months of the year. To attractively separate play from relaxation areas, try using hedges and landscaping to create play areas in the yard. Not only are these dividers decorative, they keep errant balls and other toys from interrupting the flow of conversation on the patio. In addition to sport courts, outdoor play areas allow for outdoor meditation areas or yoga nooks. Playing outside is not just for the young, but for the young at heart as well.

Whether dividing the outdoors into "rooms," or openly sharing the space for activities, it is important to be aware of how the outdoor living space will be used. Specialty landscaping and outdoor storage can be used to keep various activities from interrupting one another. However you choose to use your space, remember to take advantage of every corner, so your relaxing retreat not so far from home has everything you could possible want right in your own backyard.

Unless noted, copyright by designer/architect; Page 238, top: Plan #011S-0195; middle: Plan #026S-0018; bottom: Plan #011S-0088, Bob Greenspan, photographer; Page 239 top: Plan #106S-0046; bottom: Outdoor pool house with kitchen and living area, Green Guys, greenguysstl.com; Page 240, top: Plan #071S-0001; middle: Plan #055D-0817; bottom: Plan #065S-0033; Page 241, top to bottom: Plan #091D-0476; Backyard tennis/basketball sport court, sportcourtstlouis.com; Plan #011S-0003; Plan #071S-0002; For more photos or to purchase plans, please visit houseplansandmore.com.

Images provided by designer/architect

Plan #F08-011D-0526

Dimensions: 72' W x 65'6" D
Heated Sq. Ft.: 2,735
Bonus Sq. Ft.: 379
Bedrooms: 3 **Bathrooms:** 2½
Exterior Walls: 2" x 6"
Foundation: Crawl space or slab standard; basement for an additional fee

See index for more information

Features

- The vaulted great room with fireplace and covered porch views commands full attention when you enter this home
- A quiet home office is tucked away near the foyer
- The kitchen has an efficient angled island and breakfast bar that overlooks the great room and breakfast nook
- Two secondary bedrooms find themselves located behind the kitchen and share a full bath
- The optional second floor has an additional 379 square feet of living area
- 3-car front entry garage

STORAGE
14/2+ X 19/0+
(8'-0" CLG.)
DN.

Optional Second Floor 379 sq. ft.

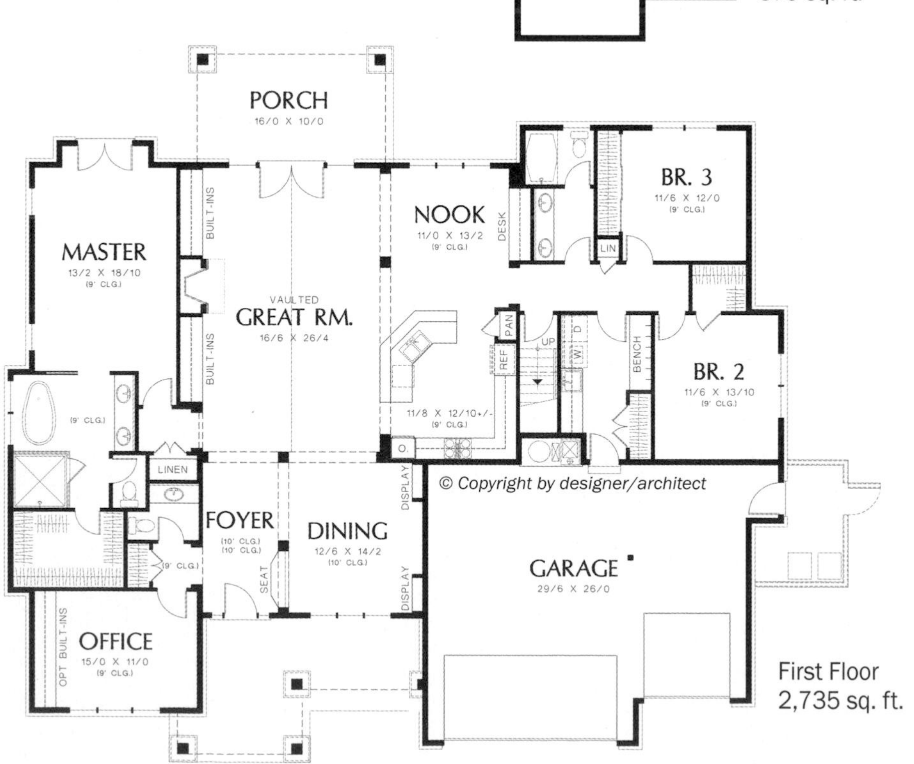

First Floor 2,735 sq. ft.

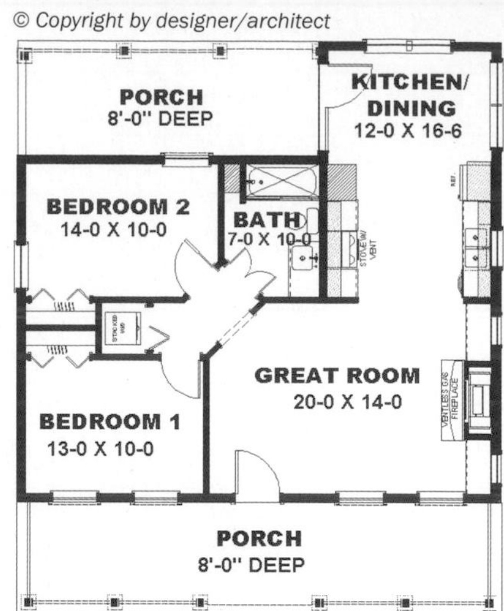

Images provided by designer/architect

Plan #F08-028D-0108

Dimensions: 33' W x 40'" D
Heated Sq. Ft.: 890
Bedrooms: 2 **Bathrooms:** 1
Foundation: Floating slab standard; monolithic slab, crawl space, basement or walk-out basement for an additional fee

Pricing subject to change

Plan #F08-164D-0044

Dimensions: 69' W x 98' D
Heated sq. ft.: 3,287
Bedrooms: 3 **Bathrooms:** 2½
Foundation: Slab

See index for more information

Images provided by designer/architect

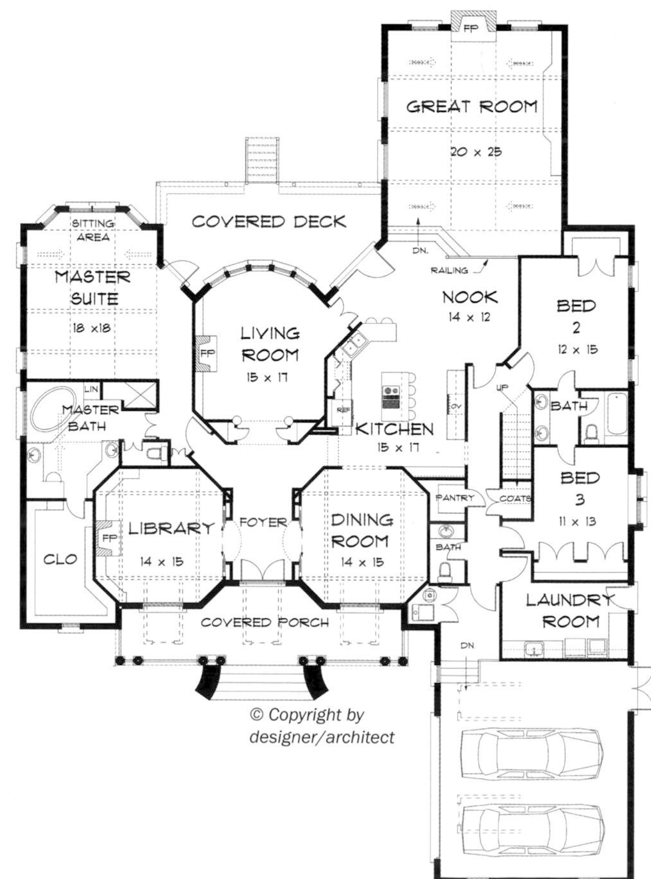

© Copyright by designer/architect

Images provided by designer/architect

Plan #F08-011D-0606

Dimensions: 94'10" W x 76'11" D
Heated Sq. Ft.: 2,301
Bonus Sq. Ft.: 355
Bedrooms: 3 **Bathrooms:** 3½
Exterior Walls: 2" x 6"
Foundation: Crawl space or slab standard; basement for an additional fee

See index for more information

© Copyright by designer/architect

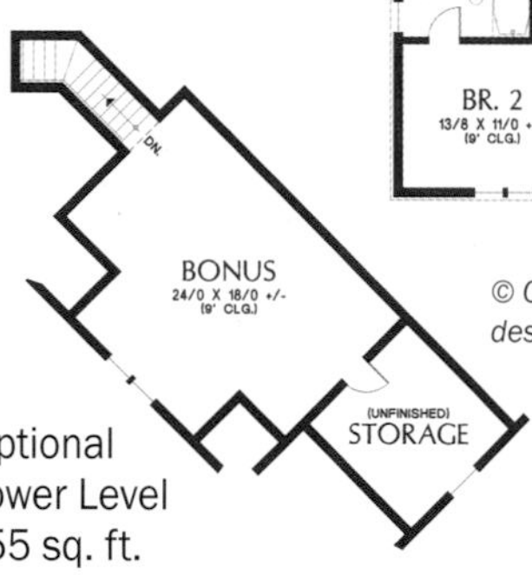

Optional Lower Level 355 sq. ft.

First Floor 2,301 sq. ft.

Plan #F08-007D-0098

Dimensions: 78'8" W x 51' D
Heated Sq. Ft.: 2,398
Bonus Sq. Ft.: 763
Bedrooms: 3 **Bathrooms:** 2
Foundation: Walk-out basement

See index for more information

Images provided by designer/architect

© Copyright by designer/architect

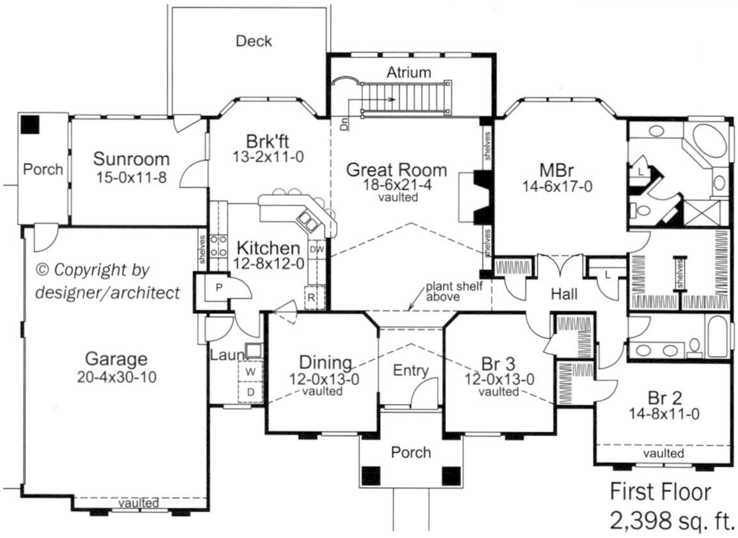

First Floor 2,398 sq. ft.

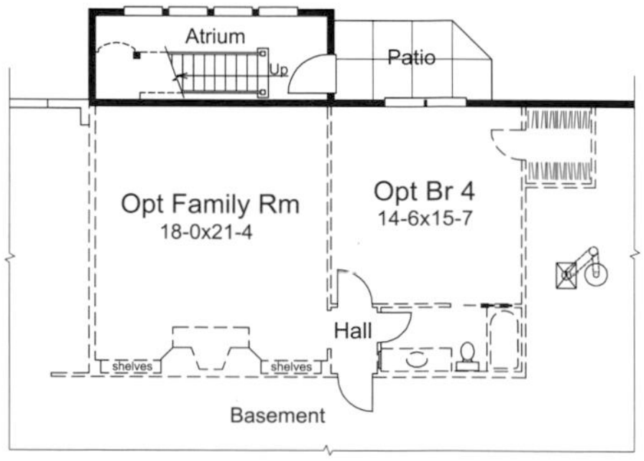

Optional Lower Level 763 sq. ft.

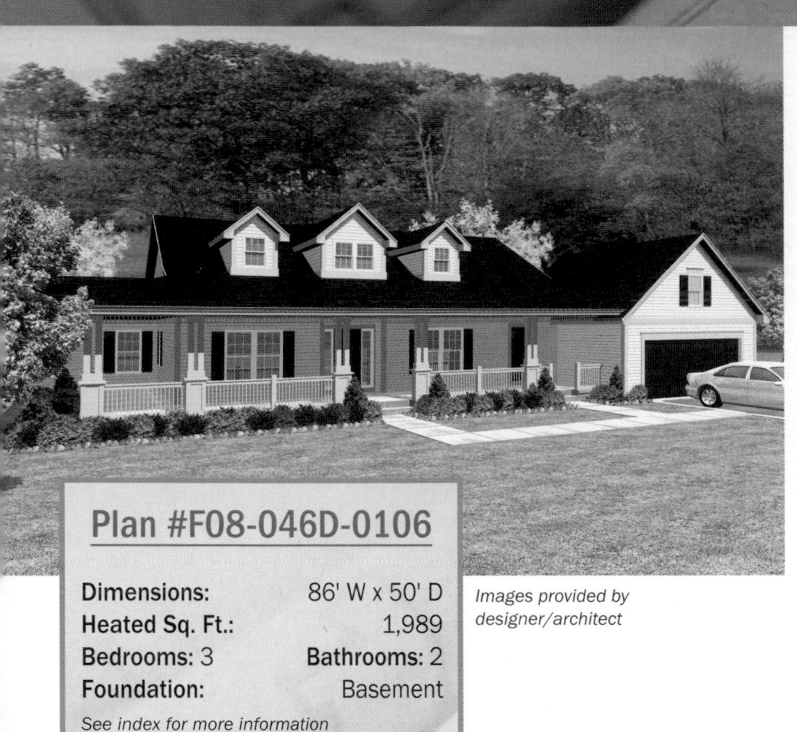

Plan #F08-046D-0106

Dimensions: 86' W x 50' D
Heated Sq. Ft.: 1,989
Bedrooms: 3 **Bathrooms:** 2
Foundation: Basement

See index for more information

Images provided by designer/architect

DECK
DECK
M. BR.
13/9X18/9
LIVING
17/4X18/6
12'-0" CLG.
BRK.
10/0X11/6
KIT.
15/5X11/1
DN
P.
L.
BR. #2
12/6X11/1
E.
DEN/
BR. #3
11/1X11/1
GARAGE
21/5X21/5
PORCH

© Copyright by designer/architect

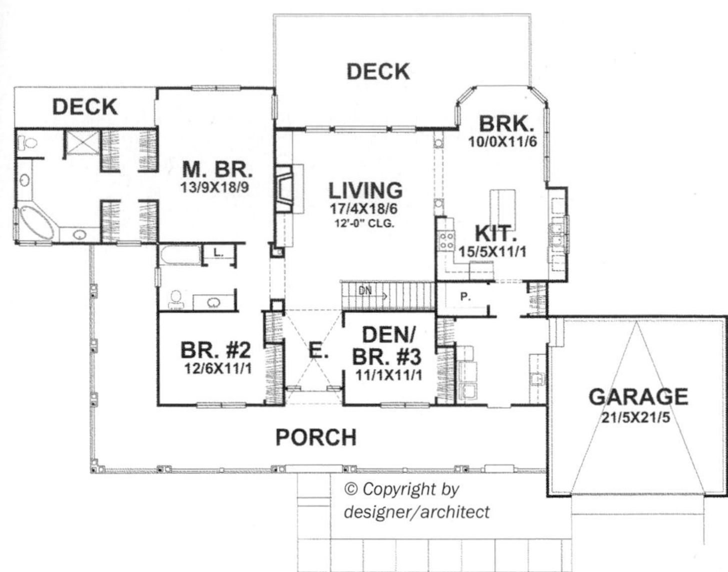

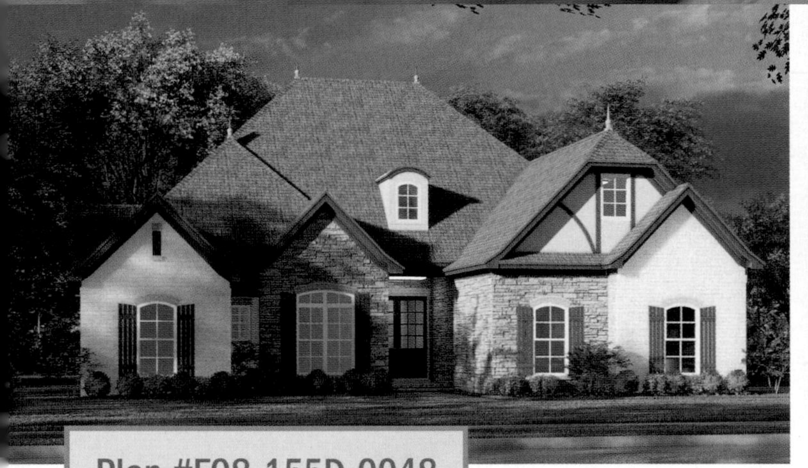

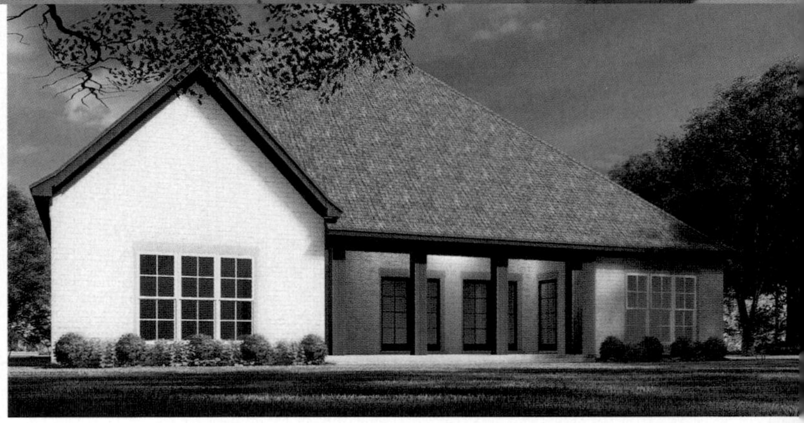

Plan #F08-155D-0048

Dimensions: 56'2" W x 57' D
Heated Sq. Ft.: 2,071
Bonus Sq. Ft.: 435
Bedrooms: 4 **Bathrooms:** 2
Foundation: Crawl space or slab, please specify when ordering

See index for more information

Images provided by designer/architect

ATTIC STRG
DN
BONUS ROOM
13'-8"X21'-0"

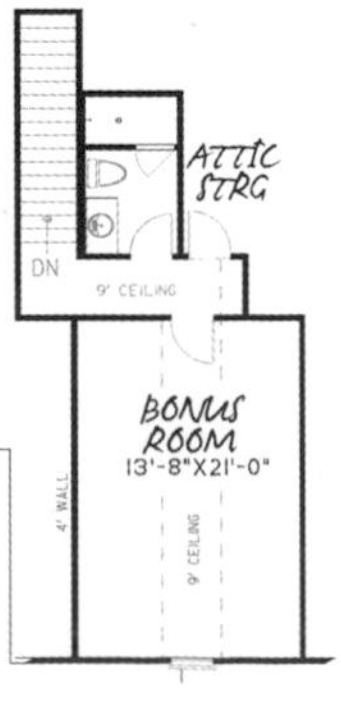

Optional Second Floor
435 sq. ft.

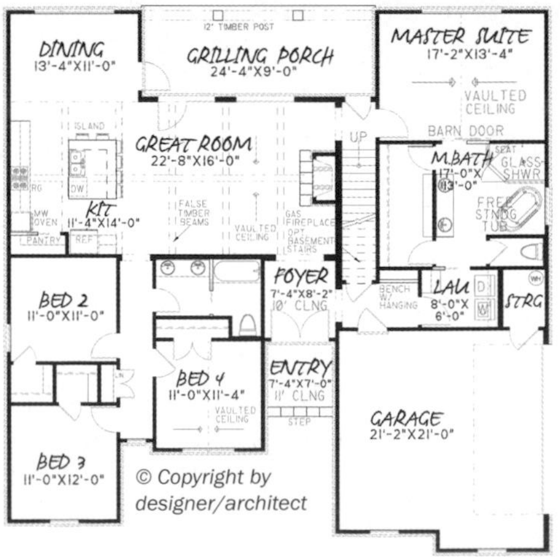

DINING
13'-4"X11'-0"
GRILLING PORCH
24'-4"X9'-0"
MASTER SUITE
17'-2"X13'-4"
VAULTED CEILING
BARN DOOR
GREAT ROOM
22'-8"X16'-0"
UP
M.BATH
KIT
11'-4"X14'-0"
FOYER
7'-4"X8'-2"
10' CLNG
BED 2
11'-0"X11'-0"
LAU
8'-0"X
6'-0"
STRG
BED 4
11'-0"X11'-4"
ENTRY
7'-4"X7'-0"
11' CLNG
GARAGE
21'-2"X21'-0"
BED 3
11'-0"X12'-0"

First Floor
2,071 sq. ft.

© Copyright by designer/architect

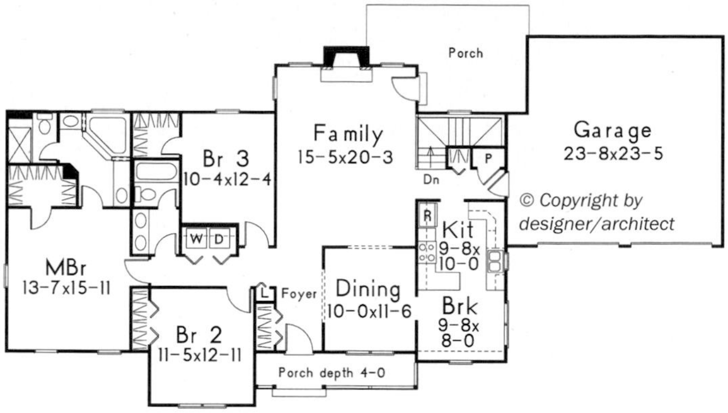

© Copyright by designer/architect

Images provided by designer/architect

Plan #F08-003D-0005

Dimensions: 80' W x 42' D
Heated Sq. Ft.: 1,708
Bedrooms: 3 **Bathrooms:** 2
Foundation: Basement standard; crawl space or slab for an additional fee

See index for more information

First Floor
2,213 sq. ft.

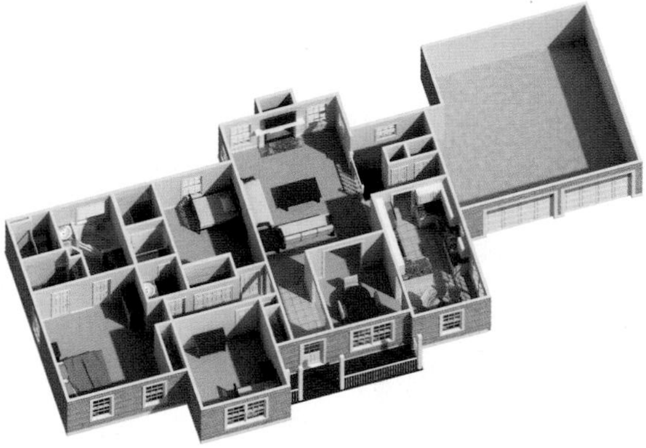

Plan #F08-007D-0235

Dimensions: 75' W x 39' D
Heated Sq. Ft.: 2,213
Bedrooms: 3 **Bathrooms:** 2
Foundation: Walk-out basement

See index for more information

Images provided by designer/architect

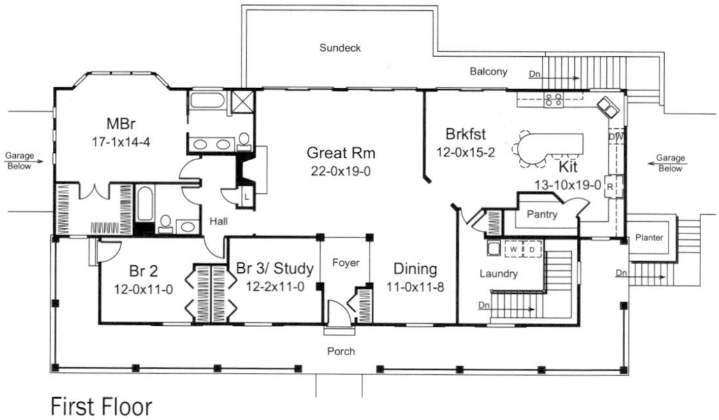

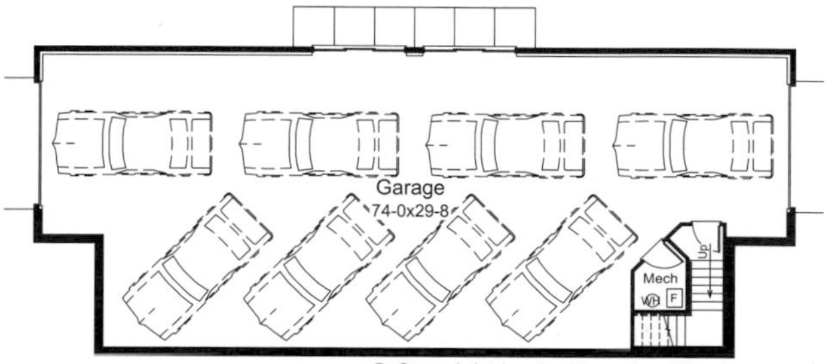

© Copyright by designer/architect

Drive-under Garage

Plan #F08-169D-0003

Dimensions: 41' W x 60'4" D
Heated Sq. Ft.: 1,762
Bedrooms: 3 **Bathrooms:** 2
Foundation: Basement standard; crawl space or slab for an additional fee

See index for more information

Images provided by designer/architect

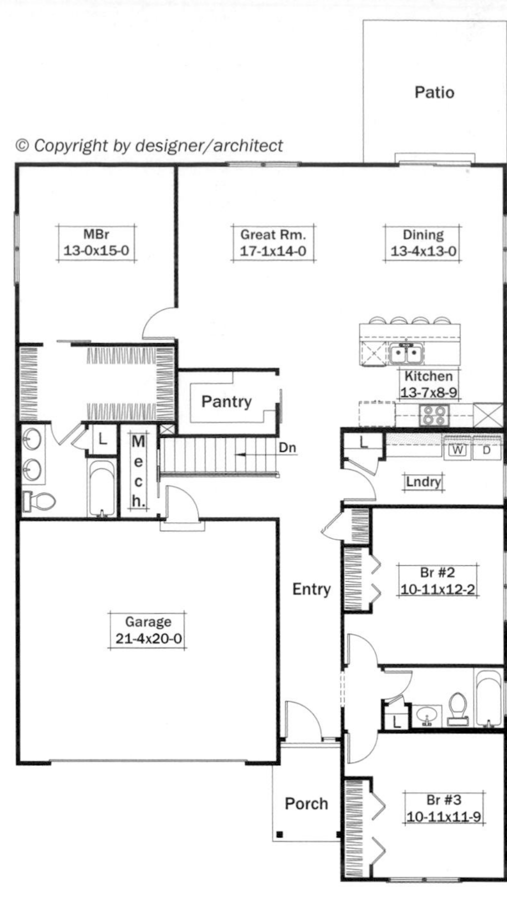

Plan #F08-013D-0245

Dimensions: 75'4" W x 59' D
Heated Sq. Ft.: 1,989
Bedrooms: 3 **Bathrooms:** 2½
Exterior Walls: 2" x 6"
Foundation: Slab standard; crawl space or basement for an additional fee

See index for more information

Images provided by designer/architect

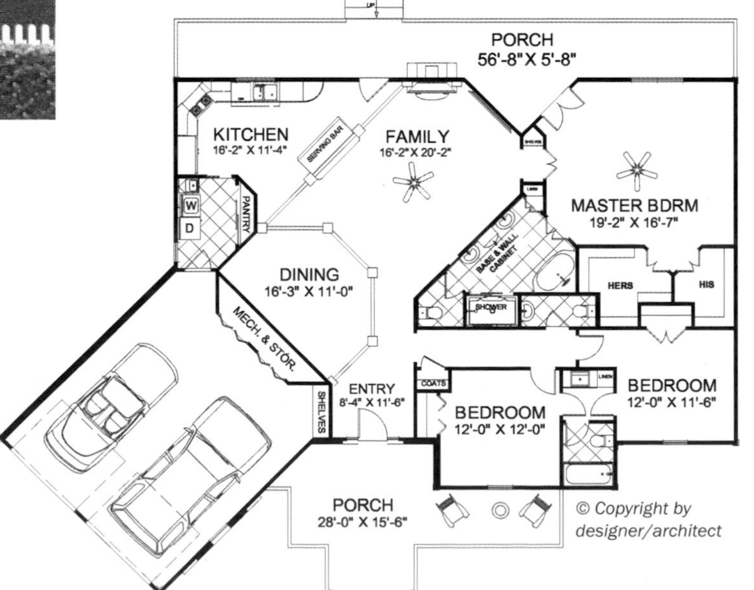

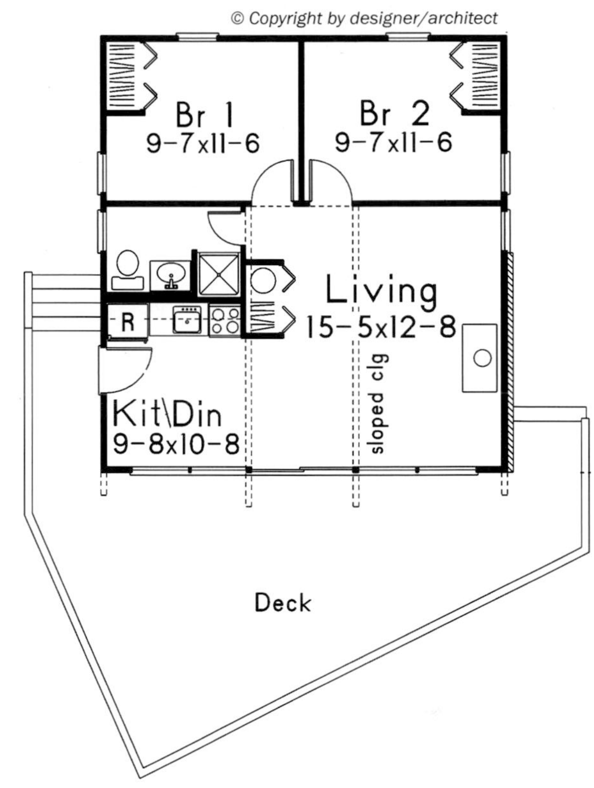

Plan #F08-008D-0133

Dimensions: 26' W x 24' D
Heated Sq. Ft.: 624
Bedrooms: 2 **Bathrooms:** 1
Foundation: Pier

See index for more information

Images provided by designer/architect

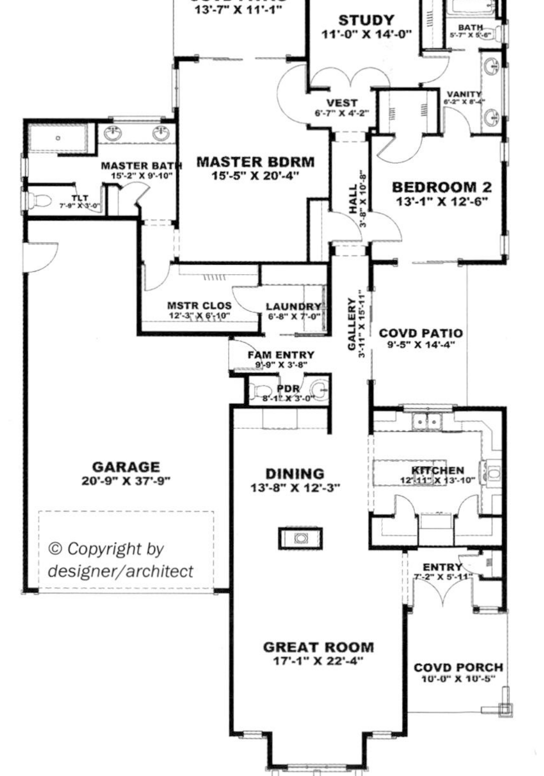

Plan #F08-166D-0001

Dimensions: 49'5" W x 84'9" D
Heated Sq. Ft.: 2,232
Bedrooms: 2 **Bathrooms:** 2½
Exterior Walls: 2" x 6"
Foundation: Slab

See index for more information

Images provided by designer/architect

Plan #F08-032D-0828

Dimensions: 40' W x 50' D
Heated Sq. Ft.: 1,040
Bedrooms: 2 **Bathrooms:** 2
Exterior Walls: 2" x 6"
Foundation: Basement standard; crawl space, floating slab or monolithic slab for an additional fee

See index for more information

Images provided by designer/architect

Plan #F08-121D-0028

Dimensions: 36' W x 54' D
Heated Sq. Ft.: 1,433
Bedrooms: 2 **Bathrooms:** 2
Foundation: Basement standard; crawl space or slab for an additional fee

See index for more information

Images provided by designer/architect

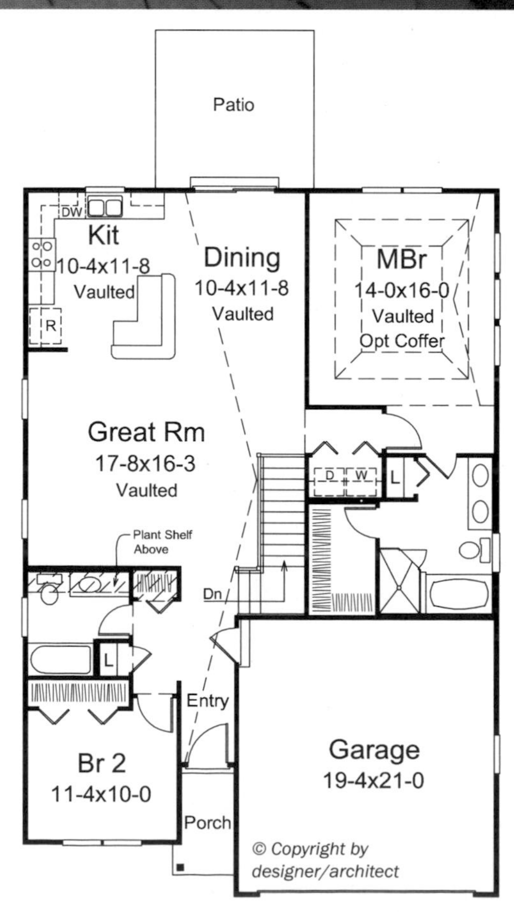

Plan #F08-058D-0249

Dimensions: 56'4" W x 42'4" D
Heated Sq. Ft.: 1,699
Bedrooms: 3 **Bathrooms:** 2
Foundation: Basement

See index for more information

Images provided by designer/architect

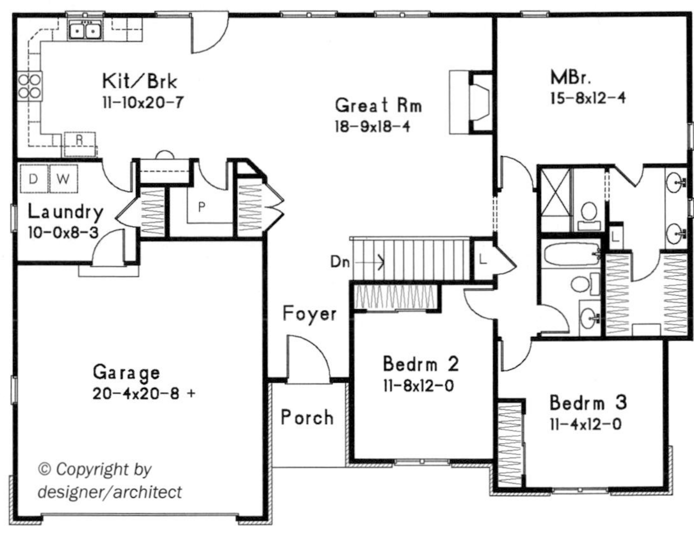

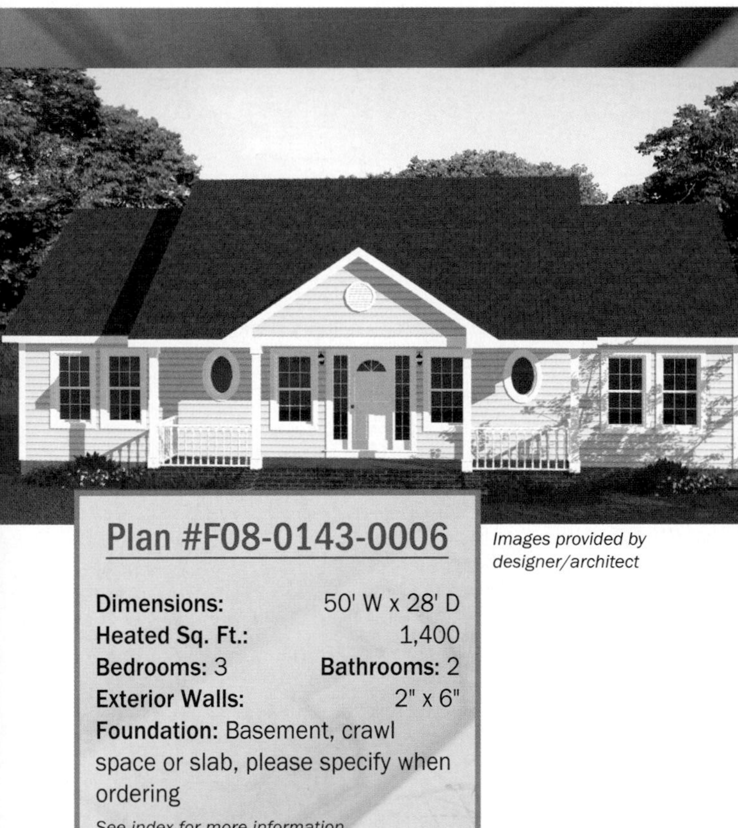

Plan #F08-0143-0006

Dimensions: 50' W x 28' D
Heated Sq. Ft.: 1,400
Bedrooms: 3 **Bathrooms:** 2
Exterior Walls: 2" x 6"
Foundation: Basement, crawl space or slab, please specify when ordering

See index for more information

Images provided by designer/architect

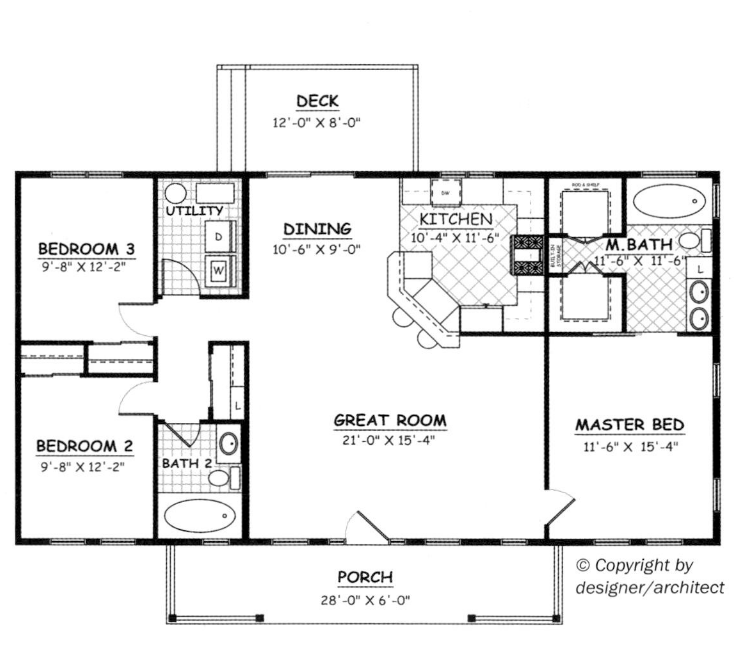

Plan #F08-055D-0196

Dimensions: 60'6" W x 91'4" D
Heated Sq. Ft.: 2,039
Bonus Sq. Ft.: 1,155
Bedrooms: 4 **Bathrooms:** 3
Foundation: Slab or crawl space standard; basement or daylight basement for an additional fee

See index for more information

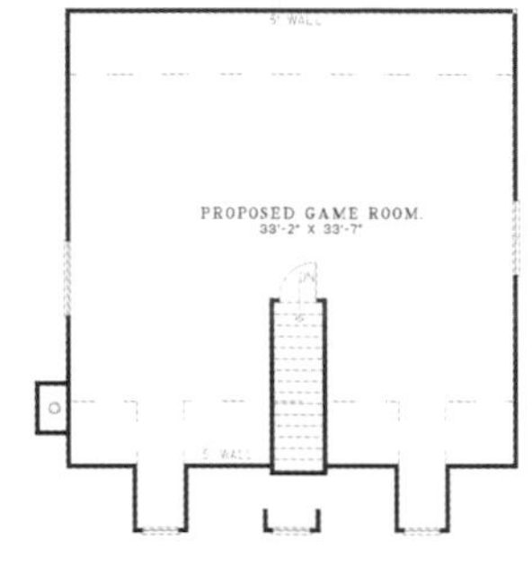

Optional Second Floor 1,155 sq. ft.

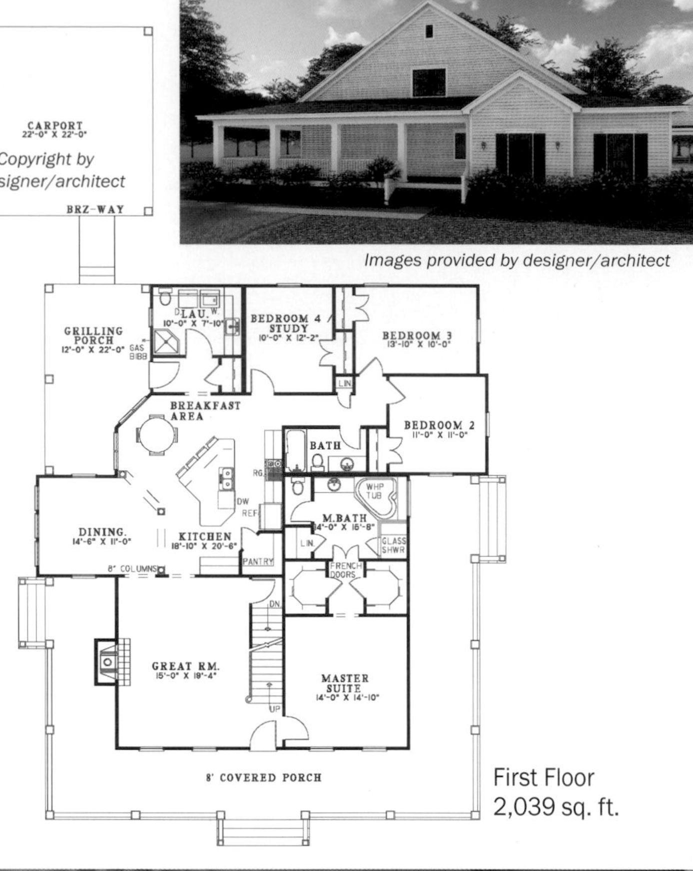

Images provided by designer/architect

First Floor 2,039 sq. ft.

Plan #F08-065D-0315

Dimensions: 60' W x 49'6" D
Heated Sq. Ft.: 1,597
Bedrooms: 3 **Bathrooms:** 2
Foundation: Basement standard; crawl space or slab for an additional fee

See index for more information

Images provided by designer/architect

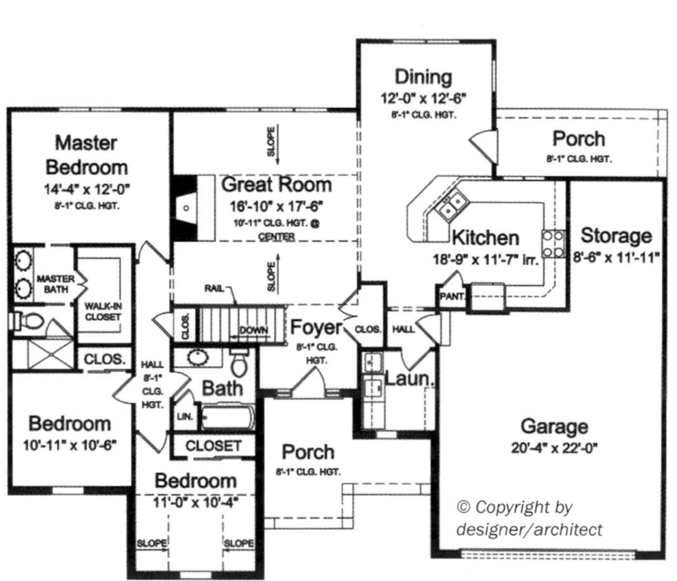

Plan #F08-007D-0196

Dimensions:	27' W x 27' D
Heated Sq. Ft.:	421
Bedrooms: 1	**Bathrooms:** 1
Foundation:	Slab

See index for more information

Images provided by designer/architect

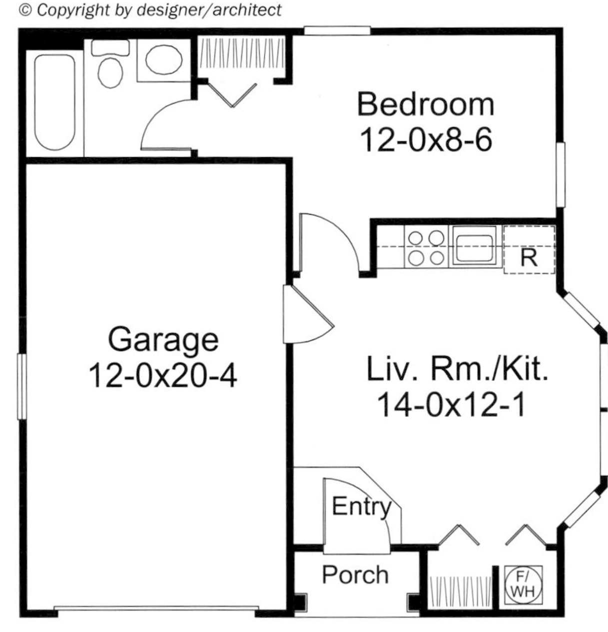

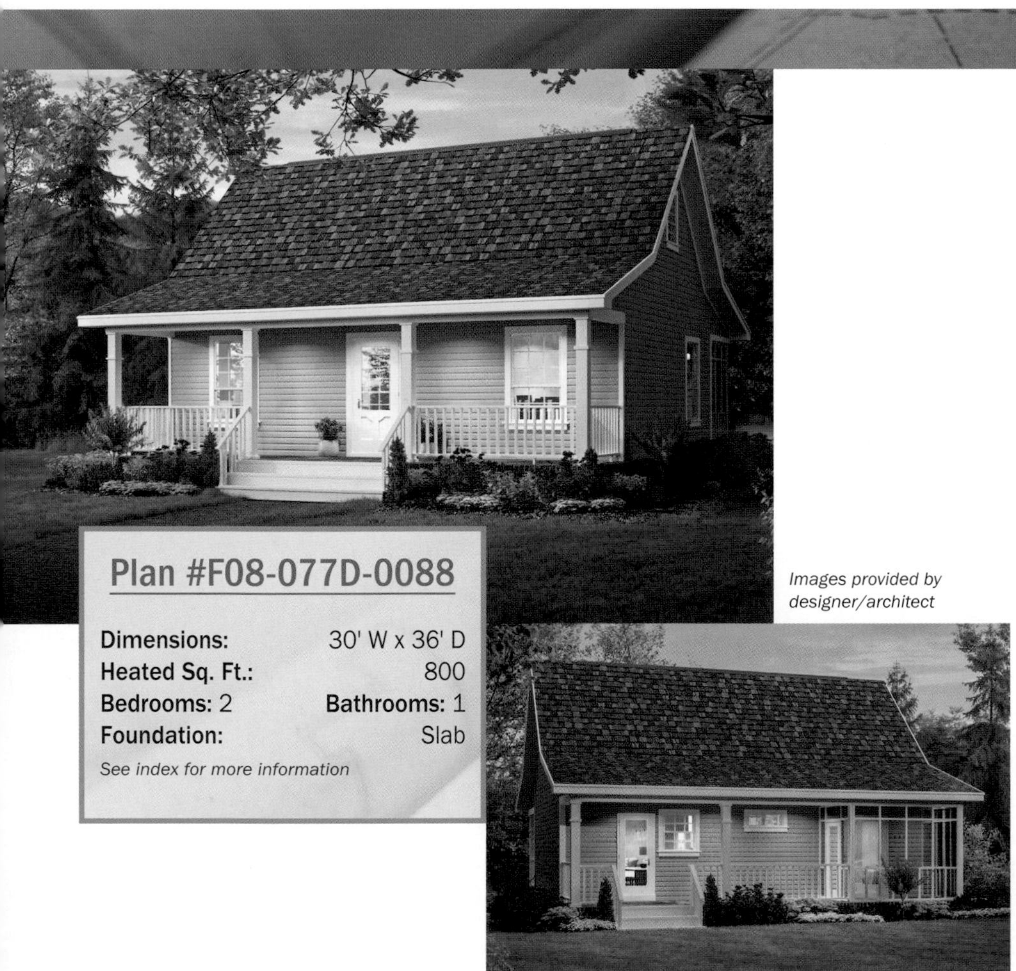

Plan #F08-077D-0088

Dimensions:	30' W x 36' D
Heated Sq. Ft.:	800
Bedrooms: 2	**Bathrooms:** 1
Foundation:	Slab

See index for more information

Images provided by designer/architect

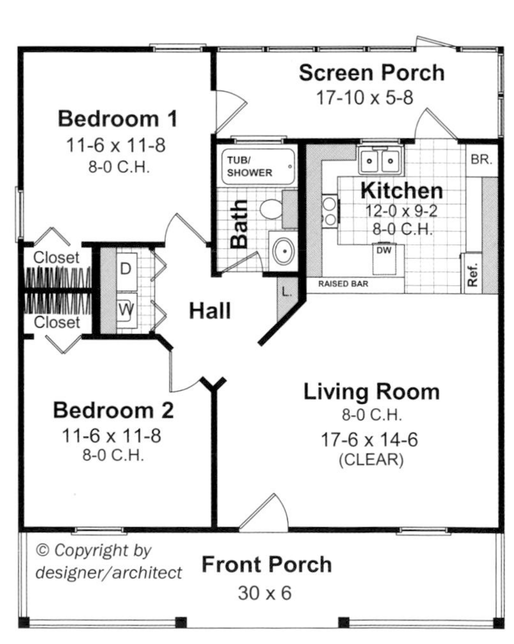

Plan #F08-121D-0017

Dimensions: 40' W x 52' D
Heated Sq. Ft.: 1,379
Bedrooms: 2 **Bathrooms:** 1
Foundation: Basement standard; crawl space or slab for an additional fee
Pricing subject to change

Images provided by designer/architect

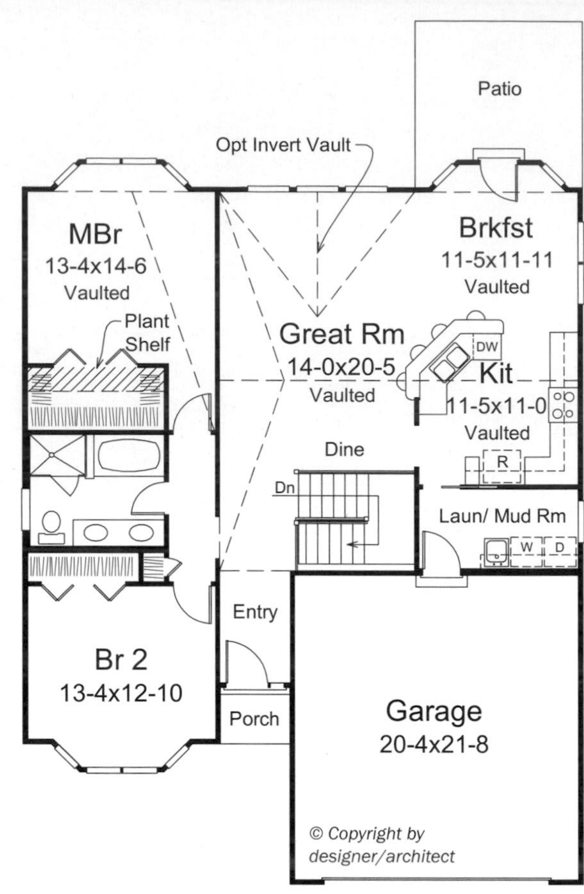

Plan #F08-013D-0048

Dimensions: 63' W x 63' D
Heated Sq. Ft.: 2,071
Bonus Sq. Ft.: 434
Bedrooms: 3 **Bathrooms:** 2½
Foundation: Basement standard; crawl space or slab for an additional fee
See index for more information

Images provided by designer/architect

Optional Second Floor 434 sq. ft.

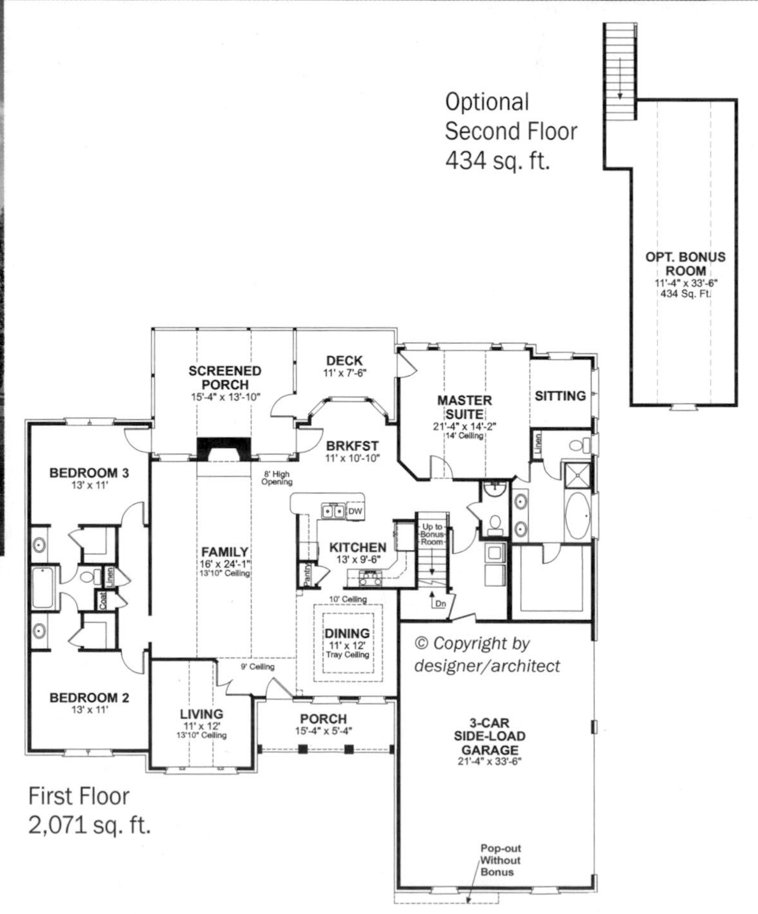

First Floor 2,071 sq. ft.

Plan #F08-058D-0053

Dimensions: 59' W x 44'4" D
Heated Sq. Ft.: 1,895
Bedrooms: 3 **Bathrooms:** 2
Foundation: Basement

See index for more information

Images provided by designer/architect

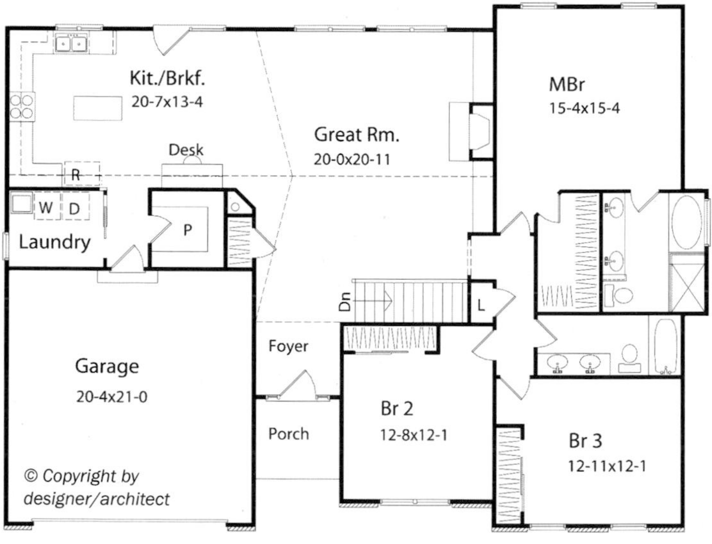

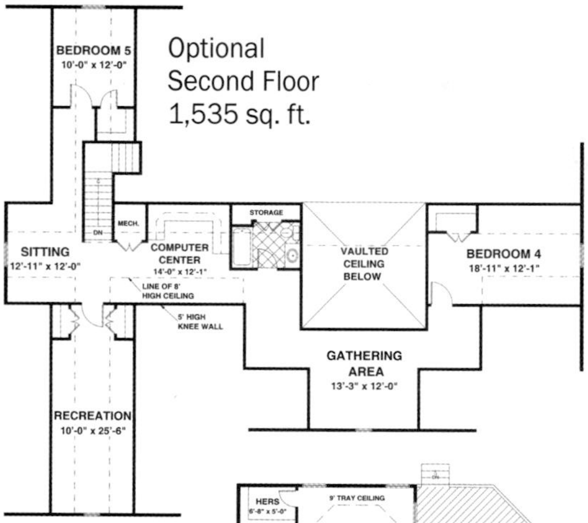

Plan #F08-013D-0235

Dimensions: 71'2" W x 64'6" D
Heated Sq. Ft.: 2,140
Bonus Sq. Ft.: 1,535
Bedrooms: 3 **Bathrooms:** 3
Foundation: Crawl space standard; slab or basement for an additional fee

See index for more information

Images provided by designer/architect

Optional Second Floor
1,535 sq. ft.

First Floor
2,140 sq. ft.

© Copyright by designer/architect

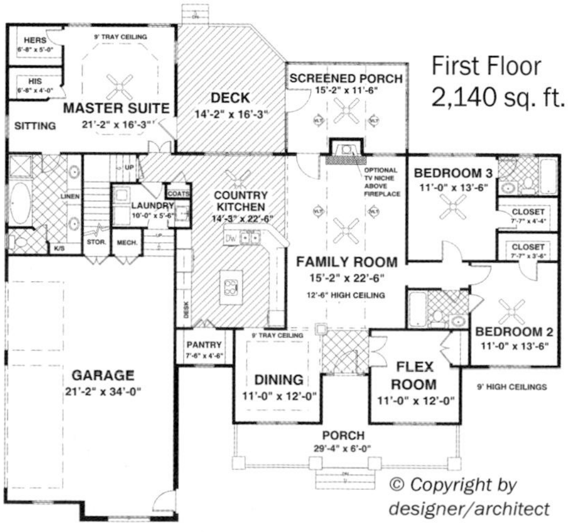

Plan #F08-101D-0118

Dimensions: 72'8" W x 85' D
Heated Sq. Ft.: 2,775
Bonus Sq. Ft.: 1,778
Bedrooms: 2 **Bathrooms:** 2½
Exterior Walls: 2" x 6"
Foundation: Walk-out basement

See index for more information

Features

- Lovely arches with stone and rustic accents create a beautiful front facade
- The entry leads to a beautiful family room with sliding glass doors leading to a covered deck
- The kitchen has a large island facing the great room
- The master bedroom has deck access, two walk-in closets, and a posh bath with a freestanding tub
- The optional lower level has an additional 1,778 square feet of living area including a rec room, media area, wet bar, two bedrooms, two full baths, and a half bath
- 3-car front entry garage

Images provided by designer/architect

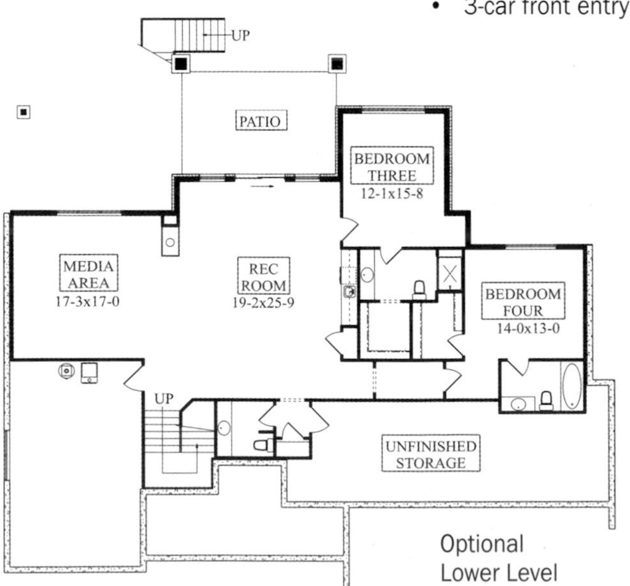

Optional
Lower Level
1,778 sq. ft.

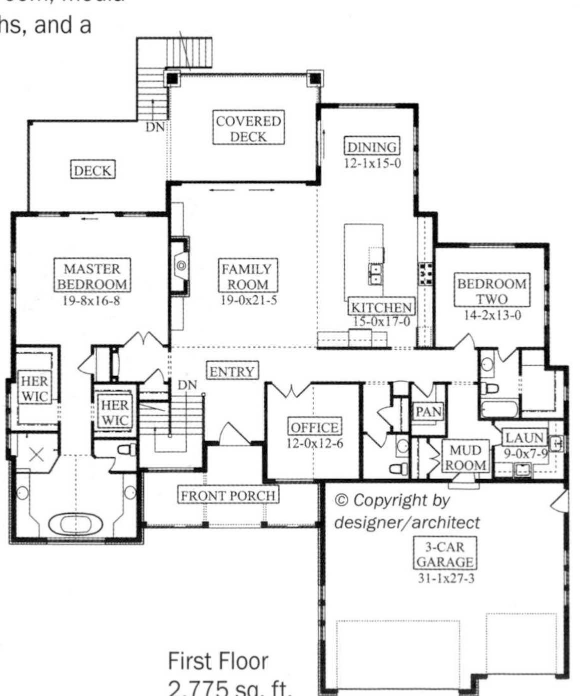

First Floor
2,775 sq. ft.

Plan #F08-011D-0684

Dimensions: 40' W x 59' D
Heated Sq. Ft.: 1,373
Bedrooms: 3 **Bathrooms:** 2
Foundation: Crawl space or slab standard; basement for an additional fee

See index for more information

Images provided by designer/architect

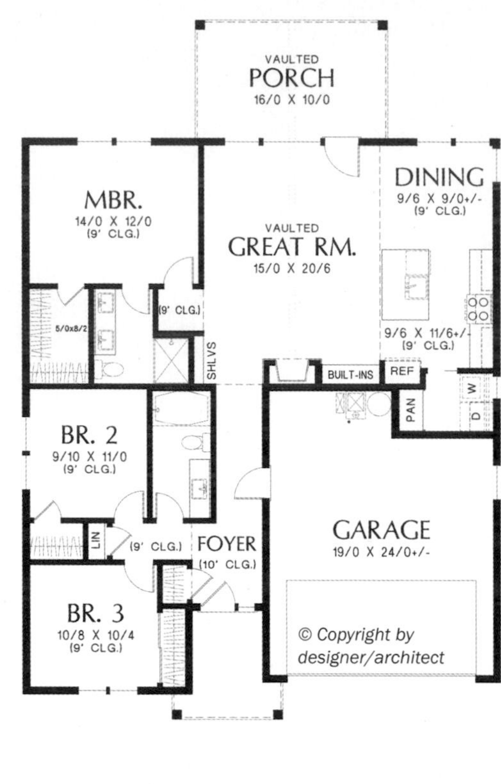

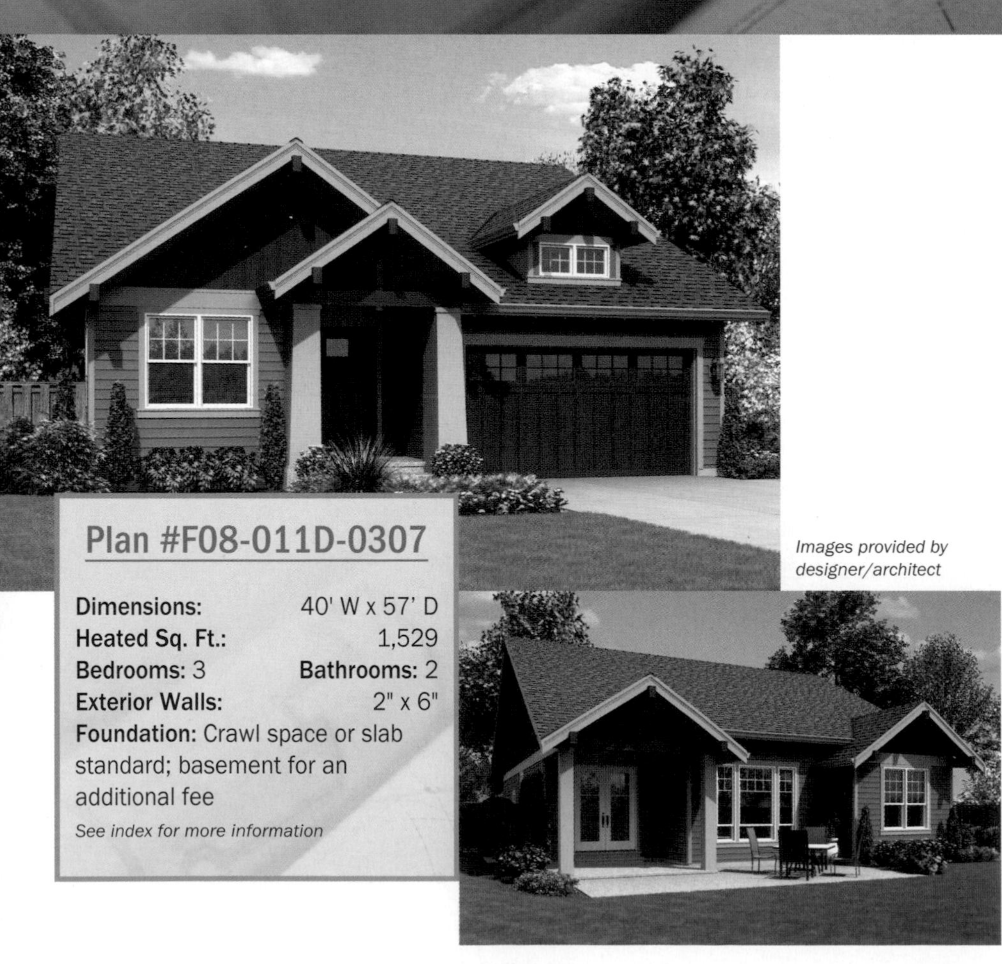

Plan #F08-011D-0307

Dimensions: 40' W x 57' D
Heated Sq. Ft.: 1,529
Bedrooms: 3 **Bathrooms:** 2
Exterior Walls: 2" x 6"
Foundation: Crawl space or slab standard; basement for an additional fee

See index for more information

Images provided by designer/architect

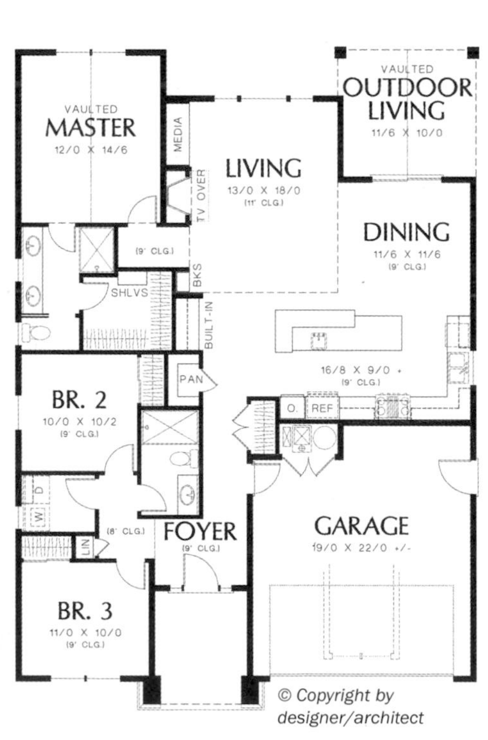

Plan #F08-177D-0006

Dimensions: 46' W x 30'6" D
Heated Sq. Ft.: 894
Bedrooms: 1 **Bathrooms:** 1
Foundation: Slab standard; crawl space for an additional fee

Pricing subject to change

Images provided by designer/architect

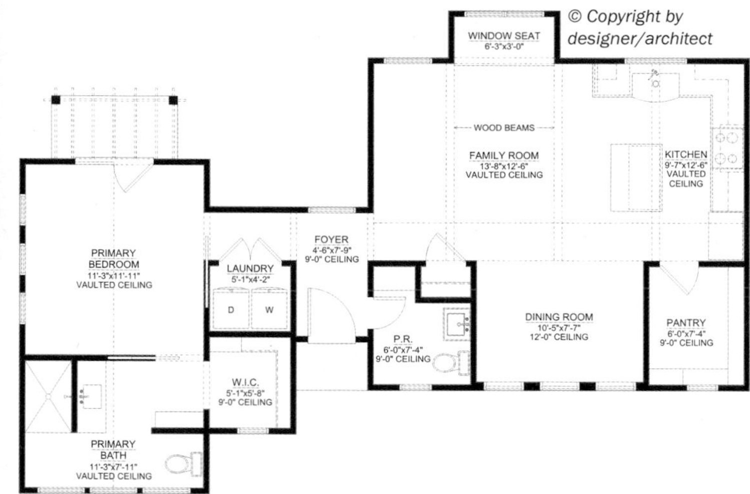

Plan #F08-088D-0267

Dimensions: 66' W x 70' D
Heated Sq. Ft.: 1,898
Bedrooms: 3 **Bathrooms:** 2½
Exterior Walls: 6" SIP
Foundation: Slab

See index for more information

Images provided by designer/architect

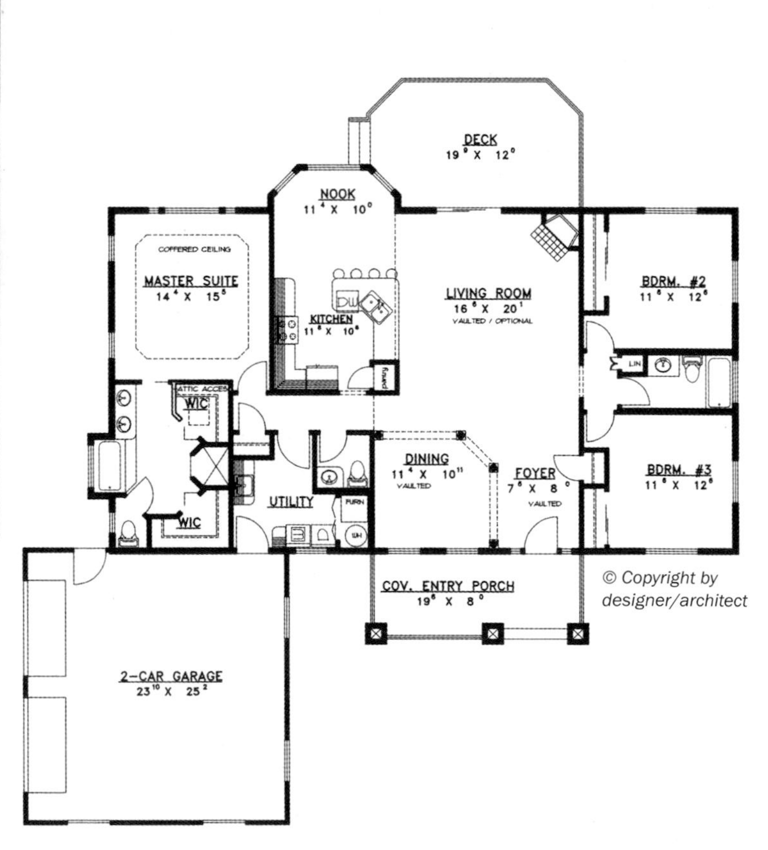

Images provided by designer/architect

Plan #F08-077D-0216

Dimensions: 55' W x 55' D
Heated Sq. Ft.: 1,640
Bedrooms: 3 **Bathrooms:** 2
Foundation: Crawl space or slab, please specify when ordering

See index for more information

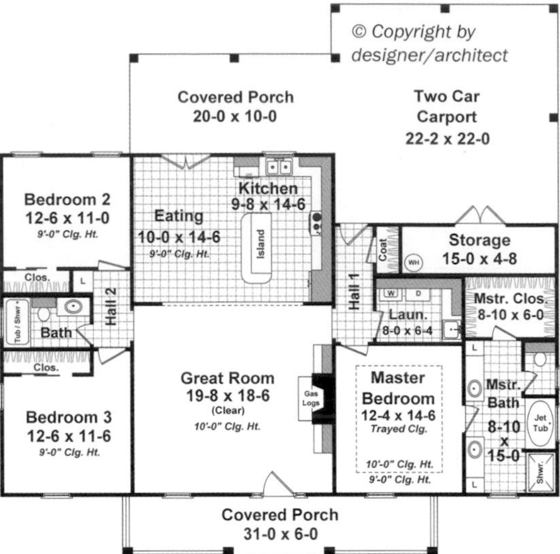

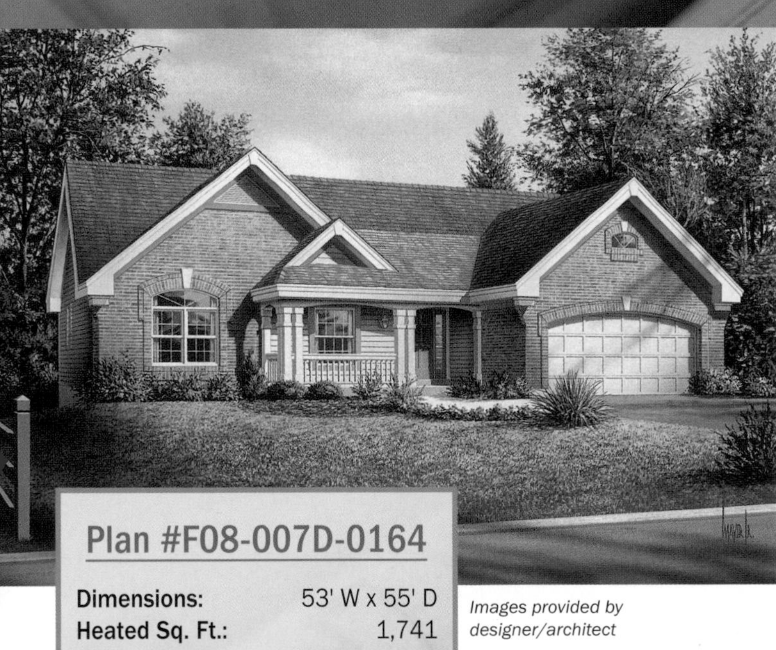

Plan #F08-007D-0164

Dimensions: 53' W x 55' D
Heated Sq. Ft.: 1,741
Bedrooms: 4 **Bathrooms:** 2
Foundation: Crawl space standard; slab or basement for an additional fee

See index for more information

Images provided by designer/architect

Patio
Patio
Din 11-0x12-0
Br 2 10-10x10-0
Kit 13-1x10-0
R
DW
P
Great Room 14-0x20-9 vaulted
Mbr 15-0x13-0 vaulted
Hall
Hall
Study 10-0x11-0
Entry
W
D
Laun.
Br 3 10-1x11-3
Br 4 10-0x11-3
vaulted
Porch
Garage 19-4x20-4
© Copyright by designer/architect

Plan #F08-121D-0048

Dimensions: 44' W x 53'4" D
Heated Sq. Ft.: 1,615
Bedrooms: 2 **Bathrooms:** 2
Foundation: Basement standard; crawl space or slab for an additional fee

Pricing subject to change

Images provided by designer/architect

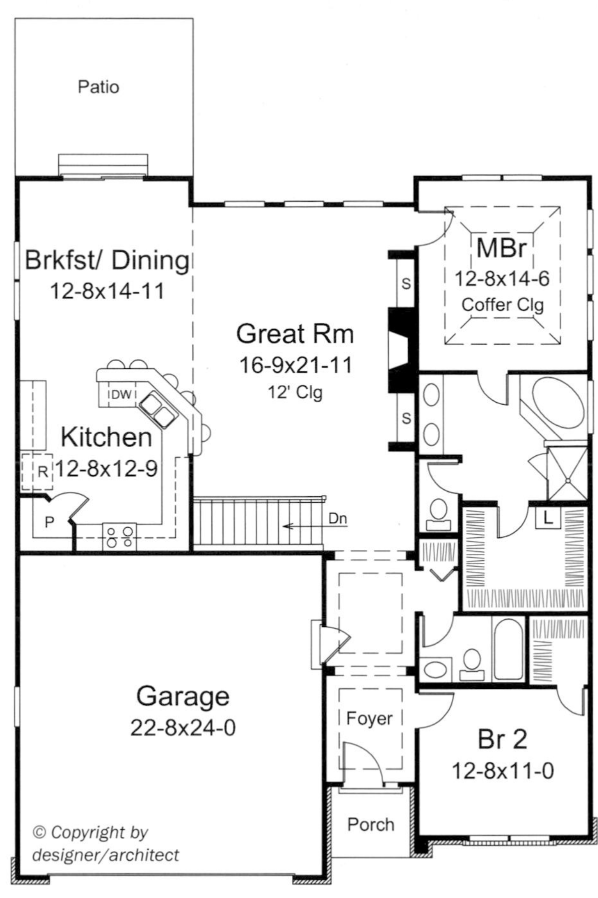

Plan #F08-076D-0213

Dimensions: 71'8" W x 79'7" D
Heated Sq. Ft.: 2,896
Bedrooms: 3 **Bathrooms:** 2½
Foundation: Crawl space or slab, please specify when ordering

See index for more information

Images provided by designer/architect

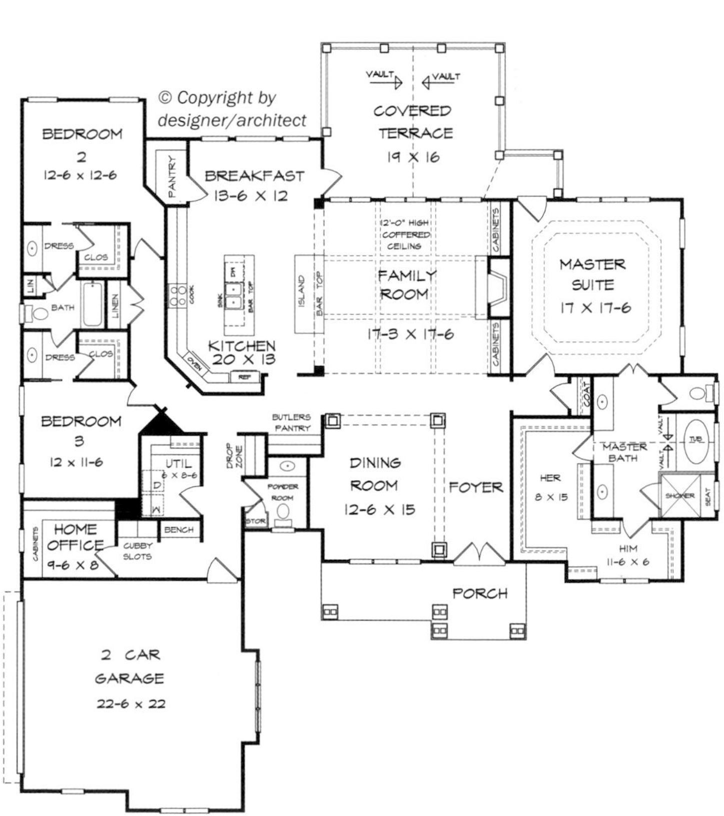

Plan #F08-128D-0209

Dimensions: 31'7" W x 64' D
Heated Sq. Ft.: 1,643
Bedrooms: 3 **Bathrooms:** 2
Foundation: Crawl space

See index for more information

Images provided by designer/architect

Plan #F08-128D-0221

Dimensions: 68' W x 63'8" D
Heated Sq. Ft.: 2,010
Bonus Sq. Ft.: 347
Bedrooms: 3 **Bathrooms:** 2½
Foundation: Basement or crawl space, please specify when ordering

See index for more information

Images provided by designer/architect

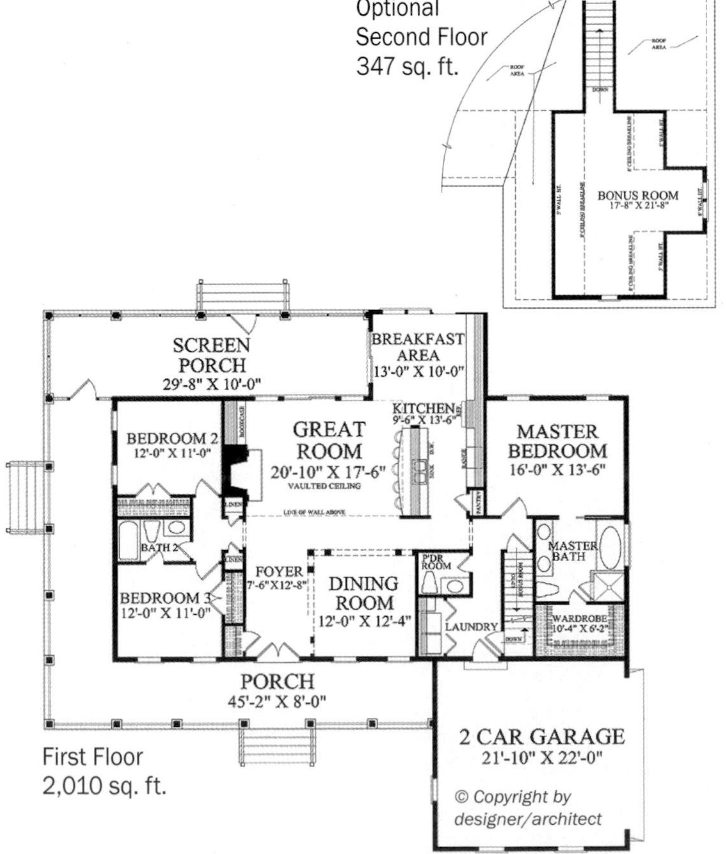

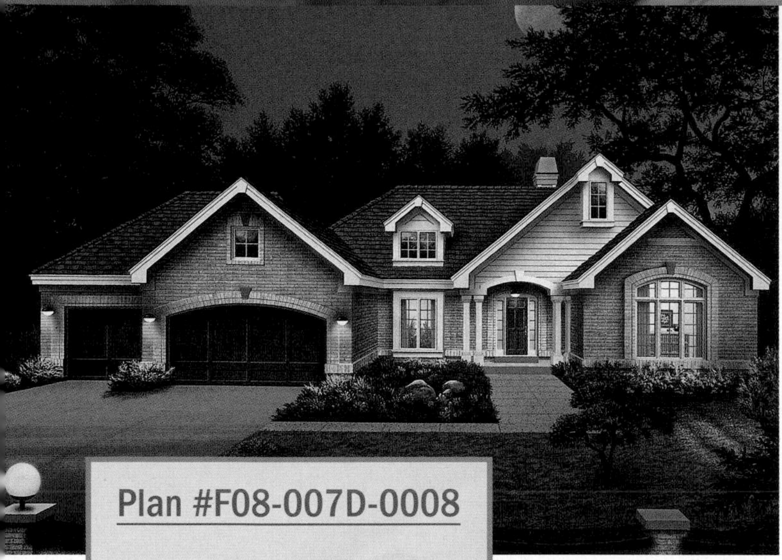

© Copyright by designer/architect

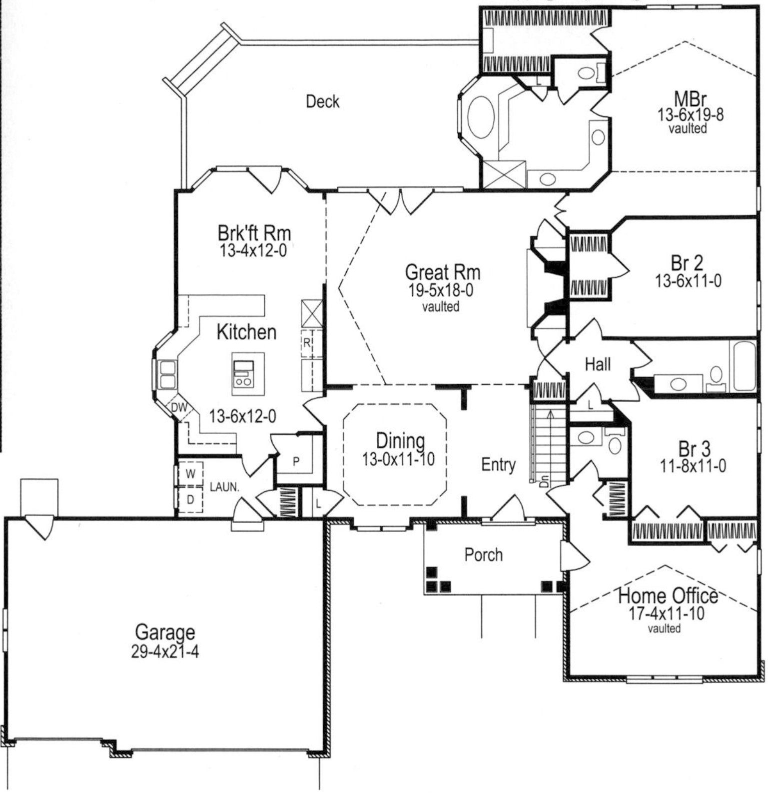

Deck
MBr
13-6x19-8
vaulted
Brk'ft Rm
13-4x12-0
Great Rm
19-5x18-0
vaulted
Br 2
13-6x11-0
Kitchen
13-6x12-0
Hall
Dining
13-0x11-10
Entry
Br 3
11-8x11-0
LAUN.
Porch
Home Office
17-4x11-10
vaulted
Garage
29-4x21-4

Plan #F08-007D-0008

Dimensions: 70'8" W x 70'4" D
Heated Sq. Ft.: 2,452
Bedrooms: 3 **Bathrooms:** 2½
Foundation: Basement standard; crawl space or slab for an additional fee

See index for more information

Images provided by designer/architect

Plan #F08-130D-0315

Dimensions: 57' W x 59'6" D
Heated Sq. Ft.: 1,988
Bedrooms: 5 **Bathrooms:** 3
Exterior Walls: 2" x 6"
Foundation: Slab standard; crawl space or basement for an additional fee

See index for more information

Images provided by designer/architect

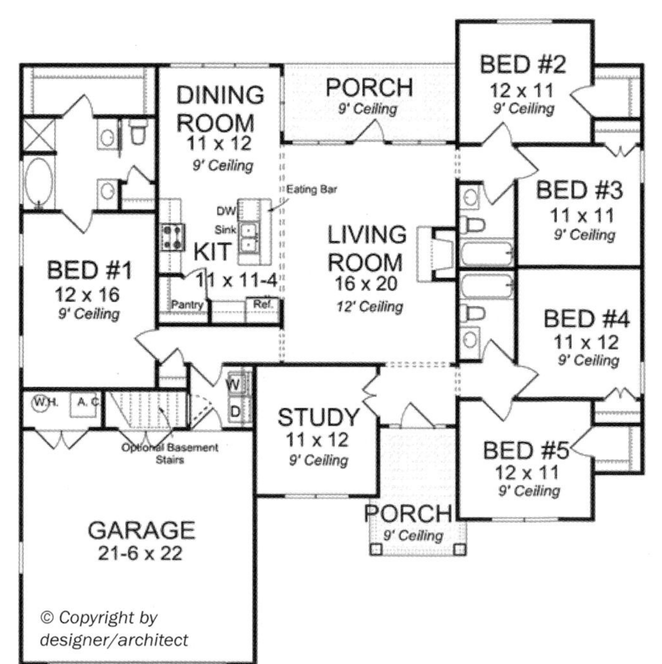

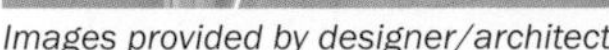

Images provided by designer/architect

Plan #F08-161D-0014

Dimensions:	78' W x 149' D
Heated Sq. Ft.:	3,832
Bedrooms:	3
Bathrooms:	3 full, 2 half
Exterior Walls:	2" x 8"
Foundation:	Crawl space

See index for more information

Features

- Great Modern style with a unique floor plan that offers plenty of space for entertaining as well as a split bedroom layout that is so popular today
- Enter the foyer and to the right is the majority of the home including the kitchen with a massive island, a living area with a see-through fireplace, an outdoor living area, a private master suite with every amenity, an office, and a laundry/mud room combo
- To the left are the two secondary bedrooms and a bonus room which is included in the square footage
- 3-car side entry garage

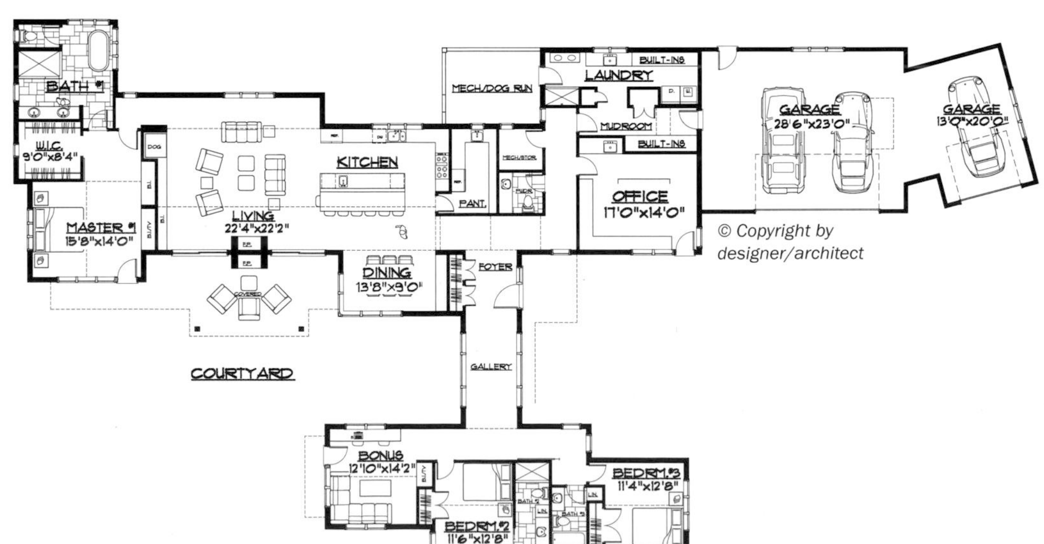

Plan #F08-026D-1939

Dimensions: 60' W x 48' D
Heated sq. ft.: 1,635
Bedrooms: 3 **Bathrooms:** 2½
Foundation: Basement standard; crawl space, slab or walk-out basement for an additional fee

See index for more information

Features

- Great style and layout in a manageable size home that still includes all of those luxurious extras
- Upon entering the home from the garage, you'll discover a handy drop zone featuring storage, a bench, and lockers
- An open family room is next to the dining room, which also extends through to the kitchen
- The kitchen overlooks the dining and family rooms and enjoys plenty of floor space, a center island, and a large walk-in pantry
- 3-car front entry garage

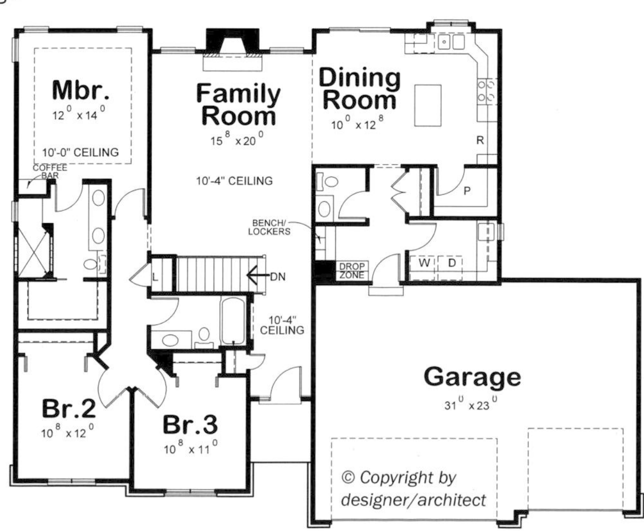

Images provided by designer/architect

Plan #F08-007D-0085

Dimensions: 59'8" W x 40' D
Heated Sq. Ft.: 1,787
Bonus Sq. Ft.: 415
Bedrooms: 3 **Bathrooms:** 2
Foundation: Walk-out basement

See index for more information

Images provided by designer/architect

Garage Below
Deck
skylights above
Great Rm
23-8x15-4
vaulted
plant shelf above
MBr
15-6x14-6
vaulted
Brk'ft
P
Kitchen
14-7x15-8
R
DW
Dining
11-1x13-8
Entry
Hall
Dn
W D
Laun.
Br 3
12-0x12-0
Br 2
12-0x12-0
Shelves
Porch
vaulted

First Floor
1,787 sq. ft.

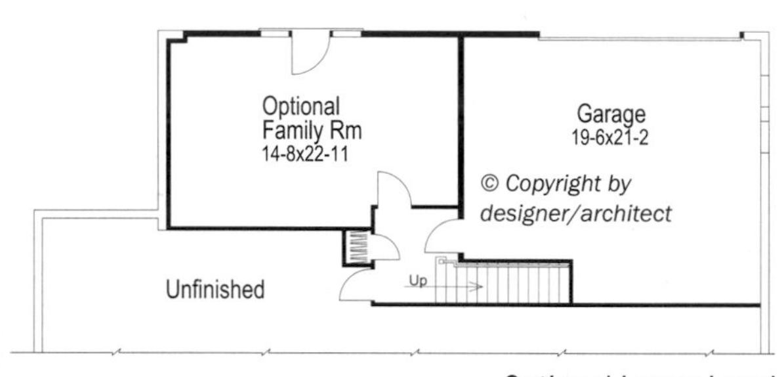

Optional Lower Level
415 sq. ft.

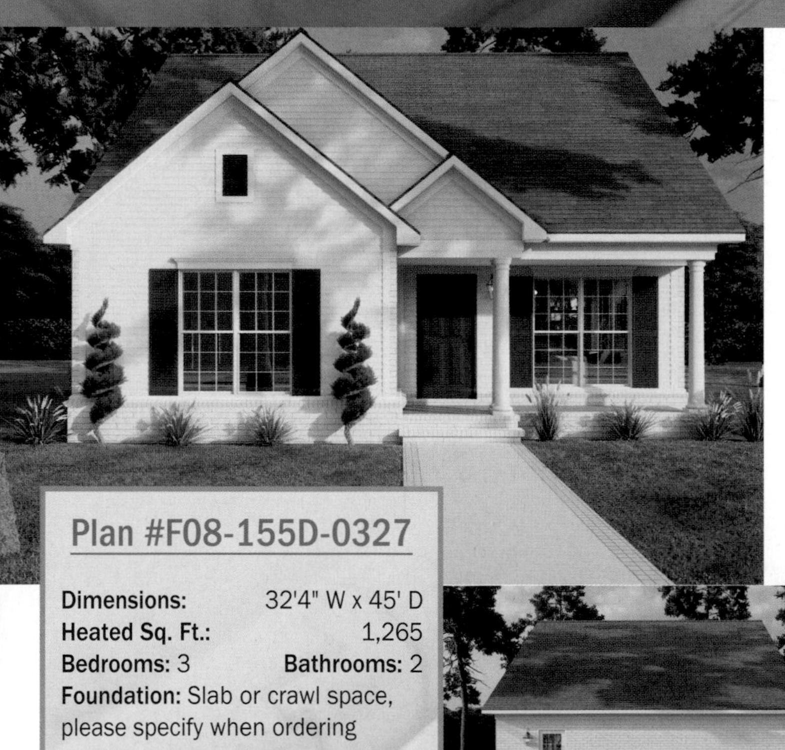

Plan #F08-155D-0327

Dimensions: 32'4" W x 45' D
Heated Sq. Ft.: 1,265
Bedrooms: 3 **Bathrooms:** 2
Foundation: Slab or crawl space, please specify when ordering

See index for more information

Images provided by designer/architect

© Copyright by designer/architect

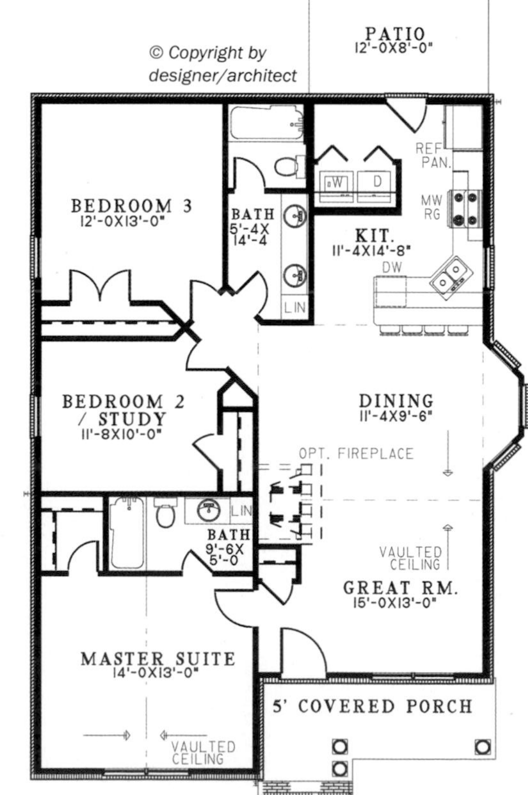

Plan #F08-011D-0682

Dimensions: 69' W x 68' D
Heated Sq. Ft.: 2,451
Bedrooms: 3 **Bathrooms:** 3½
Exterior Walls: 2" x 6"
Foundation: Crawl space or slab standard; basement for an additional fee

See index for more information

Images provided by designer/architect

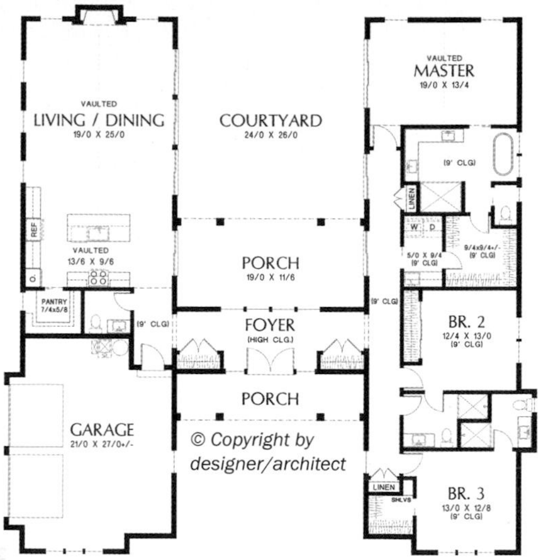

© Copyright by designer/architect

Plan #F08-001D-0072

Dimensions: 46' W x 32' D
Heated Sq. Ft.: 1,288
Bedrooms: 3 **Bathrooms:** 2
Foundation: Crawl space standard; slab or basement for an additional fee

See index for more information

Images provided by designer/architect

© Copyright by designer/architect

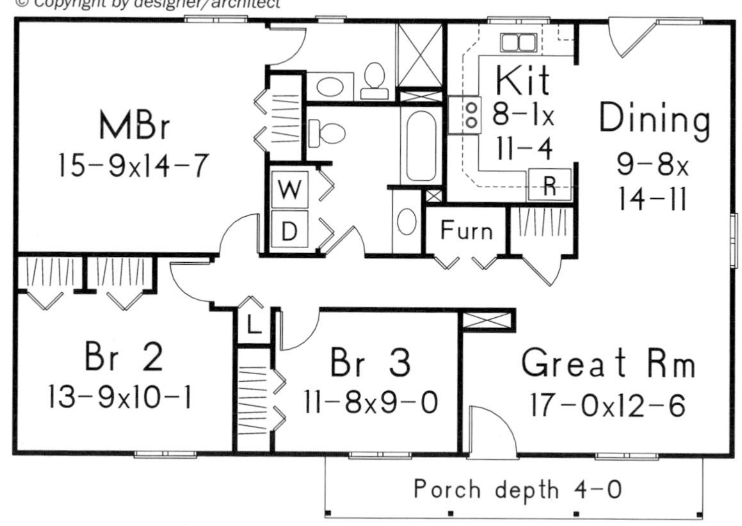

Plan #F08-101D-0056

Dimensions:	72' W x 77' D
Heated Sq. Ft.:	2,593
Bonus Sq. Ft.:	1,892
Bedrooms: 2	**Bathrooms:** 2½
Exterior Walls:	2" x 6"
Foundation:	Walk-out basement

See index for more information

Images provided by designer/architect

Features

- This stunning home has the look and feel homeowners love with its sleek interior and open floor plan
- The great room, kitchen and dining combine maximizing the square footage and making these spaces functional and comfortable
- The master bedroom enjoys a first floor location adding convenience to the homeowners
- The optional lower level has an additional 1,892 square feet of living area and adds extra amenities like a media area, billiards space, recreation and exercise rooms
- 3-car front entry garage

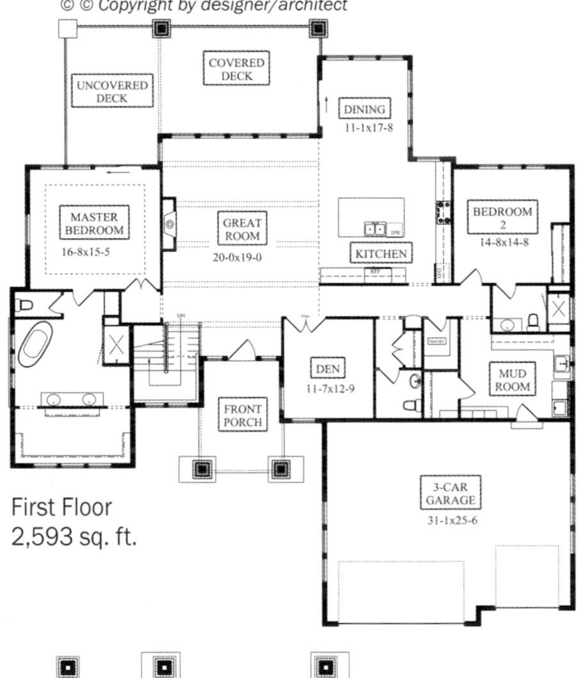

First Floor
2,593 sq. ft.

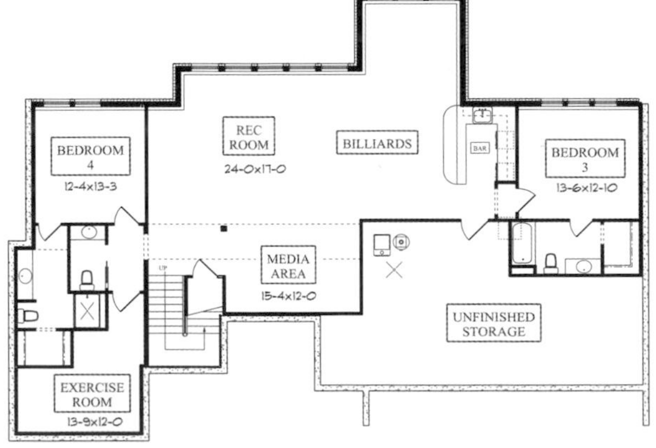

Optional
Lower Level
1,892 sq. ft.

Plan #F08-065D-0381

Dimensions: 60' W x 69'9" D
Heated Sq. Ft.: 2,336
Bonus Sq. Ft.: 2,336
Bedrooms: 3 **Bathrooms:** 2
Foundation: Basement

See index for more information

Images provided by designer/architect

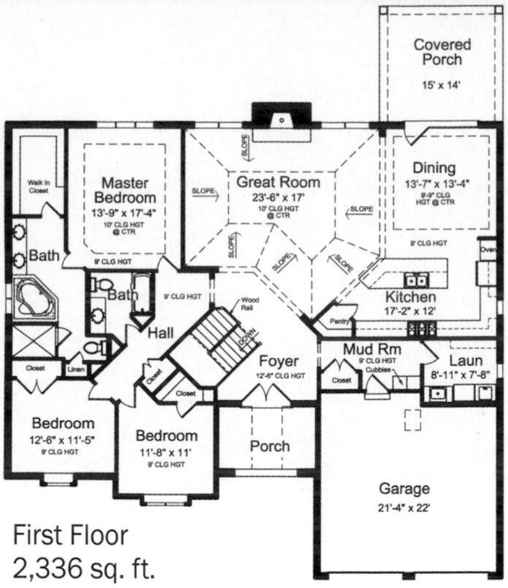

First Floor
2,336 sq. ft.

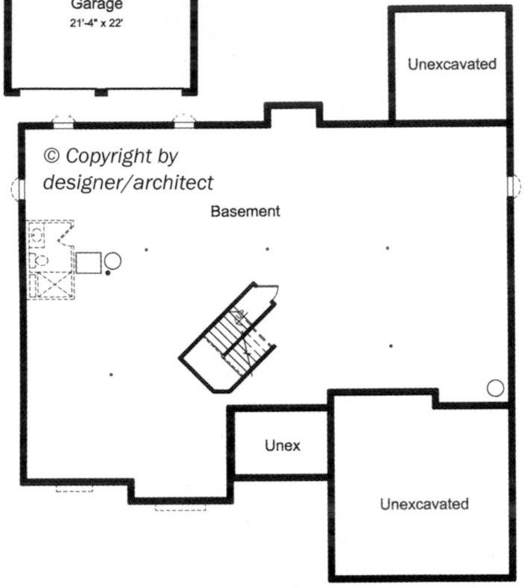

Optional Lower Level
2,336 sq. ft.

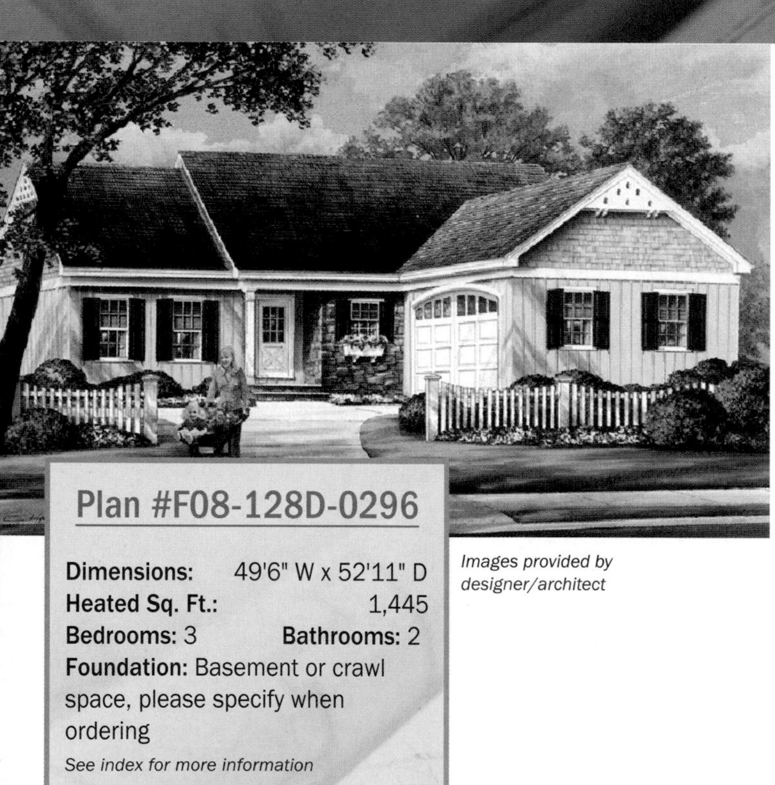

Plan #F08-128D-0296

Dimensions: 49'6" W x 52'11" D
Heated Sq. Ft.: 1,445
Bedrooms: 3 **Bathrooms:** 2
Foundation: Basement or crawl space, please specify when ordering

See index for more information

Images provided by designer/architect

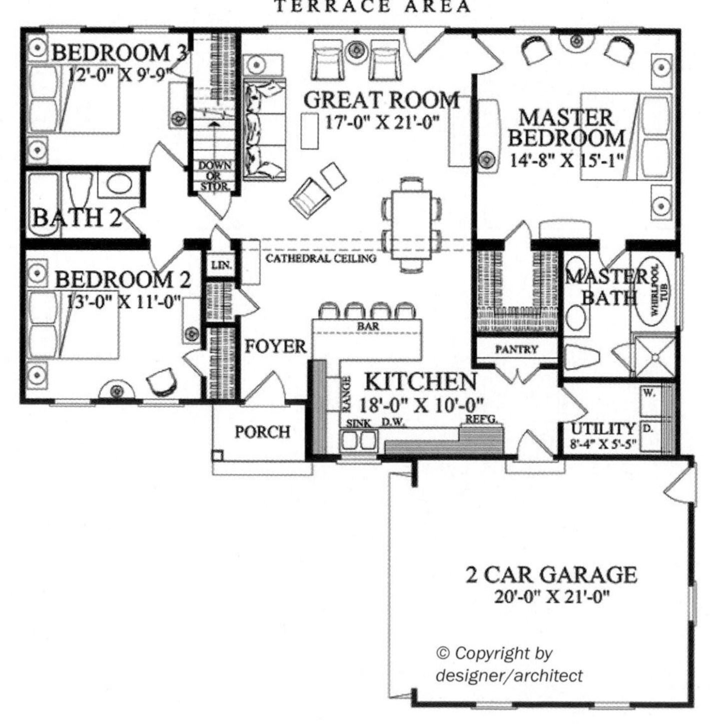

Plan #F08-013D-0201

Dimensions: 71'2" W x 64'6" D
Heated Sq. Ft.: 2,294
Bonus Sq. Ft.: 1,562
Bedrooms: 3 **Bathrooms:** 3½
Foundation: Crawl space standard; basement or slab for an additional fee

See index for more information

Images provided by designer/architect

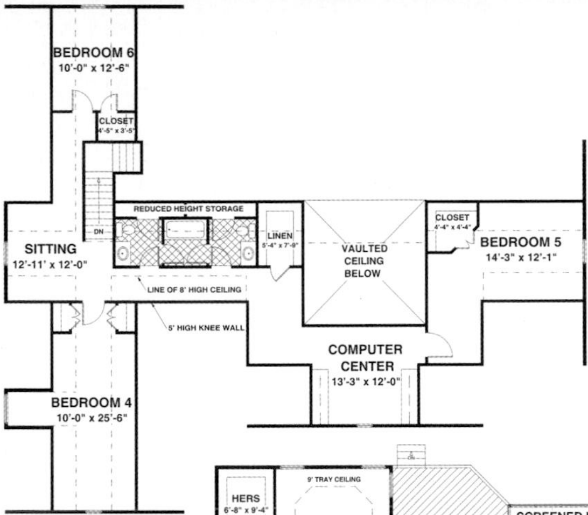

Optional Second Floor
1,562 sq. ft.

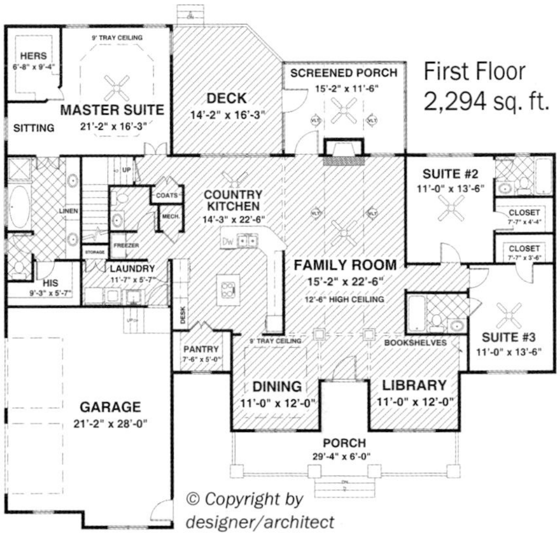

First Floor
2,294 sq. ft.

Plan #F08-001D-0088

Dimensions: 32' W x 25' D
Heated Sq. Ft.: 800
Bedrooms: 2 **Bathrooms:** 1
Foundation: Crawl space standard; slab for an additional fee

See index for more information

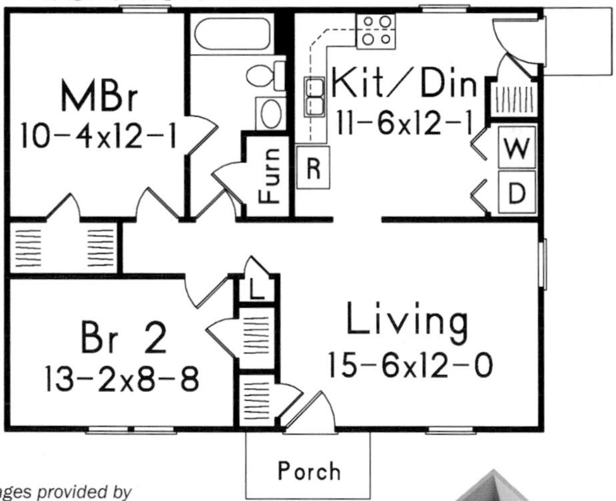

Images provided by designer/architect

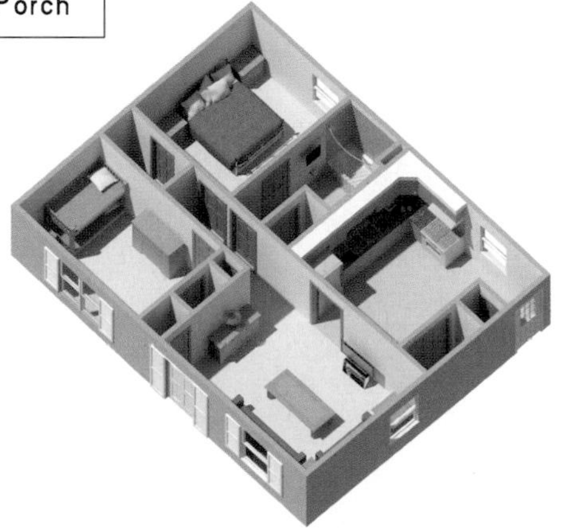

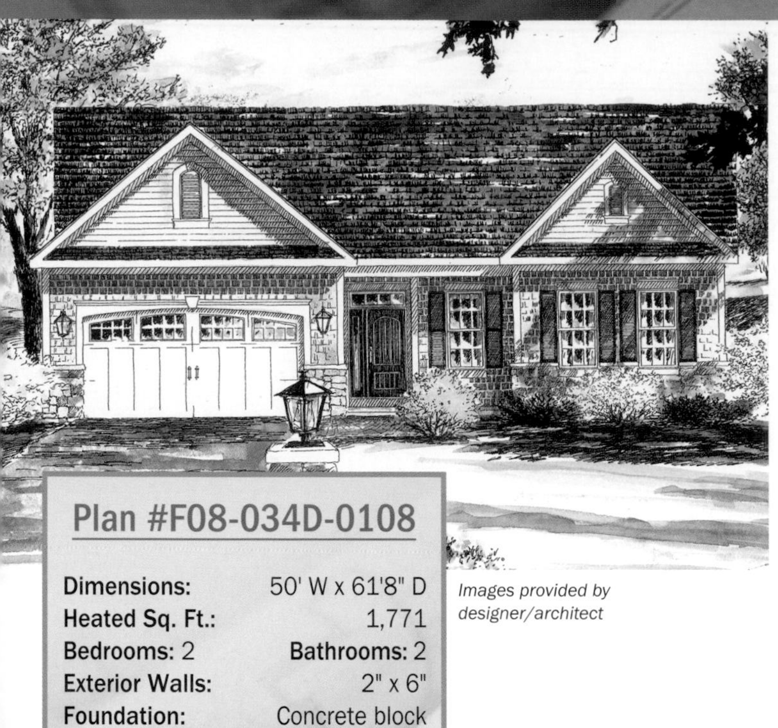

Plan #F08-034D-0108

Dimensions:	50' W x 61'8" D
Heated Sq. Ft.:	1,771
Bedrooms: 2	**Bathrooms:** 2
Exterior Walls:	2" x 6"
Foundation:	Concrete block

See index for more information

Images provided by designer/architect

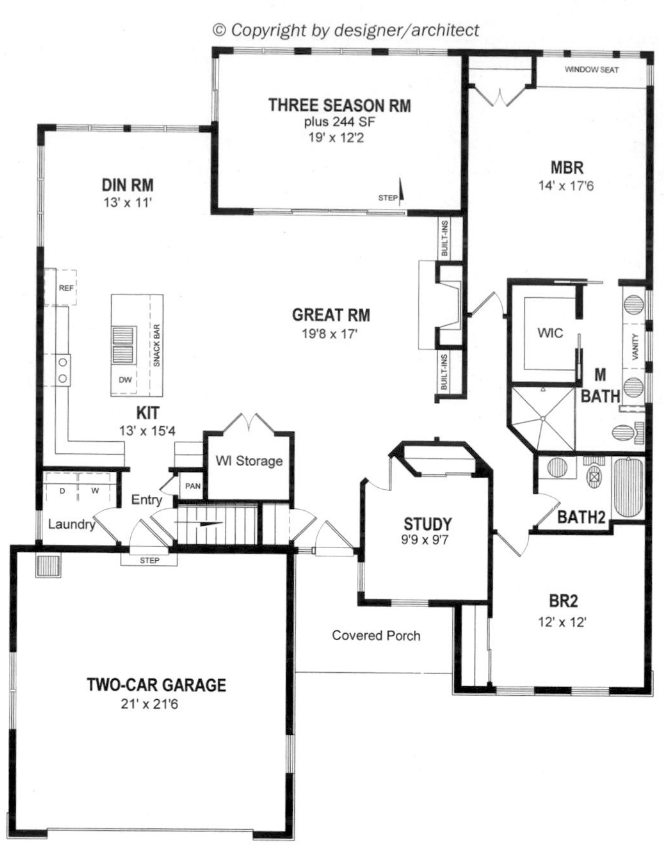

Plan #F08-048D-0008

Dimensions:	61'8" W x 50'4" D
Heated Sq. Ft.:	2,089
Bedrooms: 4	**Bathrooms:** 3
Foundation:	Slab

See index for more information

Images provided by designer/architect

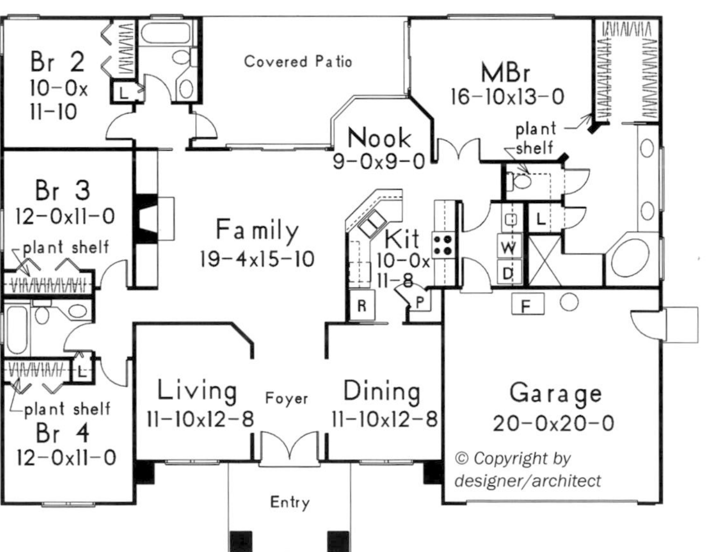

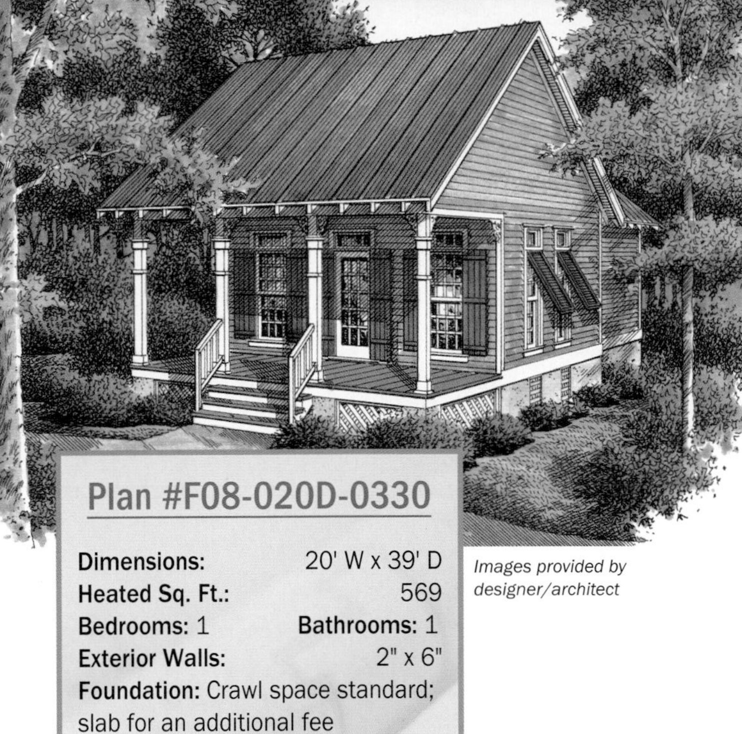

Plan #F08-020D-0330

Dimensions: 20' W x 39' D
Heated Sq. Ft.: 569
Bedrooms: 1 **Bathrooms:** 1
Exterior Walls: 2" x 6"
Foundation: Crawl space standard; slab for an additional fee

See index for more information

Images provided by designer/architect

wic
6' x 6'
bedroom
11' x 12'
bath
10' x 6'
A/C
util
& CLO.
w/d
wh
rng
snk
kit, dining, living
14' X 20'
ref
pan
© Copyright by designer/architect
porch 20' x 8'

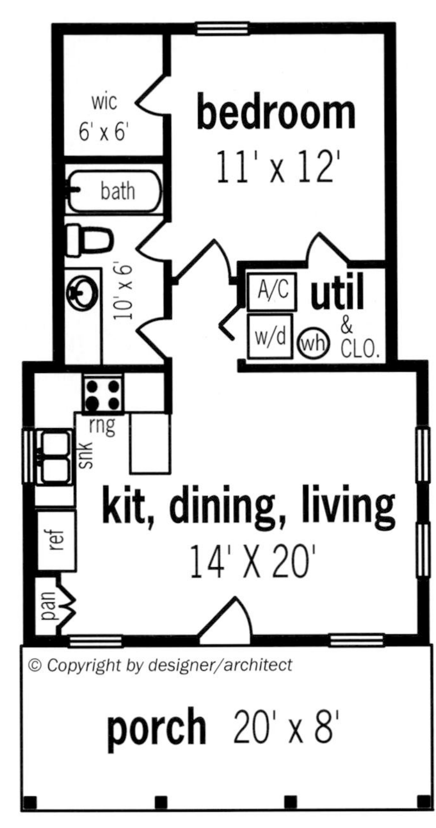

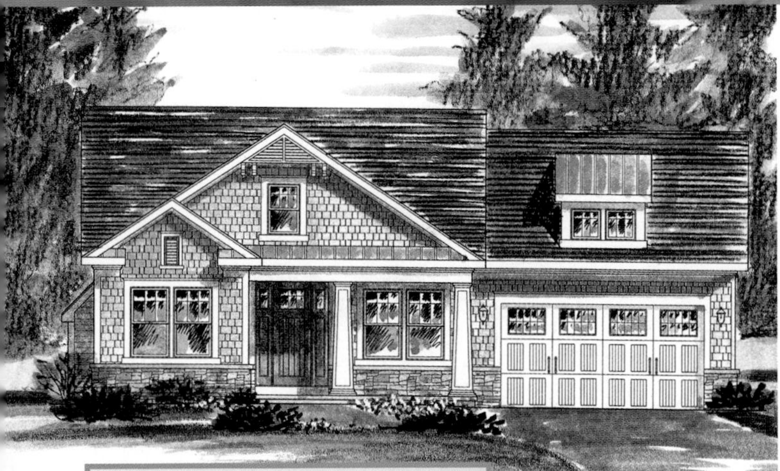

Plan #F08-034D-0104

Dimensions: 52' W x 55'2" D
Heated Sq. Ft.: 1,598
Bedrooms: 3 **Bathrooms:** 2
Exterior Walls: 2" x 6"
Foundation: Concrete block

See index for more information

Images provided by designer/architect

© Copyright by designer/architect
MBR
14' x 15'
tray cl'g
MBATH
WIC
Covered Porch
16'8 x 9'
DIN RM
12' x 12'4
PAN
Entry
Laun
BENCH
SNACK BAR
DW
GREAT RM
19'8 x 16'
KIT
9' x 12'8
REF
BATH2
LINEN
FOYER
STUDY/
BR3
10' x 10'
plus
TWO-CAR GARAGE
20'2 x 19'8
BR2
11' x 11'6
Covered Porch

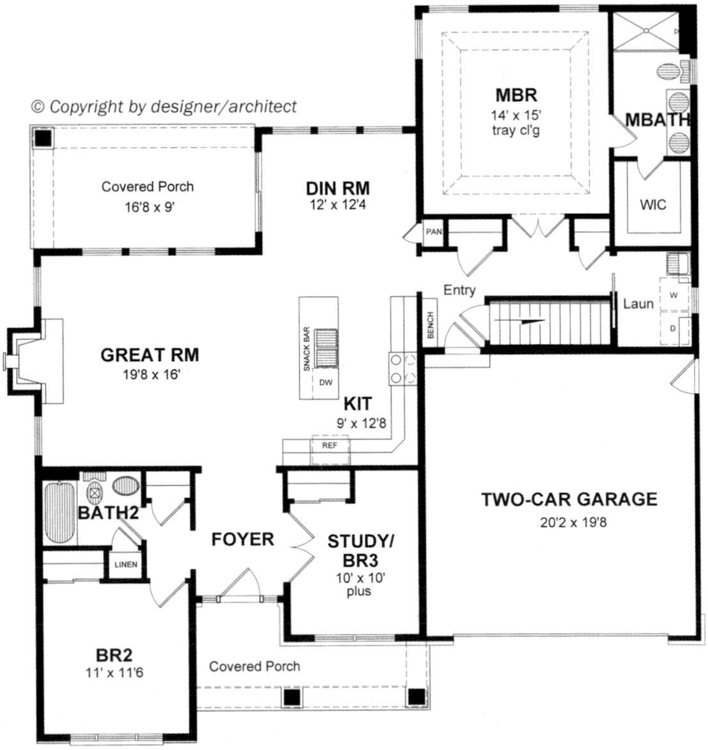

Plan #F08-055D-0651

Dimensions: 89' W x 49'4" D
Heated Sq. Ft.: 1,800
Bedrooms: 3 **Bathrooms:** 2
Foundation: Slab or crawl space standard; basement or daylight basement for an additional fee
See index for more information

Images provided by designer/architect

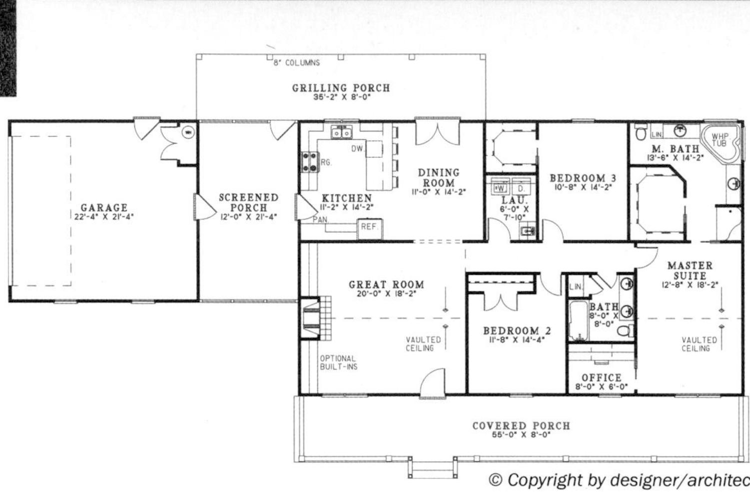

Plan #F08-077D-0052

Dimensions: 65' W x 50'10" D
Heated Sq. Ft.: 1,802
Bedrooms: 3 **Bathrooms:** 2
Foundation: Slab, crawl space, basement or daylight basement, please specify when ordering
See index for more information

Images provided by designer/architect

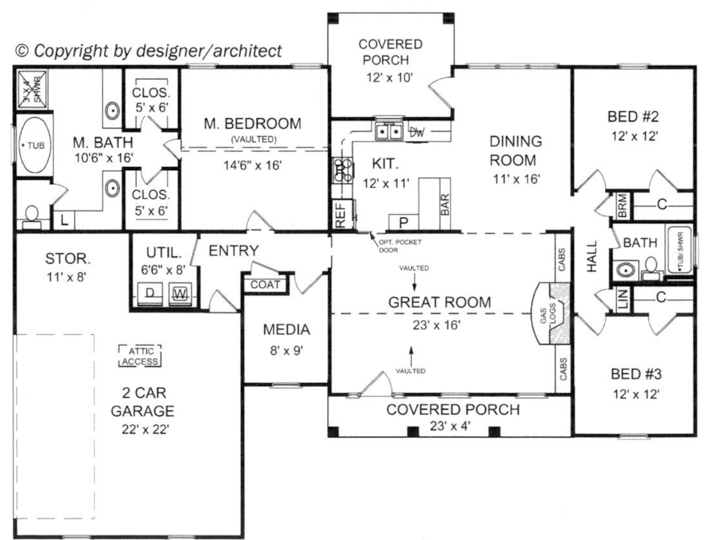

Plan #F08-128D-0313

Dimensions: 64'2" W x 52'2" D
Heated Sq. Ft.: 1,903
Bedrooms: 3 **Bathrooms:** 3
Foundation: Basement or crawl space, please specify when ordering

See index for more information

Images provided by designer/architect

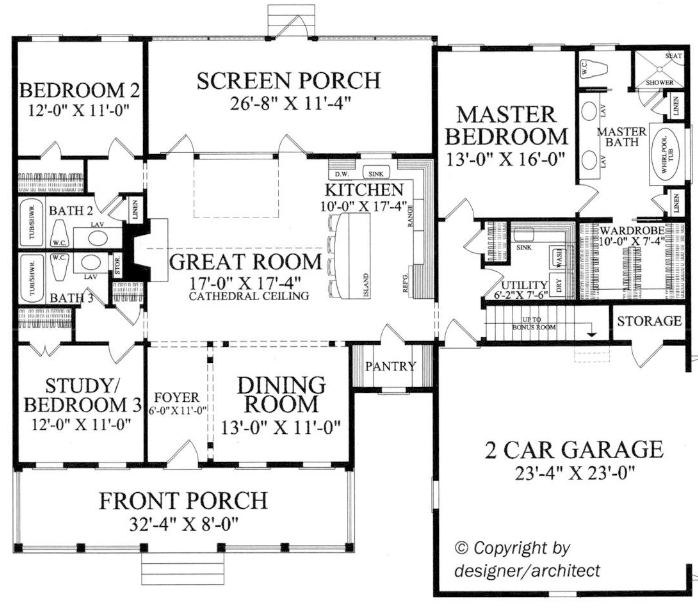

Plan #F08-065D-0398

Dimensions: 59'8" W x 62'4" D
Heated Sq. Ft.: 1,871
Bonus Sq. Ft.: 1,871
Bedrooms: 3 **Bathrooms:** 2
Foundation: Basement

See index for more information

Images provided by designer/architect

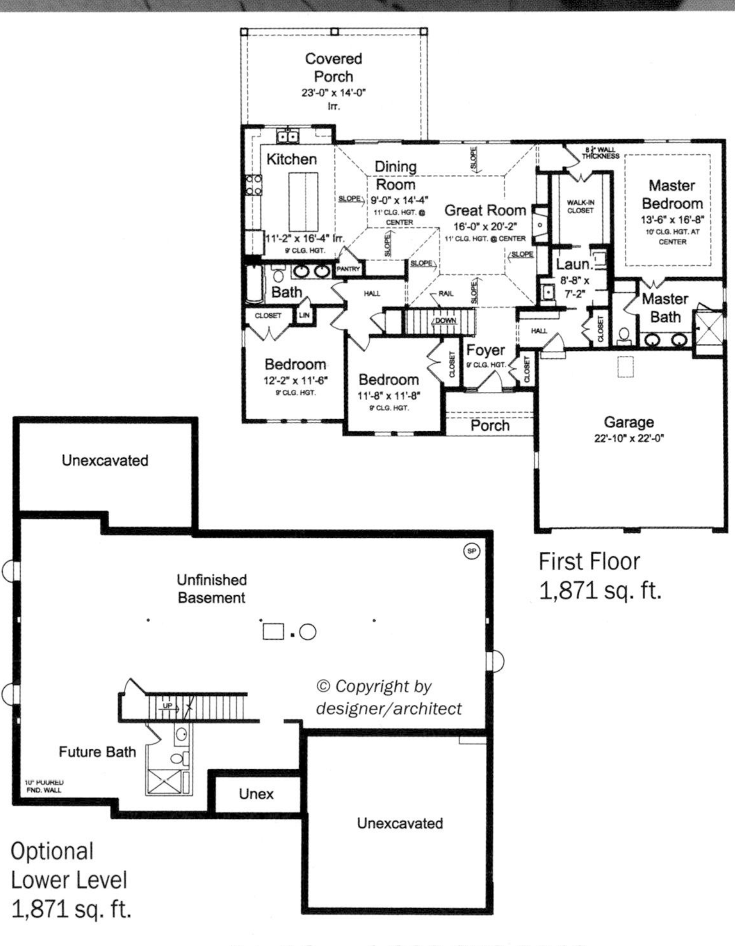

Plan #F08-101D-0214

Dimensions: 113'6" W x 62'3" D
Heated Sq. Ft.: 2,291
Bonus Sq. Ft.: 1,314
Bedrooms: 3 **Bathrooms:** 2
Exterior Walls: 2" x 6"
Foundation: Basement or daylight basement, please specify when ordering

See index for more information

Images provided by designer/architect

Features

- Craftsman details on the exterior and rustic beams on the interior creating the most open and inviting feeling in this home
- The kitchen has a cut-through directly to the dining area
- The private master bedroom has an amazing bath with an oversized tub and a separate walk-in shower
- The covered deck is ideal for relaxing outdoors in any kind of weather
- The optional lower level has an additional 1,314 square feet of living area and includes a rec room, two additional bedrooms and one and half baths
- Two 2-car front entry garages

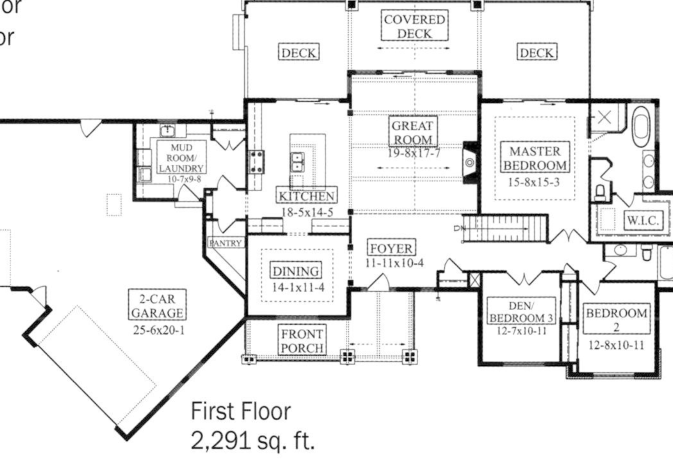

First Floor
2,291 sq. ft.

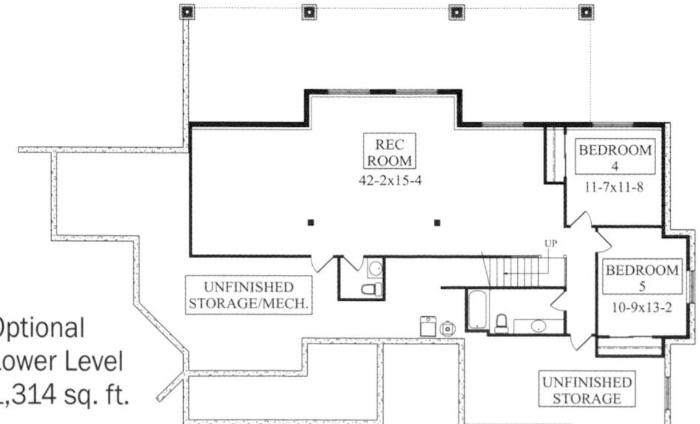

Optional
Lower Level
1,314 sq. ft.

Plan #F08-026D-2143

Dimensions: 45' W x 47'8" D
Heated Sq. Ft.: 1,642
Bedrooms: 3 **Bathrooms:** 2½
Exterior Walls: 2" x 6"
Foundation: Basement standard; crawl space, slab or walk-out basement for an for an additional fee

See index for more information

Features

- This stunning one-story has all of the essentials for comfortable living
- The kitchen features an island facing out over the dining room with views of the nearby family room
- The owner's suite has a private location and features a bath with an oversized walk-in shower and a large walk-in closet with direct access to the laundry room
- A handy mud room connects the garage to the home
- 2-car side entry garage

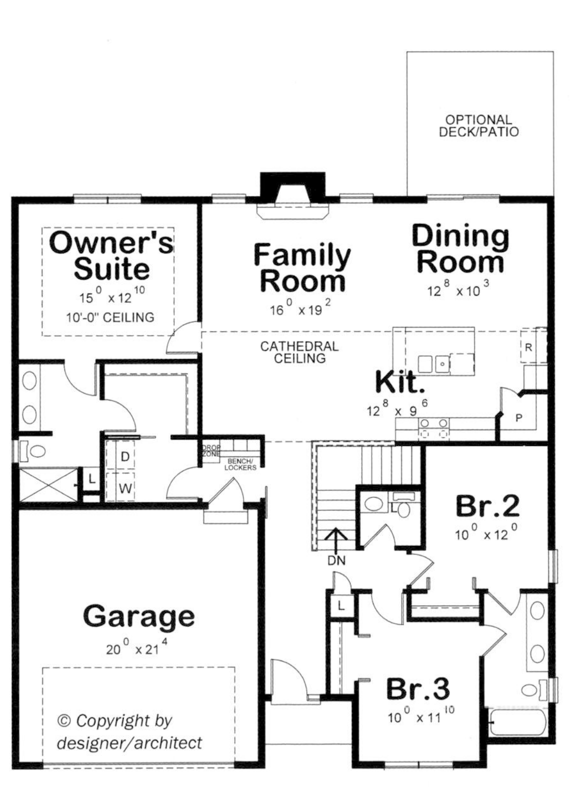

Images provided by designer/architect

Home Plans Index

Home Plans Index

why buy stock plans?

Building a home yourself presents many opportunities to showcase your creativity, individuality, and dreams turned into reality. With these opportunities, many challenges and questions will crop up. Location, size, and budget are all important to consider, as well as special features and amenities. When you begin to examine everything, it can become overwhelming to search for your dream home. But, before you get too anxious, start the search process an easier way and choose a home design that's a stock home plan.

Custom home plans, as well as stock home plans, offer positives and negatives; what is "best" can only be determined by your lifestyle, budget, and time. A customized home plan is one that a homeowner and designer or architect work together to develop from scratch, taking ideas and putting them down on paper. These plans require extra patience, as it may be months before the architect has them drawn and ready. A stock plan is a pre-developed plan that fits the needs and desires of a group of people, or the general population. These are often available within days of purchasing and typically cost up to one-tenth of the price of customized home plans. They still have all of the amenities you were looking for in a home, and usually at a much more affordable price than having custom plans drawn for you.

When compared to a customized plan, some homeowners fear that a stock home will be a carbon copy home, taking away the opportunity for individualism and creating a unique design. This is a common misconception that can waste a lot of money and time!

As you can see from the home designs throughout this book, the variety of stock plans available is truly impressive, encompassing the most up-to-date features and amenities. With a little patience, browse the numerous available stock plans available throughout this book, and easily purchase a plan and be ready to build almost immediately.

Plus, stock plans can be customized. For example, perhaps you see a stock plan that is just about perfect, but you wish the mud room was a tad larger. Rather than go through the cost and time of having a custom home design drawn, you could have our customizing service modify the stock home plan and have your new dream plan ready to go in no time. Also, stock home plans often have a material list available, helping to eliminate unknown costs from developing during construction.

It's often a good idea to speak with someone who has recently built. Did they use stock or custom plans? What would they recommend you do, or do not undertake? Can they recommend professionals that will help you narrow down your options? As you take a look at plans throughout this publication, don't hesitate to take notes, or write down questions. Also, take advantage of our website, houseplansandmore.com. This website is very user-friendly, allowing you to search for the perfect house design by style, size, budget, and a home's features. With all of these tools readily available to you, you'll find the home design of your dreams in no time at all, thanks to the innovative stock plans readily available today that take into account your wishes in a floor plan as well as your wallet.

how can I find out if I can afford to build a home?

GET AN ACCURATE ESTIMATED COST-TO-BUILD REPORT

The most important question for someone wanting to build a new home is, "How much is it going to cost?" Obviously, you must have an accurate budget set before ordering house plans and beginning construction, or your dream home will quickly turn into a nightmare. We make building your dream home a much simpler reality thanks to the estimated cost-to-build report available for all of the home plans in this book and on our website, houseplansandmore.com.

Price is always the number one factor when choosing a new home. Price dictates the size and the quality of materials you will use. So, it comes as no surprise that having an accurate building estimate prior to making your final decision on a home plan quite possibly is the most important step.

If you feel you've found "the" home, then before buying the plans, order a cost-to-build report for the zip code where you want to build. This report is created specifically for you when ordered, and it will educate you on all costs associated with building the home. Simply order the cost-to-build report on houseplansandmore.com for the home design you want to build and gain knowledge of the material and labor cost. Not only does the report allow you to choose the quality of the materials, you can also select from various options from lot condition to contractor fees. Successfully manage your construction budget in all areas, clearly see where the majority of the costs lie, and save money from start to finish.

Listed to the right are the categories included in a cost-to-build report. Each category breaks down labor cost, material cost, funds needed, and the report offers the ability to manipulate over/under adjustments if necessary.

BASIC INFORMATION includes your contact information, the state and zip code where you intend to build and material class. This section also includes: square footage, number of windows, fireplaces, balconies, baths, garage location and size, decks, foundation type, and bonus room square footage.

GENERAL SOFT COSTS include cost for plans, customizing (if applicable), building permits, pre-construction services, and planning expenses.

SITE WORK & UTILITIES include water, sewer, electric, and gas. Choose the type of site work and if you'll need a driveway.

FOUNDATION includes a menu that lists the most common types.

FRAMING ROUGH SHELL calculates rough framing costs including framing for fireplaces, balconies, decks, porches, basements and bonus rooms.

ROOFING includes several common options.

DRY OUT SHELL allows you to select doors, windows, and siding.

ELECTRICAL includes wiring and the quality of the light fixtures.

PLUMBING includes labor costs, plumbing materials, plumbing fixtures, and fire proofing materials.

HVAC includes costs for both labor and materials.

INSULATION includes costs for both labor and materials.

FINISH SHELL includes drywall, interior doors and trim, stairs, shower doors, mirrors, bath accessories, and labor costs.

CABINETS & VANITIES select the grade of your cabinets, vanities, kitchen countertops, and bathroom vanity materials, as well as appliances.

PAINTING includes all painting materials, paint quality, and labor.

FLOORING includes over a dozen flooring material options.

SPECIAL EQUIPMENT NEEDS calculate cost for unforeseen expenses.

CONTRACTOR FEE / PROJECT MANAGER includes the cost of your cost-to-build report, project manager and/or general contractor fees. If you're doing the managing yourself, your costs will be tremendously lower in this section.

LAND PAYOFF includes the cost of your land.

RESERVES / CLOSING COSTS includes interest, contingency reserves, and closing costs.

We've taken the guesswork out of figuring out what your new home is going to cost. Take control of construction, determine the major expenses, and save money. Supervise all costs, from labor to materials and manage construction with confidence, which allows you to avoid costly mistakes and unforeseen expenses. To order a Cost-To-Build Report, visit houseplansandmore.com and search for the specific plan. Then, look for the button that says, "Request Your Report" and get started.

what kind of plan package do I need?

SELECT AND ORDER THE TYPES OF BLUEPRINTS THAT BEST FIT YOUR SITUATION

PLEASE NOTE: *Not all plan packages listed below are available for every plan. There may be additional plan options available. Please visit houseplansandmore.com for all of a plan's options and pricing, or call 1-800-373-2646 for all current options. The plan pricing shown in this book is subject to change without notice.*

5-SET PLAN PACKAGE includes five complete sets of construction drawings. Besides one set for yourself, additional sets of blueprints will be required for your lender, your local building department, your contractor, and any other tradespeople working on your project. Please note: These 5 sets of plans are copyrighted, so they can't be altered or copied.

8-SET PLAN PACKAGE includes eight complete sets of construction drawings. Besides one set for yourself, additional sets of blueprints will be required for your lender, your local building department, your contractor, and any other tradespeople working on your project. Please note: These 8 sets of plans are copyrighted, so they can't be altered or copied.

PDF FILE FORMAT is our most popular plan package option because of how fast you can receive them your blueprints (usually within 24 to 48 hours Monday through Friday), and their ability to be easily shared via email with your contractor, subcontractors, and local building officials. The PDF file format is a complete set of construction drawings in an electronic file format. It includes a one-time build copyright release that allows you to make changes and copies of the plans. Typically you will receive a PDF file via email within 24-48 hours (Monday-Friday, 7:30am-4:30pm CST) allowing you to save money on shipping. Upon receiving, visit a local copy or print shop and print the number of plans you need to build your home, or print one and alter the plan by using correction fluid and drawing in your modifications. Please note: These are flat image files and cannot be altered electronically. PDF files are non-refundable and not returnable.

CAD FILE FORMAT is the actual computer files for a plan directly from AutoCAD, or another computer aided design program. CAD files are the best option if you have a significant amount of changes to make to the plan, or if you need to make the plan fit your local codes. If you purchase a CAD File, it allows you, or a local design professional the ability to modify the plans electronically in a CAD program, so making changes to the plan is easier and less expensive than using a paper set of plans when modifying. A CAD package also includes a one-time build copyright release that allows you to legally make your changes, and print multiple copies of the plan. See the specific plan page for availability and pricing. Please note: CAD files are non-refundable and not returnable.

MIRROR REVERSE SETS Sometimes a home fits a site better if it is flipped left to right. A mirror reverse set of plans is simply a mirror image of the original drawings causing the lettering and dimensions to read backwards. Therefore, when ordering a mirror reverse set of plans, you must purchase at least one set of the original plans to read from, and use the mirror reverse set for construction. Some plans offer right reading reverse for an additional fee. This means the plan has been redrawn by the designer as the mirrored version and can easily be read.

ADDITIONAL SETS You can order extra plan sets of a plan for an additional fee. A 5-set, or 8-set must have been previously purchased. Please note: Only available within 90 days after purchase of a plan package.

2" X 6" EXTERIOR WALLS 2" x 6" exterior walls can be purchased for some plans for an additional fee (see houseplansandmore.com for availability and pricing).

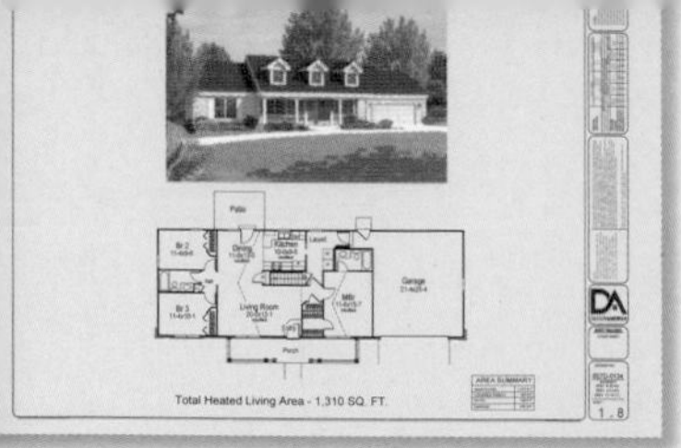
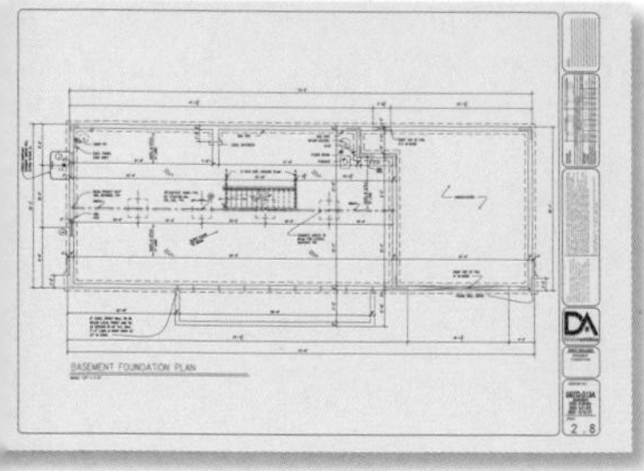
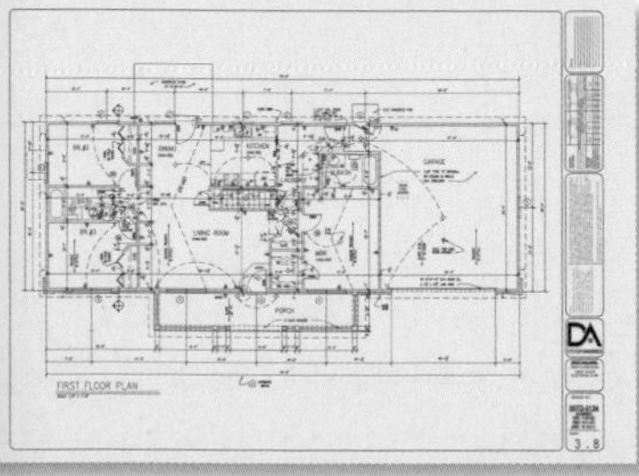
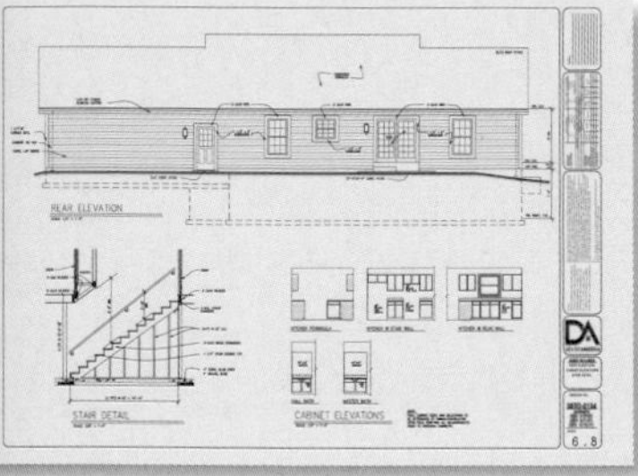
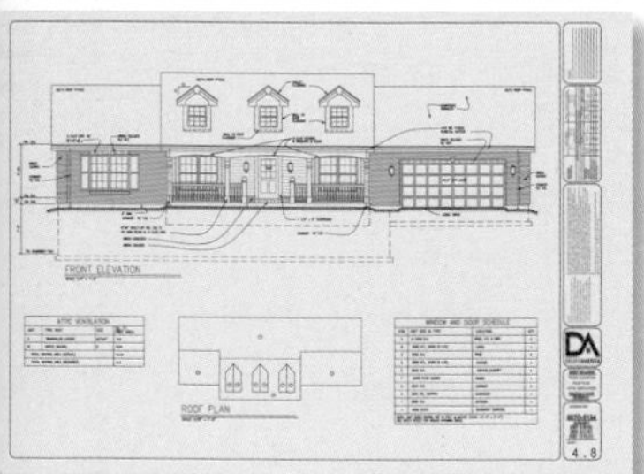
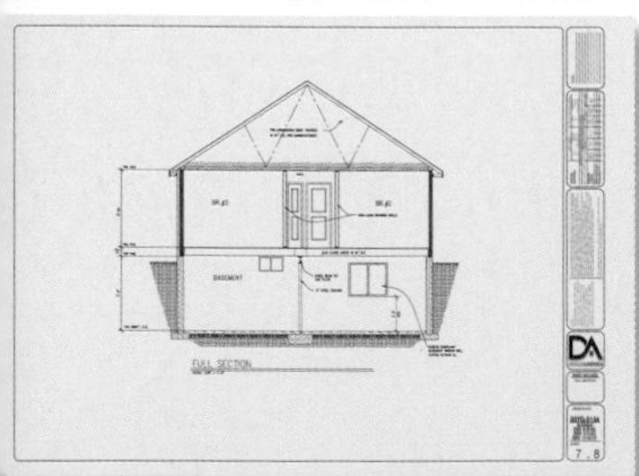
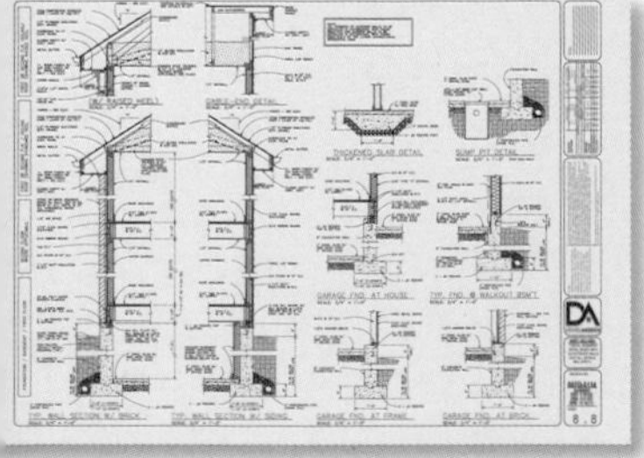

our plan packages include...

Quality plans for building your future, with extras that provide unsurpassed value, ensure good construction and long-term enjoyment. A quality home - one that looks good, functions well, and provides years of enjoyment - is a product of many things - design, materials, and craftsmanship. But it's also the result of outstanding blueprints - the actual plans and specifications that tell the builder exactly how to build your home.

And with our BLUEPRINT PACKAGES you get the absolute best. A complete set of blueprints is available for every design in this book. These "working drawings" are highly detailed, resulting in two key benefits:

- BETTER UNDERSTANDING BY THE CONTRACTOR OF HOW TO BUILD YOUR HOME AND...
- MORE ACCURATE CONSTRUCTION ESTIMATES THAT WILL SAVE YOU TIME AND MONEY.

Below is a sample of the plan information included for most of the designs in this book. Specific details may vary with each designer's plan. While this information is typical for most plans, we cannot assure the inclusion of all the following referenced items. Please contact us at 1-800-373-2646 for a plan's specific information, including which of the following items are included.

1 cover sheet is included with many of the plans, the cover sheet is the artist's rendering of the exterior of the home. It will give you an idea of how your home will look when completed and landscaped.

2 foundation plan shows the layout of the basement, walk-out basement, crawl space, slab or pier foundation. All necessary notations and dimensions are included. See plan page for the foundation types included. If the home plan you choose does not have your desired foundation type, our Customer Service Representatives can advise you on how to customize your foundation to suit your specific needs or site conditions.

3 floor plans show the placement of walls, doors, closets, plumbing fixtures, electrical outlets, columns, and beams for each level of the home.

4 interior elevations provide views of special interior elements such as fireplaces, kitchen cabinets, built-in units and other features of the home.

5 exterior elevations illustrate the front, rear and both sides of the house, with all details of exterior materials and the required dimensions.

6 sections show detail views of the home or portions of the home as if it were sliced from the roof to the foundation. This sheet shows important areas such as load-bearing walls, stairs, joists, trusses and other structural elements, which are critical for proper construction.

7 details show how to construct certain components of your home, such as the roof system, stairs, deck, etc.

do you want to make **changes** to your plan?

We understand that sometimes it is difficult to find blueprints that meet all of your specific needs. That is why we offer home plan modification services so you can build a home exactly the way you want it!

ARE YOU THINKING ABOUT CUSTOMIZING A PLAN?

If you're like many customers, you may want to make changes to your home plan to make it the dream home you've always wanted. That's where our expert design and modification partners come in. You won't find a more efficient and economic way to get your changes done than by using our home plan customizing services.

Whether it's enlarging a kitchen, adding a porch, or converting a crawl space to a basement, we can customize any plan and make it perfect for your needs. Simply create your wish list and let us go to work. Soon you'll have the blueprints for your new home, and at a fraction of the cost of hiring a local architect!

IT'S EASY!

- We can customize any of the plans in this book, or on houseplansandmore.com.
- We provide a FREE cost estimate for your home plan modifications within 24-48 hours (Monday-Friday, 7:30am-4:30pm CST).
- Average turn-around time to complete the modifications is typically 4-5 weeks.
- You will receive one-on-one design consultations.

CUSTOMIZING FACTS

- The average cost to have a house plan customized is typically less than 1 percent of the building costs – compare that to the national average of 7 percent of building costs.
- The average modification cost for a home is typically $800 to $1,500. This does not include the cost of purchasing the PDF file format of the blueprints, which is required to legally make plan changes.

OTHER HELPFUL INFORMATION

- Sketch, or make a specific list of changes you'd like to make on the Home Plan Modification Request Form.
- A home plan modification specialist will contact you within 24-48 hours with your free estimate.
- Upon accepting the estimate, you will need to purchase the PDF or CAD file format.
- A contract, which includes a specific list of changes and fees will be sent to you prior for your approval.
- Upon approving the contract, our design partners will keep you up to date by emailing sketches throughout the project.
- Plans can be converted to metric, or to a Barrier-free layout (also referred to as a universal home design, which allows easy mobility for an individual with limitations of any kind).

2 easy steps

1 visit

houseplansandmore.com and click on the Resources tab at the top of the home page, then click "How to Customize Your House Plan," or scan the QR code above to download the Home Plan Modification Request Form.

2 email

your completed form to:
customizehpm@designamerica.com,
or fax it to: 651-602-5050.

If you are not able to access the Internet, please call 1-800-373-2646 (Monday-Friday, 7:30am-4:30pm CST).

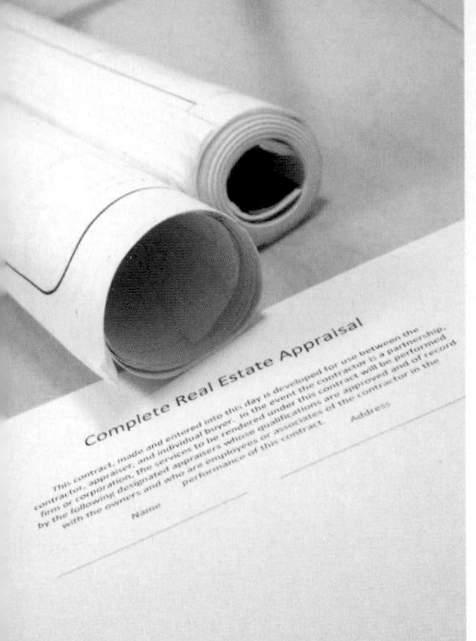

helpful building aids

Your Blueprint Package will contain all of the necessary construction information you need to build your home. But, we also offer the following products and services to save you time and money during the building process.

MATERIAL LIST Many of the home plans in this book have a material list available for purchase that gives you the quantity, dimensions, and description of the building materials needed to construct the home (see houseplansandmore.com for availability). Keep in mind, due to variations in local building code requirements, exact material quantities cannot be guaranteed. Note: Material lists are created with the standard foundation type only. Please review the material list and the construction drawings with your material supplier to verify measurements and quantities of the materials listed before ordering supplies.

THE LEGAL KIT Avoid many legal pitfalls and build your home with confidence using the forms and contracts featured in this kit. Included are request for proposal documents, various fixed price and cost plus contracts, instructions on how and when to use each form, warranty statements and more. Save time and money before you break ground on your new home or start a remodeling project. All forms are reproducible. This kit is ideal for homebuilders and contractors. Cost: $35.00

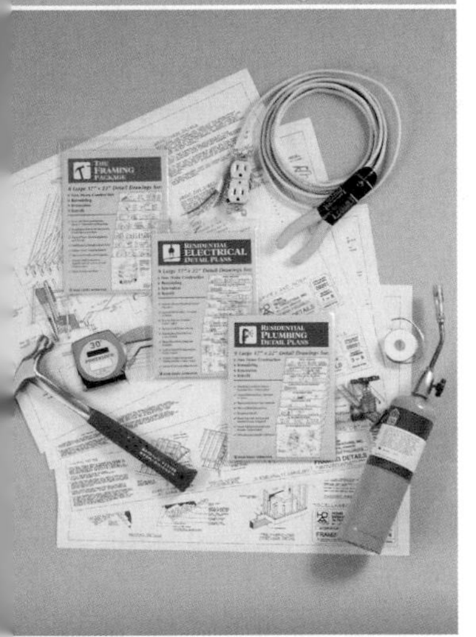

DETAIL PLAN PACKAGES - ELECTRICAL, FRAMING & PLUMBING Three separate packages offer homebuilders details for constructing various foundations; numerous floor, wall and roof framing techniques; simple to complex residential wiring; sump and water softener hookups; plumbing connection methods; installation of septic systems, and more. Each package includes three dimensional illustrations and a glossary of terms. Purchase one or all three. Please note: These drawings do not pertain to a specific home plan, but they include general guidelines and tips for construction in all 3 of these trades. Cost: $30.00 each or all three for $60.00

EXPRESS DELIVERY Most orders are processed within 24 hours of receipt. Please allow 7-10 business days for standard delivery. If you need to place a rush order, please call us by 11:00 am Monday-Friday, CST and ask for express service (allow 1-2 business days). Please see page 287 for all shipping and handling charges.

TECHNICAL ASSISTANCE If you have questions about your blueprints, we offer technical assistance by calling 1-314-770-2228 between 7:30am-4:30pm, Monday-Friday CST. Whether it involves design modifications or field assistance, our home plans team is extremely familiar with all of our home designs and will be happy to help. We want your home to be everything you expect it to be.

before you **order**

Please note: Plan pricing is subject to change without notice.
For current pricing, visit houseplansandmore.com, or call us at 1-800-373-2646.

BUILDING CODE REQUIREMENTS At the time the construction drawings were prepared, every effort was made to ensure that these plans and specifications met nationally recognized codes. These plans conform to most national building codes. Because building codes vary from area to area, some drawing modifications and/or the assistance of a professional designer or architect may be necessary to comply with your local codes, or to accommodate your specific building site conditions. We advise you to consult with your local building official, or a local builder for information regarding codes governing your area prior to ordering blueprints.

COPYRIGHT Plans are protected under Copyright Law. Reproduction by any means is strictly prohibited. The right of building only one structure from all plan packages is licensed exclusively to the buyer and the plans may not be resold unless by express written authorization from the home designer, or architect. You may not use this plan to build a second or multiple structure(s) without purchasing a multi-build license. Each violation of the Copyright Law is punishable in a fine.

LICENSE TO BUILD When you purchase a "full set of construction drawings" from Design America, Inc., you are purchasing an exclusive one-time "License to Build," not the rights to the design. Design America, Inc. is granting you permission on behalf of the plan's designer or architect to use the construction drawings one-time for the building of the home. The construction drawings (also referred to as blueprints/plans and any derivative of that plan whether extensive or minor) are still owned and protected under copyright laws by the original designer. The blueprints/plans cannot be resold, transferred, rented, loaned or used by anyone other than the original purchaser of the "License to Build" without written consent from Design America, Inc., or the plan designer. If you are interested in building the plan more than once, please call 1-800-373-2646 and inquire about purchasing a Multi-Build License that will allow you to build a home design more than one time. Please note: A multi-build license can only be purchased if a CAD file or PDF file were initially purchased.

SHIPPING & HANDLING CHARGES

U.S. SHIPPING -
(AK and HI express only)

Regular (allow 7-10 business days)	$30.00
Priority (allow 3-5 business days)	$50.00
Express* (allow 1-2 business days)	$70.00

CANADA SHIPPING**

Regular (allow 8-12 business days)	$50.00
Express* (allow 3-5 business days)	$100.00

OVERSEAS SHIPPING/INTERNATIONAL
Call, fax, or e-mail (customerservice@designamerica.com) for shipping costs.

* For express delivery please call us by 11:00 am Monday-Friday CST

** Orders may be subject to custom's fees and or duties/taxes.

Note: Shipping and handling does not apply on PDF and CAD File orders. PDF and CAD File orders will be emailed within 24-48 hours (Monday-Friday, 7:30am - 4:30pm CST) of purchase.

EXPRESS DELIVERY Since blueprints are printed in response to your order, we cannot honor requests for refunds.

Order Form

Please note: Plan package and plan option pricing are subject to change without notice. For current pricing, visit houseplansandmore.com, or call us at 1-800-373-2646

Please send me the following:

Plan Number: F08-________________

Select Foundation Type: (Select ONE- see plan page for available options).

❑ Slab ❑ Crawl space ❑ Basement

❑ Walk-out basement ❑ Pier

❑ Optional Foundation for an additional fee

Enter foundation cost here $ ______

Plan Package / Cost

❑ CAD File $ ______

❑ PDF File Format (recommended) $ ______

❑ 8-Set Plan Package $ ______

❑ 5-Set Plan Package $ ______

Visit houseplansandmore.com to see current pricing and all plan package options available, or call 1-800-373-2646.

Important Extras

❑ Additional plan sets*:

_____ set(s) at $______ per set $ ______

❑ Print in right-reading reverse:

one-time additional fee of $______ $ ______

❑ Print in mirror reverse:

_____ set(s) at $______ per set $ ______

(where right reading reverse is not available)

❑ Material list (see houseplansandmore.com) $ ______

❑ Legal Kit (001D-9991, see page 286) $ ______

Detail Plan Packages: (see page 286)

❑ Framing (001D-9992) ❑ Electrical (001D-9993) ❑ Plumbing (001D-9994) $ ______

Shipping (see page 287) $ ______

SUBTOTAL $ ______

Sales Tax (MO residents only, add 8.24%) $ ______

TOTAL $ ______

*Available only within 90 days after purchase of plan.

HELPFUL TIPS

- You can upgrade to a different plan package within 90 days of your plan purchase.
- Additional sets cannot be ordered without purchasing 5-Sets or 8-Sets.

Name ____________________
(Please print or type)

Street ____________________
(Please do not use a P.O. Box)

City ____________________ State ________

Country ____________________ Zip ________

Daytime telephone (______) ____________________

E-Mail ____________________
(For invoice and tracking information)

Payment ❑ Bank check/money order. No personal checks.
Make checks payable to Design America, Inc.

❑ MasterCard ❑ VISA ❑ DISCOVER ❑

Credit card number ____________________

Expiration date (mm/yy) ____________ CID ________

Signature ____________________

❑ I hereby authorize Design America, Inc. to charge this purchase to my credit card.

Please check the appropriate box:

❑ Building home for myself

❑ Building home for someone else

ORDER ONLINE

houseplansandmore.com

Use Coupon Code **F08OFFER** for $50 OFF your home plan order!

ORDER BY PHONE

1-800-373-2646

Fax: 314-770-2226

ORDER BY MAIL

Design America, Inc.
734 West Port Plaza, Suite #208
St. Louis, MO 63146

EXPRESS DELIVERY

Most orders are processed within 24 hours of receipt. If you need to place a rush order, please call us by 11:00 am CST and ask for express service.

Business Hours: Monday-Friday, 7:30am-4:30pm CST

Best-Selling 1-Story Home Plans

SOURCE CODE **F08**